WITHDRAWN

AMERICAN JEWISH COMMITTEE

THE JEWISH COMMUNITIES OF NAZI-OCCUPIED EUROPE

PREPARED BY THE RESEARCH INSTITUTE ON PEACE AND POST-WAR PROBLEMS

NEW YORK

Howard Fertig

1982

First published in 1944
Howard Fertig, Inc. Edition 1982
All rights reserved.

Library of Congress Cataloging in Publication Data
Main entry under title:
The Jewish communities of Nazi-occupied Europe.

   Reprint. Originally published: New York: American Jewish Committee, 1944.
   Includes indexes.
   1. Jews—Europe—Addresses, essays, lectures.
2. Holocaust, Jewish (1939-1945)—Addresses, essays, lectures. 3. Europe—Ethnic relations—Addresses. essays, lectures.   I. American Jewish Committee.
Research Institute on Peace and Post-War Problems.
DS135.E83J49   1982   940'.04924   81-5428
ISBN 0-86527-337-5   AACR2

Printed in the United States of America

The American Jewish Committee

Research Institute on Peace and Post-War Problems

THE JEWISH COMMUNITIES OF NAZI-OCCUPIED EUROPE

(Austria, Belgium, Bulgaria, Czechoslovakia, Denmark,
Estonia, France, Germany, Greece, Holland, Hungary,
Italy, Latvia, Lithuania, Poland, Roumania, Yugoslavia)

This is a collection of reports on the Jewish communities of seventeen countries under Nazi occupation in 1943, prepared between the spring of that year and 1944. Most were done at the request of a government agency; a few were added because the communities were of interest from the point of view of size or character. They were prepared by the staff of the Institute, for a number of countries with the collaboration of outside experts.

None of these reports was meant to give a complete picture of Jewish life; all were intended to answer a series of precise questions. Some important aspects of Jewish life, such as cultural activity, are not fully discussed because the emphasis was elsewhere. Other aspects were lacking because war conditions made information impossible to obtain. Most of the information we do present, however, is as complete and as accurate as was possible to get, and the reader will find some of it not readily available in other sources.

July 1944   Max Gottschalk, Director

TABLE OF CONTENTS

Each of the seventeen reports is paged separately. Preceding each report is an index to the subjects discussed.

	Pages
The Jews of Austria	1-28
The Jews of Belgium	1-16
The Jews of Bulgaria	1- 5
The Jews of Czechoslovakia	1-28
The Jews of Denmark	1- 6
The Jews of Estonia	1- 8
The Jews of France	1-23
The Jews of Germany	1-54
The Jews of Greece	1-13
The Jews of Holland	1-18
The Jews of Hungary	1-33
The Jews of Italy	1- 8
The Jews of Latvia	1-26
The Jews of Lithuania	1-18
The Jews of Poland	1-56
The Jews of Roumania	1-26
The Jews of Yugoslavia	1-20

THE JEWS OF AUSTRIA

THE JEWS OF AUSTRIA

Index

Agriculture	10	Government Posts, Jews in:	
Anti-Semitism, History of	6	Municipal	5
Nazi Leaders	25	Civil Service	5
"Aryanization"	11	Groups in Exile	28
Attitude of Government:		Health Services & Hygiene	17
Before Invasion	12	Industry	10
Attitude of People:		Insurance	9
Before Invasion	12	Judiciary	6
After Invasion	12	Languages	4
Banking	8	Leaders, Jewish:	
Bar, The	7	In Austria	28
Birth & Morality Rates	18	In Exile	27
Burials	3	Marriage	3
Catholic Church and		Minority Rights	4
the Jews	6	Motion Pictures	17
Citizenship	4	Natural Resources	9
Commerce	10	Occupational Structure	8
Foreign Trade	11	Parliament, Jews in	4
Community, Jewish	1	Physicians	15
Assets	2	Population	1
Functionaries	2	Press, General	16
Communal Organizations	2	Jewish Press	16
Cooperatives and Labor Banks	15	Anti-Semitic Press	25
Government Cooperatives	11	Public Welfare	24
Criminality	3	Child Welfare	25
Cultural Life, Jews in	5	Jewish Welfare	24
Discriminations:		Personnel	26
Before Invasion	13	Reconstruction Agencies	28
After Invasion	19-22	Refugees	1
Divorce	3	Social Security	17
Education	22	Sterilization and Liquidation	19
Economic Status after Invasion	11	Taxes and Fines	14
Employment and Wages	14	United States, Attitude toward	4
Forced Labor	15	War, Attitude toward	4

THE JEWS OF AUSTRIA

Population; Refugees.

In 1938, when Hitler invaded Austria, there were about 190,000 Jews in the country, or 3% of the population, distributed approximately as follows (census of 1933-34):

	Total population	Jews
Vienna	1,874,130	176,034
Lower Austria	1,509,076	7,716
Upper Austria	902,318	966
Styria	1,015,106	2,195
Karinthia	405,129	269
Salzburg	205,801	239
Tyrol	349,098	365
Vorarlberg	155,402	42
Burgenland	299,447	3,632
	6,715,507	191,458

The Jews were concentrated in the cities of Vienna, Linz, Gratz, Innsbruck, Neustadt, Neunkirchen, Eisenstadt, Mattersburg, Mattersdorf, and Deutsch Kreuz. The number of Jews living in Austria in 1938, according to the interpretation of the Nuremberg laws, was about 250,000.

The number of Jews left in Austria in 1943 was estimated varyingly between 5,000 and 15,000. Some 70,000 had been deported to Poland or Theresienstadt (Terezin) in Czechoslovakia. About 100,000 emigrated to other countries; approximately 50,000 to the United States; 20,000 to Great Britain and the Dominions; 15,000 to Palestine; 15,000 to South American and other countries. Many of those who escaped to Great Britain and the United States were serving in the armed forces of those countries.

Community Organization

The Kultusgemeinde (religious community) of the Austrian Jews was formed according to the law of March 21, 1890, concerning "the regulations and the conditions of the community of the religion of the Jews." The Kultusgemeinde, in which membership was compulsory, supervised worship and instruction in the Jewish religion, as well as the communal activities arising therefrom. Shehitan (ritual slaughter) was one of the functions supervised by the Jewish communities. The community could levy taxes for communal upkeep. All political activity was legally barred to it. The Constitution of May 1, 1934 (Dollfuss Verfassung) corroborated the already existing equality of all citizens before the law and affirmed the position of the religious communities as public corporations.

In Vienna, in addition to the large old synagogue on the Seitenstatten Gasse, and in other cities, there were between 300 and 400 small houses of prayer (Bethäuser), frequented largely by immigrants from East European countries. A few of them represented Hassidic groups (Hassidim are Orthodox

Jews who follow a rabbinical dynasty. Some Hassidic rabbis had emigrated
from Poland to Austria after the First World War. The Agudath Israel
(ultra-Orthodox) organization had some adherents, most of whom were of
Hungarian and Slovakian origin.

After the invasion of Austria, the Jewish communities, as of March 31,
1938, lost their character as public corporations. They were no longer
entitled to levy taxes or to claim tax exemptions; their employees lost
their civil service standing. An Ältestenrat (Council of Elders) was
reported in existence in Vienna, to care for Jewish matters.

Community Assets.

As a result of the inflation following the First World War, the assets
belonging to the synagogues and other institutions of the communities were
substantially cut, sometimes - as in the case of securities - to 1/15,000
of their former value. The income of the communities was therefore derived
largely from taxation and from contributions.

Religious Functionaries.

Rabbis, cantors and other functionaries for synagogues maintained by
private groups were appointed by the groups, but could carry out duties such
as marriages and funeral services only with the consent of the official
community. Rabbis appointed by the communities were usually graduates of the
seminaries at Vienna, Breslau or other cities; they were headed by the
Oberrabbiner (chief rabbi) of Vienna, who was elected by the community.

Communal Organizations.

Zionism had a large number of adherents in the Jewish community; the
Zionist movement had grown markedly in Austria after the Balfour Declaration
in 1917, partly under the influence of the immigrants from eastern Europe.
All groups of Zionism were represented in the Zionistischer Ländesverband,
the national union of Zionists, with the General Zionists (Allgemeine Zionisten)
in the lead. This group led also in the board and electorate of the
Kultusgemeinde.

The right to vote for the board of the Kultusgemeinde was dependent on
the payment of the minimum tax rate of the community (less than 10 shillings).
In Vienna, 49,000 Jews out of 180,000 had the right to vote. At the last
election (November 8, 1936) about 30,000 voted, of whom more than 20,000 were
Zionists. Unionists (Union Österreichischer Juden, founded in the 1880's,
and representing conservative and liberal Jews of Austrian origin) drew
13,000 votes. The Gemeinde board, following the 1936 elections, was composed
of 23 Zionists of various factions and 13 Unionists. Until the dissolution
of the Social Democratic Party in 1934, the Board had usually contained a few
members of this group (werktätige Juden). Throughout the rest of Austria,
there was more indifference toward community elections. In 1936, there were
only 17,000 voters in the rest of Austria, largely unaffiliated, but leaning
more toward the Unionists than toward the Zionists. Both the Zionist and

the Unionist groups had youth sections; the Zionists attracted more of the younger generation.

Fraternal orders and mutual aid societies included the B'nai B'rith, of which the most important body, in Vienna, had 1,000 members; numerous charitable groups, subsidized by the community; and a Hebra Kadisha (Burial Society), founded in the 18th century, which also offered aid to the sick and poor. In all these organizations membership was voluntary. Membership in the Kultusgemeinde, however, could be terminated only by an announced severance with the community.

Jewish organizations were dissolved shortly after the invasion. The assets of the Austrian Israelitic Alliance, a sister organization of the Alliance Israelite in Paris, were confiscated, as were the assets of the B'nai B'rith lodges in Austria and those of the Kultusgemeinden, particularly that of Vienna, which owned the sites and buildings of charitable and cultural institutions.

Marriage and Divorce.

The marriage rate among Jews was somewhat less than among Christians, and the average age of the couples somewhat higher. Religious ceremonies were valid, but civil ceremonies could be performed in intermarriages, when clergymen, because of the religious affiliation of one or the other of the marrying pair, would not solemnize a religious marriage. After the invasion, civil marriage was made obligatory even for Jews.

In the matter of divorce, the Jews were exempt from the severe regulations applied to Catholics in the Allgemeine Bürgerliche Gesetzbuch. Civil divorce was obtainable, and religious divorce valid.

Burials.

Vienna had two Jewish cemeteries. The Kultusgemeinde provided the simple wooden coffins prescribed by Jewish law, and the Hebra Kadishah (Burial Society) supervised all other ritualistic requirements. Burial for the poor was free. In November, 1938, the chapel of the Jewish cemeteries was destroyed by a bomb, and thereafter burials took place directly from the mortuary. In March 1941 the supervision of burials by the community seemed still to be going on, under the direction of Dr. Ernest Feldsberg, who had moved to the cemetery.

Criminality.

Per every 10,000 residents in Vienna, these were the criminality figures:

Year:	Crimes:		Minor delicts:	
	Jews	Non-Jews	Jews	Non-Jews:
1908-10	15.2	18.4	6.1	3.2
1911-13	11.4	17.8	6.2	1.6
1922-24	36.7	37.1	2.2	1.3

Languages.

All the Jews in Austria spoke German with some degree of proficiency. Those who had emigrated from other countries or other sections of the old Austro-Hungarian Empire spoke their respective languages also, particularly during the first generation. Immigrants from East European countries spoke Yiddish. French and English were spoken by the educated circles, and the young Zionist generation learned Hebrew.

Attitude toward War and the United States.

The Jews of Austria had all foreseen the portent in the invasion of Austria. With the outbreak of war a year and a half later, they hoped from the beginning for the defeat of the Nazis. Their attitude toward the United States was one of trust and friendliness, for they saw in the country a sanctuary of freedom.

Citizenship.

Before the First World War, nearly all the Jews living in Austria were Austrian citizens. After the detachment of Czechoslovakia, Hungary and Galicia from the monarchy, the Peace Treaty of St. Germain, in Article 80, provided for the acquisition of Austrian citizenship optionally by former citizens of the Austrian Monarchy. During periods when anti-Semites were in key government posts, Jews encountered difficulty in exercising this option.

After the invasion, the Jews were subjected to the same citizenship discriminations as the Jews of Germany. They were not considered citizens, and could neither hold office nor vote. The Nuremberg racial laws were applied; descendants of two Jewish grandparents were classed as Jews, as were people married to Jews.

Minority Rights.

The majority of the Jews in Austria preferred not to take advantage of the provisions of the minority clauses in the Treaty of St. Germain, Section 5 of which provided for the protection by the League of Nations of minority rights. Only the Zionists argued for the Jewish right to be a national minority.

There was in Austria no separate section for Jewish matters in the Ministry for the Interior, or in any other Ministry.

Jews in Parliament.

The Jews who served in the Austrian Parliament were representatives of the Social Democratic Party, which had no Christian or Aryan Paragraph: Dr. Victor Adler; Dr. Otto Bauer; Dr. Wilhelm Ellenbogen; Allna; Dr. Arnold Eisler; Fritz Austerlitz, editor of the Labor Party publication, Die Arbeiterzeitung; Mrs. Freundlich and others. Many of them were religiously unaffiliated (konfessionslos). They all served before the break-up of democratic representation under Dollfuss in 1934.

Municipal Posts.

Before 1934, there were several Jews in the Council of the Community of Vienna, including Hugo Breitner, city treasurer; Robert Dannenberg; Professor Julius Tandler and Julius Blum. Breitner and Tandler were city commissioners. After 1934 only one Jew, Dr. Desider Friedman, president of the Jewish Community of Vienna, served on the Council of the State (Staatsrat). Dr. Jacob Ehrlich, a member of the Board of the Jewish Community, was a member of the Council of the Community of Vienna.

Government and Civil Service.

After the shake-up under Dollfuss in February 1934 the Jews were successively eliminated from the Civil Service. The Ministry of Finance had included Ministerialrat Erich Gross, Mr. Wollheim and Mr. Manuel, a tax expert. In the public hospitals only a few Jews remained, including Maximilian Weinberger and Dr. Maurice Oppenheim. Jews remaining on the university faculty were Heinrich von Neumann, Emil Abel, Brassloff and Rudolf Pollak. Dr. Salomon Frankfurter served in the Ministry of Culture and Education. After the invasion, no Jews remained in any civil service post.

Jews in Cultural Life.

Under Franz Joseph, the Rothschilds, Koenigswarter, Gomperz, Auspitz, Figdor and other families had been known as art patrons. Even after the First World War, men like Castidioni and Bosel were liberal supporters of cultural research and accomplishment. Several Jews were well-known artists, including Kaufmann, David Kohn, Horowitz, and Strnad. Many teachers and research workers were Jews.

Arthur Schnitzler, Richard Beer Hoffman, Franz Werfel, Karl Kraus, Stephen Zweig and other writers were internationally renowned. Among composers were Gustav Mahler, director of the famous Vienna Opera House and conductor of the Philharmonic Orchestra of Vienna, and Karl Goldmark. Virtuosi included Alfred Gruenfeld, Bronislaw Huberman, and Bruno Walter. Leading actors who were Jews were Sonnenthal and Emmerich Robert; singers were Lola Beeth, Vera Schwarz, Joseph Schwarz, Schorr, Joseph Schmidt and others.

Professor Otto Loewi, of Graz, was awarded the Nobel prize for the discovery of adrenalin. He is now in the United States. Another Austrian winner of the Nobel prize was Dr. Baranyi, who now lives in Sweden.

History of Anti-Semitism.

The anti-Semitic movement in Austria began after the revolution of 1848. In the early 1880's the first racial anti-Semitic movement was that of Dr. Georg von Schoenerer and Karl Herman Wolf, who aimed at the exclusion of Jews from the public service. Their periodical was the Ostdeutsche Rundschau, edited by Wolf. The party had a few seats in the old Austrian Parliament, but was fought by all official circles except in the Sudeten territories, because they asked the union of the German-speaking countries of Austria with Germany under the rule of the Hohenzollerns. Soon afterward (1890's), Dr. Karl Lueger and Prinz Alois v. Lichtenstein founded the Christlich-Soziale Partei, declared enemies of "Jewish capitalism" and protectors of the so-called "little man" (kleinen Mann). Lueger was elected Mayor of Vienna.

The power of the Christlich-Soziale Partei, whose publication was the Reichspost, grew firm after the dissolution of the coalition with the Social Democrats. Chancellor Ignaz v. Seipel, a clergyman, was a party leader, as were Dollfuss and Dr. Kurt von Schuschnigg, the last Chancellor, who was formerly the Dauphin of the Christlich-Soziale Partei and the favorite of Dr. Ignaz Seipel. The peak of this power was reached in about 1934, when the Social Democratic Party was dissolved and banned by the Government. Dr. Schmitz, a passionate anti-Semite, became mayor of Vienna by nomination of Dollfuss. On February 14, 1934, all leaders of the Social Democratic Party were arrested, including many Jews. They were threatened by indictment for high treason, but were freed before the greater danger of National Socialism.

Catholic Church and the Jews.

Before the invasion of Austria the Catholic clergy of Austria were largely imbued with an anti-Semitic bias. The Christlich-Soziale Partei contained many clergymen; outside of Vienna the Catholic priest was usually the party leader. But this was not racial anti-Semitism; it had a religious basis. Baptized Jews were admitted to the party.

After the international economic crisis of 1929, which coincided with the rise of National Socialism in Germany, anti-Semitism in Austria, favored by the Catholic church, grew with new intensity. Members of the higher clergy agitated publicly against "Jewish influence."

A year before Hitler's attack on Austria, on March 13, 1937, the Catholic clergy attacked the Jews through Father Georg Bichelmayer, a Jesuit priest. Other attacks were made by the Federal Union of Catholic Youth, which had approximately 200,000 members. After the invasion, the attitude began to change under the influence of the Pope and German bishops like Faulhaber and Galen.

The Judiciary.

Many Jews served as judges in the higher courts of independent Austria, particularly before the shake-up of Dollfuss. Among them were S. Freundlich, member of the Court for maintaining the Constitution, and Fritz Austerlitz.

In the Criminal Court were: Dr. Orenstein (now living in the United States), Dr. Arle, (now in the United States) and Dr. Auerbach; of Jewish origin were Dr. Osio, slain in Buchenwald for having sentenced a few National Socialists, and Hofrat Dr. Stephan Moldauer. In the Civil Court was a Dr. Lelewer, who was a member of the highest Court, Oberster Gerichtshof (now living in England); Professor Dr. Heinrich Klang, one of the best civil jurists of Austria, who wrote a commentary of the Austrian Civil Code (<u>Allgemeines Bürgerliches Gesetzbuch</u>); Hofrat Dr. Bettelheim; Hofrat Dr. Loew, Hofrat Dr. Szepessy. Dr. Richard Steiner, who was of Jewish origin, served in the Commercial Court.

There were some individual cases of discriminatory judgments against Jews in the courts of independent Austria.

The German-occupying judiciary did not break the laws, but bent them, and tried to appear impartial, especially in civil cases. Their attitude was different in criminal cases, where the administrative police and judiciary were biased against the Jews. Many judges had come from Germany to be appointed in Austria, the same was true of the Gestapo. On the other hand, Austrian judges and members of the State Police were forced to move to Germany.

In political cases the Jews were severely prosecuted. Weakest evidence sufficed for an indictment, and the state prosecutor (<u>Staatsanwalt</u>) frequently made violent attacks on the Jews. Many absolutely innocent Jews were sentenced to long terms.

The plethora of cases caused by the arrest of Jews burdened the courts. According to the criminal law, the police could not keep a suspect for more than 48 hours; within that time he had either to be freed or placed under a definite charge. But the Jews were held by the police for long periods, sometimes for years, and then turned over to the courts or sent to concentration camps. Even cases which had previously been closed were reopened after the invasion.

The Bar

Only small circles of "Aryan" lawyers were unfriendly toward Jews. In general, the Bar and Christian lawyers were without prejudice. In Vienna, in 1892, there were 681 lawyers, of whom 394 were Jews, in 1934 there were 2,139 lawyers, of whom 1,825 were Jews. The president of the Chamber of Lawyers was, after 1918, a lawyer of Jewish origin, Dr. Gustav Harpner; his successor was a Zionist, Dr. Siegfried Kantor, now living in the United States. There were many free associations of lawyers, in which Jews and non-Jews sat together; only a few of these organizations did not admit Jews.

Immediately after the invasion, the "Aryan" lawyers were busy representing Jews who felt they would have fewer difficulties and the favor of judges and of the administration if they engaged "Aryans." All Jews, and non-"Aryans" were ousted from the practice of law on March 31, 1938, except those who were in practice in 1914, front fighters in the First World War or the sons of men killed in action on the German side during the First World War. After the assassination of Ernest vom Rath on November 9, 1938, the "Aryan" lawyers were forced to stop representing Jews. Jews could be represented only by admittedly Jewish practitioners, who could not accept "Aryan" clients.

In free Austria, public notaries were nominated by the Government. There were only a few Jews serving as notaries in Vienna and none in other parts of Austria. After the invasion, Jews serving as notaries were deprived of their rights.

Occupational Structure.

Statistics for the Jewish population of Vienna indicate that among the gainfully employed Jews, the occupational structure was as follows:

	Independent	Employees	Total
Agriculture	82	50	132
Industry and Trade	7,925	18,960	26,885
Commerce and Traffic	15,896	25,808	41,704
Public Service and Liberal Professions	24,988	1,114	26,102
Unemployed			18,273

Jewish women had a large share in the roster of gainfully employed. Of every 100 gainfully employed, the following were men:

Agriculture	89.40
Industry and Trade	67.64
Commerce & Traffic	87.43
Public Service and liberal professions	53.33

The Jews who had lived in Austria before the First World War lost a large part of their fortunes during the inflation. The immigrants from other countries after the war started with nothing and made some economic progress. The average economic condition of the Jews before the Hitler invasion was moderately good.

Banking.

The Kreditanstalt für Handel und Gewerbe, the most important bank in Austria, was headed by Baron Louis de Rothschild; its shareholders were the Rothschild family and British and French bankers. The Niederösterreichische Escomptegesellschaft, whose chairman was Maxim Krassny, had a board of directors consisting largely of Jews, as did the Wiener Bankverein. The Bodenkreditanstalt, which was later merged with the Kreditanstalt für Handel and Gewerbe, also had many Jews among its directors; its governor in imperial days, nominated by the Emperor Franz Joseph, was Theodor Ritter von Taussig, who was a member of the Board of the Jewish Community. He was succeeded by Rudolf von Sieghardt, a former high official of the Ministry of the Interior, nominated by the Emperor Charles. The bank was the trustee of the fortune of the imperial family, who were large stockholders. Smaller banks were the Länderbank, which was the branch of a Paris bank, and the Merkur Bank, affiliated with the Dresdner Bank in Berlin. After the invasion the Kreditanstalt and Bankverein were merged; the new bank, called Kreditanstalt-Bankverein, was owned by the Deutsche Bank. The owner of the Niederösterreichische Escomptegesellschaft, renamed the Industrie Kreditgesellschaft, was the Reichskredit Gesellschaft of Berlin, a German state bank. The Länderbank and Merkur Bank were merged and put under the control of the Dresdner Bank in Berlin.

After the invasion, all bank deposits owned by Jews, (Nuremberg interpretation) were blocked. The Jews were forced to sell their securities and place the proceeds in the blocked accounts. Later on, after December 3, 1938, Jews could dispose of their credit balances only with the consent of the Devisenstelle or Vermögensverkehrstelle. Limited disposable securities were introduced (beschränkt verfügbare Sicherungskonten). A Jew could draw only a few hundred marks monthly for living costs, medical care and for legal fees. For all other expenses the Jews were obliged to have the written consent of the Nazi authorities, even for emigration costs, which could be paid only to the Jewish communities or travel agencies with the consent of the Nazi authorities. All income had to be transferred at once to the blocked account, from which taxes could be paid, as well as the fine of atonement (Judenabgabe) and the flight taxes exacted for leaving the Third Reich. The bank had the right to buy Reich loans for the Jews.

Insurance.

Before the invasion, the Jews were greatly affected by the failure of the Phoenix Insurance Company, largely controlled by Jews. In the effort to keep the company alive, many decrees were issued by the Ministry of the Interior, and a tax on policy holders of all companies - not only on the policy holders of the Phoenix -- was introduced in order to collect a fund to meet the restricted claims of the policy holders of the Phoenix. The personnel of the Phoenix, which consisted to a great extent of Jews, was dismissed or pensioned with restricted pension claims. This had its effect on Jews employed in the other insurance companies.

After the invasion of Austria, no Jew could keep his job in an Austrian Insurance Company. Most of the Jewish policy holders let their policies lapse or surrendered them. Policies payable in foreign exchange could not be bought; and for the payment of premiums an arbitrarily low rate of exchange was established. Loans for more than 2,000 marks on foreign policies were forbidden.

Natural Resources.

Individual Jews were not known as the owners of natural resources in Austria. The largest ore mine in the country, the Alpine Montane Gesellschaft, was owned by a stock company in which a large number of shares were held by the Niederösterreichische Escomptegesellschaft. The Alpine Montane Gesellschaft also owned the coal mine of Graz Koeflach. The lead mine in Bleiberg was owned by the Bleiberger Union, on the board of which the Niederosterreichische Escomptegesellschaft was represented.

The company which owned the concrete industry was controlled by the Länderbank. The shares of the Mitterberger Copper Co. were in the possession of the Kreditanstalt. A few lumber concerns were held largely by Jewish families, such as the Glesinger, vom Groedel and Gutmann families. Coal mines in Czechoslovakia were controlled by the Rothschild and Gutmann families of Vienna.

Agriculture.

Only a few Jews in independent Austria were active in agriculture, owning farmland or living as farm tenants in Lower Austria and in Burgenland. The v. Kuffner and Wilhelm Loew families owned large tracts in Angern in Lower Austria. After the invasion, Jews were forbidden to acquire agricultural lands, and lands already owned by Jews could be subjected to forced sale.

Industry.

Jews were significant participants in the establishment and development of many industries; it was estimated that they had some connection with about 25% of the total industrial production of the country. In Vienna, where the greater part of the Jewish population was concentrated, their participation was manifestly greater than in the country as a whole. For instance, the Anker and Hammer bakeries, which produced more than 60% of the bread consumed in the city, were largely under Jewish ownership. About 65% of the fur industry was in Jewish hands. The development of the textile industry was also greatly due to their initiative; of 1,619 textile concerns, 1,186 belonged to Jews. The Treaty of St. Germain granted the right of munition manufacture to the firm owned by the Mandl family.

There was no legal discrimination against Jews in industry in independent Austria, nor by the government or government-controlled cartels. Where industries were controlled principally by banks, their representatives sat in the board of directors and the board of administration. These representatives were frequently Jewish, since the boards of directors of the large banks had many Jews as members. Alfred Hauser, a Jew, was president of the society of industrialists.

Commerce.

In independent Austria Jews were very active in commerce, chiefly in the textile, furniture and apparel lines. In 1935, there were 280 wine concerns in Austria, of which 206, or 73.60% were owned by Jews. In the oil, foodstuffs, candy, radio and perfumr lines Jews were well represented.

There was no open discrimination in commerce by national and local governments, chambers of commerce, political bodies or pressure groups and agitators. In the Chamber of Industry and Commerce there were Jewish members; the president of the professional chamber of business men (Gremium der Kaufmannschaft) in Vienna was a Jew.

The participation of Jews in commerce was finally eliminated after the invasion by the decree of November 23, 1938, which put into execution a decree of November 12, 1938. Jewish-owned concerns were either liquidated or "Aryanized". All commercial licenses issued to Jews were confiscated.

Foreign Trade.

Jews had large interests in the export and import trade of Austria, and there was no discrimination. Export firms such as Alois Schweiger, Robitschek & Reis, and Kanitz & Co. were largely owned by Jews. The import of cattle was also to a great extent in the hands of firms owned by Jews, such as Saborsky & Co. Trade with the East had been developed by Sephardic (Spanish or Portuguese) Jews since 1718 (Peace Treaty of Passarowitz).

After the invasion, the old import and export firms, were all taken over by "Aryans"; Jews were eliminated by the decree of November 12, 1938, according to which Jews were forbidden to own retail stores, mail order houses or commission houses as of January 1, 1939.

"Aryanization".

"Aryanization" was carried out by the Vermögensverkehrsstelle, under whose supervision a few banking corporations were assigned to the task; the Kontrollbank, Bankhaus Krentschker & Co., which took over Langer & Co., and the Gildemeister Organization, established for facilitating emigration and also entrusted with the "Aryanization" of the assets owned by Jews who were emigrating. All these measures were based on the decree of November 23, 1938, concerning the elimination of Jews from German economic life, and the decree of December 3, 1938, regarding the utilization of Jewish property.

The liquidation of Jewish-owned assets was completed by the decree of February 21, 1939, by which all Jews were forced to surrender all gold, platinum, silver, jewels and pearls to public purchasing offices established by the Reich. The purchase price was usually about 1/20 or 1/25 of the real value.

Government Cooperatives.

The subventions given by the Austrian government to cooperatives and other enterprises made it difficult for Jews to compete freely in certain fields and facilitated their elimination as buyers and sellers. Subventions were given principally to agricultural cooperatives, consumers' cooperatives and storage cooperatives.

Economic Status After Invasion

In July 1941, out of a Jewish population of 190,000, about 140,000 were reported to have emigrated. The assets of those who remained had been either "legally" or illegally confiscated. Pauperization was widespread. Five or six families lived together. The Jewish communities distributed food principally with the aid of funds furnished by the American Jewish Joint Distribution Committee. Since the entrance of the United States into the war only meager news has come out of Austria.

Attitude of People: Before Invasion.

Before the First World War there was a great degree of amity between Christian and Jew and widespread social intercourse. Later the poison of anti-Semitism and National Socialism infected the Austrian Christian population. Some circles withdrew from their Jewish friends. Propaganda and agitation against the Jews, carried on principally in the anti-Semitic newspapers such as <u>Deutsches Volksblatt</u> and <u>Deutsch-Osterreichische Volkszeitung</u> (DOZ), and by a few anti-Semitic politicians like Leopold Kunschek, leader of the Christian-Social Trade Union and Labor Party, were successful.

Attitude of People: After Invasion.

Some Austrians hoped that the union with Germany would bring a decrease in unemployment and improved economic conditions, and that the positions occupied by the Jews in economic life and in the liberal professions would go to "Aryan Austrians." All good posts, however, were handed to the German Nazis. Even <u>Gauleiter</u> (regional commanders) were most frequently Germans.

The young people, who enjoyed the wearing of uniforms, the carrying of weapons and Nazi encouragement of unrestricted sexual relations, were especially susceptible to Nazi doctrines. The older population was more neutral and even showed signs of sympathy for the Jews. When Jews were forbidden to occupy seats in street cars while any "Aryan" remained standing, Christians rose to give their seats to Jewish women or old men. Many "Aryans" tried to help the Jews with money and food.

Attitude of Government: Before Invasion.

After the murder of Chancellor Engelbert Dollfuss in July, 1934, the leader of the Austrian Government was Dr. Kurt von Schuschnigg, a convinced adversary of National Socialism. But his personal opposition to anti-Semitism did not prevent the government from presenting a united front in the matter of ousting Jews from public and economic life. The government consisted largely of representatives of the old Christian Social Party and included two secret Nazis, Edmund Glaise Horstenau and Guido Schmidt.

Two events gave Nazi propaganda an impetus. The first was the breakdown of the Kreditanstalt whose board consisted entirely of Jews; the second was the collapse of the Phoenix Insurance Company, which disclosed unscrupulous management and corruption involving state functionaries.

Although the government was bound by the Treaty of July 11, 1936 with Germany, it knew that its relation to the Western Powers, after the attack on democracy in 1934, could not stand the additional burden of official anti-Semitism. This ambivalence found expression in public measures which were opposed to each other; the official Government newspaper <u>Der Beamte</u> (The Official) attacked the anti-Semitic <u>Deutsche Volkszeitung</u> and called it the "Austrian Stuermer". The official <u>Wiener Zeitung</u> attacked anti-Semitic propaganda in Austria as damaging, but <u>Der Heimatdienst</u>, the official organ of the <u>Vaterlaendische Front</u>, whose leader was Chancellor von Schuschnigg himself, declared on May 7, 1937, that "we must find ways and means of putting the Jewish elements in their right place in proportion to their number. The times demand a law which would prohibit the Jews from abroad from continuing to settle in Austria." On July 8, 1937, the government prohibited the import of Hitler's Mein Kampf; later it decreed that the book could be imported, but not used for purposes of propaganda.

After his interview with Hitler in Berchtesgaden, (February 12, 1938) Schuschnigg invited the President of the Union of Austrian Jews, Dr. Herman Oppenheim, for a talk which lasted nearly two hours (February 17, 1938). The Chancellor informed Oppenheim about the events in Berchtesgaden, and asked Oppenheim to impress on the Jews of Austria the idea that the interview in Berchtesgaden and the ensuing wild rumors must be taken with reservations; there were no reasons for panic. He declared officially "that the Austrian Government has decided to abide by the constitution of May 1, 1934, which assured equal rights to all citizens. The projected law against foreigners, giving the government the right to declare inhabitants of Austria who came to Austria during the war and after the war, as stateless, is not directed against the Jews, but only against the National Socialists." Oppenheim was authorized to publish this declaration of the Chancellor in favor of the Jews, and it appeared in the Neue Freie Pressea and in the Neues Wiener Tageblatt of February 22, 1938.

Discriminations: Before Invasion

The laws of independent Austria allowed no discrimination, but universities were sovereign. The Rector of the University of Vienna, Count Gleispach, a National Socialist, was the originator (around 1930) of the first anti-Semitic decree, according to which Jews could not be admitted to the German student union. The Austrian Court for Maintaining the Constitution (Verfassungsgerichtshof) declared the decree void and invalid, and stated that all students have equal rights and duties. Afterwards, under Schuschnigg, Dr. Czermak, Minister for Education, tried to legitimatize the Gleispach order, proposing that the Jewish students form a separate group of students, but was not able to win government approval.

At the International Motion Picture Congress in Berlin in April 1937 Goebbels reported that Austrian and German producers had signed an agreement according to which Austrian producers accepted the Aryan Paragraph excluding Jews from the field of production. Actors, directors, playwrights, photographers who were Jews had to leave the cinema. This included even world-renowned artists, such as Albert Bassermann, whose wife was Jewish, and Ernst Deutsch.

On July 25, 1937, a government order declared that a graduate physician could enter practice only after one year of service in a public hospital. After 1933, however, newly-graduated physicians who were Jews were not admitted to hospital practice; consequently Jews could not practice, even after having completed their studies.

In trade, from the beginning of the economic crisis in 1929, essential limitations such as the new trade laws of 1933 and 1934 were directed against the activity of Jews. No new licenses were granted to Jews. A few periodicals, such as Der Arische Geschäftsweiser exhorted the Christian population to buy only from Christian firms. The deputy-mayor of Vienna, Joseph Kresse, participated in the agitation.

The break-down of the Kreditanstalt and the Phoenix, affected not only Jewish employees in these enterprises, but also those connected with other banking and insurance firms. Vehement propaganda began to be directed against Jews in economic life, journalism and the liberal professions. The slogan was: No subscription of newspapers under Jewish influence, no treatment by Jewish doctors and no consultation with Jewish lawyers. Professional and business organizations introduced the "Aryan" paragraph.

Taxes and Fines.

With the delivery of a passport for a Jew who was emigrating, a tax had to be paid at once. The Gestapo officer who delivered the passport, having the right to determine the amount, tried to get as much as possible.

After the death of vom Rath a decree was published (November 12, 1934) calling for an atonement fine of one billion Reichsmark to be paid by the Jews of Germany. The Jews of Austria had to participate.

Fortunes of less than RM 5,000 were free of this tax, which was imposed by the internal revenue office. The entire fortune of the Jews in Germany and Austria was estimated by the German authorities at 10,000,000,000 Reichsmark. Of this amount the Nazis would therefore have 10 percent. This tax was payable quarterly, but eventually the German authorities collected a fifth and a sixth instalment, raising the income to more than had been intended. Ruthless collection methods were used. No appeal was possible because the amount was payable on demand.

Employment and Wages.

There was only a small percentage of Jewish workers in Austria, divided as follows:

	Employees	Workers	Apprentices
Agriculture and forestry:	8.97	0.27	1.32
Industry and Trade	20.15	2.89	4.32
Commerce and traffic	25.24	7.03	16.99
Public services and liberal professions.	2.31	5.89	

Wages were the same as those of Christian workers, and were determined by labor contracts, negotiated between the organizations of the employers and the employees (Kollektiv-Verträge). For a time after the 1918 revolution, there was in Austria an index of living costs according to which wages were automatically increased or decreased. Generally wages were sufficient to cover the costs of living. There was a 48-hour work week and an 8-hour day.

Employment After the Invasion: Forced Labor.

After the invasion, most Jewish workers were dismissed. After November 1938 there were no Jews employed anywhere in Austria. On March 4, 1939, the Nazi Government introduced forced labor for Jews in the expanded Reich; later forced labor was extended to all populations of the occupied countries.

So far as Jews are concerned, forced labor has since its beginning implied not only back-breaking work but also continuous degradation. Jews were segregated in special groups, lived in barracks, and received only subsistence pay. They were not protected by general safety regulations and were barred from the social security and health insurance benefits to which other workers are entitled. All Jewish men over 16 and women over 20 who lived in Austria were subject to these regulations.

The Jews deported from Austria, who by 1943 numbered more than 50,000, had to work in deportation stations. The chief forced labor camps for Jews in Austria were at Mauthausen, Gänserndorf, Ebensee, Ischl and Gmunden.

Cooperatives and Labor Banks.

There were no Jewish cooperatives and labor banks in independent Austria. General cooperatives and labor banks practiced no discrimination against the Jews. The most important labor bank was the Arbeiterbank of Vienna, whose last president was Dr. S. Freundlich, a Jew, a lawyer and a member of the Court for Maintaining the Constitution.

There were also a few small institutions supervised by the Jewish Community for granting personal credits and small credits to Jewish tradesmen. One of them, the Gemilaths Hesed, granted interest-free credits up to 500 Shillings (about $100) on the endorsement of two other Jews. Loans were repaid in installments.

Physicians; Other Medical Practitioners.

Of approximately 7,000 physicians in Austria, about 2,000 were Jews. Of these, 1,686 were practising in Vienna, where there were altogether 3,286 physicians, and where they contributed considerably to the recognition the city had as a world medical center. Of 711 graduate physicians who were practising dentistry in Vienna, 446 were Jews; of the 1,239 dentists who were not also physicians, 385 were Jews. Jewish women who were nurses were all connected with the hospital of the Jewish Community. Very few Jews were veterinarians.

More than 30% of the medical faculty at the University were Jews. Among the leaders in the field of medicine in Austria who were Jews or of Jewish origin were Sigmund Freud, Heinrich von Neumann, Gottwald Schwarz, Victor Blum, Max Weinberger, M. Oppenheim and Robert Stein.

The Nazi regulations for Jewish physicians were stated in the 4th decree to the Reich citizenship law of July 25, 1938. Except for those who had fought in the First World War, and their descendants, Jews were virtually ousted from practice as physicians. Dentists, veterinarians and pharmacists were forbidden to practice by the 8th decree to the Reich citizenship law of January 17, 1939, which declared their licenses invalid as of January 31, 1939. The decree of September 28, 1938, applying to the nursing profession, permitted nurses who were Jews to practice only among Jews, and the Law of December 2, 1938, excluded Jews from practice as midwives.

The Jewish hospital (Hospital of the Jewish Community, formerly the Rothschild Spital), where the activities of Jews in the medical profession became concentrated was eventually expropriated by the Nazis. It is difficult to say how many Jews who were doctors and nurses remained in Vienna. Reports indicated that many of the Jews who were doctors in Vienna had been detailed for German military medical service, although in the beginning the Nazi authorities had refused to appoint Jews to medical duty. Both veterinarians and dentists who were Jews may also have been appointed. A large number of dentists emigrated; about 450 remained in Vienna in 1943. Jews in all fields of the medical profession were deported in large numbers to Terezin and to Polish centers of deportation.

General Press

The large independent newspapers in Vienna such as the Neue Freie Presse, the Neues Wiener Tagblatt, Das Neue Wiener Journal, Die Osterreichische Volkszeitung, and Die Kleine Volks-zeitung, included Jews among the owners and writers. The same was true of the more popular press (Boulevard Blätter), such as Morgen, Tag, Stunde, Telegraph am Mittag, Abend, and Echo. Most of the editors were Jews. In the provinces there were no papers in which Jews held an interest, but the Viennese press was read everywhere.

After the invasion, the Neue Freie Presse and the Neues Wiener Journal were merged with the Neues Wiener Tagblatt which changed its staff editors and administrators. The Österreichische Volkszeitung, the Tag, and Morgen Telegraph, Abend, and Echo ceased to appear.

Jewish Press.

In independent Austria, there were three Jewish weeklies in German, all published in Vienna: the Wahrheit, organ of the Union of Austrian Jews, Die Stimme, a Zionist weekly, and Der Weg, also Zionist. The Agudath Israel published a Yiddish weekly, Die Yiddishe Presse.

After the invasion, the Jewish Community published a weekly, the Jüdisches Nachrichtenblatt. It can hardly be considered a newspaper, containing only Nazi regulations, emigration information, news of emigrees in other countries, marriage and death notices. It also contained advertisements of rooms which could be rented by Jews and offers for the sale of furniture, books and other provisions of which Jews were forced to dispose. Other newspapers could not accept advertisements from Jews.

Motion Pictures.

In Vienna, Jews were very active in the motion picture field. Gradual ousting began in 1937, when the Austrian and German producers closed an agreement by which the Austrians accepted the "Aryan" paragraph. Jews who owned motion picture theatres in Austria were forced to sell them. Actors, directors, playwrights and photographers were dismissed.

Social Security.

Jews participated in the common social insurance system of independent Austria, which included sick benefits and accident insurance. The Allgemeine Arbeiterkrankenkassa (General Sick Insurance Company) handled the sick benefits and the Allgemeine Unfallversicherungsgesellschaft (General Accident Insurance Company) handled compensation matters. A general pension institution (Allgemeine Pensionsanstalt fur Angestellte) paid annuities to men over 65 and women over 60, and cared for the widows and minor children of insured employees. Contributions to the insurance funds were made partly by the employer and partly by the employee. Membership was compulsory. There were special insurance funds for various occupations -- banking, commerce, public service, law, etc.

After the invasion, Jews lost their jobs, and in consequence -- after an interval of six months -- their membership in the social insurance institutions. Previously-acquired claims of Jews against social insurance and security institutions were recognized by the Nazis; pensions and annuities were paid. But if later the claimants left Austria, their pensions were cancelled. In only a few cases was transfer allowed to the next of kin.

A qualified system of unemployment insurance, effective after a certain period of employment, existed in Austria. For a while after the invasion, Jews who lost their jobs received unemployment benefits. But after six or eight weeks they received only one-half or one-fourth of it, and finally nothing.

Health Services: Hygiene.

There was no discrimination against the Jews in the general health services in independent Austria. But the Jewish Community of Vienna maintained a Community Hospital, largely for the care of patients who wanted to observe Jewish dietary laws. The hospital contained about 300 beds, and adequate laboratory and therapeutic equipment. In 1942 the hospital was still functioning, but in 1943 there was a report that it was no longer at the service of

Jews, having been commandeered for military use. Of the few Jewish doctors permitted to treat Jews as sick-tenders (Krankenbehandler), many subsequently left or were deported from Austria. In the early days after the invasion, however, many well-known physicians, ousted from other posts, joined the staff of the Community Hospital. Among these were: Herbert Elias, Alois Strasser, Max Weinberger, Robert Bachrach, Robert Stein, Meissner, Schur and Mathias Reich.

Special sanitation and hygienic problems for the Jews arose only after the invasion. In Vienna, the Jews were crowded largely into two districts - the 2nd and 20th, where the houses were mostly more than 50 years old and without toilet or bathing facilities. For a short time, Jews were permitted access to some public bath houses, later this right was withdrawn. There were reports that a typhoid fever epidemic which had originated in the army had struck the Jewish population as well.

Birth and Mortality Rates.

The comparative number of births was as follows:

Year	Jews	Non Jews
1918	1,961	17,613
1919	2,466	22,849
1920	2,744	28,036
1921	3,080	28,687
1922	2,954	29,903
1923	2,704	27,905
1924	2,546	27,239

Figures for later years are not available, but the Jewish birth-rate had fallen even before the invasion. The population of still-births among Jews was 2.5%, among non-Jews 3.8%. There were only one-third as many illegitimate births among Jews as among non-Jews.

After the invasion, with almost all the younger members of the Jewish population gone from the country, the birth rate probably dropped to almost nil.

The comparative mortality rate was as follows:

Year	Jews	Non Jews
1918	3,852	47,645
1919	3,254	37,078
1920	2,886	25,429
1922	2,914	27,151
1923	2,565	22,915
1924	2,694	22,483

The principle cause of death among non-Jews in Vienna was tuberculosis. In 1924, the following deaths from tuberculosis occurred.

Jews	224 of 2,694 deaths, or 8.31 percent
Non-Jews	3,911 22,483 " " 17.39 percent.

The chief cause of death among Jews was cancer, for which the figures for 1924 were:

Jews   356 of   2,694 deaths or 13.62 percent

Non-Jews 2,534 of   22,483   "   " 11.27 percent.

Suicide occurred more frequently after the war among Jews than among non-Jews. From 1914 to 1920, of every 1,000 Jewish deaths, 2.52 were suicides; among non-Jews the rate only 1.91. A relatively large share of Jewish deaths were caused also by heart disease and diabetes.

The estimate of mortality among the Jews after the invasion is very high. The Nachrichtenblatt, published by the Jewish Community of Vienna, printed long lists of Jewish deaths every week. Deaths in concentration camps and in prisons were also numerous, and no figures are available for deportees. Typhoid, and dietary deficiencies due to discriminatory rationing, also contributed to a high death rate. Approximately one-third of the Jewish population of Austria, or 60,000 Jews, lost their lives under the Nazis.

Sterilization and Liquidation.

What happened in concentration camps in regard to sterilization and liquidation is unknown. In lunatic asylums such as Steinhof, all so-called incurables -- Jews and others -- were killed as early as 1941. This was also true in the general home for the aged in Lainz, near Vienna. In Jewish homes under the supervision of the Jewish Community of Vienna and with a Jewish staff (such as the home in the 9th district of Vienna under Prof. Strisover) the inmates were spared this cruelty.

Passport Regulations.

A short time after the invasion, all Austrian passports were declared invalid by the Nazi authorities. For Jewish emigrants the Central Department for the Jewish Emigration was established, with headquarters in the Rothschild home in the 3rd district of Vienna (Prinz Eugen Strasse). All government offices dealing with Jewish emigration were housed here, under Gestapo supervision and staffed largely by SS and SA men. Every Jew who applied for a passport was obliged to prove that he had paid all his taxes (state, community and Jewish community). The evidence certificate was called Unbedenklichkeitserklarung. Because of the attendant difficulties, many Austrian Jews preferred to try to cross the frontiers without a passport.

The passports which the Nazi authorities issued were German passports, containing a large red "J" on every page.

Travel Restrictions.

In general Jews were not barred from railroad travel within the boundaries of the Reich, but certain accommodations were not allowed them.

They could not travel first or second class and could not use sleeping or dining cars.

In the beginning, after the invasion, Jews were not barred from trolley cars, subways, buses and trucks. But later limitations were imposed regarding the use of these vehicles. Jews had to wait at the stops until a trolley car or bus came along on which there was unoccupied platform space. They were not allowed to take a seat until all "Aryans" were seated.

Immediately after the invasion, automobiles owned by Jews were confiscated by Nazi officials or members of the party, but the Jewish owner had to pay for fuel, garage, tires and repair. The same was true of horse carriages. After the outbreak of the war the use of taxicabs was limited, except in case of emergency or for trips to railway stations. Jews, however, were afraid to use taxicabs even in these cases, suspecting possible chicanery.

The same regulations concerning railroad travel were in force regarding the use of waterways by Jews. Jews could not reserve cabins, and had to stay in the 3rd class. For sea voyages Jews were forced to engage passage on German boats only. After the outbreak of war, Jews lost the money they had paid for these tickets because German ships no longer sailed.

In the first months after the invasion the Jews could travel by air, but later this was prohibited without exception.

Communications.

After the assassination of Ernst vom Rath in Paris on Nov. 9, 1938, the Jews were forced to deliver all radio sets to the police stations. Telephone apparatus was removed from Jewish homes on September 1, 1939, the day war broke out. They could telephone only within the city, using public telephones. Later Jews were barred from all telephone communications.

Telegraph communication for Jews was under Gestapo censorship. The messages were collected by the Jewish community or travel agencies and turned over to the Gestapo for control; consequently, messages were usually delayed for a few days or weeks.

Identification Cards.

During the second half of 1938 the Jews, like other groups of the population, were subjected to a ruling requiring them to have an identification card (Kennkarte), except that the color of the identification card for Jews was yellow. Left profile photographs were pasted on the cards, which were issued by the police. The identification cards had to contain the new "Jewish" first name or second name required by Nazi jurisdiction; Israel for males, and Sara for females. These obligatory names had to be used also in business transactions and other official dealings, but not in firm names.

General Restrictions and Curfew.

An order of July 3, 1938, by the Ministry of Agriculture barred Jews from all state-owned parks in Vienna and its environs. City parks and old family estate parks were also made inaccessible to Jews. A few squares in the city remained free, but even there Jews were plagued by the Hitler youth. Many Jews found that the only places were they could have a little fresh air were the Jewish cemeteries.

On December 5, 1938, an order issued by the police president of Vienna barred Jews from certain buildings and districts. To enter a barred district on an official summons, a Jew had to have a special police permit. Theatres, museums, cafes, concert and lecture halls and other places of relaxation and amusement were included in the restricted buildings.

In November 1938 a curfew order barred Jews from the streets of Vienna from 4 P.M. to 6 A.M. Later the curfew hour was advanced to 6 P.M. and finally to 8 P.M.

Firearm Restrictions.

Under the Nazis, Jews could not own firearms or weapons of any kind. The possession of explosives was prohibited to the entire population. Conviction on the charge of possessing firearms brought a prison sentence, followed not by release, but by despatch to a concentration camp. The possession of explosives was considered high treason, and was punishable by death. The Gestapo was known to have planted firearm evidence in Jewish homes.

Rationing.

Before the beginning of the war (up to August 27, 1939), there was no rationing at all in Austria, and immediately after its introduction, the rationing system was the same for Jews as for the rest of the population. Later rationing for Jews was limited. Their cards were marked with a "J", and they were prejudicially treated by tradesmen.

Subsequently, the difficulties for Jews became even greater. They were allowed to market only after "Aryan" population had made its purchases, and to buy only from certain specified shops. The number of Jews who ate in the feeding stations established by the Jewish Communities grew. Home cooking was still further hampered by the crowded living conditions. In the restricted Jewish areas of Vienna, one kitchen was frequently shared by numerous families.

Penal Institutions and Concentration Camps.

There were no special concentration camps or penal institutions for Jews, either before or after the invasion. At first, after the invasion, Jews shared cells with "Aryans"; later they were segregated. The main police prison in Vienna accommodated about 2,000 prisoners, but the cells were overcrowded; in the so-called "single cells" (2½x2½x6) there were often three or four prisoners. Two men were imprisoned in the offices of the Gestapo (Hotel Metropol) -- the former Chancellor Kurt von Schuschnigg and Louis de Rothschild. There were many prisoners in the so-called Landgericht Alserstrasse, which could hold 1,500 prisoners, but had to accommodate 3,000 or more. Landgericht II (Vienna) had space for 1,000 prisoners, and had to accommodate 2,000 or more. Prisons attached to district courts were also overcrowded. Sometimes all the prisons of Vienna could not hold the arrestees, who were placed under police guard in schools and other public buildings. In some of these makeshift prisons the Jews were particularly maltreated.

The head of every prison had the right to sentence prisoners to correctional punishment. Once a week a judge visited all the cells. Technically, every prisoner had the right to bring his complaints before him, but no one dared to do so for fear of the correctional punishment the prison head might impose.

Juveniles under 18 had a separate prison in the children's court (Jugendgerichtshof.) In concentration camps juveniles were kept with other prisoners.

Sanitary conditions were very bad; there was one doctor for thousands of prisoners. In the jail at Landgericht there was a so-called Inquisitenspital with about 50 beds, which had to accommodate the sick from all the prisons in Vienna. Mortality was therefore very high. After the outbreak of the war, food in the prisons and jails became even worse than before. Breakfast consisted of black "coffee", nicknamed "nigger-sweat" by the prisoners; lunch offered soup with unidentifiable "vegetables" and a quarter loaf of bread. All prisoners lost weight rapidly.

Treatment of the prisoners in official prisons was not so bad. Nobody was beaten; the Schupo (regular police) were not brutal.

The concentration camps to which Jews were sent were usually not in Austria, but in Bavaria (Dachau) and at Buchenwald near Weimar. Other concentration camps were in Sachsenhausen and Oranienburg.

Education.

The Jews of independent Austria had the unrestricted right to attend public schools of all kinds. Education was compulsory between the ages of 6 and 14. Instruction in religion was obligatory; every school attended by more than 20 Jewish children had to have a teacher of Jewish religion on its staff. High schools also had a Jewish teacher for the Jewish pupils. There were special Talmud Torah schools, supervised by the Jewish Community, in which only Jewish religious subjects were taught.

After the First World War, a few special Jewish schools were also established, all in the 2nd district of Vienna. One was an elementary and secondary school Volks und Bürgerschule, and the other the so-called Chajes Gymnasium, named for the Chief Rabbi of Vienna, Ben Zion Chajes. The Jewish schools were maintained by fees and with the aid of subsidies of the

Jewish Community, whose educational department (<u>Schulamt</u>) appointed a committee of six to regulate and supervise the schools. The committee prescribed the curricula, and selected teachers and textbooks.

On November 16, 1938, Jewish children were barred from all Austrian schools. Subsequently the Jewish Community established trade and handicraft training schools for prospective emigrants, where dressmaking, millinery, artificial flower and costume jewelry manufacture, glove and bag making and various mechanical trades were taught.

In the secondary schools of Vienna, there were (1933-34) 6,542 Jews and 24,836 non-Jews, or 20.8% Jews. At the University there were 2,295 Jews and 9,650 non-Jews (19.3%); at the Technische Hochschule, 283 Jews and 2,395 non-Jews (10.56); at the University of Forestry and Agriculture (Hochschule fur Bodenkultur) 18 Jews and 413 non-Jews (4.62%); at the Academy for World Commerce (Hochschule für Welthandel), 194 Jews and 1,027 non-Jews (15.2%), and at the Veterinary Academy, 9 Jews and 355 non-Jews (2.5%).

In the Jewish elementary school of Vienna there were about 300 pupils; the Chajes Gymnasium had eight classes with approximately 400 students. The theological seminary had about 75 students.

Elementary school teachers had to be graduates of a high school and normal school (<u>Lehrerseminar</u>). Secondary school teachers were university graduates who had passed special examinations in their subjects. There were many Jews serving as teachers in the elementary schools in Austria, under the Social Democratic regime, especially in Vienna. In Vienna the supervising teacher of every public school had to be of the same religion as the majority of the pupils; since in a few schools in the 2nd district the majority of the pupils were Jewish, a Jew had to be appointed supervisor. Altogether about 2,000 Jews were on the staffs of the Vienna schools. Many were made council to the schools (<u>Schulrat</u>).

With the establishment of a Social Democratic regime, membership in the Social Democratic party was almost a prerequisite for appointment to the school system, and the Social Democratic hold on the student body was equally great. With the shake-up of the Dollfuss regime in February 1934 those teachers who did not renounce their Social Democratic affiliations were replaced by members of the Christian Social party. Most of the Jews lost their posts. After the invasion, teachers -- to retain their jobs -- had to become members of the National Socialist party; the same propaganda was injected into the curriculum.

In independent Austria, there were about 150 teachers in the Jewish schools of Vienna, and about 50 in the Jewish schools elsewhere. In 1943, there may still have been about 50 teachers in the Jewish schools of Vienna, where the bulk of the Jewish population was concentrated,

Public Welfare

The Social Democratic administration of the City of Vienna had an exemplary public welfare system, which provided care from birth to death. Newborn children were provided with necessities; illigitimate children were kept in homes (Kinderübernahmsstelle) until foster homes could be found. There were orphan asylums. The poor were cared for by a separate organization and there were also volunteer visiting social workers. The sick had ample hospital facilities; the largest hospital was the Allgemeines Krankenhaus, established by Joseph II. There were maternity homes, old age homes, and insane asylums. To all these institutions Jews had access on a basis of equality. The famous housing program of Vienna, carried out by its treasurer, Hugo Breitner, constructed more than 2,000 houses.

Christians and Jews worked together in general welfare committees. This was true in the Allgemeine Poliklinik, a private institution; in the Franz Josef Ambulatorium; Elizabeth Heim (later Krügerheim); the Rosenhügel Sanitorium, founded by the Rothschilds; the Home for Disabled Officers in Reichenau, founded by Nathaniel von Rothschild; the Officers' Endowment in Hinterleithen; the Vienna Merchants' Hospital erected by the Gremium of Viennese Merchants under the chairmanship of Leopold Pollak von Parnegg; the Marie Theresienschlössel in the 19th district of Vienna, and the Marienspital in Baden, founded by Mme. Perliva, the daughter of Fanny von Arnstein; and other institutions.

Jewish Welfare.

The center for Jewish relief organizations was the Jewish Community of Vienna. In addition to the support and help granted by public welfare, it granted financial aid to the poor, health service to the sick in the previously-mentioned hospital of the Jewish Community, medical supplies through the Hebra Kadisha, education and homes for Jewish orphans (Itzeles Merores Stiftung), and care for the aged in the Home for Aged. After the invasion, the last-named institution was transferred to the Home for the Jewish Blind. The Jewish Community had once maintained a home for the deaf and dumb which closed in 1932 because of inadequate funds. The Jewish Community spent 2,000,000 shillings ($400,000) annually for its welfare institutions.

After the invasion, and until the United States entered the war, Jewish relief work derived its principal support from foreign organizations, especially the American Jewish Joint Distribution Committee. The income of the Community itself decreased from about 7,000,000 shillings ($1,400,000) to 300,000 shillings (about $60,000). A portion of the Jewish population took their meals at the Community kitchens. The Jewish Community paid rent for many families. The Nazi government controlled and supervised the administration of the Jewish Community. Allegedly the Community was entitled to part of the passport fee paid by Jewish emigrants, which brought in more than 5,000,000 marks. But the Community officials had to struggle for even a small share of the money. With the dollars allotted by the Joint Distribution Committee they paid travelling expenses when necessary. The Community also had the right to sell some of these dollars to emigrants who could afford to buy them at high prices. The Jewish community was badly in need of marks and the system somewhat alleviated the need.

Child Welfare.

Jewish children had access to all government child welfare agencies, especially during the incumbency of the Social Democratic Party. Government activities included public kindergartens, infant homes, orphan homes, and summer camps. For Jewish children there were special Ferienheime (vacation camps), under the direction of Sophie Gruenfeld, wife of the former president of the Union of Austrian Youth. Between 400 and 500 children were cared for here. Various other activities, including orphan homes and cultural work, provided attention for between 4,000 and 5,000 Jewish children. A society for the care of orphans had been established as early as 1861.

After the invasion, Jewish child welfare institutions, like other philanthropies, were dissolved.

Anti-Semitic Press.

The leading anti-Semitic newspaper was the Reichspost, organ of the Christian Socialist Party, which was edited by Frierrich Funder, a passionate anti-Semite. After the revolution of 1918, members of the Christian Socialist Party held seats in every government, and the Reichspost consequently became a semi-official government newspaper. Among its contributors were Dr. Ignaz Seipel, Chancellor of Austria. Dr. Kienböck, several times Ministre of Finance and until the invasion president of the Austrian National Bank, and Kurt von Schuschnigg. The Deutsche Volksblatt, edited by Virgani, a counterpart of Julius Streicher, was formerly the organ of the Christian Socialist Party; its offices were in a building called Court of Antisemites (Antisemitenhof). The name was engraved in gold on the facade. After the establishment of the Reichspost the Deutsche Volksblatt lost its influence; in order to regain its old position it became a German National and later a National Socialist newspaper. Other anti-Semitic newspapers were the Kleines Volksblatt and the Neuigkeits Weltblatt, represented by Christian Socialist opinion. The Nueigkeits Weltblatt was owned by a man named Kirsch; one of its editors, named Filsenburg, was of Jewish origin. The leading German National organs were the Wiener Neuesten Nachrichten and the Deutsch Osterreichische Tageszeitung (DöTZ), the latter a badly disguised National Socialist newspaper. After the invasion it was taken over by the Völkischer Beobachter, the official organ of the National Socialist Party. In the provinces there were always conservative clerical newspapers, as the Grazer Tagespost, Linzer Tagesbote, Innsbrucker Nachrichten, Klagenfurterzeitung, and anti-Semitci propaganda newspapers such as the Eiserner Besen in Salzburg.

Nazi Leaders.

Among the leading Nazis in Austria were Baldur v. schirach, Gauleiter of Austria and Dr. Jurie, Gauleiter of Vienna. Most of the Nazi leaders came from Germany, few were drawn from the Austrian population.

Police Force: Before the Invasion.

In the lower ranks of the police forces of independent Austria there were only a few Jews, and no discrimination was apparent against them. In the higher ranks there were relatively many Jewish officials. The former president of the criminal police of Vienna was a Jew, named Moritz Stukart. There were also a few Jews in the state police. Among Councils to the Court (Hofrat) were Gans, Pollack, Adler, Kien and Jokl, the last two now living in the United States. Many of the police doctors were Jews.

Police Force: After Invasion.

The principal Nazi organization dealing with the Jews was the Gestapo, which had a special department for Jewish affairs. One of its subsections was the Central Bureau for Jewish Emigration, with headquarters in the Rothschild palace. The first chief of this office was Fritz Eichmann, a German born in the Near East and well-versed in Hebrew; he was succeeded in Vienna by his former secretary, Brunner, 24 years old. The Central Bureau could declare a Jew expelled and set a time for his emigration, whether he had possibilities for emigration or not. In case of delay, they could imprison him and send him to a concentration camp. This Bureau also decided on the deportation of Jews to Poland or elsewhere, and supervised the regular appearances Jews had to make to the police stations. Many Jews were forced to report weekly, some twice a week, others once a day and a few twice a day.

In addition to the Gestapo departments, there were special police sections for Jews, dealing with taxes, duties, foreign currency, and criminal examinations (Zollfahndungstelle). Every Jew who possessed money, jewelry, objects of art or other valuables was suspect. If arrested and imprisoned he might be released after a trial lasting at least between four and six months.

Most of the special Nazi police were drawn from the Hitler Youth. Their ambition was to be admitted to the S.S.; to qualify they tormented the Jews during the questioning. Nevertheless graft and corruption were widespread and they tried to obtain gifts from relatives of the arrested Jews. Many of the police came from Germany, because the Nazi movement in Austria was too young and not sufficiently reliable. Every member of the Gestapo wore the equipment of the organization to which he belonged. The S.S. men wore black uniforms, black neckties and black boots, and were armed with a dagger and a revolver. On their left arm they wore a red swastika armband. The S.A. men wore brown uniforms, brown shirts and brown neckties. Their weapons were the same as those of the S.S. On their left arm they wore a white armband with the black swastika. The members of the Schupo wore the old uniform of the Austrian police but with a flat cap instead of a helmet. They carried only rubber truncheons and revolvers.

Welfare Personnel.

There were about 350 employees in the Jewish Community offices; in addition, in normal times, there were about 25 in the welfare department. After the invasion of Austria, the personnel of this section was increased by about 100 persons. In independent Austria, the welfare department worked under the supervision of a Committee of the Board of the Jewish Communities, consisting of six persons. A separate committee supervised the hospital whose director was the former surgeon-general (Generalstabsarzt) Dr. Raschkes. He headed a staff of about 150 doctors; many of the departmental heads were renowned physicians, such as Professor Braun (internal diseases); Prof. Fleischmann (gynecology); Prof. Borak (X-ray); Prof. Goldschmidt (surgery); Prof. Mathias Reich (surgery); Dr. Konrad Stein (oteology), later the assistant of Prof. Heinrich Neumann; Dr. Buchband (now in the United States); Dr. Meissner (ophthalmology); Prof. Robert Stein (dermatology); Dr. Infeld (neurology); Prof. Schur and Prof. Max Weinberger, internists.

Leaders in Exile.

The deputy-president of the Jewish Community of Vienna, Dr. Joseph Ticho, emigrated to Tel Aviv. Other leading members of the community were Dr. Leopold Plaschkes, (Palestine); Dr. Herman Oppenheim, (former treasurer of the community and a vice-president of the Austrian Staatsbank, now in New York) and Mr. Albers (New York).

Industrialists in exile were Dr. Ferdinand Bloch Bauer (Canada), E. G. Pick, Leopold Blum and Leopold Haas (New York), the brothers Askonas, - one in Canada, the other in the United States; Bernhard Altmann (United States). Others in the United States included: David Goldman; the sons and the son-in-law of Wilhelm Heller and Gustav Heller, candy manufacturers; Altmann & Kuehne, also candy manufacturers; Penzek & Rainer, fur manufacturers; Dr. Stephan Mendel, a shareholder in the Anker Bread Factory; Wilhelm Loew, agriculturist; Rudolf Loew Beer and his sons, Moravian textile industrialists (London).

Labor leaders in exile included Dr. Wilhelm Ellenbogan, for many years a member of the Austrian Parliament and Under-secretary of Commerce in the coalition government (1919); Dr. Arnold Eisler, Social Democrat and Secretary of Justice in 1919; Dr. Fritz Adler, son of the former leader of the Social Democratic Party; Dr. Victor Adler; Hugo Breitner, former Treasurer of the City of Vienna; and Allina, member of the Austrian Parliament (London).

Journalists included Dr. Schiller Marmorek, former editor of the Arbeiterzeitung, organ of the Austrian Social Democrat Party; Dr. Braunthal; Dr. Lippe; Dr. Leo Frischauer, (New York) and Mr. Loewenstein, one of the owners of Neue Wiener Journal.

Financiers include Louis de Rothschild, former president of the Kreditanstalt, (Canada); Alexander Weiner, vice-president of the Wiener Bankverein and later of the Kreditanstalt and the Bankverein; Dr. Max Sokal, former manager of the Giround Kassenverein in Vienna; Milan Reitler, banker; Paul Friedenstein, banker.

Physicians include: Prof. Glaessner; Prof. Novak, Prof. Louis Adler, Prof. Borak, Prof. Schaerf, Prof. Gottwald Schwarz (X-ray); Prof. Maurice Oppenheim (Chicago). Prof. Robert Bachrach; Prof. Porges (Chicago); Prof. Maximilian Weinberger (Chicago); Victor Blum (Chicago).

Leaders Remaining in Austria.

It may be assumed that all leaders and influential persons in the Jewish communities of Austria either left the country, were deported to Poland or Czechoslovakia, or died. It is reported that the last director of the Jewish Community of Vienna, Dr. Joseph Loewenherz, and his deputy, Dr. Murmelstein, a rabbi, were deported - Loewenherz to Terezin, Murmelstein to an unknown destination. In 1942, there were still in Vienna Dr. Ernst Felsberg, a member of the Board of the Jewish Community, who was in charge of the Jewish funerals and burials, and Weiger, also a member of the Board of the Jewish Community. The last president of the Jewish Community of Vienna, Dr. Desider Friedmann, and the deputy-chairman of the Community, Robert Stricker, were presumably in Terezin.

Groups in Exile.

There is an Austrian Jewish Council in New York, a section of the American Jewish Congress, consisting almost entirely of Zionists. It is closely connected with a group of Jewish Austrian War Veterans of the First World War, under the leadership of Mr. Stiassny. Members of the liberal and conservative group of Austrian Jews, the Union of Austrian Jews, have no separate representative in the United States, but are frequently members of the different non-sectarian Austrian groups, such as Austrian Action, Free Austrian Movement, American Federation of Austrian Democrats, the Austrian Labor Committee, and others.

The same is true in other countries. There are many Jews in the Austrian League, the Austrian Free Movement, and the Austrian Office in London. There are Austrian Unions or Free Austrian movements in Egypt, South Africa, Chile, Paraguay and elsewhere.

Reconstruction Agencies.

Among the reconstruction agencies which may aid in the rehabilitation of the Jewish population of Austria are the American Jewish Joint Distribution Committee, the American-Joint Reconstruction Foundation, the HICEM (Hias-Ica Emigration Association), the ORT Society for the promotion of trade and agriculture among Jews, the OSE World Union for health protection and the Jewish Agency for Palestine.

THE JEWS OF BELGIUM

THE JEWS OF BELGIUM

- INDEX -

Agencies
   Of Control, Nazi 10
   Of Reconstruction 16
Agriculture 9
Anti-Semitism
   History of 6
   Journals 6
   Movements 6
"Aryanization" 9
Attitude, of Jews,
   To Government. 5
   To United States 5
   To War 4

Badges 11
Banking 8
Bar 8
Births 13
Burial 3

Church 7
Citizenship 5
Commerce 9
Communications 12
Concentration Camps 12
Cooperatives 10
Criminality. 3
Community
   Assets 2
   Organizations 2
   Religious 2
Curfew 12

Discriminations, "Legal" 5
Divorce. 3

Education. 14
Employment 9

Family 3
Fines 11
Forced Labor 9

Government in Exile
   Attitude of. 6
   Attitude to. 5
Government, Posts. 6
   Judiciary 8

Groups, Communal 3

Health Services 13
Hospitals 13

Identification 11
Industry 9
Insurance 8

Languages 4
Leaders
   In Belgium 15
   In Exile 16

Marriages 3
Mortality 13
Motion Pictures. 10

Occupational Structure 8
Organizations
   Communal 2
   In Exile 15

Patriotism 4
People, Attitude of 7
Physicians 13
Police 11
Population 1
Press
   Anti-Semitic and Quisling. 6
   General 10
   Jewish 10

Rationing. 12
Refugees 1
Restrictions
   Travel 11
   Other 12

Social Workers 16

Taxes 11

Unions 10

Welfare
   Child. 15
   Public 15

THE JEWS OF BELGIUM

Population; Refugees

No official statistics on religious affiliation are available for Belgium. The figures here presented for the Jewish population are only estimates, though sober and given by persons well acquainted with the situation.

Exclusive of about 25,000 Jewish refugees arrived since 1933, there were some 55,000 to 70,000 Jews in Belgium when the Germans overran it. It is probable that the more nearly correct figure is 70,000, making a total, including post-1933 refugees, of 95,000. The population of Belgium being 8,386,000, Jews were about 1% of the total.

On the basis of nationality and citizenship, they may be classed as follows, with the caution that these figures are probably not very reliable at all: 15,000 Belgian citizens; 40,000 Stateless, mostly refugees from Russia after the First World War and Poles who had lost their Polish citizenship for having been out of Poland for some length of time; 25,000 Polish, Roumanian, French, Dutch or various other nationalities; 15,000 German Jews (of the approximately 25,000 post-1933 refugees from Germany, only about 15,000 were German Jews, the others being Polish, Roumanian, etc.).

Actually it is estimated that about 30,000 refugees had found refuge in Belgium between 1933 and 1940; but since about 5,000 had left Belgium for other destinations before May 1940, only some 25,000 were left at the time of the invasion.

The following are Jewish and general population data for important cities:

City	Population	Jewish population	Percentage
Antwerp and suburbs	about 600,000	45,000	7.5%
Brussels and suburbs	912,000	30,000	3.3%
Charleroi	27,300	7,000	25.6%
Liége	162,000	5,000	3.1%
Ghent	163,000	400	.25%

About 12,000 Jews managed to escape from Belgium: to the U.S., about 3,500; France, 3,000; South America (mainly Brazil and Argentina), 2,000; Cuba, 1,000; Great Britain (exclusive of a large number of soldiers serving in the Belgian Army), 500; Palestine and elsewhere, 2,000.

Between June 1942 and June 1943 the very great majority of the foreign Jews in Belgium were deported by the Germans to concentration camps and areas in Poland and German-held Ukraine. Of those remaining, most of the former Antwerp residents were compelled to leave their city. Only a few Jews were still living in Brussels. Some still lived in Charleroi, but practically none in Ghent and Liége. Many are in hiding from the Germans to escape deportation.

Religious and Community Organization

Most Belgian Jews were not very observant. On Passover, however, Rosh Hashanah (New Year) and Yom Kippur (Day of Atonement) the synagogues were crowded. On Yom Kippur practically no Jews worked. For obvious reasons, Jewish religious ceremonies are not now celebrated in public.

Since the independence of Belgium, in 1830, Jews have been authorized to have their own communal organization, with a central consistory (Consistoire Central) and chief rabbinate in Brussels. In 1873 state subvention, originally for the Catholic Church alone, was extended to the Jews. The Belgian community was then divided into five groups, on a geographical basis, each with its conseil d'administration (administrative council), in addition to the central consistory in Brussels. The règlement du Consistoire (consistorial regulation) of April 24, 1892, provided that the Central Consistory was to direct the affairs of the Belgian Jewish community, and was to be composed of the Chief Rabbi and lay delegates from the communities. In 1940, these lay delegates included six from Brussels, three from Antwerp, and one each from Arlon, Ghent, Charleroi and Liége. Individual membership in the Jewish community was entirely voluntary. The government allowed Shehitah (ritual slaughter).

The Jewish congregations in Belgium were either Orthodox or Conservative. The former increased in influence after the First World War as a result of the immigration of Orthodox Jews from Eastern Europe.

Rabbinical influence varied with the degree of esteem and respect in which each rabbi was held. His advice was not infrequently sought in personal matters. More rarely the rabbi was asked to serve as an arbiter among Jews in matters that would ordinarily have been taken to court. Such arbitration is known as a Din Torah (judgment according to Jewish religious law).

Judaism has always emphasized the obligations of patriotism and obedience to the lawful government. This was particularly true in Belgium, a country with a long tradition of complete tolerance.

Community Assets.

The wealth of synagogues and community institutions varied with the wealth of the communities. Some of the institutions in Brussels and Antwerp were rather richly endowed for purposes of charitable work. In Brussels the richest synagogue was that of the rue de la Régence; in Antwerp the two richest were the Hollandsche Synagogue and the Sephardic Synagogue on Hovenierstraat.

The assets of all Jewish organizations were frozen by the Germans; whether they have been confiscated is not yet known. Shehita was prohibited on October 27, 1940. On November 25, 1941 the Germans replaced the Consistoire Central by the Associations des Juifs en Belgique (Association of Jews in Belgium); unlike the Consistoire, this organization is not religious in character, and includes "non-Aryan" Christians as well as Jews. The Germans assigned to it the task of supervising compulsory registration.

COMMUNAL GROUPS.

The best organized and most influential group among the Jews of Belgium was the Zionist party. It had some 5,000 active adherents; Numa Torczyner was president. The Agudath Israel, an extreme Orthodox group, under the presidency of Mendel Haber, had some members in Belgium. Maccabi (Maccabaean) was a youth organization devoted to sports and social activities, with a Zionist ideology. It had about 6,000 members. Under the Germans, all Jewish institutions and organizations have been suppressed except the German-created Association des Juifs en Belgique.

FAMILY.

In general the Jews of Belgium were well adjusted to Belgian life, and their family relationships were much the same as among the general population. It is to be remarked, however, that family ties were rather stronger among the Jews than among other Belgians. Examples are the lesser extent of divorce among them -- though most Belgians are Catholic and consequently inhibited against divorce by their religion -- and the common support of aged or poor relatives.

Specifically Jewish tradition did tend to keep the authority of the father on a somewhat higher level than among non-Jews. Jewish women enjoyed the same independence and freedom from male domination as among the rest of the Belgian population.

MARRIAGE AND DIVORCE; BURIAL

Civil marriage was obligatory in Belgium; it might optionally be followed by a religious ceremony. A large proportion of marriages entered into by Jews were solemnized by rabbis. Under German occupation religious marriage, like other Jewish religious ceremonies, is not celebrated, except perhaps privately.

Like marriage, divorce in Belgium was a civil matter, which might optionally be followed by a religious divorce. It is believed that only few divorces obtained civilly between Jews were later confirmed by a rabbi according to Jewish religious law.

Jews were not permitted in Belgium to have cemeteries exclusively their own. Their dead were usually buried in the common cemeteries; frequently fairly large plots were acquired for the burial of Jews in one area of the cemetery. Observant Jews in Belgium had their dead buried in Holland, especially in the border town of Putte.

CRIMINALITY

The Jewish crime rate was low. Murder was practically unknown, and Jews seldom were charged with crimes of violence or theft. Most of the offenses with which Belgian Jews were charged were of a civil nature. Even in this category, however, M. Delanois, the statistician of the Belgian Ministry of Justice, estimated that the Jewish crime rate was lower than the general rate. After 1933 newly arrived refugees not uncommonly had trouble with the police in connection with residence permits.

LANGUAGES

According to the region in which they lived, the Jews of Belgium spoke French or Flemish. French was spoken by the Jews of Brussels, Liége and Charleroi, Flemish by those of Antwerp and Ghent. Even in these Flemish cities, however, many Jews, particularly those of the middle and upper classes, preferred French, as a language of greater international use, culture and prestige. Until 1919 many Antwerp Jews used to send their children to French schools in Brussels. In that year a law was passed requiring Antwerp children to attend the local schools.

In Brussels, Liége, Charleroi, Ghent, and especially Antwerp, Yiddish was spoken among Polish and Russian Jewish immigrants. Antwerp especially had a high proportion of such immigrants. In general, Yiddish was spoken by the older generation among the immigrant working and lower-middle classes. A smaller number of these immigrants spoke Polish or Russian. German refugees continued to speak German, though many tried to master French.

Patriotism

During the First World War, when the Belgian Army consisted mainly of volunteers, a great number of Belgian and foreign Jews enlisted; more than 200 were awarded military honors. One of the six army divisions was under the command of General Berheim, a Jew. In the Second World War, military service was compulsory, and Jewish as well as non-Jewish Belgian citizens were drafted. A majority of the male Jewish refugees in Belgium at the outbreak of the war tried to enlist, but it was finally decided not to accept foreigners. Among the Jews in the army held prisoner in Germany was General Wiener, head of the Corps of Engineers and former director of the Military Academy.

Jews were prominent in advancing the cultural life of Belgium, and were noted as benefactors of museums, libraries and universities. Among those known for these activities were Paul and Léo Errera, Franz Philippson, Baron Léon Lambert de Rothschild, Baron Cassel and Ambassador May.

Despite their conspicuousness, Jews remaining in Belgium after the deportations participated in all phases of underground work. Several have been reported shot by the Germans for underground activity.

Attitude to the War

The Jews of and in Belgium, like all other Jews, fervently desire a United Nations victory.

Before the war Belgian Jews very naturally were strongly anti-Nazi. Nevertheless they did not act so as to jeopardize Belgium's neutrality before she was invaded. The participation of Jews in Belgian military and underground activity against the Germans has been high. The number of Jews in the Belgian army stationed in Great Britain or training in Canada is a high proportion of those males of military age who managed to escape. The belgian government has the support of the Belgian Jews.

Attitude to the United States

As democrats Belgian Jews are unanimous in their admiration and respect for the United States. They know that America's military and industrial might will hasten the liberation of their country, and that America will probably have an important role in Belgian postwar reconstruction.

A number of the Jews from Belgium who have found refuge in this country will probably desire to remain permanently.

Nazi Legal Discriminations - General Remarks

Jews were obliged to register as such and to declare their property.

They were barred from the civil service, the bar and teaching. They were forbidden the free choice of residence; they were hampered in their traveling; they had to observe a special curfew. Ritual slaughter of meat animals was forbidden. Foreign-born Jews were compelled to prepare to return to their countries of origin at the end of 1941. All their property and belongings were turned over to a Jewish corporation under German supervision. This corporation had to be set up by Jews and to assume responsibility for property turned over. It served as a sort of central clearing house to facilitate German expropriation of Jewish property en masse. Foreign Jews, especially Poles, even though naturalized and with Belgian-born children, were deported to the East, particularly Poland.

The above describes only "legal" discriminations, and does not include all even in that category. In addition, Jews are constantly subjected to all kinds of harrassment and vexations. Whenever the occupation authorities encounter difficulties, Jews are the first to suffer reprisals. Violence can be committed against them by Germans almost with impunity. There are not unusual occurrences such as that in March 1943, when German soldiers broke into a Brussels synagogue, threatened to shoot the caretaker if he resisted, and put fire to the building.

Citizenship

Jewish citizens of Belgium enjoyed full citizenship privileges. Of those who were naturalized citizens, however, about 75% had received the "small" naturalization, which allowed them to work in municipal elections, but not to vote in national elections or to hold elective office. "Full" naturalization was granted by the Belgian government only to outstanding immigrants, and required a longer period of residence. Until 1932, the residence required for small naturalization was five years, and for full, ten years; after 1932, each waiting period was increased by five years.

Foreigners were given cartes d'identité d'étrangers (foreigners' identity cards) by the various municipalities. At the time of the German invasion an estimated 40,000 stateless Jews were living in Belgium. They had "Nansen passports" delivered by the Belgian Foreign Office, which also granted them special passports.

Under German occupation the stateless and foreign Jews have been deported to Poland and the Ukraine.

Government Posts

Several Jews had been members of Parliament and the Senate at various times. There was none in either house at the outbreak of the war. Paul May had served as ambassador to the United States.

Jews occasionally held high municipal posts. Léo Errera was for a number of years mayor of the township of Uccle (in Brussels).

Though there was no discrimination in the Civil Service before the invasion, few Jews entered it. After the invasion, a decree issued in September 1941 required that applicants for Civil Service posts produce a certificate showing that they were not registered as Jews.

Government-in-Exile

The attitude of the government-in-exile has been that all legislation and acts since the German invasion discriminating against Jews are illegal and will be voided with the coming to power again of a legitimate government. Cooperation with the Germans in persecuting and plundering the Jews will be considered acts of treason against the Belgian state. Property taken from Jews illegally or by force is to be restored to the rightful owners.

History of Anti-Semitism; Anti-Semitic Movements and Journals

The "Jewish question" can be said to have hardly existed in Belgium before the invasion. There was neither legal nor social discrimination, of the type seen in "restricted" hotels and clubs. The Belgians were by and large completely indifferent to the religious affiliations of their friends, neighbors or business acquaintances. There was no prejudice to prevent a Jew from occupying a post for which he was fitted: a Jewish general (Ernest Wiener) headed the Military Academy and was president of the Central Jewish Consistory of Belgium; a Belgian ambassador to the United States (May) was Jewish.

In the years following 1933, sections of the Belgian middle class tried to restrain competition by foreign Jews. In 1933 they succeeded in having a law passed regulating and limiting peddling in open markets, an occupation engaged in preponderantly by Jews, mostly those of foreign birth. There were also middle-class complaints about the competition of foreign Jews in other fields. These middle-class reactions were not specifically anti-Semitic, however; they were primarily concerned with minimizing competition, not with harassing Jews.

In 1939, when economic conditions compelled the restriction of the hitherto generous immigration facilities for refugees, the Belgian Government appropriated 6,000,000 francs for the care and vocational retraining of refugees already within Belgium; in 1940, 8,000,000 francs were appropriated for the same purpose. No other country had taken such measures.

Anti-Semitism as a political movement and slogan was confined exclusively to pro-Nazi organizations which served as pre-war fifth columns and provided the post-invasion Quislings. Foremost among these organizations was Léon Degrelle's Rexist Party. The Rexists published the French-language Le pays réel, of which Serge Doring, a White Russian by origin, is now one of the chief writers. Baron d'Oloneel de Heerdrinck's Volksverwering (Defense of the People) movement published a Flemish-language paper of the same name. Volk en Staat and National Socialiste Volk en Vaderland were two other Flemish-language anti-Semitic and fifth-column newspapers; the second of these two was published in Holland. Since German occupation the following have appeared: Volksaanval, a Flemish weekly published in Antwerp, of which the leading collaborators are Sagroux, Lambricht, J. Timmermans and J. Van de Wiele; Cassandre, a French weekly published in Brussels, whose editor, the brilliant traitor Paul Colin, was killed by patriots in the summer of 1943; and the French-language Nouveau Journal, published in Brussels, of whose staff Raymond de Baecker is the most important member.

As has been indicated above, the anti-Semitic movements did not have much influence among the Belgian people before the war. Their greatest appeal seemed to be to some relatively few members of the middle class, embittered and frustrated by economic hardships.

The friendship of the Belgian people for the Jews has been particularly marked since the German occupation. In Antwerp many non-Jews for a time wore the Star of David as a gesture of solidarity; the showing of anti-Semitic moving pictures is frequently disrupted by stink bombs thrown by patriots; since Jews are forbidden to carry packages on the street, their non-Jewish friends frequently carry packages for them; the Belgian Secours d'hiver (Winter relief) sometimes gives priority to the feeding of Jewish children, feeling that they have even less than non-Jews; Jewish children are often cared for by non-Jewish families; and many Jews have been hidden by their non-Jewish friends from the Germans seeking them for deportation.

Catholic Church and the Jews

The Catholic clergy in Belgium were friendly to the Jews. On the holiday of Simhath Torah (Rejoicing of the Law), the Antwerp Cathedral chimes played Hatikvah (Hope), the Jewish anthem, as an expression of good will. After the invasion the Catholic clergy interceded where it could on behalf of the Jews. At the request of Rabbi Brod of Antwerp, Cardinal van Roey, Primate of Belgium, tried to plead with the German authorities against the deportation of foreign Jews, but to no avail. Many Jews have been helped to escape by priests, or hidden in Church buildings or institutions.

Occupational Structure

A large proportion of Belgian Jews were engaged in the diamond, fur, leather and textile industries. Most of these were workers for wages and salaries, but many were independent artisans and craftsmen. Aside from these occupations, there was considerable participation by Jews in the liberal and white-collar professions and in commerce. After the invasion Jews were practically entirely eliminated from the economic life of Belgium.

The Judiciary

Few Jews served as judges in Belgium, despite the entire absence of discrimination against them. In the 1930's one judge of the Brussels Court of Justice, Mr. Busch, was Jewish.

The Bar

Until late in the 1930's there was no discrimination against Jews in the Belgian Bar. Then the presence of an increasing number of foreign-born Jewish lawyers in Antwerp began to irritate certain factions. In 1939 the Union of Flemish Lawyers and Jurists, a body without official standing, and comprising only a part of the Flemish-speaking lawyers, voted to exclude Jews.

In November 1940 Jews were forbidden by the Germans to practice law. The Brussels Bar Association, to prevent the ousting of Jewish members, did not continue its practice of periodic revision of membership lists.

Few Jews were notaries. A candidate for a notary's office, lucrative and sought after in Belgium, was named by the King after nomination by the notary he was to succeed. In most cases the nominee was a member of the incumbent's family. Since this had been the custom for generations, few Jews had entered this profession.

Banking

The following were the banks owned or controlled by Jews: F. M. Philippson and Co., Lambert and Co., and Cassel and Co.

Jews who left Belgium after the invasion could not withdraw funds from bank deposits by proxy. Those who remained were allowed to draw monthly only the interest on 10% of the amount on deposit. Safe deposit boxes had to be opened in the presence of Nazi authorities. Foreign currency and gold were confiscated and compensated for at the pre-war rate. After July 1941 banks might no longer accept deposits from Jews, who had to declare foreign exchange and transfer holdings to the National Bank.

Insurance

After the invasion Jews were barred from receiving payment on insurance policies and were ousted from the insurance business.

Agriculture

There were few Jews engaged in agriculture in independent Belgium; those few were affected exactly as all other farmers by government policy with respect to subsidies and the like. A decree of the German occupation forces, dated May 31, 1941, provided for the registration of all Jewish farm and horticultural properties for the purposes of liquidation.

Industry

The diamond industry engaged about 30,000 Jews in Belgium. About 60% of its capital was invested by Jews, and 50% of the employees were Jewish. Jews also actively participated in the fur, textile and leather industries. Under German occupation Jews are no longer active in the industrial life of Belgium.

Commerce

The participation of Jews in domestic commerce was very important. Jews owned several of the largest department stores and a good percentage of retail stores in the chief cities. Measures restricting the activity of peddlers affected Jews engaged in peddling, mostly immigrants. As has been explained, this was primarily a commercial, not an anti-Semitic, measure. In the field of foreign trade, Jews owned a number of export and import firms. Under German rule the Jews have been eliminated from commerce, domestic and foreign. Firms have been abolished or "aryanized."

"Aryanization"

All enterprises owned by Jews were required, after the invasion, to carry placards and stationery seals reading - in German, French and Flemish - "Jewish enterprise": Jüdisches Unternehmen; Entreprise juive; Joosche Ondernemming. Liquidation was instituted late in 1941; administrators (Verwalter-Commissaires) were put at the head of the enterprises and the Jewish owners ousted. Some firms were transferred to "Aryan" ownership with the permission of the occupying authorities.

Employment; Forced Labor

In independent Belgium there was no employment discrimination of any kind against Jews.

After the invasion almost all Jews were thrown out of their jobs. A special labor camp was opened for unemployed Jews on October 1, 1941, at Tervueren, near Brussels; here they were put to forced labor, working 13 hours a day. An order issued in the spring of 1942 provided that Jews must accept any job to which they were directed by the labor exchange. At the end of May 1942 the National Labor Offices in Antwerp and Brussels ordered all Jewish males over the age of 16 into the German Todt organization. Exceptions were made only for fur workers employed by non-Jewish firms working on German army contracts.

Many Jews were deported for work in German factories; those in labor camps and the Todt organization do extremely heavy road-building, drainage, construction and fortification work, mostly in Belgium or Northern France. Little regard is had for training, aptitude or physical fitness. The hardest tasks are assigned to Jews.

Jewish women have been forced into Liége armament plants, where they receive 16 francs (about 50 cents) for an eight-hour day, with no pay for overtime.

Labor Unions; Cooperatives

Before the war Jews belonged either to the Socialist unions affiliated with the Confédération générale du travail (General Confederation of Labor), with a membership of 570,000, or to the Liberal unions affiliated with the Fédération des syndicats libéraux (Federation of Liberal Unions), membership 59,000. Few Jews, naturally, belonged to the specifically Christian Trade Union Association, with a membership of 350,000. The attitude of all three with respect to Jewish workers was excellent. There were no specifically Jewish trade unions; unsuccessful attempts in this direction had been made among tailors in Antwerp.

Belgian cooperatives and labor banks were open to Jews exactly on the same conditions as to all Belgians. There were no Jewish cooperatives, but a Jewish loan bank, Ivria, organized on a semi-cooperative basis and giving small loans, functioned in Brussels during the last few years before the war.

The Press

As far as the general Belgian press is concerned, no daily or weekly paper of any importance was owned by Jews.

In Antwerp there were two Jewish weeklies: Die Presse (The Press), in Yiddish, and Hatikvah (Hebrew: Hope), in French. L'Avenir Juif (The Jewish Future), in French, was published in Brussels and Antwerp. Jewish publications were suspended by the Germans, and their printing-presses and other properties confiscated. No publications for Jews are at present allowed in Belgium.

Motion Pictures

There was no production of moving pictures to speak of in Belgium. Many of the moving-picture theaters were owned by chains, mostly foreign. Some independent motion-picture theaters, however, were owned by Jews, especially in the larger towns - Brussels, Antwerp, Liége, Tournai - and the Littoral (Seashore) - Ostend, Blankenberghe, etc. Under German occupation Jews have been ousted completely.

Nazi Agencies of Control

Under German occupation, all anti-Jewish decrees were issued by General Baron Alexander von Falkenhausen, the German military commander for Belgium, and executed by the Gestapo section for Jewish affairs in Belgium.

Police

In independent Belgium Jews were free to enter the police force on the same terms as any other Belgians. Few Jews, however, chose a police career.

In occupied Belgium there is no special police force of Jews within the Jewish community. The Gestapo headquarters in Brussels has a special department in charge of Jewish affairs which enforces all anti-Jewish measures. Its authority, scope and means of enforcement are practically limitless. Gestapo Obersturmfuehrer Bueger, a special emissary of Himmler, supervised deportation. The personnel of the Jewish section of the Gestapo in Belgium consists largely of Germans, with some Flemish Quislings. The rank and file have been trained in hatred and ruthlessness; many of the superior officers are experts in Jewish affairs and have a good knowledge, for example, of the specifically Jewish languages, Hebrew and Yiddish. Many instances of graft and corruption have been reliably reported. Gestapo men have accepted and solicited bribes for smuggling Jews out of Belgium or for extending help in other emergencies. The members of the Jewish section of the Gestapo wear civilian clothes. They wear swastika insignia in their lapel buttonholes, and most of them wear high black boots. They are armed with pistols.

Taxes and Fines

In independent Belgium there were no special taxes that had to be paid by Jews. Under German occupation, every anti-Semitic decree provides for special fines in the event of infringement. The Germans did not institute special taxes as such on the Jews, but the Association des Juifs en Belgique was charged by the Germans with responsibility for collecting taxes from the remaining Jews.

Badges and Other Identification

After the invasion Jews were required to have their identity cards stamped in red ink with the French and Flemish equivalents of "Recorded in the Jewish Register, No._____" (Fr. - Inscrit an registre des juifs, n°.....; Flem. - Ingeschreven in het Jodenregister, n...). These stamps were to be affixed above the holder's photograph. Since the Belgian authorities were not very zealous either in affixing the stamps or in making them conspicuous, the Germans themselves added a large stamp, also in red ink, with the French and Flemish for Jew -- Juif - Jood.

When the wearing of the yellow Star of David was imposed on the Jews of Antwerp, they were also required to have their papers stamped with a Star of David.

Travel and Other Restrictions

Since the fall of 1940 exit visas to cross the Belgian border have not been granted to Belgian Jews, even to those with entry visas for other countries. Jews may not own any motor or animal-drawn vehicle. In the towns of their residence they may use busses and trolleys, but the German law compels them to stand. (Friends and patriots often give up their seats for them as a gesture of solidarity and sympathy.) Jews are required to have a special permit in traveling from one town to another. They may travel on railroads only from and to large towns and after obtaining special permits. Airplane travel has been suspended in Belgium for all, as has travel on canals.

In towns where Jews are allowed to reside they are forbidden to enter cinemas, theaters, restaurants, etc.; in Antwerp they may not "loiter" in streets and public places or enter public parks and baths.

Communications and Curfew

All radio sets belonging to Jews were confiscated by the Germans. Jews may not use the telephone or telegraph. Curfew is from 8 P.M. to 7 A.M., during which hours they may not venture outside their homes.

Rationing

The Jews remaining in Belgium are in general allowed about half, frequently less, of the rations provided for the general population. Their bread allowance is 29% of the standard Belgian allowance. The percentages of required basic nutrients actually received in Belgium by the average Jew were: Carbohydrates, 27%; Protein, 20%; Fats, 0.32%. The deficiency in fats is particularly to be noted.

The average Jew, at the beginning of 1943, received about 20% of his normal pre-war caloric consumption, and about 21% of German caloric consumption during the war.

Kashrut (religious regulation of food, e.g., kosher meat, shehitah [ritual slaughter], injunction against eating meat and dairy products together, use of separate vessels in their preparation and serving) was observed before the war by a portion of the Jews in Belgium. Any strict observance of kashrut is almost impossible under the conditions of German occupation. The food situation of the Jews is made worse by their having to buy food only at certain (disadvantageous) hours and in certain (few) shops; they consequently often do not receive even the meager rations which they are theoretically allowed.

During 1942 the Germans dismissed eight mayors from their posts because of their failure to enforce Nazi food regulations for Jews.

Concentration Camps

One of the chief concentration camps in Belgium is the former fort at Breendonck, between Brussels and Antwerp. A great number of Jews of every condition and occupation were interned here. Conditions are like those of the worst concentration camps in Germany: sadism, undernourishment, brutally hard work for long hours, entire lack of medical care, etc. It is run by the Gestapo.

Prisoners are divided into two "sections": Jewish and non-Jewish. Jews wear yellow patches sewn to the front and back of their uniforms. Prisoners of the two sections are not allowed to work together or otherwise to associate.

Hospital and Medical Services; Health

In independent Belgium there were no Jewish hospitals. Jewish patients went to the general hospitals; those who wanted kosher food had it provided for them by the Jewish community. In 1938, following an increase in the number of refugees, a project was started to build a Jewish hospital in Antwerp; nothing came of it. In Antwerp there was a Jewish clinic, headed by Dr. Pruczansky.

Before the war there were about 30 Jewish physicians in Belgium, 15 dentists, a few nurses, and no veterinarians. Several Jewish physicians taught at Brussels University Medical School; Dr. Charles Cohen and Dr. Oscar Weil were heads of departments. By the time the Germans had completed their occupation of Belgium, most of the Jewish physicians and dentists had left. Those remaining are not allowed to practise.

In pre-war Belgium the health of the Jews was much like that of the rest of the population. The tuberculosis rate among Jews, however, was higher than the general rate. This higher rate was to be attributed to several factors: the almost exclusively urban residence of the Jews; the crowded quarters occupied by many poor workers; the unsatisfactory condition of many of the shops in which Jewish workers were employed. On the other hand, the tuberculosis death-rate among Jews was lower than among non-Jews, because Jews, having cause to fear tuberculosis, tended to be alert for its appearance and to seek medical help in time.

Under German occupation, tuberculosis, scurvy, rickets, anemia, dermatosis, edema and eye infections have become prevalent. In particular, the incidence of tuberculosis among Jews is startling. In the first year of German occupation the Jewish tuberculosis rate was double the pre-war rate; in 1942, it was triple. A new clinical form of acute bilateral pulmonary tuberculosis, characterized as being very deadly, has been reported among adolescents.

The health of the Jews in Belgium has deteriorated sharply as the result of very definite causes. Starvation diets have led to an average loss of weight in the Jewish adult of 16 to 45 pounds, and a hemoglobin content in the blood 25% to 35% below normal. The fact that many, if not most, live in hiding to escape imprisonment, forced labor or deportation, renders sanitation problems acute. Rejection of food because of inferior quality or actual danger to health is not practiced when food allowances are so drastically below requirements. The complete lack of medical help for Jews -- physician's attention, medicine, supplies, vaccination, etc. -- removes whatever possibility of help medical attention might offer.

Birth and Mortality

It is impossible to give a close statistical comparison of birth and death rates among the Jews of Belgium before and after invasion because of the absence of specifically Jewish statistics. In 1939, the general birth rate was 1.65%; in 1941, 0.9%. This means a decline of more than 45% in two years; it is altogether likely that the decline in the Jewish birth rate was very much greater, perhaps approaching disappearance.

It is estimated that the mortality of Jews in German-occupied Belgium is about 3%. Mortality among pre-school Jewish children is reported 4 times greater than before the invasion, especially as a result of bronchial pneumonia. Since the invasion (May 1940) many Jews have died in Belgium from violent causes. It is impossible to say how many Jews deported from Belgium have died.

No measures for the sterilization of Jews are reported.

Education

There were three types of school in Belgium: the official school, conducted by the government; the state-recognized private school, financed privately and subsidized by the government, its curriculum, methods, etc. having to be officially approved; the private school as such, entirely supported by private funds. The Jewish schools were of the second or third type. The government-approved and subsidized private Jewish school existed only in Antwerp, in both elementary and secondary educational institutions.

The majority of Jewish students attended official schools; there were only about 1,300 students and about 45 to 50 teachers in the Jewish schools of both types. There was no discrimination against students or teachers in the educational system of pre-war Belgium; the curriculum was entirely free of racist propaganda.

Except for Catholic institutions, Jewish teachers were to be found in all branches of the Belgian educational structure. Many of the most distinguished professors in the Brussels University, especially, were Jewish. They included: Jacques Errera, chemistry, 1938 winner of the biennial Francqui prize of about $20,000 for his research in molecular physics; Alfred Errera, mathematics; Herbert Speyer, colonial law, recently deceased; Serge Chlepner, public finance, now with the Brookings Institute; Max Gottschalk, research professor at the Institut de Sociologie Solvay of Brussels University, now with the American Jewish Committee, New York; Charles Cohen, recently deceased, and Oscar Weill, still in Brussels, medicine. Niko Gunsbourg, an expert in criminal law now in this country, was dean of the Faculty of Law at the University of Ghent.

Under German occupation Jewish teachers were dismissed from non-Jewish schools. In December 1941 a decree was issued limiting Jewish pupils to Jewish elementary schools. The total number of students studying in Jewish private schools consequently rose above the pre-war figure of 1300, and there should have been a proportionate rise in the number of Jewish teachers employed in these schools. Many, however, were deported, and it is probable that there are no more than about 60 teachers in the Jewish schools.

The Germans have attempted to prevent the teaching of love for democracy and liberty in the Belgian schools. The study of history has particularly been affected; all remarks considered unfavorable to Germany and to the Nazi system have had to be removed from text books. The study of National Socialist doctrine has been made compulsory.

Students are forbidden to display solidarity through such devices as wearing insignia. Teachers openly opposing Nazi measures are dismissed and frequently sent to concentration camps; nevertheless, with the exception of a few Quislings, Belgian teachers have been able to avoid teaching what the Germans would like taught. Brussels University remains closed, as a consequence of its students' and professors' opposition activity and sentiments.

The Jewish private schools have had their curriculum changed from what it was before the invasion by the compulsory addition of Yiddish.

Public Welfare and Social Security; Jewish Welfare

In independent Belgium there was no discrimination against Jews in the granting of social security payments and public assistance. Besides government institutions and private agencies, a number of specifically Jewish organizations extended help to Jews in need of it. Ezra (Hebrew: Aid), the chief Jewish philanthropic agency, was situated in Brussels and had an average annual income of 150,000 francs from individual contributions. It gave relief to Jews living in Brussels; one of its sections was active in child welfare, in conjunction with the government's Oeuvre nationale de l'Enfance (National Children's Aid). In Brussels there were also a Sociéte d'aide efficace (for loans to small merchants), an Assistance aux mères israélites (Society for Aid to Jewish Mothers), an Asyle des vieillards (Home for the Aged), a Maison de cure (Home for Tuberculars) and a Cuisine populaire (free kitchen). In Antwerp Jewish philanthropic activity was centralized in the Centrale israélite de bienfaisance (Central Administration for Jewish Philanthropy), with an annual budget of some 500,000 francs. Jewish relief organizations were also found in Liége and Arlon.

The following were some of the child welfare institutions: in Brussels, the Maurice de Hirsch Foundation (founded 1870) orphan asylum; in Antwerp, a Fresh Air Fund, a children's colony Altol in the suburbs, the Louis Landau orphanage for girls, and another for boys -- the Fresh Air Fund and two orphanages being affiliated with the Centrale israélite de bienfaisance; in Middlekerke, on the coast, a summer colony for school children, Villa Johanna (founded 1901), which annually received several hundred children, about 80% of them Jewish.

There were about 40 trained and skilled Jewish social workers in Belgium, working for government, private and Jewish organizations.

Groups in Exile

Jews from Belgium have formed no parties in exile; all of them give their support to the Belgian Government-in-Exile, in London. As regards Jewish affairs, some prominent Belgian Jews in New York are grouped in the Belgian section of the World Jewish Congress. As regards trade organizations, Belgians in the diamond industry have formed a club in New York, of which the membership is about 95% Jewish.

Jewish Leaders

The following are leaders in the Belgian Jewish community who remained in Belgium: Rabbi Salomon Ullman, formerly Jewish Chaplain in the Belgian Army, head of the Association des Juifs en Belgique until he was arrested; Marcel Blum, who succeeded him in the leadership of the <u>Association</u>; Messrs. Van Den Berg, Hellendael, A. Blum, and Benedictus; Rabbi M. Rottenberg of Antwerp, now reported in hiding in a convent; and Professor Alfred Errera, professor of sciences at Brussels University, deprived of his chair.

The following left Belgium: rabbis -- Joseph Wiener and Berman (France), Samuel Brot and J.M. Sagalowitch (New York), Israel Schapira (Cuba); industrialists -- Isidore Lipchutz, Charles Gutwirth, Numa Torczyner, Emile Bernheim (all in the U.S.A.); journalists -- Jexas (Sachs), Grégoire Koulicher, Betty Barzin; financiers -- David van Buuren, Jules Philippson; physicians -- Joseph Moldaver, Georges Kleefeld, Jules Boruchowitz, Pruczansky; professors in Belgian universities -- Serge Chlepner (Washington), Niko Gunsbourg and Max Gottschalk (New York).

Reconstruction Agencies

The principal Jewish organizations which may cooperate in reconstruction work in Belgium are: The American Jewish Joint Distribution Committee (New York); HICEM (Hias-Ica Emigration Association) (New York); and the Jewish Agency for Palestine. ORT (for vocational training) and OSE (for health and sanitation) may also be able to help.

THE JEWS OF BULGARIA

THE JEWS OF BULGARIA

Index

Anti-Semitism, History of 4
Church and the Jews, The 4
Citizenship 3
Concentration Camps 5
Cultural and Fraternal Life 2
Discriminatory Measures 4
Education 2
Identification Badges and other Restrictions 5
Jewish Community Organization 1
Occupational Structure 3
Population 1
Reconstruction Agencies 5

THE JEWS OF BULGARIA

Population.

In 1940, out of a population of 6,100,000, Bulgaria had about 55,000 Jews (0.9%). Of these, approximately 29,000 lived in Sofia (total population, 287,000), while the remainder were distributed in some 30 communities, the largest of which were Philippopolis (Plovdiv), Varna, Ruschuk and Vidin. About 45,000 of the total were Bulgarian citizens, 5,000 were aliens -- Turkish subjects, refugees from Germany and Austria, or Polish, Roumanian and Hungarian Jews -- and the balance had been added through the annexation of Dobrudja from Roumania in 1940. The Yugoslav and Greek territories subsequently added brought some 12,000 additional Jews under Bulgarian rule.

The German-inspired policy of deportations, inaugurated in Bulgarian territory in 1943, first affected the last-named 12,000 Jews, who were concentrated in five camps in Serbian Macedonia. By the end of March, 1943, about 2,000 had already been sent to Poland in sealed cattle-cars. On March 23, a Sofia announcement stated that 10,000 of an estimated 40,000 eventual Jewish deportees from Bulgaria had arrived in Germany for forced labor, with the proviso that further deportations would be directed to the eastern war front, for "army work near the fighting zones." Data regarding the success of this population clearance are unknown, except that during the same month a stay of the deportation of Jews who were Bulgarian citizens was announced by Premier Philoff, following protests by more than 100 liberal members of Parliament. Alexander Bjeleff, Commissioner for Jewish Affairs under the strongly anti-Jewish Minister of the Interior, Peter Gabrovski, resigned his office.

JEWISH COMMUNITY ORGANIZATION.

The Jewish community of Bulgaria obtained its first recognized right of organization by an ukase of 1880, investing the synagogue with strictly delimited rights as a juridical personality, represented by a Chief Rabbi. Emendations in 1900 and in 1920 granted the local communities the right to form a League of Jewish Religious Communities, represented by a Community Convention elected for a three-year term, which in turn appointed a Consistory patterned after the French model, to conduct inter-communal affairs. The Consistory was headed by a Chief Rabbi, and delegated a <u>Din Torah</u> (religious tribunal) for the settlement of controversies of a religious nature or of civil disagreements voluntarily brought before it. The chief tribunal sat in Sofia, lower tribunals in Sofia, Plovdiv and Roussa. Each court consisted of three rabbis and two lay members. Every community of more than 1,000 families was compelled to employ a rabbi. Local communities were entitled to levy direct community taxes. Only the Chief Rabbi received a salary from the government, although in other denominations all members of the clergy received such pay.

Despite the infiltration of many Ashkenazic (following the Polish or German ritual) Jews from Central Europe and Russia before the 17th century, the Sephardic Jews (following the Spanish or Portuguese ritual) became dominant. Modern Bulgarian Jewry was prevalently Sephardic.

Under the Nazis, Jewish religious and cultural life was disrupted by the dissolution of the Consistory, which was replaced by an administrative central organ under the Nazi Commissar of Jewish Affairs.

CULTURAL AND FRATERNAL LIFE.

The main language of most Bulgarian Jews was Ladino, or Judeo-Spanish, an archaic Castilian with a strong admixture of Hebrew, Turkish, Bulgarian and French words. Younger people of the present generation, however, used Bulgarian and some Hebrew (under Zionist influence). In the census of 1934, only two-fifths of the Jews gave Bulgarian as their mother tongue.

Cultural life, until the turn of the century, was in keeping with the generally backward level of the country; both secular and Jewish religious education were undeveloped. In the 1890's, the Alliance Israelite Universelle (Paris) established 14 modern Jewish elementary schools throughout Bulgaria, and later the system was expanded with the help of the Hilfsverein der deutschen Juden (Berlin). Eventually the schools were taken over by the local religious communities, under the supervision of the educational department of the Consistory.

The emergence of Zionism gave an impetus to further cultural development, and it was from Bulgaria that the Zionist influence spread to the other Balkan countries. Beginning with the 1880's, settlement in Palestine attracted the Jewish groups, and the Artuf colony in Palestine was founded by the Bulgarian Hovovei Zion group. At various times, about ten Jewish weeklies or monthlies, in Ladino, Bulgarian and French, all of Zionist orientation, had appeared. Immediately before the Hitler era, only one Jewish weekly was being published, and about 20 special organization bulletins. A publication society, Ivria, issued Jewish literature and textbooks. Several Jewish gymnastic societies were also under Zionist influence. There were a few B'nai B'rith lodges throughout the country.

Bulgarian Jews participated little in science, arts and letters. Except for violations of minor civil laws, their listing in crime was practically nil.

In 1941, all B'nai B'rith lodges were dissolved and their properties confiscated, Zionism was outlawed, Jewish papers and other publications were suppressed. Subsequently, Jewish life reached a complete standstill in Bulgaria.

EDUCATION.

Primary education was compulsory in Bulgaria, and free in the public schools; Jewish children could choose between public and Jewish schools. During the last few decades, there was no illiteracy among the Jews in Bulgaria, while as late as 1934, 20.4% of the general male population, and 42.8% of the general female population, were illiterate.

In 1939, the educational department of the Jewish Consistory supervised 15 kindergartens, 25 primary schools, 15 Sabbath schools and 5 lower gymnasiums (high schools), where more than 3,000 pupils of both sexes were in attendance. Government and municipal subsidies provided between 10% and 15% of the budgets. Under Nazi influence, the Jewish school system entered a process of dissolution, and many Jewish children were deprived of all educational opportunity. Although the anti-Jewish law of December 20, 1940, introduced a numerus clausus for all schools, a numerus nullus was actually in effect.

OCCUPATIONAL STRUCTURE.

In 1934, more than 80% of the gainfully employed general population was engaged in agriculture, mostly on small holdings of between one and six acres; 97% of the gainfully employed Jews, however, were classified as participating in occupations which were predominantly urban. There were no Jewish peasants, farmers, or farm workers. Industry was but little developed in Bulgaria; in 1931, there were 3,381 industrial undertakings in operation, largely of a small nature and including flour mills, weaving mills, cigarette and cigar factories, rose attar distilling plants, and a few mining enterprises. Altogether about 100 Jews derived a livelihood as industrial entrepreneurs, and these were small-scale operators. Government control of natural resources and other enterprises hindered the participation of Jews in investment banking, which was practically under government tutelage; only a few small money-exchange banks were owned by Jews.

No more than 600 Jews were in the liberal professions, including medicine, law and engineering. About 15% of the gainfully employed Jews (some 1,660) were engaged in manual labor, and 5% (about 560) in handicraft. Trade and commerce were the most hospitable fields of activity for the Jews, and about 75% of the gainfully employed, or 8,300, were thus engaged. However, the regimentation of foreign trade, beginning with the 1930's, served as an instrument for edging the Jews out here as well. Only about 0.7% of the Jewish population (less than 400) could have been called well-to-do; some 20% (11,000) were middle-class, and the rest were either poor workers, small traders, peddlers or paupers.

By July, 1941, only 761 out of a total of 4,272 Jewish enterprises of various categories were still functioning; later this number also disappeared almost entirely. In 1943, the Jews of Bulgaria were without any economic opportunity.

CITIZENSHIP.

After the Congress of Berlin (1878), both the First National Assembly of Bulgaria and the Organic Statute of the autonomous province of Rumelia (today an organic part of Bulgaria), carried the principle of full and equal citizenship into the constitution of the country. All Jewish inhabitants, therefore, unless expressly persevering in some foreign citizenship, automatically became citizens of Bulgaria. The anti-Jewish law (officially termed the Law for the Defense of the Nation) of December 20, 1940, barred Jews from Bulgarian citizenship and drastically curtailed their rights.

The prohibition of Jewish participation in public service contained in the law was merely a formal confirmation of a situation which had been long in existence, despite the stipulations of equality in the constitution.

HISTORY OF ANTI-SEMITISM.

Although according to the terms by which the principality of Bulgaria was created at the Congress of Berlin (1878), the Jews were granted actual civil and political rights on a constitutional basis, anti-Semitism nevertheless forced the gradual disappearance of Jews from public service and from public affairs. In contrast to the equality with which they had been treated under Turkish rule, in 1884 and 1890, the Jews were attacked in Sofia and Wratza under the pretext of ritual murder accusations; even more serious excesses occurred in 1895 in Pasardjik, in 1903 in Lom and in 1904 in Kustendil. Government discrimination remained constant despite the wholehearted participation of Jews in the many wars in which the country engaged. No Jew was made an official, teacher, judge, or admitted to any other public service. In 1939, with the exception of 20 Jews serving as panel physicians, there were no Jews in any kind of government or municipal service. There were no Jews serving as deputies, and except for one member in Sofia, no Jews on municipal councils.

Yet the situation was immeasurably worsened with the establishment of Nazi influence in the Balkans, after the fall of Austria in 1938. The agitation of Nazi-Fascist groups, such as the Army League <u>Rodna Zashtita</u> (Home Guard), and the <u>Ratnitzi</u>, assumed a violent anti-Jewish character. In 1939 the <u>Ratnitzi</u> conducted a strong economic boycott. The government compromised with these groups by ordering the expulsion of foreign Jews, including those whose ancestors had lived in the country for generations, and by manipulating the issuance of trade licenses and orders. Anti-Semitic factions derived their support from commercial and industrial interests, younger army officers and university students. The large peasant population, industrial workers and the intelligent remained generally sympathetic to the Jews.

THE CHURCH AND THE JEWS.

Although the dominant Greek Orthodox Church proved to be one of the decisive forces behind the reactionary trend, there is no evidence of the leading participation of the official Church in direct anti-Jewish activities. Many members of the lower clergy participated in reactionary and anti-Semitic groups. The Bulgarian Holy Synod formally denounced the anti-Jewish law on its adoption in December, 1940.

DISCRIMINATORY MEASURES.

The first anti-Jewish law was adopted on December 20, 1940. It barred Jews from citizenship, public office, army service, the ownership of rural property, the publication of newspapers, film production, intermarriage, and the employment of non-Jewish domestic servants. Jewish participation in commerce, industry, the professions and educational opportunities were limited to the population ratio. Forced labor for Bulgarian Jews was introduced. Jews were prohibited from residing in the capital, which had contained the largest Jewish population. Registration of property owned by Jews was ordered.

On January 31, 1941, the government announced that for six months no actual steps would be taken toward the execution of the law; this was a concession to liberal opinion. The subsequent fall of Yugoslavia and Greece, however, prevented further equivocation, and the measures were enforced, even beyond legality. Four concentration camps were established, and deportations inaugurated. In June, 1943, it was reported that 19,339 Jewish residents of Sofia had been deported to provincial concentration areas. The majority of the Jewish population may be assumed to have been living in these concentration areas toward the end of 1943.

Additional discriminatory measures which followed the execution of the primary law included: On July 16, 1941, the imposition of a special 20% levy on Jewish-owned property, and the prohibition of Shehitah (ritual slaughter); July 30, conscription of foreign Jews for forced labor; December 10, confiscation of Jewish-owned pharmacies; January 1, 1942, confiscation of Jewish-owned mining property; February 19, the forced sale to "Aryans" of Jewish-owned houses, unless used as personal residences, and the confiscation of stocks, bonds and insurance policies owned by Jews; April 19, confiscation of the total property of Jews residing abroad; December 15, the limitation of practising lawyers of Jewish descent to 21, physicians to 21, dentists to 7, chemists to 3 and architects to one -- all allowed to practice because they were either decorated war veterans or converts to Christianity.

IDENTIFICATION BADGES AND OTHER RESTRICTIONS.

Special identification cards for Jews were introduced on January 1, 1942; on August 28, 1942, Jews were ordered to wear a yellow Star of David on their sleeves (foreign Jews and war veterans were to wear red circles). In July, 1941, Jews were ordered to surrender their radios and telephones. On April 3, 1942, travel was forbidden to Jews. There were also special restrictions regarding marketing hours, Jews were barred from certain streets and from street cars, entry to places of amusement was forbidden, and there were extraordinary curfew limitations.

CONCENTRATION CAMPS.

The first concentration camps for Jews were set up in the occupied Serbian Macedonian areas. Later, with the expulsion of Bulgarian Jews from the capital, four concentration areas were established (February, 1943), to which more than 19,000 Jews were conveyed. They were allowed to take only small sums of money and not more than 50 pounds of luggage; the rest of their property was reported seized. In the concentration areas, the Jews were fed in Communal kitchens, subjected to military discipline and permitted to move about only during certain hours. The location of these areas could not be ascertained.

RECONSTRUCTION AGENCIES.

The foreign organizations which may aid in the reabilitation of the Bulgarian Jews are the American Joint Distribution Committee (New York): the American Joint Reconstruction Foundation (New York): the HICEM (Hias-Ica Emigration Association) (New York); the ORT Society for the promotion of trade and agriculture among Jews, the OSE World Union for Health protection and the Jewish Agency for Palestine.

THE JEWS OF CZECHOSLOVAKIA

THE JEWS OF CZECHOSLOVAKIA

Index

Agriculture	8	Industry	9
Anti-Semitic Parties	17	Insurance	8
"Aryanization"	9	Jewish Groups-in-Exile	28
Attitude of People towards Jews	17	Languages	4
After Occupation	18	Medical Practitioners	11
Background, Social and Cultural	3	Minorities	4
Banking	6	Mortality Rate	12
Bar, The	11	Municipal Posts	5
Birth Rate	12	Natural Resources	8
Christian Churches and the Jews	16	Political Activities	4
Citizenship	5	Population	1
Commerce, Foreign	9	Press	
Communal Organization		Anti-Semitic	19
Before the Occupation	2	General	16
After the Occupation	2	Jewish	16
Concentration Camps	27	Reconstruction Agencies	28
Cooperatives and Labor Banks	11	Social Security	12
Discriminatory Measures	21	Taxes	24
Basic Anti-Jewish Laws	20	Trade Unions	10
Economic Structure	5	Welfare, Child	15
Education	12	Welfare, Jewish	14
Fascist Parties and Leaders	19		
Government-in-Exile	28	Welfare, Public	13

THE JEWS OF CZECHOSLOVAKIA.

Population.

In 1930, there were in Bohemia, Moravia and Silesia 117,551 persons of the Jewish faith, and 136,737 in Slovakia, or a total of 254,288 out of a general population of 14,729,536 (1.7%). According to the census law of 1930, nationality was determined by the mother tongue of the parents. Jews, however, could declare themselves as belonging to the Jewish nationality regardless of the parental mother tongue. In Bohemia, Moravia and Silesia, 36,778 (31.3%) of the Jews declared Jewish nationality, 42,669 (36.7%) declared Czechoslovak nationality and 35,657 (30.3%) German nationality. In Slovakia, 72,644 (53.1%) declared themselves as being of Jewish nationality, 44,009 (32.1%) of Czechoslovak, 9,945 (7.3) of German and 9,728 (7.1%) of Magyar. More than 70,000 were transferred to Hungarian rule in the adjustments following the Munich pact (1938).

On October 1, 1939, a census taken in the Protectorate of Bohemia and Moravia showed that according to the Nazi specifications, there were 90,147 Jews, of whom 80,319 (89.1%) were of the Jewish faith and 9,828 (10.9%) were not. Of the 90,147 Jews, 64,488 (71.5%) were in Bohemia and 25,659 (28.5%) in Moravia. There were 131 Jewish communities in the Protectorate, 93 of which were in Bohemia and 38 in Moravia. Prague, with 46,170 Jews, constituted the largest community; Brno (Bruenn) had 9,726 and Moravská Ostrava 4,185. As under the Republic, Jews still remained concentrated in large communities; out of the 131 communities, 84 had fewer than 200 members.

In Slovakia, according to the 1940 census, 101,005 persons were adjudged to be Jews, on the basis of racial standards which were close to those of the Nazis. Of the total number, 88,951 were of the Jewish faith.

The 1930 census showed 93,341 Jews in Carpatho-Ruthenia, constituting 15.4% of the general population, or the highest percentage in Eastern Europe. Between 1921 and 1930 the Jewish population of Carpatho-Ruthenia increased by 10.25%.

Since 1939, the following changes may be assumed to have occurred in the Jewish population figures for the Protectorate:

```
Legal emigration (1939) . . . . . . . . . . . . . . .   1,000
    "         "     (1940) . . . . . . . . . . . . . . .  31,000
    "         "     (first five months of 1941) . . . .   7,000
Total legal emigration . . . . . . . . . . . . . . .    39,000

Unregistered emigration (1939-1941) . . . . . . . . .    8,000
Deportation (1939-1941) . . . . . . . . . . . . . . .   12,000
Deportation (first three months of 1942) . . . . . .     6,000
Total . . . . . . . . . . . . . . . . . . . . . . . .   26,000

Number of Jews in Protectorate on October 1, 1939 . . . 90,147
Total emigration and deportation . . . . . . . . . . .  65,000

Number of Jews in Protectorate in 1942 . . . . . . . .  25,000
```

The majority of the Jews who remained in the Protectorate in 1942 have since been sent to Terezin, once known as an internment camp for political prisoners and now designated as the final concentration center for Jews prior to deportation. The number of Jews in Slovakia in 1943 may be estimated to be 16,000. Carpatho-Ruthenia became part of Hungary in 1939.

Jewish Communal Organization: Before the Occupation.

There was no legal general regulation of Jewish community life; Jewish communal organization was entirely voluntary, as was the support of the educational and welfare institutions the community chose to maintain. But on the basis of the Congrua Law of 1926, the municipalities aided in the collection of taxes assessed by the community on those who declared themselves as being of the Jewish religion. The communities throughout the country were grouped in regional associations linked by language (German, Czech or Slovak), but all of them were somewhat under the guidance of the old Prague community. . There was a Supreme Council of Jewish Communities of Bohemia and Moravia, with headquarters in Prague. The other regional associations cooperated with it in matters of common interest. In Slovakia and Carpatho-Ruthenia, the original Orthodox and Congressional, or Neolog (Moderate Reform) communities survived.

Communal activities consisted mostly of religious and welfare work. In 1935, after the influx of refugees from Germany, the Prague Jewish Community founded the Jewish Welfare Institute, which had additional work to do when refugees from Austria, and later from the Sudeten area, poured into the city. The Prague community owned many valuable buildings, including the Alt-Neu Synagogue, the Jewish Council House, a museum, library and archives. It had considerable funds, part of which were earmarked for the construction of a Jewish hospital.

Jewish Communal Organization: After the Occupation.

Immediately after the occupation, the attack on the Jewish communities was instituted. The Jewish Council Hall in Prague was repeatedly raided by the Gestapo, searching for valuables and for lists of German and Austrian refugees. Officials and employees were cross-examined and arrested. The Jewish Welfare Institute was closed, but subsequently reopened at the behest of official Czech circles. The Prague Jewish Community was forbidden to grant relief to refugees; meetings of the executive were forbidden, and Dr. Erich Kafka, president, had to act entirely on his own initiative and responsibility.

With the inevitable decrease in the income of the community, even before occupation, and the increase of refugee relief demands, the American Jewish Joint Distribution Committee had to establish free kitchens, where thousands were fed, and to contribute $28,000 per month to the Prague Jewish Community during the time between the Munich Pact and the establishment of the Protectorate. At the same time, $10,000,000 was put at the disposal of the Prague Government by Great Britain for refugee aid.

At the end of August 1939 Gestapo Obersturmführer Fritz Eichmann, who was of Palestinian birth and knew Hebrew and Yiddish well, was sent to Prague, where he set up an office of Jewish immigration. The Jewish Community was called on to assist the Gestapo in matters of immigration, deportation, forced labor, and even in the presentation of data that facilitated the plunder of Jewish-owned property.

In the Protectorate, and particularly in the provinces, synagogues were ravaged, destroyed and burned. The synagogue in Uherské Hradiště was completely destroyed. Some Jewish communities, in order to save their synagogues from destruction, offered the buildings for use to the local municipalities, often without avail.

Synagogues provided a favorite weapon of propaganda for the Nazis. An article in the Czech Fascist <u>Vlajka</u> (Prague), on May 17, 1940, called synagogues the source of all evil, and stated that according to the percentage of the Prague population professing the Jewish faith (4.2%), there should be only two synagogues in the city. However, it generously suggested that four out of the nine existing ones might continue to serve as synagogues, and the others be converted into museums, galleries, used for storage of theatrical equipment, and as club houses containing permanent anti-Semitic exhibitions.

In October 1941 all Prague synagogues were reported closed. In the fall of 1942, the use of synagogues or houses of worship was forbidden everywhere, as were religious services even in private homes.

Social and Cultural Background.

The social and cultural structure of the Jewish population differed regionally. In the "Historic Lands" (Bohemia, Moravia and Silesia), it was akin to that of neighboring Austria, showing a high degree of assimilation of the local languages and culture (Czech or German) and upper-middle class social stratification. The Jewish population, as a rule, was better off economically, and on a higher cultural level, than the non-Jewish.

Observance of Jewish traditional rites was lax; in Prague where - before Munich - there were 70,000 Jews, half of whom declared themselves as being of Jewish nationality, there was only one butcher selling kosher meat. The meat had to be brought from Česká Třebora. Yom Kippur was observed by some people, but many stores owned by Jews remained open even on that day. Small groups of Orthodox Jews were found in Brno, Moravská-Ostrava and several other centers; they were mostly refugees from Poland who had entered Bohemia and Moravia during and after the First World War. But by far the greater part of the Jewish population could trace its ancestry in the region back many centuries. Ties with the population-at-large were very close; there was a high rate of intermarriage. In 1933, of all marriages in which Jews were a partner in Bohemia, 23% were mixed marriages; in Moravia-Silesia, 15%.

The Jews of Slovakia were subject to three major influences: Magyar, German, and Yiddish. The majority of the Magyar - and German - speaking Jews were in the larger cities; most of the Yiddish-speaking groups were in the smaller towns in the Northeastern part of the provinces. During the 20 years of Czechoslovak independence, the younger Jewish generation had attended general schools and learned the Czech and Slovak languages. But the older Orthodox element in the smaller Eastern towns remained isolated from the general population, and resembled, in a social sense, the Orthodox groups in Poland and Galicia. In Carpatho-Ruthenia, Hassidic rabbis (<u>Hassidim</u> are followers of a rabbinical dynasty) exerted great personal influence.

Languages.

The older Jewish generation used German most frequently, even in communities whose entire population was Czech, but they also knew the Czech language. The majority of the younger generation attended Czech schools and used the Czech language. The fact that a portion of the Jews spoke German was one of the causes of anti-Semitism in the Czech National groups.

In Slovakia, Hungarian occupied the same position among the Jews as did the German language in the Czech provinces. In Carpatho-Ruthenia, Yiddish was the most commonly-spoken language, with Ruthenian and Hungarian as the additional media.

Political Activities.

Part of the Jewish population, taking advantage of the minority rights granted by the Treaty of St. Germain and of the principles expressed by the Czechoslovak Constitution, according to which the citizen is entitled to maintain and develop his particular national individuality, were attached to one of the three Jewish parties -- the Jewish Party, the Hassidic (Hassidim are Orthodox Jews who follow a specific rabbinic dynasty) Jewish Agricultural Party (which cooperated with the Czechoslovak Agrarian Party), and the Jewish Handicraft Party. Of these, only the Jewish Party, supported by the Supreme Council of Jewish Communities in Prague, had any great significance.

Many Jews, however, preferring not to opt Jewish nationality, identified themselves with one or another of the general parties. A few weeks prior to the proclamation of Czechoslovak independence (1918), a Jewish National Council was formed in Prague. Later, before the formation of the Jewish Party, the Jewish minority was represented in the town councils of the City of Prague, and in the provincial councils. After 1929, two representatives to Parliament were elected by the Jewish Party.

The Jewish Party consisted of Zionists, non-Zionists, and some Orthodox Jews who might have belonged to either of the first two classifications. It worked in cooperation with the Labor Zionist group - Poale Zion.

Among the "Czech Jews," who considered themselves Czech nationals of the Jewish religion, there were some who were affiliated with the Czechoslovak Small Traders Party, the Social Democratic Labor Party and the Czech National Socialist Party (which was in no way related to the German National Socialist Workers Party). Jews speaking Hungarian usually supported Hungarian minority groups. A large number of Orthodox Jews in Carpatho-Ruthenia and Slovakia belonged to the Czechoslovak Agrarian Party. A number of Jewish intellectuals belonged to the Communist Party.

Minorities.

The final Article in the Czechoslovak Constitution prohibited any form of "forcible denationalization" of minorities (Article 134). All nationalities were guaranteed equality in the right to establish, support, and administer private institutions of a philanthropic, religious, or social nature, to use their own languages and to worship according to their own religious ceremonies (Article 130).

In districts where linguistic minorities formed a "considerable fraction" of the population, the public schools were to provide suitable opportunities for instruction in minority languages with the provision that the Czechoslovak language be made a required study (Article 131). A proportionate share of public moneys budgeted for education, religion, or philanthropy in such places was to be allotted to the minorities in question (Article 132). A special constitutional law of February 28, 1920, established detailed provisions for the use of Czechoslovak and minority languages in "central and local" administrations and in the courts.

In accordance with the minority rights secured by the Constitution, the Jews in Slovakia also had full possibilities for cultural and economic development. Wherever Jewish settlements existed, Orthodox and Neolog Jewish congregations were maintained. The Jews had their representatives in town, district, provincial and state councils. They maintained Jewish national Schools, some of them using Hebrew as the language of instruction. They had their own sports and scout organizations and lectures. The Zionist movement also played a significant part in the Jewish life in Slovakia. This picture changed entirely when, after the Munich agreement Slovakia became autonomous and later, after the Nazi occupation of Bohemia and Moravia, an "independent" state.

In the last two elections, 1934 and 1938, two representatives were elected to Parliament by the Jewish Party: Dr. Angelo Goldstein, prominent Prague lawyer, and Dr. Chaim Kugel, naturalized Polish Jew, and director of the Hebrew High School in Mukacevo, Sub-Carpatho Ruthenia. In the last election (1938) the Jewish Party and the Czechoslovak Social Democratic Party ran on one ticket.

Citizenship

There was no discrimination regarding citizenship. After the occupation, Jews still remained citizens of the Protectorate of Bohemia and Moravia. During the first two years after the occupation, Jews emigrating legally received ordinary Czechoslovak passports.

Municipal Posts

At various times during the existence of the Czechoslovak Republic, there were between six and ten Jews in the City Council of Prague, two of whom were elected by the Jewish Party, and the others by general parties. The mayor of Plzen (Pilsen), was a Social Democrat of Jewish descent.

Economic Stratification

The majority of the Jews in the Czech provinces belonged to the middle and upper-middle class. They comprised 1.3% of the gainfully employed population, but only 0.5% of the wage-earners. Among "proprietors," they constituted 2.2%, and among salaried employees, 3.5%. More than half (56.1%) of the Jews were proprietors of business enterprises, independent professionals, or persons of independent means, as compared with 32.4% among the non-Jewish population. Among gainfully employed Jews, 20.8% were salaried employees; among non-Jews 7.8%. Wage-earners comprised only 23.1% of the gainfully employed Jews, but 60.1% of the non-Jews.

Income levels among Jews were therefore comparatively high. In 1927, the per capita income tax paid by Jews (according to nationality) in Bohemia was 201.26 crowns, as compared with 89.30 crowns paid by Czech nationals and 90.02 crowns paid by Germans. Here the income tax payments of Jews was 125.5% higher than that paid by the others; in Bohemia and Moravia-Silesia together, it was 69.8% higher than that of the Czechs, and 60.4% higher than that of the Germans.

In 1930, the percentage of proprietors in various types of business enterprise who were Jews was as follows:

```
General total . . . . . . . . . . . . . . . . 2.2%
Agriculture . . . . . . . . . . . . . . . . . 0.1%
Industry (total) . . . . . . . . . . . . . . .1.9%
     Mining . . . . . . . . . . . . . . . . . .16.3%
     Chemicals . . . . . . . . . . . . . . . .15.9%
     Foundries . . . . . . . . . . . . . . . .10.0%
Finance and Insurance . . . . . . . . . . . .18.3%
Wholesale and Retail trade . . . . . . . . . 9.3%
```

****

Other classifications were:

```
Liberal professions  . . . . . . . . . . . . .13.5%
Domestic and personal service . . . . . . . . 0.5%
Other occupations and without occupation  . . 2.2%
```

The Jews of Carpatho-Ruthenia constituted the economically poorest group in Europe. Small farmers and tenants made up 26.9% of the Jewish population, but most of them were so badly off that they had to cut timber for wages. About 80% of them were on a permanent near-starvation level, and forced to draw on Jewish relief and charitable organizations, notably the American Jewish Joint Distribution Committee. Not much better was the predicament of the craftsmen and artisans whose primitive workshops were being swept away by the wave of industrialization moving eastward. In 1926, according to an investigation made by the Joint Distribution Committee, 17% of the Jews in Carpatho-Ruthenia were small artisans, 6% carters, 16.5% petty traders and innkeepers, 6% religious communal employees, 7.9% merchants and intellectuals. The rest had no definite occupation. For the youth, emigration offered the only hope. Between 1933 and 1936, 60% of the Jewish immigrants from Czechoslovakia were from Carpatho-Ruthenia.

Banking.

There were 50 banks in Czechoslovakia. "Aryanization" was required, after the occupation, when one or more members of the executive committee of the board of directors were Jews, when more than one-fourth of the capital belonged to Jews, and when Jews controlled more than 50% of the number of votes. On the basis of one or another of these provisions, eight banks, with joint stock capital totalling 662,000,000 crowns (the crown is the equivalent of $.029) were "Aryanized" in 1939. Subsequently a total of 39 banks, with joint stock capital totalling 1,431,000,000 crowns (or 85.4% of the total value of the joint stock capital in the country), fell to the Nazis.

These steps obtained for the Germans the possession of vital economic units. Late in April, 1939, the Bohemian Discount Bank, which had a staff consisting 99% of Jews, replaced them with Sudeten and Reich Germans. An "Aryan" department proceeded to transfer commercial and industrial enterprises owned by Jews to German hands. The Bohemian Discount Bank, the Bank of Trade and Industry, and the Credit Bank of Bohemia all came under the control of the Dresdner Bank. The Deutsche Bank of Berlin acquired the Union Bank of Bohemia, the second largest concern engaged in financing the export trade of Czechoslovakia.

Other banks "Aryanized" were the General Cooperative Bank (Všeobecha Druzstevní Banka), the Mortgage Bank (Hypotečni a Zemska Banka v Praze), the Agrarian Bank of Moravia (Agrarni Banka Moravska), the Cattle and Meat Bank (Dobytči a Masna Pokladna Praze), the Czech Bank Union, the Bank of the Czechoslovak Legions (Banka Csl. Legii), the Bohemian Industrial Bank (Ceska Průmyslova Banka), Länderbank (Banka pro Obchod a Průmysl), and Anglo-Czech and Prague Credit Bank (Anglo-Csl, a Průmyslova Urerni Banka).

Jewish-owned capital and assets in financial institutions were frozen from the very first day of German occupation. The German army which occupied Bohemia and Moravia issued a decree on March 29, 1939, forbidding Jews to dispose of their real and personal property. This measure was designed to prevent the flight of Jewish-owned capital abroad and the transfer of Jewish-owned assets into non-Jewish hands. Further regulations ordered the Jews to combine all money they had on deposit in various places in a single blocked account, to which all payments due them for rent, real estate and previously-incurred commercial obligations were to be made. Finally an order was issued by the "autonomous" Government's Ministry of Finance on January 23, 1940 that all sums payable to Jews or to Jewish enterprises, whether Jews or non-Jews were the debtors, be deposited in the blocked Jewish accounts.

By an order of the same Ministry on March 9, 1940, all payments made for previous obligations, savings' deposits entered in bank-books, securities, etc. were to be frozen when the owners were persons married to Jews. Thus, in mixed marriages, the restrictions of financial character imposed on Jews in the Protectorate were also applied to their non-Jewish spouses. Financial institutions had to make an investigation and inform the Ministry of Finance of accounts opened after March 15, 1939 by persons married to Jews.

The regulation of March 9, 1940, also provides that a married Jewish couple, or a couple with one Jewish spouse only, are entitled to withdraw from their blocked accounts not more than 1,500 crowns (about $50) weekly. On December 6, 1940, by order No. 73.537/IV, the Ministry of Finance greatly reduced the amount permitted to be withdrawn weekly from the blocked accounts of Jewish families. Single persons or widowers were allowed no more than 2,000 crowns a month ($66) from their blocked accounts. Married couples could withdraw 3,000 crowns a month ($100) and 500 crowns more for each additional member of the family; or, if such "members of families" had their own money on deposit, they were entitled to withdraw 500 crowns a month, provided that the head of the family did not collect this amount from his own account. Under local regulations in Moravia, an even stricter procedure was required before Jews were permitted to withdraw money from their own accounts. According to executive order No. 25761/29/VI of January 23, 1940, of the Moravian Office of Financial Administration, withdrawals by Jews from their blocked accounts could be made only upon presentation of special licenses issued by the Financial Administration in Brno.

Insurance.

There were 28 insurance companies with capital of more than 1,000,000 crowns each. Fifteen companies, with a total joint stock value of 337,700,000 crowns, of which 287,200,000 crowns (or 85%) was owned or controlled by Jews, were "Aryanized."

Natural Resources.

In 1939 there were 66 mining enterprises; the joint stock capital of corporately-owned mines totalled 1,659,000,000 crowns ($55,300,000). Of the corporately-owned mines, a total of 48, with joint stock capital amounting to 1,042,700,000 crowns ($34,750,000), were "Aryanized." The soft coal mines of Czechoslovakia belonged entirely to the Petschek (originally a Jewish family) banking house.

Even before Munich, the largest mining enterprises owned by Jews closed down their affairs in the Sudeten area, and moved into the interior of Czechslovakia. The Petschek firm sold its lignite mines (Nordkohle and Bruexerkohle), valued at 2,000,000,000 crowns ($67,000,000), and employing 7,500 workers, to the Živnostenská Banka (Trade Bank) in Prague and to British capital for 600,000,000 crowns ($20,000,000). The Ed. J. Weinman firm sold its Western Bohemian Mining Share Association (West Kohle) for 125,000,000 crowns ($4,167,000).

Agriculture.

In Slovakia about 90% of the population as a whole was engaged in agriculture. Although the percentage of Jews in agriculture was not nearly so great, their participation in the field is one of the characteristics of Slovak Jewry. According to statistics published in 1941 by the Slovak Land Reform Board, there were in the country 4,693 Jewish landowners, owning 41,172 hectares of agricultural land, 45,883 hectares of forest, (38% of the timber industry was in Jewish hands), and 11,168 hectares of uncultivated land (about 247,000 acres altogether). About half of the Jewish landlords or farmers possessed medium-sized estates, ranging from 400 to 500 cadastral jochs (550-700 acres); the rest owned estates of between 500 to 2,000 cadastral jochs.

According to a report in the Bulletin of the Czechoslovak Economic Advisory Council (London), #28, March 1942, at least 224,000 acres of land owned by Jews in Slovakia had been confiscated. Another report stated that 15,000 landed estates, valued at approximately 1,250,000,000 Slovak crowns ($42,500,000) had been taken from Jews in 227 Slovak communities. These properties were partly sold, and partly distributed among the Slovak peasantry. In the district of Trnava - the most fertile region of Slovakia - one-sixth of the land, or 1,466 cadastral jochs (2,085 acres) was taken away from the Jews and given to Christians.

In the Protectorate, Jews owned 148,266 acres of plow-land, gardens and forests. All possessions were ordered registered by July 31, 1939, and the land was confiscated. Together with Czechoslovak state estates, the land provided the basis for German colonization of the Protectorate. In Carpatho-Ruthenia, dwarf farming and tenantry occupied 26.9% of the Jewish population, but did not make them self-supporting.

Industry.

In 1939, there were 990 large industrial establishments in Czechoslovakia, with stock capital of more than 1,000,000 crowns each. In 605 of these companies (67.7%) Jews served on the boards of directors, or controlled more than 50% of the capital. All such enterprises were "Aryanized."

In Slovakia the Jews were pioneers in industrialization, which began on a large scale with the establishment of the Czechoslovak Republic. They were active in the sugar, lumber, paper and textile trades, and were prominent in the development of spas and watering places (Pieštany, Banská Štavnice), which were important in Slovak economy.

Foreign Commerce.

Approximately 72% of all the industrial manufacturing production of Czechoslovakia (according to a 1938 estimate by the Ministry of Finance) was for export. Jews played an especially important role in this field; the majority of large export enterprises were in Jewish hands, and more than half of the smaller enterprises were either Jewish holdings or had Jewish participation. The Bohemian Discount Bank (known as Bebka), the Czech Bank Union, the Länderbank and the Anglo-Czech and Prague Credit Bank were the chief financing institutions for the export business. Export enterprises also received government subsidies.

Enterprises that were considered Jewish holdings were the first to be "Aryanized."

"Aryanization"

In the Protectorate, no special corporation for "Aryanization" was established, but a special German agency, Hadega (Handelsgesellschaft) was set up in Prague for the registration of property and jewelry owned by Jews.

The Nazi legislation permitted the Reichsprotektor or his agents to appoint "trustees" to liquidate, manage or supervise Jewish businesses in the interests of the Reich. This function the Germans reserved for themselves; and any "trustees" already appointed by local Czech authorities had, after June 21, 1939, to secure the approval of the Reichsprotektor for their further functioning. The "trustees" appointed with the Reichsprotektor's approval were empowered to act for the affected businesses in all legal questions. To facilitate their work, such "trustees" were not only freed from the ordinary restrictions imposed on Jewish business but were granted equality with managers of non-Jewish establishments, with regard to the placing of orders by government bureaus, the allocation of government-controlled supplies, bank dealings, etc.

The coup de grace was given by the Reich Protector's decree of January 26, 1940 "for the elimination of the Jews from the Protectorate economy" (Vdg. des Reichsprotektors... zur Ausschaltung der Juden aus der Wirtschaft d. Protektorates von 26 Januar 1940) and by the orders which followed and implemented it at intervals thereafter. This decree made it "legal" for any business to be closed to "Jewish enterprise" (as defined in the June 21, 1939 decree) and consequently also for Jewish enterprises or handicraft shops already established in any line to be ordered liquidated or, with special permission, "transferred" to non-Jews. Subsequent ordinances barred Jewish business from a wide variety of commercial and financial lines, ranging from the whole moving picture field to marriage brokerage, from retail and wholesale trade, "independently or as agents", to the keeping of penny arcades.

Enterprises were "Aryanized" either by being turned over directly into German hands, or, more frequently, by the appointment of German "trustees" (Treuhänder) by the Oberlandrat. These trustees usually brought with them their secretaries and assistants, German officials, and thousands of German employees. Their salaries were charged to the firm and were invariably higher than customary salaries. In most cases, these commissars had no idea how to conduct the business of the "Aryanized" enterprises. They were, therefore, obliged to retain the former owners and the old administrative personnel for a short time. The commissars were more interested in mulcting the "Aryanized" enterprises of as much as possible than in maintaining and carrying on their business. This was in full accord with the economic policy of the Germans in the Protectorate, which was aimed, insofar as was compatible with the industrial needs of the war, at the destruction of the industrial structure of the country, and the replacement of industrial pursuits by agriculture.

Most of the "Aryanized" firms were turned over to Germans. There are also instances of the transfer of Jewish firms to Czechs. Their number cannot be stated at the present time.

The "Aryanization" and liquidation of Jewish property in Slovakia was completed during 1941. In January 1942, Augustin Morávek (President of the Slovak Economic Office) stated in a radio broadcast from Bratislava that the Jewish problem in Slovakia was practically solved. This official reported that the Jewish property in Slovakia had amounted to 3,950,000,000 Slovak crowns (about $135,000,000), of which sum 250,000,000 crowns had been blocked by the Government. Some 6,000 buildings owned by Jews and 12,300 Jewish-owned business enterprises, which had employed 13,000 Jews, were already in the possession of "Aryans."

Trade Unions.

Trade unions played an important role in the political life of Czechoslovakia. There were occupational, national and -- in the case of the Catholic unions -- religious divisions. The majority of the trade unions were affiliated with the Social Democrat or the Czechoslovak National Socialist parties (the latter bore no resemblance to the German National Socialist Party, but had a program similar to that of the Social Democrats. There were no separate Jewish trade unions. But one of the most important organizations, Ústřední Svaz čsl. Soukromých Zaměstnanců (Central Union of Private Employees) was headed by Robert Klein, a Jew and a Social Democratic member of the Czechoslovak Parliament. Before the establishment of an independent Czechoslovakia, Klein had been one of the organizers of the Poale Zion (Zionist Labor Party). The union which Klein headed was comprised largely of Jews. After the occupation, Klein was sent to the concentration camp at Dachau, where he died early in 1942.

In the Czechoslovak Government-in-Exile, the Czechoslovak trade unions are represented by Bělina, a member of the International Labor Organization.

Cooperatives and Labor Banks.

There was no discrimination against Jews in cooperatives and labor banks, except for an organization set up shortly before the Munich Pact -- Kooperativa, a state-supported concern for the purchase and redistribution of agricultural products. The president of Kooperativa was Dr. Feierabend, later minister of the Czech "autonomous" government under the Nazis. Subsequently he escaped to London, where he joined the Government-in-Exile. He is known to have strong anti-Semitic tendencies.

The Bar.

During the Second Republic, fascist influences had succeeded in making the Bar associations and the Czecho-Slovak Government take measures to restrict the number of Jews in the legal profession. Nevertheless, when the Protectorate was established, the number of Jewish lawyers still remained relatively large in comparison with the total number of lawyers.

According to the 1930 Czechoslovak census, there were 12,192 lawyers in the Czech provinces, 2,786 (22.9%) of whom maintained their own offices. The number of lawyers in the Protectorate maintaining their own offices

in March 1939:

	Total No. of lawyers	No. of Jews
Bohemia (1939)	2800	800 - 900
Prague (1939)	1200	378 (38.9%)
Moravia	640 - 780	250
Brno	289	110 (39.0%)
Total	3440 - 3580	1050 - 1150

The elimination began without waiting for the enactment of enabling legislation. On March 16, 1939, the day after the proclamation of the Protectorate, the Czech Bar Association excluded Jewish lawyers. "Aryan" lawyers were to wind up the business of the Jewish lawyers and to inform their clients of the new situation so that they might choose new "Aryan" lawyers. Simultaneously, the Ministry of Justice instructed all courts to postpone lawsuits conducted by Jewish lawyers until they were replaced by "Aryans". Mimeographed circulars regarding this decision were sent to all lawyers.

Physicians

Although Jewish physicians had already been excluded from hospitals and from the panels of the Sick Benefit Insurance Fund, they still comprised a relatively large proportion of the medical profession when the Protectorate was established. According to the 1930 census, there were 6,063 physicians in the Czech provinces, including both Jews and non-Jews. The Czech Medical Association in Prague estimated that there were about 2,000 Jewish physicians in Bohemia and Moravia when the Protectorate was established. These, with a few exceptions to serve the Jewish population, were barred from practice. No data on Slovakia and Ruthenia are available.

Education.

There were no restrictions at all for the Jews in the Czechoslovakian educational system. Moreover, Prague and Brno were centers of university education for many Jewish students from Poland, Roumania, Hungary, Yugoslavia and Bulgaria between the end of the First World War and 1938.

In Bohemia and Moravia the number of pupils of Jewish faith in the secondary schools was as follows (1937-1938):

In Bohemia, there were 2,104 pupils who declared themselves as belonging to the Jewish faith. Of these only 34 pupils, or 1.6% identified themselves with the Jewish nationality, as compared with 20.3% of the whole population of Jewish faith which claimed Jewish nationality, according to the 1930 census. In Moravia and Silesia, the number of secondary school pupils of Jewish faith was 1,312. Of these, 443 pupils, or 33.8%, declared themselves as belonging to the Jewish nationality, as compared with 51.7% in the whole Jewish population (1930).

In the Protectorate and in "independent" Slovakia Jewish children were not admitted to Czech, Slovak or German schools. Even private lessons by "Aryans" to Jewish children were prohibited with threats of severe punishment to both. Some educational facilities for Jewish children were provided by the Jewish Community Center in Prague, but this did not have much value since the parents were afraid to concentrate many Jewish children in one place.

Social Security.

Czechoslovakia had exemplary social legislation, with an 8-hour working day in industries and commerce, and a 7-hour working day in offices. Social insurance, sickness benefit, and accident insurance were obligatory. There was no discrimination against the Jews.

Birth and Mortality Rates.

There are indications that the Jews of the Czech provinces were, biologically speaking, a "declining population."

The following table shows the birth rate, mortality, and "natural increase" of population per 1,000 of the Czechoslovak, German, and Jewish nationalities in Bohemia and Moravia-Silesia during 1937 and 1938.

	Nationality					
	Czechoslovak		German		Jewish	
	1937	1938	1937	1938	1937	1938
Birth-rate	14.84	15.43	6.9	7.11	9.62	10.43
Mortality	12.82	13.20	11.13	10.76	19.92	24.04
Natural increase	+2.02	+2.23	-4.23	-3.65	-10.30	-13.64

Thus, in addition to the decreasing identification of the younger generation with the "Jewish nationality," the group was declining because of an excess of deaths over births. (The same phenomenon appeared in the "German nationality," but to a smaller degree.) The low birth rate and high death rate of the "Jewish nationality" were probably characteristic of the "Jewish religion" also. This is indicated by the fact that in 1930, 44.4% of the total number of Jews by faith in Bohemia and Moravia-Silesia were more than forty years old.

There are no statistics available regarding the birth rate among the Jews in Czechoslovakia under Nazi rule. It is, however, evident that the birth rate has practically dropped to zero. The Jüdisches Nachrichtenblatt for 1942 reported almost no births.

Public Welfare.

Public welfare in Bohemia, Moravia and Silesia was based on the Poor-Law (1864-1868) taken over from old Austria. The eastern parts (Slovakia, Ruthenia), with a large Jewish population, were administered according to the old Hungarian laws.

The Poor-Law placed the final responsibility for the poor and destitute upon the community of domicile. Thus, for instance, every underprivileged person could receive treatment in a public hospital free of charge and the community of domicile was responsible for the incurred hospital bills. Where the community was unable to pay the full amount, or its share, the balance was covered by a special fund of the province.

Social services which were beyond the technical and financial possibilities of individual local communities were maintained by the county -- child welfare bureaus, hospitals, infirmaries, children's homes, labor offices, etc. Social service institutions serving yet larger territories were maintained by provinces -- maternity hospitals, hospitals for the insane, correctional institutions for chidren, etc. The state, through the ministries of public welfare and public health, prepared and put into practice social legislation of the most advanced type. The state also undertook certain social service tasks of large scope, such as migration, international labor market, large scale combat of social disorders and defects, scientific research in all fields of social and health service, and administration of institutions of statewide importance (specialized hospitals, prisons, etc.).

All citizens of the Czechoslovak Republic could use the social services. No discriminations were made against citizens of any faith. Cooperation between public services and Jewish social services was close. The Jewish religious communities of Prague, for instance, had an extensive social service department. With financial support from the municipality and the state the Jews of Prague administered relief to their local poor and to transients. On the other hand a large number of Jewish foundations were administered partly by the City Social Service Department and partly by the Ministry of Welfare.

Before the occupation there were perhaps 1,500 trained social workers in the public and private social services of Czechoslovakia. About 25 of them were Jewish. There were Jews amongst the rest of personnel, especially among the physicians. Jewish physicians, economists and social scientists were employed by the central offices of the state wide social insurance, as well as by many other public and private agencies.

Jewish Welfare

Czechoslovak citizens of Jewish faith had the same right to participate on all public assistance as the rest of Czechoslovak citizens. The state-wide scheme of pensions and social insurance included citizens of all faiths, as contributors and recipients of benefits. Several kinds of social insurance were compulsory for public as well as private employees - for all persons gainfully employed.(old age pensions, widows and orphans pensions, veterans' pensions, insurance for case of accident, sickness, maternity, invalidity, old age). All public institutions were open to citizens of Jewish faith; the Central Social Service Institutions of the city of Prague had a number of Jewish inmates. Pensions and insurance benefits were based on the insured person's income.

Private relief work among Jews was carried on by a large number of Jewish charitable organizations. In smaller religious communities there was at least one such society. Large religious communities had many. Prague had about 150 charitable Jewish organizations, most of them the usual type of voluntary charity organization with no permanent office of their own. Their sources of income were: membership fees, donations, bequests, income from cultural and social events, collections, etc.

Some of them offered services as well as relief (employment service, medical service, home visiting, child placement, scholarships, etc.). The majority limited themselves to relief which was mainly financial, taking the form of either regular allowances to families or individuals, or occasional gifts to local poor or transients, or gifts of money at special occasions (such as New Year, weddings, etc.). Relief in kind included free meals, shelter, clothing, special groceries for holidays, gifts for children on Hanukah, books for students, etc.

Some of the larger organizations maintained their own institutions (orphanages, homes for the aged, infirmaries). In Prague there was a special home for apprentice boys and another home for Jewish students. Many foreign students from countries where a numerus clausus had been introduced studied in Prague and received free room and board in this home.

In 1935 the religious communities of Prague founded the Jewish Social Service Institute. It was the first attempt to coordinate services of several religious communities in a large city. Beside other departments the Institute had a special department of Child Welfare with a Bureau of Vocational Guidance and a special department for refugees. Some of the rudimentary services of the Institute are reported still to be functioning.

Most of the work for the Jewish charitable organizations was done by volunteers; only a few of the larger organizations used paid personnel. The executives of larger Jewish organizations were usually graduate lawyers. Other professionals employed were physicians, nurses and teachers. Before the occupation, the Prague Jewish Communities employed three fully qualified social workers and one psychologist The rest were lawyers and persons with business or other training who acquired some knowledge of social service routine thru long years of experience.

Information on Jewish relief personnel today is not at hand. It is believed that the rudimentary social services for Jews still existing are concentrated in the Prague Jewish Town Hall. It is also believed that some of the Jewish employees and a Jewish executive are still working there under close supervision of the German police.

Child Welfare.

Czechoslovak child welfare was organized on a state-wide basis, cooperated closely with public social services, and was an example of a coordinated branch of social service of a semi-public character. There were units of child welfare in local communities, but the main working centers were the county child welfare bureaus. Larger territorial units were the provincial child welfare bureaus, united in one state-wide Child Welfare Federation linked up with international child welfare groups. The child welfare service included all stages - expectant mothers, lying-in-mothers, mothers and infants, mothers and small children, children of pre-school age, children of school age (6-14) and youth between 14 and 18 years. No difference was made between children of married and unmarried mothers. A large number of institutions for children with physical, mental or moral defects were also administered.

Jewish children and young people were active members of all except Catholic recreational organizations. They took an active part in the state-wide gymnastic associations (e.g. Sokol) and in all sporting clubs.

Jewish child welfare organizations in Czechoslovakia, in the majority of cases, formed a part of the general Jewish charities, although a number of organizations had child welfare as their main program. These ranged from small groups of a few members to large organizations maintaining the Prague Jewish orphanages. The Prague Jewish orphanage for girls was one of the most modern institutions in the country in regard to building, equipment and methods of child care. It offered maintenance to girls from 5 years of age and within its scope of individualized care was able to see its inmates through high school or even through university. Jewish institutions used public educational facilities.

General Press.

Jews were very active in the general press of Czechoslovakia, particularly in the German language press. But with the establishment of the Second Republic after the Munich Pact, Jews holding editorial posts in the German language newspapers began to be dismissed. Five were discharged from the staff of the Prager Tageblatt, one of the largest and most influential papers in Central Europe. Dismissals also occurred on the staff of Bohemia and other publications.

After the occupation, the existing German newspapers and periodicals were shut down and replaced by new ones, such as Der Neue Tag and Die Zeit. The various newspapers in the Czech language, hitherto representing different political groups, became instruments of German propaganda and administration. Articles were written by German writers and translated into the Czech language, so that the Czech press became virtually a Nazi German press.

Anti-Semitic propaganda in the Czech press began shortly before the Munich Conference. At the beginning of August 1938 the most popular bourgeois Czech newspaper, Národní Politika (National Politics) launched an anti-Semitic campaign, directed particularly against the Jewish refugees from Germany and Austria in the country. The agrarian Večer (Evening) and other papers, owned by the fascist publishing house of Stříbrný, followed in the same vein. With the establishment of the Second Republic (October 5, 1938), anti-Semites gained the upper hand, particularly in the press of Bohemia and Moravia.

Jewish Press.

There were three periodicals of Jewish interest in Czechoslovakia; Židovské Zprávy (Jewish News), of Zionist orientation and published in Czech; Rozvoj (Development), also published in Czech and the organ of the Czech Jews, and Selbstwehr (Self-Defense), a Zionist periodical published in German. All these ceased publication immediately after the Munich Pact.

At the end of 1940, the Jewish Community Organization in Prague began to issue a weekly in German and the Czech language: Jüdisches Nachrichtenblatt--Židovské Listy, the purpose of which was to keep the Jewish population informed about anti-Jewish legislation and regulations. Before mass deportations were instituted in the autumn of 1941, the paper also provided information about emigration possibilities to neutral countries and vocational courses maintained by the Jewish Community Organization.

In Bratislava, Slovakia, a weekly: Vestník Ústredné Židov, similar to the Prague publication, made its appearance in March, 1941.

The Christian Churches and the Jews.

The Christian Churches, as such, were not direct participants in the internal or foreign policy of the country. However, many clergymen, as individuals, were politically active in many groups. The present Prime Minister of the Czechoslovak Government-in-exile is Monsignor Šrámek, a Catholic priest. The present "president" of "independent" Slovakia, Dr. Tiso, and Andrej Hlinka, a leader in the Slovak autonomy party, were Catholic clergymen.

There was no influence of the Catholic Church apparent in anti-Semitic movements. The clergy, like the rest of the Czech population, was friendly to the persecuted Jewish population. So outstanding a church leader as Abbot Zavoral was reported to have sent New Year greetings to several Jews in 1941. At about the same time the Prague Catholic newspaper, Lidoré Listy, was obliged to publish an article by a German, demanding that the Catholic Church stop being friendly to the Jews, and demanding an uncompromising solution of the Jewish question. There were numerous instances where Catholic and Protestant clergymen were known to have issued ante-dated baptism certificates to Jews, thus saving the recipients from deportation. In Slovakia, John Pruskas, a Hungarian Protestant pastor, was sentenced to a long prison term for having issued hundreds of ante-dated baptism certificates.

Anti-Semitic Parties.

There were a few anti-Semitic parties; including a fraction of the Czechoslovak National Socialist Party headed by Jiří Střibrný: and a Czech Fascist party the "Czechoslovak Legion", headed by Rudolf Gajda and founded in Brno in 1935-1936. Both of these parties were insignicant, having together only five members in the House of Representatives (400 members). After the Nazi occupation of Czechoslovakia, elements of those parties helped to constitute anti-Semitic organizations.

Attitude of People.

There was no Jewish problem of importance in Bohemia and Moravia prior to Munich. By the end of the First World War, mainly under the influence of the elder Masaryk and his circle, the Czech people had developed a remarkable degree of tolerance; Jews and non-Jews lived peaceably side by side. However, there were evidences of hostility to the Jews based on economic or national motives, the latter arising from resentment against the Jews for their allegiance to the Austro-Hungarian monarchy, and later to German culture.

Nearly one-third of the Jewish population in the Czech countries had considered themselves members of the German-speaking minority. A considerable portion of those who claimed "Jewish" nationality also made use of the German language, which had, for centuries past, been the language of the majority of the Bohemian and Moravian Jews. The fact that the majority of the Jewish population belonged to the upper social and economic classes was another prod to anti-Semitic feelings.

After about 1000 years of Magyar rule, Slovakia joined Bohemia and Moravia in a common independent Czechoslovak state in 1918. Until the first World War the Slovak Jews had developed their activities in a liberal atmosphere according to the agreement reached in 1867 between the representatives of the Hungarian people and Franz Josef I. There were three types of Jews on Slovak territory. One group had through a long period of years merged with the language and culture of Hungary, and belonged largely to the upper-middle class of merchants, industralists and professionals. Another group had originated in neighboring Galicia; they were very

Orthodox, used the Yiddish language, and were occupied in handicraft, or as seasonal workers in agriculture and forestry. A third group, in the Austrian region, spoke German.

There were two reasons for such hostility to the Jews as existed in Slovakia. The Jews were engaged in the development of the natural resources of the large estates owned in Slovakia by Magyar aristocrats; and a large number of Jews had been entirely magyarized. The transitional period after the First World War did not pass without heavy losses in lives and property for the Jews in Slovakia. Unorganized anti-Jewish riots had taken place in Nové Mesto nad Váhom, Myjava, Ružemberok, Senkevice, Previdza, Starotura and other localities. The Jews were forced to move to larger communities and towns. In many parts of Slovakia small Jewish communities ceased to exist and the Jewish population in larger cities increased substantially. Under Czech influence, the anti-Jewish riots were eliminated. The prejudices against the Jews did not entirely disappear among Slovaks; nevertheless, common confidence between Slovaks and Jews was established and they came closer to one another.

Attitude of People: After Occupation

After the Nazi occupation of Czechoslovakia, the Government measures directed against Jews and the repeated efforts of the Germans to isolate the Jews from the rest of the population failed to destroy the old friendly feelings between the Czechs and the Jews. During the early period of the Protectorate, Czechs continued their private friendliness to the Jews, persistently crowding the cafés and restaurants in the Jewish sections as a demonstration of their hostility to the Germans.

The National Solidarity Party, which had to maintain "normal" relations with the Germans, could not remain indifferent to this demonstration on the part of the Czech population. Josef Nebeský, then Party Chairman, therefore forbade all social intercourse of its members with Jews. At the same time, he demanded that the Government issue a decree for the protection of Czech "Aryan" blood and honor.

Although 99% of the Czechs belonged to the National Solidarity Party, they paid scant heed to its instruction. In the Czech provincial cities the friendly attitude toward Jews was openly manifested. In the large cities, like Prague, where the German control was more stringent, the Czechs still found many ways of showing their friendship for Jews, such as reading Jewish authors openly in street cars and public places, and by leaving the books on the tables and seats so that others could read them too. These quiet demonstrations went on even after the Germans announced that they would treat those suspected of being friendly to Jews in the same way as those who showed their sympathy for the enemies of the Reich, notably, Britain and the Benes Government.

In preaching anti-Semitism in the Protectorate the Nazi sympathizers were confronted with the fact that the whole terminology and spirit of their efforts to win the Czechs to anti-Semitism were regarded with suspicion as a form of German propaganda. "Anti-Semite" and "Nazi" became synonymous in the eyes of the Czechs. The Germans then tried to convince the Czechs that anti-Semitism was not new in Bohemia, that in the Middle Ages Jews were regarded as parasites, and that the Czechs had tried to get rid of them. The new anti-Semitism was defended as only a logical continuation of the old Czech anti-Semitism. The Czechs, however, persisted in their coldness to the anti-Semitic philosophy.

An opportunity to aid the Jews who were forced to emigrate was given to the Czechs when Reichsprotektor Heydrich renewed the deportation of Jews from the Protectorate to Poland. The deportation orders were accompanied by a heightened anti-Jewish campaign in the Nazi-controlled Czech press, directed not only against Jews but also against the Czech population for trying, in every possible way, to show its friendly attitude toward the Jews. The press accused the Czechs of furnishing the Jews who were to be deported with food and clothing, in spite of repeated warnings against such acts, thus committing a double crime: damaging the German economic situation and, showing a lack of confidence in German victory.

After the imposition of the Star of David badge law on September 18, 1941, many Czechs manifested their resentment by wearing the badge. Threats of severe punishment, including subjection to all the disabilities forced on the Jews, were made by the German authorities.

Fascist Leaders: Press: Publications.

Before the Protectorate was established there had been two relatively important fascist leaders, General Rudolf Gajda and Jiří Stříbrný, whose followers, together with the members of the extreme rightist-agrarian groups (all of whom had previously been an insignificant factor in Czech politics) assumed real importance under German rule. Some, led by Gajda and Stribrny themselves, joined the National Solidarity Party. Others, especially the more radical fascists in Moravia, refused to accept Gajda's and Stříbrný's version of anti-Semitism, and also refused to join the National Solidarity Party. These latter groups were supported by the Germans, who were not entirely satisfied with the activities of the National Solidarity Party. Renouncing the title of a political party, they formed a "national movement" under the name of the "Czech National Camp," or the National Aryan Culture Association, consisting largely of disreputable characters. A subsidiary organization, the Svatopluk Guards, copied not only the Nazi salute, but the functions and methods of the Nazi Storm Troopers.

The fascist anti-Semitic press in the Protectorate is represented by the following newspapers and periodicals: Vlajka (Banner), Štít Národa (The Peoples Shield), Arijská Fronta (The Aryan Front), Boj (The Struggle), Náradní Výzva (National Appeal, Prague) and Národni Tábor (The National Camp, Brno).

The most important is Vlajka, which follows the leadership of the Czech fascist, Jan Rys. It demands that all laws and decrees directed against Jews as a race be strictly enforced, and that the Jews be isolated completely from the Czech people. Vlajka did not hesitate to revive the old ritual slaughter slander, spreading over its pages the story of the ritual murder trial in Polná, that same trial in which the young Thomas G. Masaryk won his spurs as a champion of liberal principles.

Of special interest is the journal Štít Národa, the Czech counterpart of the Stürmer. Karel Kasanda, editor-in-chief, published a violent anti-Semitic program in its first issue on May 12, 1939. A portrait of Hitler was on the front page. Every issue of "Štít Národa" seethes with anti-Semitism. The program of Arijska Fronta, published by the Czech Aryan Association, is self-evident from its motto "Against the Jews until the last Jew."

The rest of the anti-Semitic press wages a continual petty campaign against Jews. The leader among these lesser journals is Nástup Červenobílých (Red-White Attack), published by Zdeněk Zástera.

Odžidovštiti (Out with the Jews) a book by Jaroslav Veverka, (Odžidovštiti, Prague, 1939) has the following motto: "If you want your garden to bloom you must extirpate the weeds, root and all." The religious "philosophy" of anti-Semitism is expounded by the editor of Vlajka, Emil Šourek, in a book entitled "Origin of Christianity, according to the opinion of a Talmudic Jew." In another volume entitled Malé národy Nové Europe, (Small Nations in the New Europe), by Emil Vajtauer, (Orbis, Prague, 1941) the author takes up the Jewish question from the racial point of view.

The controlled, one-sided Czech press is dependent for its existence upon the goodwill of three groups: the German authorities in the Protectorate; the National Solidarity Party, especially in the beginning (later the party lost its hold on the press; whereas at first all Czech newspapers had appeared with the subtitle "Organ of the National Solidarity Party," fewer and fewer did so as time passed), and a group of anti-Semitic journalists including such persons as Emanuel Moravec, Vladimír Krychtálek, E. Vajtauer, and Karel Laznovský. Many periodicals were shut down, and those that remained were obliged to publish the anti-Semitic ordinances of the Reichsprotektor and the "autonomous" Government, and, in general, to write to please their German masters. It is, therefore, natural that the Czech press reflects German racial policies in the Jewish question.

Basic Anti-Jewish Laws.

A decree was issued on June 21, 1939, establishing regulations concerning Jewish property rights, defined what persons were to be considered "Jews." 1) Persons descended from three "full-blooded" Jewish grandparents. Grandparents were designated as "full-blooded Jews" if they belonged at any time to a Jewish religious community. Therefore, anyone with three such Jewish grandparents was regarded as a Jew even if he himself and both his parents were without religious belief or of some other than the Jewish religion. 2) Persons descended from two Jewish grandparents, who belonged to Jewish religious communities on September 15, 1935 (the date of the Nuremberg laws) or joined such communities thereafter. 3) Persons descended from two Jewish grandparents, who were married to "Jews" on September 15, 1935, or entered such marriages thereafter. (According to the law, persons with only one Jewish grandparent or with no Jewish grandparents at all were not subject to its provisions. But in practice the Germans did not take the strict meaning of this paragraph into consideration and, in carrying out anti-Jewish measures of economic character in the Protectorate, applied them to all persons, without distinction, who were married to Jews). 4) Persons with two Jewish grandparents, and born of a marriage contracted after September 15, 1935, in which one of the partners was a Jew by virtue of three Jewish grandparents. 5) Persons descended from two Jewish grandparents, and illegitimately born of an illegitimate relationship, in which one of the partners was a Jew by virtue of three Jewish grandparents.

The first of the basic anti-Jewish decrees to be announced was the law of June 21, 1939, establishing oppressive regulations concerning Jewish property rights. It was one of the most important instruments used by the Nazis both in eliminating the Jews and achieving effective control of the Czech economy.

The second anti-Jewish law was the decree of the "autonomous" Government of the Protectorate published on April 24, 1940, but dated July 4, 1939, which restricted the number of Jews in the public service professions. By the time it was made public, the effects it was nominally intended to produce had already been accomplished by other means.

The third basic anti-Jewish decree was issued on July 5, 1941 by the Reichsprotektor, and dealt with the enforcement in Bohemia and Moravia of the Nuremberg law of September 15, 1935 for the "protection of German blood and honor." According to that decree the "protection of German blood and honor" became part of effective law in Czechoslovakia, retroactive to the establishment of the Protectorate on March 16, 1939.

Discriminatory Measures.

With the establishment of the Second Republic in October 1938 various professional associations started to ask for the introduction of "Aryan" clauses in civil service and in public life.

Jewish physicians were denied the right to treat patients in hospitals and to serve on the panels of the Sick Benefit Insurance Fund. On March 1, 1939, without any administrative or legal ground, all Jews were discharged from state and municipal positions. Dismissals from financial, commercial and industrial establishments followed.

However, despite demands from pressure groups, the government of the Second Czecho-Slovak Republic did not issue a single formally anti-Jewish decree. Two decrees, however, without mentioning the word Jew, were directed primarily against Jews. One of the decrees gave the administration discretionary powers to limit the number of lawyers of non-Czecho-Slovak or non-Ruthenian nationality admitted to practice (November 16, 1938): the second ordered a revision of the status of naturalized Czechoslovak citizens (January 27, 1939), which deprived a considerable number of Jews of their status as citizens.

In the Protectorate numerous measures, generally following the German pattern, were adopted against the Jews.

A police decree of August 14, 1939 (#19.334) forbade Jews to frequent the majority of restaurants and cafés, and required proprietors to post Juden nicht zugenglich notices. Proprietors of public bath-houses were ordered to separate Jews from non-Jews. Later, Jews were permitted to bathe only at certain hours. They were barred from beaches and forbidden to bathe or fish in streams or rivers. In Brno after September 20, 1939, and in Prague after May 15, 1940, Jews were denied the use of public parks and gardens.

The managements of hospitals, sanatoria and homes for the aged were ordered not to accept Jewish patients unless they could be segregated (September, 1939). Some hospitals set aside special rooms for Jews. During that same month, all business enterprises owned by Jews had to be marked Jüdisches Geschäft; 2,300 such inscriptions were issued by the police and the Chambers of Commerce in Prague alone.

According to a Gestapo order of April 22, 1940, Jews were forbidden to appear on the streets after 8 o'clock in the evening or before 6 o'clock in the morning. In may, 1940, the Prague General Hospital (Vseobecna nemecnice) refused entirely to treat Jewish patients.

Although foodcards were allotted to the Jews when rationing was instituted, cards for clothing and footwear were not granted. Jews were not allowed to buy commodities directly from the producer, or to buy fruit or tobacco at all. They were also forbidden to buy lottery tickets. All radio sets were declared confiscated and the Jews had to deliver them to the authorities. Inter-city travel was forbidden; exceptions were not made even for funerals of near relatives. Jews were not allowed to enter the front car of street cars; where only one car was used, they could not enter at all. Taxicabs, automobiles and bicycles were forbidden.

Public libraries and similar public institutions were barred to the Jews. Jewish children were not allowed to attend public schools and Czech teachers were forbidden to give them private lessons. According to regulations of September 24, 1941, affecting the postal and telegraph system, Jews could submit mail only by appearing personally between 1 and 5 p.m. at specially designated postoffices.

All Jews in the Protectorate had to register, as of April 30, 1941, and to carry their registration cards with them. According to a decree on September 1, 1941, effective as of September 19, 1941, the German Minister of the Interior, who was empowered to issue regulations in the Protectorate of Bohemia and Moravia, ordered all Jews over six years of age to wear an identifying badge "over the heart." This badge was to consist of a six-pointed star, as large as the palm of a hand, on a yellow background bound in black and containing the word Jude in black letters. No exceptions were allowed; failure to comply was punishable by a maximum fine of 150 Reichsmark or six weeks imprisonment.

On September 26, 1941, in the Jüdisches Nachrichtenblatt, the Jewish Community Organization of Prague published a Jewish Time-Table, listing the restrictions and limitations to which Jews were subjected in public appearances. Included in the listing were the following regulations: Jews could make purchases in retail stores only between 3 and 5 p.m. Only one health-insurance clinic remained accessible to them; this they were allowed to visit between 1 and 2 p.m. Barber shops, unless catering exclusively to Jewish patronage, could be visited between 8 and 10 a.m. only. Municipal buildings were accessible between 8 and 9 a.m. and the Pension Bureau between 1 and 2 p.m. Banks and insurance offices could be visited between 8 and 9 a.m.

Provincial towns from which Jews had not yet been either deported or transferred to Prague issued their own time-tables. In the district of Prostejov, Jews could enter the market for the purchase of food only between 10 a.m. and noon during the period of fairs, and between 11 a.m. and noon in the winter. Afternoon hours for marketing, in Olomouc as well as Prostejov, were between 3 and 5 p.m. The same regulations applied in Brno with regard to purchases in "Aryan" stores or cooperatives. Failure to comply with these regulations was punishable by a fine of from 10 to 5,000 crowns, or a maximum of two weeks imprisonment.

Jews were not allowed to see, donate, pawn, deposit, diminish or deteriorate their assets or property without the permission of the authorities (April, 1942).

They could not visit beauty parlors or summon "Aryan" hairdressers and barbers to their homes (June, 1942). A decree of June 30, 1942 specified that anyone who wanted to employ a Jew had to apply at the Arbeitsamt (Labor Bureau) for permission before July 31, 1942. Further rules relative to the employment of Jews (decree of July 17, 1942) were that Jews could not apply for payment in case of illness, overtime, night, Sunday or holiday work; they were not entitled to bonuses or to special allotments for extraordinary occasions, such as births or funerals; they were not entitled to paid vacations; and a Jewish worker was subject to dismissal at one day's notice, but could himself give notice only according to legal requirements.

The law determining the new position of the Jews in the professions, when finally published on April 24, 1940, established the following provisions: Jews were barred from all governmental, communal and "public" activities. They could no longer, as a general rule, be teachers in elementary or secondary schools or in universities, or members of scientific institutions, lecturers, or contributors to scientific periodicals, administrative or judicial officers and employees, actors or editors, lawyers, patent attorneys, notaries or brokers, doctors, dentists, or veterinarians. Infractions of the rules were punishable by a fine of up to 100,000 crowns (about $3,300) and six months in jail. Exceptions to the rule were provided, in general, only to supply the needs of the Jewish population itself, and under the strict regulation of the Government of the Protectorate.

Jewish lawyers, doctors, and other professionals were limited to 2% of the total number in their professions, and to Jewish clientele. In the case of lawyers, notaries (only graduates of law schools possessing the same qualifications as lawyers or judges could become notaries in Czechoslovakia) and similar professions under its jurisdiction, the Ministry of Justice, at the suggestion of the Supreme Court, was empowered to grant or withhold the permission to practice. The Czech Ministry of Health and Welfare had to determine who might be allowed to practice as a Jewish physician. To attend the medical needs of the Jews in Prague (over 46,000 according to the October 1, 1939 census) twenty Jewish physicians were permitted to practice.

Although, until 1941, the Jews of the Protectorate were not segregated in ghettos, as in other countries under Nazi rule, they were permitted to reside only in certain sections of the cities of Prague and Brno. After September, 1940, Jews were no longer allowed to rent vacant apartments, even in the sections where their residence is permitted, but could move only into apartments already inhabited by other Jews. The housing problem was doubled in intensity by the fact that about 40,000 Jews from the provinces were ordered to remove to Prague. By order of the Prague police on September 10, 1940, a total of the hostels for transients in Greater Prague was reserved for Jews exclusively. They were not admitted to any of the others. According to the decree of October 7, 1940 regarding the renting of "Jewish apartments," apartments or places of residence rented to Jews, or occupied by Jews after expiration of the contract, or unoccupied apartments from which the last tenants moved later than June 30, 1941, may be rented only with the approval of the Central Office for Jewish Emigration. An order of the Prague police on October 25, 1940 forbade Jews to change their permanent residence, or even to be temporarily absent from Greater Prague, if they reside permanently in Prague.

Slovakia.

In Slovakia the sale of kosher meat was prohibited on July 5, 1939. Ritual slaughter (shehitah) was prohibited by a law of June 19, 1940.

On the basis of decree No.190) 1939 Sl., the Minister of the Interior, Sano Mach, laid down the following regulations for Jews on July 18, 1941: They were forbidden to attend public baths and visit public parks, to buy food in the markets or from dealers before 10 a.m., to appear on the streets after 9 p.m., and to have any kind of social intercourse with "Aryans," which included not only visiting each other's homes, but casual conversations on the streets or in public places. Violations of this order were punishable by fines of from 10 to 5,000 crowns, twelve hours to fourteen days imprisonment, or both.

After September 19, 1941, all Jews in Slovakia had to wear yellow armbands bearing a Star of David. An order of March 12, 1942, increased the width of the star from two to three inches.

Jews were forbidden to appear in the streets in groups, to frequent theatres, movies or restaurants, to use telephones and to ride bicycles or automobiles. They were also forbidden to enter synagogues except for religious services. Beginning with November, 1941, the curfew as applied to Jews was extended to fifteen hours -- from 3 p.m. to 6 a.m. Jews were forced to turn over to the authorities all radio sets, fishing and photographic equipment, field glasses, phonographs and phonograph records.

On the pretext that since they were not being called for military service, Jews had to be drafted for forced labor, labor battalions were established in various parts of the country. When Slovakia decided to enter the war against Russia, it was ordered that when they had completed their compulsory term of "service" in labor camps, the Jews should not be released, but should be assigned as laborers to the families of mobilized soldiers. This was tantamount to a new slave status. However, as late as February, 1942, Prime Minister Tuka was reported to have sent 204 officials of the Hlinka Guards to Germany to study the question of Jewish forced labor battalions. New forms of forced labor service were established and the Jews were ordered to register in municipal offices by March 10, 1942. Both the Ministry of War and the Hlinka Guards were reported to be in charge of labor battalion formations. The Hlinka Guards, an organization similar to the German S.S., had always been empowered to enforce anti-Jewish measures, and to search Jewish households.

Emigration and Expropriation: Special Taxes.

While working toward the elimination of the Jews, the Gestapo also took care that they left their goods behind and departed under circumstances and at times satisfactory to the Nazis. Systematic work in that field began when Obersturmführer Fritz Eichmann was brought to Prague from Vienna in July 1939 to take over the job of controlling Jewish emigration. Eichmann, born in a German colony in Palestine, was regarded as the Gestapo expert in "Jewish affairs" and had accomplished "remarkable" results in "solving the Jewish problem" in Austria.

Under his supervision, the Zentralstelle für jüdische Auswanderung (Central Office for Jewish Emigration) was organized, and began to function at the end of

August 1939. The Office, attached to the Jewish Community Organization, housed the Czech tax and passport officials and the Jewish community officials who had to pass on all applications for emigration. The Central Office was a clearing house for all formalities concerning Jewish emigration and was strictly supervised by the Gestapo. Its legal status and competence were defined by a decree of the Reichsprotektor on March 5, 1940, after the Office had been operating for six months.

By the provisions of that ordinance "regarding the care of Jews and Jewish organizations", the Jewish Community of Prague and, more particularly, the Central Office for Jewish Emigration, working under the Gestapo, were given broad powers to "care for" all Jews, including those of non-Mosaic confession, looking towards their emigration. For its services, the Central Office could collect fees from the Jews. Subject to its direction were all Jewish religious communities and associations. The Central Office was empowered to dissolve, transfer to other "Jewish organizations" or incorporate in them all Jewish religious communities, organizations, foundations, and funds, except purely business enterprises already being cared for under the law regarding Jewish property; the assets of such associations could be transferred to a public fund of the Central Office, bearing the name of the "Emigration Fund for Bohemia and Moravia." When such assets were transferred the Fund would not be held legally responsible for the liabilities of such associations. The fund was controlled by the chief of police in the Reichsprotektor's Office.

Since all the arrangements for emigration were handled by the Central Office for Jewish Emigration in Prague, the Gestapo set about concentrating the Jews of the Protectorate in that city. The Jewish Community of Prague was thus confronted with the difficult problem of finding lodging and food for a constant stream of newcomers, under the restrictions which the Nazis imposed upon Jews with regard to both residence and supplies. Those transferred to Prague included, in addition to the members of the provincial Jewish communities of the Protectorate, also Jewish refugees from Germany, Austria and the Sudeten area, and, in accordance with the German definition of the term "Jew," Jews without religion or of Christian faith.

All the Jews of 123 communities out of the 131 listed in the October 1, 1939 census, or a total of about 40,000 persons were transferred, over a period of years, to Prague.

Little formality attended the removal of the Jews from any town. Orders were transmitted orally. The Nazi regional governor (Landrat) simply invited the rabbis or the heads of the Jewish Community to his office, and instructed them to transfer the Jews to Prague immediately, holding them responsible for carrying out his commands. In many cases, the Jews were given only twenty-four hours to leave their homes. Except for a few personal belongings, all their property was left behind and confiscated by the Nazis. Upon arrival in Prague the Jews of the provinces were registered immediately at the Central Office for Jewish Emigration.

Although emigration was the ultimate result at which the Jewish policy of the Nazis was aimed, great difficulties were placed in the way of the prospective emigrant. No emigrant was permitted to leave until he had obtained an exit-permit from the Gestapo, in addition to the ordinary passports and visas. During the first three months of the existence of the Protectorate, the Gestapo in Prague granted hardly any exit-permits to Jews. In the hall of the Prague Gestapo department where exit-permits were granted, an announcement was hung stating that no Jews were admitted. Despite the announcement, among the thousands who stood in line at the Gestapo office were also Jews, risking serious injury at the hands of the Storm Trooper guards.

After Obersturmführer Eichmann organized the Central Office for Jewish Emigration, the Gestapo at first demanded that three hundred Jews emigrate daily from the Protectorate. This represented an excellent pretext for the Gestapo to despoil the Jewish population. Without any consideration as to the actual possibilities of emigration, Jews, particularly those who were well-to-do, were ordered by Nazi authorities to leave the country within three weeks. When the persons in question were unable to secure the necessary visas and transportation within the time-limit, they were, as a rule, fined 50,000 crowns. After this, the time-limit was usually extended to three months. If, after expiration of this period, the Jews were still unable to secure the required visas and documents, they were fined again.

If a Jew found an opportunity to emigrate, he had to apply to the Gestapo for an exit-permit through the Central Office for Jewish Emigration. There he had to fill out about eighteen questionnaires, containing questions regarding property, taxes and total possessions, as well as of a personal character. The Germans frankly admitted that the purpose of these questionnaires was to obtain as much money as possible from Jews who were granted the "privilege" of going abroad.

Just as no passport was issued until the Czech officials, working under German control, were satisfied that all general taxes were paid, so the Gestapo issued exit-permits only after the payment of special taxes imposed on Jews. It was the duty of the Jewish community to fix the so-called "Jew-Tax" to be paid to the Gestapo in cash before obtaining the exit-permit. If someone had, for instance, 300,000 crowns (the value of the crown was $.029), the "Jew-Tax" was payable according to the following scale:

Jew-tax	5% - 15,000 crowns
Flight-tax (Reichefluchtsteuer)	25% - 75,000 crowns
Duties on baggage and belongings valued at 10,000 crowns	6,000 crowns
Total	96,000 crowns

Thus, there remained at his disposal 204,000 crowns. When he called to collect his exit-permit, the Gestapo demanded an additional "voluntary" payment of 200,000 crowns. No consideration was given to the objection that if he paid the amount in question, he would be unable to emigrate, because he would have no money left to transfer, and his visa would be withdrawn.

As a rule, it was far easier for poor people to emigrate than for the rich. For a property worth up to 6,000 crowns, the tax was 3 Reichsmarks

" " " " " "	10,000 " " " "	1%
" " " " " "	20,000 " " " "	2%
" " " " " "	50,000 " " " "	3%
" " " " " "	200,000 " " " "	4%
" " " " " "	500,000 " " " "	5%
" " " " " "	1,000,000 " " " "	10%

For each additional 100,000 crowns the rate rose 1% more, up to 20%.

If the total property exceeded 200,000 crowns in value, a flight-tax (Reichsfluchtsteuer) of 25% of the value of the property had to be paid, in addition to the Jew-Tax.

Duties were also levied on goods the emigrant proposed to take with him. For the license to take clothes and underwear, a tax varying between 50% and 120% of the estimated value was paid. If jewelry, silver, rugs, and furs had been previously exported with the approval of the Ministry of Finance, despite the fact that duty had already been paid once, these articles were again subject to duty up to 300% of the estimated value.

After paying the sereral varieites of taxes and imposts, there was generally very little left for the emigrant to take along. In practice, the Gestapo did not limit itself by the tax-laws, but found ways to take everything the Jews owned.

Terezin; Other Concentration Camps.

In the spring of 1942, the town of Terezin (Theresienstadt) was transformed into a concentration settlement for Jews by the Reich Protector of Bohemia-Moravia. Its 7,000 non-Jewish inhabitants were evacuated to make room for a large number of Jewish internees from the Reich, Austria and the Protectorate.

According to reports, Terezin differed greatly from all the other ghetto areas of Eastern Europe, and especially from the confinement areas in Poland where large numbers of old people had been permitted to starve or to die of disease even before the period of outright extermination. In Terezin large numbers of elderly Jews, men and women alike, are reported to be living under comparatively satisfactory conditions. Under German supervision, a well-organized Jewish welfare committee is said to take care of the feeding and the medical treatment of the more than 40,000 inhabitants of the crowded ghetto town. The welfare committee is also under the guidance of Jewish public leaders and welfare experts who are themselves Terezin internees.

While the population consists of prevalently old people, the various public services are manned by some 7,000 younger, able-bodied Jews who are paid at a fixed scale of salaries, half of which is deducted "for the aged." There are even said to be salaried Jews among the white collar workers of the various services. An adequate number of Jewish physicians are in charge of public health which, in spite of a shortage of medical supplies, is reported to be satisfactory.

During the early part of July 1942 some 8,000 Jews between the ages of 65 and 85 were transferred from Prague to Terezin; an additional 7,000 were scheduled to be evacuated later that month.

The unique example offered by Terezin may perhaps be explained by the realization, among Nazi leaders, that they must have an alibi at hand when they are confronted with the evidences of mass Jewish destruction. The maintenance of Terezin as a model ghetto is in line with the Nazi efforts to efface the traces of mass graves around Warsaw, Lublin, Tremblinka and Grodek in Poland.

In Moravia, a ghetto was set up in the town of Uhersky Brod, and settled with the Jews from the surrounding districts. According to a report in March 1942 those Slovak Jews who had not been deported to Poland had been put into fourteen concentration camps, the most important of which was at Oremlaz.

Government-in-Exile.

In the Czechoslovak Government-in-Exile, the following persons are of Jewish faith or of Jewish origin: Jaroslav Stransky, Minister of Agriculture and Public Works, an outstanding journalist and liberal politician (christened Jew); Ernest Frischer, of Moravská Ostrava, President of the Czechoslovak Zionist Party, and appointed by President Beneš at the beginning of 1942 to represent the interests of the Jewish Party in the Czechoslovak State Council; Julius Friedman, leading official in the Economic Section of the Czechoslovak Ministry of Foreign Affairs, and appointed to the Czechoslovak State Council as an economic expert.

Jewish Groups-in-Exile.

Although the majority of the Czechoslovak refugees in England are Jews, most of them are not active politically. The only Czechoslovak Jewish groups-in-exile are a small group of between 20 and 25, constituting the Czechoslovak Jewish Committee affiliated with the World Jewish Congress, a small organization of Czech Jews in London, with membership of between 20 and 30, and the organization called the Czech National Jew, in London, with 100 members.

Reconstruction Agencies.

Among the foreign reconstruction agencies which might help in the rehabilitation of Czechoslovak Jewry are the American Jewish Joint Distribution Committee, the American Joint-Reconstruction Foundation, the ORT Society for the promotion of trade and agriculture among Jews, the OSE World Union for health protection, the HICEM (Hias-Ica Emigration Association) and the Jewish Agency for Palestine.

JEWS OF DENMARK

JEWS OF DENMARK

Index

	Page
Age Distribution	2
Anti-Semitism	6
Attitude of Jews to the United States	4
of Government to Jews	5
of People to Jews	5
Birth	2
Church and the Jews	5
Citizenship	4
Community Structure	1
Divorce	2
Education	3
Health Services	4
Languages	3
Marriage	2
Mortality	2
Occupation Measures, German	6
Occupational Distribution	3
Patriotism	4
Population	1
Press	5
Reconstruction Agencies	6
Refugees, Danish, in Sweden	6
Religious Organization	1
Social Structure	2
Welfare Services	4

JEWS OF DENMARK

Population

Since 1921 no statistics on religious affiliation have been available for Denmark, so that the figures here presented are estimates. Before Denmark was occupied by the Germans its Jewish population was between 6,000 and 6,500. They constituted about 1% of the Copenhagen population, where more than 95% of all Danish Jews lived, and about 1.5 per thousand of the total Danish population.

After 1933 many German Jews sought refuge in Denmark. Entry was very difficult for refugees who intended to remain, but not so difficult for those who intended to remain only temporarily, until they could get visas for the United States, Palestine, etc. 1,500 to 2,000 were in Denmark when the Germans occupied it.

In August 1943 the Germans imposed total military control on Denmark and the Danish government resigned. Early in October the Germans began to round up the Jews for deportation. Of the 14,000 who had escaped to Sweden from Denmark by January 1944, some 7,000 were Jews, including refugees.

No Jews were left in Denmark. All those who did not succeed in escaping were sooner or later deported to Terezin (Theresienstadt), Czechoslovakia.

Religious and Community Structure

Since the beginning of the twentieth century the Jewish community had not existed outside of Copenhagen. In the nineteenth century there had been flourishing communities in provincial cities, some with their own rabbis (e.g., Randers, Aalborg, Faaborg). By the beginning of the twentieth century the younger generation had moved to Copenhagen and these communities ceased to exist. All that was left of them was the Jewish cemeteries in a chain of provincial towns.

The Jewish community received the major share of its income in the form of taxes, which it continued to levy on its members in accordance with long established privilege. The tax assessment, which was subject to the approval of the Copenhagen city council, normally ran between 1% and 1½% of the declared annual income. The Community also had assets of about 8,000,000 Kroner (approximately $2,000,000), largely derived from legacies and earmarked for philanthropic purposes. The main Copenhagen synagogue was erected in 1833; its one hundredth anniversary was celebrated at a ceremony attended by King Christian X. (The Copenhagen Jewish community itself had been founded in 1684.) Since 1920 Dr. M. Friediger had been chief Rabbi.

Danish Judaism was strongly conservative; there was no Reform movement. This despite the extremely emancipated character of the older community and the high incidence of intermarriage and abandonment of Judaism. Among the newer immigrant group many were very observant.

In Copenhagen there were a Zionist society, a B'nai B'rith lodge, a branch of the Alliance Israelite Universelle, and the headquarters of the union of Jewish youth organizations of all the Scandinavian countries. There were about

400 members of the youth organization, besides a large number who belonged to the athletic society Hakoah (Heb. -- "Strength"), which was very active and some of whose members were outstanding as wrestlers.

Social Structure

The Danish Jewish community was composed of two fairly distinct groups: the descendants of Dutch Sephardic and German Jews who had settled in Denmark in the seventeenth century at the invitation of the Danish king, who hoped thereby to stimulate trade; and immigrants from Eastern Europe since 1905 who were driven from the Russian Empire by pogroms, together with their children. By the middle of the 1920's, the latter element was the more numerous.

The immigrant group was much more religious than the other, and was more active in Jewish affairs. It constituted the bulk of the Danish Zionist movement.

A study of incomes of Danish Jews showed a fairly large number of Jews in the lower income groups and a substantial proportion among the wealthy, with surprisingly few in the middle brackets. By and large, the immigrants and their children had the low incomes, and the members of the long-established community were the wealthy. During the 1930's there was a growing bridging of the social and economic gap between the children of the new immigration and the longer-established group.

Age Distribution; Birth; Mortality

The age distribution of the Danish Jews resembled that of the total Copenhagen population. Before the arrival of the East European immigration, the oldtime Jewish community had a smaller proportion of young people and a larger proportion of old than the general population; the immigrants restored the balance.

The age distribution being similar to that of the entire Danish population, the Jewish mortality was also similar. No data are at hand for the number of Jews who died in Nazi internment either in Denmark or in the places in which they had been deported.

The proportion of births among Jews was about the same as among the rest of the Copenhagen population. The Danish birthrate had been declining for a number of years; the decline was felt in the Jewish community (including the newer elements) too, perhaps to a greater extent.

Marriage; Divorce

The distribution of the Jewish community according to marital status was very similar to that of the Copenhagen population as a whole, as was the divorce rate.

Since the nineteenth century the proportion of mixed marriages entered into by Jews was very high; throughout the twentieth century it averaged almost 50%. The bulk of these mixed marriages were contracted by members of the older community. As in other countries, men tended a little more than women to marry out of their faith. Most of the children of such marriages were not brought up as Jews.

Languages

The older Jewish community was entirely Danish in its culture and speech. Most of the members of this group were of the Danish upper class with respect to education, status and wealth, and they were familiar with the major foreign languages of educated Danes: German and English. Very few knew Hebrew; Yiddish, being primarily an East European phenomenon, was unknown to them.

Most of the immigrants knew Danish, and for their children Danish was the mother tongue. A large part of the immigrants continued to speak Yiddish at home, and it was understood by their children.

Education

At the beginning of the nineteenth century two elementary schools, one for boys and one for girls, were founded by leaders of the Jewish community to give Jewish youth a modern Danish education. These schools still existed at the time of the German invasion, with a total student body of some 250. In the middle of the nineteenth century a religious school was founded, which had about 150 students in 1940.

A large majority of Jewish children attended the public schools.

In 1931 it was estimated that about fifty Jewish men and women were teachers, with a little more than half in higher education.

Occupational Distribution

The following were the occupations in which Jews were engaged, in the order of their importance: 1) handicrafts and industry; 2) trade and commerce; 3) professions. In this distribution the Jews resembled the general Copenhagen population, with the one exception that whereas about 10% of all the Copenhagen gainfully employed were engaged in transport and communications, only about 1% of the Jewish gainfully employed were so engaged. The ratio of Jews in all occupational categories who were owners and directors was higher than the general ratio, and the ratio of salaried employees and workers lower. This had an income significance in commerce and the professions, but very little in handicrafts and industry, in which the owner of a small tailor's shop was considered in the same category with the owner of a large industrial plant.

In handicrafts and industry, more than 20% of all male Jews gainfully employed were tailors, constituting 10% of all tailors in Copenhagen.

In trade, the largest number was that of wholesalers. Of the professions, the following were the categories in which Jews were engaged, in the order of their importance: 1) arts and science (i.e., journalism, music, etc.); 2) law and accounting; 3) education; 4) medicine.

The largest group of Jewish women were in the home. Those employed outside the home tended to work in the professions, stores and offices.

During the 1930's a considerable number of the children of the immigrants were able to establish independent enterprises, especially in the textile, shoe and leather trades; a fair proportion of these businesses grew considerably.

Citizenship

The process of emancipation of the Danish Jews began at the end of the eighteenth century, when restrictions against their entering certain crafts were removed, and continued until 1849, when the constitution was granted; by its terms full and equal citizenship rights were conferred on them.

In the early 1930's, about 65% of the Jewish population had been born in Denmark and the rest were immigrants. About 75% of all Jews were Danish citizens, with one half the remainder being children who would probably attain citizenship on their majority. By the end of the 1930's the only Jewish non-refugee non-citizens were a few of the aged immigrants.

Non-Scandinavian immigrants applying for naturalization were required, among other things, to have lived in Denmark for fifteen years (Scandinavians, ten years).

Patriotism

The Jews of Denmark were loyal Danes concerning whose devotion to their country there was no question. A significant number of the men who had made major contributions to the welfare of Denmark and added to her fame throughout the world were Jewish; the eminent nineteenth-century literary critic, Georg Brandes, was the most outstanding of these.

Attitude to the United States

Like the rest of the democratic Danish nation the Jews had a favorable attitude towards the United States. After the Germans occupied Denmark this attitude was intensified.

Health Services

There were no special Jewish hospitals, although there was a society for the needy sick. About forty physicians were Jewish; the three most outstanding were O. M. Henriques, L. S. Fridericia and Erik Warburg. There were few Jewish nurses.

Welfare Services

Until about 1930 it was the responsibility of the Copenhagen community to provide for all its members in need of assistance. Funds for this purpose came from the taxes levied by the community. The welfare institutions owned by the community were two homes for the aged.

Of the German refugees admitted to Denmark very few were given the right to work, as a consequence of widespread Danish unemployment. These refugees were almost entirely dependent on assistance from the Jewish community, the funds for which were provided out of annual collections and contributions from the Joint Distribution Committee.

In cooperation with non-Jewish organizations, the Jewish community made it possible for Jewish children from Germany, 300 at a time, to live in Danish homes or camps until they were ready to join the Youth Aliyah to Palestine.

For the assistance of the estimated 5,000 who escaped to Sweden, a central organization was established by the Danish legation in Stockholm, under the leadership of Professor Stephan Hurwitz, of the University of Copenhagen, to supervise all camps and the distribution of all assistance, to provide for the schooling of children and to assist the able-bodied to find employment.

Press

A monthly Danish-language paper, Israeliten, had originally been published by the Jewish youth organizations but later became the official organ of the Copenhagen Jewish community. The Yiddish semi-monthly Kopenhagener Tribune ceased publication in the 1930's.

A certain number of Jews were journalists of the general Danish press.

Faedrelandet ("Fatherland") and Nationalsocialisten were the two largest anti-Semitic newspapers. They were both organs of the German propaganda machine.

Church and the Jews

The Danish Church, like the rest of the Scandinavian churches, was opposed to anti-Semitism and Nazism. In October 1943, after the Germans had started to deport Jews to Poland, a pastoral letter of strong protest was read in all the pulpits of the country.

Attitude of People and Government

Since the nineteenth century Denmark had been a very democratic country, and no significant native anti-Semitism existed there.

After 1933 a considerable number of halutzim (pioneers) from Germany were admitted to Denmark, where they received agricultural training before going to Palestine. The Danish government and Danish farmers were very helpful in this program, which was initiated by the Zionist organization in Copenhagen.

In April 1940 the Germans invaded and overran Denmark. The German occupation authorities allowed the Danish government to continue functioning. When they demanded the introduction of anti-Jewish measures, the King and the Government refused. In 1943, after long occupation and in intense propaganda campaign, the Germans allowed an election to take place, and 98% of the population supported the democratic parties.

Increasing sabotage and popular resistance led the Germans to make demands for intensified suppression. Following the refusal of the King and Government, the Germans imposed their own total military dictatorship. The Government resigned and the King was put under house arrest. Among the prominent Danes arrested by the Germans were leaders of the Jewish community. Some, like Dr. Erik Warburg, the King's physician, were later released through the influence of the King or other highly placed Danes, and of those released some later escaped to Sweden.

On October 1, 1943, the Germans began to round up all the Jews of Denmark for deportation. Most Jews had been warned and had left their homes before the Nazis came for them. About half of all those who reached Sweden from Denmark were Jews. Only the wholehearted help of the Danish population -- fishermen, policemen, etc.--

enabled them to escape the Gestapo and to make their way in small boats across the Oresund strait.

Anti-Semitism

No native anti-Semitic movement of any significance existed in Denmark. After Hitler came to power in Germany several Danish Nazi organizations were founded, with a membership mostly of Danes of German origin from Slesvig. Fritz Clausen was Fuehrer of the largest of these parties; others were headed by Aage Andersen and Vilfred Petersen. Shortly before the war only three Nazis were elected to the lower chamber, of a total of 150. In 1943 the democratic parties received 98% of all votes.

German Occupational Measures

In the beginning of the German occupation the German authorities allowed the Danish government to continue functioning, and no attempt was made to impose the Nuremburg racial laws or similar anti-Jewish measures. Jews were able to continue living almost as they had lived before; the Jewish organizations were not interfered with. The Germans were successful in having a new Danish government formed which was to be friendly to the Germans, but it refused to accede to German demands for the introduction of anti-Jewish legislation.

Not all who attempted to escape to Sweden in October 1943 succeeded. Some were caught and shot, and others were drowned or machine-gunned in their boats. Those who were caught before they could try to escape, including the aged and the sick, were interned in various prison camps, from which they were subsequently deported to a concentration camp near Terezin, in Czechoslovakia. Among them was Dr. Friediger, the chief rabbi. About 600 Jews from Denmark were in Terezin at the beginning of 1944.

The property of Jewish individuals and organizations was confiscated.

Danish Refugees in Sweden

The Swedish government gave radio assurance of welcome in Sweden for all who succeeded in escaping the Germans in Denmark. When they arrived they were received with the greatest hospitality by the government and people. For the majority of the refugees, penniless and without prospects of self-support, the Swedes established several camps where they were fed and given shelter. The attitude of the Swedish people was admirable.

Contributions for the maintenance of these refugees came from the Swedish people, from Jewish organizations in Sweden and other free countries and from Danish organizations throughout the world. By 1944 most of the refugees from Denmark were employed and living in private homes.

Reconstruction Agencies

The principal Jewish organizations which may cooperate in reconstruction work in Denmark are: The American Jewish Joint Distribution Committee (New York); HICEM (Hias-Ica Emigration Association) (New York); and the Jewish Agency for Palestine (Jerusalem).

JEWS OF ESTONIA

JEWS OF ESTONIA

Index

	Page
Age Distribution	3
Agriculture	5
Anti-Semitism	6
Banks	5
Birth	3
Citizenship	5
Commerce	4
Communal Organizations	1
Cooperatives	5
Criminality	2
Divorce	2
Economic Position	3
Education	2
Family	1
Government, Jews in	6
Health Services	6
Industry	4
Insurance	5
Labor	4
Languages	2
Leaders, Jewish	7
Marriage	2
Minority Rights	6
Mortality	3
Occupational Distribution	3
Population	1
Press	3
Reconstruction Agencies	8
Religious Organization	1
Social Services	6
Sovietization	7
Taxes	5

JEWS OF ESTONIA

Population

On March 1, 1934, the 4,434 Estonian Jews constituted .4% of the total population of 1,126,410. Almost all lived in cities and towns, representing 1.3% of the urban population. Nearly one half of all Estonian Jews lived in Talinn and more than one fifth in Tartu. Of the rest, the majority lived in the following towns, in the order of size of their Jewish communities: Valga, Pärnu, Narva, Viljandi, and Rakvere.

Since Estonia was overrun by the Germans later than the other Baltic countries, it is likely that some Estonian Jews had a chance to escape to the Soviet Union. It was reported that no Jews were left in Estonia by August 1943.

Family

Jewish tradition perhaps made for greater family stability among Jews than non-Jews. There were no legal differences, with respect to the authority of the father, the position of the wife, etc., between Jewish and other families.

Religious Life and Organization

There was complete separation of Church and State. Jewish religious functions and institutions were considered the private concern of those interested.

Of the 4,434 Jews by nationality, 4,302 declared themselves Jews by religion. The community was small and not long-established. Synagogues were Orthodox. There was a larger group that was not observant than might be deduced from the figures on religious affiliation, but there was no conflict between the observant and non-observant groups. Rabbis had little influence in the non-religious activities of the communities.

Communal Organizations

There were no very marked or bitter party divisions within the community. The Zionist groups were the largest and most active, and they dominated the Jewish cultural administration. Among the Zionists, the General Zionist group was most influential. The "Yiddishist" minority, in opposition to the dominant Zionists, was composed of groups and individuals without very clear-cut party affiliations. The influence of the (anti-Zionist, Socialist and Yiddishist) Bund was slight.

The following is a partial list of Jewish cultural organizations, with the dates of their founding: Bialik Society, Tallinn, 1918; Kadima, Tallinn; Yiddish School Organization, Tallinn, 1928; Likht Society, Tallinn, 1926; Dramatic Circle, Tartu, 1917; Jewish Dramatic and Literary Society, Narva, 1930; Eiges Library, Tartu, 1906; Friends of Yiddish, Tartu, 1930; Achdut Society, Pärnu, 1919; Culture Society, Viljandi, 1935; Jewish Archives in Estonia, Tartu, 1920.

Marriage; Divorce

No statistics are available for marriage and divorce among Jews. A civil ceremony for marriage and a civil decree for divorce were compulsory; they might be followed, in each case, by their religious equivalents. It is likely that the proportion of religious marriage rites to the total number of marriages entered into by Jews was higher than religious divorce decrees to the total number of divorces.

Criminality

No data are available for the criminality of Jews, except for prostitution statistics in 1929. In that year the Jewish and German groups had the lowest proportion of prostitutes.

Languages

The 1934 census listed Yiddish as the customary language of 2,381 persons and an additional language for 1,142. Hebrew was customary for 88 and additional for 380. Probably every Jew had some knowledge of Estonian. Russian was known at least to the older generation, as was German. Swedish was confined largely to the Swedish group.

Education

From the founding of the Estonian state all citizens were allowed to educate their children in their own language. Twenty or more children in a locality, speaking a minority language, were entitled to have a state school in that language. Machinery was also provided for the cultural development of minorities, exclusive of schools. The 1925 law on cultural self-government was the most liberal in Europe, and a proof that political cohesiveness did not require the inhibition of the rights of minorities. The law allowed every ethnic group of 3,000 or more to be legally organized as a cultural administration receiving state support for its institutions in proportion to its numbers. Much care was exercised to safeguard cooperation between the administrations and the state authorities while not jeopardizing the full autonomy of the cultural administrations. Over and above state subsidies for the educational institutions of minorities, the imposition of special taxes by the cultural administrations on their own groups was allowed. In May 1934, at the beginning of the authoritarian regime, the law on secondary schools was changed, with administration being more centralized than previously in the Ministry of Education.

In the first few years of the Republic a radical Yiddishist policy was followed in the Jewish elementary and secondary schools. With the election of a Zionist cultural administration Hebrew became the chief language of instruction. As a result of the dissatisfaction of the opposition Yiddishist elements in the cultural administration, and the founding of a private school in which Yiddish was stressed, equality between Hebrew and Yiddish was introduced into the schools. (The private school was later absorbed into the cultural administration school system.) This condition lasted throughout the 1930's, until the Soviet regime suppressed the teaching of Hebrew.

More than 11% of the Estonian Jewish population were well educated, and more than 37% had received a secondary education. In 1926 there were 188 Jewish students at the University of Tartu; in 1934 there were 96. 51 students attended the University school of medicine in 1926, but only 18 in 1934. By the latter year it was said that discrimination was being practiced against Jews in the form of more rigorous entrance examinations. In 1934 there were 104 Jewish students of law at the University; in 1937 there were 44.

Of the 86 secondary schools in existence during the school year 1928-29, two were Jewish, with 148 students. Probably almost all of the 42 Jewish teachers in the elementary and secondary schools were employed by the Jewish schools. The very large majority of Jewish children attended the Jewish schools.

Dr. Lazar Gulkovitch was the only Jewish professor at the University. He occupied the chair of Jewish history and philosophy. A non-Jewish "non-Aryan," Dr. Agatha Lasch, taught Germanic philology at the University after she was compelled to leave the University of Berlin.

Press

There was only one Jewish publication in Estonia, the periodical Yediess fun der Yidisher Kulturfarvaltung in Esti (Yiddish -- "Estonian Jewish Cultural Administration News"). Weekly supplements devoted to the Estonian scene were regular features of the Riga (Latvia) Haynt (Yid. -- "Today") and Frimorgen (Yid. -- "Morning"), and the Kaunas (Lithuania; also known as Kovno) Yidishe Shtimme (Yid. -- "Jewish Voice").

Age Distribution; Birth; Mortality

The census of 1934 showed proportionately fewer Jews than other Estonians in the age brackets 0 - 20 and over 60. Comparison with the 1922 census indicated that the Jewish group as a whole had been aging.

The Jewish birthrate was substantially below that of non-Jews. In 1928 the proportion of Jewish births to the total was .22%, whereas the Jews constituted .4% of the population.

Infant mortality among Jews was lower than among any other ethnic group.

Economic Position; Occupational Distribution

The general economic position of the Jews in Estonia was sound. Most Jews were self-maintaining. Jewish emigration was considerably lower than it would have been had strong economic factors operated.

According to the census of 1934 Jews were particularly active in industry, commerce, administration and the professions. In 1935 the Jewish Cultural

Administration made a survey which indicated that 56% of the total Jewish population were gainfully employed. They were categorized as follows: commerce, 30.4%; employers, 24%; artisans, 14.8%; workers, 14%; professionals, 9.5%; industrialists, 5%; landlords, 1.4%; religious functionaries, .9%.

Labor

Workers and (white-collar) employees thus constituted 38% of the entire number of Jews gainfully employed. Of the employees, more than 70% worked in offices and stores. Their wages and salaries were average for their occupations.

Commerce

In commerce, which constituted the largest field of occupation for Jews, the most numerous group of Jews was composed of wage-earners and salaried people; the next largest group worked for themselves; then came employers of paid help, and finally the independents who worked together with their families. The Jewish Cultural Administration 1935 census estimated that only about 2% of Estonia's commerce was in the hands of Jews. There was an emphasis on timber, textiles, fur and drygoods. The export of chocolates was mostly in Jewish hands. Most of the Jews in commerce were in retail trade. 30% of Jewish retailers conducted enterprises characterized as "modest" in size. Between 1925 and 1933 the number of commercial enterprises owned by Jews declined about 25%. By 1938 the export of butter, eggs, bacon, flax and meats had become a government monopoly, and the export of grain and lumber had increasingly come under government control. Actually this large measure of government intervention did not undermine the economic position of the Estonian Jews, but the possibility that it might do so, like government intervention in other East European countries, affected the feeling of security of the Jews.

Industry

After commerce, industry of various kinds, including artisan handicrafts, was next in importance as a source of livelihood for Jews. The largest industrial group consisted of wage-earners and salaried employees; next came employers; the self-employed were third, and independents working with their families were last. Among the artisans, about 60% had no employees at all, and only about 8% had three employees or more. The number of shops owned by Jewish artisans represented about 6.5% of all such shops in the country. 31% of all tailors in Estonia, 16% of all furriers and 15% of all tinsmiths were Jews. Artisans who were not employers were not required to be licensed. Those who did need licenses did not complain about discriminatory licensing. It was believed, however, that members of minority groups, including the Jewish group, were discriminated against when they sought entrance to the Tallinn School of Arts and Trades.

Agriculture

In 1934 only 38 Jews were listed as being occupied in agriculture, of whom in turn only four were farm-owners. In 1937 a <u>hachsharah</u> (training) farm for about 30 <u>halutzim</u> (Palestine pioneers) was established.

Banks

There were three Jewish banks: 1) the Tallinn Jewish Cooperative Bank, with a (1936) capital of 103,000 kroon (the kroon was worth between $.20 and $.25); 2) the Tartu Jewish Cooperative Bank, with a capital of 50,000 kroon; and 3) the Narva Jewish Loan and Savings Bank. There was no discrimination against these banks. They were so small because the important Jewish merchants and industrialists dealt with non-Jewish banks. The Jewish banks were primarily concerned with providing credit for small businessmen, who would have found it impossible to interest the larger banks in their needs.

Insurance

Two Jewish insurance companies were affiliated with the Jewish bank of Tallinn. One was for life insurance; the other, called <u>Ezra</u> (Heb. - "Aid"), provided insurance against transportation risks.

Cooperatives

A number of cooperatives were established in the 1920's and 1930's. Particularly after the establishment of the authoritarian regime in 1934 they had government support. The largest of them, known as ETK, entered into the production of such commodities as dyestuffs and cosmetics, competing in part with Jewish entrepreneurs. But the government did not practise economic discrimination against the Jews.

Taxes

No discriminatory taxes were levied against Jews.

Citizenship

The Jews living on Estonian territory when the new state was established became Estonian citizens without any difficulty. Five years of residence were required of immigrants who desired to be naturalized. There was no discrimination against Jews. In 1935, 3,305 Jews were citizens; 336 were stateless with Nansen passports; the rest were nationals of other countries, especially of the two other Baltic republics, Latvia and Lithuania.

Minority Rights

In addition to the autonomy granted to the Jewish community in matters of culture and education, Jews were allowed to use Yiddish in communication with local authorities in areas where they constituted a majority. Unlike other language minorities, however, they were not allowed the use of their minority language in correspondence with the national authorities. The Jews being a very small proportion of the total population even in the cities, the question of separate representation in the municipalities was not raised.

Jews in the Government

In 1937 H. Gutkin, vice-president of the Jewish cultural administration, was appointed to the Senate. He was the only Jew in Parliament. There were no Jewish judges.

Social Services

Because the Estonian Jewish community was small and relatively prosperous there was no great development of the social services. In 1935 only 21,000 kroon (kroon = approximately $.23) were distributed to those in need. Delinquency presented no important problem.

Health Services

Jewish physicians constituted 8.9% of the total number in Estonia.

Anti-Semitism

The Estonians were comparatively free of anti-Semitism. By temperament rather more sober than other peoples in Eastern Europe, they also had a more sturdy democratic and civic tradition, dating back to the days of opposition to the Czars and, before that, to Swedish times. Finnish cultural influence was strong, and the Finns were regarded as older, more advanced and more successful ethnic brothers. The number of Jews in Estonia being small, their usefulness as scapegoats in times of crisis would not have been perhaps very great. Nor were the Jews so outstandingly successful in their economic life as to arouse popular jealousy and enmity.

The minorities provisions and practices of the Estonian state were outstandingly liberal, and in the economic sphere, even after the institution in 1934 of an authoritarian government, there was no specifically anti-Jewish discrimination. As late as December 1938 the Minister of Economics declared that the "Estonization" of industry would not be accomplished by a forcible change of ownership and that minorities would be given an opportunity to collaborate. This promise was not broken, though naturally the trend of events was not reassuring to the Jews. They were particularly disturbed by the harsh attitude of the government with respect to refugees from Germany and Austria in 1938 and 1939. In July 1938 O. Kask, Minister of Public Welfare, announced that Jewish refugees would not be admitted, adding that the Jewish problem became acute in countries where a small number of Jews had a disproportionately strong influence on economic life.

The first Estonian constitution, promulgated in 1920, had been very democratic. In response to the tensions and frictions in the rest of Europe, however, unrest began to grow noticeably. The rise of the Nazi movement in Germany particularly encouraged the Estonian War Veterans' Movement to demand the institution of the "leadership" principle to supplant the "decadent" parliamentary system. This movement later adopted the name "Fighters for Freedom" (VAPS). Its ideologist was Dr. Mäe, its candidate for the presidency General Larka, and its real leader Arthur Sirk, a lawyer. Others prominent in it were: Captain Reha, Colonel Seiman and General Törwand.

When Hitler came to power in Germany, in 1933, the VAPS gained sharply in strength. Its opponents were terrorized. Repressive measures, including the dissolution of its Tartu branch, were unavailing. In August 1933 the government declared a state of emergency, outlawed the VAPS, and confiscated its property. Nevertheless the influence of the VAPS continued strong. In the October elections a referendum which it had introduced received a majority of the votes, and a new authoritarian constitution went into effect.

In this juncture the former president, K. Päts, took the initiative in proclaiming an authoritarian regime. The VAPS movement was suppressed and finally eliminated in the trials of 1936. All other parties were also suppressed, and the freedom of the press was circumscribed. Estonia became a one-party state, with the Fatherland Party declaring as its aims the promotion of civil peace, national ideals, and class collaboration.

Since, however, this authoritarian regime had been instituted primarily to ward off a worse one, and since many of its leaders continued to hold fairly liberal sentiments, the liberal elements in Estonia did not fare nearly so badly as in some neighboring countries. The position of Jews, too, did not deteriorate so sharply as elsewhere. Indeed, by comparison with the lot of the Jews in Germany, Austria, Poland, Roumania, etc., the Jewish situation in Estonia was quite good. The Päts government neither advocated nor introduced a measure, advocated by the VAPS group, that ethnic Estonians constitute at least 90% of all workers and employees in each industrial and commercial enterprise. In the more-or-less fascist organization of industry and commerce the various "chambers" into which the economy was organized were not used as instruments of anti-Semitic policy.

Sovietization

Jewish "bourgeois" interests were affected in the same way as others like them; there was no discrimination against Jews as such. Hebrew was suppressed because of the long-standing Soviet hostility to it.

Jewish Leaders

Some of the prominent figures in the community were: H. Gutkin, vice-president of the cultural administration, a Zionist, appointed to the Senate in 1937;

G. Aizenstat, president of the cultural administration for many years, a General Zionist; N. Genss, a Zionist; and J. Halbreich, J. Genss and A. Rochlin, "Yiddishists." The fate of all of them is unknown.

Reconstruction Agencies

The principal Jewish organizations which may cooperate in reconstruction work in Estonia are: The American Jewish Joint Distribution Committee (New York); HICEM (Hias-Ica Emigration Association) (New York); and the Jewish Agency for Palestine. OSE (for health and sanitation) may also be able to help.

THE JEWS OF FRANCE

THE JEWS OF FRANCE

Index

Affiliations, Political	5	Marriage	3
Anti-Semitism, History of	8	Medical Services	19
"Aryanization"	14	Minority Status	8
Assets, Community	3	Motion Pictures	14
Banking	11	Occupational Structure	10
Bar	12	Organization -	
Burial	3	Community	2
		Religious	2
Church	9	Organizations, Communal	4
Citizenship	6		
Communications	16		
Concentration Camps	18	Parliament	7
Criminality	4	Patriotism	6
Curfew	16	People, attitude of	22
		Population	1
		Press -	
Discriminatory Measures	17	Anti-Semitic and Quisling	13
Divorce	3	General	13
		Jewish	12
Education	19	Prisons	18
		Prostitution, Forced	18
Fines	17		
French Committee of National		Rationing	16
Liberation	10	Reconstruction, Agencies of	23
		Refugees	1
Government, Posts	7		
Judiciary	11	Social Security	19
Groups in Exile	10		
		Travel Restrictions	15
Hospitals	19		
		Unions	15
Industry	11	United States, Attitude to	23
Languages	4	Welfare -	
Leaders -			
in Exile	21	Jewish	19
in France	21	Public	19

THE JEWS OF FRANCE

Population; Refugees

This report deals with Metropolitan (European) France only; neither Algeria nor any other part of French North Africa, although the home of a substantial Jewish population, is treated here.

On the eve of the war, in 1939, there were about 320,000 Jews in France. The German campaign in Holland and Belgium drove before it an estimated additional 15,000 into France. About 25,000 French Jews were taken prisoner, were killed or disappeared during the period from the German invasion of the Low Countries to the armistice of June 22, 1940. We may therefore estimate the number of Jews in France at that date as about 310,000, or a little less than .75% of the total population (1936 census, 42,000,000).

Of these 310,000, about half were French citizens by birth or by naturalization, the other half being foreigners. About 50,000 were refugees from Germany, Austria or Czechoslovakia. The other foreigners were divided among various other nationalities, primarily Roumanian, Polish and Russian. Among those of the last three nationalities a good many were stateless, having been deprived of their citizenship by revolutionary upheavals in their home countries (e.g., Russia) or by legislation specifically, if not ostensibly, designed to deprive Jews of their citizenship (e.g., Roumania, Poland). The French authorities provided them with a carte d'identité and registered them, in most instances, as nationals of the countries of their birth, paying little heed to the statelessness decreed by the governments of their home countries. Among the Russian Jews, however, those who were not Soviet citizens were generally classed as "Russian refugees" and usually were in possession of the "Nansen passport." Among foreign Jews there was one special category - numerically not negligible, especially in Paris and Marseilles - of "Jews from the Levant," mostly from Greek Salonica and the countries of the Near East. They were considered only "half-foreign," because in their homelands they had traditionally been, like other non-Moslems, "wards" of the French government in the face of Turkish oppression before the First World War. They enjoyed certain benefits not usually accorded to foreigners.

The Jews were an urban element, concentrated in the large cities: Paris, in which there lived about one half of the total Jewish population of France; Lyons; Bordeaux; Marseilles; Strasbourg; Nancy; Lille. There were some Jewish plantations in the south of France; and training farms throughout France, since about 1925, to provide agricultural training for young people, most of whom wished to emigrate to Palestine.

From June 1940 to the end of 1942 the Jewish population of France was probably reduced by considerably more than 100,000, so that it numbered several thousand less than 200,000. This reduction in population was brought about by various means: deaths in concentration and labor camps in both the (pre-November 1942) occupied and "unoccupied" zones; executions of foreign Jews; deportations en masse, both by the Germans and the Vichy government, after July 1942; the execution of Jewish hostages; and the voluntary emigration overseas of those Jews who were fortunate enough to be able to emigrate.

Before the mass deportations, Jews lived mostly in Paris, Lyons, Toulouse, Marseilles, Nice and Grenoble. After total German occupation of France, following the Allied landings in North Africa in November 1942, the Jews of Marseilles and the German-occupied Mediterranean coast were driven into the interior or put into concentration camps. Jews who had fled to the French region occupied by Italian troops (Nice, Grenoble, Chambéry, Aix-les-Bains) do not seem to have been very badly treated. Their relative immunity lasted only until the Germans took over.

Religious and Community Organization

The majority of the French Jews were not very observant. Solemn holidays, however, like Rosh Hashanah (New Year) and Yom Kippur (Day of Atonement) were generally observed. After the German conquest, many Jews, fearing to draw attention to themselves, did not observe even those holidays.

A certain number, principally among the wealthy, belonged to the "Reformed" group (prayers in French, etc.). Among the immigrants from Eastern Europe there was a relatively high proportion who observed Shabbat (Saturday Sabbath) and the other injunctions of Orthodox Judaism. About the same proportion obtained for the Jews of Alsace. The latter, however, were not immigrants, but had lived in Alsace for centuries and were completely integrated into French life, both socially and spiritually. Before the war there was a relatively strong movement for religious revival among youth groups, especially the Eclaireurs Israélites de France (Jewish Scouts of France).

The laws of the Third Republic made no distinction among religions, and no religious body was given special privileges. The function of the Jewish community was to look after the religious and spiritual needs of the Jews and offer specifically Jewish philanthropy. The responsible central organization was the Consistoire Central des Juifs de France (Central Council of the Jews of France), composed mostly of laymen. The Consistoire ratified the choice of rabbis by the various communities and supported synagogues, the rabbinical seminary and various philanthropic institutions. A rabbinical tribunal, to adjudicate disputes in matters touching on religion, was attached to the Consistoire. Membership in the consistorial structure was not obligatory, but very few refused to contribute when approached.

From 1905, when the law on separation of Church and State was passed, the Jewish religious organization, like all other religious organizations, had the status of a private body. Its finances had to be provided by individual contributions. (An important part of the finances had traditionally been furnished by the Rothschild family.) The French rabbi's influence was limited to the religious sphere.

The Levantine Jews had a religious organization of their own, the Association Cultuelle des Israélites du Levant. Its rabbi was authorized by the Ministry of Foreign Affairs to exercise a certain amount of civil authority. He was empowered to determine who should be considered a Levantine Jew and to issue certificates for births, deaths and marriages that had taken place abroad.

When the Germans occupied Paris they immediately shut down all synagogues except the Grand Temple, on the rue de la Victoire. Later a few were reopened. In the occupied zone acts of desecration were committed against synagogues in Bordeaux and Amiens. The hoodlums responsible were Doriotists (members of the Parti Populaire Français) who enjoyed the full cooperation of the Gestapo.

In the unoccupied zone the Vichy government repealed the 1905 law on separation of church and state. A law of November 1941 provided for the dissolution of all existing Jewish organizations and for the transfer of their funds to an Union Générale des Juifs de France, to be created on the Nazi model, with membership compulsory. Nevertheless, the Consistoire apparently was able to continue a legal existence. Indeed, the Chief Rabbi of France and other rabbis who had fled to the unoccupied zone continued to exercise their religious functions freely until the end of 1942. They were, however, severely hampered in their work because of lack of funds and the general crisis affecting the Jews.

Until the summer of 1942 the official attitude of Vichy to the Jewish religion was rather fair. For example, the Minister of Supplies allowed Jews to turn in their bread rations for matzot (unleavened bread) instead of bread during the Passover, and 500 tons of flour were allocated for baking matzot.

Despite the relative absence of violence and official disapproval many Jews refrained from synagogue attendance, fearing anti-Jewish outbursts at any moment. In the autumn of 1942 such an outburst did occur: under pretext that "communistic literature" had been discovered there, the Grande Synagogue in Nice was ravaged by the S.O.L. (Service d'Ordre Légionnaire - Pétain's Legionnaire Police). In Nice a synagogue was wrecked by a bomb planted by Doriot elements.

Shehitah (ritual slaughter of meat animals), permitted under the Republic, was not banned in the unoccupied zone. In practice, however, the meat shortage made it next to impossible to obtain kosher (ritually prepared) meat.

Community Assets

Under the Republic, religious organizations might own only such funds and property as were necessary for the discharge of their functions. However, the buildings, the sacred vessels and the libraries belonging to synagogues and related institutions were sometimes very valuable. (For example, the Paris synagogues of the rue de la Victoire or the rue des Tournelles were known to be quite wealthy.)

After the Armistice of June 1940, the funds of the Consistoire were confiscated in the occupied zone, and the libraries (totaling 60,000 volumes) of the Consistoire, the Alliance Israélite Universelle and the Paris Rabbinical Seminary were transferred to the Nazi Institute of Research on Jewish Problems in Frankfurt.

Marriage and Divorce; Burial

Before the invasion the marriage rate was somewhat higher among Jews than among non-Jews. French law was extremely severe in insisting on a civil marriage ceremony at the Town Hall, performed by a functionary of the State. This obligatory civil marriage might optionally be followed by a religious service. Not all Jews had their marriages solemnized by a rabbi; the proportion that felt the need of a religious in addition to the civil ceremony was about the same as that of similarly placed non-Jews married by a priest or minister.

Mixed marriages, between Jews and non-Jews, were quite common, especially among the wealthier classes. After the Statut des Juifs of October 3, 1940, and the supplementary law of June 2, 1941, civil authorities were instructed to place as many obstacles as possible in the way of mixed marriages. Among Jews the marriage rate decreased sharply as a result of the unfavorable conditions of existence.

Like marriage, divorce was a civil matter. A substantially smaller proportion of Jews asked for a subsequent rabbinical divorce (Get) than for rabbinical solemnization of marriage.

Jews were buried with appropriate religious ceremonies in common cemeteries that had sections reserved for Jews.

Criminality

The participation of Jews in crimes of violence was almost non-existent; those violations of which Jews were guilty were largely in the civil categories. Alcoholism was less frequent among Jews than among the general population.

Languages

The large majority spoke French. Among immigrants Yiddish continued to be spoken, as also Russian, Polish and - after 1933 - German. Most Levantine Jews spoke French adequately, but among themselves they tended to use their own Ladino (Judeo-Spanish).

Communal Organizations

Most Jews were not affiliated with any groups within the Jewish community. Among those who were affiliated, the Zionist movement was strongest, especially among elements more recently from Eastern Europe. Pro-Palestine sentiment, as distinguished from the Zionist movement with a relatively clearcut ideology, had in the years preceding 1940 become more popular, as a result of Palestine's achievements in refugee-absorption, among elements previously indifferent or even hostile to Zionism. All wings of Zionism were represented in France, from the religious (Mizrachi) through the general to the Labor wing. General Zionists were the most numerous, but the Labor groups were the most active and influential.

Two groups of importance in the Jewish community in some other European countries were comparatively unimportant in France: The Agudath Israel, the extreme Orthodox wing; and the Bund, or the General Alliance of Jewish Workers, with a pro-Yiddish and anti-Zionist attitude.

Particularly in Paris there were a number of Jewish societies, known as Amicales, each composed mainly of immigrants from the same area. Many, perhaps most, were founded about 1923 or 1924, a period of relatively large-scale immigration from Eastern Europe; a few had already been in existence for some time. They conformed to the requirements of the French law of 1901, and were active in social affairs (parties, lectures, etc.) as well as in mutual aid. A few burial societies existed, in addition to the Amicales.

A French section of the B'nai Brith was affiliated with the central French Masonic organization.

The Alliance Israélite Universelle had been formed toward the middle of the nineteenth century. Its purpose was to combat discrimination against Jews in the Near East and in backward European countries like Roumania. Its emphasis had become increasingly educational, and it maintained a network of schools in the Near East and North Africa.

Naturally, French Jews were also active in general French organizational life, embracing fraternal orders, sport clubs, mutual-aid societies and civic organizations.

Youth organizations had been founded not many years previously. For the most part, they had their origin in the need for united action in the face of the campaign of race hatred incited in France by the agents of Goebbels. The most important of the Jewish youth groups was the Eclaireurs Israélites de France, affiliated with the central scouts' organization, the Fédération des Eclaireurs de France. The Eclaireurs Israélites achieved remarkable success during the short period of its existence.

The Vichy government dissolved all Jewish communal and social organizations and ordered their assets to be transferred to the Union Générale des Israélites de France. "Illegal" Jewish organizational activity continued at least until 1942, however; the Zionist movement continued a restricted and undercover existence, and the Eclaireurs Israélites was kept going by the sacrifice and bravery of its leaders. In some regions, underground "cells" of the Eclaireurs were formed, and boys and girls were given an education stressing Jewish, French and democratic values.

Political Affiliations

The very great majority of the Jews of France were republican and democratic. A very small group far to the right was composed of a few wealthy Jews who were antagonistic to republicanism and democracy because of what they considered the interests of their class or because of a desire to conform to the political pattern dominant among certain circles of the French upper class.

The large proportion of French Jews were in the lower and middle-class. Their allegiance was to the parties traditionally supported by those classes among the French: the radicals and radical-socialists -- non-socialist and historically the bulwark of a democratic republic.

Most Jewish workers belonged to the socialist Confédération Générale du Travail (C.G.T.) Whether or not they were actually members of the Socialist Party, they and a certain number of Jewish intellectuals regularly voted for Socialist candidates.

The number of Jewish Communists was small, and their influence in the Jewish community nil.

Patriotism

In general, Judaism preaches devoted patriotism. In France especially, the rabbis constantly exhorted to the scrupulous fulfillment of the citizen's obligations to his country, in peace as well as in war. At frequent intervals and on all solemn holidays special prayers were said in the synagogues for the French Republic, the President and his family.

In practice the Jews of France have repeatedly given proof of their intense patriotism. In the war of 1870 a regiment of Algerian Jewish sharpshooters (Tirailleurs) particularly distinguished themselves. In the First World War thousands of foreign Jews living in France enlisted under the French colors, and were decimated in the early battles. About a quarter of the famous Zouaves were Jewish. The memory of Rabbi Bloch has become legendary; he was a Jewish chaplain who was killed while holding out a crucifix to a dying French soldier who had taken him for a priest. In all, about 6,000 Jewish soldiers of the French army were killed in the First World War.

After the Munich agreement of 1938 the Jews of France were worried. Their fear of what would happen with the extension of Hitler's power coincided with a concerted campaign from reactionary quarters, directly inspired and paid for by the Nazis, accusing the Jews of being warmongers. The Jews of France consequently abstained from any act which might have appeared to justify the demagogy of the French Nazis. Furthermore, they sincerely wished to avoid war, being, like other Frenchmen, lovers of peace.

When war broke out, the response of the Jews in France was even more marked than in 1914. A greater number of foreign Jews enlisted in 1939 than twenty-five years previously; they constituted a large percentage of the foreign regiments, which made an excellent record. Jewish citizens were called up to their units like all other Frenchmen. The famous Corps Francs, which served as a model for the British Commandos, were recruited to a large extent among Algerian Jews. The Germans learned to fear them in their special night missions during the winter of 1939-1940.

The number of World War II French Army Jewish casualties, in dead and prisoners, probably exceeds 15,000.

After the Pétain armistice of June 1940, a great many Jews managed to join the Fighting French forces. Many others are active in the French underground.

Citizenship

The law of August 10, 1927, continued in force the principle that citizenship was determined by place of birth (jus soli) and by family (jus sanguinis). All those born on French soil, even though of alien parents, were French unless they explicitly renounced their French citizenship upon coming of age. An alien woman marrying a French citizen became French unless, prior to the marriage, she made a declaration of her contrary desire.

The 1927 law liberalized the old procedure by reducing from ten years to three the length of residence required before application could be made for naturalization, while for the possessor of a diploma from a French university the period was one year. In practice the officials in charge of naturalization were rather less eager to facilitate it than the liberal provisions of the law itself would indicate. Nevertheless, about 60,000 Jews were naturalized between 1927 and 1939.

The Vichy law of July 22, 1940, ordered a review of all naturalizations obtained since 1927; actually, it was aimed almost exclusively at Jews so naturalized. By the end of 1942, several thousand had been deprived of their citizenship. A more recent law, signed by Laval and effective in June 1943 collectively revoked all naturalizations of Jews since 1927. With this accretion of new stateless Jews, the total imminently liable to deportation to the East became about 100,000.

Jews in Parliament.

The following were members of parliament at the conclusion of the armistice, and as Jews were declared to have lost their offices by a Vichy decree of November 1941: Louis Alphand, Pierre Bloch, Léon Blum, Salomom Grumbach, Robert Lazurick, Charles Lucy, Georges Mandel, Pierre Mendès-France, Jules Moch, Georges Oulmot, Abraham Schrameck, Jean Zay.

Jews in Government Posts.

Among the Jews who had held major government posts in the last decades were: Léon Blum, Prime Minister in the Popular Front government, head of the Socialist Party, sponsor of many reforms, some of which even the Vichy government has not felt able to abolish, and a symbol of republican resistance to the Germans and their French collaborators as a result of his intrepid conduct at the Riom "war-guilt" trial in 1942; Georges Mandel, who had served in many ministerial posts; Abraham Schrameck, Minister of the Interior; and Jean Zay, Minister of Public Education.

Under the Republic there were no legal restrictions on the admission of Jews to public office and the civil service. The only requirements for the latter were French nationality and passing a competitive examination. After 1927, however, a naturalized citizen was not eligible for public office until ten years had elapsed from the date of his naturalization. There were Jews in nearly all public services: post office, ministries, police, etc.

The *Statut des Juifs* of October 3, 1940 and June 2, 1941 banned all Jews from public office. Some exceptions were made, however, and apparently there were still a few Jewish or half-Jewish functionaries in the Vichy administration as late as March 1943.

Minority Status.

There was no bureau for Jewish affairs in the government before the invasion. In March 1941, the Vichy government set up the <u>Commissariat Général Aux Questions Juives</u>. Its functions were the following: 1) to propose to the government legislation for the execution of the government's policy toward the Jews, their civil and political status, their employment and their occupations; 2) to coordinate the various governmental agencies to this end; 3) to manage and liquidate Jewish enterprises "in accordance with the requirements of the national economy," where such action was prescribed by law; 4) to appoint and supervise agents for the management and liquidation of Jewish enterprises; and 5) to initiate police measures with regard to Jews "as required by the national interest."

The Commissariat exercised a fatal role in the economic and physical destruction of the Jews in France. It was the instrument of the Gestapo in the unoccupied zone.

History of Anti-Semitism.

After the acute crisis of the Dreyfus affair (1894-1906) French anti-Semitism, and the French anti-Jewish movements which had been formed during the struggle between the <u>Dreyfusards</u> and the <u>anti-Dreyfusards</u>, underwent a marked decline.

Only the royalist <u>Action Française</u> (movement and newspaper of the same name) survived, continuing to be pronouncedly anti-Semitic. Its man of action was Léon Daudet, who died not long after the armistice; its philosopher and ideologist remains Charles Maurras, who has always deliberately stressed anti-Semitism. Maurras' ideas and influence are not to be overlooked as factors subversive of the military and political security of France. A large proportion of his followers were to be found among army officers of high rank. Reputed to be fiercely anti-German, he was the behind-the-scenes mentor of Pétain and many of Pétain's subordinates.

French anti-Semitism almost disappeared during the first years after World War I, perhaps largely as a consequence of the excellent war record of the Jews, native and foreign. A kind of latent anti-Semitism continued to exist in the drawing rooms of the reactionary right; and among the middle classes it persisted among some practitioners of the liberal professions, especially among lawyers, who as a group were rather far to the right. Nevertheless, the great mass of the French people were sincerely devoted to the principles of democracy and religious tolerance.

It was the rise and coming to power of the Nazi movement in Germany which gave new vigor to anti-Semitism in France. In part it was the outcome of a renewed hope for success, stemming from the example of the Nazi victory beyond the Rhine; but much more important was the flow of money and propaganda from Germany. There was a sustained and well financed campaign of propaganda and incitement. (Much of the literature was actually labelled printed in Germany.) In addition to the Action Française, previously long in existence, new publications appeared: <u>Je Suis Partout</u>; <u>La France Enchaînée</u>; <u>Le Franciste</u>; <u>Le Cri du Peuple</u>, founded by the perfume millionaire Coty and falling into step with more directly Nazi-sponsored sheets. <u>Gringoire</u>, the newspaper of de Carbuccia and Béraud, began to take a violently anti-Jewish line.

The Maison Brune was opened in Paris, and the agents of Goebbels gave financial and "spiritual" sustenance to the anti-Jewish campaign. New parties with anti-Semitic platforms were created: The Jeunesses Patriotes of Pierre Taittinger, a rightist deputy from Paris; Coty's Solidarité Française; the Parti National Socialiste of Coston; Bucard's Francisme; and, most dangerous of all, Doriot's Parti Populaire Français, the backbone of the French Nazi movement. (After the armistice Doriot publicly boasted that he had been in the pay of the Germans for years.)

Anti-Jewish demonstrations broke out in Paris, especially in the Latin Quarter and on the Champs-Elysées. After Munich they assumed threatening proportions. Members of the Ligue Internationale Contre l'Antisémitisme (LICA) vigorously combatted physical and verbal attacks on the Jews. The Munich surrender, however, had created great moral confusion. Thus, Darquier de Pellepoix, then a Paris alderman and the founder of a street-fighting anti-Jewish group, was sentenced to jail. (In the summer of 1942 he succeeded Xavier Vallat as head of the Vichy Commissariat for Jewish Affairs.) At the same time, however, there were judges who punished a "too active" resistance against anti-Semitic hoodlums by some members of the LICA with severe sentences.

Premier Daladier did not issue a decree against racial and religious incitement until a few months before the outbreak of war.

After his armistice, Pétain created the Légion Française des Combattants as the one party, on the Nazi model. It was to be composed of veterans of the two World Wars and supporters of the "new order" and the "national revolution," known as "national volunteers." It rapidly developed into an agency for the repression of Frenchmen indifferent or hostile to the "national revolution." One of its chief tasks soon came to be making incessant anti-Jewish propaganda through personal contact, the press and the radio. The Service d'Ordre Légionnaire (S.O.L.) was created within the Legion; it was made up of the Legion's most fanatical elements, and may be considered the French counterpart of the German S.S. It was the S.O.L. which attempted to organize a large-scale pogrom in such cities as Casablanca, Rabat and Fez when the American troops landed in North Africa.

Within France the leading anti-Semites are: Henri Béraud, Marcel Bucard, Henry Coston, Joseph Darnand, Louis Darquier de Pellepoix, Jacques Doriot, Pierre Laval, Jean-Charles Legrand, Charles Maurras and Xavier Vallat.

Some notorious French anti-Semites were in North Africa and have recently been interned by the French National Committee of Liberation: Pierre Pucheu; Marcel Peyrouton; Marcel Boisson; and Pierre Tixier-Vignancourt.

The Church and the Jews.

Before the invasion the Catholic clergy, both higher and lower, condemned anti-Semitism. Their attitude with respect to the Jews was one of understanding and tolerance. The relations between the Chief Rabbi and the Cardinal Archbishop of Paris were usually very cordial.

By and large, after the invasion, the clergy maintained their previous attitude. (There were one or two exceptions, of politically-minded cardinals who became collaborators.) Especially in the unoccupied zone the attitude of the lower clergy in many places can be characterized only as courageous and noble. In that zone, however, the higher members of the hierarchy, inevitably influenced by the favorable position set aside for the Church by Pétain, did not overtly come out against the anti-Jewish measures until the imposition of the yellow badge in the occupied zone (June 1942) and, above all, the barbarous deportations to the East (occupied zone, July 1942; unoccupied zone, August 1942) of foreign and stateless Jews, some of the latter being denaturalized Frenchmen. From that time on the higher clergy waged an open struggle against the Pétain-Laval regime. Particularly strong and courageous was the reaction of the Cardinal of Lyons, Archbishop Gerlier, Primate of the Gauls, and of the Bishops of Montauban and Toulouse. The Bishop of Toulouse, Monseigneur Saliège, from the very beginning of the anti-Jewish discriminatory policy had given proof of a truly admirable attitude. In his sermons, his pastoral letters and in his behavior he refused to recognize the anti-Semitic "new dogmas" preached by Vichy.

The attitude of Protestant clergymen is no less worthy of praise. The Rev. Marc Boegner, president of the Protestant Federation, sent a strong letter of protest to Pétain against the deportation of Jews.

Jews in the French Committee of National Liberation

Early in 1944 René Mayer was Commissioner of Communications and Merchant Marine, and Pierre Mendès-France was Commissioner of Finance. René Cassin had been Commissioner of Justice in the French National Committee in London.

Jewish Groups in Exile.

By and large, only those Jews from France who were affiliated with Jewish groups in France itself belong to Jewish groups in exile. A number of French Jews in exile, some of them very distinguished, have not joined any Jewish groups at all. In the United States, Jews from France -- both citizens and foreigners, the latter constituting a majority -- have organized the Union des Juifs de France. In general, French Zionists who managed to flee France have continued their Zionist affiliations abroad; and so on.

Occupational Structure.

Since official censuses and statistical surveys in France ignored religious affiliation, it is difficult to give an accurate picture of the occupational distribution of the Jews of France. Unofficial estimates, however, are available for Paris; and since about half of all the Jews in France lived in Paris, these estimates may be considered more or less valid for the Jewish population of France as a whole: 45%, commerce and industry; 30%, workers, craftsmen, white-collar employees; 10%, professions; and 15%, pensions, investments, etc.

The economic situation of the Jews was fairly stable. With few exceptions, there were no great fortunes; but neither was there great poverty. Unemployment was not a grim problem. The white-collar workers were probably the poorest group.

Immigrants who had arrived since about 1910 were to be found mostly in the crafts, the retail trade and small business. In the crafts, the majority were tailors, hatmakers and furriers, usually working where they lived. The workers, strictly so-called, were employed chiefly in factories and shops.

Industry.

The Paris clothing and leather-goods industries were largely Jewish. The textile industry in France owed its start in some measure to Jews, but in more recent years could not be considered predominantly Jewish. The outstanding enterprise of a heavy-industry character was the naval construction company, <u>Les Chantiers et Ateliers de St. Nazaire</u>, owned by the Fould family. (Alphonse Fould, father of René, the present owner, had provided the steel for the Eiffel Tower.) Citroën, "the French Ford," was Jewish.

Banking.

In Paris the following banks were controlled by Jews: Banque Rothschild; Banque Louis Dreyfus et Cie; Banque Heine et Cie; Banque Cahen d'Anvers, Propper et Cie; Banque Spitzer et Cie; Banque Georges Lévy et Cie; Lazard Frères.

Several major banks had important, if not majority, Jewish investments; an example is the Banque de Paris et des Pays Bas, whose director, Horace Finaly, was in New York in 1943.

There were several important Jewish foreign-exchange establishments in Paris: Perquel, Level, Crémieux. A number of Jews were also active as stock market brokers.

Outside of Paris, there were some Jewish banks of secondary importance in Nancy, Strasbourg, Bordeaux and Marseilles. Of these the most important was the Banque Gomez, active throughout the Southwest of France.

After the armistice, in the occupied zone the Germans immediately seized all the currency, bonds and, subsequently, deposits of the Jewish banks. The Jewish owners were expropriated and their ownings, in shares or otherwise, were sold, often to dummy purchasers acting for the Nazis.

In the unoccupied zone the banking profession was one of the first forbidden to Jews by the first <u>Statut des Juifs</u>, of October 1940. Since, however, almost a year elapsed between the promulgation of the statute and the law of July 22, 1941, authorizing the appointment of provisional administrators for Jewish enterprises, there is reason to believe that some Jewish bankers were able to make arrangements for partly safeguarding their interests.

The Judiciary.

Under the Republic there was no discrimination against the Jews by or in the courts. Jews served throughout the court structure: civil, criminal, etc. They were not numerous, but they generally enjoyed considerable prestige. The same is true of other functions under the jurisdiction of the Ministry of Justice, notably that of attorney for the State.

The Bar.

Outside of Paris the general attitude of lawyers toward Jewish colleagues was on the whole friendly. In Paris the Bar Association numbered about 3500 lawyers and law clerks. Of this number some 300 were Jews, of whom 25, in turn, were naturalized foreigners. The general attitude toward the latter was, to say the least, cold.

The French Bar was traditionally conservative, with a fairly strong reactionary wing. Action Française recruited many of its members among lawyers, especially the younger ones. The Jeune Barreau, a professional organization composed of young lawyers adhering to Action Française, constantly adopted resolutions to prevent naturalized Frenchmen from becoming lawyers. It was largely the influence of the Jeune Barreau which led in the 1930's to the passage of a law requiring a candidate for admission to the bar to have been a citizen for at least ten years, like a candidate for a civil service position. This law very drastically restricted the opportunity of foreigners to become French lawyers. It was not, however, retroactive in its effect.

Anti-Semitic incidents and brawls began to flare up in 1934 in the Paris bar. The moving spirit behind them was usually Georges Calzant, a fervent disciple of Maurras. Calzant's legal activity consisted largely of finding or inciting incidents. He was one of the chief militant anti-Semites.

With respect to Jewish lawyers born in France and practising in Paris, the attitude of their colleagues was about as friendly as could be expected in a very crowded calling in which professional jealousy was keen. But even they were subject to certain discriminations. For example, a Jew had never been elected president of the Paris Bar Association. A concerted campaign, conducted as well by the older and more sedate elements as by the Jeune Barreau, kept Pierre Masse from that office, although he was a man of extraordinary distinction and even social status, whose worth was conceded by his opponents. (Masse was interned by the Germans first in Drancy and then in Compiègne; he was probably deported to the East.) A tacit understanding always kept a few Jews on the Council of the Paris Bar Association.

While there was still an "unoccupied" zone the proportion of Jewish lawyers to the total was fixed at 2%; under the Germans none is allowed to practice.

There were practically no Jewish notaries.

Jewish Press.

In September 1939 there were in Paris: one daily -- Pariser Haint (Yiddish, "Today"); two weeklies -- Les Archives Israélites (founded 1840) and L'Univers Israélite (1844); four monthlies -- Le Rayon (organ of the Reformed sect, founded 1913), Paix et Droit (organ of the Alliance Israélite Universelle), Le Droit de Vivre (organ of LICA-Ligue Internationale contre l'Antisémitisme), La Terre Retrouvée (organ of the [Zionist] Jewish National Fune); and one learned quarterly -- La Revue des Etudes Juives (founded 1880 by the Société des Etudes Juives).

There appeared in Nancy the monthly Revue Juive de Lorraine; and in Strasbourg the monthly Tribune Juive (in French and German).

All these publications were prevented from appearing after the armistice. In April 1941 the Comité de Coordination des Organisations Juives began to publish the bi-weekly Information Juives, devoted to questions of relief and readjustment.

General Press.

The extent to which Jews shared in the ownership of the general press was not great. L'Intransigeant (Paris, conservative, several editions daily) had once belonged to Louis Louis Dreyfus, and Charles Lévy later held an interest; L'Information was owned by the Banque Lazard; and L'Agence économique et financière and L'Agence Fournier were owned by Robert Bollack.

There were some Jews active in editorial and administrative capacities on large dailies: Louis Forest, Le Matin; Marcel Hirsch (Huttin), L'Echo de Paris; Fernand Weil, administrator, Le Journal; Lazarus (Gallus), L'Intransigeant; and Léon Blum, director of the Socialist Le Populaire, which had some other Jewish collaborators as well.

After the armistice newspapers appearing in the occupied zone were nazified. In the unoccupied zone the Statute on Jews forbade them to engage in directorial or editorial work on newspapers or magazines, with the exception of publications having a strictly religious or scientific character.

Anti-Semitic and Quisling Press.

This subject has been partly discussed under History of Anti-Semitism, above.

In the occupied zone newspapers were nazified, the old titles being kept to fool the readers. A Nazi Humanité duly made its appearance; it obviously was not the organ of the Communist Party, as of old. There was also a rash of new papers and magazines of Nazi inspiration. A list (far from exhaustive) of prominent Nazi and collaborationist publications in the occupied zone follows: all are anti-Semitic, but some are more especially and vigorously so: L'Oeuvre (Marcel Déat, a leading collaborationist); Paris-Soir (H. Saison); Le Matin (Bunau-Varilla); La France au Travail (new, completely Nazi-- Charles Dieudonné); Le Cri du Peuple (Jacques Doriot); L'Emancipation Nationale (weekly, also appears in Marseilles -- Jacques Doriot); Les Nouveaux Temps (new, Nazi -- Jean Luchaire, a prominent collaborationist); Aujourd'hui (new, collaborationist -- Georges Suarez); La Gerbe (new, collaborationist -- Alphonse de Chateaubriant); Le Fait (new, Nazi, viciously anti-Semitic -- Drieu de la Rochelle); Au Pilori (new, Nazi, specializing in anti-Semitism -- de Lestandi).

In the unoccupied zone the most prominent collaborationist newspapers were: L'Action Francaise (anti-Semitic -- Charles Maurras); Gringoire (anti-Semitic -- Henri Béraud); L'Alerte (anti-Semitic, collaborationist -- Gustave Hervé); L'Emancipation Nationale (Jacques Doriot, Jacques Ploncart); L'Effort ("socialist," collaborationist -- Paul Faure, Charles Spinasse); Le Moniteur du Puy-de-Dôme (Pierre Laval).

The rest of the press is Pétainist -- some sincerely, and some because the semblance is necessary for continued publication.

Motion Pictures.

Jews had been active in all branches of the French film industry since the 1920's. Among producers the Nathan brothers (Pathé), Georges Haik and the Osso Company may be cited. The role played in production of films by Jewish stage-designers, directors, actors, decorators and sound engineers was important, but it was in the distributing end in which they were especially prominent. Two large moving-picture theatre chains belonged to Jews in Paris. In other large cities -- Marseilles, Lyons, Bordeax -- Jews owned important movie houses.

In the occupied zone Jews were immediately forced to yield possession of their movie theatres. Only a very small proportion were paid. In the unoccupied zone, the Statute on Jews forbade the employment of Jews in the production, photographing and staging of movies. Toward August 1942 Jewish actors were excluded from the film industry.

The decline of the French cinema since 1940 may be in part attributed to the ban on Jews.

"Aryanization"

In the occupied zone there was a sort of competition between Vichy and the Germans. The Vichy Ministry of Industrial and commercial Production, established in Paris immediately after the armistice, had administrators named for the most important Jewish enterprises in the occupied zone, especially Paris. State Counsellor Bichelonne was at the head of this ministry. In certain cases Jewish owners had taken precautionary measures and had had administrators of their own choice approved by the Tribunal de Commerce de la Seine. In general the Germans replaced these administrators by their own men after a certain length of time. The Germans were primarily interested in the largest enterprises, those which offered the best opportunities for gain. They had their own administrators named to these businesses, or else arranged for their sale to buyers whom they approved. Aryanization quickly developed into a racket on a large scale, with the Germans profiting most. The Germans maintained a special service for Jewish affairs, which supervised aryanization. Its head was a Dr. Blanke, a fanatical Nazi.

In the unoccupied zone, starting with the summer of 1941, aryanization was the province of the <u>Commissariat aux Questions Juives</u>. Special offices, called Bureaux d'aryanisation économique, were opened in the large cities: Marseilles, Lyons, Toulouse, Limoges, Clermont-Ferrand and Nice. They were directed by fanatical members of the <u>Parti Populaire Français</u> (PPF - Doriot's party) or of Pétain's <u>Legion Française des Combattants</u>. Administrators for small and middle-sized businesses were named by the PPF and the Legion; Vichy kept for itself the more "promising" enterprises. Indeed, everything connected with "aryanizatiion" was quite lucrative for the "aryanizers." The administrator granted himself, or saw to it that he was granted, "administrative fees" at least equal to the incomes of the actual managers or the dispossessed owners. The first thing the administrator usually did was to dismiss Jewish employees and, frequently, to raise the wages of the non-Jewish employees so as to win their favor and undermine any feeling of loyalty to their Jewish employer. The administrator's function was either to "aryanize" the enterprise by sale to a non-Jew of to liquidate it.

In the occupied zone all Jewish enterprises had been aryanized by the end of 1942. In the unoccupied zone there were not many eager to buy. The Russian resistance, the de Gaullist propaganda and the activity of the underground had persuaded the average Frenchman as early as 1941 that German victory was not at all certain, and that prudence in such matters as buying Jewish businesses was indicated. Consequently liquidation was much more common than aryanization. Certain administrators distinguished themselves by particularly scandalous conduct, such as compelling the former Jewish proprietor, by threatening to have him declared guilty of fraudulent bankruptcy, to turn over sums realized as income months before an administrator was installed. This is only one facet of the very widespread racketeering, involving grafters in and out of the government, that was bred by aryanization.

All Jewish bank accounts were blocked. In the occupied zone deposits were turned over to the Germans to go toward making up a collective fine of one billion francs imposed on the Jews.

Labor Unions.

In both the Confédération Générale du Travail (C.G.T. -- socialist) and the Confédération Générale de Travail Unifiée (C.G.T.U. -- with Communist tendencies) there was no discrimination against Jews. Even during periods of economic crisis the attitude of the labor unions remained liberal. The C.G.T. was not even very strict about barring foreign workers, whether Jewish or not, whose papers were not entirely in order in the eyes of the Police and the Ministry of Labor.

There were a few special Jewish groups, of workers and employers, in the apparel and leather trades. They were not very important, and the workers' groups were generally affiliated with the appropriate C.G.T. trade unions.

Travel Regulations.

In the occupied zone the Germans made no distinction between foreign and French Jews. By the end of September 1940 all Jews had been forbidden to cross over into the unoccupied zone, whatever the means of transportation at their disposal. By the end of 1940 Jews had been forbidden to enter or to leave Paris or the Seine Department without special permission. Finally Jews were not allowed to travel on the railroads without special permission. On the Paris Métro Jews were confined to special cars, usually the last of the second class.

The Germans confiscated automobiles owned by non-Jews as well as Jews. They requisitioned horses and all means of transportation capable of being used by their army.

In the unoccupied zone, until the end of 1942, a clear distinction was made between foreign and French Jews. The French were allowed to travel freely, except by airplane, for which special permission was required, and except to several départements forbidden to Jews. Foreigners, by the terms of a war regulation issued before the armistice, were not allowed to leave the commune of their residence without a special travel pass issued by the police or the gendarmerie, and which, in fact, could be obtained only with much trouble. This regulation applied to non-Jewish as well as to Jewish foreigners. In practice, difficulties were experienced primarily by Jews. On November 9, 1942, a law was promulgated specifically applying the ban on leaving the <u>commune</u> of residence to foreign Jews.

If only for lack of gasoline, Jews were unable to use automobiles. In addition, permission to use them was not given to Jews, except physicians. Soon, however, the number of Jewish physicians was drastically reduced by the <u>numerus clausus</u> of 2%. Theoretically Jews had the right to own and to use horse-drawn vehicles and bicycles, but after the law of July 22, 1941, even these means of transportation could be taken away by the nomination of a provisional administrator. Cases were known of the appointment of administrators for household goods owned by Jews.

Communications.

In the occupied zone, the Germans immediately barred the use of private telephones to Jews and confiscated their radios. In July 1942 the use of public telephones by Jews was also forbidden.

In the unoccupied zone, both foreign and French Jews were allowed to use public telephones on presentation of identity papers. There were no restrictions, at least until the end of 1942, on the use of private telephones.

In order to send telegrams, foreigners -- Jewish and non-Jewish alike -- had to have them approved by the police or the gendarmerie, whether they were sent within France or abroad. French citizens -- whether Jews or not -- were free to send telegrams within France, but had to have them approved if they were sent abroad.

Curfew.

In the occupied zone, Jews were forbidden to be out of doors from 10 P.M. to 6 A.M.; violations were punishable by internment, deportation or even execution. In the unoccupied zone there were no special curfew hours for Jews.

Nothing is known here of developments since the total German occupation, late in 1942.

Rationing.

Until November 1942, when the Germans imposed total occupation on France, Vichy theoretically controlled rationing for all of France; after that date the Germans took charge. Until then there had been no substantial food discrimination against Jews. (It must, however, be remembered that the Jews on the average probably fared worse than the rest of the population because there were no agricultural elements among them, to speak of; and it is those elements which are best fed in times of food shortages.) After December 1942 Jews in the previously unoccupied zone were required to have their ration cards stamped with a "J." The subsequent extent of discriminatory rationing is not known here.

Fines

Both the Germans and Vichy imposed high collective fines on the Jew. In Paris, General von Stulpnagel compelled the Jews to pay a fine of one billion francs for the alleged participation of Jews in attacks on German soldiers. Vichy ordered the Jewish community of Nice to pay a fine of one million francs for allegedly hiding "communist literature" in the Grande Synagogue, allegedly there discovered by the Service d'Ordre Légionnaire (which profaned the Synagogue).

Review of Discriminatory Measures

Occupied Zone: The first de facto discriminatory measures were instituted by the Germans in July, 1940, when Jews returning to their homes in the occupied zone were taken from the trains at the line of demarcation and returned to unoccupied territory. A decree of September 27, 1940, forbade Jews to reenter the occupied zone. Subsequent decrees ordered that identification cards be marked with the word Jew; business enterprises owned by Jews were ordered so identified, and "Aryan" administrators were assigned. Decrees of April and May, 1941, barred Jews from all professions and employment which might provide contact with the public; safe deposit boxes belonging to Jews were ordered opened and bank accounts blocked. At the end of 1941 it became illegal to shelter a Jew even for one night. Jews from Paris and the Department of the Seine were required to have authorization to travel; this was followed by mass arrests in Paris and its environs and the dispatch of Jews to Drancy, the nearby concentration camp. In June, 1942, the Star of David badge was made compulsory for Jews over the age of six. Jews were refused entry to all public places. They could shop and market only between three and four o'clock in the afternoon. "Jim Crow" cars - the last second-class car - were assigned to them in the Métro. In July and August, 1942, the mass deportations were begun.

Unoccupied Zone: Until June 1941 the Vichy government moved slowly. On July 22, 1940, citizenship revision was ordered for all those naturalized after August, 1927. In August and September 1940 laws restricting the practice of medicine and law were ordered. The first Statut des Juifs (October 3, 1940) defined Jews according to a religious, not racial, criterion. The second law, passed the same day, authorized the prefects to intern or confine to special residences all alien Jews deemed superfluous from the point of view of the national economy. In March, 1941, the Commissariat Général aux Questions Juives was created, under Xavier Vallat, who was superseded in May, 1942, by Darquier de Pellepoix. On June 2, 1941, two additional laws were promulgated, the first further restricting the activities outlined in the first Statut des Juifs, and barring Jews from acting as bankers, foreign exchange dealers, business solicitors, general and stock exchange brokers, real estate or loan agents, middlemen, gambling concessionaires, publishers, newspapers or periodical managers, editors or correspondents (except as contributors to scientific or religious publications), and from all positions in the motion picture or radio industry. The second law ordered a census of all Jews in the unoccupied zone. On July 22, 1941, a third law barred the participation of Jews in practically all commerce and decreed the liquidation of Jewish-owned property. Expropriation proceeded under the Bureau of Economic Aryanization. Subsequent laws instituted a 3% numerus clausus in the higher schools and 2% in the practice of the liberal professions. In November 1941 Jews serving as deputies and senators were deprived of office. In February 1942 foreign Jews were forbidden to leave their communes of residence. In June 1943 all Jews naturalized after August 1927 had their naturalization automatically revoked.

Forced Prostitution

There was some evidence that after July 1942 young Jewish women were being deported from both the occupied and unoccupied zone to German army brothels.

Concentration Camps and Prisons

There were no special prisons or jails, properly so called, for Jews; but there was a whole series of concentration camps set up by Vichy in France and in North Africa. In this matter Vichy was swifter than the Germans. On July 7, 1940, Jewish refugees from Germany and Austria were ordered interned. In September 1940 a decree was promulgated given the prefects power to intern any foreign Jew in a special camp or to impose forced residence on him. The prefects of certain departments -- especially Haute-Garonne (Toulouse), Bouches-du-Rhône (Marseilles), and Alpes-Maritimes (Nice) -- were not sparing in their use of this power.

There were about fifty concentration camps in Metropolitan France, of which the most notorious are: Gurs, Rivesaltes, Recebedou, Le Mille, Noé and Nexon. (In North Africa the worst were Colombe-Bechar, Saida and Sidi el Ayachi.)

Conditions in camps are horrible: indiscriminate and extreme overcrowding in vermin-infested barracks, with almost no light and air, and without the most elementary sanitary provisions. Food is very insufficient in quantity, repulsive in quality. Most internees became so weak they were hardly able to walk. This was true before November 1942; since then conditions, at least so far as food is concerned, must have become even worse, with the generally deteriorating food position of France. In the labor battalions (compagnies de travailleurs) things were not much better, with this aggravating circumstance, that those serving in these units were forced to do extremely hard work, of which the usefulness was frequently not apparent at all, on roads and forests and in salt mines. The food situation was better in the compagnies agricoles, as was, in general, the behavior of those in charge.

The above refers to the Vichy-run camps; conditions were far worse in the occupied zone. There the camps with the worst reputation were: Drancy, about 13 miles from Paris, known as the "French Dachau," in which the commandant, Lieutenant Danacker, had distinguished himself among competent competitors for savageness and sadism; Pithiviers and Beaune-la-Rollande, both in the Loiret Department; and Compiègne. From these camps men and women from both zones were deported to the East for forced labor - behind the lines in Russia or to the coal and salt mines of Upper Silesia, there to work until killed -- or to the extermination camps in Poland.

In the occupied zone the camps were administered by the Gestapo; in the unoccupied zone, by the Ministry of the Interior (Peyrouton, Darlan, Pucheu), and more especially by the Police and the Sûreté Nationale (Bousquet). The personnel was chosen from among the most hardened functionaries of the colonial penal administration and the Doriot party.

Education

There were a number of general and trade schools supported by the Consistoire, with the usual primary or secondary curriculum, and courses in Hebrew, religion and Jewish history in addition. Such schools were the orphan asylums at Boulogne-Sur-Seine, Strasbourg and Haguenan, where general and trade education was given; the Ecoles de Travail at Paris and Mulhouse; the Ecole des Arts et Métiers at Strasbourg; Ecoles professionnelles for girls at Neuilly-Sur-Seine and Bischoffsheim. The Alliance Israélite Universelle maintained in Paris the Ecole Normale Israélite Orientale to train teachers for the schools maintained by the Alliance in North Africa and the Near East.

There were rather few Jews among the body of instituteurs. The instituteurs remained strong in their republicanism and became the backbone of French resistance. There was a somewhat higher proportion of Jews among lycée and university teachers. In the nineteenth and twentieth centuries some of France's most eminent scholars were Jews. In recent years Jewish lycée and university teachers seemed to be attracted, in general, to the teaching of foreign languages and mathematics.

Resistance was neither so early nor so strong among the secondary and higher school teachers as among the instituteurs.

Hospitals and Medical Services

There were numerous Jews on the roster of French physicians, some with international reputations. Among hospitals, the Rothschild Hospital in Paris, established in 1852, received both Jewish and non-Jewish patients. In 1926, a tuberculosis preventorium was opened by the Baroness de Rothschild in Hauteville (Ain). There was a Jewish hospital in Strasbourg and Jewish homes for the aged in Paris, Lyons, Nancy, Strasbourg, Lunéville and Metz.

Social Security and Public Welfare

Jews shared without discrimination in the social security and public welfare advantages of the French republic. Hospitalization and other public welfare assistance was highly developed. Foreigners were so generously treated that anti-Semitic periodicals raised an outcry whenever statistics were published. French citizens and all others possessing working permits were entitled to social security privileges.

Jewish Welfare Activity

In the large cities -- Paris, Lyons, Marseilles -- there were Jewish relief societies and committees. The oldest of these was the Comité de Bienfaisance Israélite de Paris, which had been functioning since 1809. Relief was given in kind (food and clothing coupons) and in money; small loans to enable the borrower to become self-sustaining were also made. The Comité functioned under the control of the Consistoire. In Paris, since after 1918, there had also been in existence a Comité Central d'Assistance aux Emigrants, supported by private contributions and by American Jewish relief organizations.

Jews from Eastern Europe and the Mediterranean littoral -- of the latter, mostly those from Salonika, in Greece -- had their own societies and committees for relief and mutual aid. The sphere of activity of these groups was naturally limited. Financially they were supported by <u>Amicales</u> (usually equivalent to "Landsmannschaften") which raised the necessary sums by balls, raffles, private contributions and the like.

Besides these organizations for direct relief, there functioned the large-scale Jewish organizations more especially concerned with long-term assistance: ORT workshops, training schools and training farms; OSE clinics and children's colonies; HICEM emigration assistance -- advice, help in obtaining passports and visas, contributions toward travel expenses.

(HICEM played a role of primary importance in Jewish life in France after the armistice. It was because of its efforts that thousands of Jews, otherwise doomed to concentration camps, were able to leave France and find refuge overseas. It was HICEM, too, which enabled thousands of Jews and non-Jews - the latter mostly Spanish Republicans - to be freed from camps in which they had already been interned and to leave France.)

These organizations depended for their funds, to a large extent, on American Jewish relief organizations, especially the American Jewish Joint Distribution Committee. The French government did not contribute to any private relief agencies.

In the beginning of German occupation the internal administration of the Jewish community and its relief organizations was in the hands of the <u>Consistoire</u> and the <u>Fédération des Sociétés Juives.</u> In the occupied zone (Paris), Grand Rabbi Julien Weil was in charge; in the unoccupied zone, Jacques Heilbronner, Conseiller d'Etat and Pétain's aide during World War I, and Grand Rabbi Issaye Schwartz, Chief Rabbi of France. To cope with the new and crushing burden of relief to Jews in both zones (internees in concentration camps, refugees from the occupied zone and those who had been deprived of their jobs and possessions), special relief committees were set up under the direction of a <u>Commission centrale</u> with offices in Vichy and Marseilles. Help was given in the form of direct relief (money, food in free kitchens -- especially in Paris) and long-term assistance (vocational retraining in the ORT's workshops, schools and farms, in the unoccupied zone). About 25,000 benefited by this help in the unoccupied zone during the months following the conclusion of the armistice, and their numbers continued to grow. Probably equal numbers received help in Paris. In the unoccupied zone the monthly expenditures of the organizations affiliated with the <u>Commission Centrale</u> amounted to some 4,200,000 francs (about $100,000, at the official rate of exchange).

All Jewish organizations, relief and other, were supposed to be dissolved and merged in the <u>Union Générale des Israélites de France</u> after March 1942. As has been indicated, the dissolution was largely nominal, and most Jewish organizations continued to function as before. But their task was made more difficult, both by the administrative control, especially financial, to which they were subject and by the fact that the <u>Union</u> delegated to its "constituent" organizations inexperienced men constantly harrassed by the presence of the <u>Commissariat aux Questions Juives</u> in the background. Considerable trouble was also caused for the Jewish organizations after March 1942 by Vichy's requiring the dismissal of foreign employees, even those in possession of work cards in good order.

According to the terms of the Vichy law, the <u>Union</u> was supposed to receive a certain share of the funds realized by liquidating Jewish-owned property, in order to be able to meet its relief requirements. Actually, however, it realized no money from this source; instead, Darquier de Pellepoix issued a decree (September 1942) taxing the <u>Union</u> a monthly sum of 6,000,000 francs, to be obtained from Jewish families in both zones. The organizations continued to live on their own funds, largely obtained from American sources and private contributions.

The total German occupation of France, the break in relations between the United States and Vichy, the hermetically sealed Spanish and Swiss borders, all must have created a desperately critical situation for the entire Jewish relief work in France. Nevertheless, according to recent information from France, Jewish relief committees continued to function, especially in Marseilles, in which all the central Jewish organizations had come to be located before total occupation. Since that time most of the organizations which escaped abolition moved to the interior, especially to Lyons and to Brive.

Jewish Leaders in France

The deportations and persecutions executed against the Jews of France in the past years make an accurate listing of Jewish leaders left in France impossible. This reservation applies to the following list:

The Rothschild family, banking and industrial enterprises; Wolf Levitan, furniture manufacturer; Rosengart, automobile plants of the same name; Lévy-Finger, chemical products; Bloch, airplane manufacturer; Weil, iron works; Charles Lévy, sugar refineries; Ballman, Strasbourg flour mills; Paul Helbronner, <u>Forges et Acieries de Pompey</u>; Henri and Emile Deutsch de la Meurth, Henri Goldet and Baron Pierre de Gunzbourg - all of the <u>Société des Pétroles Jupiter</u> (the Deutsch de la Meurth family were well known as patrons of French aviation); Albert Lévy, André Baur and Raymond Raoul Lambert, of the <u>Union Générale des Israélites de France</u>; Myrtil, lawyer, president of the French Section of the (Zionist) Jewish National Fund; Leonce Bernheim, on the Executive of the French section of the Palestine Foundation Fund; Pierre Parof, journalist; Schah, director of the HIAS-ICA Emigration Association (HICEM); Weissmann, president of the <u>Association des Anciens Combattants Juifs</u>; Dr. Weil-Hallé and Dr. Zadoc-Kohn, both very eminent physicans; Grand Rabbis Liber and Berman; and Grand Rabbi Issaye Schwartz, Chief Rabbi of France.

Jewish Leaders in Exile

In the United States are:

Pierre Dreyfus, industrialist, son of the famous Captain Alfred Dreyfus; Isaac Naiditch, sugar refineries; Baron Pierre de Gunzbourg, industrialist, Baron Edouard de Rothschild, financier; Robert Bollack, financier and publisher; Ado Dreyfus, of the Paris <u>Galeries Lafayette</u>; Horace Finaly, banker, André Spire, poet; Gustave Cohen, professor of French literature, and Jacques Hadamard, professor of mathematics, both of the <u>Sorbonne</u> and of the <u>Collège de France</u>.

Present Attitude of the People to the Jews

Three periods should be distinguished since June 1940:

1) The first lasted about six months in the occupied and about a year in the unoccupied zone. As a result of incessant German and Vichy propaganda, hostility to Jews became widespread. The elimination of the Jews from the French economy appealed especially to certain sections of the middle class, which were glad to see the disappearance of competitors. In the unoccupied zone popular anti-Semitism was a by-product of the great prestige in which Pétain was then held, and of the blind confidence of the French masses in him. Pétain publicly supported the anti-Semitic campaign of the Légion Française des Combattants, which blamed the Jews for all the misfortunes that had befallen France.

2) The second lasted until about October 1942. In the occupied zone German misconduct and exploitation fairly quickly aroused the French, with the exception of professional pro-Nazis and profiteers. Reacting against the Germans, the French rejected their anti-Jewish propaganda, and began to sympathize with the suffering Jews. Concrete proof of solidarity and sympathy was demonstrated in open protest against the yellow-badges requirements, mass raids, internment and deportation. Jews were frequently hidden to protect them against persecution.

In the unoccupied zone this development was somewhat slower. The decrease in anti-Jewish sentiment was a function of the decrease in popular esteem for Pétain. By August 1942 most Frenchmen had come to the conclusion that Pétain was consciously playing the Germans' game. With the clear realization of the spurious nature of the theory of German invincibility -- on which Petain's appeal was primarily based --, the Vichy anti-Jewish slogans ("The Jews run the black market; the Jews are responsible for our defeat.") lost their potency. The attitude of the people became more and more sympathetic. When the deportations en masse began to the East, in July and August 1942, all Frenchmen reacted with indignation.

3) The third period began about November 1942. Solidarity between Jews and non-Jews was strengthened by the Germans' total occupation of France, the systematic extermination of Jewish citizens and foreigners alike, the increased moral and physical suffering of the entire population and the deportation of French workers to German war plants.

With the possible exception of Holland and Belgian, anti-Jewish propaganda proved less successful in France than in any other country under German occupation. It should not, however, be assumed that the "French" (Pétain - Laval) anti-Jewish propaganda has left no impress on the French population; on the other hand, it should not be an insuperable task to eliminate anti-Jewish feeling after the liberation of France and the restoration of her republican liberties, before such sentiment has had time to naturalize itself in the French spirit.

Attitude to the United States.

Like other Frenchmen the Jews of France were traditionally pro-American. After 1939 French Jews looked with increasing hope to the United States as the great power that would be able to deliver the decisive blow to Hitler and save France. After the armistice the Jews were naturally the element most strongly opposed to collaboration with the Germans and most pro-British and pro-American. It was their conviction that the arrival of American troops anywhere on Nazi-dominated soil would automatically bring with it the restoration of democratic liberties and the abolition of racial discrimination.

The fact that more than eleven months were allowed to intervene between the American and Allied landings in North Africa and the restoration of citizenship to the Jews of Algeria must have caused great disappointment among the Jews of France.

Reconstruction Agencies.

The principal non-French Jewish organizations which may cooperate in reconstruction work in France are: The American Jewish Joint Distribution Committee (New York); HICEM (Hias-Ica Emigration Association) (New York); the Jewish Agency for Palestine; ORT; and OSE.

THE JEWS OF GERMANY

THE JEWS OF GERMANY

Index

Agriculture 20	Languages 8
Anti-Semitism, History of 10	Leaders, Jewish 51
"Aryanization" 22	Liquidation 36
Badges and Other Identification 46	Marriage 5
Banking 19	Medicine
Loan Banks 27	Physicians 36
Bar, The 17	Other Practitioners 36
Birth Rate 35	Minorities 15
Cemeteries 6	Mortality 35
Christian Church and the Jews 11	Motion Pictures 22
Citizenship 14	Natural Resources 20
Commerce and Trade 21	Occupational Structure 18
Communities, Jewish 2	Penal Institutions 49
Assets 4	Police Force and the Jews 43
Communal Organizations 7	Political Structure 9
Functionaries 5	Population 1
Concentration Camps 49	Press
Cooperatives 27	General 23
Criminality 8	Jewish 24
Discrimination, Extra-Legal 12	Reconstruction Agencies 53
Divorce 5	Refugees 1
Education 29	Restrictions
Fines 28	Communications 48
Government Posts, Jews in 16	Curfew 46
Fire Department 45	Passport 47
Judiciary 17	Rationing 48
Municipal 16	Travel 47
Police 42	Social Security 38
Reichstag 16	Social Service
Groups in Exile 52	Child Care 41
Jewish 52	Jewish Welfare 39
Political 52	Mutual Aid 42
Health Services 32	Public Welfare 39
Hospitals 32	Welfare Workers 42
Hygiene 34	Sports 8
Industry 21	Sterilization 36
Insurance 20	Taxes 28
Judiciary, The 17	Underground Movement 10
Labor	War and Peace, Attitude Toward ... 9
Employment 24	Women, Position of 7
Forced Labor 26	
Trade Unions 26	
Wages 24	

THE JEWS OF GERMANY

Population; Refugees.

According to the census of June 16, 1933, when some 50,000 Jews had already left Germany under Nazi pressure, there were in Germany 499,682 persons of the Jewish faith, representing 0.77% of the total population of 61,340,000. Their citizenship was divided as follows:

Germany, 400,935; Poland, 56,480; Austria, 4,647; Czechoslovakia, 4,275; Hungary, 2,280; Roumania, 2,210; Russia, 1,650; Holland, 1,604; Lithuania and Latvia, 1,730; England, 532; Turkey, 753; other European countries, 1,692; United States, 536; countries outside of Europe and the United States, 398; stateless, 19,746; not ascertained, 214. A little less than 20% were therefore foreign-born. About 1/5 of this number were stateless.

The distribution of the Jews within Germany took the following form: Prussia, 361,826; Bavaria, 41,939; Baden, 20,617; Saxony, 20,584; Württemberg, 10,023; Hamburg, 16,973; Hesse, 17,888; Thuringia, 2,882; other states, 6,950.

The seven largest Jewish communities in Germany in 1933 were: Berlin, 160,564; Frankfort, 26,158; Breslau, 20,202; Hamburg, 16,885; Cologne, 14,816; Leipzig, 11,564; Munich, 9,005.

Inadequate data makes only an estimate of the number of Jews living in Germany in 1943 possible. On January 1, 1940, the number was approximately 202,400. In 1940 and 1941, 29,000 of these emigrated from Germany. The excess of deaths over births in these two years may be estimated approximately at 14,000. On January 1, 1942, the number of Jews in Germany was therefore approximately 159,400.

Mass deportations to the East and the systematic annihilation policy of the Nazi government have reduced the Jewish community to such extent that by 1943 no more than 30,000 probably remained. Jews still living in the Reich then were economically valuable to the country, and included technical specialists, skilled war workers, doctors, and Jews living in a so-called privileged mixed marriage, that is, a mixed marriage with living descendants who were Christians.

The last reliable figures on the distribution of Jews in Germany were of January 1, 1940, when there were district offices of the Reichsvereinigung (Central Organization) in 20 larger cities, not including Sudetenland. One may assume that the small number of Jews living in Germany at a later date were concentrated in a few larger communities, such as Berlin, Hamburg and Breslau, and in a number of labor camps, mostly situated in North and Central Germany.

Between 1933 and 1941, 310,900 persons were able to leave Germany by emigrating to other countries. Reliable official figures regarding Jewish immigrants are available only for the United States and Palestine. Other important countries of immigration, especially those in South America, have not issued statistics classifying the Jewish immigrants by their countries of origin.

Between July 1, 1932, and June 30, 1942, 81,328 Jewish immigrants from Germany were admitted to the United States; between 1933 and 1941, 50,424 Jewish immigrants from Germany were admitted to Palestine. After 1938, Jewish refugees from Austria were included in this number; moreover, the figures refer only to those who came directly from Germany, not to the many refugees who found temporary refuge in other countries before their arrival in the United States or Palestine. Immigration tables published for the United States list many immigrants according to the countries of birth or the countries to whose quota the immigrant is charged; frequently, therefore, immigrants who came directly or indirectly from Germany, but were born outside Germany, were not registered as immigrants from Germany. The figures for the United States also did not include holders of temporary visitors' visas and non-quota visas. A study published by the Committee for Selected Social Studies gave an estimate of 106,017 refugees as having come to the United States from Germany during the period between 1933 and 1941, but this figure covered non-Jews and non-"Aryans" as well as Jews.

A number of Jews escaped to the Soviet Union between 1933 and 1936; some technical experts and professionals received specific invitations and employment contracts from the Russian Government. The exact number of Jews from Germany in the U.S.S.R. in 1942-43 is not known, but it is probably very small.

The age structure of the Jewish population of Germany was:

	1925	1933	1938
Below the age of 20	26%	21%	16%
Between 20 and 45	41%	39%	30%
Over 45	33%	40%	54%

German Jewry had already entered on a state of senescence, even before the advent of Hitler and especially before the violent campaign of annihilation was instituted in November, 1938.

COMMUNITY ORGANIZATION.

Under the Weimar Constitution, there was no State Church in Germany. Neither was there complete separation between the church and state as in the United States. The law of July 3, 1869, granted freedom of religion; thereafter all creeds were entitled to gather for religious worship and to organize public religious corporations Articles 135-141 of the Weimar Constitution continued this freedom. The corporations were granted subordinated and limited powers of legislation; they could levy taxes for communal expenses, and like municipalities, they were autonomous in the administration of their own affairs. Institutions, functionaries and properties of religious public corporations enjoyed special privileges, such as exemption from civil taxation and special protection under the criminal laws: libelous attacks against them were prosecuted as public offenses. Together with the Christian churches, the Jewish religious communal bodies in Germany received financial assistance from the state and were subject to its financial control. There were thirteen provincial committees (Landesverbände), representing local communities. These Landesverbände formed a national board (Reichvertretung der Gemeindeverbände).

Jewish groups of all religious factions and beliefs -- Orthodox, Liberal and Reform -- made up the communal organizations (Einheitsgemeinde). In some German states - Prussia, Bavaria, Hesse - groups of extreme Orthodox communities (Gesetzestreue Gemeinde) - were separately organized, and had their own national committee (Reichsbund der gesetzestreuen Gemeinden). In 1933 there were about 1,600 Jewish communal bodies in Germany. Community districts were usually identical with the municipalities. Every Jew within a district automatically became a member of its Jewish communal body; if he wanted to leave it, he was required to declare his intention before a municipal court. A decree of March 31, 1938, deprived the Jewish communities of their rights and character as public corporations, but they continued to exist as private corporations.

The largest and most influential of the religious groups (Orthodox, Liberal and Reform) in most of the communities was the Liberal group, nationally organized in the Vereinigung fur das religiös - liberale Judentum. It published a weekly paper, Jüdisch-Liberale Zeitung. Liberal Jews were willing to accept only a modified Orthodox ritual. Their religious interest found expression in the life and organization of the community which attained a state of organization and effectiveness in Germany (before 1933), unparalleled in any other country. Orthodoxy provided the second largest Jewish group in Germany, and was divided into community (Gemeinde) Orthodoxy and the separatist Orthodoxy (Trennungsgemeinde). Most adherents of the latter group belonged to the Agudath Israel, which published the weekly Der Israelit. The smallest religious body in Germany was the Reform group, which was a section of religious Liberalism, but had abolished nearly all the ceremonies of the Jewish ritual. There were a few Hassidim in Germany, but the group was not important. Reports from Germany show that in the winter of 1942-43 there were still Orthodox, Liberal and a few Reform services being held in Berlin and other Jewish communities.

State officials, soldiers, students and school children were allowed time off on Jewish holidays and for divine services. State institutions, hospitals and prisons were obliged to provide Jewish services for the Jewish inmates; in Prussia, for instance, Jewish prison chaplains took care of Jewish prisoners. Jewish religious education was part of the prescribed curriculum for Jewish students in public and private grammar schools, colleges and high schools. Orthodox children were freed from writing at the Sabbath services of the public schools. The Jewish religious teacher, usually appointed or selected by the local Jewish community, was a full member of the government school staff, with the rights and privileges of other teachers. Each religious group in Germany observed the Jewish holidays according to its respective principles.

Dietary laws as prescribed by the Jewish religion were strictly observed in Germany only by the Orthodox minority and by many of the Jewish institutions. Matzoh was generally eaten during Passover and some fast days were observed, especially Yom Kippur.

No law against Shehitah (ritual slaughter) existed for Germany before 1933, although Bavaria had barred it in 1931. One of the first discriminatory measures of the Hitler government was a law making Shehitah a criminal offense (Gesetz über das Schlachten von Tieren, April 21, 1933.)

There were no other legal restrictions in Nazi Germany against the Jewish religion as such and its profession. Having lost their privileged status as public corporations in 1938, the Jewish communities first became ordinary associations under the civil law and later, in 1939, were incorporated into the Reichsvereinigung, which thereafter controlled all Jewish affairs in Germany.

Observance itself did not change fundamentally under Hitler, but persecution and pressure evoked a Jewish renaissance from within. Many who had been indifferent, and sometimes even hostile, toward the Jewish ritual before Hitler, found new strength and comfort in the message of religion. Destruction of between 300 and 500 synagogues in the pogrom of November, 1938, made the unbroken and orderly observance of Jewish services much more difficult.

A voluntary Din Torah (Jewish Court of Arbitration) existed in Germany but was used in pre-Hitler days only by Orthodox Jews. Under the Nazi government, voluntary arbitration courts continued to arbitrate differences among Jews in some of the larger Jewish communities, as for instance in Berlin.

COMMUNITY ASSETS.

No exact figures are available as to the wealth possessed by synagogues and institutions, but some of the older and larger communities and institutions had substantial real and personal property, part of which was a total loss during the inflation after the First World War. The major source of income for the Jewish communities were the taxes which they, like municipalities, were entitled to levy on the incomes of all Jews living in their district. In 1936 the Jewish communities in Germany derived an income of 25,000,000 marks (about $10,000,000) from taxes alone.

The largest and most representative Jewish community, that of Berlin, had -- in 1937 -- an income of 7,700,000 marks from taxes and 3,900,000 marks from other sources. The expenditures of the Berlin community for 1937 amounted to 12 million marks. The same year the community owned 21 apartment houses, the total value amounting to 2,100,000 marks; 17 synagogues (the newest and most modern synagogue in Prinzregentenstrasse was built at the cost of 6,000,000 marks); six school buildings, several administrative buildings, one museum, one hospital, three modern athletic stadiums, ten gymnastic halls, eight homes; one hospital for the aged; two orphanages and two large cemeteries with more than 30,000 graves under permanent care. A number of independent Jewish institutions had substantial property of their own.

Properties owned by the Jewish communities and institutions were transferred to the Reichsvereinigung in 1939, when the organizations ceased to exist as independent groups, but many Jewish buildings were destroyed by Nazi vandalism and the sites later confiscated. No legal excuse was being given for the confiscation of Jewish properties in 1942-43, but during the first years of the Hitler regime the Nazi government tried to preserve at least the semblance of law and order, so sabotage evidence was planted, or "fabricated" if necessary, to provide legal grounds for confiscation.

FUNCTIONARIES.

The census of June 16, 1933, showed 1,792 Jews to be employed by congregations as rabbis, cantors, or other religious functionaries. The rabbi was the recognized spiritual leader of the community, although his authority and his influence were firmer in Orthodox than in Liberal groups. Both Liberal and Orthodox rabbis supervised the religious education of their respective communities, and lectured on religious topics in public and private schools. The rabbis were directly employed by the local communities, many receiving lifetime contracts.

Smaller communities shared a district rabbi; some of the smaller German states (like Anhalt and Mecklenburg) had a state rabbi (Landesrabbiner). In some German states, rabbis held the same privileged position as Christian ministers, in Württenberg older rabbis even received the title of church counselor (Kirchenrat). A rabbi in Germany was required to have a general college education, good academic training and a diploma from one of the three rabbinical seminaries: the Academy for the Science of Judaism (Hochschule für die Wissenschaft des Judentums), in Berlin; the Orthodox seminary (Rabbinerseminar), Berlin, and the conservative seminary in Breslau (Jüdisch Theologische Seminar).

One general organization united all the rabbis of Germany -- the Allgemeine Rabbinerverband in Deutschland; there were also separate organizations for Orthodox and Liberal rabbis. Cantors were organized in the Allgemeine deutsche Kantorenverband. Almost every community, large and small, had a shohet (ritual slaughterer), who was supervised by the local or district rabbi. One man frequently served as shohet and Jewish teacher; a special school for the training of shohetim was located in Berlin. Those few rabbis and religious functionaries who were still in Germany in 1942-43 became the spiritual leaders of German Jewry's fight for survival.

MARRIAGE AND DIVORCE.

Until 1933, marriage in Germany demanded a prior civil ceremony, legally performed by a public official, such as the registrar (Standesbeamte). Religious ceremonies were permitted but not essential for validity. There were no restrictions regarding inter-marriages between people of different color, creed or religion. Religious marriages, without civil registration, performed in other countries were recognized in Germany when they were valid under local law at the place of performance.

In Germany, in 1926, of a thousand non-Jews, 7.7 got married, but of a thousand Jews, only 5.9. In 1927, the corresponding ratio was 8.7 non-Jews to 6.3 Jews for a group of a thousand persons. But the most striking feature in Germany was the steady decline of Jewish marriages compared with the increase of mixed marriages (the first figure indicates Jewish marriages, the second, mixed marriages):

1923: 4833, 2008; 1924: 3310, 1547; 1925: 2904, 1413; 1926: 2656, 1315; 1927: 2789, 1505; 1928: 2983, 1604; 1929: 2817, 1663; 1930: 2851, 1644; 1931: 2484, 1405; 1932: 2307, 1378; 1933: 2174, 1693; 1934: 2522, 792; 1935: 2751, 503; 1936: 2665, 90.

For each 100 Jewish marriages there was an average of 60 mixed marriages annually from 1929 to 1935. The peak of the development came in 1933, when 35.5% of all Jewish men married in Germany took non-Jewish wives. In 1935, with the decree for the protection of German blood and honor of September 15, which outlawed mixed marriages, the trend came to a sudden end. There were no restrictions against Jewish marriages in Germany in 1942-43.

The Constitution of the Weimar Republic provided for complete equality between men and women. But in the family, the husband and father enjoyed a number of important prerogatives. The father was the sole guardian and representative of his children; it was he who determined their membership in a religious community and directed their religious education -- a prerogative of particular importance in mixed marriages. In Prussia, in a given year, 25.8% of the children born to a Jewish father and a non-Jewish mother were given a Jewish upbringing. In marriages where the mother was Jewish, only 23.7% of the children received a Jewish education in the same year.

The Jewish citizens of Germany were subject to the divorce statutes of the German civil code (Bürgerliches Gesetzbuch). Dissolution of marriage by the divorce writ (Get) of a rabbinic court was not recognized by German courts, except insofar as the lex loci prevailed for citizens of countries where religious divorces were recognized, as for instance in most parts of Poland. The Nazi government did not establish special divorce laws for Jews, but the new law of marriages (Ehegesetz) of July 27, 1938, facilitated divorce in general and the dissolution of the numerous mixed marriages between "Aryans" and Jews in particular. No Agunah (deserted wife) problem existed. The husband who absented himself for more than ten years and could not be traced, could be declared dead by judicial decree, automatically dissolving the marriage. This naturally failed to solve the problem in the case of practicing Orthodox Jews, who would not permit the remarriage of a woman whose husband's whereabouts were unknown.

CEMETERIES.

Even the smallest Jewish community in Germany had its own cemetery, of which the oldest was the famous cemetery of Worms (1000 A.D.) Communities cared for their respective cemeteries, providing their own undertakers and burial services. The cemeteries were considered imperishable (Beth Olam). Even communities which had ceased to exist provided for the care of the old cemetery before their dissolution. Cremation was resorted to only by Liberals; there was no Jewish crematory. A Hebrah Kadisha (burial society) was formed in each community; usually it was a voluntary association assisting in the observance of Jewish rites at funeral services. The community cemeteries were used by all Jewish factions, Orthodox and Liberals alike, but there were also a few cemeteries used exclusively by the Orthodox. Many Jewish cemeteries were destroyed after 1933.

POSITION OF WOMEN.

Jewish women, although frequently holding important public posts, still had to fight for equality in the Jewish community. Until 1930, women were not permitted to vote in community elections. A few extremely Orthodox communities continued to refuse the electoral franchise to women, others granted them the right to vote, but barred them from community offices. Jewish women were very active in social work. The largest Jewish women's organization was the Jüdischer Frauenbund, founded in 1904, which united 450 clubs and associations comprising more than 50,000 members.

COMMUNAL ORGANIZATIONS.

Among themselves the Jews were divided into assimilated German Jewish groups and Zionist Groups with Jewish nationalist tendencies. The Centralverein deutscher Staatsbürger jüdischen Glaubens was the leading organization of German Jews, without interest in Zionism; it was followed in importance by the Verband national deutscher Juden. Zionists were organized in the Zionistische Vereinigung für Deutschland, the Poale Zion, and Mizrachi. The Revisionist group were called the Staatszionisten. The Agudath Israel (ultra-Orthodox, non-Zionist group) was well represented in Germany, with centers in Berlin, Frankfort, Breslau and Halberstadt.

In 1933 there were 97 Jewish youth organizations registered in Germany, their program and structure following the pattern of the German youth organizations (Jugenbünde), founded on ideals of comradeship, friendship, dramatic work, athletics, dancing and mutual self-education in Judaism. There were three main youth groups - Zionist, German-Jewish and Orthodox.

All Jewish youth organizations were united in 1933, in the Reichsausschuss der jüdischen Jugendverbände, with 55,000 members. Most of the non-Zionist organizations were dissolved between 1937 and 1939. The status of the few Jewish youth organizations remaining in Germany in 1943 is not known.

All Jewish organizations in Germany, with the exception of the official Jewish Community, were organized on the basis of voluntary membership. Membership in the Reichsvereinigung der Juden in Deutschland -- the central Jewish organization functioning in the Hitler regime, was obligatory; special permission from the Minister of the Interior was required for a cancellation of membership.

In 1933, there were about 100 major Jewish organizations, fraternal orders and societies in Germany, of which the most important were:

The B'nai B'rith lodges, (12,000 members, 100 lodges); Central Verein deutscher Staatsbürger jüdischen Glaubens; Zionistische Vereinigung für Deustschland; Reichsbund jüdischer Frontsoldaten, (30,000 members, 350 branches); and the Reichsbund der jüdischen Kulturbünde, devoted to the development of Jewish culture (140 organizations, 600 employees, 110,000 members). Before the advent of Hitlerism some Jews were Freemasons; after 1933, they were forced to leave the Masonic lodges. Fraternal organizations were most active among students.

SPORTS.

Many Jews had been active in German sport and athletic associations, before the Nazi regime. About 25 Jewish athletes were German champions, some were world champions. Among these was Helene Mayer, world fencing champion at the Amsterdam Olympic Games, 1932.

LANGUAGES.

The German Jews all spoke German. Even in parts of Germany predominantly populated by national minorities (Polish, Danish or Lithuanian), the language was German. Yiddish was spoken only by immigrants from Eastern Europe. Most German Jews had some knowledge of Hebrew, educated people could speak French and English and understood some Latin.

The Jewish renaissance under Hitler evoked a new interest in modern Hebrew and in the study of English, Spanish and Portuguese in preparation for emigration. In 1941, in addition to many private language courses, the following courses in foreign languages were offered by the Reichsvereinigung in Berlin: 14 in English, 9 in Spanish, 3 in Portuguese, 3 in Russian, 7 in English stenography, 1 in Spanish stenography.

CRIMINALITY.

That the Jews in Germany were law-abiding citizens was evidenced by comparative crime statistics for the years from 1882 to 1917, when the practice of classifying criminals according to religion was discontinued, until the Nazi regime reinstated it. The Jews of Germany contributed only one-fifth of one percent of Germany's criminals, although they made up one per cent of its population. The criminality of Jews was lower than among non-Jews for most of the serious crimes against life and property. According to the statistics for 1903-1906, the following serious offenses were committed more frequently by non-Jews: robbery, 5.6 times as frequently, homicide, 4.3 times as frequently, accidental homicide, 2.6 times as frequently, theft, 2.8 times as frequently, arson, 2.9 times as frequently, assault, 2 times as frequently.

On the other hand, the Jewish population, engaged to almost half its number in trade, showed a larger proportion of criminality for certain types of crimes related to business or property dealings. Involvement of Jews was higher for the following categories (1903-1906); usury, 29 times as frequently, fraudulent bankruptcy, 12.6 times as frequently, fraud, 2 times as frequently, forgery, 2.3 times as frequently.

The general change of conditions under the Hitler regime brought about a change in the Jewish criminality record.

Of 100,000 Jews in 1916, 589 were convicted for criminal offenses, but in 1936, of 100,000, 1,026 were convicted, 1,268 in 1937 and 1,194 in 1938. To understand the real meaning of these figures, an analysis of the individual offenses is necessary. Of 4,104 Jews convicted in 1936, only 1,756 were found guilty of a violation of the Penal Code, which enumerated and included all real crimes. The rest, 2,348, were convicted of violating other laws, the majority of which were specific anti-Jewish or discriminatory laws. The average convictions per 100,000 persons, from 1936 to 1938, were as follows: serious crimes (murder, assault, sex crimes), 55.82 Jews, 95.70 non-Jews; light crimes and misdemeanors (violations of industrial regulations, traffic laws, etc.), 89.33 Jews, 50 non-Jews; political crimes, 3.71 Jews, 9 non-Jews; violation of discriminatory and anti-Jewish laws (racial pollution, foreign exchange restrictions, passport rules), 350.19 Jews, 16.40 non-Jews.

In the use of alcoholic beverages and tobacco, there was no substantial difference between the general population of Germany and the Jews. But alcoholism was less frequent among Jews, as proved by the statistics of crime committed under the influence of alcohol. Delirium tremens was very rare among Jews; of the inmates of Prussian asylums for mental diseases in 1898-1900, 7.5% of the Protestants had been committed for delirium tremens, 5.1% of the Catholics, 12.3 of the religiously unaffiliated and only 1.1% of the Jews.

ATTITUDE TOWARD WAR AND PEACE.

The Jews of Germany shared no common opinion toward war; among them were militarists and pacifists, chauvinists and cosmopolitans. Like many outstanding Germans after Goethe and Kant, there were pacifists among German Jews who dreamed with Kant of "eternal peace". But even the pacifists among the Jews did not fail their country in time of war. The first member of the German Reichstag to be killed in action during the First World War was a Jewish Socialist, Dr. Ludwig Frank; in all German wars after 1813, the time of the emancipation, German Jews distinguished themselves.

About 100,000 German Jews - 18% of the total Jewish population - were in the German Army in the First World War. Some 75,000 fought on the front; 12% had volunteered and more than 12,000 Jews died on the battlefield. About 35,000 Jewish soldiers were decorated for bravery, 23,000 were promoted and 2,000 received commissions as officers, an achievement particularly remarkable in view of the fact that they had to overcome the traditional prejudices of the Prussian caste system. This prejudice was influenced by the idea that the power of the state should never be represented by Jews; it prevented Jewish soldiers from becoming officers in the German army before the First World War, but there were a few exceptions in the particularly liberal southern states like Bavaria and Baden.

POLITICAL STRUCTURE.

Since the Jews were enfranchised in the German Reich, and in the various German states, they belonged to all political parties which did not exclude Jews from membership. They did not constitute a political block or belong to one party; they were members of those parties which represented their individual beliefs and which protected their economic and cultural interests. Naturally no Jews were found in the anti-Semitic -- the National Socialist and German National -- parties. Jews of the bourgeois classes joined the progressive parties -- the Democratic Party (later called Staats-partei) and Stresemann's National Liberal Party (Deutsche Volkspartei); some Jews, particularly those who were extremely Orthodox, even voted for the Center, which was Catholic. Jews who supported Socialist ideas and theories belonged to the Socialist parties.

Since a secret ballot prevailed, it is impossible to quote figures showing the division of the Jewish vote among the various parties, but it seems safe to estimate that the democratic and social democratic parties received the majority. There were one or two deputies of Jewish descent among the Communists, but out of the total of 81 Communist deputies of the Diet of 1933, dissolved by Hitler, there was not a single Jew.

UNDERGROUND MOVEMENT.

German Jewry, under Hitler, experienced a kind of nationalist renaissance and dreamed only of a new life in Palestine or of migration to other parts of the globe, disclaiming any interest in the internal affairs or politics of a country where they were pariahs and outlaws.

Nevertheless, many Jews were active in the underground movement, mostly those who had participated in labor groups and in socialist party activities. These people continued the fight side by side with their old comrades, not as Jews but as socialists. If arrested, a worse fate awaited them -- stiffer sentences from the courts, and more brutal treatment from concentration camp guards. As Jews, they were under closer observation and suspicion and more exposed to the ever-present danger of denunciation by a "neighbor" or "friend." But despite all these hazards, many Jews refused to submit and gave their lives in the silent war of the German underground.

There were even underground workers on the staff of Jewish organizations. In 1937, a female secretary of the Hilfsverein in Berlin was convicted for participation in underground activities.

HISTORY OF ANTI-SEMITISM.

Apart from finding the Jew a convenient scapegoat for all German miseries, certain theories helped to form the Weltanschauung which provided Hitler with the ideological foundation for his anti-Semitic movement. The foundation had two bases: economic and racist. Numerous publications which appeared during the last few decades of the 19th century played up the putative connection between economic "freedom" and anti-Semitism.

The racist element entered somewhat earlier, with the launching -- and subsequent misinterpretation -- of various theories on human origins and development. Almost every study that touched on racial history, from the work of Renan through Gobineau to Darwin, was perverted for their own use by the protagonists of false theories of racial superiority. Surprising artistic ramification was provided in the artistic field, by Wagner and the Bayreuth Circle, who deserted the realms in which they could speak with authority and talent for regions to which they could offer neither. Houston Stewart Chamberlain's Foundations of the Nineteenth Century, which appeared in 1899, added the ultimate fillip to the concept of superiority with which the Teutons were plying themselves.

With the economic disasters brought by the end of the First World War, and the disgrace which was a consequence of Germany's defeat, both the economic and the racist incitements became empowered. The Nazis expected that the looting of the Jews and bestial persecution of them would offer gratification to the need to obtain economic solace and at the same time to serve the Fatherland.

The first anti-Semitic parties were founded in Germany, in 1878, in connection with Hofprediger (court preacher) Adolf Stoecker's Christian-social movement. In 1889 Liebermann Von Sonnenberg formed the first anti-Semitic party based on race anti-Semitism -- the so-called German social party: Deutsch soziale Partei, which was united in 1894 with Böckel's anti-Semitic party to form the German Social Reform party (Deutsch soziale Reform Partei). A short time before the outbreak of the First World War, all anti-Semitic groups combined in the Deutsch Völkische Partei. Under the Weimar Republic, there were two anti-Semitic parties in addition to the National Socialists: the great conservative party, Deutschnationale Volkspartei, under the leadership of Count-Westarp and Alfred Hugenberg, and the Deutsch Völkische Freiheitspartei, led by Graefe, Wulle and Henning.

The National Socialist German Workers Party was founded in 1919. Its first program, adopted on February 25, 1920, pledged the elimination of Jews from Germany's political, social and economic life, establishing anti-Semitism as the cornerstone of the movement. Most of the large and influential German student organizations (Burschenschaften, Korps, etc.) had practiced anti-Semitic principles since 1830, and did not accept Jews as members, especially the Verein deutscher Studenten. Other student organizations, however, and even some Burschenchaften, condemned anti-Semitism and accepted Jews as members.

Additional anti-Semitic organizations were the Bund deutscher Landwirte (Farmers Association) founded in 1893, and the Deutscher Schutz und Trutzbund. The leading independent anti-Semitic publication was the Hammer (1902), edited by Theodor Fritsch, who had since 1884 published the Handbuch zur Judenfrage, a compendium of the Jewish question. The most important anti-Semitic newspaper outside the Nazi party press was the Deutche Zeitung of Berlin, although with the beginning of the 20th century, almost every province had its outspokenly anti-Semitic periodical.

CHRISTIAN CHURCHES AND THE JEWS.

After 1870, Germany was identified with Prussia, and much of German nationalist propaganda was identified with Prussianism and Protestantism. It cannot be said, however, that the Catholic Church in Germany was less nationalistic than the Protestant. Some Catholic laymen were leaders in the ultra-nationalist movements which helped the National Socialist doctrine take hold. The official attitude of the Catholic Church was particularly friendly to the Jews in the Protestant parts of Germany, where the Catholic Church often looked on Jews as allies in the fight against religious intolerance. Many prominent Catholics, among them Cardinal Faulhaber, Archbishop Jacobus von Hauck (Bamberg), Professor Carl Maria Kaufman, editor of the influential Catholic magazine, Fels, and many Catholic newspapers, attacked anti-Semitism as un-Christian and un-Catholic.

Similarly, the Protestant Church as a whole was not anti-Semitic, but some Lutheran leaders, tending toward extreme Germanism, again abetted Nazi infiltration. Frequently the Germanism of certain pagan Germans was unjustly attributed to the Protestant Church. The nationalist aspects of the Nazi beliefs were not unpopular with leading Protestants who believed that the Nazis would not interfere with the Church. Prominent in the antagonism to the Hitlerian policies as a group, however, was the Bekenntniskirche of the Protestant Church; among its leaders, Gotthelf Bronisch, Gerhard Jacobi and Dr. Otto Dibelius, were outspoken in their opposition to Nazi policies, including the policy toward the Jews.

In general, both churches, Catholic and Protestant, have defied National Socialism on ethical issues and where the Christian faith was challenged. But sustained and emphatic protests against the treatment of the Jews, if any, were negligible.

EXTRA-LEGAL DISCRIMINATION: BEFORE AND DURING NAZI REGIME.

While the German people, before the advent of Hitler, never completely overlooked differences between various religions, there were but few social and economic restrictions of an anti-Semitic nature between 1918 and 1933. The great number of mixed marriages and intimate friendships between Christians and Jews, the economic success of Jews, especially in the professions, and many other facts were evidence of a far-reaching rapprochement between the German Jews and the rest of the German population.

Nevertheless, a substantial remnant of anti-Semitism was always to be found in Germany, but that it was originally not a spontaneous expression of the majority of the German people was confirmed by Hitler himself, who wrote in Mein Kampf -- "In 1918 there was no such thing as systematic anti-Semitism in Germany." Modern German anti-Semitism was skillfully manufactured and stirred into flame by the Nazis, in a campaign that began in 1920, when Hitler and his followers recognized that the economic and social conditions in defeated Germany were favorable for a revival of anti-Jewish agitation and the creation of a Jewish scapegoat for all German troubles. Both presidents of the Reich between 1918-1933, Friedrich Ebert and Paul von Hindenburg, condemned anti-Semitism and discrimination against Jewish citizens. In a letter written August 12, 1932, four months before Hitler took power, Reichspresident von Hindenburg decried all attempts to limit or to violate the constitutional, political and religious rights of German Jewish citizens and condemned attacks upon Jews or their property.

Yet, there was unofficial discrimination against the Jews of Germany even before Hitler. Hardly any Jews were to be found in the army (as officers), post office, customs department, the Reichsbank (Federal Reserve Bank) and the German State Railways. It was quite difficult for a Jewish doctor to be appointed to the army or police medical corps, or to the medical staff of state institutions like prisons, asylums or hospitals. Only a few outstanding Jewish business men, engineers or chemists managed to obtain high-grade posts with the large business firms, such as Siemens, I.G.Farben or Krupp. Even firms which were founded and developed to a state of international importance by Jews, such as the <u>Allgemeine Elektrizitäts Gesellschaft</u> (Rathenau), Hamburg-American Line, (Ballin) and Orenstein and Koppel became more and more restricted, not officially, but <u>de facto</u>. A Jewish professor had to possess exceptional scientific attainments to be admitted to the faculty of one of the leading universities.

Anti-Jewish legislation in the third Reich had but one goal -- the complete elimination of Jews and of certain Christians of Jewish ancestry from all public and semi-public professions and institutions, from the liberal professions, as well as from the intellectual, cultural and economic life of the German nation. The basis of the structure of legislative discrimination was the law for the restoration of the professional civil service of April 7, 1933, whereby all Jews and thousands of Christian non-"Aryans" were excluded from civil service. Similar laws were applied to all other avenues of the political, economic, social and cultural life of the country. They were codified into numerous and voluminous laws, and culminated in the tenth amendment to the Nationality Act of July 4, 1939, which decreed that henceforth no Jew was entitled to relief or assistance from the government or any other public institution.

Nazi Germany's supreme law, superior even to the public statutes, was the will of the Führer and of the Nazi party as expressed in the party program. Many important discriminations against the Jews were never embodied in formal statutes. There were no restrictions on travel by Jews prior to 1938, yet hundreds of little townships, hamlets and villages erected signs barring Jews from their boundaries; the city of Coburg, as early as 1933, issued an order forbidding Jews the use of street cars. In some towns Jews were not permitted to attend the fairs. From some markets Jews were completely barred, in others they were segregated in special stalls or limited to certain days and hours. While many Jewish firms were still in business in 1935, the German State Railways, a semi-official corporation, refused to accept advertisements of Jewish firms. While Jewish firms did continue to do business and certain groups of Jewish doctors and lawyers were legally admitted to practice until 1938, the Nazi party and their affiliated organizations used threats of official punishment and mob violence to provoke the boycott of such people. There were no legal restrictions on lodging and shopping before 1938, yet many hotels were forced -- in some instances against their will -- to reject Jewish guests and buyers; an increasing number of stores refused to sell to Jews.

There were provincial sections and towns where pharmacies were closed to Jews and the most essential necessities of life, such as bread and milk, were unobtainable. After the outbreak of war in 1939 the situation was aggravated. While some factories treated their Jewish forced laborers decently, others made them wear yellow bands, relegated them to separate latrines and rest rooms and denied them the right to eat or to buy in the factory canteen. There was no law forbidding Jews to use the services of barbers and beauty shops or to buy newspapers, yet the police in Berlin issued orders to that effect. There was no law against Jewish ownership of domestic animals, but the police issued orders forbidding Jews to keep pets. Aside from suffering under the extensive and intensive discriminatory legislation of Hitler's government, the Jews were subjected to the whims and fancies of thousands of local Hitlers.

The German people, entirely subdued by their Nazi masters, had no means of showing their real attitude. Millions of Nazis and their sympathizers were definitely and violently anti-Jewish. But according to the experience of those who lived in Germany under Hitler, judging by the repeated provocative outbursts and threats against Jewish "sympathizers" in the German press, and considering the reports of numerous expressions of apologetic sympathy toward Jews in subways, street cars and public places (New York Times, November 2, 1941), there seems reason to believe that at least a part of the population did not agree with official anti-Semitism.

CITIZENSHIP.

The legal status of German citizenship before 1933 was defined by the Nationality Act of July 22, 1913, which was based on the Constitution of the German Reich of 1871, and confirmed and guaranteed by the Constitution of Weimar. There was no discrimination on the basis of nativity or religion; all citizens were equal before the law and enjoyed all the rights, privileges and benefits of citizenship. German citizenship was acquired either by birth, legitimation, marriage or naturalization.

In determining citizenship by birth, the German law was governed by the jus sanguinis and not by the jus soli of the Anglo-Saxon law. Each child of a German citizen, born in wedlock, acquired his father's German citizenship, whether born on German soil or elsewhere. The same was true for a child born out of wedlock to a mother who was a German citizen. Each child born out of wedlock acquired German citizenship by subsequent marriage of the parents, if the father was a German citizen. Adoption did not confer German citizenship upon the adopted child. A woman acquired German nationality by marrying a German citizen. The governments of the various German states had the right to naturalize foreigners. In June, 1933, out of a total Jewish population of 499,682, 400,935 were German citizens.

The German Nationality Act of September 15, 1935, deprived Jews of their citizenship. Section 2 of this law included the following specifications: "A citizen is only that subject of the state who is of German or related blood and who proves that he is willing and able to serve the German people and empire faithfully. Only the citizen enjoys full political rights as granted by the law." Paragraph 4 states expressis verbis, "A Jew cannot be a citizen."

The former Jewish citizens of Germany retained a limited status, or second-class citizenship. Its possessors were deprived of all the essential elements of citizenship, such as the right to vote for representation in the Reichstag and to vote for or to be elected to public office. The fact that persons of Jewish blood were, by deprivation of citizenship and by denationalization, placed in the position of "aliens" to the German State, and therefore not entitled to its diplomatic protection, was internationally recognized as early as December 25, 1935, in the letter of resignation sent to the League of Nations by James G. MacDonald, High Commissioner for Refugees. A decree of November 25, 1941, effective the following day, deprived all German Jews living abroad of their limited status as German subjects of the second class. By this decree -- which also confiscated the property of emigrated Jews -- all German Jews outside of Germany proper became stateless.

There had been about 20,000 stateless Jews in Germany in 1933, most of them of Russian or Polish descent. Stateless refugees from Russia received the so-called Nansen passport, issued by the Nansen office of the League of Nations -- an internationally recognized identification paper which gave its possessor a slightly more advantageous position than provided by an ordinary stateless passport. All other stateless persons received a stateless passport from the aliens' department of the German police. In the pre-Hitler period, stateless persons were fairly well treated; they were required to have a general or individual permit to work, but were entitled to welfare or other public assistance and to court rights as paupers. Many stateless persons -- Jews included -- were naturalized in Germany under the Weimar republic.

Under a law passed on July 14, 1933, all naturalizations of "undesirable elements" naturalized between November, 1918, and January, 1933, could be revoked. The law characterized as "undesirable" criminals and Jews from Eastern Europe, with the exception of those who had served as "front fighters" in the German or Austrian armies or had rendered especially valuable services to Germany. Many Jews could meet these requirements, but a considerable number, nevertheless, were deprived of their citizenship and became stateless. Not only foreign Jews but also many German-born children of foreign parents naturalized after 1918 were denaturalized. Many denaturalized Jews were expelled or deported from the Reich.

MINORITIES.

There were no national minorities under German law; there were only German nationals speaking a foreign tongue (<u>Fremdsprachige</u> <u>Volksteile</u>) whose right to use their own languages in school and in public life was guaranteed by the Weimar Constitution (Article 133). German Jews, speaking only German, did not come within this classification, and were therefore not recognized as a national or religious minority, except under the terms of the Upper-Silesia treaty of May 15, 1922, between Poland and Germany. This covenant was under the guarantee and control of the League of Nations. The famous Bernheim petition of 1933 forced Germany -- then a member of the League of Nations -- to recognize and to respect Jewish rights in Upper-Silesia until the termination of the treaty in 1937. For four years (1933-37) the anti-Jewish laws of the Reich were not in effect in Upper-Silesia. Jews who were judges and government officials retained their positions, professionals and business men remained undisturbed, and even <u>Shehita</u> -- which was forbidden in Germany after April, 1933 -- was permitted in Upper-Silesia under the terms of a special agreement between the government of the Reich and the association of Upper-Silesian synagogues of August 27, 1934.

Since there were no minorities under the Weimar Constitution, there were no Jewish divisions under the Ministry for the Interior, and no minority offices of any kind in Germany.

JEWS IN THE REICHSTAG.

Out of a total of 576 deputies elected to the German Reichstag in 1930, there were thirteen members of Jewish descent -- one Communist, one Democrat and eleven Social Democrats. In the Reichstag of 1932 there was one Jew out of a total of 608 deputies, and in addition there were thirteen religiously unaffiliated members of Jewish descent -- eleven Social Democrats, one Democrat, and one Communist. One deputy was half-Jewish. There were six deputies of Jewish descent in the Reichstag of 1933 -- all Social Democrats. Very few Jews served in the parliaments of the various German states. In the last Prussian parliament of 1932, out of a total of 423 deputies, there were two Jews and two religiously unaffiliated members of Jewish descent -- all Social Democrats.

JEWS IN GOVERNMENT POSTS.

In the federal, state, and communal administration of Germany and its states in 1933, there were 1,827 Jewish officials (0.22% of the total). Although the number of Jews in state and municipal positions was relatively small, legal or official discrimination was absent, but a certain degree of unofficial discrimination was found in the selection and appointment of officials, especially within the Department of the Interior. Many officials in charge of personnel management were brought up under the old prejudices of the Empire, and believed that a Jew should never be vested with state power.

The caste system and *esprit de corps* of the higher bureaucracy was almost as potent in the German Republic foreign service as it had been under the Kaiser. In the last three German cabinets before 1933, there was no Jew; altogether there had been two Jews and four men of Jewish descent out of about 250 ministers serving in twenty German cabinets between 1918 and 1933. There were altogether only about fifteen Jews of higher rank out of 500 officials in the federal government. In the government of Prussia, ten officials in the higher ranks of the various Prussian departments were Jews. In 1932, there was no Jew among the twelve provincial governors, 35 district presidents and 400 county presidents in Prussia. There was no Jew on the executive board of the German State Railways or the Reichsbank.

MUNICIPAL POSTS.

In pre-Hitler Germany there were no restrictions against Jews in municipality organization, but there was unofficial discrimination in the selection and appointment of municipal officials and employees. Nevertheless, there were some Jews among the officials and representatives of high rank in local governments between 1918 and 1933; the deputy mayors of Frankfort (Max Michel), and Cologne (Albert Kramer), were Jews, as were also the comptroller (Dr. Asch) and other officials of the city of Berlin and high officials in the city administrations of Breslau (Georg Less) and Leipzig. There were Jewish mayors in Würzburg (Freudenberger) and Luckenwalde (Hermann Solomon). Jews had no part in local government under Hitler. After 1938, no Jews could be found in the German Civil Service, police force or post office.

THE JUDICIARY.

There were 286 Jewish judges and public prosecutors in Germany in 1933. Eduard von Simson, a converted Jew, had been president of the Reichstag from 1867 to 1873, and from 1879 to 1891 the first president of the German Supreme Court (Reichsgericht). Hugo Preuss, Minister of Justice under President Ebert, drafted the Weimar Constitution. Many Jews contributed to the structure of German jurisprudence as professors of law, as judges, and as private practitioners. Two non-Jews of Jewish descent were both judges and later ministers of the Reich -- Eugen Schiffer (1919 and 1921) and Bernhard Dernburg (1919). There were two Jews in the German Supreme Court, Justices Salinger and Jacob Friedrich Behrendt. In various departments of the highest court of Prussia (Kammergericht), Victor Ring and Freymuth were presidents, and a few others were justices. A few Jews were presiding justices of various departments of the Supreme Courts of Berlin and elsewhere; still others served in the courts proper. Alfred Neumeyer was justice of the highest Bavarian court, and several Jews were justices of the Court of Appeals in Cologne and Breslau.

Under the Weimar Republic, there was no discrimination against Jews in trials on the part of the judiciary.

THE BAR.

There was no official discrimination against Jews in the German Bar before Hitler, nor as notaries. Notaries were selected from the members of the local Bar and appointed by the state. Occasionally Jewish lawyers, especially in the provinces, found it difficult to get an appointment.

There were 3,030 Jewish lawyers (including notaries) in Germany at the time of Hitler's advent to power, comprising 16.25% of the total of the German Bar, which numbered 18,641. The non-"Aryans" subsequently added brought the first total to approximately 4,100 (22%). 60% of all non-"Aryan" lawyers were notaries in 1933. In addition, there were 79 Jews acting as patent lawyers (13.28%), 986 judges and district attorneys (2.76%), 165 (5.40%) counsellors (lawyers admitted to practice only in municipal courts), and 515 auditors and public accountants (13.6 %).

Under the "law regarding admission to the profession" of April 7, 1933, the admission of all Jews and non-"Aryans" who had neither served on the front during the First World War nor been admitted to law practice on or before August 1, 1941, was cancelled. Thus, 1,080 of the younger lawyers lost their right to practice in Prussia alone, but 2,736 non-"Aryans" were still admitted to practice on January 1, 1935; the majority of this number continued to practice until September 27, 1938, when a new decree cancelled admission of all Jews, effective as of November 30, 1938. Non-Jewish lawyers were in 1943 not permitted to represent Jews. A limited number of Jews were readmitted not as full-fledged attorneys but as konsulenten - counsellors allowed to represent Jews in court. Of these counsellors, 172 were practicing in 1939, at the outbreak of war, 40 of them in Berlin, while in many large circuits there was only one counsellor who had to travel from court to court and from town to town to represent his clients. These counsellors could charge the same fees as the non-Jewish attorneys but were forced to transfer the greater part of their earnings to the German Bar Association. A counsellor whose fee was less than 500 marks ($200) had to pay more than 30%; on earnings between 500 and 1,000 marks, 50% and on amounts above 1,000 marks, 70%. Jews could be appointed as attorneys for Jewish paupers or as public defenders for Jews and receive a statutory compensation for their work; they were also entitled to collect costs from their client's adversary when he was liable for costs.

OCCUPATIONAL STRUCTURE.

The occupational structure of the Jewish population in 1933 was as follows:

Economic group	Persons gainfully employed	Percentage	Including dependents
Agriculture	4,167	1.7	5,124
Industry and handicraft	55,655	23.1	95,472
Commerce and transportation	147,314	61.3	262,223
Public and private service	29,974	12.5	53,443
Domestic service	3,377	1.4	3,494
Total	240,487	100.0	419,756
People without occupation	60,941		79,926
Total	301,428		499,682

Before 1933, German Jewry was largely economically independent; one-half of the total Jewish population of 499,682 was gainfully occupied. Of these, 240,487 (48.12%) were employed and 60,941 (12.2%) could be classified as "independents without profession". 23,824 were laborers and white collar employees. Employees constituted 33.5% of all gainfully employed Jews, laborers 9.9%; together the percentage was 43.4%. Some 40% of the gainfully occupied Jews in Germany were in lower-income bracket working classes.

The majority of the German Jews were members of the middle classes, which included professionals and other independent practitioners and the better paid employees. Some belonged to the well-to-do bourgeoisie, a few possessed large fortunes. Jews had their share in the increasing unemployment; in 1933, there were 33,661 unemployed Jews. As early as 1925, about 1/3 of all the Jews in Berlin were exempt from both general and Jewish community taxes because their incomes were less than 1,200 marks ($480.00). Some 31% of the Jewish tax-payers in Berlin were in the low-income bracket (from 1,200 to 2,400 marks a year). In 1934, 31,000 Jews in Berlin required relief.

The remnants of German Jewry which survived in the Reich in 1943 were almost paupers. In 1933, 41% of the Jews in Germany were gainfully employed, but in the fall of 1939, only 16% received their livelihood from employment or independent occupations. Fines and special taxes imposed on Jews had depleted the accumulated resources possessed by Jews so that in 1939 only 16% of the once well-to-do German Jewish population had resources of more than 5,000 marks ($2,000). But these Jewish "capitalists" were not at liberty to dispose of their property; it was subjected to "security" blocking and was levied and administered by the foreign exchange office. Jews under "security" lost all control of their money and were allowed only to draw between 200 and 600 marks per month for living expenses, the amount depending on the size of the fortune and of the family.

No statistics are available for conditions after the persecutions and deportations of 1942-43. Aside from the Jews drafted for forced labor (about 50,000 in 1940), a numerically small category of wage-earners and professionals still existed who had a somewhat higher income and retained some sort of economic independence. These were the persons employed by the Reichsvereinigung and by Jewish institutions, also the few doctors, dentists, masseurs and attorneys permitted to practice for an exclusively Jewish clientele. Their income was subject to many Jewish strangulation taxes.

BANKING.

The principal private banks owned by Jews and their respective owners were: Arnhold Brothers, Berlin-Dresden: Hans Arnhold, Heinrich Arnhold, Kurt Arnhold, Mayer and Fritz Merzbach; Aufhaeuser, Munich: Geheimrat Aufhaeuser and Siegfried Aufhaeuser; J. Dreyfuss and Co., Frankfort and Berlin: Willy Dreyfuss, Landsberg, Flarsheim and Dr. Wallich; Simon Hirschland, Essen: Kurt Hirschland, Dr. Georg Hirschland, and Hanff; A. Levy, Cologne: Louis Hagen and Leubsdorff; Mendelssohn and Co., Berlin: Franz von Mendelssohn, Loeb, Paul Kemperer, Robert von Mendelssohn; M.M. Warburg and Co., Hamburg: Max M. Warburg, Dr. Fritz M. Warburg, Erik M. Warburg and Dr. Spiegelberg; A. E. Wasserman, Bamberg-Berlin: Dr. Siegmund Wasserman and Count Bernstorff.

After the establishment of Nazi rule, the Warburg firm was taken over by a Kommandit Gesellschaft, which corresponds to a limited partnership. The general partners were Rudolf Brinkmann and Paul Wirtz; the special partners were some leading industrial firms, such as Siemens and Gute Hoffnungshütte. J. Dreyfuss and Co. was acquired by the Munich bank, Merck, Finck and Co. Simon Hirschland in Essen was taken over by the Deutsche Bank, Berlin. The Mendelssohn Co. firm in Berlin was liquidated; the Arnhold bank was taken over by the Dresdener Bank. A. E. Wasserman and Co. was taken over by one of its partners, Count Bernstorff, in company with a new partner, von Heinz; the name of the firm was changed to Bankhaus v. Heinz, Jecklenburg and Co.

INSURANCE.

In 1933, there were 1,908 Jews engaged in the insurance business in Germany, some holding leading positions with such companies as the Victoria and Phoenix. There were no Jews in the insurance business in Germany in 1942-43; they were eliminated from this branch of business as from others.

It would seem that although Jews still living in Germany were permitted to maintain their insurance policies, some companies refused to have business relations with Jewish insurance clients. Jews holding insurance policies payable abroad, or in foreign currency, were sometimes forced to change to payments inside Germany in German currency. After the riots of November, 1938, following the assassination of Ernst vom Rath in Paris, insurance companies were released from the obligation to pay for Jewish property destroyed.

NATURAL RESOURCES.

Jews were not generally prominent as the owners of natural resources in Germany, but a few Jews did own substantial properties of this type. Fritz von Friedlander-Fuld had a number of coal mines, largely situated in Silesia. The Petschek concern of Prague controlled and owned a number of coal mines in Lausitz and middle Germany. Aron Hirsch (Hirsch Copper) was the greatest producer of copper; Moritz von der Porten, a converted Jew, created the aluminum industry. Philip Rosenthal made the famous Rosenthal porcelain, Paul Silverberg and Simon Loewy owned coal and other mines. Maximilian Kempner and H. Gumpel were important potash experts, Moritz Becker was a leading amber industrialist. The number of Jews in "big business" and in the heavy industry concerns which together owned almost all of Germany's natural resources, was always very small and of no importance.

AGRICULTURE.

No restrictions on the ownership of land by Jews existed in pre-Hitler Germany. There were a number of large Jewish country estates (Rittergüter) but only a few farms. A total of 808 Jewish farmers were engaged in agriculture in Germany in 1933, besides 395 gardeners and 331 persons working in other fields of agriculture.

While the legislation of September 29, 1933, excluded persons of Jewish or colored blood from the ownership of an inherited estate, Jews were permitted, until the end of 1938, to own farms or farmland. By a decree of December 3, 1938, "regarding the utilization of Jewish property", a Jew could be ordered to sell his farming or forest land and real-estate wholly or partly within a specified period of time. The few remaining Jewish landowners were thus forced to sell their property, frequently at arbitrary prices much lower than the real value. Buyers were usually party officials or their friends and relatives. It seems that at least until 1941 the Reichsvereinigung was able to maintain some of the numerous

Jewish training farms: Gross Breesen, Winkel, Gross--Gaglow and Garzau, also the gardeners' school in Ahlem.

There were no Jewish agricultural cooperatives in Germany.

INDUSTRY AND PUBLIC UTILITIES.

In 1933, there were 55,655 Jews engaged in industry in Germany, or 23.1% of the gainfully employed Jewish population, as follows: garment industry, 33,035; food and luxuries, 19,568; metal & trades, 7,220; building industry, 2,771; textile, 3,517; chemical, 2,223; miscellaneous 7,332. The majority belonged to the skilled labor and small business groups.

The Allgemeine Elektrizitäts Gesellschaft, one of the largest power companies in the country, was established by Emil Rathenau. Ludwig Loewe was the founder of one of the leading machinery and armament plants. The largest copper smelting plant in the country was named Hirsch Copper after the Hirsch family. Orenstein and Koppel established the great locomotive and railway car foundry which still bears their name. The prosperity of the German shipbuilding and steamship industry was closely connected with the success and development of the Hamburg-American Line, created by Albert Ballin. The Weinberg family, originally Jewish, sponsored the organization of the enormous dyes concern I.G. Farben. Other well known firms were Cassirer Cable and Casella Chemistry.

There was no official discrimination against Jews in the numerous government-owned cartels, but some unofficial discrimination existed in the field of employment and the selection of business connections. Cases of open discrimination were speedily remedied by appeal to the proper authority when sufficient evidence could be offered. Only a few Jewish industrialists were employed in the numerous foundries and power utilities of the Reich, the Prussian state, the other states and the communities.

Among the leading officials in charge of public utilities in Berlin were: Dr. Kaufman and Dr. Walter Meyer, of the Bewag (Berliner Elektrizitäts Werke Aktien Gesellschaft), and Dr. Alexander, who was in charge of the Berlin Gas Works. Some local government and other political bodies preferred to deal with non-Jews, but when it could be adequately established that a Jewish competitor was discriminated against, an investigation was held and in many cases the situation was remedied. But only in rare cases was convincing evidence obtainable.

COMMERCE AND TRADE.

After the end of 1938, Jews were completely eliminated from industry, commerce and trade in Germany. Only a few small Jewish establishments, as for instance Jewish bookstores, were permitted to remain for exclusively Jewish trade. Many German enterprises advertised that they would not sell to Jews or do business with them. But there were a few exceptions, especially in the field of travel and emigration, where German non-Jewish firms as late as 1940 made it known that they were still able and willing to do business with Jews.

That Jews had been very active in foreign commerce was acknowledged even by firms which did not employ many Jews, such as for instance Siemens, the leading power concern. These firms had many Jews as their representatives and as branch office managers in foreign countries, and maintained long-standing and well-established business relations with Jewish-owned firms all over the world.

The elimination of Jews as executives and as other employees in the field of commerce, under the Nazi regime, did not halt on the frontiers of the Third Reich, although foreign trade was the last to be "Aryanized." A few more level-headed Nazis like Schmidt and Schacht recognized that a too-speedy introduction of anti-Jewish laws in this field would bring more harm than benefit to German commerce. They therefore warned against radical methods. Many firms engaging in foreign trade were at first permitted to retain their Jewish business representation and relationships in foreign countries on the ground of "indispensability." But after 1938, the Nazi party, and the increasing influence of the foreign branches of the party, forced the majority of these firms to dissolve their Jewish business connections; even foreign citizens had to be dismissed and eliminated from enterprises affiliated with German industry.

"ARYANIZATION".

"Aryanized" Jewish property was in most instances taken over by well-known "Aryan" firms of the same business branch for a fraction of its worth. An outstanding example of a special corporation established to succeed an "Aryanized" Jewish firm occurred when the Simson armament plants in Suhl, Thuringia, were expropriated and the ownership transferred to a new corporation, the Wilhelm Gustloff Foundation, established in the personal interests of Marshal Goering.

The majority of Jewish firms were not "Aryanized", but simply ceased to exist. Of 3,750 Jewish retail establishments in Berlin on August 1, 1938, only 700 were transferred to "Aryan" hands; 3,050 disappeared. Adefa, a cooperative of German "Aryan" clothing manufacturers, was established in 1934 for the purpose of eliminating Jewish firms from the clothing industry. It organized a complete boycott of Jewish business and refused to sell or to buy from Jewish firms or to deal with Jewish agents, buyers or other middlemen. All merchandise sold by members of Adefa bore the trademark "Adefa, the sign of merchandise made by Aryan hands." Adefa, consisting of 500 member firms, was incorporated in 1938 in Adebe, a cooperative of apparel and leather material manufacturers which comprised 4,000 "Aryan" firms, covering almost all apparel industries; it successfully drove the few remaining Jewish firms out of business. Mr. Jung, a director of Adebe, reported on January 11, 1939, that more than 200 Jewish firms in the women's and men's apparel line had been forced to close by the end of 1938, and that only five Jewish firms of this type were left.

MOTION PICTURES.

Many Jews helped to establish the fame and reputation of the German motion picture industry. Ernst Lubitsch, Alexander Korda, Fritz Lang and Emil Pommer head the list of producers, but Jews were even more numerous among the directors, actors, producers and scenario-writers. The largest German movie organization, Ufa, was non-Jewish; only a few minor companies were owned by Jews, including the Mia May, Ellen Richter and Richard Oswald Film companies. Heinrich Brueckmann, a Jew, was a pioneer in talking pictures, founding the Tobis, which led in the field of talking pictures in Germany. Klangfilm GmbH was headed by Emil Meyer. Some of the best known movie theatres in Berlin and other cities were owned by Jews.

Participation of Jews in the film industry as producers, actors or production company owners came to an end with the creation of a film chamber on September 22, 1933, which was made one of the seven divisions of the Chamber of Culture. All Jewish officials and employees of movie corporations were dismissed from their posts; Jewish owners of production companies had to sell or close their business. The purchasers were generally the large German film concerns, such as Ufa or Tobis (already "Aryanized") which swallowed the Jewish enterprises at bargain prices. A number of the smaller companies were liquidated; some of the owners succeeded in transferring their business to other countries.

GENERAL PRESS.

In 1932 there were 4,703 newspapers in Germany with specific political orientations. Of these, 1,266 newspapers were conservative or right-wing, 603 were Catholic, 2,456 (mostly provincial or small-town newspapers) professed political neutrality, and only 378 represented the view of either the democratic parties or left-wing groups. Newspapers owned by Jews were generally of the democratic type.

The Leopold Ullstein publishing firm was founded by a Jew; the Rudolph Mosse and Frankfurter Zeitung concerns by converted Jews. Later the latter two also passed into the ownership of professing Jews. Rudolph Mosse published the Berliner Tageblatt and the Berliner Volkszeitung. Ullstein was the publisher of the Vossiche Zeitung, Berliner Morgenpost, BZ am Mittag and many important magazines, including the Berliner Illustrierte, Dame, and Uhu. A few provincial and smaller newspapers were owned by Jews, such as 8 Uhr Abendblatt and Neue Zeit (Charlottenburg). The papers published by the Ullstein and Mosse presses, and the Frankfurter Zeitung, were very influential; their editors, for more than half a century, advocated liberal and progressive ideas throughout Germany. The Frankfurter Zeitung was taken over by a concern owned by the I.G. Farben interests; it ceased publication in September, 1943.

Jews who were publishers of general newspapers were forced in 1933 and 1934 to "Aryanize" their firms, which were taken over either by Hitler's own publishing house, Franz Eher, Nachf. (Munich), the publisher of Mein Kampf and the Voelkischer Beobachter, or by dummy concerns organized and owned by the government or the Nazi party. Some compensation was paid in the beginning, but in practice "Aryanization" amounted to little more than confiscation. The Mosse publishing house in Berlin, for example, assessed at 14,000,000 marks by the revenue authorities, had to be sold for 5,000,000 marks.

JEWISH PRESS.

In 1934 there were 60 Jewish newspapers and periodicals in Germany, with a total monthly circulation of 1,180,000, distributed as follows: political publications, 755,000; community publications, 315,000; religious publications, 47,000; professional and fraternal publications, 28,000; cultural and scientific publications, 22,000; miscellaneous publications, 15,000.

The most important Jewish periodicals were: 1) C. V. Zeitung, weekly organ of the Centralverein, 40,000; 2) Jüdische Rundschau, Zionist bi-weekly, 37,200; 3) Hamburger Isrealitisches Familienblatt, unaffiliated, 36,500; 4) Der Schild, organ of the Jewish War Veterans, 20,000; 5) Der Israelit, organ of Orthodoxy, 4,015. Of the various Gemeindeblätter, monthly or semi-monthly periodicals circulated without charge by local communities, the largest was in Berlin, with a monthly circulation of 50,000.

Between 1933 and 1938, Jewish newspapers and periodicals were often temporarily suspended; at the end of 1938 they were permanently banned. After 1939, only one Jewish newspaper appeared in Germany, published by permission of the Propaganda Ministry, and strictly censored. It was a weekly, originally called Jüdisches Nachrichtenblatt, and edited by Leo Kreindler, former editor of the Berlin Jewish community paper. Being the only Jewish periodical in greater Germany, it experienced a certain boom at first, publishing articles, community announcements, pictures and advertisements in its 8 to 16 page issues.

In 1941, the Nachrichtenblatt became the victim of the new wave of terror. Significantly, its name was changed from Nachrichtenblatt to Mitteilungsblatt, indicating its transformation from a newspaper to an announcement sheet. In January, 1943, it consisted only of one small and poorly-printed page, which revealed graphically the pitiful state of German Jewry. There were no news items, but only official announcements about taxes, contributions and the many new restrictions, one or two articles on strictly religious matters, the time-table of Jewish religious services and a list of institutions and rationing offices. There were also a few birth, death and marriage announcements, a number of furnished room notices and advertisements of doctors and other professionals, but there was nothing to brighten the spirit of the doomed community.

EMPLOYMENT AND WAGES.

With the approach of Hitlerism, the employment situation in Germany deteriorated rapidly. In the last two months before Hitler, the number of unemployed increased from 5,109,000 in October, 1932, to 5,773,000 in December, 1932. In 1928, there were 2,969 unemployed registered with the Jewish employment agencies in Berlin; in 1929, -- 3,616; in 1930, -- 5,795; and in 1931 -- 6,013. Most of these people had previously been engaged in industry and commerce, which were restricted by expanding state capitalism and by the increase in the number of cartels and trusts. In addition, the aggravation of anti-Semitic influence in the entire economic life of the country made it more difficult for Jews to find employment. In 1933, there were 33,661 Jews unemployed.

The outbreak of the war had an unexpected effect on the Jewish workers left in Germany. Germany's economic dictator, Hermann Goering, rediscovered the value and possibility of Jewish manpower, as stated in an official decree of March 4, 1939. Large numbers of Jews were incorporated in the industrial army of Germany. Men between the ages of 16 and 55 and women under 45, drafted by a labor office especially created for this purpose, were sent to factories, workshops and public projects to perform the hardest menial tasks. At the end of 1940, 50,000, or nearly all the able-bodied Jews in the country, had been pressed into this service. Many young people trained in agriculture and handicraft to prepare them for emigration had to use their newly-acquired knowledge and experience within Germany. Despite the difficulties and humiliations attending the situation, it had its advantages for Jewish workers. For many, this was the first opportunity in years to work, to earn a petty livelihood and to fill out the endless hours of their empty days with activity. Such work meant also a temporary respite from the constant fear of deportation to Poland and death. A small number of Jews were permitted employment in Jewish institutions, households, etc.

Before 1933, Jewish workers in Germany received the same wages as other German workers. The official hourly wage rate, in German pfennig, for 17 groups of industry was as follows:

Yearly Average	For skilled male workers	For unskilled male workers
1928	95.9	75.2
1929	101.1	79.4
1930	102.8	80.7
December, 1931	94.2	74.1
", 1932	79.2	62.8
", 1933	78.3	62.1

At the depression level of 1932, immediately before Hitler's rise to power, the average hourly wage of a skilled male worker was 79.2 pfennig (31.68 cents); that of an unskilled worker 62.8 pfennig (25.12 cents). Hourly wage rates for female workers were between 18 and 21 cents. According to the official statistics for disability insurance, which was compulsory for all workers and for almost all salaried employees, the distribution for the various income brackets for 1932 was as follows:

Monthly income in marks	0-100	1-200	2-300	3-500	over 500
	31.57%	30.73%	18.30%	14.93%	4.47%

The average annual wage per employed person in 1932 was about 1,347 marks ($538.80).

The average number of working hours per week and per person in German industry rose from 41.6 in 1932 to 47.04 in 1939. Jewish workers had to meet the same requirements.

TRADE UNIONS.

There were never any Jewish labor unions in Germany. Labor unions (Gewerkschaften) had been well established in Germany since 1865, and were an important and influential force in politics and economy. There were three main types of unions: 1) The Socialistic free trade unions, 2) The Christian Trade Unions, 3) The Liberal (Hirsch-Duncker) trade unions.

The free trade unions, united in 1868 in the Allgemeine deutsche Gewerkschaftsbund (ADGB) had the largest number of members and the strongest political influence. All the unions within a city or district formed a flexible organization to further their respective interests, and all the locals together formed the national organization, which had 5,749,763 members in 1923. White-collar employees were organized in the AFA bund (Allgemeine freie Angestelltenbund), a national organization with 658,234 members in 1922. The public officials affiliated with AFA and ADGB were organized in the Allgemeine deutsche Beamtenbund (ADB). These three organizations were officially independent, but de facto very closely connected with the Social Democratic party.

The Hirsch-Duncker unions (Deutsche Gewerksvereine), liberal workers' organizations affiliated with the Liberal Democratic party, were founded by Max Hirsch, a Jew who was a wealthy industrialist and social reformer. They were opposed to the Marxian theory of class warfare and sought to maintain amicable relations between employers and employees; at the end of 1923 they had 230,261 members. The Liberal white-collar employees were organized in the Gewerkschaftsbund der Angestellten (GDA), with 300,000 members. These two organizations were closely affiliated with similar organizations of Liberal railwaymen and public officials.

Proximate politically to the parties of the right wing were the Christian Trade Unions, with 806,992 members in 1923. In 1919 they formed the Deutsche Gewerkschaftbund (DGB), together with Gedag, a Christian national employees' organization, which had 460,000 members in 1922. These two organizations were closely affiliated with an organization of Christian national public officials and civil service employees.

All the trade unions in Germany were dissolved early in 1933; their assets and their membership were transferred to the German Labor Front, which did not accept Jews as members. Before 1933, Jews could join the free and the Hirsch-Duncker trade unions, which were opposed to anti-Semitism and any kind of discrimination. Some 35,000 to 40,000 Jewish white-collar employees and the majority of the 15,000 to 20,000 Jewish workers were organized members of these unions. By the dissolution of the trade unions in 1933 Jewish members lost about 5,000,000 marks previously paid in membership dues.

FORCED LABOR.

While at the beginning of the war, Jewish workers in forced labor were treated fairly well, the situation became worse in 1941. From 1939 to 1940 they were paid about the same wages as non-Jewish workers, after 1941 they received wages far below the generally established scales; in addition they were denied pay for legal holidays, the paid vacation any German worker is entitled to, and other benefits granted to non-Jewish workers. General deductions for taxes and social insurance amounted to 25% for all workers, but Jews had to submit to deductions totalling to between 40 and 50% of their pay. Other benefits enjoyed by non-Jews such as the use of factory canteens and supplementary food rations for heavy labor were denied to Jews.

Reliable reports from Germany state that in 1941 the net weekly wages of Jewish men were between 18 and 20 marks ($7.20 to $8); of Jewish women between 16 and 18 marks ($6.40 to $7.20). Other reports cite figures some 10 to 12% higher. The Jews working in labor camps or in forestry or agricultural projects received nominal pay or none at all.

The Jews remaining within Germany itself in 1942-43 seem to have been concentrated in a few large cities, such as Berlin, Hamburg, Breslau and Leipzig, where they were kept at factory work. There were also some Jews to be found in a few agricultural and forestry projects, as for instance Landwerk Neuendorf, Garzau, Gross-Gaglow and in the Jüdisches Forst-Einsatzlager Kersdorf.

COOPERATIVES.

Cooperatives did business mainly with their own members. Socialistic cooperatives and labor banks in Germany had Jewish members and clients and practiced no discrimination. Cooperatives maintained by Christian labor unions accepted only Christian workers as members, but did business with Jewish firms. Discrimination against Jews was practiced by one of the largest employee organizations, the Deutsch nationale Handlungsgehilfenverband, with 260,527 members in 1933 comprised of nationalistic business employees. Other cooperatives, such as the cooperative of the association of commissioned German army officers, Deutscher Offiziersbund, had Jewish members and were officially not anti-Semitic.

The Iwria, a Jewish peoples' bank, established in Berlin in 1928, maintained branch offices in five German cities and catered to small businessmen and middle-class people; it went bankrupt in 1937 as the result of bad management. The second Jewish cooperative was the Kreditverein für Handel und Gewerbe, catering to artisans and craftsmen, with an office in Berlin. In 1938, it was still in operation, but doing business only on a small scale.

There were only a few Jewish cooperatives in Germany before 1933, whether they received government grants or not is indefinite. Under certain conditions, public funds made loans to encourage and to start small business enterprises. A number of Jewish firms received such loans; before Hitler there seems to have been no discrimination in this field.

LOAN BANKS.

In 1933 there were 35 Jewish loan institutions -- Kassas, -- possessing funds totalling 750,000 marks, largely established with funds given by the American Joint Reconstruction Foundation. At the beginning of 1938, there were 45 Kassas in operation, 35 operating with credits of the Foundation. On September 30, 1938, the total capital owned by these <u>Kassas</u> was 1,200,000 marks, approximately one-half of which was derived from a credit fund advanced by the Joint Reconstruction Foundation. On December 2, 1938, the German commissioner for credits ordered the Jewish central welfare office to liquidate the <u>Kassas</u> on January 1, 1939. Only a small total loss from outstanding loans was shown. The funds of the <u>Kassas</u> were transferred to the <u>Reichsvereinigung</u>.

TAXES AND FINES.

There was no special department in the Nazi legislature dealing with Jews. Jews were largely under the control of the Minister of the Interior, who issued the laws dealing with the Jews in general or with the supervision of Jewish organizations. Laws involving Jews and dealing with particular problems such as health, justice or finances were issued by the respective ministers, usually in cooperation with the Minister of the Interior and the Gestapo.

The German penal code enumerates many fines for various crimes, either in addition to a prison sentence or as a substitute for a prison sentence. Under Nazi "justice", higher fines were often imposed on Jews than on others for the same petty delict. There are many special fines for "Jewish crimes", such as not showing the Jewish badge or identification card, travelling on a bus, tram or train without special permission, and entering a banned area without previously obtaining a police permit. The most important fine was the "atonement" fine of one billion marks imposed on Jewry after the assassination of Ernst vom Rath in Paris in November, 1938. All German and stateless Jews had to pay 20% of the value of their property as their share of the fine.

Jews not only had to pay special Jewish taxes and exceedingly high general taxes, they were also subjected to the highest tax rates by being placed in the highest brackets and not being granted ordinary exemptions and reductions. This was effected by the Adaptation Act of October 16, 1934, which provided that taxation statutes must be construed according to the National Socialistic "<u>Weltanschauung</u>." As a result of this and subsequent laws, Jews were denied exemptions for married persons, credits for dependents and other considerations granted to "Aryans."

All Jewish charities were outlawed and lost their statutory exemptions from taxation, on the ground that support of persons of a foreign race did not serve the welfare of the German people. Tax exemptions were denied to trust funds for Jewish crippled and blind children, to Jewish scholarship endowments, orphan asylums and nurseries and even to a foundation for the preservation of Jewish graves. On February 17, 1939, an amendment to the income tax law bracketed all Jews as unmarried persons. Artists, teachers, agents or writers are exempted from the special tax on turnover when the income is less than 6,000 marks a year, Jews did not have the benefit of this exemption after January 1, 1939. The flight and defense taxes, while not exclusively "Jewish" taxes, were predominantly applied to Jews. The flight tax, enacted in 1931 under Chancellor Bruening, imposed a tax of 25% on all property assessed in excess of 200,000 marks, of each emigrant of German nationality. Originally directed against the flight of big business and industry from crisis-stricken Germany, this tax became, after 1933, a sort of property levy directed practically exclusively against Jews. While from 1931 to the middle of 1933 this tax netted only 2,876,000 marks, the first four years of the Nazi regime brought 170,970,000 marks into the Reich treasury through the tax, or an average annual tax income of 42,000,000 marks. During the last three months of 1938 alone the tax amounted to 92,000,000 marks, more than double the income of previous years. The "defense tax", enacted July 20, 1937, was imposed on all persons of draft age not drafted for active service; Jews were excluded from active service in Germany as "unworthy", and the tax was therefore applied especially to Jewish males between the age of 18 and 45. Beginning with February 1, 1941, the Jewish population had to pay a surtax of 15% as a so-called "social equalization tax." Enforcement of collections was exceedingly severe, failure of payment led to attachment proceedings and in cases of intentional noncompliance to fines and imprisonment. Special considerations allowed some taxpayers in assessing property, as for instance consideration of real estate devaluation in certain areas and decrease of rentals, were not extended to property owned by Jews.

Taxes levied by the Reichsvereinigung for the expanded needs of the Jewish community continued. In 1941, the Reichsvereinigung tax amounted to 30% of the national income tax paid by the Jews.

All Jews possessing more than 5,000 marks ($2,000) were under blocked "security", in the Hitler regime; their funds were blocked as security against the flight tax. Control was rigorously exercised by a special department of the foreign exchange office; the owner could draw only a fixed monthly amount for living expenses. This amount was fixed in 1941 at about 200 marks for a single person and 500-600 marks for families. The owner of a "blocked" bank account could not receive cash payments in person. Taxes, legal and medical fees, and expenditures in preparation for emigration could be paid out of the blocked account without special permission.

Jews leaving the country could take only 10 marks (4 dollars) out of the country. Theoretically special permission to transfer more money was obtainable from the foreign exchange control, but this permission was hard to get even during the first five years of the Hitler regime and was given only in rare and exceptional cases after 1938. Until the outbreak of the war, emigrating Jews who had paid the flight tax and other taxes could transfer their remaining funds to a blocked account (Sperrmark) and were entitled to sell this blocked account abroad. But the exchange value of these blocked mark funds had so deteriorated that the Jewish emigrant could not receive more than 4 or 5% of the original value of his funds. After November 26, 1941, all Jews leaving Germany or living abroad were considered expatriated by the German government; their funds remaining in Germany were subject to confiscation.

EDUCATION.

Before 1933, there were no legal and official restrictions against Jews in the field of education in Germany. Only a limited number of Jewish schools existed. German law under the Republic of Weimar looked with disfavor on separate schools established on lines of creed, and favored the community school (Gemeinschaftschule), which accepted pupils of all religious beliefs. In general, only Orthodox Jews and some Zionist parents sent their children to Jewish schools. The result was a steady decline in the number of Jewish schools and their pupils.

In 1921 there were in Prussia 153 Jewish public schools with 3,029 pupils (26.1% of all Jewish school children). In 1926 the number of schools had declined to 96, the number of pupils to 2,828 (20%). There were 26 Jewish public schools in Bavaria in 1926, and only 21 in 1933, with a required curriculum of at least eight school years. There were also private Jewish primary, grammar and high schools, of which the most important were: the High School of the Adath Yisroel, Berlin; the large municipal grammar school in Cologne; the Talmud Torah School in Hamburg; the Jacobson School in Wolfenbüttel; the Philanthropin in Frankfort.

Under the law, the greater part of the financial burden of the public schools -- non-Jewish and Jewish alike -- was carried by the respective municipalities, which received financial assistance from the state when they were unable to raise necessary funds. The private Jewish schools organized and controlled by the Jewish communities were financed by the communities, which devoted a substantial portion of their annual budgets to educational purposes; the Berlin community in 1926 spent about 18% of its outlay, or 1 1/2 million marks, for schools and other educational purposes. But the Jewish communities and their national associations received assistance in the maintenance of their school work from public funds as well; before 1933 the Jewish communities in Prussia received 400,000 marks annually from the State of Prussia as a subvention for Jewish private schools. The 95 public Jewish schools in Prussia were entirely supported by the state and municipalities. The Jewish communities in Bavaria received 60,000 marks in 1932, and two Jewish public schools were entirely financed by the state. The state continued to finance Jewish public schools, even under Hitler, until 1938, and also subventioned Jewish private schools; the community in Berlin received a subvention of 10,000 marks for their schools from the Prussian state in 1937. After 1933, the Reichsvereinigung built up a Jewish school system of its own and took over most of the Jewish private and even some of the public schools; in 1938 this organization appropriated 350,000 marks, -- or 7% of its annual budget -- for the maintenance of Jewish schools. After 1939, the Reichsvereinigung was in sole charge of Jewish education. Consequently, the appropriations must have been higher, but exact figures are lacking. In the year 1933-1934 there were 44,500 Jewish students in the elementary schools, colleges and secondary schools of Germany, and 18,500 Jewish students in Jewish schools in Germany.

Between 1933 and the end of 1938, Jewish children could still attend public schools, but were limited to 1.5% of all new admissions in secondary schools. Many were forced by various administrative measures and petty chicaneries to yield to anti-Semitic pressure and to transfer to a Jewish school. The number of Jewish schools increased to 140 in 1936, with 20,000 pupils; in 1938 there were about 170 Jewish schools in Germany. On November 15, 1938, the Minister of Education issued a decree excluding Jewish children from German public schools because "German teachers can no longer be expected to give instruction to Jewish pupils; German students find it unbearable to share classrooms with Jews."

At the outbreak of war in 1939, there were still 15,000 Jewish children under the age of 15 in Germany. Under the supervision of the school department of the Reichsvereinigung, there were in existence 125 primary schools, one grammar school and six public schools. There were also a number of professional schools for training in arts and crafts, a school for chemistry, and nine training farms and schools for gardeners and farmers, where 5,000 young people were prepared for emigration.

After 1933, the Reichsvereinigung issued instructions regarding a curriculum for Jewish schools, the goal of which was to give the children a good Jewish background, to train them professionally, especially in manual occupations and agriculture, and to prepare them for a new life outside Germany -- in Palestine or elsewhere. Although the program was only a framework, it covered the minimum requirements and gave the school boards the possibility to develop their own curricula in accordance with their character as Orthodox, Liberal, or Zionist schools. The curriculum was extended from 8 to 9 and 10 years, to provide more time and opportunity for the study of Hebrew and foreign languages, and for practice in arts, crafts, agriculture and other useful vocations.

There had been a number of isolated cases of discrimination in German schools before 1933, provoked by anti-Semitic teachers or pupils. In general, however, there was no discrimination in the curriculum or daily routine of German schools. The school administration or the Minister of Education took necessary steps in eliminating any excesses, by reinstating the victim and punishing the guilty, whenever cases were brought to official attention.

All courses taught in German schools, from mathematics to art and from physics to history, were after 1933 permeated by the National Socialist philosophy. "Racial" instruction had to be given in all classes; the children were taught to love everything German and to despise everything foreign, especially the Jews, who were pictured in the German schools as "the eternal menace of mankind." Streicher's pornographic sheet, the Stürmer, which reported almost nothing but alleged sexual outrages, bedroom gossip and scandal, was read in the schools to children between 6 and 14. The teaching of religion and Christian traditions was often taken out of the hands of the clergy and entrusted to apostles of Nordic paganism.

In the teaching of history, special emphasis was laid on the "injustice" done to Germany by the terms of the treaty of Versailles; another favorite topic was the suffering of German minorities abroad and the need of protecting Germans all over the world. The propaganda of the Verein für das Deutschtum in Ausland (Association for Germanism abroad) was particularly effective in schools. The problem of Germany's rearmament and of the return of the territory lost after the First World War were also frequently discussed.

According to the official statistics for 1933, there were 1,323 Jews serving as elementary and high school teachers in Germany, or .053% of all the teachers. This included the 306 teachers in Jewish public and about 300 in Jewish private schools. To qualify for appointment in an elementary public school, a teacher was required to graduate from a special state seminary for teachers and to pass a state examination. High school teachers had to be graduates of a college or university and to have passed a special examination. There were also a number of teachers who had graduate degrees, including Ph. D's.

Theoretically, teachers were elected and appointed according to merit and their success in the examinations, but in practice there was considerable discrimination against Jewish teachers, who found it exceedingly hard to obtain employment, even before 1933. A Catholic investigation in 1930 showed that to effect the equality and parity granted by the Constitution, 300 additional Jewish teachers would have to be employed in high schools in Prussia. The proportion for young teachers in preparatory service was even worse, demanding the appointment of an additional 391 Jewish male and 205 Jewish female teachers before parity could be achieved.

The selection of teachers in Germany after 1933 depended not on scholastic records or scientific attainments, but on National Socialistic activities. The National Socialist teacher had to be "educated" by the Hitler Youth movement, or by membership in the stormtroops or elite guards. He must also have been a graduate from one of the so-called political academies, National Socialist seminaries for teachers.

In 1937 there were 700 Jewish teachers employed in 165 Jewish schools (public and private). In 1938 there were still 165 Jewish teachers employed in 68 Jewish public schools and about the same number in 72 Jewish private schools.

On January 1, 1940, there were under the supervision and administration of the Reichsvereinigung 142 primary, secondary and higher Jewish schools in Germany, employing approximately 300 to 400 teachers. For 1942-43 not even an estimate is possible, but it is known that many of the remaining Jewish schools had to be closed in 1942, because many teachers and all boys over the age of 12 had been forced into labor service.

HEALTH SERVICES AND HOSPITALS.

In pre-Hitler Germany, and under the Nazi government until 1938, a separate Jewish health service was of no more than supplementary importance, because the Jewish sick were cared for by the public health service in the general hospitals. There were twelve Jewish hospitals, and a number of convalescent homes. Some of these institutions had been established by endowment, and derived their main support from similar sources, but the majority were administered and financed by the local Jewish communities. Before 1933, and even for a time under Hitler, they received financial support also from public funds; many of the Jewish sick were entitled to financial assistance from public welfare funds and the various social insurance agencies. These funds paid the costs of Jewish patients in Jewish institutions; in addition, there were always a number of non-Jewish patients, assisted by public funds, in the Jewish hospitals.

In 1937, an average of 220 beds were occupied per day in the Berlin Jewish Hospital, which employed 34 doctors, 12 resident physicians, 54 licensed nurses, 3 licensed children's nurses, 4 technical assistants, 2 midwives and 2 social workers. A second Jewish hospital in Berlin, containing 56 beds, was used largely by Orthodox patients.

In 1937, the Jewish Hospital polyclinic treated 9,511 persons, for the first time, and 39,523 patients on return visits. In the second polyclinic of the Jewish community in Berlin, 7,512 patients were treated for the first time, and 43,750 patients on return visits. That same year the community paid the expenses for 454 adults sent to health resorts and convalescent homes throughout Germany and for 60 persons treated in family care. Some 500 Jewish patients treated in public hospitals and institutions in 1937 received additional assistance and special benefits from the community, which also maintained a special hospital for ailing old people and incurables, with 167 beds.

In 1928 there were 12 Jewish hospitals in Germany, 47 homes for the aged, 7 institutions for the blind, deaf-mute and insane, 2 tuberculosis sanatoria, 29 convalescent homes for children, 24 convalescent homes for adults. The 12 Jewish hospitals were located in the following cities: Berlin (2), containing approximately 270 and 56 beds, respectively; Breslau, 250 beds; Hamburg, 150 beds; Frankfort, 120 beds; Mainz, 43 beds; Fürth, 45 beds; Gailingen, 26 beds; Cologne, 180 beds; Leipzig, 85 beds; Würzburg, 81 beds; Hanover, 70 beds.

On January 1, 1939, there were 14 Jewish hospitals in Germany, located in the following cities: Berlin (2), 456 beds; Breslau, 180 beds; Frankfort (2), 250 beds; Fürth, 45 beds; Gailingen, 26 beds; Hamburg, 250 beds; Hanover, 70 beds; Cologne, 140 beds; Leipzig, 91 beds; Mannheim, 37 beds; Munich, 39 beds; Wurzburg, 15 beds.

There were also the following Jewish homes: 67 homes for the aged, 3565 beds; 6 homes for the ailing aged, 303 beds; 2 convalescent homes for adults, 135 beds; 1 convalescent home for children, 35 beds; 19 children's homes, 1,076 beds; 8 various other homes, 442 beds.

In 1939, the situation became particularly difficult in the various fields of health protection. General hospitals were closed to Jews and the few Jewish hospitals in existence were not sufficient. There was no place to which tuberculosis patients could be sent for cure because the Jewish sanatorium in Soden was closed. Some were treated in special departments of the Jewish hospitals, which could in no way replace the therapy provided in a modern tuberculosis sanatorium.

For the 2,500 to 3,000 Jewish insane needing institutional care, only one institution remained, with 190 beds. All Jewish convalescent homes with the exception of one had to be closed. It became almost impossible for Jews to go to health resorts and spas, so that the larger part of the Jewish population had no possibility for treatment.

On January 1, 1940, there were in Germany 90 homes for the aged; 23 more than in the preceding year. 600 new accommodations for old people had to be created in 1939. There were 25 children's homes and 9 other homes for blind, deaf mutes and mental defectives. The existing Jewish hospitals were quite modern and exemplified the highest standards in modern medicine, but they were insufficient for the increasing demands.

Reliable information concerning the situation in 1942-43 is not available, but there were reports that the Jewish hospitals in Leipzig and Breslau were requisitioned for the army. The Jewish hospital in Berlin was in operation in October, 1942. Jews were excluded from the protection and benefits of the general health service and left entirely to the care of the few remaining Jewish physicians, hospitals and other institutions.

Drugs, serums, and other medical supplies were being strictly rationed in Germany in 1942-43, for the population in general and for Jews in particular. In 1941, the Jewish hospital in Berlin had to keep sedatives in reserve for only the most serious cases. After 1938, many provincial pharmacists refused to sell to Jews.

The law of April 4, 1874, made vaccination against smallpox obligatory in Germany. Each person had to be vaccinated during the first year of his life and all school children at the age of 12. From an announcement in the official Jewish publication in Berlin of October, 1942, it is evident that Jewish communities still received vaccination supplies.

Immunization against other diseases was voluntary, except at the outbreak of certain epidemic diseases. Schools were immunized when a case of measles was reported among students. These laws applied equally to Jews and non-Jews, and the situation seemed to be unchanged under Nazi rule. Persons suffering from sexual diseases, Jews and non-Jews alike, were forced to receive treatment under a special law.

HYGIENE.

Because of the high prevailing standard of hygiene and preventive medicine, there were no epidemics among Jews in Germany before the outbreak of the war. Restriction and crowding within a limited area, and insufficient living space, especially in some quarters of Berlin and in deportation centers like Lublin, Litzmannstadt (Lodz), and Theresienstadt (Terezin), abetted by insufficient nourishment, may have provoked epidemics, which spread rapidly under such conditions. But no information is available about such occurrences, although there are reports that prisoners in overcrowded concentration camps were attacked simultaneously by epidemic diseases like dysentery and typhus fever.

There were in 1942-43 no ghettos in Germany. It may be assumed that in the interest of public hygiene, the municipal sewage services served Jewish households. There was no prevalence of flies, lice or other vermin in Germany. But in overcrowded concentration camps and prisons, lice and bedbugs were prevalent. Under the Nazis, Jews in Germany had their own exterminators, it seems that they were not permitted to employ non-Jewish exterminators.

Housing conditions in Germany were always fairly adequate; if they did not include all the conveniences of the American home, they were healthful and satisfactory from the hygienic point of view. After the outbreak of the war, Jews were in many instances being expelled from their own apartments and herded with other Jewish families. Public baths were barred to Jews but there were a few Jewish bath houses. Advertisements in the October, 1942, issues of the Jüdische Nachrichtenblatt offered furnished rooms with all modern conveniences in many parts of Berlin and in a few other German cities.

BIRTH RATE.

After 1870 the number of Jewish births steadily decreased, from an annual average of 11,349 in Prussia to 6,833 between 1906 and 1910. Berlin, the largest Jewish community, containing about one-third of all the Jews in Germany, showed a decrease typical and characteristic for German Jewry.

	Births		Deaths		Increase or Decrease	
	Jews	Non-Jews	Jews	Non-Jews	Jews	Non-Jews
1922-23	10.1	10.9	11.9	13.5	-1.8	-2.6
1933	5.3	12.	15.8	11.4	-10.5	0.6

In Prussia, where 72% of all the Jews in Germany lived in 1933, the number of births in Jewish marriages were as follows: 1925, 4,680; 1926, 4,135; 1927, 3,729; 1928, 3,675; 1929, 3,283; 1930, 3,004; 1931, 2,712; 1932, 2,024. The number of Jewish children born in mixed marriages and out of wedlock was estimated at about 2,500 for the period from 1925 to 1932.

The Jewish birth rate reached new lows under the Nazi government. In 1928, there were 10.5 Jewish children per 1,000 births in Berlin; in 1933 there were only 6.4 per 1,000 and in 1935 only 5.2. In 1930, 3,004 children were born of Jewish marriages in Prussia; in 1935, only 1,553. The decrease was even greater in certain districts or localities; in Frankfurt, for instance, there were only 67 Jewish children born in 1934 as against 257 in 1929 and 464 in 1932.

The Nazis declared publicly that a decrease in the Jewish birthrate was in the German interest. In spite of the severe prosecution of abortion cases in Germany, Jewish doctors who performed abortions on Jewish women were not prosecuted because their acts were "in accordance with Germany's population policy."

MORTALITY.

Estimates show that the most frequent causes of death among Jews in Germany included: heart disease, arteriosclerosis, diabetes, kidney diseases, cancer, mental diseases, infectious diseases and suicide. Cases of death from external causes, especially suicide, were at the bottom of the list in 1924-1926 in Berlin, but in 1932-1934 they increased considerably and rose to fourth place. Before the rise of Hitler to power, there was an annual average of 250 Jewish suicides in Germany; this figure was somewhat higher than among Protestants and 3 to 4 times that of Catholics. The increased persecutions during the first six months after the outbreak of the war resulted in new waves of Jewish suicides; during this time 460 Jews committed suicide in Berlin alone. In 1934, 1.21% professing Jews died of violence -- suicide, executions, accidents, etc., while the proportion of Jews in the general population was 0.77%.

After 1911, the mortality of the German Jews exceeded the birth rate as follows:

		Excess of deaths over births
Prussia	1911-1924	18,252
	1925-1932	18,407
All Germany	1933-1939	38,400

At the outbreak of the war and the beginning of an unrestrained policy of extermination there was a tremendous increase in mortality among Jews. From September, 1939, to March, 1940, there were 1,844 Jewish deaths recorded in Berlin, showing an increase of about 26% compared with the 1933 total (1933: 15.8 per thousand; 1940: 40.9 per thousand). In 1936 there were 2,483 Jewish deaths in Berlin as against 494 Jewish births, or a ratio of 5 to 1; for the first six months of 1939 we find 1,844 Jewish deaths in Berlin as against only six births, or more than 300 times as many deaths as births.

LIQUIDATION AND STERILIZATION.

Reliable reports state that about 100,000 persons were "liquidated" in Germany during 1939-1940, on the basis of being incurable mental cases. More detailed information is lacking but in a number of cases relatives of mentally diseased Jews were informed that their kin had been liquidated as incurables. Certain types of habitual sex criminals were castrated in Germany. Nazi sources report that from 1,500 to 2,000 individuals were castrated between January 1, 1934 and the outbreak of the war. Jews were included, but the exact figure could not be ascertained.

The law of May, 1933, provided that any person suffering from hereditary disease may be sterilized by means of a surgical operation. Sterilization orders were issued by 206 sterilization courts, each court consisting of a judge and two medical men. Comprehensive figures not available, but in 1934, 56,344 persons were sterilized. Wallace R. Deuel estimated that prior to the outbreak of the Second World War, approximately 375,000 persons were sterilized in Germany. (People under Hitler, New York 1942, page 221). It seems safe to assume that there were a number of Jews among these unfortunates, but no precise figures are available.

PHYSICIANS AND OTHER MEDICAL PRACTITIONERS.

In 1933 there were 5,567 Jewish doctors in Germany, or 10.88% of all physicians practicing in the Reich (51,067). If "non-Aryan" physicians are added, the number would be 6,480, or approximately 13%. There were 1,041 Jewish dentists (8.6%), 653 Jewish dental technicians (2.1%), 660 pharmacists (3.61%), and 98 veterinarians (1.55%). In 1925, seventeen communities had Jewish homes for nurses and 234 resident nurses, but about 1,000 had been trained in the homes.

The elimination of Jewish physicians and other medical professionals in Germany was effected step by step between 1933 and 1938. The "decree regarding admission of physicians to practice for compulsory health insurance, of April 22, 1933" terminated health insurance practice for Jewish doctors, with certain exceptions. Some physicians thus lost 75% of their patients. Exemptions were made for "front fighters", for fathers or sons of men who lost their lives in the First World War and for the elderly doctors who had been in practice on or before August 1, 1914. The number of Jewish physicians able to comply with these rules was surprisingly high. Of 4,800 "non-Aryan" doctors in 1935, 3,600 (75%)

had to be admitted to compulsory insurance practice. Of these, 2,800 were Jews.

Until the end of 1937, these Jewish doctors still admitted to practice were relatively undisturbed, although subject to many discriminations. Partnership between Jewish and non-Jewish doctors was forbidden; non-Jewish doctors were not permitted to assign non-Jewish patients to Jewish specialists, all Jewish doctors were ousted from positions in public hospitals, clinics and universities. But on January 1, 1938, the Kassenärztliche Vereinigung (Central physicians' organization of the compulsory insurances) suddenly dismissed all Jewish physicians, even the war veterans. For Jewish welfare patients a small number of Jewish doctors were admitted to welfare practice.

The 4th decree of the Reichbürgergesetz of July 25th, 1938, cancelled the licenses of all Jewish physicians then still admitted to practice in Germany, as of September 30, 1938. Nazi sources reported that in July, 1938, there were still 1,561 "Non-Aryan" physicians practicing in Berlin alone, or 22.4% of all Berlin physicians. A Jewish doctor could be admitted to practice for Jewish patients only as a so-called sick-tender (Krankenbehandler). There were 416 such sick-tenders in Berlin, about 60 in Breslau and Silesia, about 40 in Frankfort and its environs, 20 in Hamburg and Munich, 10 in Nurnberg and Leipzig, out of a total of 709 permitted to practise. In some provinces, there were no Jewish doctors at all. For the population of some 320,000 Jews (1938), dispersed over an area of 200,000 square miles, the ratio in October, 1938, was only one sick-tender for every 450 Jews. In Bavaria, which is twice as large as Holland, there was only one Jewish surgeon, one gynecologist, one skin specialist, and one eye specialist. There was not a single specialist in X-ray, nervous diseases, neurology or pediatrics.

It seems that military necessity ultimately exempted a number of Jewish doctors and dentists from deportation. In the winter of 1941-42 there were still 12 Jewish dentists (Zahnbehandler) practicing in Hamburg. In October, 1942, advertisements of Jewish doctors and dentists residing in various cities appeared in the Jüdisches Nachrichtenblatt of Berlin. To humiliate these doctors and to make them more conspicuous, they were forced to stamp their name plates and their prescription forms with a Star of David and with the statement: "admitted only to practice for Jews."

While in Berlin most of the "sick-tenders" were permitted to work in their own offices, the Jewish doctors outside of Berlin could work only in Jewish community clinics or ambulatories. In Hamburg, there were in 1940 only two such ambulatories, which meant that the Jewish population from every part of the ckty had to go to one or the other of these centers.

The elimination of dentists and dental technicians followed the same pattern as the elimination of the physicians; their licenses and diplomas were cancelled as of January 31, 1939, by a decree of January 17, 1939. A few Jewish masseurs were admitted to practice, but only for Jews. After December 21, 1938, Jewish women were not permitted to act as midwives except for Jews. Another law "regulating the profession of nursing" of September 28, 1939, permitted only persons with a certificate of the health department to practice nursing, and this certificate was unobtainable for Jews. Jewish nurses were permitted to practice nursing only for Jews. The licenses of all Jewish veterinarians were cancelled by a decree of January 17, 1939, effective the same day.

SOCIAL SECURITY.

Under Bismarck, Germany was one of the first countries to undertake the gigantic task of solving the social problems evoked by the industrial revolution. Bismarck did not revive or modernize already existing laws for the poor, but adopted the principle of insurance, distributing the risks and exigencies of industrial life among large numbers of workers exposed to similar hazards. For the non-insured population, public assistance and social care was widely regulated. Under the Weimar Republic, the existent insurance laws were modernized and adapted to new conditions.

In 1927, an unemployment insurnace plan was created along Bismarckian principles, giving all salaried employees the protection of compulsory unemployment insurance. The uninsured sections of the population obtained the right to public assistance in cases of need (Decree of December 4, 1924). Communities, towns and villages had to bear the financial and administrative burden of the public welfare organization, but they received subventions and contributions from the state and federal governments. Public assistance and social insurance were granted without distinction as to religion or nativity. Foreigners could belong to social insurance institutions and also receive public assistance. There was no legal or official discrimination against Jews in this field.

The federal law of 1927 made insurance against unemployment obligatory for all wage-earners earning up to 300 marks a month and for all salaried workers earning up to 700 marks a month. The rate of contribution was originally 3%, but rose to $6\frac{1}{4}$% of the basic wage in October, 1930. Contributions were shared equally by employers and employees, the employer deducting the worker's share from his wages. There were regular and emergency benefits.

The worker who had exhausted his claim for regular benefits was eligible for emergency benefits when in actual need. The conditions governing these benefits, their duration and amount, were subject to occasional regulations by the Minister of Labor. Administration of the unemployment insurance system was entrusted to a public corporation known as the Federal Institute of Employment Exchanges and Unemployment Insurance.

Until 1933, the insurance funds were administered by representatives of the insured and the employers. On entering an insurable employment, the worker automatically became a member of the insurance fund, but he could select another private insurance out of a number of voluntary insurance institutions. The insured could choose his doctor from the selected panel of insurance doctors, to which any duly licensed physician could apply for admission, Jews and non-Jews. The insurance also included funeral benefits.

Old age and disability insurance was available to the same group of wage-earners and salaried employees as health insurance and was part of this system. Men and women received an old-age pension at the age of 65, if they had paid to an insurance fund for 60 months in the case of salaried employees, or for 200 weeks if they were wage-earners. Wage-earners receive 240 marks per year, plus an annuity equal to 20% of all contributions paid after January 1, 1924; salaried employees received 480 marks, plus an annuity of 15%.

Disability insurance was combined with old-age insurance. Insured people received a disability allownace after their rights to benefits under sickness insurance were exhausted. Permanent disability pensions were granted to workers when their earning ability was reduced by at least 2/3; salaried employees when their earning capacity was reduced by only 50%.

Extra allowances for children were paid to all civil employees of the government, and to many workers and employees in private industry, on the basis of collective agreements between the employers' associations and the unions.

PUBLIC WELFARE.

Public welfare granted the amount necessary for a modest living, including lodging, food and clothing, depending on personal circumstances and particular conditions. It also included medical care and maternity benefits. Special provisions took care of the needs of deaf mutes, cripples and the blind. War victims and persons who had lost their fortunes during the inflation received special consideration and extra grants.

JEWISH WELFARE WORK.

In a country with such extensive social rights, only limited need for specifically Jewish welfare work existed; yet there was a widespread system of Jewish philanthropic organizations. This was due to the fact that the Jews presented problems which could not always be handled by public welfare. Jewish employment agencies were necessary to contend with anti-Semitic prejudices in the field of employment, and to provide jobs for Orthodox Jews who would not work on the Sabbath. In the care of the sick and indigent, the Orthodox group faced the problem of dietary laws. German Jewry was also confronted with the great task of helping the Jews from Eastern Europe.

In general, it may be said that before the advent of Hitler, the Jews in Germany could rely on public assistance in case of need; for their particular problems, however, they could turn to their own philanthropies. But the scope and the amount of public relief and assistance to Jews became more and more limited under the Nazi regime, until at the end of 1938, Jews were compoetely eliminated.

Social service in Germany - Jewish and non-Jewish alike - distinguished between "open," "closed" and "semi-closed" welfare work. "Open" care maintained the client in his own home, and consisted mainly of family assistance, financial help, day nurseries, clubroom facilities and child care. Sanatoria and children's homes constituted the "semi-closed" welfare work; the "closed" welfare work was performed in institutions for the insane, blind and deaf-mutes, in reformatories, hospitals and homes for the aged.

In 1927 a Central Welfare Office of German Jewry was founded, to co-ordinate the work of the various Jewish welfare groups. This office controlled seven state offices, twelve provincial bureaux and 89 other offices in as many important German cities; it supported or maintained 35 welfare institutions in Berlin and about 65 hospitals and similar institutions throughout the country. The organization cooperated with other public and general welfare bodies and received financial support from the federal government and other public funds.

A number of the older institutions owned substantial property and capital; one provincial orphanage in Paderborn (Westphalia), which cared for about sixty children, owned real estate, its buildings and other equipment, and had 800,000 marks in cash and securities (1938). Although Jews were still entitled to relief and assistance from public funds until the end of 1938, more and more segments of the Jewish population were reduced to pauperism and became partly or entirely dependent on Jewish welfare. As early as the winter of 1936-37, 82,067 persons had to receive relief from the Jewish Winter Relief Fund.

The radical and enormous changes for the worse in the general situation of the Jews in Germany at the end of 1938, created a new and almost unbearable burden for Jewish welfare work. From serving as a supplementary aid, it became a sole and unique source of public relief when the Jews were completely excluded from any public assistance. For 1938 the total amount needed for public relief and assistance to Jews in Germany was estimated at about 36,000,000 marks. More than 90% of the need had once been supplied by public funds. Progressive impoverishment of the Jewish population (24.6% needed winter relief in 1938 - 1939) made it absolutely impossible to raise the needed sum of money. The amount given to each recipient in the Jewish Winter Relief of 1938-39 had to be cut 20% compared with the amount given the preceding year. While 20% of the whole Jewish population had to be supported by public funds in the middle of 1938, the number amounted to 26% in 1939. At the end of the year, 52,000 persons received their entire support from Jewish funds.

All Jewish welfare organizations, foundations and philanthropic societies were dissolved in 1939, and their property transferred to the Reichsvereinigung, which had to carry the entire burden for needy Jews. The annual report of the Reichsvereinigung for 1939 stated: "the amount of assistance is based on local allowances made by the public welfare funds, taking into consideration any support received by other members of the family. Rent relief was given according to the regulations of public assistance. Extraordinary grants to alleviate special emergencies were only given in exceptional cases. In the larger communities, there are community kitchens. A number of Jewish communities undertake the distribution of clothing in neediest cases. Many of the Jewish poor had to be helped with clothing when emigrating." At the end of 1939 the Reichsvereinigung had the following facilities for institutional care at its disposal: 90 homes for the aged, 26 children's homes, one home for the tuberculous, one home for the blind, two homes for the deaf, one convalescent home, one children's hospital, one home for juvenile delinquents and one special home. There were also 14 Jewish hospitals and 16 Jewish residential homes for boys and girls. The larger communities had soup kitchens, for instance there were 17 soup kitchens in Berlin in 1942. Jewish welfare offices functioned in all of the 20 Bezirkstellen (district offices) of the Reichsvereinigung. There were also special departments for war victims who were still privileged to some extent, having reduced rates in railways and other means of commutation.

CHILD CARE.

The Weimar Republic was particularly interested in the organization and welfare of youth. The Youth Welfare Law of July 9, 1922, created a special agency, the Jugendamt (Youth office) to supervise the health, education and protection of the young. This office, in most instances associated with the public welfare authorities, cared for all religious denominations, combining the functions of the surrogate, probation officer, and children's welfare agencies. It also acted in close cooperation with the juvenile courts created by the law of February 27, 1923, one of whose sponsors was a Jewish juvenile court judge named Koehne. The public welfare office cooperated with the Jewish institutions and welfare offices of the Jewish communities; there were many Jewish children under public care and in public institutions, and there was no official or legal discrimination in this field.

The foundation, in 1924, of the National Committee of Jewish Youth Societies (Reichsausschuss der jüdischen Jugend-Verbände) implemented Jewish child welfare work in Germany, and gave it a new impetus. The committee took special interest in social service, and worked in harmony with the public welfare offices and the Federation of German Jewish Social Agencies (Zentral Wohlfahrtstelle der deutschen Juden). Twenty of the larger Jewish communities set up youth welfare boards, others instituted children's homes, playgrounds, day nurseries, kindergartens and homes for juvenile delinquents.

The National Committee of Jewish Youth Societies, which embraced all Jewish groups and factions, helped create Jewish solidarity in this branch of endeavor, and trained leaders whose guidance was particularly valuable after 1933, when the plight of German-Jewry demanded aggressive and schooled Jewish leadership. The Berlin community was especially cooperative, placing a special building at the disposal of youth organizations, and setting aside means to help young peoples' clubs and societies. In 1926, the Berlin Jewish community had a budget of 1,550,000 marks for youth and general welfare.

In 1935, there were 67 Jewish day nurseries and kindergartens; 26 Jewish children's homes and 55 educational homes and institutions in Germany. Berlin alone had, in 1937, 40 homes for youth, 3 athletic stadiums, 7 playgrounds, 10 gymnasiums, 2 orphanages and other institutions. Until 1939, there was also a school for Jewish sport and athletic teachers in Stuttgart.

The last reliable data and statistics for child welfare work in Germany are for the year 1939, when there were 25 children's homes in various parts of Germany, but the overstrained budget of the Reichsvereinigung could allot only 31,195 marks for youth activities and sports.

The situation was much worse in 1942-43 than in 1939. A most optimistic estimate can grant the existence of only a skeleton of the once-flourishing organization of Jewish child welfare, providing for a minimum of housing, feeding and education and medical care for children under 16. Older ones were drafted for forced labor.

WELFARE WORKERS.

According to the census of June 16, 1933, there were 104,512 registered workers in the field of public welfare in Germany, but only 91,066 of these gave welfare work as their sole profession and source of income. Of the latter figure, 61,165 were women; social service in Germany was a predominantly female occupation. Out of the professional group, 13,345 were state employees (Beamte) and 58,644 were employed either by public or private welfare.

According to the census of June 16, 1933, 1,307 Jews were registered as being employed in public welfare, or 1.25% of all persons so engaged. A number of Jewish social workers were employed in public and general welfare; others in Jewish welfare work. The plight of the Jews of Germany after 1933 created a great demand for trained social workers, and the Reichsvereinigung organized effective special courses to train social workers. A number of the older, as well as some newly trained social workers, were still on the job in 1941; how many were left in 1942-43 is impossible to ascertain or even to estimate.

MUTUAL AID GROUPS.

The most important organizations for mutual self-help in pre-Hitler Germany were the German student groups, which had founded loan banks for students. Special offices for economic aid and relief were in operation in all universities. For a number of years, Jewish students were very active in this field, and received loans and economic assistance like all other students. There was no official discrimination, but the anti-Semitic attitude of many students who administered the funds often resulted in practical discrimination in the distribution of benefits.

There were a number of Jewish relief groups. The Jewish students of Leipzig organized a committee in 1932 for mutual financial and economic aid. Various Jewish parents' groups had committees to help the Jewish education of children from poorer families. Many larger communities had societies for Hauspflege (home nursing) to help those Jewish sick who could not afford to engage a regular nurse. Most of the nurses working in these committees were volunteers; in Berlin there were, in 1937, about 200 such volunteer nurses. In 1936 they had cared for 431 cases.

The most prominent relief group was the Hilfsverein der deutschen Juden, founded in 1904 for aid to Eastern European Jews, particularly pogrom victims and immigrants in transit through Germany. The Hilfsverein maintained offices in the more important frontier stations to the East and in emigration ports like Hamburg and Bremen. In the Slavonic lands the Hilfsverein established elementary schools, supported Talmudic academies, provided medical care for children and sheltered war and pogrom orphans. After 1938, the Hilfsverein became the chief agency for the emigration of Jews from Germany to all countries except Palestine.

POLICE FORCE : BEFORE HITLER.

Legally there was no discrimination against Jews in the German police forces of the pre-Hitler republic. But only a few Jews managed to enter the police of the various German states; the federal Government had no police force of its own.

Prussia, the largest and most important German state, had 80,000 men in its police force. In the lower bracket of 77,000 police officers and detectives there were only two Jews. Among the 2,400 lieutenants, captains and higher ranking police officers of the uniformed police, there was one Jewish lieutenant; of a total of 120 police sergeants, there was one Jew. Among higher police officers, police commissioners and administrators, there was one Jew who served as police commissioner in a city of 157,000 residents; he was a lawyer with previous experience in colonial administration. Dr. Bernhardt Weiss was for a number of years vice-president of the Berlin police, an office held by Jews even under the King of Prussia. Six Jews were supervisors or staff officers in various departments of the public safety administration. Among the 37 ranking officers of the police general staff of the Ministry of the Interior in Prussia, there was only one Jew, who served in the capacity of general legal counsellor. There were therefore about ten Jews among the 2,600 commissioned police officers and higher executives. There were about half a dozen Jews in the police forces of the other German states, whose forces totalled more than 40,000 police officials.

This was tantamount to a practical exclusion of Jews from the field of public safety, partly due to hesitation among Jews in entering an occupation opened to them only in 1919. But the decisive obstacle was the mental attitude of the persons in charge of the selection and appointment of police officials, reared in the traditions of the Imperial army, which did not favor representation of the state by a Jew. (Part of the information for the above data is taken from the forthcoming book by Robert M. W. Kempner, The German Police System.)

POLICE FORCE : UNDER HITLER.

The Gestapo (Geheime Staats Polizei: Secret State Police) - was the special Nazi police handling Jewish matters. No other instrument of the Nazi government was as effective in destroying German Jewry as the Gestapo, the very name of which drove Jews to suicide. The Gestapo was established by a Prussian law of April 26, 1933, as a Prussian government agency to take charge of the duties of the political police and to destroy the enemies of the state in accordance with the program and the views of the Nazi party and its leader. This praetorian guard of National Socialism, after June 17, 1936, under the command of Heinrich Himmler, chief of the SS (Schutz Staffel, elite guard) and the German police, developed this apex of power within the state, the greatest known in the modern history of mankind, to an instrument of efficient brutality.

The Jewish policy of the Gestapo may be divided into three periods. From 1933 to 1935 the aims were complete elimination of the Jews from German life. During the second period, from 1936 to 1939, the goal was to drive the Jews out of Germany by forcing them to emigrate. After 1939, not emigration, but extermination of the Jews became the object of Gestapo policy.

After 1933, all Jewish men, women, and children were under permanent Gestapo surveillance, even abroad; Jews who left Germany for a short business trip or vacation were often arrested after their return, for the "crime" of having bought an anti-Nazi newspaper in a foreign country or of having spoken to a so-called "enemy" of the Reich. Many, asked to appear for a hearing before the Gestapo, were never seen again; some were taken to concentration camps after these hearings. The Jews directly or indirectly murdered by the Gestapo are beyond numbering.

The Gestapo main offices and headquarters were in Berlin, where they were known as the famous Prinz Albrechtstrasse; district offices (Staatspolizeistellen) were located in the administrative center of each larger district. The Berlin headquarters housed the central administration of the concentration camps, the Inspecteur der Konzentrationlager, and included a special department for Jewish affairs, which handled matters of general policy towards the Jews, such as emigration, and which supervised and directed the central Jewish organizations, such as the Reichsvereinigung. Every district headquarters also contained one or two experts on Jewish questions, to supervise the local Jewish population and to deal with the Jewish organizations and communities within the district. These district officers controlled all Jewish meetings, lectures and other assemblies, and took charge of all investigations of specific Jewish "crimes", such as race pollution or the violation of one of the numerous anti-Jewish laws.

In addition to the Gestapo, there were three branches of the police which dealt especially with Jews: the aliens' division, the passport police, and the special police force of the foreign exchange control.

The aliens' division was in charge of all foreigners in Germany; it was of particular importance to the great number of stateless Jews, who were entirely at its mercy, because the only valid and internationally recognized identification paper -- the stateless passport -- was issued by this office to everyone but the Russian refugees, who could obtain the Nansen passport of the League of Nations.

The passport police was in charge of the issuance of passports to German nationals, including Jews. The personnel of both these two police forces represented the ability and thorough training which characterized the ordinary German police official and detective; their morale was fair and cases of graft and corruption were not numerous in spite of the very small salary they received. There were incidents indicating an anti-Semitic bias on the part of the passport and aliens' police even before Hitler, but no general, official or systematic policy of discrimination. Even under the Hitler government, especially during the first years of the regime, members of the regular police force (Schutzpolizei) were known to have protected Jews against excesses by stormtroopers and even to have tried to help them against the Gestapo. In 1937 general instructions were issued to the regular police to treat Jews with extreme harshness. At the end of July, 1943, a law was promulgated excluding Jews from all court jurisdiction, and committing them to police control.

Under Hitler, the morale of the police force in general and of the special branches in particular deteriorated more and more. The Nazis infiltrated all police services with their own trusted men; many regular police officers were dismissed; the remainder, prompted by a sense of insecurity, became more susceptible to corruption and bribery, which had been rare before, but which now became a common feature of the Nazi police system. The attitude of the officers towards Jews grew increasingly intolerant and harsh, partly in self-interest, partly because they had to obey orders and to follow the general trend of the times. All this held true also for the special police of the foreign exchange control, which included a number of trained experts in economics and in the field of foreign currency.

The rank and file of the Gestapo was selected from police officers with strong Nazi sympathies and a satisfactory party background; the higher brackets were chosen from a group of younger judges and public prosecutors who were party members of long and good standing. A typical example of this group was Commissar Eichmann, successively in charge of the Jewish departments of the Gestapo main office in Berlin and Vienna. This young man, then about 30 years old, spoke, read and wrote Hebrew and Yiddish fluently, and could read an Aramaic text. His amazing knowledge of Jewish matters and the comprehensive nature of the Gestapo files on Jewish affairs was demonstrated on many occasions. At the end of 1937, the Reichsvereinigung was ordered to submit to the Gestapo a report on American Jewish organizations, their aims, structure and leading personalities. The report was carefully prepared with the assistance of the newest issue of the American Jewish Yearbook, which had appeared in the last quarter of 1937. A few days after the report was handed in Eichmann pointed out to representatives of the Reichsvereinigung that changes had occurred in the leadership of some American Jewish organizations after the publication of the Yearbook. People of Eichmann's type approached the Jewish problem with the scientific calm of the vivisector; the killing of a Jew was to them neither murder nor even an act of brutality, it was the solution of a problem, the attainment of a political objective.

The aliens' and passport police officers in Germany wore no uniforms, but often carried pistols. Where they had to make an arrest, they were assisted by regular uniformed police officers, who wore blue uniforms, a black shako, and carried side-arms and pistols, sometimes also police sticks. The regular blue-uniformed police (Schutzpolizei) were not permitted to have heavy arms under the disarmament clauses of the Treaty of Versailles, but they had guns, machine guns and armored cars, also a few planes. Under Hitler, the police were equipped with heavy arms, tanks, cannons and additional airplanes. Commissioned police officers wore the insignia of their rank, similar to those of the regular army officers. Foreign exchange police were not uniformed, but were often assisted by the olive-green uniformed armed custom guards. Gestapo officials usually acted in mufti but carried pistols. They were assisted by the regular police or by the SS, which were also in charge of the Gestapo headquarters in Berlin, of the Gestapo prisons and of all the concentration camps. The SS elite guards wore black uniforms and a black cap or steel helmet, often bearing the death head insignia. The SS was excellently armed with automatic guns, pistols, machine guns and side arms; later they received cannons, tanks, airplanes and the best equipment of the regular army. Reliable reports in 1942-43 stated that the SS was a fully trained and equipped combat army of possibly 250,000 men, consisting of picked youths.

FIRE DEPARTMENT.

There were no restrictions regarding the services of Jews in fire departments in Germany before 1933, but figures showing the extent of Jewish participation in this branch of service are not available; the number was in all probability very small. A number of Jews were members of auxiliary voluntary fire companies in smaller towns and rural districts, but they were excluded in 1933. Since there were no ghettos in Germany in 1942-43, the question of fire departments in segregated quarters did not arise.

BADGES AND OTHER IDENTIFICATIONS.

After January 1, 1939, all Jews of German nationality and stateless Jews living in Germany were required to show identification cards, containing left profile photographs taken in police fashion. For new-born babies an application for an identification card had to be filed within three months. Every Jew more than 15 years of age was obliged to carry this domestic passport on himself in order to be able to establish his identity at any time. The identification card number was to be added to any letter or petition addressed by the Jew to a court or to a government official; where a Jew was represented by a third person, the representative had to give the number of his client's identification card and emphasize that he was representing a Jew. These identification cards were prerequisites for ration cards; the Jewish housewife, in addition, had to show a special yellow "household card" issued only to Jews.

By police decree of September 1, 1941, all Jews over six years of age were forbidden to show themselves in public without the Jewish Star. The law stated: "the Jewish Star consists of a six-pointed star outlined in black on yellow cloth the size of the palm of a hand, with a superscription in black, reading Jew. It must be worn visibly and firmly sewed to the left breast of the clothing."

Only Jews living in a mixed marriage were exempt from the Badge Law. For disregarding this law, fine or imprisonment was threatened, and even concentration camp. The same law deprived the Jews of the right to wear orders, decorations or other insignia which were given chiefly to veterans of the First World War, a degradation which had previously been inflicted only after conviction for a particularly dishonorable crime under the German Penal Code. Enforcement of these laws was very strict, even Jews who were working in their gardens in shirt sleeves or opening their apartment doors in answer to the bell had to wear the star.

CURFEW AND OTHER REGULATIONS.

Under curfew regulations in force in 1942-43, Jews could not appear on the street after 8:00 o'clock in the evening or before 7 in the morning. At any hour of the night Jews might expect one of the frequent Gestapo or regular police visits to control the compliance with curfew regulations.

In pre-Hitler Germany a license (Waffenschein) was necessary for the purchase of or to carry a gun outside the home (Weapon law of April 12, 1928). No discrimination was practiced against Jews; many of them possessed the license. A new weapon law of March 18, 1938, excluded Jews from the right to manufacture or to repair firearms. By a decree of November 11, 1938, Jews were forbidden to acquire, possess or to carry firearms, ammunitions and other weapons, such as sabres and swords. All such weapons and ammunition had to be surrendered immediately to the local police, to avoid confiscation and severe punishment.

PASSPORT AND TRAVEL REGULATIONS.

Until 1938, Jewish subjects of the German state were technically entitled to the same passports as other citizens, but after 1936 it had become more and more difficult for them to obtain a passport at all. Jews received passports only for emigration purposes or for business trips which were deemed essential to German trade and economy. By the decree of October 5, 1938, all passports held by Jews of German nationality were declared invalid and had to be returned to the police. Jewish passports were issued only for emigration and characterized by the letter "J". They were "one way" passports, entitling the holder to leave the country but not to return. German consulates in foreign countries in many instances refused to prolong or to renew these passports. Stateless Jews living in Germany who were refused visas to enter foreign countries were in many instances given German passports by the police, to facilitate their leaving the country. Until the outbreak of war in 1939, there were no restrictions on railroad travel by Jews within Germany, but in 1942-43, Jews living in Germany needed a permit to travel on railroads. This permit was issued only for emigration purposes, and for certain emergencies, such as medical treatment, attendance at funerals or going to work. There were special compartments marked "For Jews Only" in many German trains. Jews were not permitted to use sleeping cars, dining cars, public waiting rooms, or station restaurants.

Under the Nazi regime, Jews were not permitted to own or drive buses or trucks, and needed a travel permit to ride on buses as passengers, even within the limits of their own residential communities. Jews were also generally forbidden to use buses for excursions, recreation, or to travel on extra buses running on national holidays and other special occasions. Cross-country buses run by the government (Landposten) were largely barred to Jews.

Until 1938, there were no restrictions regarding the ownership or use of motor cars by Jews in Germany. Then automobile license plates issued to Jews in Berlin were given numbers higher than 350,000, so that every traffic policeman could readily identify a Jewish car owner and impose a fine or arrest the driver for the slightest traffic violation. A police decree of November 4, 1938, forbade all Jewish subjects of the German state to own or drive automobiles and motorcycles; their driving licenses were confiscated.

Whether restrictions were imposed on the ownership of horsecarriages could not be ascertained, but it may be assumed that Jews were not permitted to use such vehicles. Jews needed a special permit to take a taxi; such permits were granted only in cases of exceptional emergency.

General restrictions applied to travel by Jews under the Nazi regime were enforced also on waterways. Jews could not use excursion boats and could travel on other ships only when there was no possibility of reaching a particular destination; in any case they needed a travel permit. There seemed to be no law forbidding the use of rowboats, canoes or sailing boats, but the existence of so many other restrictions on traveling in general and on visits to restaurants and public beaches, rendered the use of pleasure boats by Jews impossible or highly improbable.

Until 1938, no air travel restrictions were imposed. After the outbreak of the war in 1939, all civilian air travel became severely restricted. Jews were given permits for air transportation solely for emigration purposes, and only when such accommodations were not needed by other passengers.

A law of November 28, 1938, dealing with "the appearance of Jews in public" authorized police authorities to impose "upon Jews, both subjects of the German state and stateless Jews, restrictions as to place and time, that they may not enter certain districts or may not appear in public at certain times." On December 5, 1938 a police order for Berlin was issued, banning Jews from certain areas in that capital, especially the so-called government district around Wilhelmstrasse and Unter Den Linden; it also excluded them from all places of entertainment, theatres, movies, cabarets, public concerts and lecture-houses, parks, museums, fairs, athletic fields, and all private and public bathing places.

By a police decree of September 1, 1941, Jews were forbidden to leave their residential precinct without a written permit from the local police authority. Jews of German citizenship had to notify local police headquarters of each change of residence even within their residential precincts. Jews were permitted to leave Reich territory only with permission of the police. For a violation of these regulations, imprisonment and other severe punishment by the Gestapo were threatened.

Jews living within restricted areas first had to have a special police permit for entering and leaving the forbidden zone; on July 1, 1939, they had to leave the area entirely. Jews who had to appear at government offices or elsewhere within the restricted area could obtain a permit, valid for 12 hours, from the local police precinct. On national holidays and other special occasions Jews were confined to their homes all day. The laws were not too strictly enforced in the beginning, but subsequently Jews were made so conspicuous by their yellow badge and the Star of David that violation of these restrictions seemed almost impossible or at least improbable.

A report of August 30, 1943, stated that Heinrich Himmler had forbidden Jews to use any means of transportation, under any conditions.

COMMUNICATIONS.

At the end of 1938, all Jews had to turn their radios over to the police. In 1942-43, the only Jews still allowed to have telephones were physicians (practising only for Jews), Jewish lawyers, and the offices of Jewish institutions, including the Reichsvereinigung, hospitals and welfare offices. Special permission was needed for the sending of a telegram or cable.

RATIONING.

During the first months of the war, the official German news agency Deutsches Nachrichten Büro (DNB) stated that "the Jews in Germany receive food cards and rations equal to those of the entire population." This was certainly not true in 1942-43. Jewish food cards were marked with the letter "J", or the word "Jew". Jews were permitted to make purchases during one or two specified hours a day, and only a few stores were open to them.

Out of eleven basic rationed items -- bread, milk, cheese, fat, meat, eggs, cereals, coffee, potatoes, sugar and jam, Jews received only four -- bread, potatoes, sugar and jam. And even of these they received only a fraction of what other consumers could have. Jews were denied all essential protective and vitamin foods, including poultry, fish, game, milk, fresh and dried vegetables, flour, white bread, rice, fruits, sweets, coffee and tea and their substitutes.

Jews were barred from restaurants, public kitchens and cafés. With so little protein and only a fraction of the essential vitamins, they faced slow and systematic starvation. Jews were also excluded from extraordinary special rations (weddings, births, etc. and for particularly arduous work.) Jewish mothers and children received no milk, and were not allowed to purchase unrationed foods.

After December, 1940, the Jewish population was denied clothing ration cards; even burial shrouds were withheld. In January, 1942, they were compelled to surrender their winter coats, furs, muffs, boots, woolen articles and blankets for shipment to the Russian front. During the first months of the war, Jews received coal and fuel rations, but in 1942-43 these were evidently refused them, according to a decree by the Mayor of Berlin on March 30, 1943. For a long time tobacco was not rationed in Germany, but supplies were low and most of the stores selling tobacco carried signs on their windows "No Sale to Jews."

PENAL INSTITUTIONS AND CONCENTRATION CAMPS.

Neither before nor under Hitler were there separate penal institutions or concentration camps for Jews; Jews were kept in the general institutions. Before Hitler, however, Jewish convicts were usually concentrated in a few prisons, to give them the benefit of Jewish religious services. There were 5 different types of imprisonment: <u>Zuchthaus</u>, severe punishment with hard labor; state prison; jail (municipal); <u>custodia honesta</u> (fortress imprisonment for political prisoners); military arrest. The punishment of criminals was under the jurisdiction of the different states, the federal government controlling only military prisons. Control over prisons was exercised by the ministers of justice of the states; in Prussia it was exercised by a special office in each judicial district (<u>Strafvollzugsamt</u>).

Institutions ranged from small local jails, accommodating a few dozen prisoners, to large penitentiaries with from 2,000 to 3,000 inmates. Men and women were separated, and there were special prisons in Wittlich and Eisenach for juvenile delinquents under the age of 25. The tendency before Hitler was to limit the number of prisoners in any institution; 500 was considered a maximum. Under Hitler, all prisons became terribly overcrowded; institutions which were designed to house 500 to 700 men had to accommodate 2,000 to 3,000, and local jails with a normal capacity of 30 had 160 prisoners. Those prisons which contained the largest number of Jewish inmates in 1938 were the Zuchthaus in Brandenburg-Goerden; Zuchthaus in Luckau; Zuchthaus in Waldheim, Saxony; Zuchthaus in Straubing, Bavaria; Zuchthaus in Wartenburg, East Prussia; penitentiary in Berlin - Tegel; penitentiary in Berlin - Ploetzensee; penitentiary in Berlin - Lehrterstrasse; penitentiary in Berlin-Spandau; penitentiary in Berlin-Moabit; the large police prison in Berlin - Alexander Platz. Women were sent to Jauer, Lubeck, Waldheim and Berlin - Barnimstrasse. The concentration-camps were: Sachsenhausen (Oranienburg), near Berlin; Dachau, near Munich;

Buchenwald, near Weimar; Papenburg und Esterwege, near Osnabrueck; Lichtenburg, near Torgau; Columbia Haus-Gestapoprison, Berlin. The concentration camps in Brandenburg and Sonnenburg, notorious during the early years of the Hitler regime, were later dissolved. The concentration camp for women was first located in Moringen (near the Harz mountains), later it was transferred to Lichtenburg near Torgau. The concentration camps were under the supervision of the Gestapo <u>Generalinspecteur der Konzentrationslager</u>.

It is almost impossible to arrive at the number of prisoners in the Third Reich in 1942-43. Estimates range as high as 2 million. Before Hitler, nearly 300,000 persons were annually sentenced to prison in Germany for ordinary crimes; there can be no doubt that this figure increased considerably after 1933. The number of prisoners in concentration camps fluctuated constantly. At the end of June, 1938, there were about 8,000 people in the large Buchenwald concentration camp, but mass arrests in June and toward the end of 1938 brought the number to about 20,000. Altogether, at the end of 1938, there were approximately 25,000 Jewish prisoners in various German concentration camps. Several estimates placed the number of political prisoners in custody in Germany during the years between 1936 and 1942 as 500,000 to 600,000 -- a figure which is probably exaggerated. But one may be justified in estimating that the total number of political as well as ordinary prisoners in German prisons and concentration-camps was between 500,000 and 600,000.

The basic idea behind Nazi penology was that every spark of individual initiative must be extinguished in the convict. The prison regime of the Third Reich was particularly harsh on political prisoners, special care being taken to separate them from ordinary criminals to prevent contact between the regular prison population and "subversive political elements." Solitary confinement on bread and water was applied for the slightest violation of one of the numerous petty regulations. In ordinary prisons, Jewish inmates were in general not separated from other prisoners, but in concentration camps they had to live and work in separate Jewish blocks and companies and were usually assigned the hardest menial tasks.

In the hastily constructed concentration camps, under an administration which was not at all concerned with the health and welfare of the prisoners, even primitive sanitary facilities were lacking. Water was scarce and lavatory equipment insufficient. SS physicians, entrusted with the care of the camps, were the scum of the medical profession; at least as many prisoners died as the result of the lack of proper hygiene, medical attention and undernourishment as from brutal treatment and general exhaustion. Typhus, dysentery, and other epidemics were frequent in concentration camps. The physical violence and brutality, which were part of the daily routine and practice in every concentration camp, are so well known that further detailed description seems unnecessary.

Prisoners of the Gestapo and prisoners in concentration camps were divided into several classes, in accordance with their putative crimes; Class A consisted of those charged with high treason, Class B, attacks against the Führer or other National Socialist leaders, Class C, industrial espionage, Class D, cases not under special suspicion, and Class E, caught smuggling money across the border. The treatment in these classes differed considerably. Prisoners in concentration camps had a number sewed on both coat and trousers and had to wear on their breast a triangle indicating their classification. Ordinary criminals wore green triangles and stripes; homosexuals, pink; religiously unaffiliated (<u>Bibelforscher</u>), violet;

workers accused of sabotage, black; general political cases, red. Jews wore two superimposed yellow triangles forming the Star of David and had yellow stripes on their uniforms. The treatment of female prisoners and of juvenile delinquents was much more lenient, even in concentration camps.

JEWISH LEADERS; IN GERMANY AND IN EXILE.

It is impossible to list the Jewish leaders living in Germany in 1942-43. In October, 1942, the executive board of the Reichsvereinigung consisted of the following six persons: Dr. Paul Epstein, Rabbi Leo Baeck, Dr. Moritz Henschel, Leo Kreindler, Dr. Arthur Lilienthal and Dr. Philip Kozower. A Jewish Telegraphic Agency report from Stockholm on February 28, 1943 stated that seven leading members of the Reichsvereinigung and the Hechalutz leader, Alfred Selbiger, were executed in November, 1942, and that all Jewish leaders in the Reich were considered hostages, and held under arrest. Earlier, the deportation to Terezin of Rabbi Baeck, chief rabbi of Germany and president of the Reichsvereinigung, of Heinrich Stahl, former president of the Berlin community (who died in Terezin), and of Cora Berliner and Hannah Karminsky, leaders in the women's movement, had been reported.

Among the leaders who left Germany, and some of whom have since died, were:

Industrialists: Hermann Aron, Nora Radio Works; The Berglas brothers, textile manufacturers; Arnold Bernstein, Bernstein Shipping Co. & Palestine Shipping; Dr. Herman Fleischer, pulp factories; Moritz and Eugene Garbaty, Garbaty Cigarettes; Dr. Gruenfeld, linen; Dr. Georg Haberland; builder and architect; Dr. Hahn, Hahn tube factories; Siegfried Hirsch, Hirsch copper; Georg Jacobowitz, builder and architect; Dr. Georg Lewandowsky, Vineta Chocolates; Guido Neustadt, chemical factories; Dr. Orenstein, Orenstein & Koppel-Railway material; Dr. von der Porten, aluminum manufacturer; Herman Schocken, textile; Seemann, Nurnberg screws and machine factory.

Labor Leaders: S. Aufhauser, Kurt Rosenfeld, Toni Sender, Friedrich Stampfer, Hedwig Wachenfeld.

Journalists: Raoul Auernheimer, Georg Bernhard, Margarete Edelheim, Julius Elbau, Manfred George, Arno Herzberg, Alfred Hirschberg, Hans Jacob, Richard Katz, Rudolf Kayser, Alfred Kerr, Egon Erwin Kisch, C.Z. Kloetzel, Anton Kuh, Karl Misch, Rolf Nuernberg, Heinz Pol, Kurt Riess, Franz and Hermann Ullstein, Berthold Viertel, Ernst Wallenberg, Robert Weltsch, Theodor Wolff.

Bankers: Hans Arnhold, Arnhold Brothers, Dresden-Berlin; Siegfried Aufhauser, Aufhauser & Co., Munich; Willi Dreyfuss, I. Dreyfuss & Co., Frankfurt-Berlin; Jacob Goldschmidt, Darmstaedter & National bank; Wilhelm Kleeman, Dresdner Bank, Berlin; H. Leubsdorff, A. Levy, Cologne; Prof. Stein, Strauss, Karlsruhe; Max M. Warburg and Fritz Warburg, M. M. Warburg & Co., Hamburg; Sigmund Wasserman, A. E. Wassermann & Co., Bamberg-Berlin.

Rabbis: Dr. Galliner, Berlin; Dr. Gottschalk, Berlin; Dr. Gruenewald, Manheim; Dr. Hugo Hahn, Essen; Dr. Kober, Koeln; Dr. Max Nussbaum, Berlin; Dr. Joachim Prinz, Berlin; Dr. Rosenthal, Berlin; Dr. Manfred Swarsensky, Berlin.

Physicians: Alfred Adler, Ernst Bibram, Prof. Ferdinand Blumenthal, Gustav Bucky, Prof. Leopold Casper, Rudolf Cohn, Prof. Hugo Falkenheim, Prof. Heinrich Finkelstein, Ludwig Halberstaedter, Rudolf Hoeber, Prof. Alfred Kanotorowitz, Prof. Ludwig F. Meyer, Max Meyerhof, Prof. Rudolf Nissen, Prof. Rosenow, Prof. Paul Rosenstein, Prof. Erich Seeligmann, Prof. Bernh. Zondek, Prof. Herman Zondek.

Jewish Political Leaders: a) Leading executives of the Reichsvereinigung: Adler-Rudel, Dr. Fritz Aron, Dr. Friedrich Brodnitz, Dr. Rud. Callmann, Dr. H. Lubinski, Dr. Franz Meyer, Dr. Werner Rosenberg.

Zionist Leaders: b) Kurt Blumenfeld, Dr. Kreuzberger, Dr. Landauer, Felix Rosenblueth, Michael Traub, Robert Weltsch.

C. V. Leaders: c) Herman Berlak, Kurt Braum, Julius Hirsch, Alfred Hirschberg, Eva Jungmann, Julius Loewenstein, Hans Reichmann, Moritz Rosenthal, Bruno Weil, Alfred Wiener.

POLITICAL GROUPS IN EXILE.

Only two German political parties after 1933 set up any kind of organization outside Germany, the Communists and the Social Democrats. Among the German Communists active in the Soviet Union there were a few religiously unaffiliated members of Jewish origin; in the Social Democratic movement there were a number of Jews, including Friedrich Stampfer, Kurt Rosenfeld, Toni Sender and Siegfried Marck.

JEWISH GROUPS IN EXILE.

Jewish immigrants from Germany have established a number of different organizations and institutions in the various countries of refuge. As a rule, fraternal benefit organizations play a major role among refugee groups, but sport-clubs, political associations and groups of the Landsmannschaften type, have also appeared. Many organizations have their own newspaper or publish regular circulars. In New York City, there are two newspapers published by Jewish immigrants, the Aufbau and The Jewish Way (Der Weg). Immigrant newspapers were also established in London, Johannesburg, Buenos Aires, Sao Paolo, Shanghai and in other cities.

The following list is composed chiefly of organizations established in the United States, most of them in New York:

1. New Worlds Club (formerly known as the German-Jewish Club), founded in 1924. This is a fraternal organization and social club with many branches, including women's and youth divisions, professional groups, etc. The club has about 2,000 members and publishes the weekly Aufbau, with a circulation of about 20,000. Organizations similar to the New World Club exist in Chicago (New Home Club), Newark (Jewish Unity Club), Philadelphia (Central Club), Pittsburgh (Friendship Club), and in Baltimore, Los Angeles and San Francisco.

2. The Self-Help of Emigrés from Central Europe, Inc. is a non-sectarian

organization composed of German-speaking volunteers who interpret American ways to newcomers and offer them employment, guidance and necessary support. Self-Help has a branch-office in Chicago.

3. American Federation of Jews from Central-Europe, Inc. unites a number of smaller groups and organizations for representation and protection of their interests.

4. Landsmannschaften, organized along lines of regional or community origin, have groups representing, among others, Berlin, Baden and Württenberg.

5. Professional organizations, such as, for instance, The American Association of European Lawyers, which is composed of lawyers of almost all European countries.

6. Fraternal organizations, including The New Yorker K.C., a club of former university students, similar to the American Greek letter associations. The K.C. has local groups in Great Britain, Argentina, Brazil, Chile, South Africa, Bolivia, Uruguay, Australia, East Africa and Palestine.

7. The Theodor Herzl Society, comprised of Zionists from Germany.

8. Veterans of the First World War, organized in the Jewish Immigrant War Veterans.

9. Sport clubs, including the Makabbi A.C. and the Hakoah A.A.C.

10. Social circles, like the Prospect Unity Club in New York.

11. Between 15 and 20 Jewish congregations in New York were founded by Jews from Germany. These congregations have their own rabbis. The majority are Orthodox, but the largest one, Congregation Habonim, is a Liberal Synagogue maintaining a school for adult education, a summer camp for children and the usual sisterhoods and brotherhoods. Congregations have been established also in Philadelphia, Cincinnati and other cities.

The above list, while not exhaustive, gives an idea of the type of organizations set up by Jewish immigrants from Germany in almost all the countries where German Jews are to be found, even in modest numbers.

RECONSTRUCTION AGENCIES.

The foreign relief organizations which were the bulwark of comprehensive and vital relief and reconstruction work in Germany and which are most familiar with the situation are: the American Jewish Joint Distribution Committee of New York; the Jewish Colonization Association, formerly of Paris; the Hicem (Hias-Ica Emigration Association), Paris and New York; the Council for German Jewry, London, and the Jewish Agency for Palestine.

For vocational retraining after the war, the experience of the ORT Society for the furtherance of crafts and agriculture among the Jews and the OSE, Society for the Protection of Health among the Jews, might be of help. Both these organizations had their headquarters in Germany for a number of years; an ORT training school, accommodating 200 students, was in operation in Berlin as late as 1940. The economic experience gained by the Refugee Economic Corporation of New York in resettling Jews from Germany in various parts of the world might also be useful.

THE JEWS OF GREECE

THE JEWS OF GREECE

- INDEX -

Age 4	Groups, Communal 3
Agriculture 5	Health Service 7
Anti-Semitism 10	Hospitals 7
After the Invasion 11	Housing 8
Before the Invasion 11	Hygiene 8
History of 9	Identification 12
Army 1	Industry 5
"Aryanization" 6	Insurance 5
Banking 5	Languages 3
Labor Banks 6	Leaders
Bar, The 5	In Exile 12
Birth Rate 7	In Greece 12
Characteristics, Cultural and	Marriage 2
Social 3	Mortality 7
Church 9	Motion Pictures 7
Citizenship 4	Natural Resources 5
Commerce 6	Occupational Structure 4
Communities, Religious 1	People, Attitude of 10
After the Invasion 2	Physicians 7
Assets 2	Population 1
Functionaries 2	Press 7
Concentration Camps 12	Anti-Semitic and Quisling . . . 7
Cooperatives 6	
Curfew 12	Rationing 12
Divorce 2	Reconstruction, Agencies 13
Economic Stratification 4	
Education 8	Taxation 12
Employment 6	Travel, Regulations 12
Fascism 10	
Funerals 3	Unions 6
Government	
Attitude of 10	Wages 6
Jews in Cabinet 4	
Jews in Civil Service 4	Welfare
Jews in Judiciary 4	Child 9
Jews in Parliament 4	Public 8

- - - - - -

THE JEWS OF GREECE

Population.

The Jewish population of Greece, according to the official census of 1928, was 72,791, out of a total population of 6,204,684 (1.17%). In 1939, however, the Jews numbered about 85,000, the difference being due to natural increase and to immigration from countries to the East. According to the 1928 census, the Jews resided mainly in the following cities: Salonica -- 55,290; Cavalla -- 2,135; Jannina -- 1,970; Corfu -- 1,819; Attique -- 1,781; Athens -- 1,578; Comotini -- 1,148; Volo -- 959; Larissa -- 767; Xanthe -- 718; Drama -- 672; Castoria -- 655; Demotika -- 651. The Jewish population of Salonica formed three-quarters of the total Jewish population of Greece, and 22% of the total population of Salonica.

It is estimated that with the exception of 5,000 Jews of Turkish and Italian nationality who lived in Salonica, and 10,000 Greek Jews living in southern Greece, all other Jews had by 1943 been either deported to Poland, placed in concentration camps or drafted for forced labor camps in Germany. The remaining Jews were located in the following cities: Athens, Piraeus, Volo, Larissa, Patras, Chios, Arta, Trikkala, Attique, Corfu, Chalcis, Jannina, Xanthe and Castoria. Very few Jews from Greece escaped immediately before or after the German invasion. Those few went to Turkey, Palestine and Egypt.

Jews in the Greek Armies.

The exact number of Jews in the Greek army prior to the invasion by Germany in 1941 is not available. However, it was officially stated that 7,000 Jews from Salonica enlisted in the Salonica division and fought in Albania in 1941, together with more than 3,000 Jews from other parts of Greece. When the Greek army was reorganized in Egypt in November, 1941, 700 Greek Jews residing in Palestine enlisted. Some 9,000 Jews are estimated to be fighting in the Greek guerrilla armies. They have a newspaper, **Zion**, published in Ladino (Judeo-Spanish).

Jewish Religious Communities.

The Jews of Greece were all of Sephardic affiliation, having come originally from Spain and Portugal during the 15th and 16th centuries. They followed the Spanish or Portuguese ritual. Some immigration of Ashkenazim (followers of the German or Polish ritual) had occurred from Central and East European countries in the 19th century, but these Jews had been entirely absorbed by the Sephardic elements. There was still in Salonica a synagogue known as the Ashkenazic synagogue, in which the ritual differed somewhat from the Sephardic. The Jewish population was entirely Orthodox; about 90% observed the dietary laws and high holidays.

Under the Greek Constitution, the Greek Orthodox Church was recognized as the dominant church of the State. However, all other denominations enjoyed an official status. The government subsidized the Jewish communities in their philanthropic, religious and educational activities, and the communities themselves were empowered to tax their members. Community taxes were assessed annually by a special board, taxpayers being allowed a period of grace during which assessments could be protested. When the assessment was made final, it could be enforced by law -- this was the total of State cooperation in community tax matters. All Jews were assumed to be members of the Jewish community.

The municipality of Salonica contributed $15,000 a year to the Jewish community philanthropic institutions; and the national government $17,000 a year for the support of its schools, paying in addition the salaries of the instructors in Greek, who were chosen by the community.

Freedom of religion was constitutionally guaranteed, and proselytizing forbidden. Jewish dietary laws were recognized, and the Jewish communities had the right to regulate <u>Shehitah</u> (ritual slaughter). A tax, payable according to the number of cattle slaughtered, and known as the <u>Gabella</u>, provided a source of income for the community. By reason of an obscure old decision of the rabbis, three families in Salonica enjoyed the exclusive right to act as <u>Shohetim</u> (ritual slaughterers), and to charge for their services: the Molho, Beraha and Estrumsa families. The decision relating to this succession is known as <u>Askama</u>.

Community Assets and Functionaries.

Before the invasion, the synagogues and Jewish institutions, though running at a deficit, were able to maintain their activities. In addition to its synagogue buildings, hospitals and other philanthropic institutions, the Jewish community of Salonica owned income-yielding property to the value of $500,000. It was all confiscated by the invaders.

The most important religious functionaries were: the Chief Rabbi, who was the head of a large community; the <u>dayan</u>, a religious scholar who served on the <u>Beth Din</u> (Jewish religious court); the <u>haham</u>, a religious leader or rabbi; the <u>hazan</u>, or cantor; the <u>shohet</u>, the <u>mohel</u>, who performed circumcisions, and the <u>sofer</u>, or scribe.

The Jewish <u>Beth Din</u> had official recognition and exclusive jurisdiction in religious, marriage and divorce matters, with power to subpoena parties and to render decisions which were enforced by the State. In other matters the court acted as voluntary arbitrators. Many Jews had recourse to these courts in family and commercial disputes, since they offered the opportunity for prompt and inexpensive decisions.

Communities After the Invasion.

Following the Nazi invasion, all synagogues in Greece were closed and the properties confiscated. The Jewish community of Salonica was fined 1,000,000 drachmas ($10,000) in May, 1941, on the pretext that the Jews of the city had inspired a Greek demonstration against the Nazis. All Jewish communities in the country ceased to operate.

Marriage and Divorce.

Prior to the invasion, the Jewish communities had exclusive supervision of marriage. Religious ceremonies were obligatory, and were registered with the civil authorities for the purposes of vital statistics. In those localities where Jews remained after the invasion, it may be assumed that marriages were being performed in the same manner, except that there were no attendant celebrations.

Divorce was also delegated by the State to the various religious denominations, and Jewish divorces were therefore regulated by Jewish religious laws, granted by the Beth Din, and registered with the local authorities.

The Agunah proscription, barring a Jewish woman from remarriage if her husband's death cannot be proved and his whereabouts are unknown, brought about a number of difficult situations after every war.

Funerals.

All funerals were conducted by the Jewish communities. They were a public function, at which the officiating rabbis were uniformly attired. What remained of this practice after the invasion cannot be ascertained, but it is fair to assume that all corteges were eliminated, and that funerals were conducted as inconspicuously as possible.

Cultural and Social Characteristics.

The Jews of Greece were characterized by strong family attachments and a paternalistic family structure. Their participation in violent crime was practically non-existent, and they were also noticeably absent among violators of civil regulations.

Languages.

In Macedonia and Thrace the Jews spoke Ladino (Judeo-Spanish) and Greek, while the educated class also knew French, Italian and some Hebrew. In the port cities the population -- especially those engaged in the maritime trades -- had a smattering knowledge of Italian, which was spoken by the Jews of Corfu as well. The Jews of southern Greece and the Greek Islands did not speak Ladino, but only Greek; the educated class knew French and Italian.

Jewish Communal Groups.

Within the Jewish communities, Zionists and Socialists had the strongest organizations. The Zionists were subdivided into general Zionists, Mizrachists (Orthodox), who were predominant, and the Poale-Zion (Labor group). The great majority of the Jews were Zionists. Among the workers were a number of socialists, and there was a small but militant communist minority. There was a B'nai B'rith lodge in Salonica and one in Athens. The Jews also belonged to a number of cooperatives organized by the different trades and occupations, including consumers' cooperatives, building and loan associations, and sick, old age and unemployment benefits. All Jewish activities and organizations went out of existence after the invasion, including the well-known Maccabe, a youth sport organization with a Zionist program.

Citizenship.

Prior to the invasion, the Jews enjoyed full and unqualified citizenship. Theoretically this status was retained in every part of Greece, even after the invasion.

Jews in Parliament and Cabinets.

During the period of validity of the Venizelos law establishing a special electoral college for the Jews (1924-1934), the Greek Chamber of Deputies included two Jewish deputies and the Senate one Jewish senator. Subsequently, one or two Jews were usually elected to the Chamber of Deputies.

Peppo Mallah served as minister of finance under Gounaris.

Civil Service; the Judiciary.

There were very few Jews in Civil Service in Greece, mainly because the bulk of the Jewish population was not annexed until 1913, after Macedonia and Thrace had been conquered during the Balkan War. The intervening period had been too short to allow the Jews of these regions to become integrated in the country's political life. In Old Greece there were a small number of Jews serving in the judiciary.

Municipal Posts.

In Salonica a Jew once occupied the post of vice-mayor, and several members of the city council were Jews.

Age and Occupational Structure.

The age composition of the Jewish population of Greece was as follows: under 14 years of age -- 32.78%; between 15 and 39 -- 41.28%; between 40 and 59 -- 18.19%; over 60 -- 7.75%.

The gainfully employed were divided as follows: workers and employees -- 40%; small businessmen -- 30%; artisans -- 15%; industrialists, financiers and large-scale merchants -- 10%; professionals -- 5%.

Economic Stratification.

About 10% of the Jewish population, before the invasion, could have been classified as wealthy, and these consisted of bankers, large-scale importers and exporters, agents of foreign firms and government contractors. The middle-class, which comprised about 70% of the population, had a variable economic status, depending on the condition of the country as a whole; here were included wholesalers, smaller-scale importers and exporters, and retailers. About 10% of the Jews could have been considered poor -- artisans, factory workers, employees, workers in the maritime trades, and at the bottom of the ladder, the <u>hamal</u>, or colporteur, a human van.

In Jewish community affairs, the wealthy class was very influential, since their contributions to the support of the community, through taxation, were substantial. Among factory workers there was a marked degree of class consciousness; they were generally adherents of socialist movements and formed a militant part of the country's trade unions.

With the invasion, all distinction between the various economic classes ceased to exist. The wealthy were stripped of their possessions. It may safely be said that practically the whole Jewish population has been deprived of the means of livelihood, not only as the result of discrimination but because of the disappearance of foreign commerce, on which most Jews were directly or indirectly dependent.

The Bar.

There were about 50 Jews engaged in the practice of law in free Greece. No discrimination was evident in the Bar, or in the appointment of public notaries. Jews practicing law were among the first to suffer from the effects of the invasion; it may be assumed that there are none in practice in 1943.

Banking; Insurance.

In Salonica the Banque de Salonique was controlled by the family of the late Emanuel Salem, a lawyer, and by French capital; the Banque Amar was controlled by the family of Saul Amar, and the Banque Union was owned by Joseph Nahama. In Jannina, Samuel Matza was a well-known financier, and in Athens, Abraham Constantinis. There is no information available regarding Nazi regulations or policies on the withdrawal of funds by Jews.

Nor are data available on regulations regarding insurance policies owned by Jews, or Jews in the insurance business.

Natural Resources.

The principal Jewish owners of natural resources were Peppo Mallah and Gabriel Almoslinos, who held interests in coal mines and forests.

Agriculture.

Jews were not directly identified with agriculture or farm ownership in Greece. Their only connection with agriculture was in the purchase and the financing of crops.

Industry.

The Jews played an important part in the development of the tobacco, textile, leather, glass, chinaware, paper and alcohol industries. All their interests were confiscated by the Nazis.

Commerce.

The Jews were important in domestic commerce, and were not subjected to any government discrimination. Certain agitators and the Greek refugees from Asia Minor, who considered the Jews competitors in business, were able to effect extra-legal measures. Under the Nazis, the Jews were entirely eliminated from domestic commerce.

In the field of foreign commerce, their knowledge of foreign business and foreign languages, as well as their many contacts in foreign countries, facilitated their participation. Many foreign firms, as well as shipping and insurance companies, were represented by Jews. The isolation resulting from the invasion, barring contact with any but German-controlled countries, removed every opportunity for foreign trade from the Jews.

"Aryanization."

No special corporation for "Aryanization" was established by the Nazis, but a special office was created to liquidate the property owned by Jews.

Employment and Wages.

The employment situation of the Jews in independent Greece was on a par with that of non-Jews. Wages varied between 50 and 150 drachmas a day ($.50 to $1.50), on the basis of six 8-hour days per week. The war had a ruinous effect on Jewish workers, who were engaged mostly in trades connected with export and import. Restriction of shipping brought idleness to those Jewish workers who had been in the maritime trades. Those who could remain working, in any field, were subjected to sub-standard wages, because the regulations were decided on by Germany or the Nazi-controlled countries for which the products were destined.

Prior to the invasion, the Jewish workers were congregated mainly in Salonica, Drama, Kavalla, Serrea, Attique, Comotini and Xanthe. After the invasion, a large number of Jewish workers were deported for forced labor in Germany, but their more exact destinations were unknown. The only fields remaining open to Jews within Greece were menial labor and petty trading.

Trade Unions.

Before the war there were 14 labor federations in Greece, and one General Confederation of Greek Labor, with a total membership of more than 100,000. Including civil employees, the figure was sometimes put as high as 300,000. The first industry to have been unionized was the tobacco industry. There was no discrimination against Jews in the labor unions, and there were no special Jewish labor unions.

Labor Banks and Cooperatives.

There were no labor banks, but many unions maintained insurance funds against unemployment, sickness, and old age, and some unions had savings plans. Jews participated equally in all these undertakings. In conjunction with some Jewish trade associations, there were Jewish consumers' cooperatives, building and loan associations, and sick benefit societies.

The Press.

Two French dailies published in Salonica were owned by Jews: <u>Le Progrès de Salonique</u> and <u>L'Indépendant</u>. Three dailies published in Ladino (Judeo-Spanish) were appearing in Salonica at the time of the invasion: <u>El Liberal</u>, <u>Avanti</u> (Socialist) and <u>La Renascenzia Judia</u>. At various times about five weeklies in Ladino and one in Greek (also of Jewish interest) had appeared in Salonica. All these publications ceased with the invasion. There were no papers of Jewish interest published elsewhere in Greece.

Anti-Semitic and Quisling Press.

The only periodical that was clearly anti-Semitic in independent Greece was <u>Makedonia</u>, owned and published by Leonidas Phardis. There were two Quisling papers: <u>Eleftheron Vima</u> (Free Platform), edited by Lembrakis, and <u>Athenaika Nea</u> (New Athens), editors unknown.

Motion Pictures.

There was no motion picture industry in Greece. All films were imported from the United States, France, Italy and Germany. A number of Jews were engaged in the import and distribution of these films.

Physicians and Other Medical Practitioners.

There were about 100 Jewish physicians in Greece, about 60 dentists, and between 200 and 300 nurses. There were no veterinarians. No information is available about Nazi regulations regarding these practitioners.

Hospitals and Health Services.

Salonica had two Jewish hospitals: the Hirsch Hospital, containing 97 beds, and a hospital for mentally diseased, containing 75 beds. There was also a community clinic with facilities for maternity deliveries. These were all partly subsidized by the municipality. Other cities in Greece had Jewish clinics, but no hospitals. After the invasion, the Jewish hospitals were occupied by the Nazis.

Birth and Mortality Rates.

The birth rate among Jews before the invasion was 20.55 per 1,000. Information is not available regarding the birth rate after the invasion. There are no data regarding the death rate among Jews.

Housing and Hygiene.

The living conditions of the Jews before the invasion was generally fair, except for the poorer classes, who lived in crowded and sometimes dark apartments. The Jews of Salonica, however, suffered from a serious housing problem for many years, because of two serious fires. In 1917 a conflagration ravaged the Jewish quarter, and thousands of families were sheltered in hurriedly constructed and unsanitary barracks. In June, 1931, anti-Semitic riots resulted in the burning of the new Jewish quarter, again forcing the residents to take shelter in temporary barracks. These two fires lowered the standard of living of the Jews of Salonica for many years.

Greece had a modern sewage disposal system, except in the villages, where the cesspool is still very much in vogue. But in Salonica the temporary barracks in which many Jewish families lived for long periods after the fires offered no sewage facilities.

Public Welfare.

The Jews maintained their own private relief organizations, supported mainly by community funds, but with the aid of private contributions. The city of Salonica had an institution offering free meals, Matanot Laevionim, a home for the aged and an organization to provide dowries for poor unmarried girls. Similar organizations existed in practically every Jewish community of importance, and where organizations were lacking, the needy had recourse to the community itself. The welfare personnel consisted largely of volunteers; the limited number of paid workers were not specially trained. Since the invasion, the Jewish communities, deprived of their resources, have been unable to provide for the needy.

Education.

Jews had equal access to the government educational facilities in independent Greece, and were required by law to devote a minimum of 10 hours per week to the study of Jewish subjects and religion. There is no evidence that the Quisling government has been able to introduce any discrimination into the school system.

Every Jewish community, even the smallest, had a Talmud Torah -- a Jewish elementary school supported by the community. In Salonica there were a number of elementary schools and also a number of high schools, all maintained directly by the community, but with the aid of subsidies from the municipality and the national government, which also paid the salaries of Greek language teachers, who were selected by the community. No figures are available for the annual expenditure per Jewish student, but the annual expenditure per student for the whole of Greece was $58, or 6.55% of the national budget. In addition to the communal schools, there were in addition in Salonica a number of private Jewish elementary and high schools. Jewish schools of all grades were closed by the Nazis.

In 1938, there were about 16,000 Jewish students in Greece, 14,000 of whom attended Jewish schools.

Few Jews were found on the teaching staffs of the Greek schools. Where they did serve, they usually taught foreign languages. There were about 400 Jewish teachers in the Jewish schools.

Child Welfare.

The only child welfare institutions known in Greece were orphan asylums, maintained by the various religious groups. There were two Jewish orphan asylums in Salonica, <u>Allatini</u> and <u>Aboav</u>. Elsewhere orphans were cared for by private families. No information is available as to what happened to the orphan homes after the invasion.

History of Anti-Semitism.

In 1913, as a consequence of the Balkan War, Macedonia and Thrace were annexed to Greece. Under the instigation of the local Greeks of Salonica, who sought an opportunity to injure their Jewish competitors, rioting broke out, and resulted in the murder of two Jews. The government of Athens brought the outlawry to an end.

The Jews of Salonica participated in the Greek national elections for the first time in 1916. They supported Gounaris, the monarchist, and contributed to the defeat of Venizelos and his Liberal Party. Although Venizelos could not be called an anti-Semite, the rancor he bore against the Jews for their opposition in the elections resulted eventually in his establishment of a special electoral college for the Jews of Salonica, allowing them two seats in the Chamber of Deputies and one in the Senate. This law remained in effect from 1924 to 1934, when it was declared unconstitutional and repealed. Further antagonism during the same period provoked a change in the market day from Monday to Saturday, which the Jews of Salonica had always observed as a day of rest. The policy of trying to Hellenize Macedonia and Thrace through the settlement of large numbers of Greeks moved from Asia Minor and Istanbul in a population exchange with Turkey precipitated commercial competition which militated against the Jews. The situation was further aggravated by crowded housing conditions.

The refugees from Asia Minor were so numerous that they gained municipal control. It was to them that the riots of June, 1931, can also be traced, when the entire Jewish quarter was burned to the ground.

The only anti-Semitic party ever organized in Greece was the EEE (Three Epsilons), which again derived its support largely from the resettlement immigrants to Macedonia and Thrace. Organized in 1931 under the stewardship of Leonidas Phardis, editor of the anti-Semitic Salonica newspaper, <u>Makedonia</u>, the party was subsequently dissolved by the government on March 28, 1935, when all racial propaganda was also prohibited.

The connection between Fascism (viewed as a movement which disregards franchise) and anti-Semitism has not always been direct in Greece. Metaxas, who came to power in 1936 and eventually dissolved the Chamber of Deputies and suspended the constitution, was always friendly to the Jews, as were his associates. On the other hand, some of the former Venezelists have remained to serve as Quislings, such as John Rhallis, puppet governor of Athens.

The Church and the Jews.

The Orthodox Church, representing 96% of the Greek population, had always been friendly toward the Jews, and had made no attempts at conversion. After the invasion, the Church wholeheartedly came to the defense of the Jews. Priests refused to obey an order to preach an "inferior race" doctrine; as a result, many were reported to have been executed. When, in September, 1941, the Germans threatened to deport many Jews from Macedonia to a ghetto to be established in Crete, the Patriarch of the Greek Church protested, and succeeded in temporarily halting the deportations. Many priests kept Jews in hiding at the risk of their own lives. The Patriarch of the Church in Athens undertook the representation of the Jews during the occupation, and leaders of the Greek Church throughout the world came out with public and unequivocal statements against discrimination and persecution.

Attitude of Government.

The attitude of the free Greek government was fair and cooperative toward the Jews. Whenever signs of race hatred or rioting arose, the national government promptly took steps of prevention and relief. Immediately after the riots of June, 1931, which resulted in the destruction of the entire Jewish quarter of Salonica, the government paid $60,000 to the Jewish community as compensation, and extended a loan of $300,000 for relief. By dissolving the only anti-Semitic party (EEE), and by making it a criminal offense to preach race hatred or to libel any religion in the press, the government made an attempt to stop anti-Semitic propaganda. The special electoral college for the Jews of Salonica, established by Venizelos in 1924, was declared unconstitutional by the Court and repealed in 1934. Jewish community institutions received subsidies from the government. Grain imported for matzoth (unleavened bread) and sugar also imported for Passover were exempt from import duty. Jewish pupils in elementary schools had to devote a minimum of 10 hours a week to the study of Jewish subjects and religion.

Attitude of People.

Except for Macedonia and particularly Salonica, where bitterness had been aroused by the electoral campaigns of 1916 and by the subsequent arrival of large numbers of trade-seeking Greek refugees from Asia Minor, the attitude of the Greek people toward the Jews was friendly. As a result of the present war, this friendliness has increased, partly because of the patriotism and sacrifice shown by the Jews. In April, 1943, Greek students in the University of Athens started to wear the yellow badge imposed on the Jews, as a protest against anti-Jewish discrimination. The Council of Athens University petitioned the Nazi headquarters to treat the Jews equally with all other Greek citizens. King George II and all other Greek leaders in exile, of both parties, have acknowledged the patriotism of the Greek Jews in the regular army and as guerrilla fighters, and the aid rendered the Greek cause by Greek Jews within the country and abroad.

Greek Fascists and Anti-Semitism.

It is difficult to define a Greek Fascist. Some of the supporters of Metaxas were considered Fascists, on the theory that the Metaxas administration was totalitarian. Among these supporters were Admiral Alexander Sakellariou, commander of the fleet under Metaxas; Col. Dimetrious Xenos, Greek military attaché to the United States and a high official in the Security Division of the Metaxas administration; George Skylakakis, who had frequently voiced his opposition to parliamentary government; Costas Kodjias, former mayor of Athens, and George Maniadakis, head of the Security Division under Metaxas, and now in South America. It is significant, however, that none of these people have ever identified themselves with anti-Semitism, and their alleged Fascistic leanings must be viewed in the light of the internal political fight between the Venizelist and the monarchist groups. Col. George Tsolakoglou, who surrendered to the Nazis, and Constantin Logothetropoulos and John Rhallis, who replaced him as Quislings, may be definitely classed as Fascists.

Discrimination Before the Invasion.

There were no legal discriminations before the invasion. The most identifiable case of extra-legal discrimination was the change effected by the municipality of Salonica during the 1920's, when the market day was shifted from Monday to Saturday, handicapping the Jewish merchants who observed the Sabbath. This was done over the protests of the Jewish population and the intervention of the national government, and was provoked by the newly-arrived refugees from Asia Minor, who had gained control of the municipal government by weight of number.

Discriminatory Measures: After the Invasion.

In August, 1941, the Nazis kidnapped 8,000 Jews from Salonica and transported them to the Macedonia hills, where a ghetto was to be established. In June of that year the Jewish community of Salonica was fined 1,000,000 drachmas ($10,000), on the alleged charge that they had been instrumental in inciting a Greek demonstration against the German military occupation, and the community was ordered to supply 3,000 Jews daily for forced labor. Those refusing to be drafted were taken in sealed trains to unknown destinations, and their properties confiscated. During 1941, also, some 200 intellectuals and 7,000 workers were arrested in Salonica for being pro-democratic. In October, 1941, all Jews were required to register and to wear yellow armbands with the Star of David emblem. In July, 1942, all Jews were ordered to leave the seaports, which happened to be where they lived in the largest numbers. In March, 1943, all Jews between the ages of 17 and 55 were mobilized for forced labor, to erect fortifications on the Greek borders. In March, Bulgaria applied all the discriminatory laws against the Jews residing in the territory occupied by it. By April, 1943, 3,000 Jewish families had already been deported from Salonica to Poland; their arrival was confirmed in the Lwow concentration camp, where they had been brought in cattle trains, 80 persons to a car, supplied with one loaf of bread each and allowed a maximum of seven kilos (17½ pounds) of luggage per person, for food and clothing. Each car was also supplied with one petrol can of water and one empty can for sanitation purposes. In the town of Demotika all Jews were rounded up in the main square in May, 1943, publicly lashed, and packed into cattle trains for deportation to Polish ghettos. In two other towns the Nazis collected all Jews, men and women alike, forced the men to strip bare, march nude through the streets to the railway stations, and be herded into cattle trains for concentration camps in Poland. After the Jews left, their homes were ransacked and everything of value was confiscated. Much of the loot, especially the kitchen utensils, was sent to Germany. Many Jews died during the trip to the concentration camps. In August, 1943, 1,245 of the Jews remaining in the country were tried for alleged violation of occupational laws. Four hundred were given jail terms, 800 were sent to concentration camps and 45 were set free. All property owned by deported Jews, or otherwise confiscated by Germans, is administered by a special office and is considered the property of Germany. There have been many outright executions of Jews on flimsy, false charges.

Taxation.

There was no tax discrimination of any kind against the Jews in independent Greece. Since the government was trying to encourage commerce, the tax strain on urban and commercial populations was not great. Evaluation and assessment were impartial. Except for the tax of 1,000,000 drachmas imposed on the Jews of Salonica by the Nazi authorities, there is no evidence of discriminatory taxation after the invasion.

Curfew; Travel Regulations; Identification Cards.

All Jews are subject to the general curfew regulations, which prohibit appearance on the street after sunset. Jews are especially watched in connection with the general regulations forbidding the possession of firearms. No evidence is available regarding special restrictions on circulation and travel, except that Jews have been forced to move from all seaports into the interior. There are no data regarding special identification cards.

Rationing.

The Nazi policy was to deny food to those who refused to do forced labor for Germany. Even when compliant, they were allowed $4\frac{1}{2}$ lbs. of olives, 2 or 3 kilos of lentils or beans, some rice and vegetables, 2 loaves of bread and 2 eggs for one month's labor. The rest of the population was left largely to its own resources; The Nazi ration of bread was 3 to 4 ounces daily per person. Jews were particularly affected because they did not live on farms, where foodstuffs could be raised. Until food was distributed impartially by the Red Cross, the mortality rate was very high.

Concentration Camps.

Soon after the invasion, a large number of Jews from Salonica were removed to concentration camps in the Macedonia hills, but with the Bulgarian occupation of that part of Greece, these camps seem to have been vacated, and the Jews removed either to the Polish ghetto or to forced labor in Germany.

Jewish Communal Leaders in Greece and in Exile.

The Jewish communal leaders who, it is assumed, remained in Greece after the invasion, include the Chief Rabbi of Salonica, Zwi-Hirsch Coretz; Chaim Cohen, ex-president of the Jewish Community of Salonica; Leon Gattegno, last president of the Jewish community of Salonica; Canetti, president of the Jewish community of Athens; Sabatay Saltiel, secretary of the Salonica community; Adolphe Arditti and Solomon Mordoh, journalists; Joseph Nahama, writer and banker; Jacob Aroeste, manufacturer; Abraham Constantinis and Samuel Matza, financiers; Mentesh Bensantchi, editor, community leader and former deputy; Trabouh, cotton yarn manufacturer; Raoul Torres and Fernandes, jute manufacturers; the Salem family, financiers; the Alhadef brothers, textile manufacturers; Isidore Kalamaro, hosiery manufacturers; J. Salem, Bloch and Merpourgo, owners of the Cassandra lead and other mines; Gabriel Almoslinos, coal mine concessionaire; Ovadia, Jack Benzonana and David Arditti, tobacco manufacturers; A. Veissi and Joseph Angel, editors; and Ventura, former deputy.

Some of the leaders who had left Greece just before the invasion were: Peppo Mallah, former senator, industrialist and minister of finance; Fernandes, industrialist; Amar, banker; the sons of Allatani, industrialists; Albert Matarasso, banker and editor; and Nissim Sakitudis, department store owners -- all of whom were presumably in France. Leon Rekanati, communal leader and former president of the Zionist organization, may be in Palestine.

Reconstruction Agencies.

The only Jewish relief personnel left in Greece today are the few communal leaders who have not been deported to ghettos or concentration camps or taken to Germany for forced labor. The Central Sephardic Jewish Community of New York, with offices at 225 West 34th Street, New York City, the Joint Distribution Committee, the American-Joint Reconstruction Foundation, the HICEM (Hias-Ica Emigration Association), the ORT Society for the promotion of trade and agriculture among Jews, the OSE World Union for health protection and the Jewish Agency for Palestine are some of the foreign Jewish organizations which may possibly work in the field of post-war relief in Greece.

THE JEWS OF HOLLAND

THE JEWS OF HOLLAND

Index

Agriculture	9	Government Posts, Jews in	7
Anti-Semitism, History of	13	Groups-in-Exile	18
Army, Jews in	2	Hospitals	11
"Aryanization"	16	Housing	11
Banking	8	Hygiene	11
Bar, The	7	Industry	9
Birth Rate	11	Jewish Religious Community	2
Christian Churches and the Jews	14	Assets	4
Citizenship	7	Functionaries	4
Civil Service	6	Judiciary, The	7
Commerce	9	Languages	6
Communal Groups	4	Marriage	6
Criminality	6	Mortality	12
Cultural Life	5	Motion Pictures	10
Deportations	1	Parliament, Jews in	7
Discrimination: Before the Invasion,	16	People and Government, Attitude of	
After the Invasion: Communications,	17	Before Invasion	14
Concentration Camps,	17	After Invasion	15
Forced Labor	17	Physicians	11
Forced Prostitution,	17	Population	1
Identification Badge	16	Press, The	10
Public Places	16	Jewish Press	10
Registration	16	Public Welfare	13
Sterilization	17	Reconstruction Agencies	18
Transportation	17	Refugees	1
Divorce	6	Stock Exchange	9
Economic Stratification	8	Taxes	7
Education	12	United States, Attitude toward	5
Family Life	6	War, Attitude toward	5
Funerals	6	Women, Position of	6
Government-in-Exile	7		

THE JEWS OF HOLLAND

Population; Deportations; Refugees

On January 1, 1931, there were in Holland 111,917 Jews, or 1.41% of the population (but it is assumed that many, having no connection with a Jewish community, did not register as Jews). Of the known number, 5,186 were Sephardic Jews (followers of the Spanish or Portuguese ritual), 4,547 living in Amsterdam and most of the others in The Hague. The rest were Ashkenazim (followers of the German or Polish ritual). The most important Jewish centers (1930), were: Amsterdam, with 65,523 Jews (8.65% of the population; in 1939 the percentage was between 10 and 15); Rotterdam, 10,357 (1.76%); The Hague, 10,224 (2.34%); Groningen, 2,398 (about 2%). The remaining Jews lived in several other towns in smaller numbers.

With the establishment of the Hitler government in Germany, Jewish refugees began to arrive in Holland; about 25,000 were said to have come in, although some estimates gave the number at 15,000. Nazi racial standards estimated that at the outbreak of the war there were 180,000 Jews in Holland (2.4% of the population).

After the invasion (May 10, 1940) Jews were first expelled from the smaller places and crowded into Amsterdam, where in May 1942 they were confined in three ghettos. Deportations to Poland began in June 1942. In December 1942 some 12,000 Dutch Jews were transported to Poland from the concentration camp in Westerbork. There were 1,010 people in each group of deportees; it was assumed that 10 would die during the trip. The Jewish Council (Joodsche Raad) warned the Jews to have small bags packed and their documents ready, for deportation at any time. In November 1942 Chief Rabbi Sarlouis of Amsterdam and Max H. M. Bolle, secretary of the Jewish Council, and their respective families, were believed to have been deported to Poland.

In March 1943 eight provinces were reported cleared of Jews. Completion of evacuation was ordered to begin in April 1943. The last 5,000 Jews, including the members of the Jewish Council, were reported to have been removed from Amsterdam in October 1943.

According to information received in November 1943, three classes of Jews were exempt from deportation from Holland. They were

1. Those who had Palestinian immigration certificates.
2. Those who had original South American visas.
3. Jews for whom a ransom was paid by "Aryan" friends which amounted to 25,000 Swiss francs per person.

The first group were sent to a special camp in central Germany. About 150 Jews who previously had been functionaries and those who were in the camp in Barneveld for privileged Jews who had rendered special service to the Netherlands, were also sent to central Germany, including the members and the staff of the Jewish Council. The Nazis state that there are still 15,000 Jews hiding in the Netherlands, but Swiss reports give the figure at 20,000. A large number have recently been arrested by the Nazis.

Very few Jews were able to escape. It was impossible to go south because the invaders cut off all means of conveyance. A maximum of 500 were believed to have been able to escape by boat and ship to England. However, at the time of the invasion many Dutch Jews were either in Belgium or in France. Those, of course, had a chance to escape overland toward the south. During the time that part of France was "occupied" there seems to have been considerable traffic for getting Jewish people across into the unoccupied part. Others going south went either to Switzerland or through Spain and Portugal to North Africa and then to the Americas. Most of them came to the United States, others went to South America, and a smaller number to the Dutch colonies in the west: Curacao and Surinam. The Dutch government also helped to transport Dutch Jews from Lisbon to the Dutch East Indies (Java) in 1940 and 1941.

After the occupation, many Jews tried to escape "illegally," since a few received permits from the Germans to emigrate. It has been reported that more than 50% lost their lives in the attempt, while others reached Spain or Switzerland, where there is now said to be a colony of about 800, many of whom are interned. Some are waiting in Cuba or Jamaica to enter the United States. There are also a few in Canada. Very few reached Palestine.

Before 1939 a number of German Jews became naturalized Dutch citizens; these were supposedly the first to be taken back to Germany.

Jews in the Army

There are no statistics of Jews in the Dutch Army. A few are in the Navy and a few more in the Air Forces. Dutch Jews who had arrived in England were called to the Dutch Army. Many who had escaped to the United States or Canada also joined the Dutch Army, were trained for a short period in Canada, and were then sent overseas.

The Government appointed Rabbi S. Rodrigues Pereira, formerly Chief Rabbi of the Sephardic Community in The Hague, to be Chaplain to the Dutch forces and Adviser to the Government on Jewish questions. He is now in England.

Jewish Religious Community

Freedom of religion was granted to all creeds in 1579. After the French occupation, equal rights were guaranteed for all religions by the New Constitution of 1815; these have been maintained.

The highest administrative and representative body of the Ashkenazic Jews, since 1870, has been the Centrale Commissie tot de Algemeene Zaken van het Nederlandsch-Israelietisch Kerkgenotschap (Central Commission for the General Affairs of the Dutch Israelite Communities). Although a general right of supervision was reserved by the state, it was hardly ever exercised. The state paid a grant to the rabbis. The affairs of the local communities were regulated according to the Statues of the Central Commission (the last one was dated March 25, 1917). Within the limitations imposed by these Statutes, each community was autonomous.

In 1927 there were 146 communities, which sent delegates to the provincial or district committee. The latter elected the Chief Rabbi. Districts were usually identical with the provinces of the Netherlands. The Chief Rabbi lived in the capital of the province or district and made regular pastoral visits to the other communities. Some communities had their own rabbi; in the small congregations the hazan (cantor), teacher or shohet (ritual slaughterer), who were often combined in one person, looked after the religious interests. Amsterdam had a Chief Rabbi (L. H. Sarlouis) and three assistant rabbis. All ecclesiastical matters were under rabbinical supervision. Each Jewish community was ruled by its own council.

The Ashkenazim had a seminary in Amsterdam for the training of rabbis with a separate department for the training of teachers and shohetim. Before Hitler there were no restrictions on Shehitah (ritual slaughter).

The Sephardim had two congregations, one in Amsterdam (with two rabbis) and one in The Hague. Sephardic communities were independent, and had their own seminary, Ets Haim, in Amsterdam. They were headed by a Hoofdcommissie.

All chief rabbis, including the Sephardim, met periodically in conference to discuss religious questions and to promote united action and attitudes. This was a voluntary arrangement.

All communities were officially Orthodox - synagogues had Orthodox services and Orthodox rabbis, and all official functions were according to the Orthodox customs and rules, but individually the members were not necessarily all Orthodox or observant. Unsuccessful attempts had been made to organize a Reform community in Amsterdam and The Hague. When German refugees began to arrive, special arrangements were made in Amsterdam for their affiliation with the Jewish Community. These efforts, also intended to prevent the formation of a special (German) Reform community, were very successful.

Jewish religious holidays were observed in the synagogues and homes. There was no public display except that in the Jewish districts no markets were open on the Sabbath and on Jewish holidays. Special arrangements were made by the school authorities to have schools with predominantly Jewish student bodies closed on the Sabbath. Soldiers were allowed as much as was possible to observe the Sabbath and arrangements were made for them to have kosher food. When meals to school-children were introduced, certain schools in predominantly Jewish districts provided kosher meals. For Jewish refugee children and in internee camps kosher food was provided. There were many kosher restaurants. Under REOR (ritual food on journeys) it was possible to have kosher food in many towns and villages (in restaurants and with private people).

The attitude of the Jewish religion to the state was intensely loyal. Dutch Jews deeply appreciated their freedom of religion and remembered that Holland was the first country to grant such freedom constitutionally (1579). They also recognized the part played by the reigning House of Orange in safeguarding this freedom.

After the invasion, a Jewish Council (Joodsche Raad), headed by Abraham Asscher and Dr. David Cohen, was formed in Amsterdam to see that all new laws and regulations were obeyed. Shehita was abolished in August 1940. In December 1941 it was reported that synagogue services were no longer permitted on Friday evenings. The Council was also required to supply all information demanded by the Nazis and forced to assist in deportations. The members of the Council were among the last Jews to remain in Amsterdam and were removed with the last group in October 1943. After the deportation of Rabbi Sarlouis, Rabbi Dasberg was appointed in his place. Rabbi Frank, of Haarlem, one of the youngest Dutch rabbis, was reported shot as a hostage.

Religious Functionaries.

The most important functionaries were the rabbis; requirements for the occupancy of a rabbinical post were high. Of late, almost all rabbis were native Netherlanders. Cantors and shohetim (ritual slaughterers) who were not also the rabbis of small communities had little importance. Mohelim (performers of circumcision) did not -- as is the custom in other countries -- receive payment for their services, but on the contrary, sometimes donated gifts if the family was poor.

Community Assets.

The Sephardic Community of Amsterdam was originally very wealthy; many rich members had left considerable legacies to the synagogue. But the number of Sephardim had declined gradually, and they were subsequently outnumbered by the Ashkenazim. The value of the various funds left to the Synagogue had also declined, except for the Dotar, which was intended to provide dowries for a selected group of Sephardic girls.

The Sephardic Synagogue of Amsterdam (and in a lesser degree of The Hague) possessed a number of old Torah Scrolls and many valuable scroll ornaments, such as crowns, bells and embroidered cloaks. In later years the Ashkenazic synagogues were also the recipients of many gifts from the congregants, especially covers for the ark. Legacies were also left them. It is feared that all valuables have been taken away.

The Sephardic Seminary in Amsterdam had a valuable library, which was transported to Germany together with the Rosenthaliana (Jewish division of the Amsterdam University Library), the Seeligman collection, and the collection of the Nederlandsch Israelietisch Seminary (Ashkenazic).

In September 1942 the Synagogue of The Hague was forcibly entered by storm troopers who destroyed ceremonial objects and furniture. Books, except for scrolls, were burnt. Jews and Gentiles drove off the storm troopers. It seems that this resistance, especially on the part of the Gentiles, prevented destruction elsewhere.

Communal Groups.

The Agudath Israel (ultra-Orthodox) did not have a large following. Zionists were well organized and raised a great deal of money; comparatively the Mizrachi (Orthodox Zionists) were very strong.

Youth organizations were active. There were religious groups such as Toutsous Haim in Amsterdam, where there was also a Youth Synagogue and several strong Zionist youth groups.

B'nai B'rith was rather "young" in Holland; it had a small but influential membership. There were two B'nai B'rith lodges, one in Amsterdam, one in The Hague.

There was also an order of Foresters, but in general fraternal organizations were not customary. Masonry was also not well-rooted among the Dutch in general and there were hardly any Jewish Masons. There were Hebra Kadishas (Burial Societies), and the so-called Cemetery-Societies (Kabranim) were quite significant. Some of these also gave financial assistance. A Society for Jewish Science held regular meetings at which scientific Jewish problems were discussed.

Attitude toward War; toward the United States.

The Jews share the feelings of their fellow-citizens towards the war, which was forced on them by the invasion of the Nazis. Jews defended the country with the others against the invaders. The Germans are hated and despised by Jews and Christians alike.

Since the United States has always been a champion of freedom, it has always been much admired by the Dutch Jews.

Cultural Life.

Among the Jews who were well-known as professors were: L. S. Ornstein - chemistry, David Cohen - history, H. Fryda - economics, I. Snapper - medicine (now in the United States), van Embden - law, Ed. Meyer - law, J. L. Palache - Semitic languages, and Leo Polak.

Art: The famous Josef Israels (d. 1911) had a son named Isaac Israel, also a painter. Other artists were Eduard Frank, Benjamin Prins, B. Lopes de Leao Laguna, Martin Monnichendam, S. Garf, and Marinus van Raalte; Joseph Teixeira de Mattos (graphic art), Samuel Jessurun de Mesquita (woodcuts and etchings), Joseph Mendes da Costa (sculptor), Harry Elte (architect and designer of several synagogues), Staal (architect), Lea Halpern (ceramics; now in the United States).

There was a Jewish Historical Museum in Amsterdam. The library of Baron Rosenthal, which was presented by his son in 1880 to the University of Amsterdam, remained known as the Bibliotheca Rosenthaliana.

Theatre: Louis de Vries and Louis Davids. Rabbi Meyer de Hond wrote a number of Jewish plays.

Literature: Herman Heyermans (d. 1924), Israel Querido (dec.), Siegfried van Praag (now in London), Emanuel Querido (who wrote under the name of Joost Mendes). There is now a Querido publishing house in New York. Carry van Bruggen, a sister of Jacob Israel de Haan, was an excellent novelist; her brother was a poet (both are dead). Many Jews were engaged in the book trade.

Music: Sam Swaap (violinist), Max Orobio de Castro (cello), Sem Dresden, composer and choir director.

Medicine: J. de Bruin (children's diseases), Abraham Hartog Israels, medical historian, Prof. van der Bergh, internist.

Under the Nazis, the Netherlands Kulturkammer was established; no Jew was admitted to any artists' guild.

Family Life; Position of Women.

The "authority" of the father was much the same among Jews as among other Dutch citizens. There was no restriction on the activities of women, but the Dutch Jewess spent much of her time in her home. Jewish girls were given an excellent education. Many attended universities; there are many doctors, nurses, lawyers and teachers among the women. Women had their own organizations, the most significant of which was de Joodsche Vrouwenraad (Council of Jewish Women), and their own branches of Zionist groups. They did excellent work for hospitals, orphanages and other homes.

Marriage and Divorce.

A civil marriage ceremony was obligatory; a religious ceremony optional. The same was true of divorce decrees. Intermarriage was on the increase.

Funerals.

Jews had their own cemeteries. Mourners and friends gathered at the house of the departed and walked behind the bier to the synagogue past which the body was taken for a last farewell. In the case of prominent men, the body was carried on the shoulders through the streets to the synagogue. Very rarely, however, was the body taken inside the synagogue; this was done only for rabbis, when a special service was held.

Languages.

Jews in Holland did not speak Yiddish, except for a small group of Polish Jews. During the First World War many Jews emigrated from Antwerp and other parts of Belgium, settling mostly in Scheveningen, but with the return of peace practically all went back. After 1933 many German Jews came to Holland and continued to speak German. They tried to form separate congregations, especially in Amsterdam, but efforts of a special committee of the Amsterdam Congregation resulted in the integration of the new arrivals into the Jewish community. Only occasionally were German sermons given.

Criminality.

Murder and other violent crimes occurred in low percentage among Jews.

Civil Service.

No total statistics are available for the number of Jews in the civil service. Out of 73 sheriffs in the larger cities, 5 were Jews. It is known that Jews were included in the (approximately) 65,000 civil servants in Holland who were put on half pay in May 1940. In October 1940 the civil service was completely closed to Dutch Jews or to Christians who were married to Jews. Among those barred were 800 Jews in Amsterdam.

Citizenship.

The granting of nationality required the passing of a special decree by Parliament, but there was rarely any difficulty. Many German refugees who had entered the country during and after 1933 became citizens after the required period of residence had elapsed (five years was the minimum), and after going through the necessary formalities.

Taxes.

Taxes were considered rather high in Holland, and urban residents were subjected to even higher rates. Since Jews lived largely in cities, they belonged to the higher-taxed portion of the population. Those Jews who voluntarily affiliated themselves with a Jewish community paid taxes also to the community.

Jews in Parliament; Government Posts.

In 1937, of the 100 members in the Second Chamber (Lower House) five had Jewish mothers, but only three were full Jews. Of the 50 members of the First Chamber (Upper House), five had Jewish mothers. Among the members elected to the Second Chamber in the elections of May 1938 were seven Jews or part Jews; the First Chamber had three. Of the 65 members of the provincial executive boards only four were Jews. The provincial councils constituted the local government for the provincial areas, and were also the electors for the members of the First Chamber. Of the 590 members of these provincial councils 30 were Jews. There were 73 aldermen in Holland, five of them Jewish; three of these served in Amsterdam. There was no Jewish burgomaster, but some Jews served on municipal councils. J. Limburg was a member of the State Council and represented Holland at the League of Nations Assembly.

Government-in-Exile.

Dr. A. H. Drilsma, a Jew, was named Public Prosecutor of one of the Dutch District Courts set up in Britain. Dr. G. H. C. Hart, who has since died, was Secretary General of the Ministry of Colonies. M. Sluyser is a member of the Netherlands Extraordinary Advisory Council. Several Jews have been elected to special committees preparing post-war legislation and other measures, both in New York and London.

The Judiciary.

Some of the Jews who served as judges were: I. van Creveld, N. de Benedetti, S. G. Kanes, L. S. Hartog, Mr. Parser, and L. E. Visser, who was vice-president of the Supreme Court. Out of a total of 990 judges, 46 were Jews.

The Bar.

There was no discrimination against Jews in the Bar. Professor Eduard Maurits Meyers was an internationally-known jurist, a professor at Leiden University and teacher of Princess Juliana. When, after the invasion, he was ousted, the occasion was made a public demonstration. His successor, Professor Cleveringa, made a speech which was widely-quoted. He said "The Netherlands Constitution does not distinguish between creed and race. According to Article 43 of the International Law, the occupying power is bound to respect the country's laws except in such cases where the absolute necessity of safeguarding his own military interests prevents him from doing so. There was no reason whatever why the authorities could not have left Dr. Meyers in the place he occupies."

T. M. C. Asser, who died in 1913, was a famous authority on international law; in 1911 he won the Nobel Prize.

Notaries were appointed by the Queen on the proposal of the Minister of Justice and their number was restricted, but a Jew was always appointed when a Jewish incumbent resigned.

Economic Stratification.

The majority of the Jews belonged to the middle classes. Extreme poverty was not prevalent, but there were poor as well as wealthy Jews. The Jewish poor received support and free services like all poor, and in addition were helped by Jewish organizations.

Some of the leaders of trade unions and socialist groups were Jews, such as Henri Polak and A. B. Kleerekoper.

Banking.

The most important banks owned or controlled by Jews were: Lippman, Rosenthal & Co. (Amsterdam), S. van Dantzig & Co. (Rotterdam), Lisser and Kann (The Hague). In 1938, only two banks in Holland had Jewish directors. A Mr. Rabbie was assistant director of the Rotterdamsche Bank.

On August 8, 1941, a decree was issued by Seyss-Inquart, Reich commissioner, regarding Jewish-owned capital in the Netherlands. All Jews had to deposit their cash and checks, including those until then held in other credit institutions, in a special account with the bank of Lippman, Rosenthal & Co., which now became "Aryanized" and German-controlled. Each depositor was allowed 1,000 gilders. Those with a capital of less than 10,000 gilders were not subjected to the ruling. Imprisonment, fines and confiscation of all property were punishments for violation.

By a decree of September 20, 1941, all capital belonging to German Jews who had taken refuge in Holland was frozen. They were not allowed to dispose of their possessions within the Reich unless they had the consent of officials in the foreign exchange department. During the summer of 1942, Jewish-owned assets and property passed legally into the hands of Lippman, Rosenthal. Jews no longer had the right to open their own deposit vaults or to handle the contents. After January 1, 1942, Lippman, Rosenthal made no more payments to Jewish depositors. Those who had applied to the bank for payments had to renew their applications and address them to the Jewish Council.

Stock Exchange.

About 18% of the members of the Stock Exchange were Jews. In November 1941 they were all ordered to resign.

Insurance.

According to an official Nazi decree, all insurance policies contracted by Netherlands Jews were terminated as of June 1, 1943. If a policy contained a redemption clause, the insurance company had to pay the redemption value to the bank of Lippman, Rosenthal. In all other cases, the insurance companies had to deposit 75% of the total premium and all unpaid dividends with Lippman, Rosenthal "to the account of the insured."

Industry.

About 37% of the Jews in Holland were engaged in industry. Most of them were in the diamond industry, which occupied 8% of the Jews of Holland. Of the total number of people engaged in the diamond industry, 90% were Jews. About 27% of all Jews employed were in the diamond-cutting industry, as against $2\frac{1}{2}$% of the employed non-Jews. The Diamond Exchange was closed on Saturdays and open on Sundays; the restaurant in the Exchange provided only kosher food and there was a special room for prayers inside the Exchange. The Exchange had 900 Jewish members, mostly small jewelers; the most prominent of these was Abraham Asscher who, together with Prof. David Cohen, was at the head of the Jewish Council. Asscher also had the best diamond-cutting factory in Amsterdam; it was there that the King of England sent the Cullinan, which was almost entirely prepared by Jews.

The artistic silk industry in Holland was founded by J. C. Hartog. Jews named Van den Bergh and Hartog were also active in the development of the pearl industry. N. J. Menco was a textile manufacturer in Enschedi. The Van den Bergh and Zwanenberg families built up an important dairy industry which manufactured margerine and similar products.

Agriculture.

About 0.1% of the Jews in Holland were engaged in agriculture (1930), and there were some Jews in the cattle trade. But movement toward the cities was widespread. In June 1941 all agricultural land owned by Jews had to be registered and could be appropriated before September 1st. Leaseholders of Jewish-owned property were allowed to continue the leases but were permitted to postpone the payment of rent and mortgages. Any change in the ownership of Jewish-owned land had to have the approval of the Reich commissioner.

Commerce.

About 45% of the Jews of Holland were engaged in commerce, mostly as small merchants. In an article written by a Mr. van der Beugel, before the invasion, a protest was voiced against statements published by Nazi circles that the whole of Dutch commerce was in the hands of the Jews. Very few large commercial concerns were dominated by Jews.

Some Jews were engaged in foreign trade, especially as small import and export merchants. Here also there was no discrimination.

In September 1940 Jews were barred from acting as merchants in the Amsterdam public markets. Toward the end of 1941, within one month, 1,400 Jews who were textile dealers were forced to close their shops; the stocks were requisitioned by the State Bureau for Textile Products. In December 1942, about 9,000 Jews were forcibly seized in Amsterdam stores, and together with all the personnel of Amsterdam stores and shops who were Jews, were deported to an unknown destination.

The Press.

The Dutch general press was on a very high level, with excellent news services and foreign articles. Before the invasion, there was no anti-Semitic press although occasionally there may have been an item in which some anti-Semitic tendency might have been discerned.

Algemeen Handelsblad, which was read by many Jews, contained most of the Jewish advertisements, and had a number of Jews on its staff, kept its independence as long as it could against Nazi rule.

The important Nazi papers now appearing in Holland are: Nationale Degblad (pre-Hitler), founded by Dutch Nazis; Volk En Vaderland, also pre-Hitler, a weekly published by Mussert; Deutsche Zeitung in den Niederlanden, a daily issued by Germans; Misthoorn (Foghorn), edited by Jan Nysse; De Zwarte Soldaat (Black Soldier) Storm-trooper periodical; De Waag, a weekly.

The two oldest underground papers are: Vry (free) Nederland, founded August 19, 1940 (there is a London weekly of the same name edited with the help of the Dutch Government) and Oranje Krant (Orange paper). There are also Paraat (Ready), Nederland Ontwaakt (Netherlands Wakes Up), Je Maintiendrai (Motto of House of Orange) and De Geus (Beggar).

Jewish Press.

There were the following Jewish papers in Holland: Nederlandsch Israelietsch Weekblad (Netherlands Jewish Weekly), Amsterdam, edited by Staal; Centraalblad voor Israelieten in Nederland, (weekly, Amsterdam), edited by Creveld; Joodsche Wachter (Jewish Watchman), a Zionist paper; Weekblad voor Israelietische Huisgzinnen (Weekly for Jewish Families), Rotterdam.

The Jewish press was stopped by the forces of occupation, and the Joodsche Raad (Jewish Council) then issued a weekly newspaper called Joodsche Weekblad.

Motion Pictures.

The motion picture industry was rather undeveloped in Holland, and the participation of the Jews in it was very small. An attempt was made by a Jew named

Barnstein to create a Dutch Hollywood near Amsterdam. The most beautifully-equipped motion picture house in Amsterdam was owned by a Jew named Tushinsky.

Physicians.

There are no specific statistics available about the number of doctors who were Jews, but the percentage of Jews studying medicine was rather high. Many Jews were also dentists and nurses. In the thickly-populated Jewish districts of Amsterdam, three Jews were physicians in the municipal health services.

Hospitals.

There were a number of well-known Jewish hospitals in Holland, staffed largely by Jews. In Amsterdam the Nederlandsch Israelitsch Ziekenhuis accepted patients at a very low fee, according to their income. Christian patients were also treated there when they were sent in by the municipality, which paid a daily allowance. The P. I. Z. (Portugeesch Israelitsch Ziekenhuis) was maintained by the Portuguese Congregation. A hospital for paying patients was the Centraal Israelitsch Ziekenhuis (C.I.Z.).

There was an excellent insane asylum in Apeldoorn, and a special convalescent home in Hilversum.

After the invasion, the Jewish hospitals were the first to be taken over. The Apeldoorn insane asylum was converted into the Nazi Ministry of Education.

Housing.

General living conditions were good. There was no ghetto in Holland. Jews were voluntarily concentrated in certain districts around the synagogues. In Amsterdam, where living conditions gradually became bad, the Municipal Government organized an excellent slum-clearing scheme. Most of the Jews living in old houses in the Jewish centers moved to the newer districts.

Hygiene.

Although the control measures of the government in Holland were excellent, Jewish communities had their own supervision. Kosher milk, meat, butter, cheese, and many other items, such as biscuits, jams, chocolates, soaps and bread, were available all the year round. Most Jewish people bought bread from Jewish bakers. As late as February 1943 a German paper complained that kosher cheese and butter was still being manufactured in Holland.

The Jewish congregations in the large towns maintained their own ritual baths (mikvehs); those who used them paid for their use.

Birth Rate.

The number of births among Jews in Holland was considered to be 250 per year.

Mortality.

In the years 1926-30, 23% of the deaths among the Jews was due to heart disease, while among the non-Jews it was 13.7%. The percentage of Jews dying of cancer was 14.7. The percentage of suicide and death by violence was lower among Jews than among non-Jews.

Education.

There has been a compulsory education law in Holland since the defeat of Napoleon. All children had to attend the public schools, which were free. There was no discrimination in the appointment of teachers. Under the leadership of the Catholics, an agitation was started for private schools; finally Parliament decided that the state would support private schools which met the necessary requirements. The Jews subsequently took advantage of this. There had already been a private Jewish school, of the parochial class, in Amsterdam, founded by H. Elte, but after the change in the law a number of Jewish schools were established, including a Jewish high school which won an excellent reputation.

Public schools gave due consideration to Jews and the requirements of Jewish children. In predominantly Jewish quarters, schools were closed on the Sabbath and on Jewish holidays. In other schools only gymnastics, drawing and other unessential subjects were taught on Saturday. Certain schools which provided meals for poor children had kosher kitchens.

According to a report on Jewish schools, there were in 1936 five "preparatory" schools with 600 pupils, two "elementary" schools with 410 pupils and one "intermediary" school. There were also Jewish kindergartens. The parents paid the fees, but the schools were government-controlled. Accommodations and equipment had to satisfy certain requirements. The general school curriculum was followed, for the children had to take regular examinations. Jewish subjects were distributed throughout the week, so that two or more hours a day were devoted to Jewish instruction. There were a considerable number of Jewish teachers (no statistics). All schools respected religious objections to attending sessions on Saturdays.

After the invasion, a German official decree forbade the coeducation of Dutch and Jewish children in elementary schools. Jewish teachers had been eliminated from all Dutch schools by November 1940. On September 1, 1941, 6,000 Jewish school children were removed from primary and other schools in Amsterdam and placed in special schools, where Jewish pupils would be taught only by Jewish teachers.

In October 1941 it was announced that under the new decree of segregation three Jewish preparatory schools were to be opened in The Hague, and also a Jewish lyceum for classical and modern languages, sciences and commercial education. In November 1941 it was reported that the municipality of The Hague had established a Jewish girls school for domestic science.

The City Council of Amsterdam had allocated 282,000 gilders for Jewish schools for the first half of 1942, but an order decreed that the Jews had to pay the entire cost of their special schools; hence the Jewish Council was ordered to refund the allocation.

In the provinces nothing was done for the Jewish children; Jewish teachers were not allowed to teach anywhere, and the children were often forced to remain at home and receive private instruction. Gradually deportation made the need for Jewish schools unnecessary.

Public Welfare.

In general, welfare services were under national or local government supervision. The Jews had their own organizations supported by the congregations with funds received from annual contributions. These were tantamount to a "tax," except that there was no compulsion. The members paid a sum fixed by the different boards in proportion to what they paid on government tax.

There was a central Jewish orphanage in Utrecht. Rotterdam and Leiden also had orphanages. The Sephardic Jews had their own orphanages for boys and girls respectively and homes for the aged, in Amsterdam. The Joodsche Invalide (Home for Incurables), in Amsterdam, was a model institution. Gouda had a home for the aged. The Berg Institution housed children who had been taken away from parental supervision. The Board of Guardians of the Jewish Community of Amsterdam supplied most of the needs of the Jewish poor of the city.

There were loan societies and Jewish vacation homes. The Council for Jewish Women did excellent work, and the Maatschappytot Nut der Israelieten in Nederland (Society for the Benefit of the Jews in the Netherlands) supported students and maintained other cultural activities.

History of Anti-Semitism.

The National Socialist movement, called N.S.B. (Beweging) in Holland, was founded in 1931 by Anton A. Mussert, who was a civil engineer in government service, and a second-rate demagogue. His colleague and co-worker was Rost van Tonningen, a financial expert who was for a number of years in charge of the Netherlands Bank, but who was also a great fanatic.

The N.S.B. followed the German example, organizing drills and the usual pattern of anti-Semitism. During the depression, they used prevailing conditions as an argument to spread discontent among the people. As a result, at the 1935 provincial council elections, they obtained 8% of all votes cast, which was the highest they ever reached, because subsequent events in Germany aligned the people of Holland strongly against the N.S.B., and caused them to rally around the House of Orange and the legitimate government. In the 1939 elections for provincial councils, the N.S.B. drew no more than 3.7% of the votes. They never had more than four members out of the 100 in the Lower Chamber.

A special racial approach was used in Holland. Dutch nationality was talked of in a wider sense, to embrace the Flemings and the South Africans, but exclude Jews and others. The argument was never very successful.

Christian Churches and the Jews.

Before the Hitler attack, the attitude of the representatives of the different churches in Holland to Jews was very friendly. Since the invasion, warm cooperation has been extended by the churches and strong protests against the deportations of Jews from Holland have been made by the heads of Catholic and Protestant communities. Public protests were read in all churches.

The churches have also constantly supported resistance against anti-Jewish legislation by secretly distributing pamphlets calling for resistance. On October 24, 1940, they sent the following message to Nazi-Commissar Seyss-Inquart: "The sufferings which the execution of this measure will inflict on thousands of men, women and children and their entire families and the realization that it contravenes the profound moral and ethical feelings of the people of Holland, compel us urgently to request that this measure shall not become effective."

In September 1941 a pastoral letter of the General Synod of the Dutch Reformed Church stated: "The Jews have lived among us for centuries and are bound with us in a common history and a common responsibility." And in 1942 they said: "The Church would fail grossly to do its duty if it did not call on the authorities to halt these measures."

On February 17, 1943 a delegation of representatives of Protestant Churches of all denominations and of Roman Catholic Bishops of Holland saw Reichs-Commissar Seyss-Inquart, and protested against persecutions of Jews. On May 16, 1943 another protest was voiced to Seyss-Inquart against the newly-instituted sterilization of Jews in Holland. This protest was made by the Netherland Reformed Church, Roman Catholic Church, Calvinist Churches, Baptist Society and Evangelical Lutheran Church. They wrote: "There is now taking place in our country something so monstrous".... and exhorted Seyss-Inquart "to prohibit these infamous practices at once."

Attitude of People and Government: Before Invasion.

The traditional attitude of the Dutch toward freedom of religion expressed itself very clearly in their actions in regard to their Jewish fellow-citizens, as well as on behalf of the Jewish victims of persecution outside the country. The Queen changed her broadcasts from Friday nights to another time so that her Jewish subjects would be able to listen in. The rabbis and representatives of the Jewish communities and important organizations attended the annual audiences of the Queen. The Queen visited Jewish institutions and synagogues. After the advent of the Hitler regime, the Dutch government put at the disposal of a special committee, for a very small amount, some new land just reclaimed from the Zuyderzee, to be used as a training camp for victims of Nazi persecution who planned to migrate to Palestine.

In May 1934 an act was introduced by which the instigation of racial and religious hatred was made punishable. In March 1936 an anti-Semitic propagandist was ostentatiously punished with 100 days imprisonment.

During the Nazi persecutions it was easy to pass the Dutch borders, and although the number of emigrées increased abnormally, the borders were never closed for those whose lives were in danger. In March 1938 some immigration restrictions were applied, partly because of pressure from the Nazi party within.

After the November 1938 pogroms in Germany, 100,000 gilders were collected in one day for a special fund for the persecuted, and the Dutch government demanded compensation for damage done to property of Dutch Jews residing in Germany. At the same time the borders were re-opened, and between November 10th and December 4th, 4,000 refugees entered the country. A special camp for illegal entrants was established, and in some of the camps, inhabited parctically by Jews only, arrangements were made for the provision of kosher food.

Attitude of People and Government: After the Invasion.

There are numerous examples of the aid and sympathy offered by the Christian people to their Jewish compatriots. They have protected Jews in their houses, keeping them in hiding at the danger of their own lives; they have given them all kinds of support in the way of food when it was not in abundance. They have organized strikes, as in Amsterdam, to protest against anti-Jewish measures. Many boycott the theatres, cinemas and cafés where Jews are not allowed to enter. The populations of several Dutch towns have defied the orders of the German occupation authorities to rename streets named for Jews.

When Jews were ordered to don the yellow star, many non-Jews also attached it to their clothing, and showed conspicuous respect for Jews in the street. Non-Jewish doctors remained loyal to their Jewish fellow-practitioners. Professors and teachers protested widely against the anti-Jewish measures.

Christians secretly took photographs of disfigured synagogues and other buildings belonging to Jews, and distributed the prints on a large scale throughout the country. In January 1942 fifty butchers banded together to aid a Jewish butcher whom the German authorities had excluded from receiving meat for his clients.

In November 1942 a yellow pamphlet was distributed by Holland's underground asking that the mass deportation of Jews be sabotaged. When the first group of Jews was sent off the Germans, fearing disorders, were obliged to call out extra police protection. Jews were reported receiving the aid of Dutch physicians in obtaining certificates of lunacy, which saved them from deportation.

On September 11, 1942, (the eve of the Jewish New Year) Prime Minister Peter Gerbrandy broadcast a message of sympathy from London. The Queen repeatedly spoke of her indignation; she awarded the Distinguished Service Cross to a Dutch Jew for sabotage against Nazis in Holland. A special service was held at the Dutch Protestant Church in London for Dr. Henri Polak, a Jew, who had been a labor leader and member of the Senate, and who died in March 1943 after imprisonment by the Nazis.

In general, the friendship and assistance of Dutch non-Jews towards Jews has never been stronger than it is today.

Discrimination Before the Invasion.

There was no legal discrimination at all against the Jews in Holland. On the contrary, everything was done to help the Jews keep their Jewish laws and observances, especially as regards the Sabbath. For instance, weekly tramway tickets for high school students and others were valid on Sundays instead of the Sabbath.

There was some unofficial anti-Semitism. Some very important clubs would not admit Jewish members. But these cases were very rare.

"Aryanization."

The April 1943 report of the German Chamber of Commerce in Holland gives details of the "Aryanization" of Jewish concerns. The Chamber was to investigate the qualifications when trustees for Jewish firms were appointed. The total value of Jewish-owned real estate, business and capital confiscated by the Germans was estimated by the Frankfurter Zeitung at half a billion gilders. This does not include all collections of art, precious stones and other valuables which were to be deposited in the bank which deputized for the Nazi control. In June 1942 the Frankfurter Zeitung stated that of 21,000 Jewish enterprises, 10,000 must be liquidated. Of the remaining 11,000, 8,000 had accepted "Aryanization" voluntarily and the remaining 3,000 were to be transferred by the authorities. According to this newspaper, the value of Jewish concerns which were "Aryanized" was estimated at 150,000,000 gilders. The value of the real estate "taken over" from Jews was estimated at 200,000,000 gilders.

Registration.

Early in 1941, registration of Jews or those who were partly Jewish was ordered. Identification cards were given and marked with the letter J for those who were full Jews. Part Jews were stamped B-I or B-II (B standing for bastard) if descended from only one Jewish grandparent. But the Dutch people were so indignant at this terminology that a few weeks later the terms were changed by the German authorities to G-I and G-II, G standing for gemengde, which means mixed.

All Jewish-owned business concerns had to register in October 1940. About 30,000 fell within the ruling, determined by Nuremberg definitions.

Public Places; Identification Badge.

On September 17, 1941, a decree was published barring Jews from libraries, museums, swimming pools, beaches, theatres, cinemas, sports events, pullmans, dining cars, restaurants, cafes, public parks, hotels and boarding houses. Jews were permitted to leave their residence only by special permission.

On April 30, 1942, the Nazis in Amsterdam decreed that all Jews over the age of six were forbidden to appear in public without a yellow Star of David. At the same time, Jews were not permitted to wear military decorations or other insignia.

Transportation.

In May 1942 Jews were forbidden to travel in trains or to use any other public transportation facility. They were commanded to give up horses and vehicles in their possession, including bicycles. This was a severe blow, because hardly anywhere in the world is the bicycle so much used as a means of transport.

Communications.

Jews were not allowed to own radio sets. They were not allowed to use telephones without special permission.

Sterilization.

The Germans ordered the sterilization of all Jewish men or women who had married non-Jews, but Dutch doctors refused to perform the operation and German military doctors were dispatched to do the work. According to reports in November 1943, 25,000 Jews were sterilized in one week. Then, "since they were no longer harmful to the purity of the Nordic race" they were no longer obliged to wear the Star of David.

Prior to the Hitler regime, there had been no sterilization at all, not even of feeble-minded.

Forced Prostitution.

In 1942 there were reports that several 16-year-old Jewish girls from Amsterdam had been sent to German army camps.

Concentration Camps.

Dutch Jews were kept in concentration camps at Buchenwalde (where at first the treatment was reported as not bad, but where later deaths were numerous). Many Jews also died in the camp at Mauthausen, Austria, where they were assumed to have been working in the mines. In Holland there were concentration camps at Westerbork, Vught and Barneveld. Barneveld was said to contain privileged Jews, and conditions here were somewhat better.

Forced Labor.

Hundreds of young Dutch Jews were reported to have been sent to work in white lead factories, where many died. The salt and sulphur mines at Mauthausen also took the lives of hundreds.

Jewish Groups-in-Exile.

The largest group of Dutch Jews is in the United States, with a few thousand living in New York City. There is a Netherlands Jewish Society, of which Rabbi D. A. Jessurun Cardozo is the President. Most of the Dutch Jews in England live in London and are organized in a Kring van Nederlandsche Joden in Engeland (Circle of Netherlands Jews in England). The Kring publishes a <u>Rondschrijven</u> (circular letter). There is also a group in Switzerland.

The Jewish congregations in the Netherlands West Indies remain active since the colonies are still independent. A small influx of Jews from the mother country has come to this region and Jewish life has been strengthened, particularly in Curacao, where the rabbi is Is. Jessurun Cardozo of the Congregation Mikveh Israel. The Sephardic colony here is more than three centuries old, and includes some important bankers and shipping agents, such as the Maduro family. Surinam (Dutch Guiana) has a Jewish population of about 800; there are two congregations in Paramaribo.

Reconstruction Agencies.

In addition to groups of Dutch Jews in other countries, foreign reconstruction agencies which might help in the rehabilitation of the Jews of Holland are the American Jewish Joint Distribution Committee, the American Joint-Reconstruction Foundation, the HICEM (Hias-Ica Emigration Association), the ORT Society for the promotion of trade and agriculture among Jews, the OSE World Union for health protection and the Jewish Agency for Palestine.

THE JEWS OF HUNGARY

THE JEWS OF HUNGARY

Index

Age Structure	9	Judiciary, The	8
Agriculture	12	Languages	5
Anti-Semitism, History of	24	Liquidation	19
"Aryanization"	14	Marriage	4
Attitude toward War and toward the United States	5	Medical Practitioners	18
		Minority Rights	6
Banking	11	Mortality Rate	19
Bar, The	9	Motion Pictures	16
Birth Rate	19	Natural Resources	12
Child Care	23	Occupational Structure	
Christian Churches and the Jews	26	Before Jew Laws	9
Citizenship	6	After Jew Laws	11
Commerce	13	Parliament, Jews in	7
Communal and Fraternal Groups	3	Police	28
Cooperatives	16	Political Affiliations	7
Criminality	5	Population	1
Discriminatory Measures	27	Press	
Extra-Legal Discrimination	27	Anti-Semitic	26
Divorce	4	General	16
Economic Structure		Jewish	16
Before Jew Laws	9	Public Service, Jews in	8
After Jew Laws	11	Rationing	29
Education	19	Reconstruction Agencies	33
Employment	14	Refugees	1
Family Life	4	Regulations	
Fascist Parties and Leaders	25	Commercial; Passport; Travel	29
Fines	30	Religious Community Organization	2
Forced Labor	29	Assets	4
Funerals	4	Functionaries	4
Government Agencies for Jewish Affairs	6	Social Insurance	17
		Sterilization	19
Groups-in-Exile	31	Taxes	30
Health; Housing; Hygiene	17	Trade Unions	15
Hospitals	18		
Identification Cards	29	Underground Movement	7
Industry	13		
Insurance	12	Wages	14
Jewish Court of Arbitration	3		
Jewish Leaders		Welfare, Jewish	21
In Hungary	31		
In Exile	32	Welfare Workers	23

THE JEWS OF HUNGARY

Population; Refugees.

According to the last official census (1930), the number of confessing Jews in Hungary was 444,567, or 5.1% of the total population. Territorial changes following the Munich agreement augmented the Jewish population under Hungarian rule approximately as follows:

Some 75,000 Jews in Southern Slovakia (in Hungarian terminology, the "Upper Land") were shifted from Czechoslovakia rule; about 90,000 were added with the occupation of Carpatho-Ruthenia; some 160,000 came in the transfer of Northern Transylvania from Roumanian control, and 15,000 were added after the Nazi attack on Yugoslavia.

The available data on conversion to Christianity cover only the pre-Munich territory, and are not complete. After the Communist regime and the counter-revolutionary period of 1919, which brought acute anti-Semitism, 11,146 Jews became Christians. Between 1919 and 1937, official estimates state that an average of 400 were converted annually, a number almost counterbalanced by an annual average of 300 to 350 conversions of Christians to Judaism. In 1938, the vain hope of escaping the consequences of the First Jew Law prompted another 8,584 Jews to assume Christianity. Regarding the annexed territories, the total number of conversions that took place there after 1930 may be estimated 35,000.

According to the census of 1930, 204,371 Jews, or 46% of the total pre-Munich Jewish population lived in Budapest, the capital, where they made up 20.3% of the population. By the end of 1935, their number had decreased to 201,069. In the most important regions under Hungarian control in 1943, the percentages of Jewish population were: Transdanubia: 2.3%, the Hungarian Lowland (incl. Budapest 6.9%, Zemplen county: 8.5%, Szabolcs and Ung counties: 6.5%, Szatmar, Ugocsa and Bereg counties: 6.2%, former Slovak territory: 4.1%, former Carpatho-Ruthenia: 14.1%, Transylvania: 4.2% and former Yugoslav territory: 1%. The average percentage of Jews in the general urban population in 1930 was 14.8%, in the rural population 2.8%.

The Jewish population in Hungary began to decrease in 1920, with the inception of anti-Semitic policies. From 1920 to 1930, the total number of Jews dropped from 473,355 to 444,567, or a decrease of 28,788, while the general population increased by 698,117. During this period, the natural increase among the Jews was only 2,256.

The number of confessing Jews under Hungarian rule in 1942-43 may be estimated as follows: In pre-Munich Hungary, 444,000; in the annexed territories: Slovakian, 75,000; Carpatho-Ruthenia, 90,000; Northern Transylvania, 170,000; Northern Yugoslavia, 15,000. Deducting from this total of 794,000 an estimated natural decrease for twelve years of an annual average of 1,600, which amounts to 19,000, and an estimate of 35,000 conversions since 1930, a remaining total, in 1943, of 740,000 is reached.

However, anti-Jewish legislation considered as Jews all persons who had themselves, or whose one parent or two grandparents had at any time, belonged to the Jewish religious fold. This category brought about 60,000 or 70,000 additional people into the Jewish listing, so that the total number of victims of anti-Jewish legislation in Hungary was probably about 800,000.

Greater Budapest, with 232,212 Jews in 1930, had the second largest Jewish community in pre-war Europe. After the destruction of the Jewish community of Warsaw, Budapest took first place. While in 1930 it had contained more than half the Jewish population of Hungary, the addition of the annexed territories brought the proportion down to 23%. Other large Jewish communities were: Ujpest (near Budapest), 11,396, or 13% of the population of the city; Miskolc, 10,862 (19%); Munkacs (Carpatho-Ruthenia), 10,500 (60%); and Debrecen, 10,044 (13%).

Between 1937 and 1942 some 6,500 Jews from Hungary and the annexed territories came to the United States. Between 1938 and 1941, about 2,000 went to Palestine. No more than 2,000 reached other countries. The total number of Jews who left pre-Munich Hungary and the annexed territories during the period of Hitler influence was probably around 10,000.

RELIGIOUS COMMUNITY ORGANIZATION

The Reception Law (1895: XLII) declared the Jewish religion to be one of the "incorporated and recognized" denominations, enjoying full privileges of the other denominations so recognized, which were the Roman Catholic, Evangelical Reformed, Evangelical Protestant, Greek Orthodox Serbian and Greek Catholic Roman. It excluded encroachments of any kind on the part of any religious confession upon any other confession, provided for compulsory Jewish religious education in all public educational and welfare institutions as well as in the army, and for the proportionate participation of Jewish religious or educational institutions in public subsidies. Membership in the recognized religious community was compulsory.

Law 1895: XLIII, guaranteed full free exercise of religious practices and declared the exercise of civic and political rights to be independent of religious affiliations.

Jewish members of the armed forces were allowed to observe Jewish holidays, and Jewish pupils in the public schools could be excused from writing on the Sabbath. Until 1938, the right to observe ritual slaughter laws was never interfered with.

In February, 1869, the Jewish religious community of Hungary was granted the right to form its own organic statute and representative organization, to maintain public confessional educational institutions and to levy specific Jewish community taxes, in the collection of which the state tax collection service would cooperate. As early as 1855, Jewish religious and educational institutions had received annual state subsidies.

The Law 1926: XXII provided for the official representation of the Jewish religious community in the Upper House of the Hungarian Parliament by two rabbis elected by the Jewish community to be life-long members. In October, 1940, this representation was abolished by decree. In December, 1941, the Reception Law of 1895 was revoked, reducing Judaism to one of the "non-recognized" minor religious denominations. Freedom of worship was not affected, but communal life was handicapped by the withdrawal of state assistance in the collection of communal taxes, and of state subsidies to Jewish religious institutions. Membership in the community was evidently still compulsory.

The community organization of Hungarian Jews was divided into three officially recognized groups: the Congressional (neolog-progressive), the Orthodox, and the Satus Quo Ante center organizations. The Congressional organization, consisting largely of intelligensia and economically significant circles, led in importance. It was centered in Budapest, and had affiliated communities in most of the larger cities. The Orthodox organization was concentrated in the northeastern sector of the country, and derived its constituency from smaller conservative communities. The Status Quo organizations comprised only a few provincial communities. Each group had a so-called National Chancery, authorized to handle internal and official matters. Only the Congressional and Orthodox groups had obtained representation in the Upper House. In the 1930's the three groups, while remaining separate, cooperated in political matters, largely under the guidance of the Congressional faction.

Religious observance was widespread. The Jewish high holidays brought even the community of Budapest to a standstill; many baptized Jews observed them. Nazi oppression strengthened this religious steadfastness. Hassidism was of minor importance, being almost entirely confined to Carpatho-Ruthenia.

JEWISH COURT OF ARBITRATION

A Din Torah, or Jewish religious arbitration system, was restricted to rabbinical jurisdiction in matters of religious practice or to arbitration in civilian matters voluntarily submitted by the litigants. Decisions had no legal validity. The three National Chanceries representing the three leading factions within the Jewish religious community could sit in litigation between Jewish communities and religious functionaries. For this purpose, the Congressional and Status Quo Chanceries maintained elected district courts, whose decisions were appellable to and enforced by the Minister of Cults and Education.

COMMUNAL AND FRATERNAL GROUPS

Despite the fact that Theodore Herzl, the founder of political Zionism, and Max Nordau, one of its greatest proponents, were both born in Hungary, political Zionism did not make significant inroads among Hungarian Jews until the beginning of the Hitler era, when there was a noticeable increase in the acceptance of the Zionist idea.

Most important Jewish fraternal groups were the Hebra Kadisha, which not only provided religious burial ceremonies and cared for the graves of its members, but undertook the charitable support of the poor, members and non-members alike. In Budapest the society maintained two large cemeteries, a general hospital, a hospital for incurable diseases and a home for the aged. Lodges like the B'nai B'rith or the B'rith Abraham did not exist in Hungary. Several smaller self-help societies in Budapest were devoted largely to sick relief. Further relief work was carried on by special groups, including cultural societies, literary societies, an agricultural and handicraft society, various orphanages, hospitals and other institutions. The Jewish womens clubs had projects of their own.

COMMUNITY ASSETS; FUNCTIONARIES.

Although the Jewish community budgets in Hungary were based on compulsory taxation, freeing the communities from dependence on capital property, the Budapest Jewish community was one of the wealthiest in Europe, both in regard to the importance of its institutions and their real value. No confiscations of Jewish communal property seem to have resulted from the Hitler influence, except that, together with a number of non-Jewish medical institutions, the three Jewish hospitals in Budapest were commandeered by the army early in 1943 for use as military hospitals.

Neither rabbis nor lesser functionaries in the religious setup of Hungary could be regarded as having an active role in politics or any other field outside that of religious leadership.

MARRIAGE AND DIVORCE

For legal purposes, both religious marriage and religious divorce were irrelevant, since only civil proceedings were valid in both cases. The Hungarian marriage law of 1874: XXXI, forbade the solemnization of a religious wedding without presentation of a civil marriage certificate. There was no legal impediment against intermarriage.

In December, 1941, an anti-Semitic marriage law was passed, forbidding mixed marriages as well as extra-marital relations between Jewish men and "decent" non-Jewish women. As the news of the proposed bill became known, the number of conversions of Christian women to Jewish faith increased conspicuously; official figures show that 546 conversions of this kind occurred in 1942 when mixed marriage was barred. Prosecution for extra-marital relationships between Jewish men and "decent" non-Jewish women frequently led to a classification of all but publicly registered prostitutes as "decent", and the subsequent punishment of the man.

FUNERALS

The Reception Law (1895: XLII) provided that members of any religious community could be buried without hindrance in any burial ground. In practice, however, separate burial grounds had always been assigned to the Christian and Jewish communities; cemeteries for Jews were put at the disposal of the Jewish communities by the local municipalities. In this situation and in Jewish religious funeral practices no change is known to have occurred after the establishment of Hitler's influence over Hungary. Several Jewish cemeteries, however, were damaged by vandalism.

FAMILY LIFE

Paternal authority among the Jews of Hungary was generally the same as is found in average middle-class society. In ultra-Orthodox groups, the father was more assertive, sometimes even to the extent of choosing mates for the children.

Similarly, the position of the wife was substantially the same as in other middle-class groups, except that in some ultra-conservative circles, her prestige depended on whether she had succeeded in bearing a son or not. Jewish parents, as a whole, were considered more attached to their children than non-Jewish Hungarian parents, and there was closer economic solidarity among the members of a family, and a greater degree of readiness for mutual aid.

LANGUAGES

Almost every Jew in Hungary speaks Hungarian well. In the annexed territories, where the younger generation had been educated in Ruthenian or Slovak, there was some deficiency in Hungarian. Long association with Austria made German the most widely used second language among Hungarian Jews, between 80 and 85% of whom mastered some degree of German. In Carpatho-Ruthenia, in the Eastern section of the Slovakian territory, and in Northern Transylvania, the mother tongue of the great majority of the Jewish population was Yiddish. Elsewhere in Hungary, Yiddish had become almost unknown. English was a favorite third language of the intelligensia, Jewish and non-Jewish alike. Jews, however, commanded more languages than other citizens. With the advent of Hitlerism, the study of English among Hungarian Jews became even more widespread. Although the Jews always spoke some degree of the language of the particular section of Hungary in which they lived, language conflicts did not arise until after the frontier disputes which followed the First World War and the Munich Pact.

CRIMINALITY; ALCOHOLISM

The degree of probity found among the Jews was very high. Although, under the economic pressure of Nazi influence, the involvement of Jews in the so-called "intellectual delicts", like fraud or forgery (notably of documents of citizenship) increased, their share in violent crimes remained practically nil. Propaganda statistics published by the authorities were doctored to include the charges made against Jewish writers and journalists for resisting reactionary forces, and against other Jews for violating currency restrictions, which violation offered almost the only expedient for the purchase of foreign raw material.

Jewish restraint in the use of alcoholic beverages was proverbial in Hungary. Tobacco was widely used, but there was no data on the use of narcotics.

ATTITUDE TOWARD WAR AND THE UNITED STATES

The attitude of Hungarian Jews toward the present war can hardly be questioned, since for them the victory of Hitler would mean death and the victory of the allies salvation. That the victory of Hitler would also be tantamount to the end of Hungary is no small factor in their ardent allegiance to the allied cause. The United States is to them a great power viewing European matters unselfishly and fated to save democracy and civilization for a better world. The number of Jews convicted for spreading news favorable to the Allied cause, for anti-German agitation and for sabotage is proof of the deep alignment Hungarian Jews have for the democratic victory.

CITIZENSHIP

Before the submission to Hitlerian pressure, the citizenship status of Jews was determined by Law 1867: XVII, which confirmed the equality of the "Jewish inhabitants" of Hungary in the exercise and enjoyment "of the same civil and political rights as the Christian population." The Jew Laws of 1938 and 1939, although curtailing drastically some of the civic and political rights of the Jews, did not reduce them to the level of mere subjects. All regulations applied also to the residents of the annexed territories.

Although the acquisition of citizenship through naturalization, marriage or adoption was forbidden by the law of 1939, it was not retroactive. More serious was the power of denaturalization granted for any Jew and his dependents "whose circumstances do not necessitate their stay in the country," for this was a matter allowing much interpretative license. In practice, however, little use had been made of this weapon.

Statelessness, before the discriminatory laws went into effect, had little application. Some Jews, opting for Hungarian citizenship after the frontier realignments that followed the First World War, failed to obtain official papers. Under Goemboes, Jews were required to produce citizens' certificates for any administrative procedure. This was made difficult not only because of frequent failure to follow through opted citizenship, but because official matriculation had been introduced only in 1895. Between 40% and 50% of the Jews in Hungary were therefore unable to authenticate their citizenship. In the summer of 1941, a combination of Nazi dissatisfactions resulted in the rounding up of the 18,000 Jews mentioned above chosen from among those who could not "authenticate" their citizenship, and their deportation to Galicia, for almost complete extermination.

MINORITY RIGHTS

The Jews had persistently refused to avail themselves of the minority rights clauses in the Peace Treaty of Trianon, on the ground that their long history of equality in Hungary demanded that infractions be remedied on the basis of equality and not of minority rights. The special treatments outlined in the Jew Laws have not brought minority rights, but minority disabilities.

Since minority rights had never existed, political gerrymandering was indirect. The system of the open ballot in the provinces made franchise a farce. In addition, provincial districts were so delimited as to make a constituency of a few hundred people, while in the cities -- where secret balloting was practiced -- 10,000 to 20,000 voters were necessary for the election of a representative to parliament. This served to diminish the value of votes cast by Jews and other liberal groups, who were congregated largely in cities. By the specification that active and passive franchise could be exercised only by those Jews whose parents and grandparents had been born in Hungary, the Second Jew Law cut down the number of enfranchised Jews in Budapest from 288,000 to 100,000.

GOVERNMENT AGENCIES FOR JEWISH AFFAIRS

Since Jews were not a minority, but a religious community, their affairs were handled -- until the promulgation of the Jew Laws -- by the Ministry of Cults and Education, an arrangement which continued into 1943. Anti-Jewish legislation and its execution were put into the hands of a Government Commissar of the Intellectual Professions, directly responsible to the Minister of the Interior. Penalties for infringement were administered by ordinary police and court procedure, with the assistance of the Government Commissar.

POLITICAL AFFILIATIONS

Before the Hitler influence became acute, Jews participated widely in the activities of the National Liberal Party (Nemzeti Liberalis Part), which was founded in 1920 and headed by Representative Charles Rassay, and in the National Democratic Party (Nemzeti Demokrata Part) which was founded by William Vaszonyi, a Jew who was Minister of Justice. After Vaszonyi's death the two groups united, under Rassay's leadership, in the National Liberal Party, which had the support of the Jewish middle-class and intelligensia. The largest number of representatives this party ever had in parliament was 17, among whom were five Jews. In 1943, it had five representatives, including one Jew, Ernest Brody. The Social Democratic party (Szocial Demokrata Part) had the support of Jewish workers and Jewish socialistic intellectuals; in 1943 it had five representatives in parliament. During the conservative-liberal Bethlen government (1923-30) the Jewish upper middle-class and industrialists supported the government party; representative Geza Desi, a Jew, was considered Count Bethlen's liaison officer with the Jewish population. No specific Jewish political parties ever existed.

UNDERGROUND MOVEMENT

The existence of a quasi-parliamentarian system, even under Nazi influence, did not favor the development of underground political activities to the same extent as in other Eastern European countries. However, the large number of political trials, the sentencing of many common people -- including an exceptionally high proportion of Jews -- for political offenses, and the frequency of unsolved sabotage incidents seems to indicate the presence of an underground combination of the democratic and patriotic anti-Nazi political groups. There can be no doubt that Jewish support is resolutely behind this tendency. In 1943, the strength of the communist underground seemed to be limited, although during 1942 a few communist groups had been apprehended by the regime. Under the pressure of rapidly deteriorating social conditions, the communist movement might expand considerably.

JEWS IN PARLIAMENT

During the Horthy regime, the average number of Jews in the House of Representatives varied between 10 and 12, including 5 or 6 liberals and democrats, the rest Social Democrats and one government party (Bethlen group) representative. The most outstanding parliamentarians of the period who were Jews were William Vaszonyi, previously Minister of Justice and secret court councillor, and founder and head of the National Democratic Party, and Representative Paul Sandor. Two Jews were appointed members of the Upper House, and two rabbis were elected by the Jewish religious confessions. The Jew Laws annulled the appointments of the two appointed members to the Upper House, but not the rabbinical representation. This was later abolished by a decree lacking legal foundation.

JEWS IN PUBLIC SERVICE

During the liberal era which came to an end with the First World War, the participation of Jews in public service was not numerically large, but it included representation in almost every field. Several ministers of finance and of commerce were Jews or former Jews. Jews also held the posts of minister of justice and undersecretary of justice; there were several Jewish generals, one of whom -- during the First World War -- was minister for the Hungarian army under the Minister of War; there were at various times at least four Jews in the Supreme Court, one who was assistant attorney general, and numerous judges in both the higher and lower courts. A number were university professors (the universities were state institutions). Both a Jew and a former Jew were chairmen of the State Railways, a Jew was head of the State Statistical Office and another of the Patent Court. In Budapest a Jew held the post of Lord Mayor and another vice-mayor. In the lower brackets, the number of Jews was not great, partly because of the absence of a marked trend among Jews for public employment, and partly because the gentry of officialdom were not hospitable to Jews. Under the Horthy regime, many of the Jews serving as officials were weeded out, so that by the beginning of the Hitler era, only a few dozen remained in inconspicuous jobs.

In the county governments, a part of the council was chosen without election, on the basis of high tax payments. Thus, although provincial counties rarely elected Jews to their councils, a number of wealthy Jews nevertheless found places on them.

In Budapest, before the Horthy regime, about 1/3 of the city council consisted of Jews. There were several Jews who served as city commissioners. Under the Horthy regime, the number of Jews serving as municipal council members considerably declined, but prior to the execution of the Second Jew Law, there were still some 25 Jews or former Jews on the Budapest municipal council. The Second Jew Law provided that Jews could not be members of municipal councils unless elected. Although the principle allowing high taxpayers to serve on the councils remained, Jews could no longer be so appointed. A large number of elected municipal council members were deprived of their seats because they could not prove that they themselves, their parents or grandparents had lived on Hungarian territory consecutively since December 31, 1867.

Only Jews exempt from the specifications of the Second Jew Law remained in public service in 1943. These included war veterans with at least one decoration, war invalids more than 50% incapacitated, war widows and orphans, those who risked their lives in the anti-Communist struggles of 1919, secret councillors, university professors, ministers of a Christian religion and Olympic champions. In 1943 no Jew held any significant position in public service.

THE JUDICIARY

Jews had held prominent judicial posts during the liberal era, but had been almost eliminated under the Horthy regime. The last Jew to hold a high judiciary post was Dr. Charles Foedy, until 1938 a member of the Administrative Supreme Court and head of the religious tribunal of the Congressional National Chancery. Discrimination against the Jews by the judiciary could be effected only through loopholes. A series of laws dealing with matters like the "defamation of the nation" and offenses against the "order of the State and of Society" permitted the judiciary to deal harshly with Jewish political offenders, although the measures were not directed specifically against Jews.

THE BAR

Hungarian Lawyers' Chambers were not conspicuously anti-Semitic before the Hitler era. The Budapest Chamber had been fairly liberal; its chairman for many years, Dr. Joseph Pap, opposed anti-Semitic tendencies within the Chamber and also in the Upper House, of which he was a member. During the Horthy regime, however, the younger generation of lawyers turned to a more flagrant anti-Jewish attitude, under the influence of the unofficial National Lawyers' League. A Numerus Clausus law for lawyers, restricting admission to professional chambers and therefore to professional practice, was enacted in 1934 or 1935. But this was not openly directed against Jewish lawyers; its avowed purpose was to limit the admission of all lawyers, and thus to prevent further professional overcrowding. The result, however, was unquestionably a reduction in the number of new Jewish lawyers.

Under the Jew Laws, the legal status of Jews who had been members of the Lawyers' Chambers before the enactment of the laws was not changed. Article 9 of the Second Jew Law stipulated that no additional Jews may become members of the Lawyers' Chambers until the percentage of Jews in the membership roster has fallen below 6% of the total. So numerous were Jews in the legal profession that it would take many years for this percentage to be reached by natural processes. In October, 1941, the National Lawyers' League demanded that Jewish and Masonic office-holders be barred from the Chambers; the demand was rejected by a majority of the Chambers. In April, 1942, they proposed that non-Jewish lawyers should wear special badges in court to identify themselves before the judge as racial and ideological comrades. This proposal was rejected by both the Chambers and the government. By a decree of September 13, 1941, Jews who were pensioned judges and state attorneys were ordered admitted to the Lawyers' Chambers. No special lawyers were appointed to plead for Jews, as was done in other countries under Nazi control.

The position of public notary was much coveted, very lucrative and socially distinguished; it was in effect a monopoly given by the governments to a limited number of "distinguished partisans." Even in the liberal era, few Jews were notaries; during the Horthy regime, none was appointed.

AGE STRUCTURE

The census figures of 1930 already showed that a process of decline in the young age group was well under way among Hungarian Jews; Jewish children under six years of age represented only 2.9% of all Hungarian children of that age group. In 1938 the percentage was only 2.4%, instead of 5.1, in accordance with the proportion of Jews in the total population. Without doubt, there was even more of a drop after 1938.

OCCUPATIONAL AND ECONOMIC STRUCTURE: BEFORE JEW LAWS

In 1920, Jews represented 5.4% of the gainfully employed population of Hungary; in 1930, 5.1%. In 1930, their principal categories of occupation, and the percentages they held in each category, were as follows: trade and credit (incl. banking and insurance), 40.0%; pensionists, rentiers and house-owners, 9.1%; public service and independent (liberal) occupations, 8.9%; industry, 8.3%; other occupations, 5.7%; transportation, 3.7%; day labor 1.4%; domestic service, 1.0%; mining, 0.8%; agriculture, 0.3%.

In a prevalently agrarian country, the Jews were almost completely absent from agricultural occupations, ... and were active in commercial and financial life. Between 1920 and 1930, however, economic anti-Semitism lowered the percentage of Jews engaged in trade and credit from 45.1 to 40.0. During that period, Jewish participation in "other occupations" rose from 5.1 to 5.7% and in day labor by 0.1%. Both increases showed the obstacles which Jews were finding to participation in commerce and other traditional Jewish means of livelihood. Their disproportionate involvement in the commerce, trade, and professions of Hungary had been abetted by 1) their exclusion--following emancipation--from landownership, agricultural labor, public and military service; 2) their adaptability to economic and intellectual enterprise; and 3) the lack of initiative among Hungarian non-Jews for economic functions. The last-named fact was attested to as late as December 24, 1942, by the <u>Völkischer Beobachter</u> (Berlin), which described the difficulties of finding "Aryan" successors for the economic life of Hungary, and stated: "In spite of all efforts of responsible factors, [Hungarian] youth still does not want even to hear of commercial or industrial pursuits."

Within the various occupations, Jewish participation was as follows (1930):

In trade and credit: independent, 45.6%; office employees and salesmen, 47.6%; physical workers, 29.1%.

In industry: independent, 11.0%; office employees, engineers, etc., 33.4%; physical workers, 5.6%.

In the independent (liberal) occupations: independent (lawyers, physicians, engineers), 34.2%; office employees, 7.4%; physical workers (office boys, etc.), 3.1%.

The participation of Jews in independent undertakings and white-collar work was obviously far greater than their percentage in the general population, but in trade and credit and in physical labor they were also represented in larger proportion. In 1930, the Jewish and Christian populations were divided in the three main social categories as follows:

	Jews		Christians	
Middle Class	91,840	43.1%	1,670,000	44.1%
Intellectual	53,478	25.1%	199,475	5.3%
Labor	67,917	31.8%	1,916,187	50.6%

Of 21,138 houses owned by physical persons in Budapest in 1930, 72.6% were owned by Christians, 26% by Jews (the percentage of Jews in the total population of the capital was 20.3) and the ownership of 301 houses remained unknown. It was highly probable that the percentage of Jewish ownership in the more valuable categories of real estate was higher than 26. Of a total of 16,173,178 cadastral acres of land and property, 790,173 acres, or 4.9%, were said to have been owned by Jews. These were mostly large holdings in the hands of wealthy families.

Although the above facts seem to indicate a strong middle-class position for a large part of the Jewish population, they reflected the situation only in small pre-Munich Hungary. In the annexed territories, the Jews were less favorably placed. Moreover, even in pre-Munich Hungary, the situation of the white-collar workers, of whom the Jews constituted a large portion, was hardly better than that of labor.

Many of the Jewish independent businessmen were small retailers even more precariously placed than laborers. As early as 1935, 100 Jewish breadwinners had to provide for 79 dependents; among the non-Jews the number was 73. In 1930, Jews already comprised only 18.3% of the total earning population of Budapest, while their percentage in the population was 20.3. At the end of 1934, access to gainful occupations began to be reserved -- through government pressure -- for Gentile applicants among the youth. The adoption of the First Jew Law in 1938 started the wholesale demolition of the rights and positions still held by the Jewish population.

ECONOMIC STRUCTURE: AFTER JEW LAWS

In June, 1940, the Jewish community of Budapest published a preliminary estimate of the social devastation inflicted upon the Jews of pre-Munich Hungary by the Second Jew Law (Law 1939:IV), whose measures were largely to be carried out before December 31, 1942. According to this estimate, and including dependents, 73,487 white-collar employees, 30,268 salesmen and other commercial representatives, 2,741 professionals, 13,500 possessing special monopoly licenses, and 20,400 possessors of trade licenses were earmarked for statutory elimination from social life. The total, 140,396, represents 31.5% of the Jewish population of pre-Munich Hungary. Together with those deprived of livelihoods before the Jew Laws, the total may be put at between 45 and 50%, which would leave some 400,000 Jews in Hungary without subsistence in 1943. It must not be forgotten also that the welfare of the other 50% of the Jewish population was in a sense interdependent on the ousted half, and also that an artificially-promoted anti-Jewish boycott must have had some bearing on the situation of the Jews.

Compared with the radical anti-Jewish measures adopted in other Eastern European countries under Nazi pressure, the Hungarian system bears certain distinguishing features. It did not affect property owned by Jews, except rural landed property expropriated by a law of July, 1942, and paid for in blocked, non-negotiable government bonds at $3\frac{1}{2}$%. By January, 1943, some 500,000 acres had been expropriated, affecting a relatively small group of landowners. Certain occupational categories were permitted limited continuation, including the professions, independently owned commercial and industrial enterprises. In private employment, 12% might remain Jewish. This 12% stipulation applied, however, not only to the number of employees but to the amount of the payroll. This frequently provoked the voluntary resignation of a high salaried Jewish manager in favor of a number of small salaried Jewish minor employees. The selection by the Jewish owners of business enterprises of non-Jewish license holders to represent them was evidently tacitly countenanced. Mob excesses and extra-legal interpretations of the Jew Law were not tolerated.

BANKING

Modern banking in Hungary was developed almost exclusively by Jews. The only exceptions were the hypothecary credit banks which were brought under state control by the grant of state subventions. The largest hypothecary credit bank was a typically non-Jewish establishment, but the four leading commercial and industrial banks were considered "Jewish banks." A "Jewish" bank was not necessarily one entirely owned by Jews. Stock ownership was scattered, and the Jewish management was in partnership with a number of aristocrats and non-Jewish capitalists. The largest commercial bank in Hungary is the Hungarian General Bank of Credit, formerly a branch of the Österreichische Credit Anstalt of Vienna, the Austrian branch of the Rothchild banking firm. In addition, the Baron Kornfeld and the Baron Ullmann families had been important in its development. The second largest commercial bank in Hungary was the Hungarian Commercial Bank of Pest, until recently headed by Philip Weiss and a group of managers who were or who had been Jews. The third of the leading group was the British-Hungarian Bank, Ltd., operating partly with British capital, and under the management of Jews.

With the inception of the Jew Laws, many of the bankers were forced to abandon their active role in the management of their institutions, and to transfer their functions to non-Jews they had themselves selected. Stock ownership was not affected, except in the Hungarian General Bank of Credit, the majority syndicate of which is reported to have been acquired by German banking interests. Only 12% of the personnel of the banks was allowed to be Jewish under the Jew Laws.

In general, Jews retained the right to free disposition of their bank deposits in Hungary. Deposits owned by persons who resided abroad for more than six months without government permit were sequestered; a measure obviously aimed at Jewish emigrés, without actually specifying them. No information was available about the confiscation of such funds.

INSURANCE

There was no change regarding the acquired rights of Jews who held insurance policies. Within the insurance business itself, the provisions of the Second Jew Law regarding percentages of employment were rigidly enforced. In 1943, no Jew held any leading position in any insurance company, and only 12% of the office staffs were Jews. This in spite of the fact that most of the important Hungarian insurance companies had been founded and managed by Jews.

NATURAL RESOURCES

Most of the important natural resources of Hungary are corporate property, but Jews were active in their development. The major mining enterprise is the Hungary General Coal Mine Co., Ltd., which belonged to the Hungarian General Bank of Credit, formerly managed by Jews. Its president, Eugene Vida, who was a Jew, was forced to resign in 1942. Since Germany took over control of the bank, the mining enterprise was also probably transferred to German supervision. Rimamurany-Salgotarjan Ltd. is the largest coal-iron-steel combine, controlled by the Hungarian Commercial Bank of Pest. Dr. Franz Chorin, who headed the management of the concern, was a vice-chairman of the bank. The Baron Weiss family held a large interest in the combine, which controlled Hungary's bauxite deposits, the largest in Europe. As far as could be ascertained, Dr. Chorin was still conducting the affairs of the concern in 1943, actually if not formally. According to recent news, some of the important natural resources, among them the bauxite mines and aluminum works, were "purchased" by Germany.

AGRICULTURE

In 1939, Jews constituted only 0.3% of Hungary's agricultural population, and owned 4.9% of the landed property, or 790,173 cadastral acres out of a total of 16,173,178. Land owned by Jews consisted mostly of middle-size estates (between

500 and 1,000 acres) and large estates (between 1,000 and 20,000 acres). A substantial part of this land was utilized in beet, potato, flax and hemp production, providing opportunities for corresponding agricultural industries. During the parliamentary debate over the Second Jew Law, even Nazi deputies admitted that the average Jewish-owned estate was better managed than other property, and that the economic position of the farm laborers employed by Jews was higher than average.

The Second Jew Law (#16) provided that Jewish landowners "may be obliged to make over all their landed property, for the purpose of property transfer or small tenancy." It also gave the state the sole right to purchase such land. Until 1942, this power was not used. Then a new law was promulgated ordering the expropriation of all landed property owned by Jews against the issuance of government bonds paying no capital, only an annual interest of 3%. In December, 1942, it was officially reported that some 550,000 cadastral acres had already been taken over by the government. Only members of the "Heroes Order", a militaristic political creation of Regent Horthy, were scheduled to obtain land from this pool; the genuinely landless peasantry was evidently ignored. Late in June, 1943, Premier Kallay reported that by the end of the year, all landed property owned by Jews would not only have been taken over, but distributed.

There were no Jewish agricultural cooperatives in Hungary.

INDUSTRY

Definite discrimination against Jews in industry by the government or by municipalities occurred only during the first period of the Horthy regime, ending in about 1924. It was manifest in the field of public supplies and bids. Later, and especially under the Bethlen government, the need for industrial development curtailed anti-Jewish discrimination in this field. Government-controlled cartels and monopolies were not directly discriminatory, excluding all private competition. Public monopolies, including alcohol, tobacco and salt, had been established in the 1880's, and Jewish business enterprise had long since adjusted itself to this limitation. Moreover, the licensing of a number of Jews as retailers in the monopoly fields provided some business opportunity.

The share Jews had in the development of industrial property was very high. In 1935, out of a total of 3,207 factories, 1,507, or 47%, were "owned or managed by Jews," according to statistics published in support of the First Jew Law. These figures may have been doctored; since most of these factories were corporately owned, the actual Jewish share in ownership was probably lower. Even when the majority of the stockholders were non-Jews, the managers were often Jews, and the firms were therefore classified as "Jewish." By 1943 most of the Jews in management had been ousted; only 12% of the office personnel was Jewish, instead of 33.4%, as in 1930. On the other hand, property rights of factory owners and shareholders who were Jews were not affected. Some of the major industries, however, were reported to have been taken over by German syndicates.

COMMERCE

In 1930, 45.6% of the total number of independent merchants in Hungary were Jews, and 47.6% of the commercial employees. Of 153 wholesale distributing houses, 120 were owned by Jews. In Budapest the proportion of participation may have been higher.

German anti-Semitism came to the aid of domestic anti-Semitic tendencies in 1936, after the Goemboes government had already coerced Jewish owners of firms into padding their payrolls with Christian employees. Early in 1936, the German Reichsstelle informed the Hungarian government that they would not further permit Hungarian Jewish cattle merchants to supply military horses. Horse export was promptly centralized in the agrarian cooperatives. Other German prohibitions provoked further withdrawals of export trade from Jews. This policy would have had disastrous results even before the introduction of the Jew Laws in 1938 and 1939, had the Hungarian government not tried, at the same time, to bolster the commercial connections held by Jews with French, British and American trade.

The Second Jew Law imposed a series of restrictions on the participation of Jews in domestic commerce, forbidding the issuance of new trade licenses to Jews until their proportion of held licenses had dropped to below 6% of the total. In practice, the rule was extended also to expired licenses still held by Jews, the renewal of which had always been a mere formality. Jews could not participate in deliveries to the state or to the municipalities beyond the following percentages of the value of supplies: 1939-40, 20%; 1941-42, 10%; beginning with 1943, 6%. Exceptions could be made when no bids were offered by non-Jews, or when such bids were obviously disadvantageous. All licenses in monopoly trades were withdrawn from Jewish license-holders.

Exclusion of Jews from the trade-license system affected foreign commerce as well. The absorption of some 80% of Hungary's foreign trade by Germany and Italy added to the fatal effect. According to the Völkischer Beobachter of December 24, 1942, Jews had been entirely eliminated from the animal fodder, tallow and grease, wine, paprika, onion and garlic, and textile waste export lines; and almost entirely eliminated from the export of eggs and live animals. The Nazi paper complained of the continued predominance of Jews in the textile and firewood business.

"ARYANIZATION".

No corporation for "Aryanization" existed in Hungary. Execution of anti-Jewish legislation was entrusted to the Government Commissar for Intellectual Occupations.

EMPLOYMENT AND WAGES.

According to Dr. Aloysius Kovacs, former president of the Central Office for Statistics of the Hungarian government, 31.8% of all Jews gainfully employed, or 67,917 persons, were physical laborers in 1930. They worked largely in commerce, serving as movers, packers, delivery men, etc; here their proportion reached 29.1% of all physical workers. In industry, they comprised 5.6% of labor. Data for the annexed territories were not available.

The Jew Laws did not generally affect Jews employed as physical laborers, because they were directed at the position of Jews in "economic and intellectual life." Nevertheless, several grotesque interpretations are recorded. Waiters and restaurant workers, for example, were classified as "intellectual workers," to subject them to the 12% limit. The war proved advantageous to Jewish workers, because a shortage in manpower forced the employment of more Jews. Some Jewish students, intellectuals, white-collar employees and merchants had turned to factory jobs after the enactment of the Jew Laws. Their probably limited number is not known; it is likely that they were safe from compulsory labor service. In 1941, a total of $63,000 was spent by Jewish welfare organizations in Hungary on industrial and agricultural retraining of several thousand young Jews, mostly students and white-collar workers. Figures for 1942 are not available. The American Jewish Joint Distribution Committee aided in the organization and support of this service.

The average annual wage of the Hungarian industrial worker was pengo 1,330 in 1926 and pengo 1,137 in 1936, or a drop of almost 15% in 10 years. At the official exchange rate, the two figures are $266 and $227 respectively, but in buying power they might be estimated at $530 and $455. A drop in the cost of living from 117.4 in 1937 to 89 in 1934 accompanied the drop in income. These conditions held true for Jewish workers, as well as for others, except that the number of Jewish workers who succeeded in advancing themselves to higher wage ratings was somewhat higher than average. The equality of treatment for Jewish and non-Jewish workers was due partly to the share of Jews in industrial ownership and partly to the egalitarian attitude of the predominant Socialist trade unions.

Working hours were long. In 1936, only 40.6% of the industrial workers had achieved a six-day week of eight hours (and this for the summer months only); 16.7% worked $8\frac{1}{2}$ to 9 hours; 22%, $9\frac{1}{2}$ to 10 hours; 5%, $10\frac{1}{2}$ to 11 hours and 6.5% more than 12 hours a day, six days per week. Of the total number of workers, only 9.2% worked fewer than 7 hours a day. No information is available regarding discrimination against Jewish workers in wages and hours, after the outbreak of war. Labor was concentrated around Budapest.

TRADE UNIONS.

The largest portion of Hungary's industrial workers belonged to the Socialist trade unions, which were economic projections of the Social Democratic Party, and followed liberal and egalitarian party policies. Although the proportion of Jewish workers only slightly exceeded the proportion of Jews in the general population, their superior education brought them more frequently to directive posts in both party and unions. Before and during the First World War, the Christian (Catholic) labor unions marshaled only an insignificant segment of Hungarian labor, drawn from the lower strata of unskilled workers, but aided by a number of independent craftsmen, for whom the industrialization in which Jews played so large a part boded danger. Horthy cooperated with the Christian labor movement, allowing certain categories of state employees to become members. Socialist trade unionism, however, remained staunch, and the Hungarian leaders of the movement notably remained free of leanings to the extreme left or right. This firmness, with its resistance to anti-Semitic agitation, maintained the labor unions of Hungary as a surviving factor for reconstruction.

COOPERATIVES.

The labor cooperative movement, which had been of long duration in Hungary, and frequently under the management of experts who were Jews, was forced to liquidate under the pressure of the inimical Horthy regime in 1926. One savings bank for Socialist laborers remained in Hungary, and its treatment of Jews was faultlessly egalitarian. No Jewish labor cooperatives or labor banks existed, but there were a few small cooperative sick benefit and obsequial groups.

GENERAL PRESS.

At the end of the First World War, seven Budapest dailies were owned by Jews, and two by non-Jews. The entire press of Budapest had until then been liberal, with the exception of Alkotmany, the mouthpiece of the Catholic political and Christian Socialist movement. With the inception of the reactionary era in 1919, anti-Semitic papers began to emerge. Yet at the time of the promulgation of the Jew Laws, the following Budapest dailies were under Jewish ownership: Pesti Naplo, Az Est and Magyarorszag, which three formed the Est concern (Liberal); Az Ujsag (Liberal); and Pesti Hirlap (Conservative-Liberal). Pester Lloyd, a German daily morning and evening paper, was the property of the Lloyd Society, a club made up largely of Jewish industrialists.

The Second Jew Law provided that Jews could not be editors, or publishers of any publication, or determine policies, but it did not affect property rights. However, indirect methods of change were applied: Pester Lloyd was tacitly transformed into a government mouthpiece; the three dailies published by the Est concern were seized under the pretext of tax debts. Only Ujsag and Pesti Hirlap were in 1943 still owned by Jews or baptized Jews. In February, 1943, Dr. Andrew Zsilinsky, leader of the Democratic Wing of the Independent Labor Party, became editor of Ujsag. Since they could not be admitted to the Journalists' Chamber, created after the enactment of the First Jew Law, almost all Jews who were journalists were unemployed in 1943. A few indispensable editors of Pester Lloyd were allowed to remain at work.

JEWISH PRESS.

Before the era of Hitler influence, four Jewish religious or communal weeklies and one illustrated monthly appeared in Hungary.

Of these only Magyar Zsidok Lapja, a religious weekly, was tolerated in 1943.

MOTION PICTURES.

The Hungarian film industry, the oldest and best developed in Eastern Europe, owed its existence to a great extent to the initiative of Jews. During the silent film era, Alexander Korda (today Sir Alexander Korda) and Michael Kertesz (today Michael Curtiz of Hollywood) founded the Corvin Film Company, which later became the Hunnia Film Company. After 1934, it produced between 40 and 50 full length sound films a year. The following motion picture companies were also founded by Jews: Muveszfilm (Horowitz), Harmonia (Pless), Kinofilm (Farago) and Hirsch and Tsuk. In Budapest as well as the provinces, the network of motion picture theatres was founded and owned largely by Jews: Hirsch and Tsuk, Corvin Film, Winter, Ungerleider, Upor, Guttman, Lederer, etc. In 1920-21, the Horthy regime cancelled the licenses of all motion picture theatre owners who were Jews, but since most of the non-Jewish successors lacked capital and experience, the Jews were invited to stay on as partners. Producers, directors and writers were also most frequently Jewish. The position of the Jews in the Hungarian film industry remained undisturbed until the enactment of the Second Jew Law.

Paragraph 11 of the Second Jew Law provided that only members of the Chamber of Theatrical and Motion Picture Arts may be film producers or directors. This Chamber was created solely for the exclusion of Jews. In practice, not only these leading posts, but every job and function connected with motion pictures was barred to Jews. Film production was concentrated in the Hunnia and Hungarian Film Bureau firms, both lucrative sub-agencies of the Hungarian Telegraph Bureau and a source of income for grafters like Frederic Wuenscher, Szabados, and others. All theatre licenses were in the hands of non-Jews, who usually paid rent to the Jewish owners of the buildings. Yet Jews evidently had to be called into service because of their experience and ability. In 1942, thirteen Jews who were film directors, script writers, idea men and cameramen had been "accused" by the Nazi press of having secretly written, directed and photographed films under the names of non-Jewish "film experts." All were put into concentration camps, but the "Aryanized" film companies and the "dummies" were not touched.

SOCIAL INSURANCE.

Jewish industrial workers benefited from compulsory membership in the National Office for Social Insurance. Other employees belonged to the Insurance Institute for Private Employees; where they were not discharged as the result of the Jew Laws, they continued to derive these benefits. A certain degree of unofficial bias existed in the attitude of some physicians and officials connected with these institutions. There was no special system of social insurance for Jews.

HEALTH, HYGIENE, HOUSING.

Vaccination against smallpox before the age of six was compulsory for all residents of Hungary. Jews serving in forced labor battalions were vaccinated against typhoid, typhus fever and cholera, just as were soldiers. No restrictions or discriminations were imposed on the accessibility of vaccines, serums and other medical supplies for Jews.

There were no major epidemics in Hungary or among the Jews of Hungary during the 1930-40 decade. Nor did any special endemic diseases exist among the Jewish population, whose health average was somewhat higher than among the rest of the people. A greater inclination to diabetes, gastric ulcer and gastritis was found among the Jews, but these are common to Jews in all countries, and are usually attributed to the inherited effect of the specific circumstances under which Jews have lived for several centuries.

In the sections inhabited by the poorer stratum of Budapest Jews, old structures with obsolete sanitary equipment constituted the only approach to special sanitation problems, but these were no worse than sanitation and housing problems created in any old city district inhabited by poor people. In provincial towns, the sanitation and housing problems faced by the Jewish populations were primitive, but no different from those of the rest of the population. In Carpatho-Ruthenian towns and villages sanitary conditions were very poor for the Jews, and even worse for the rest of the people.

All food consumed by Jews was subject to the same control and inspection as other food. To this control was added the special dietary regulations of the Jews, such as ritual slaughter, which was prohibited in 1938, but which continued to be performed surreptitiously.

A special aid to sanitation among the Jews was the maintenance of ritual baths (mikvoth) by many of the communities.

MEDICAL PRACTITIONERS.

In pre-Munich Hungary, in 1930, 34.4% of all physicians and dentists were Jews, a decline from 46.3% in 1920. Estimates for 1939 were that in Greater Hungary there were then some 6,000 Jews out of a total of 14,000 physicians and dentists. In 1930, 24% of the veterinarians were Jews, but no concrete figures are available. Nor are there data for nurses. Both physicians and dentists had to have an M.D. degree.

Those Jews who were already members of the professional chambers were allowed to continue in practice by the Jew Law, therefore a decrease in their number could be brought about only through death or voluntary retirement. New candidates were not admitted. The estimated number of Jews practicing as physicians or dentists in Hungary in 1943 was at least 5,500.

HOSPITALS.

There was no outright Jewish health service in Hungary, but there were a number of separate health institutions maintained chiefly by the Budapest Jewish community. There were four modern, well-equipped Jewish hospitals in Budapest: the Hospital of the Jewish Community, with 700 beds, the Charity Hospital of the Budapest Hebra-Kadisha (Burial Society), with 150 beds, the Orthodox Hospital (150) and the Jewish Hospital in Buda (30). There was a small Jewish hospital in Szatmar, and one in Munkacs (Carpatho-Ruthenia). The Hospital of the Jewish Community of Budapest was one of the best in the country, and was used by many upper-class non-Jews. During the war all Jewish hospitals were taken over by the army, and civilian patients were no longer admitted, although the equipment remained the property of the sponsoring groups. Jewish hospital needs were greater than the facilities, and Jews had always been admitted on an equal basis into public hospitals, where the Jewish community had provided ritual food to those Jewish patients who wanted it. This equality of treatment is presumed to have continued even into 1943. Industrial workers who were Jews received equal treatment in social insurance and affiliated hospitalization services.

BIRTH AND MORTALITY RATES.

The total number of live births in Hungary in 1921 was 255,453; in 1930, it was only 219,748, or a drop of 14%. In 1921, there were 7,776 live births among the Jews; in 1930, only 5,533, or a drop of 28.8%, more than double that of the general population. By 1935, the number of live births among Jews decreased to 4,720, and by 1938, the rate of reproduction was less than 10 per 1,000 souls, a rate at which the stock can no longer be maintained. Jewish births then represented only 2.2% of the total number of births, as compared with the 5.1% share of Jews in the population. After 1938, though no statistics are available, it may safely be estimated that in the Jewish population of enlarged Hungary, which numbered some 740,000, there could not have been more than 3,000 or 4,000 births annually, or a rate of 4 to 5 births per 1,000.

During the fifteen years between 1921 and 1936, the number of deaths among Jews decreased slightly, from 6,780 to 6,196. After 1927, the number of live births never equalled the number of deaths; between 1931 and 1935, the number of deaths exceeded the births by 1,324 per year; in Budapest, by about 1,500. No statistics are available regarding the comparative incidence of fatal diseases among Jews.

Conditions in 1943 indicated that a substantial increase in Jewish mortality had occurred after 1938, resulting from the economic and psychological difficulties imposed under Nazi influence. Press reports also showed a highly increased rate of suicide among Jews after 1938. Without accurate statistics being available, indications are that the biological deficit of the Hungarian Jewish population between 1940 and 1943 will have been about 12,000 -- a serious, but of itself not a catastrophic condition. If it is allowed to continue, however, the sinking population trend will reduce the Jewish stock in Hungary by half within less than two generations.

STERILIZATION AND LIQUIDATION.

Sterilization or liquidation of incurables and others was not introduced in Hungary, either for Jews or other residents.

EDUCATION.

Elementary education was compulsory and free of tuition fees for Jews as well as for the rest of the population, and remained so after the introduction of anti-Jewish measures. Secondary schooling was free only to especially gifted children. No limitation on the attendance of Jews was set in the elementary and secondary school systems, and generally speaking, there were no disturbances regarding Jewish attendance. Two numerus clausus laws limited the attendance of Jews at universities to 6% of the total enrollment, as discussed earlier. At some universities, anti-Jewish demonstrations occurred as late as 1942. In Kolozsvar, Transylvania, one Jewish student was killed during an anti-Semitic riot in the spring of 1942.

Public education was and remained under the control of the Hungarian government, represented by the Minister of Cults and Education, whose authority extended also over confessional and private schools. Nazi influence expressed itself in the establishment of an additional number of German-language primary and secondary schools in all German-inhabited parts of the country, where full defiance of Hungarian educational interests prevailed. Where Hungarian was the language of education, no infiltration of the Nazi spirit had been permitted until the end of 1941; after 1923 -- when the Bethlen government suppressed the anti-Jewish bias instilled in textbooks during the early years of the Horthy regime -- there were no anti-Semitic tenets or references in the curricula. On the other hand, a large number of reactionary teachers had continued to be admitted to the public school system, and their personal influence was subversive. Compulsory Catholic and even Protestant religious instruction had been misused for the propagation of an anti-Jewish bias. One of the protectors of these tendencies was -- from 1934 until the spring of 1943 -- Valentine Homan, a Swabian-German lieutenant of Premier Goemboes. The German minority, which had come to enjoy the privileges of a State within a State, followed Nazi tenets in its growing school system.

Only scattered index figures are available for the number of Jews in the elementary and secondary schools and the universities. In 1920-21, 4.4% of the pupils of elementary schools were Jews; in 1935-36, only 2.5%, representing a reduction of 13,700 as against an increase of 105,000 in the total number of pupils in the elementary schools. In apprentice schools the percentage fell from 10.5% to 6.6%, in the so-called "civic schools" (a school between the elementary and high school type), from 19.9% to 9.6%, a reduction of 6,300, as against an increase of 15,500 in the total enrollment. In secondary schools, the enrollment of Jews fell by 3,000, from 25% to 16.3%; in commercial schools, by 1,700, from 35.1% to 18.9%.

It may be said with certainty that the drop in the enrollment of Jews in the school system continued into the 1940's, although there was no obstacle to the admission of Jews to secondary schools, and elementary schooling remained compulsory.

The Budapest Jewish religious community maintained about 15 religious elementary schools, two high schools and one technical high school. About 50 larger provincial religious communities in pre-Munich Hungary had their own Jewish elementary schools, and the community of Delrecen had a high school. Many of these provincial schools were in bad straits in the 1940's, as the result of the economic pressure exerted on the Jews. The Orthodox communities, especially in the northeast part of the country, maintained a number of traditional Hebrew schools (Hadorim), and there were several Yeshivoth (talmudical academies). Sunday religious schools were provided in some progressive communities. All Jewish students in public, Christian confessional or private elementary and high schools were required to take two hours of religious instruction a week and a Sabbath afternoon religious service. Teachers were provided by the Jewish communities.

There was one Jewish theological seminary in Hungary, the Francis Joseph Central Rabbinical Seminary in Budapest. It was founded in 1867 by the Congressional group of communities, with the aid of one million gold crowns put at the disposal of Hungarian Jews by a royal decision to turn back a collective fine imposed by the Austrian military rule in 1849, as punishment for the support Jews gave to the Hungarian war of independence in 1848-49. The seminary also maintained a Jewish teachers' institute.

As far as is known, the curricula of Jewish schools remained unchanged, even in 1943; it consisted of the general curricula of the public schools, supplemented by additional religious subjects, such as Bible study in Hebrew, Jewish religious ethics and history. The total number of students in attendance in these schools in 1943 may be put at between 5,000 and 6,000.

The support of the various types of schools in Hungary was divided, with the Catholic Church predominant. During the school year of 1935-36, the Catholic Church maintained 41.3% of all the elementary schools, the state 18.5%, the municipalities 12.1%, while the remaining 28.1% were supported by Protestants, Jews and other groups. The Catholic share in the maintenance of secondary schools was 24.3%, that of the state 37% and the municipalities 20.4%. Before 1941, a number of Jewish schools obtained state or municipal subsidies, or both. The Francis Joseph Rabbinical Seminary was also aided by state subsidies until 1941.

Even during the liberal era which came to an end in 1919, the number of Jews serving as teachers in primary and secondary schools was insignificant. There were a comparatively large number of university professors, however, notably in the fields of economics, history, mathematics, medicine, physics and literature. During the Horthy regime, Jews who were teachers of all grades had been consistently retired on pension. In 1943, there were probably between 1,500 and 2,000 Jews teaching in the public schools, including teachers of religion.

Teachers are appointed by the Minister of Cults and Education, or by municipal and confessional councils, with the consent of the Minister.

JEWISH WELFARE.

Social insurance was a state function in Hungary, and public welfare was in the hands of the municipalities and private organizations. In the liberal era, there had been no anti-Jewish bias in either the municipal or private welfare organizations; during the Horthy regime, however, many of the organizations in both categories had stopped helping Jews. Jewish welfare agencies had to take over their care.

No family, old age or unemployment relief existed, except such as was granted by Socialist Labor Unions for limited periods. Official social insurance covered only medical care, hospitalization, and daily allowances for curable disabilities or temporary injuries. No relief of any kind existed for agricultural workers. War invalids and widows were pensioned. Civil service jobs had their own pensions, as did many private business concerns. There was never any discrimination against Jews in any of these fields.

The most important relief work undertaken by the Jews was the distribution of alms and food among the needy by religious communities, Hebra Kadisha societies and women's organizations. In Budapest, in addition to four Jewish hospitals, there was a home for the blind, a home for deaf-mute children, three homes for the aged, and three orphan asylums -- all large, modern institutions. The Jewish Patronage Society (Zsido Patronage Egyesület) provided for the care of delinquent children, and for summer vacations for poor children. The Jewish Cultural Society (Zsido Közmivedödesi Egyesület) maintained a Mensa Academica and a home for poor university students. There was also a Mensa Academica in Pecs and one in Szeged. The Jewish Committee to aid Jewish Students Abroad (Külföldi Zsido Diakbizottsag) paid tuition fees and sent allowances to Jewish students forced out of Hungary by the Numerus Clausus laws. The Jewish Handicraft and Agricultural Society (Zsido Kezmües Földmives Egyesület) sheltered and educated Jewish handicraft and agricultural overseer apprentices. Since the 1920's, these organizations had been financed exclusively by the Jews of Hungary.

With the enactment of the First Jew Law in 1938, the increase in the numbers of Jews who, having been made jobless, would be thrust on public support resulted in the establishment of the Central Jewish Assistance Committee, about whose accomplishments only scant data are available. During the first five months of 1939, 4,382 persons applied for jobs and 3,068 people sought retraining at the retraining schools maintained by the Committee. In 1938, only 8,630 persons had applied to the Committee for aid in emigration; during 1939, 56,066 persons applied. Only 620 persons were aided in emigrating by the Committee in 1939.

In 1940 the activities of the Committee included: industrial vocational retraining in 200 retraining centers and trade schools, and for prospective farmers, on several large estates; the maintenance of several apprentice homes; aid to some 10,000 needy Austrian, German, Polish, Slovakian and Roumanian Jewish refugees; aid to some 30,000 impoverished Jews in Carpatho-Ruthenia; child care; the maintenance of soup kitchens in a number of localities, and the distribution of clothes.

During 1941, the American Jewish Joint Distribution Committee contributed $141,000 toward the work of the Central Jewish Assistance Committee, including $42,000 for refugee aid. The total expenditure of the Hungarian committee on refugee aid alone in 1941 amounted to $140,500. The committee also sent $6,000 worth of food to the Hungarian-Polish border for a group of Jewish deportees from Hungary. For aid to Jews in the poverty-stricken areas of Carpatho-Ruthenia, Upper Hungary and Transylvania, $87,000 was expended in 1941. Vocational training took $22,000; assistance to unemployed Jews in Budapest, $105,000. The dollar has a purchasing power of at least 12 pengos.

The Jewish Cultural Society undertook the support and encouragement of Jewish students, scientists, writers and artists. Feeding stations for these people were maintained, books by Jewish writers were published, lectures, concerts, theatrical and operatic performances were sponsored. No information regarding either the Central Jewish Assistance Committee or the Jewish Cultural Society was available for 1942 and 1943. American aid was withdrawn, of course, after Pearl Harbor. It is uncertain whether even the large, well-established Jewish welfare institutions were able to keep themselves going. In general, there was no government interference. Administrative assistance was given to the extent that permits were granted for fund collections, etc.

CHILD CARE.

Foundlings and children born out of marriage were cared for by the state, orphan asylums were maintained mainly by municipalities and religious communities. Disabled and handicapped children were largely cared for by private organizations and religious groups. The League for the Defense of Children (Gyermekvedö Liga) provided summer vacations; the Free Masons of Budapest, although officially dissolved, provided free bread and milk among poor children of the city, and also sponsored a home for crippled children.

During the Horthy regime, child welfare was left more and more to the Jewish communities. There were three large Jewish orphan asylums in Budapest, and two smaller ones in the provinces. The Jewish Patronage Society (Zsido Patronage Egyesület) cared for a few hundred delinquents, and sought to improve home conditions in the poorer quarters. Destitute Jewish children were sent to summer camps. A Jewish branch of the Boy Scout movement ran a number of Jewish Scout Camps. How many of these undertakings and institutions have remained functioning, in view of the strained economic conditions of the Jews of Hungary, is problematical.

Juvenile delinquency was not a major problem in Hungary, despite the grave social condition of the landless peasantry. First and second minor offenders were entrusted to the care of semi-official Patronage Societies maintained by the Catholic, Protestant and Jewish groups respectively. The Societies either put the children on probation into the temporary charge of volunteer foster parents, or with paid guardians. Third offenders, or those guilty of grave crimes, were sentenced to state institutions of correction. Anti-Jewish discrimination was hardly evident in the matter of juvenile delinquency; the courts cooperated with the Jewish Patronage Society on the same terms as with the Catholic and the Protestant societies.

WELFARE WORKERS.

Almost all the welfare institutions in Hungary were creations of the liberal era. Many of the pioneers and sponsors in the field had been Jews. During the Horthy period, all Jewish welfare workers serving state, municipal or general non-sectarian institutions were eliminated. Many of them entered the employ of Jewish welfare institutions. Directorates, also, had included Jews during the liberal era, but under Horthy the leadership became almost exclusively non-Jewish.

HISTORY OF ANTI-SEMITISM.

Until the First World War, the population of Hungary was an island of resistance against two separate anti-Semitic currents: the anti-democratic anti-Semitism of Czarist Russia, and the middle-class anti-Semitism of Germany. Hungary resisted the first because it was tantamount to resisting Russian influence in the Balkans, and also because the Jews -- with their quick orientation to Hungarian ways and the Hungarian language -- provided a weight against non-Hungarian minority groups. Economically the Jews were important because the Hungarians had little adaptability or training in commercial and professional fields. The peasant population resisted anti-Semitism, offered as a bait instead of land reform, because they soon learned that it was a useless sop. Among the urban population, middle-class agitation was able to win considerable support. It may be said, however, that the bulk of the Hungarian population -- including peasants, industrial workers, members of the aristocracy and most of the really educated group -- did not become converted to anti-Semitic doctrines.

The government attitude toward Jews, beginning with the establishment of the Horthy regime, was determined by several interactive factors. Anti-Semitism remained a permanent implement in the political arsenal of the Horthy government because 1) urban German and Catholic middle-class Jew-baiters in Budapest wanted to take over the economic positions of the Jews; 2) the landed gentry had fought off land reform, leaving popular dissatisfaction to be appeased by the sacrifice of a substitute victim: the economic position of the Jews; 3) there was need of a common platform (i.e. anti-Semitism) to be shared by the urban reactionaries and the rural gentry; and 4) the crimes of the Bolshevik regime under Bela Kun (who had been a baptized Jew) needed to be permanently exploited as a justification for the maintenance of a reactionary political trend; and 5) despite the fact that the Jewish populations had suffered most under the short-lived Communist dictatorship, they were nevertheless propagandistically identified with the dictatorial groups.

In 1900, Premier Goemboes, the founder of the racial anti-Semitic political tendency in Hungary, inaugurated the slow but sure retrenchment of the economic bases of Jewish existence in Hungary. After 1938, the Horthy regime tried to use its anti-Semitic prestige as a means of barter with Hitler, hoping that radical anti-Jewish legislation would serve as a substitute for other concessions to the Nazis. The First Jew Law of 1938 was the first measure of its kind outside Germany. As the success of this barter became dubious, and even more after Allied persistence grew manifest, the official mind of Hungary began to waver.

Between 1937 and 1943, there was almost no mob violence against the Jews, with the exception of some atrocities committed in the annexed territories. Although the bulwark of anti-Semitic conviction lay in the middle-class, there were evidences of good will and cooperation even here. A surprisingly high number of non-Jewish employers, for instance, were indicted for refusing to dismiss their Jewish employees after the enactment of the Jew Laws.

The official anti-Semitic party of Hungary in 1943 was the large government party, called the Party of Hungarian Life (Magyar Elet Partja) whose 185 members in the Lower House were committed to support of the official anti-Jewish government policy. The prime agitators, however, of anti-Semitic doctrines were the outright Nazi groups. There were, in 1943 in the Lower House 42 representatives belonging to one or the other of the four National Socialist parties, of which the largest were Major Ferenc Szalassi's Arrow Cross Party (Nyilaskereszt), and Premier Bela Imredy's Party of National Rebirth (Nemzeti Ujjaszuletes Partja). Although mutually inimical on other issues, these Nazi groups agreed on anti-Semitism. In May, 1943, Imredy introduced a no-confidence vote in the government, on the ground that the government refused to settle the Jewish question drastically. The motion was rejected. During the summer of 1943, German efforts were concentrated on forging a solid pro-Nazi bloc out of the various Nazi groups. Recriminations against Hungary for its obstinacy in not eliminating Jews from its economic and political system were repeatedly directed at the Hungarian government by the German press, which threatened action if a more satisfactory line was not taken.

FASCIST PARTIES AND LEADERS

There were several categories of Nazis, Fascists and anti-Semites in Hungary. The first category consisted of confessed Nazis openly labeling themselves as such in their party denominations. Four such parties existed, with a combined strength of between 30 and 36 parliamentary seats (in 1939 they had 42 seats). The Arrow Cross (Nyilaskereszt) Party under the leadership of Ferenc Szalassi, who was himself 'führer" and not a member of parliament, was the strongest. In 1939 they won 30 seats, but in 1942 had only 16, and the number was probably even lower in 1943. Some members of the party resigned, others were convicted of treason and some joined other groups, usually Imredy's Party of National Rebirth (Nemzeti Ujjaszuletes Partja), which seems to have won Hitler's confidence most. The National Socialist Party (Nemzeti Szocialista Partja), headed by Representatives Charles Meisler and Matthew Matolocsy obtained 9 seats in 1939; the National Socialist Party of Count G. Festetich and Zoltan Mesko 2 seats, and the National Socialist Party of Count Fidel Palfy one seat in 1938. All gained adherents subsequently from the Szalassi followers. Internecine quarrels make any estimate of their relative strength in 1943 difficult. They were used by Hitler as pressure groups against the Horthy regime, which -- in Jewish affairs as in others -- struggled to retain its own precarious existence and some shred of Hungarian independence. An Imredy government would probably submit entirely to that part of the Nazi program dealing with Jews, and would completely subordinate Hungary to the service of Hitler's war.

The leading anti-Semites in the Imredy Party of National Rebirth are, in addition to its leader, Stephen Milotay and Francis Rainiss, both members of parliament, newspapermen, and vicious pro-Nazi agitators. Others are Anthony Kunder, former army officer and Minister of Commerce in the Imredy cabinet, Andrew Jaross, Count Dominik Festetich, Francis Ulain and Bela Jurtsek. Many of them had belonged to the Goemboes junta.

Radical anti-Semites within the government ranks include William Brand, Henry Muschong, Anton Muehl, J. Zerinvary, Bela Teglassy, B. Torkos, Bela Huszovszky, George Biro, Nicholas Bonczos, John Szeder and George Bobory. Andrew Mecser was one of the Goemboes aides, in the early 1930's, in early scheming with Hitler. Michael Kolozsvary-Borcsa, chief of press in the Goemboes cabinet, was for a time chairman of the Journalists' Chamber. In April, 1943, Nicholas Lazar, a Jewish journalist, furnished evidence in court that the chairman had embezzled the Chambers' funds.

CHRISTIAN CHURCHES AND THE JEWS.

Both the Catholic and Protestant clergy of Hungary have been represented in reactionary as well as liberal attitudes toward the Jews. An anti-Jewish trend among the Catholic clergy became noticeable as early as the 1880's; it was part of the anti-Semitic movement launched by Mayor Lueger of Vienna in the 1870's. After 1900, it was led mainly by several members of the Jesuit order who happened to be of Slovak or German extraction. Before the rise of the first anti-Jewish regime in 1919, however, the official attitude of the Catholic church, as represented by its Archbishop-Primates, was benevolent. In 1920, Catholic followers of the anti-Semitic factors of the clergy cooperated with the Protestants surrounding Regent Horthy in enacting the first educational numerus clausus. Only an overwhelmingly liberal popular sentiment managed to keep the anti-Semitic agitations in check between 1920 and 1938. In 1938, at the promulgation of the first Jew Law, the Primate Dr. Justinian Seredy, and Bishop Langfelder, in the name of Bench of Bishops, approved the proposed legislation in the Upper House. The Bench of Bishops also approved the enactment of the Second Jew Law in 1939, except that at this time the high clergy protested against penalizing converted Jews. Late in 1941, the official Catholic attitude changed. Various moves were made by leading members of the clergy on behalf of converted Jews and Jews in military labor units. In December, 1942, Seredy himself denounced racial, national, birth and class privileges. Nevertheless, anti-Jewish agitation continued among other representatives of the clergy.

The Hungarian Protestant churches, strongholds of religious liberalism, underwent a change with the establishment of the Horthy regime. Among the leaders of the reactionary group were Bishops Ladislas Ravasz of Budapest and Imre Szabo. Other Calvinist and Evangelical leaders retained the liberal tradition. Bishop Alexander Raffay took an open stand against the Jew Laws. Bishop Nicholas Jozan of the Unitarian church and Elemer Gyori, Calvinist Bishop of Transdanubia, also upheld the liberal tradition.

ANTI-SEMITIC PRESS

The chief Catholic anti-Jewish dailies of the early reactionary era had been Nemzeti Ujsag and Uj Nemzedek. Both had adopted a mollified tone by 1941. Szozat, organ of the Goemboes junta, went under in 1925. In 1943 the most brazenly anti-Semitic dailies, maintained by German subsidy, were Magyarszag, mouthpiece of the Arrow Cross Party, and Uj Magyarsag, organ of the Party of National Rebirth. Oliver Ruprecht was editor-publisher of the first; Stephen Milotay and Franz Rainisch of the second. These three men were the leading demagogues and corruptionists of the Hungarian press. Other dangerous Nazi publicists were Koloman Hubay (Huber), Franz Vajta, Andrew Jaross, Charles Megay-Meisler, John Huettner, Edmund Malnasi, Franz Fiala, Paul Szvatko and Koloman Ratkay. The smaller Nazi groups published weeklies, edited largely by their respective leaders, such as Mesko, Festetich, and Palfy. The official government press struggled between keeping pace with the Nazi press as regards anti-Semitism and explaining the government's resistance to the extremist anti-Jewish proposals of the Nazi factions. Fuggetlenseg, Reggeli Magyarorszag and Esti Magyarorszag were government organs, edited by journalistic mediocrities.

EXTRA-LEGAL DISCRIMINATION.

Extra-legal discrimination was practically unknown between 1867 and 1919, except for a short period around 1900, when Baron Barkoczy, state secretary of education, tried to obstruct the appointment of Jewish high school teachers. The competition of agrarian consumers' cooperatives against Jewish village merchants may also be so classified. In 1919, the counter-revolutionary regime pensioned off -- and thus retired -- Jewish public officials in a wholesale fashion; hundreds were pensioned in the Budapest municipality alone. Between 1928 and 1930, under Bethlen, a few were reappointed by the national government. The period of reaction also introduced economic discrimination, including the refusal to renew expired trade licenses and the exclusion of Jewish business from public deliveries. This was also brought to an end by the Bethlen regime. Under Goemboes (1932-35), discrimination was aggravated. Private enterprise, including Jewish-owned firms, were forced to employ non-Jewish white-collar workers, and the export-import license system was manipulated to eliminate Jewish business.

The most important extra-legal discrimination under the Hitler influence was the maintenance of a Jewish compulsory labor service, to be dealt with in detail later. Concentration camps, in which were confined thousands of Hungarian and refugee Jews, were also extra-legal. Mass deportation was practiced only once, in July, 1941, when some 18,000 Jews who could not authenticate their citizenship were rounded up and sent to German-occupied Eastern Galicia. When some 12,000 were killed by Ukrainian bands under German command, the remaining 6,000 were hurriedly returned to Hungarian concentration camps by order of the Hungarian army command. Minor extra-legal discriminations include prohibitions against giving Jewish children "archaic Hungarian" first names; the reservation of Jewish-owned World War bonds over the value of 5,000,000 Pengo (paying neither capital or interest) for the purpose of a Jewish emigration fund; the elimination of all Jews from the service of the Chambers of Commerce and industry; the prohibition of Jews from selling newspapers; the withdrawal of Jewish taxi-drivers' licenses; the prohibition of the sale of real estate owned by Jews unless to the National Bank, and the conclusion of a Hungarian-German agreement on the exchange of "personal data" of individuals suspected of Jewish descent.

DISCRIMINATORY MEASURES.

Before the promulgation of the First Jew Law, the only measures which were directly aimed at anti-Jewish discrimination were the first Numerus Clausus law (1920: XXV) and the second (1928: XIV). The first law, while ostensibly applying to all national groups, and specifying that their attendance at the universities should correspond to their proportion in the population, or to 9/10 of it, was actually applied only to the Jews, whose attendance was set in practice at 6%. Until 1923, the proportion was rigidly adhered to in all the universities; later, because of poor attendance at the three provincial universities, only the University and Technical University of Budapest adhered to it literally. The second Numerus Clausus law, enacted in 1928 under the liberal Bethlen regime, was intended to palliate resentment abroad and to ease negotiations for an international loan. Race or nationality were eliminated as criterions for university admission, and the occupational status of the parents largely substituted. War orphans, children of war veterans and of public employees were also given priority status. Before the enactment of the 1920 law, 11.6% of the university students were Jewish. By 1927-28, the proportion was 8.3%, the difference between that and the "legal" 6% being due to the higher rate of admission in the provincial faculties. The more liberal policy instituted by the second law raised the proportion in 1932-33 to 12%. After 1934, under Goemboes, restrictions tightened again, and in 1936-37, the proportion was only 7.4%, with 6.1% among freshmen. The Second Jew Law (1939: IV) supplanted the second Numerus Clausus law, limiting the admission of Jewish students to the first terms of universities to 6%, and in the economic and commercial department of the Budapest Technical University to 12%.

The Second Jew Law (1939) was an implementation of the various measures the First Jew Law (1938) had contained, providing that: Jews could not acquire Hungarian citizenship through naturalization, marriage or adoption; Jews and their dependents whose "circumstances do not necessitate their stay in the country" could be denaturalized; active and passive franchise could be exercised only by those Jews whose parents and grandparents had been born in Hungary; Jews could not be public officials, judges, teachers, public notaries, panel experts, translators, patent attorneys or public accountants, publishers, editors, producers or directors of plays and movies.

POLICE.

During the liberal era, Jews occasionally rose to positions of importance in the police force. Toward the end of the era, one of the two assistant police commissioners of Budapest was a Jew, and there were a few Jews serving as policemen and detectives. No Jews were in the service of the state police or the gendarmerie in the provinces. During the Horthy regime, all Jews, except two or three specially trained detectives, were dismissed, even in Budapest.

No special police force was established or detailed to handle Jewish affairs in Hungary after the submission to Nazi influence. The average police official, however, frequently representing the most narrow-minded, provincial nationalist and reactionary type was an excellent potential Jew-baiter. The attitude of most of the police was definitely malevolent toward the Jews, and mass injustices went far beyond the disciplinarian regime of the Minister of the Interior. Though corruption was not conspicuous in Hungary, a widespread system of graft developed in relation to the execution of the Jew Laws. In many cases, deportation was escaped through bribery.

The functions of the police in regard to the execution of the Jew Laws were mainly over the following violations: failure to report the employment status of Jews; false reports concerning their employment status; continued employment of Jews, contrary to the provisions of the Jew Law; clandestine participation of Jews in the conduct of newspapers, theatres, motion picture houses, etc.; proceedings against non-Jews for acting as "dummies" for Jews in the sale of monopoly articles or in the procurement of contracts for public supplies, and administrative procedures against Jews who could not "authenticate" their citizenship, and whose stay in the country was not regarded as "motivated by their circumstances," which called for confinement in concentration camps or deportation.

TRAVEL, PASSPORT AND COMMUNICATION REGULATIONS.

With the outbreak of the war, travel abroad for all Hungarians required a special permit from the Minister of the Interior.

There were no special passports for Jews, even under Nazi pressure. On the contrary, the Hungarian government in 1939 eliminated from passport forms the question regarding the religious confession of the bearer. This was intended to facilitate the admission to other countries of Jewish emigrants inclined to conceal their religion, and was in accordance with the policy of the Second Jew Law, which authorized the government to promote Jewish emigration. There were no known restrictions for Jews regarding railroad travel, the use of public highways and parks, street car, bus or truck travel, ownership of motor cars and horse carriages, or the use of waterways or air transportation.

In 1940 the ownership of radio sets was prohibited to Jews. Nevertheless, the majority of those indicted for listening to and disseminating foreign news favorable to the Allies -- a crime for all Hungarians -- were Jews. There were no known restrictions on the use of telephone or telegraph facilities.

FOOD AND RATIONING.

The prohibition of the ritual slaughter of cattle in the First Jew Law of 1938, inaugurated a period of food deficiency for observant Jews, although in most communities the ritual slaughter of poultry was continued and in some localities even the ritual slaughter of cattle tolerated. There was no indication of discrimination in food or fuel rationing. The attempt of the administrative head of Pest County to forbid the sale of edible fats to Jews was revoked by the government. Although local administrative discrimination may have been practiced in remote parts, Hungary was the only country in Eastern Europe where the Jews were not restricted to specific, inadvantageous shopping hours. Their difficulty lay in finding the wherewithal to buy the food they were allowed.

IDENTIFICATION CARDS.

There were no special identification card requirements for Jews, even after 1938. The possession of citizenship papers was made the criterion in the raids on "alien" Jews, as well as in applications for various official documents. This was the method used to list the Jews who could be classified as "alien." There no restrictions of any kind for Jews regarding travel within the country.

FORCED LABOR.

Between 60,000 and 150,000 Jews (so widely did reports vary) were engaged in compulsory work in labor camps and battalions under military command. Able-bodied men between the ages of 18 and 60 were drafted for this service. They obtained food, shelter and the regular military pay, which had only token value. Clothing, however, was not provided, as for the military; the Jews had to report for service in their own civilian attire, and with their own blankets. They wore yellow armbands, without the Star of David. Non-Jewish forced laborers wore white armbands; this latter group was recruited from the ranks of unskilled laborers, while the Jewish labor squads consisted of overwhelmingly middle-class elements, and a large percentage of former reserve officers of the Hungarian army. In exceptional cases, according to a decree, Jews could be put into military service, but there was no evidence that this had been done. The labor battalions were used for general construction and fortification work within Hungary, and on the Russian front, where there were many casualties. One report indicated that a number of Jews had been put at the disposal of the German Todt organization, to build fortifications for the Germans on Russian territory.

TAXES AND FINES.

Jews bore a larger burden in ordinary government taxation because the greater strain was deliberately laid on industry and commerce as compared with landowning. Moreover, non-Jewish business men were frequently treated with obvious leniency by the tax-collecting authorities. Discrimination in the levying of taxes was more difficult, because Jews participated in the work of the tax commissions, especially in Budapest.

Until December, 1941, government agencies could collect taxes for the Jewish religious communities in cases of default. This cooperation was then withdrawn.

Special penalties were provided for violation of the Second Jew Law and the Marriage Law. For "misdemeanors" in the violation of the Second Jew Law, maximum fines of 8,000 pengo (about $1,500 in pre-war nominal value) could be imposed; for "offenses", imprisonment for a maximum of one year and a maximum fine of 20,000 Pengo, for "felonies", imprisonment for three years, a fine of 20,000 pengo, the loss of public office and the suspension of political rights. A "felony", for instance, consisted of furnishing authorities with false data concerning the employment status of a Jew. The penalties were applicable to both Jewish and non-Jewish offenders.

Christian-Jewish marriage, and illegal relations between Jews and "decent" Christian women could impose on the Jewish partner imprisonment for a maximum of three years, a fine of 20,000 pengo and the loss of political rights.

The only special levy imposed upon the Jews of Hungary was a decree, promulgated early in 1943, setting a 10% levy as a "hypothecary loan" on the taxable value of all taxable urban real estate property owned by Jews. The proceeds were to be used for national defense; the idea was that Jews, being barred from active combat service, should be taxed instead. In May, 1943, the discriminatory levy lost its sting with the imposition of a general property levy of 10% affecting all categories of private property owned by all Hungarian subjects.

GROUPS-IN-EXILE.

There are three Hungarian political groups abroad, intent upon having a role in the political life of post-war Hungary. In the middle of 1941, Representative Tibor Eckhardt, head of the Small Farmers' Party in Hungary, arrived in the United States with the purpose of forming a Hungarian political group for the support of Hungary's post-war interests. Although the Small Farmers' Party is at present a staunch opponent of Nazism, Eckhardt's anti-Semitic and reactionary past proved an insuperable obstacle in the way of his ambitions. Under the pressure of American democratic public opinion, Eckhardt was soon forced to liquidate the "Free Hungary Movement" he had started. Jewish support of this movement remained limited to the Chairman and Rabbi of a small and new New York Hungarian Jewish Community (New Light Community).

In London, Count Michael Karolyi, the leader of the long defunct Hungarian Republic of 1919, is at the head of a Hungarian movement counting on British and Russian support. His support in Hungarian circles in London is limited to some radical intellectuals, among them a number of Jewish refugees. The "Federation of Democratic Hungarians", a group founded in the United States by Prof. Rustem Vambery, may be regarded as an American auxiliary of Karolyi's movement. The group enjoys the support of the small leftist Hungarian groups, and of a small number of Hungarian Jewish radicals.

In London, there is a small, democratic middle-of-the-road group which was founded by Dr. Anthony Zsilinszky, former secretary of the Hungarian legation in London. After the suicide of Zsilinszky, Andrew Revay, a journalist took over leadership. The general tendency of the group seems to be closest to the aims of the U. S. government. In the U. S., Dr. Anthony Balasy, a former diplomat, is considered the outstanding representative of the democratic, middle-of-the-road, constructive trend among Hungarians.

The bulk of Hungarian Jewish refugees in the U. S. and in Britain have hitherto withheld their support both from the Eckhardt and the Karolyi-Vambery groups. In 1943, no important Hungarian Jewish groups had yet been organized either in Great Britain or in the United States.

JEWISH LEADERS IN HUNGARY.

The official head of the "National Chancery" of the organization of Congressional Jewish communities, and, at the same time, chairman of the large religious community of Budapest, was Court Councilor Samuel Stern, a food processing inddustrialist. The religious head of Congressional Jewry had been, until his death in February, 1943, Dr. Simon Hevesi, chief rabbi of Budapest and chairman of the Rabbinical Assembly of Hungary. His son, and successor, Rabbi Dr. Francis Hevesi, of Budapest has repeatedly visited the United States and speaks English well. The head of the Orthodox National Chancery was Samuel Frankl-Kahan, (Budapest); of the Status Quo group, Rabbi Dr. B. Bernstein (Nyiregyhaza).

The Board of the Jewish Community of Budapest consisted of the following members: Samuel Stern, chairman; Dr. Ernest Boda, lawyer, vice chairman; members: Dr. Charles Wilhelm, corporation lawyer; Dr. Leo Buday-Goldberger, textile industrialist, and former member of the Upper House of parliament; Coloman Frey, former chairman of the Budapest Stock and Commodity Exchange; Henry Kalman, president, British-Hungarian Bank; Emil Vertes, former chairman, Association of Budapest Merchants; Dr. Emil Zahler, physician; Dr. Ernest Brody, lawyer, member of parliament; Prof. Max Rosenak, physician; Dr. Louis Lang, lawyer, former member of Upper House.

Jewish political figures include: Dr. Bela Fabian, former member of parliament; Dr. Geza Desi, former member of parliament, and a partisan of the conservative-liberal leader, Count Stephen Bethlen. (Dr. Desi is at present acting chairman of the Budapest Hebra Kadisha)

Labor leaders who are Jews include: Dr. Imre Gyoerky, John Esztergalyos, Alexander Propper and Daniel Varnay, all former Social Democratic members of parliament. Leading industrialists are: Baron Alphonse Weiss, head of Manfred Weiss, Ltd., a heavy industrial concern employing between 35,000 and 40,000 workers; Eugene Vida, chairman, Hungarian General Coal Mines Co., Ltd., a leading enterprise; Baron Andrew Hatvany, sugar industrialist; Alexander Deutsch, chemical industrialist; Gustave Lang, machine industrialist; Geza Drucker, Alexander Fobath and Emanuel Agoston, textile industrialists. Baptized Jews: Dr. Francis Chorin, former chairman, National Association of Industrialists, head of the Rimamurany-Salgotajan coal, iron and steel combine; Dr. Paul Biro, his chief aide; Dr. Joseph Hiller, chairman, Bauxite Industry, Ltd.

Leading Jewish bankers: Dr. Emil Stein, former president, Commercial Bank of Budapest; Dr. Stephen Perenyi, former director Hungarian General Bank of Credit; Emanuel Halasz, former director, General Savings Bank; Baron Marcel Madarassy-Beck, chairman, Hungarian Bank of Escompte. Baptized: Baron George Ullmann, Joseph Bun, Otto Conrad.

Leading Jewish journalists: Max Markus, until the Hitler regime, chairman of the Association of Hungarian Journalists; Thomas Kobor, former editor of Az Ujsag; Imre Salusinsky, former editor of Az Est, Pesti Neplo and Magyarorszag; Nicholas Lazar, former editor of Reggeli Ujsag; Dr. George Kecskemeti, former editor of Pester Lloyd; Dr. Bela Agai, former publisher of Az Ujsag; Bela Zsolt, Simon Kemeny, Joseph Vago, George Kemeny, Dr. Charles Sebestyen and Samuel Nagy.

Among thousands of Jewish lawyers, the most noted are the following: Dr. Charles Wilhelm, Dr. Andrew Gluecksthal, Dr. Erwin Doroghy, Dr. Ignace Friedman, Dr. Elias Hevesi and Dr. Bela Berend.

Of the large number of Jewish physicians the following may be mentioned: Prof. Max Rosenak, Prof. Ludwig Levy, Prof. Z. Aszodi, Dr. Bela Molnar, Dr. Imre Fodor, Dr. Eugene Biederman, Dr. Ignace Farkas.

JEWISH LEADERS IN EXILE.

Community representatives: In the United States; Berthold Magyar, textile industrialist, former member of the Board of the Jewish Community of Budapest, (New York); Eugene Hevesi, son of the chief rabbi of Budapest, former Hungarian commercial attache in the U. S., at present connected with the American Jewish Committee; in Canada; Dr. Desider Rakonitz, former attorney of the Orthodox National Chancery.

Prominent Jewish businessmen in the United States; Berthold Magyar, Albert Ungar, Henry Fleischman, George Popper -- all textile industrialists; Alexander and Siegfried Lindenbaum, oil industry; in Canada; Joseph Schober, textile industry.

Journalists, writers: In the United States, Franz Molnar, the famous playwright; Dr. Ladislas Boross, former editor of Esti Kurir, and former secretary general of International Association of Journalists as well as of the Society of Hungarian Journalists; Hans Habe, writer (the latter is baptized).

Prominent physicians in the United States; Dr. Henry Lax, Dr. Gideon Eroes, Dr. Bela Koevesi, Dr. Julius Hollo (internal diseases), Dr. Stephen Rosenak, Dr. Alexander Baron (surgery), Dr. Arthur Linksz (ophthalmology), Dr. Julius Baron (X-ray).

At the end of the war, the original staff of professional welfare workers remaining in Hungary, expanded as it may have been by recruits from the general welfare field working under the aegis of the Central Jewish Assistance Committee, may be turned to as the foundation of reconstruction activities. Only American and British Jewish welfare organizations will probably be in a position to cooperate. The American Jewish Joint Distribution Committee is likely to assume leadership in the field, but may be aided by the American Joint Reconstruction Foundation; the ORT Society for the promotion of trade and agriculture among Jews; the OSE World Union for health protection; the HICEM (Hias-Ica Emigration Association) and the Jewish Agency for Palestine.

THE JEWS OF ITALY

THE JEWS OF ITALY

Index

Anti-Fascist Italians in Italy and Other Countries.....8

Banking and Bank Deposits............................6

Catholic Church and the Jews.........................4

Community Structure..................................2

Discriminatory Measures............................4-5

Education..7

History of Anti-Semitism.............................3

Jews in Fascist Movement.............................2

Occupations and Professions........................5-6

Periodicals and Press................................6

Population...1

Reconstruction Agencies..............................8

Stateless Jews.......................................4

Social Security......................................7

Welfare Institutions.................................7

THE JEWS OF ITALY

In 1938, there were approximately 45,000 Jews in Italy, 0.1% of the total population. The introduction of racism, however, raised this number to about 60,000 by categorically including as Jews all those whose two parents had been Jewish, whether they were subsequently baptized or not.

To the total number must be added more than 10,000 foreign Jews, mostly immigrants who entered from Germany, Austria, Roumania, Poland, Hungary and other East European countries after the First World War. There were also about 5,000 Jews from Turkey and Greece who lived largely in Milan, Turin and Genoa.

The census of 1931 showed that more than 85% of the Jews in Italy lived in the large cities: Rome, 14,000; Milan, 7,000; Trieste, 4,500; Turin, 3,800; Florence, 3000; Genoa, 3,000; Leghorn, 2,000; Venice, 1,800; Fiume, 1,600.

There were between 30,000 and 34,000 Jews in the Italian colonies: Tripolitania, 22,000; Cyrenaica, 4,000; Eritrea, 300; Somaliland, 100; Dodecanese Islands, 6,000-7,000; Ethiopia, 1,000-2,000.

After the enactment of Fascist anti-Jewish legislation in 1938, the Jewish population decreased as a result of emigration or baptism, although the latter was of no legal consequence unless one parent had not been Jewish. While official statistics are not available, the total emigration may be put at 5,000 Italian Jews and 5,000 foreign Jews. Against the emigration of foreign Jews, however, should be set the immigration of several thousand Jews from Yugoslavia, who were in 1942-43 living in concentration camps or as civil internees in Italy. No statistics are available for the number of Italian Jews who were baptized as the result of Fascist persecution. Baptism seems to have been prevalent mostly among professionals and the wealthier classes; according to an estimate, it affected more than 10% of the Italian Jewish population.

Between 1938 and 1943, emigration of Jews from Italy was directed mainly towards the United States (3,000); Palestine (1,000); and Latin America (500). Some Jews also found their way to the French Riviera and to Switzerland.

Anti-Jewish legislation had a definite effect on the structure of the Jewish population, both from the point of view of age and of occupation. Young people, their education or careers blocked by the new laws, emigrated in large numbers.

The Jewish communities were regulated by the Royal Decree of October 30, 1930, No. 1731, which established the compulsory organization of Jewish communities in centers containing numerous Jewish groups. The communities were united in the Unione delle Communita Israelitiche Italiane (Union of the Italian Jewish Communities), with headquarters in Rome. Each community held regular elections for its council. The president of the Jewish community in Rome in 1943 was Dr. Almansi. The Chief Rabbi was Prof. Israele Zolli (Zoller), former Chief Rabbi of Trieste.

Compulsory contributions, based on the State income tax, were levied on every Italian Jew for the maintenance of the Jewish community and its subsidiary institutions. The Communities were public corporations authorized to possess real estate, cash and securities, and to receive gifts and legacies. The councils of the Jewish communities, like those of other public corporations recognized by the State, acted under the control of the prefetto, the Chief Executive of the province. Except in a few old communities, the property owned by synagogues and other Jewish institutions and organizations was not great. Educational, religious and welfare needs were covered by the levy and voluntary contributions. Even after the reorganization of the Jewish communities according to the above-mentioned Royal Decree of 1930, financial difficulties continued to harass several localities.

As a consequence of the Royal Decree, rabbis practicing in the legally-recognized communities were authorized to perform marriages between Jews in the capacity of public officials. Marriage certificates issued by rabbis were transcribed as official papers. Like other Italian citizens, however, Jews had the right to choose civil marriage. Anti-Jewish legislation imposed no change on this procedure, except to forbid marriages between Jews and "Aryans". Before 1938, mixed marriages had become increasingly frequent (80% of the marriages recorded in Trieste in 1935-36 fell under this classification).

Being of Sephardic (Spanish) affiliation, the Jews of Italy were generally observant of the Jewish ritual. Important holidays were widely observed. Shehitah (Jewish method of slaughter) was maintained by the community. Jewish children, even when they attended public schools, were usually given a Jewish education in addition. After 1938, Shehitah was forbidden, but reports indicated that those Jews remaining within Italy who wanted to observe this ritual found it possible with the aid of bribery.

The religious freedom and civic emancipation granted the Jews with the formation of a united Italy in 1870 inaugurated a long period of Jewish participation in the activities of the country that did not come to an end with the establishment of the Fascist regime. With some Jews, as with other citizens of Italy, the Mussolini doctrines seemed for a time to promise progress for the country. Because the system of party coercion which Fascism invoked meant that Italian citizens had to be -- or make believe they were -- Fascists, there were Jews among them, and a number of these were sincere believers in the government. Massimo de Castiglioni, commander of the army garrison in Rome at the time of Mussolini's march on the city in 1922, gave the freedom of the city to the marchers. Edoardo Polacco, general secretary of the Fascist party in the province of Brindisi and Dr. Aldo Finzi, later undersecretary of the Ministry of the Interior, also participated in the march. Other leading early Fascists were Professor Carlo Foa, who became editor of La Gerarchia, an extreme Fascist review, Dr. Maurizio Mandel and Enzo Ravenna, mayor of Ferrara until the beginning of anti-Jewish practices. A Jew named Bolaffio was one of the "martyrs" of Fascism whose tombs were transferred to the Cathedral in Florence in 1936. Another Jew, whose name was Mandolfi, was killed even before the March on Rome and is also considered a "martyr"; he is buried in Fiume. After the promulgation of the anti-Jewish laws, 724 Jewish families were declared exempt from their application as regards property because members of the family had taken part in the March on Rome, joined the Fascist party immediately after the murder of Matteotti in 1924, or were decorated or killed in the Libya war, the First World War or the two wars conducted by Mussolini in Ethiopia and Spain. Like many other Italians, many Jews were attracted to Fascism in its early stages because its doctrines included the repudiation of Italy's participation in the First World War, with the ensuing "mistreatment" of Italy by the other victorious powers.

Before Fascism, no anti-Semitic parties or organizations existed in Italy. The most flagrantly anti-Semitic paper was La Vita Italiana (Milan and Rome) which had few readers and little influence. Its editor was Giovanni Preziosi, a former Catholic priest, who first published the Protocols of the Elders of Zion in Italian in 1921, and issued a mimeographed copy of the book. Later, in 1937, government funds helped Preziosi to establish La Nuovissima, a publishing house interested chiefly in propagating the Protocols. He also issued a Spanish version for distribution in South America. The popularity of the fabrication grew overnight when the Italian anti-Jewish laws adopted after Italy joined the Axis put Preziosi and his magazine into the lime-light. Even before that, anti-Semitic trends had been in evidence among leading Fascists. After 1938, several Italian papers published anti-Semitic articles under government order or suggestion. A new magazine, La Difesa della Razza, preaching racism, was founded in Rome in 1938 by Telesio Interlandi, a newspaperman, who became Hitler's mouthpiece in racial questions in Italy. Interlandi is said to have received 14,000,000 lire from the Nazis to organize his campaign and his magazine. He was later made chief of the racial division of the Italian Ministry of Interior. Other publications which propagated anti-Jewish doctrines after 1938, and in many cases, even before, were: Il Legionario (Rome), organ of fascists abroad; Il Giornalissimo (Rome); Il Tevere (Rome); Il Regime Fascista (Cremona); Popolo d'Italia (Milan) and Quadrivio (Rome).

The acknowledged leader of the Italian anti-Semitic politics was Roberto Farinacci, a former secretary of the Fascist party. Farinacci was surrounded by a group of political profiteers who grabbed the spoils and occupied the positions formerly held by Italian Jews. In the United States the best known Italian anti-Semite was Domenico Trombetta, owner and editor of *Il Grido della Stirpe*; he was interned and deprived of his American citizenship.

The Catholic clergy did not commit itself openly or clandestinely to any anti-Jewish policies in Italy. After 1938, Catholic priests were in several instances known to have helped Italian Jews. The Vatican itself set a precedent by admitting to the Pontifical Academy several Italian Jewish scientists dismissed from Italian universities. Obviously, this support of the Catholic clergy was intended to encourage the conversion of the Jews. The process of "Aryanization" of converted Jews was often abetted by Catholic priests, who seem to have supplied ante-dated baptismal certificates to be used as evidence of "Aryan" descent.

Before 1938, Italy did not have extra-legal or *de facto* anti-Semitic discrimination. With the exception of a few clubs frequented by the old aristocracy, Italian Jews were welcome in practically all social strata.

Official discrimination against Italian Jews, as legalized by the laws of 1938-39, followed the Nazi pattern. Laws excluding Jews from every phase of public life were vigorously applied in Italy. The laws depriving the Jews of their real estate property (Royal Decree, November 17, 1938, #1738), were not actually enforced until much later. The extent of the confiscations was not known. Frequently, Italian Jews were protected by the intervention of Italian non-Jewish friends, in whose favor the title was changed. Sometimes, customary bribery helped. It is hard, however, to judge how far this sort of protection could be carried on under the new conditions created by the war.

As a consequence of the anti-Semitic laws, the Italian Jews were practically segregated from the rest of the population. However, judging from the attacks printed in the fascist papers against fair Italians, one is inclined to conclude that the segregation had its exceptions.

Before 1938, the attitude of Italy toward stateless Jews was friendly. After 1938, those who did not succeed in leaving within the time limit of six months, were either confined to concentration camps or made civil internees (in small localities). The chief concentration camps were near Naples. Treatment was comparatively humane; as far as is known, there were no cases of murder. A report in the middle of 1943 stated that 16,000 Jews of all nationalities had been moved from concentration camps in the South of Italy to the North.

From the occupational point of view, anti-Jewish legislation brought a real revolution in the composition of Italian Jewry. Jews were practically excluded from professions which characterized them: from the legal profession, from the practice of medicine, from the direction or trusteeship of commercial or industrial enterprises, from employment in several lines of business (i.e. books, magazines, etc.), from teaching in government or government-controlled universities or schools. (Royal Decrees September 5, 7, November 15, 1938. Also Royal Decree, November 17, 1938, #1738.) According to official statistics published in 1938, there had been 100 Italian university professors of Jewish extraction.

Only lawyers of Jewish extraction who obtained "reclassification" were admitted to the bar. Reclassification was accorded for achievement in pro-Fascist politics or distinguished service in one of Italy's wars: (World War I; Ethiopian or Spanish campaigns). Even such admission, however, was of ephemeral character, because Jewish lawyers were barred from cases of special importance, or cases involving government or government-controlled agencies. Jewish lawyers, whose names were included in a special roll, could continue to plead for Jewish clients. Jewish physicians, in 1942-43, could treat only Jewish patients. They were allowed also to treat non-Jewish patients in an emergency; "emergencies" were therefore arranged to cover almost every case in which a non-Jewish Italian wanted to remain under the care of his Jewish doctor.

Several Jews who were forced to relinquish control of important commercial firms preferred to sell them; obviously the terms of sale were not favorable to the sellers. It does not appear, however, that special organizations were created for the "Aryanization" of all categories of enterprise. The <u>Ente di Gastione e Liquidacione Immobilare</u> (Institute for the Administration of Immovable Property) handled the transfer of real estate owned by Jews to "Aryan" or "Aryan"-dominated corporations.

After 1938 only minor clerical jobs were left open to Italian Jews, no matter how high their training, skill and previous experience; the retention of even these posts depended on the good-will and generosity of the employers.

Before 1938, there was no discrimination against the Jews in either the Italian Army or the Italian Navy; Jews held high posts in both, especially in the Navy. After 1938, no Jew was allowed to remain in service (Royal Decree, December 22nd, 1938, #2111). Admirals Ascoli and Moroni were both dismissed with the introduction of the anti-Jewish law; Admiral Sinigaglia had been retired only a few years before. A few irreplaceable technicians were later re-admitted into the services, possibly after baptism or "documentation" of "Aryan" descent.

Jews have long participated in the federal and local governments of Italy. At the time of the March on Rome, there were 11 Jews serving as deputies and 10 as senators. Jews were active in all phases of the municipal governments. For many years before 1930, the master of ceremonies for the Governor of Rome was a Jew named Levy; it was only after the conclusion of the Lateran Treaty that the presence of a Jew as the arranger of various ceremonials involving high Catholic dignitaries began to seem strange enough to provoke his friendly dismissal. In 1938, the promulgation of the anti-Jewish laws ousted three incumbent Jewish mayors from their posts; the mayors of Ferrara and of two small cities.

Until the introduction of racial legislation, the Italian Civil Service had been open to Jews without discrimination, and Jews were found in small number in the mail, telegraph, railway and other departments. This included moderately high posts, especially in the professional fields, such as engineering. All Civil Service employees who were Jews were ousted in 1938, even those belonging to privileged Fascist families.

No special taxes on Jews seem to have been levied after 1938, nor does it appear that Italian Jews have been taxed more heavily than the rest of the Italian population. No information is available concerning the confiscation of bank deposits as such of Jews. It appears, however, that after Italy entered the war, the Fascist government conducted a survey on the property of the Italian Jews who had emigrated, as a measure preparatory to confiscation. The theory was to confiscate the property of those who might have acquired enemy citizenship, whether or not such citizenship was actually acquired.

No important banking institutions under direct Jewish control ever existed in Italy. There were a few small private banks in several Italian cities owned by Jews. The most important of these, however, had disappeared long before 1938. Generally speaking, the financial situation of the Italian Jews was not outstanding enough to make it conspicuous before the Italian public. Jews had a certain control, more technical than financial, in the most important insurance companies in Trieste.

No special limitations were imposed upon Italian Jews in the withdrawal of funds from banks beyond the usual restrictions applicable to all clients.

No special limitations were established against Jewish insurance policy-holders. The capital of Jews who had emigrated to foreign countries was blocked; this included insurance claims. Technically, this was the result of emigration, not of racial origin.

No special limitation was imposed on Jewish exporters as such. Jews, however, were barred from the management of corporations hiring more than 100 employees, or corporations working on defense contracts.

Jews were not prominent in the ownership or directorship of the general press in Italy. There were, however, a number of leading theatre, art and literary critics who were Jews, as well as sports editors. Enrico Rocca was theatre and literary critic for Lavoro Fascista, Paolo Milano, who escaped to the United States, was on the staff of Scenario. Pier Filippo Tagiuri was one of the editors of the sports paper Il Littoriale.

There was a weekly of Jewish interest published in Italian; Israel, with publication offices in Rome. The same editorial office issued a monthly review, the Rassegna Mensile del Israel, which was established about 1930. Both publications ceased to appear in 1938, with the introduction of the anti-Jewish laws.

In the public school system of Italy, before 1938, there was no discrimination against Jewish pupils. But the preponderance of Catholic religious instruction prompted the establishment of Jewish schools, maintained by the communities of Rome, Florence, Leghorn and Turin. These schools, run on a co-educational basis, covered the elementary classes. If recognized by the government, they were exempt from taxation and a government inspector assured the fulfillment of state requirements in curriculum. After the introduction of anti-Jewish laws, when Jewish school children were excluded from the general school system, these Jewish schools provided almost the only educational facilities for them. Classes were open in other cities also. Many Jews who had been employed in the public elementary and high school system joined the faculties of the Jewish schools, and there was a resulting increase in both teachers and pupils. In some cases, baptism was resorted to for the sake of continued educational opportunities in other schools, where Catholic priests were known to have admitted baptized Jewish children in defiance of government regulations. This state of affairs gave impetus to conversions among Jews after 1938 and was probably used by some priests as an inducement to gain proselytes.

The most important higher school of Jewish learning in Italy was the Collegio Rabbinico Italiano (Italian Rabbinical College), which had been established in Padua in 1829, was subsequently situated in Rome and Florence, and returned to Rome in 1932. Its student body consisted largely of Jews from other countries. Though definite information is not available, the College was probably closed during the period of anti-Jewish laws.

Italy had an elaborate and rather progressive although not too efficient system of social security (assicurazioni sociali, assicurazioni infortuni sul lavoro, etc.). No discrimination existed in the public welfare organizations against non-Catholic citizens before 1938. Catholic charitable institutions generally did not discriminate against non-Catholics, either before or after 1938.

The several relief and public assistance measures in Italy, such as family, old age, unemployment, disabled veterans', workers' compensation for accidents and occupational diseases, etc. were extended, prior to 1938, to every person entitled to them without any discrimination. No exclusion of Jewish workers as such seems to have taken place after 1938. Jewish workers and employees, however, in consequence of the anti-Jewish legislation, were excluded from every government or government-controlled job, their pensions being liquidated at the moment of their dismissaal. A small number of Italian Jews seemed to be working in 1942-32 in jobs where they were were classified as "indispensable" or "Aryanized." Relief or public assistance does not seem to have been denied in these cases.

To ramify general public welfare agencies, the Jewish communities maintained various public welfare institutions of their own. In 1934, for instance, 600 Jewish families in Rome, or 3,000 individuals, received aid for the Passover holiday. The existence of a Jewish proletariat in Rome, Leghorn, and Venice imposed a somewhat heavier strain on the charitable institutions of the Jewish communities in those cities. The Rome community also offered maternity aid, which was occasionally subventioned by the government, aid to the sick, and other assistance. There was an orphan asylum and a home for the aged in the city. The Associazione Donne Ebraiche d'Italia (A.D.E.I.), the organization of Italian Jewish women, carried on various philanthropic activities of its own.

After 1933, two Hechalutz Hachsharah (Pioneer training) camps for Palestine pioneers were established, mostly for non-Italian Jewish young men and women, on land given by the Italian government. The camps were located near Florence and near Padua, respectively. The Revisionist-Zionist group maintained a marine school at Civita Vecchia, also with government support, and under the direction of a naval officer detailed by the government. All these institutions were closed in 1938. The Convegno di Studi Ebraici was a cultural organization, with groups for Jewish studies in many communities.

Italian Jews who migrated to the United States and who -- being mainly of Sephardic (Spanish rite) origin -- gathered around the Spanish and Portuguese synagogue, do not take an active part in political movements. Numerous Jews, however, participated in various anti-Fascist organizations. Among the Italian Jews who reached the United States after the inauguration of the anti-Jewish program were: Dr. Guido Bachi, Turin lawyer (New York); Prof. Bruno Foa, with the Office of Coordinator of Inter-American Affairs in Washington; Prof. Mario Forti, former professor of gynecology in Milan; Dr. Kalman Friedman, former chief rabbi of Florence (Quincy, Mass.); Edward D. Kleinlerer, journalist (New York); Prof. Enzo Rava, professor of Labor legislation in Florence (New York); Fausto R. Pitigliani, professor of economics at the University of Rome (New York); and Dr. Mario Volterra, former professor of medicine at Cagliari and Florence (New York).

Among the Jewish leaders who found their way to Palestine were Enzo Sereni, Zionist leader and brother of an active anti-Fascist; Dr. Yakir Behar of Milan, born in Constantinople but a naturalized Italian; Guido Lodovico Luzzatto, engineer; Dr. Pacifici, former editor of Israel; Chief Rabbi David Prato; Prof. Bacchi, statistician; and Prof. Cassuto, Biblical authority. Remaining in Rome were Dr. Roberto Algranati, and Arrigo Tedeschi, engineer.

The Jewish Agency for Palestine and the Joint Distribution Committee are among the Jewish organizations which may possibly work directly or through affiliated agencies in the relief and reconstruction of post-war Italy. The Italian Jewish Club of New York, the only organization of Italian emigrees abroad, may be of considerable assistance in this field, because of its connections with leading American circles and because of its complete knowledge of the Italian Jewish communities.

---ooOoo---

THE JEWS OF LATVIA

THE JEWS OF LATVIA

Index

Alcoholism	4	Industry	9
Anti-Semitism, History of	22	Jewish Religious Communities	2
Birth Rate	16	Functionaries	3
Citizenship	7	Judiciary, The	9
Civil Service	7	Languages	5
Commerce	10	Marriage	4
Criminality	4	Medical Practitioners	15
Discrimination, Extra-Legal	25	Minority Rights	8
Divorce	4	Mortality	16
Education	18	Occupational Structure	8
Employment	13	Population	1
Family Life	3	Press, The	14
Government, Attitude of	24	Reconstruction Agencies	26
Departments of Jewish Affairs	8	Taxes	7
Groups-in-Exile	7	Trade Unions	14
Health Services	14	Underground Movement	6
Hospitals	15	United States, Attitude toward	6
Housing	18	Wages	13
Immovable Property, Appropriation of	26	War, Attitude toward	6
		Welfare Institutions	22

- - - - - -

THE JEWS OF LATVIA

Population.

According to the last official census (1935), there were 93,479 Jews in the country, out of a general population of 1,950,502 (4.79%). In 1939, the estimated Jewish population was about 95,000; the general population was estimated at 1,990,700 (Latvia in 1939-1942, Washington, D. C., 1942, p.29).

There was in Latvia practically no difference between the number of Israelites (adherents of the Mosaic faith) and Jews in the ethnic (nationality) sense. According to the census of 1935, these two groups in the five administrative districts into which the country was divided were tabulated as follows (the capital city of Riga, though geographically in Vidzeme, was considered a separate administrative unit):

	Jews by Nationality	Of Mosaic Faith	Percentage of Jews in Latvia	Percentage of Jews in relation to the general population
Riga	43,672	43,558	46.72	11.34
Vidzeme	2,458	2,460	2.63	0.60
Kurzeme	12,012	12,002	12.85	4.11
Zemgale	7,363	7,382	7.88	2.46
Latgale	27,974	28,004	29.92	4.93
Latvia	93,479	93,406	100.00	4.79

(A. Maldups, ed., Latvija Skaitlos, Riga, 1938, pp. 67, 68, 69, 71.)

After the First World War, Latvia emerged as an independent state out of several components, each with a different historic heritage. The city of Riga, though outside the Jewish Pale in Russia, contained a number of "indigenous" Jews and another group of "tolerated" ones who had settled to the districts of Kurzeme and Zemgale. Vidzeme was outside the Pale and even under subsequent Latvian rule never attracted a large portion of the Jewish population. Latgale, on the other hand, belonged to the Pale (province of Vitebsk) and had a comparatively dense Jewish population.

These pre-First World War conditions are still reflected in the returns of the census of 1935, though it should be stressed that the general trend of the Jewish population movements during the twenty years of Latvian independence was toward concentration in the capital of Riga. In 1920, 24,863 out of 79,368 Jews lived in Riga; in 1930, 42,328 out of 94,588; in 1935, 43,672 out of 93,479.

In 1935 a total of 86,555 Jews lived in urban settlements in Latvia, and only 6,924 in rural settlements. In the nine largest cities and towns of the country, the figures for the total population and for the number of Jews were as follows:

City	Total	JEWS Absolute	Percentage
Riga	385,063	43,672	11.3
Daugavpils (Dvinsk, Dünaburg)	45,160	11,116	24.6
Liepāja (Libava, Libau)	57,098	7,364	12.9
Rēzekne (Ryezhitsa, Rositten)	13,139	3,338	25.4
Jelgava (Mitava, Mitau)	34,099	2,043	6.0
Ludza (Lyutsin, Ludsin)	5,546	1,522	27.4
Krāslava (Krislavka, Kraslava)	4,276	1,445	33.8
Ventspils (Vindava, Windav)	15,671	1,246	7.9
Krustpile (Kreytsburg, Kreuzburg)	3,658	1,041	28.4

(Yidishe Ekonomik, published by the Yivo, I, 1937, p. 195: from IV ième Recensement de la population en Lettonie, Riga, 1936/37)

The population of Latvia in 1935 was divided as follows according to nationality:

Nationality	Number	Percentage
Letts	1,472,612	75.50
Russians	206,499	10.59
Jews	93,479	4.79
Germans	62,144	3.19
Poles	48,949	2.51
White Russians	26,867	1.38
Lithuanians	22,913	1.17
Estonians	7,014	0.36
Others	8,946	0.46
Unknown	1,079	0.05
Total	1,950,502	100.00

Jewish Religious Communities.

The Latvian constitution adopted in the early 1920's established only the equality of all citizens before the law without specifying details. When admitted into the League of Nations, Latvia pledged fair treatment of her minorities and lived up to her obligations. Religious freedom never constituted a problem, either under the democratic rule or under the authoritarian regime established on May 15, 1934; as a matter of fact the dictatorship even played up religious tolerance and gave pronounced support to the Jewish Orthodox party, the Agudath Israel.

Nevertheless, no Jewish religious community (Kehillah) was established in Latvia. In Riga there was an institution known as the Jewish Kehillah (located at Jēkaba Iela 8), which registered births, marriages and deaths as an agent of the municipality, but this Kehillah was considered a private institution, not a public corporation.

In general it may be said that the Jews of Kurzeme, Zemgale and Vidzeme were Mithnagdim (followers of the letter of the law, without fidelity to any rabbinic dynasty). Their origin led to Prussia and partly to northern Lithuania. The Jews of Latgale were most frequently Hassidim (followers of a rabbinic dynasty) of the Habad school. In Riga both sects were represented. In the life of the younger generation, the division between the Mithnagdim and Hassidim played a rather insignificant part. No clashes between the sects were recorded even during the earlier part of the nineteenth century. The dividing line between observant and non-observant Jews did not coincide with the difference between Hassidim and Mithnagdim.

It is hard to evaluate exactly the degree of Jewish religious observance, but it was no doubt fairly strong. At the end of the 1920's the arrival of the Lubavitcher Rebbe from Soviet Russia, brought about by the Agudath Israel leader, Mordecai Dubin, helped to rally the Orthodox group. With the establishment of the authoritarian regime which turned over the Jewish school system to the Agudath Israel, religious observance began to be definitely encouraged by the state, whereas pronounced anti-religiosity was bound to be considered characteristic of leftism.

The Agudath Israel representatives in the Saeima (Diet) steadily supported all government coalitions, but in the course of time grew nearer to the Peasants' Union, of which Kārlis Ulmanis was leader; when Ulmanis established his dictatorship the Agudath Israel was given practical control of Jewish cultural life and became identified with the authoritarian form of state.

Religious Functionaries.

Some rabbis of the traditional type exerted considerable influence within their sphere on the basis of their personal qualities. No modern rabbis after the German model were found in independent Latvia. The Lubavitcher Rebbe had great influence among his followers, from Czarist times on. It was increased when the Rebbe was brought to Latvia from the Soviet Union and maintained even when the Rebbe left for Poland in the 1930's.

Family Life.

The Jews in Latvia had kept pace with the general westernization of the country during the last sixty years, so that there was no marked difference between the family position of Latvian Jewish women and those in the non-Jewish populations of Latvia or even of the United States. To an increasing degree, women were represented among the gainfully employed; practically no difference existed between the elementary and secondary education offered to boys and girls. In social and political life women were also quite active. The role of the father or of the large family in the Jewish group was therefore not extraordinary.

If impressions may be accepted as evidence, the Jewish family, owing to its traditional coherence, seemed to be somewhat more stable than the average. It may be appropriate to cite the figures for extra-marital births in 1938, according to ethnic groups, in relation to the general number of births in the respective groups: Poles, 33.8; Lithuanians, 23.3; Russians, 12.7; Letts, 7.3; Germans, 6.4; Jews, 3.1.

Marriage.

Jewish marriages could be registered either directly with the municipality or with its Jewish agency, the Kehillah. In the latter case, a religious ceremony had preceded the registration.

In 1935, 1,008 Jewish men and 999 Jewish women were married. In 1937 the corresponding numbers were 857 and 859. The average number of marriages for every 1,000 inhabitants in 1937 was 16.23; i.e. 8.12 marriages; for the Jews the corresponding figure was 18.32 (9.16).

The extent of mixed marriages in 1937 was as follows: 839 Jews married Jewish women, 4 Jews married Lettish women, 5 Jews married German women, 6 Jews married Russian women, 1 Jew married a Lithuanian woman, 2 Jews married women of other or unknown nationalities; 14 Jewish women married Letts, 3 Jewish women married Russians, 1 Jewish woman married a German, 1 Jewish woman married a Pole, 1 Jewish woman married a man of unknown nationality.

Divorce.

The total number of divorces in the country listed for 1938 was 1,601, including 979 Lettish couples and 134 Jewish couples.

Criminality.

In 1937 a total of 13,738 persons were convicted by civil and military courts. They were divided as follows:

	Number	Percentage
Letts	9,314	67.8
Russians	2,349	17.1
Poles	681	4.9
Jews	572	4.2

The average number of convictions by the civil or military courts, for every 1,000 inhabitants, was 7.0, but according to nationalities, the ratio was as follows:

Germans	3.8	Russians	9.8
Jews	6.1	Lithuanians	10.6
Letts	6.3	Poles	13.7
Estonians	7.9		

Alcoholism.

The Riga municipal health center for alcoholism in 1933 treated a total of 281 persons: 219 Letts, 29 Germans, 14 Russians, 11 Poles, 4 Jews, 2 Lithuanians, 2 Frenchmen. Jews, therefore, comprised 1.42% of the patients in the city where they formed 11.34% of the population.

Languages.

In the province of Kurzeme and in the city of Riga, some sections of the Jewish population had, during the latter part of the 19th century, begun to acquire the German language instead of Yiddish; in the 1890's, Russian was also acquired. The Russian census of 1897 showed Yiddish to be the mother-tongue of those affiliated with the Jewish religion in the following proportions: Province of Kurland (comprising Kurzeme and Zemgale), 73.8%; Vidzeme (including Riga), 80.0; Latgale, 92.0. In the whole of what later became Latvia, 81.9% of all the Jews reported Yiddish as their mother-tongue in the census of 1897.

Censuses taken during the period of Latvian independence contained no questions regarding linguistic backgrounds. Many Letts by nationality spoke Russian or German as a mother-tongue and the Latvian government did not want to offer figures that would diminish the prestige of the state language. In the case of the Jews, conclusions can be drawn from the numbers of pupils who attended Yiddish and Hebrew schools.

Language conflicts were largely avoided by the school legislation of Latvia which conceded schools in their respective languages to every minority group. For the same reason conflicts between adherents of Yiddish and Hebrew were greatly reduced. Requests for the recognition of Yiddish as an official language were never put forward as the number of the Jews in the country did not warrant it. In the municipal government, particularly in Latgale, where the Jews formed a rather conspicuous part of the urban population, Yiddish did enjoy some rights during the democratic regime.

Multilingualism in Latvia was not limited to the Jews. To understand conditions in the country correctly, one must bear in mind that Lettish was young, not only as an official language, but also as a language of civilization in general. German, the official language in the country until the 1880's, and Russian, the language of the government and schools between that time and the First World War, consequently enjoyed much more prestige even among the Letts themselves than they would have as languages of rather inconsiderable minority groups within the country. Even the Lettish intellectuals, including the founders and leaders of the state, had received their education in one of these languages. During the period of independence many Letts still had to use Russian or German in business dealings.

The variegated language picture of the country is reflected in the following figures (1930):

Average Number of Languages Known by One Person

Nationality	% in the whole country	% in cities and towns
Russians	1.28	1.72
White Russians	1.50	1.83
Letts	1.54	1.88
Poles	2.40	2.60
Estonians	2.47	2.89
Lithuanians	2.51	2.09
Germans	2.70	2.79
Jews	2.91	2.93

Several conclusions of a more general nature may be drawn from these figures.

1. Members of smaller language groups in a country (Poles, Estonians, Lithuanians) must know a greater number of languages.

2. Members of language groups (for instance the Germans) who are preeminently city dwellers must know a greater number of languages. This is particularly true of the Jews who as a rule seem to approach every person in his own language. The conclusion as to the Jews is substantiated even further by the figures referring to the capital of Riga, whereas for the Russians and Germans, conditions in the capital appear to deviate from those in the country as a whole.

Of the 369,212 inhabitants of Riga in 1930, 39.79% knew three languages; 28.73% knew one language; 26.70% knew two languages; and 10.56% knew four languages. The particular nationalities, however, differed greatly as to the number of languages known. The following table referring to the city of Riga in 1930 is illuminating:

Nationality	Number of Languages			
	1	2	3	4
Jews	9.93	17.11	26.11	36.68
Russians	9.78	23.7	47.65	13.92
Letts	36.23	28.44	29.26	4.72
Germans	42.41	33.03	18.44	4.44

Attitude Toward War; Toward the United States.

In spite of their many adversities, the Jews of Latvia knew that war would infinitely worsen their position. Russian conquest meant nationalization of trade and industry, standardization of education along Communist lines and ostracism, if not liquidation, of all those suspected of bourgeois leanings. Nazi conquest meant physical extinction. Now that both conquests have successively materialized, it has turned out that the worst expectations were by no means exaggerated.

The attitude of the Jews in Latvia toward the United States, as of those in the whole of Europe, has always been enthusiastic. Many of their compatriots had immigrated to the United States; their social and economic advance had been duly noted, and many persons and institutions benefited directly from material support coming from America.

Underground Movement.

No information about an underground movement in the Latvia of today has seeped through. Soviet reports speak of a partisan movement in this region, but in view of the early and complete segregation of the Jewish population by the Nazis, it appears doubtful whether any considerable number of Jews could have joined the partisans.

Groups-in-Exile.

No attempt to set up a Latvian government-in-exile has been made. At the end of 1939, after signing the Moscow pact of mutual assistance, the Latvian government decided that in case it should be deprived of its freedom of action, all its powers would be transferred to the Latvian envoy in London and should he prove unable to carry out his mission, to the Latvian envoy in Washington, D. C., Dr. Alfred Bĭlmanis. A union of Latvians abroad set up during this war in New York has as its vice-president a Dr. Danenberg.

Citizenship.

The citizenship law of Latvia gave the opportunity of naturalization to anyone who had resided in the country for five years. In 1935 the Jews of Latvia were classified as follows: Latvian citizens, 86,427; aliens, 3,625; stateless, 3,313.

After the coup d'état of 1934, naturalization became much more difficult. In view of the relatively small number of stateless Jews involved (26% of the stateless residents of the country were Jews), statelessness did not constitute a serious problem, the chief difficulty being that stateless persons had to pay a rather heavy tax for the right to stay in the country and that the permission to stay had to be renewed every six or even every three months.

Civil Service.

There were practically no Jews in the civil service of the country even under democratic rule. Margers Skujeneiks, known as a socialist economist in Czarist days, later the leader of the "New Farmers" and for many years the chief of the state statistical department, one of Ulmanis' lieutenants during the coup d'état and an ardent advocate of Lettization, publicly pointed to this absence of the Jews from civil service as one of the signs of the privileged economic positions held by the minorities. According to him, they stubbornly refused to enter the low-salaried civil service because more brilliant careers were oepn to them in the professions and in private business.

Taxes.

Since the urban population bore the chief burden of taxation in the country and persons engaged in commerce and industry were the chief taxpayers, the Jews paid more taxes than their proportion in the general population would have warranted. But no particular complaints of discriminatory assessment of taxes were known to have been made by Jewish taxpayers before Ulmanis embarked upon a program of depriving the Jews of their economic strongholds. In this undertaking he made use of more effective means than the exaction of excessive taxes.

As the Jewish Kehillah was not a public corporation, no special Jewish taxes were collected by the state. Yiddish and Hebrew schools, though completely tax-supported, were maintained out of the general funds of the Ministry of Education.

Minority Rights.

Minority rights in Latvia were in the main school rights, providing opportunity to educate children in their own languages. Latvia did not sign the Versailles minority treaties, since the country was recognized de jure considerably later, but in a declaration issued on its admission to the League of Nations, Latvia promised fair treatment of minorities. The democratic government fully lived up to these promises; even the totalitarian government of Ulmanis, though it aimed at uprooting the minorities economically, infringed upon the autonomy of the minority groups in the educational field without abolishing the minority schools as such.

The school laws of democratic Latvia gave parents the right to send their children to a school conducted in the language they preferred. The state, or for that matter the municipalities, had to provide the necessary number of classes. Administration of the minority schools was granted to the Russian, the German and the Jewish departments respectively of the Ministry of Education. The directors of these departments were responsible to the Minister of Education and were entitled to be present at the meeting of the Council of Ministers when questions relating to their fields were to be discussed. Appointments were recommended to the Minister by the Saeima (Diet) members of each respective nationality; a consultative body of educational leaders of each nationality was to assist the director of each department. As far as is known, no conflicts in carrying out these regulations occurred.

Under Ulmanis the minority departments as well as the consultative bodies were abolished; instead, individual officials (referents) for each minority school system were appointed. For the Jewish schools, Morduch Khodakov, an active member of the Agudath Israel, was chosen.

A limitation imposed by the Ulmanis government upon the minority schools was that parents could no longer arbitrarily choose a school for their children; children could attend either a school in their family language or a Lettish school.

Government Departments for Jewish Affairs.

Except for the Jewish department in the Ministry of Education, there was no office devoted to Jewish affairs in any ministry.

Occupational Structure.

The occupational distribution of the gainfully employed Jewish population according to the census of 1935 was as follows:

	Number	% of gainfully employed Jews.
Agriculture	457	1.11
Industry	11,838	28.74
Trade and commerce	20,021	48.63
Communications	903	2.19
Public administration	610	1.48
Professions, education, art, etc.	3,046	7.40
Public health, hygiene	1,642	3.99
Domestic service	838	2.04
Others	1,819	4.42
Total	41,170	

For the purpose of comparison it may be useful to quote the respective figures for the German minority group which, particularly after the agrarian reform of the early twenties, was also predominantly an urban group (the total number of Germans in 1935 was 58,113; of these 51,106 lived in urban settlements):

Occupation	No. gainfully employed	%
Agriculture	5,917	15.97
Industry	9,915	26.77
Trade and commerce	7,310	19.74
Communications	1,523	4.11
Public Administration	1,165	3.15
Professions, etc.	4,527	12.22
Public health	1,844	4.98
Domestic service	2,416	6.52
Others	2,423	6.54
Total	37,040	

(A. Maldups, *Latvija Skaitlos*, 1938, p. 77)

The Judiciary.

As far as known there were no Jewish judges in independent Latvia.

Industry.

Latvian statistics deal with crafts (artisan) and industries together, so that there is no way of distinguishing them in the following discussion except that the statistics regarding the number of persons employed in an enterprise may offer some clue. Although gathered a year after the establishment of the authoritarian regime, the 1935 figures essentially reflected pre-Ulmanis conditions since the new economic policy gained momentum only later.

The statistics differentiate between individual enterprises and corporations of all kinds. No detailed classification of the corporates is given. In 1935, 49,774 individual enterprises were existent in Latvia, of which 35,416, or 74%, were owned by Letts; 67% of the employees were Letts. The total value of industrial and craft production in 1935 was 476,000,000 lats ($95,200,000). The value of the production of all four forms of companies was 204,500,000 lats ($40,900,000) which would leave to the individual enterprises 271,500,000 lats ($54,300,000). There were 213 corporate enterprises owned by Jews; their total production was valued at 72,798,000 lats ($14,559,600), or 35.6% of the total production value of the corporate firms.

The number of Jewish enterprises according to the number of workers employed was as follows:

Size of enterprise by no. of workers.	Total no. of enterprises in the country	Total no. belonging to the Jews Absolute	%	Percentage in relation to the no. of Jewish enterprises
I 0 - 4	46,404	4,627	9.97	92.62
II 5 - 9	833	193	23.17	3.86
III 10 - 19	369	93	25.20	1.86
IV 20 - 49	224	56	25.00	1.12
V 50 - 99	61	17	27.87	0.34
VI 100 and over	30	10	33.34	0.20
Total	47,921	4,996	10.43	100.00

Division by craft and industry was as follows:

Branch	Total number of enterprises	Total number of enterprises owned by Jews Absolute	%	Percentage in relation to number of enterprises owned by Jews
I Mines and quarries	30	-	-	-
II Ceramics, stone products	790	30	3.80	0.60
III Metallurgy, mechanical construction	6,545	646	9.87	12.93
IV Chemical industry	290	87	32.00	1.74
V Leather industry	798	135	16.92	2.70
VI Textile industry	1,317	77	5.85	1.54
VII Lumber industry	6,346	198	3.12	3.96
VIII Paper industry	72	31	43.05	0.62
IX Graphic arts	755	128	16.95	2.56
X Food industry	4,075	343	8.12	6.87
XI Clothing, shoe industry	18,947	2,967	15.66	59.39
XII Building industry	7,923	353	4.46	7.07
XIII Public Utilities	33	1	3.03	0.02
Total	47,921	4,996	10.43	100.00

Of the total number of enterprises in crafts and industry, 53.66% were located in urban settlements and 46.34% elsewhere. The enterprises owned by Jews were predominantly urban, the corresponding figures being 92.61 and 7.39% The distribution according to districts was as follows: In Riga the Jews owned 23% of all individual enterprises, in Vidzeme, 2.54, in Kurzeme, 13.51, in Zemgale, 6.78, in Latgale, 27.14. The distribution of these enterprises according to districts showed that Riga had 58.85% of all individual enterprises owned by Jews; Vidzeme, 2.88; Kurzeme, 12.48; Zemgale, 5.44; Latgale, 20.35.

Commerce.

In 1935, statistics concerning commercial enterprises included the following:

	Absolute	Percent	Persons Employed	Percent
Enterprises owned by Letts	27,164	58.8	51,757	54.5
Enterprises owned by Jews	11,295	24.4	23,943	25.2

The number of persons employed in Jewish enterprises is by no means identical with the number of Jews employed in commerce. The latter figure may be approximately obtained by deducting the number of Jewish owners of commercial enterprises (11,295) from the total number of Jews engaged in trade and commerce (20,021), leaving 8,726. In Latgale, the percentage of commercial enterprises owned by Jews was as high as 60%. In 1937, 11,242 trade licenses were issued to Jews which, however, constituted no more than 28.9% of the total number of licenses issued.

Trade license statistics also show that the number of large enterprises owned by Jews had dropped during the years 1933 to 1937:

Licenses of the First and Second Category Issued

	1933	1937
To Letts:	27.3%	33.6%
To Jews:	48.6%	45.8%

Other figures, however, show that 11,166 commercial enterprises were owned by Jews and 22,405 by Letts. The percentages, according to the latter data, are:

Enterprises	Letts	Germans	Jews	Poles	Russians	Others
1st and 2nd categories (larger)	30.0	16.3	47.9	0.5	1.4	3.9
3rd, 4th and 5th categories (smaller)	58.0	4.2	27.8	2.1	6.0	1.9

The total commercial turnover during 1936 amounted to 1,170,000,000 lats ($234,000,000). After deducting the turnover in state monopolies in rye, sugar, spirits and wood, the figure of 897,000,000 lats ($179,400,000) is left. Of this, 496,300,000 lats ($99,260,000) were provided by the large enterprises, of which 149,000,000 lats ($29,800,000) were provided by enterprises belonging to Letts. Altogether Lettish-owned enterprises provided 381,500,000 lats ($76,700,000) and those owned by Jews 349,000,000 lats ($69,800,000).

The policy of Ulmanis, before his access to power, was openly directed toward eliminating the minority groups from economic life and of giving the Letts access to all positions in the national economy. But since the development of this policy seemed too slow and events in Europe seemed to justify a prodding of the historical process, Ulmanis and his group seized power and started to use the state machinery for the purpose of creating a "Lettish Latvia". More than once Ulmanis emphasized that "government in business" was not contemplated as a permanent policy and that eventually private enterprise would be returned its full measure of rights. In the meantime, however, 'social justice' demands "a rearrangement of the hitherto existing position" (Ulmanis in a speech, February 5, 1937) by which the Letts had been presumably underprivileged in their own country. Birznieks, the Minister of Agriculture, in a speech delivered in Ventspils on January 26, 1936, was much more outspoken: "The Letts are the only masters of this country; the Letts will themselves promulgate the laws and judge for themselves what justice is." This passage refers to the economic laws of December 31, 1935 and January 11, 1936 which together with subsequent laws and regulations succeeded in establishing in Latvia an economic order that in respect to state interference was second only to Soviet Russia.

These laws provided for the establishment of a chamber of commerce and industry. "To fulfill particular tasks and in order to cultivate activity of businessmen and industrialists", business and industrial associations were created which were to function under the direction of the chamber. "In every town with a population of over 10,000 inhabitants one such association is to exist...Apart from...associations under the control of the chamber no associations or organizations are to be founded for protecting and furthering the interests of commerce and industry. All hitherto existing commercial and industrial non-profit associations, alliances and organizations of different types have to cease their activities within three months after this law comes into force..."

The point was clear. All minority associations were to disappear in favor of a state-supported, government-supporting chamber of a fascist brand, to consist of 90 members and 45 substitutes to be appointed by the Minister of Finance for three years. Four Jews were among the appointees but they had no influence. All non-profit business and industrial associations previously in existence had to surrender their whole property to this newly-created, Lettish body.

In close cooperation with the chamber of commerce and industry, the government proceeded in its ruthless policy. As J. Bokalder, a member of this chamber, wrote in "The Industry and Home Trade of Latvia" (The Latvian Economist, Riga, 1937, p. 75): "In accordance with these necessities and the guiding principles of an authoritarian state, the government on July 9, 1936 promulgated a special law . . . concerning craft and industrial enterprises...to correspond with the correctly and objectively understood interests of national economy. . . Thus the Ministry of Finance will be able in the future to prevent the opening of new branches of enterprise in which there is already over-production or at least the danger of overproduction...In every enterprise there has to be a . . . manager . . . responsible for the rationality and utility of the enterprise . . . The Minister of Finance can by special decree determine which industrial enterprises or industrial groups require a technical manager with professional rights acknowledged in Latvia, or with a special education."

The Latvian Credit Bank (Latvijas Kreditbanka) has been founded even earlier, by the law of April 9, 1935. It was modestly presented as a private credit establishment which at the beginning had a capital of only 10,000,000 lats ($2,000,000). No restrictions customarily applied to commercial banks were imposed; according to the by-laws of the bank, the functions of the board and of the general meetings were transferred to the Minister of Finance.

Thus instruments were created by which the government could "take possession of any commercial enterprise in the country, should this be in the interest of the state." A number of the most important textile plants, breweries and distilleries, tanneries, chocolate factories, tobacco factories, plywood, brick and cement factories owned by Jews were taken over by the Credit Bank or by corporations assigned by it. L. Ekis, Minister of Finance, did not entirely deviate from the truth when he wrote (Latvian Economist, Riga, 1937, p. 17): "In many cases where the credit bank has taken over private economic enterprises, this has been achieved by free-will sales." He could even have added that the Credit Bank, or for that matter the government, paid good prices and that in spite of severe restrictions in exporting money, the sellers, at least in some cases, obtained their money in foreign currency abroad. The only thing he failed to say was that the "free will" was created by coercion. In many places, enterprises were combined; for instance, of eleven plywood plants only three remained. Competition was reduced and frequently eliminated.

Banking was one of the chief objects of Lettization. According to some computations, about 90% of the credit establishments in Latvia were in Lettish hands in 1939, as against 20% in 1933.

Foreign trade was also controlled. Imports were subjected to a rigid system of concessions or even monopolies. A state-supported association of import cooperatives was founded under the name Turība (Prosperity) with a founding capital of 7,000,000 lats ($1,400,000); its secondary purpose was to endeavor to distribute cooperatives equally throughout the whole country. Shortly after May 15, 1934, the export of butter, one of the chief items in Latvian economy, was concentrated in the hands of Centralais sviesta eksporta; the export of bacon and other basic products of the country was handed over to an organization called Bekone eksporta; other agricultural products, too were similarly handled. Fixed prices, on a considerably higher level than on the world market, were established and guaranteed to the producers. Import companies for coal (Ogla) and other products also started functioning under government guidance, which meant the elimination of non-Lettish capital, management and labor. The names of the same officials, Peasant Union bosses, and professionals close to the government appeared on the boards of more and more commercial and industrial enterprises.

To round out the fascisation of the country and its transformation into a "cooperative state", a chamber of professions and another of literature and art (May 5,1938) were established. A general law concerning non-profit-making societies enacted on February 11, 1938,implied the liquidation of all associations not complying with the law relating to the chambers.

Employment; Wages.

No figures were published regarding Jewish employees and workers. The Department of Statistics did, however, tabulate the number of persons, not indicating nationality employed in 1935 by individual enterprises belonging to Jews. The general number of employees in the country is given as 95,486, out of which 15,664 (16.41%) were employed by Jews.

As a rule, Jews could get work only in enterprises owned by Jews. There was, however, a proportion of Jewish workers in highly developed plants that came into being in the 1930's as a result of the rigid anti-importation laws.

Jewish workers were paid the same wages as their non-Jewish colleagues where they worked together, although the promotion of Jewish workers even in Jewish-owned enterprises was somewhat slower. In the small artisans' shops where no more than one or two Jewish workers were employed, their average income was certainly lower than in the industrial enterprises.

Trade Unions.

There were no separate Jewish trade unions in Latvia. In the democratic era some Jews did achieve prominence in the socialist or the communist unions (before the latter were suppressed). The unions created by the Ulmanis regime were compulsory for all workers and as far as the larger enterprises were concerned this rule was strictly adhered to, but the leadership everywhere was confined to Letts.

The Press.

The impact of the totalitarian regime upon the Yiddish press is best presented in the following figures of publications in Yiddish:

1933 - 11   1935 - 2
1934 - 14   1936 - 2

In 1937 one Yiddish daily and two weeklies were in existence.

The large Russian newspaper Sevodnia, which appeared twice daily and was quite influential all over the Baltic countries and widely read as far as Warsaw, was published by a Jewish-owned concern, the Riti corporation. This publishing house also issued several weeklies, magazines, books, etc. in Russian, Yiddish, German and Lettish. Under the new economic laws the whole concern was taken over by the government.

In the highly developed Lettish press the Jews as a rule did not play any part worth mentioning. Jaunakas Zinas, which enjoyed the widest circulation, had some foreign correspondents who were Jewish.

Health Services.

In democratic Latvia there seems to have been no discrimination against the Jews in state or municipal health services. A Jew for many years headed the Health Department of Riga. Under Ulmanis not only was he removed, but most of the Jewish physicians who worked for the Health Insurance (Slimibas Kasa) were dismissed. As far as is known, no particular complaints were voiced about the treatment of the Jews as patients.

Jews also had their own supplementary Jewish agencies, centralized by the OSE World Health Union in Riga. According to the report published in the Paris Revue OSE (March 1939) the Latvian OSE was at that time maintaining 41 different health institutions caring for between 4,000 and 5,000 children in eight towns; two health centers in Riga and Daugavpils (Dvinsk, Dünaburg); two summer camps for 800 children; one summer camp for adolescents, and other institutions. About 300 families suspected of being tubercular were under constant observation; a number of backward children were cared for and the medical and dental care of the whole Jewish school population was entrusted to the OSE. At least part of its income was derived from municipal funds.

Medical Practitioners.

There were 1,589 physicians in Latvia in 1938, including 967 Letts. Earlier and detailed figures give the following information:

District	1927 Total No.	1927 No. of Jews	1932 Total No.	1932 No. of Jews	1934 Total No.	1934 No. of Jews
Riga	1,006	438	1,205	490	1,251	496
Vidzeme	194	28	261	35	294	31
Kurzeme	195	95	246	107	263	104
Zemgale	131	37	202	65	215	60
Latgale	150	78	211	99	230	90
Total	1,676	676	2,125	796	2,253	781
Of these, the following number were dentists	524	372	694	443	754	441

Hospitals.

Data regarding Jewish hospitals and sanatoriums in Latvia in 1938 are as follows:

Hospital	No. of Beds	Number of patients during the year
In Riga		
1. Bikur Holim (organization)	100	1,799
2. Linas Hacedek (organization)	50	1,505
3. Shenfeld	30	62
4. Dubinski	15	371
5. Chackelson	10	132
6. Hercfeld	12	262
7. Berniker	10	247
8. Naichin	10	101
9. Ickin	7	406
10. Kushner	5	89
11. Aronshtam	10	58
12. Minc	21	485
In Jelgava (Mitava, Mitau)		
13. Bikur Holim (organization)	40	324
14. Chanal	10	139
In Ludze (Lyutsin, Ludsin)		
15. Gurevic	20	251

The total number of beds available in the hospitals and sanatoriums of the country in 1938 was 13,218; the number of patients admitted to these institutions during the year was 130,871.

Birth Rate.

The number of births among Jews was:

Year	Number of births	Percentage of Jewish births in relation to total number
1925	1,755	4.2
1930	1,515	4.0
1935	1,290	3.8
1936	1,204	3.4
1937	1,261	3.6

There was a similar decrease among the Germans, Russians and Lithuanians in the country. Per 1,000 Jews the birth rate was:

1925	18.34
1930	16.5
1935	13.79
1936	12.86
1937	13.46

The corresponding figures for the other nationalities in 1937 were

Letts	17.09	Lithuanians	13.73
Germans	11.69	Russians	24.24

The Russian birth rate for 1925 (34.88) for every 1,000 Russian inhabitants of Latvia, shows a decrease by 10.64, or more than 30% in 12 years, while the decrease among the Jews in the same period was 4.88, or 26%. The birth rate for the country as a whole during the decade in question decreased by 4.53.

The number of children born to an average Jewish family are shown by the following figures (1931):

Children born in wedlock (by order of birth)

	1st	2nd	3rd	4th	5th	6th	Over 6
Total	33.52	23.01	15.07	9.86	6.70	4.15	5.63
Jews	39.22	24.13	16.01	9.40	5.62	2.63	2.28

Mortality.

The mortality rate for 1938, according to nationalities, was as follows:

Total number of deaths

Nationality	Absolute Number	Out of 1,000 persons of each nationality
Germans	1,079	17.8
Poles	765	15.3
Letts	19,946	13.4
Russians	3,217	13.3
Lithuanians	281	12.3
Jews	1,111	11.8

In infant mortality (children under one year), the Jews occupied the lowest place.

Out of every 100 children born alive, there died in

Nationality	1931	1938
Jews	3.49	3.2
Germans	6.07	5.5
Letts	7.92	6.0
Lithuanians	8.18	9.8
Poles	10.29	9.4
Russians	12.93	10.4
Average	8.63	

There were considerable differences in infant mortality among the non-Jews as to the districts; significantly, however, there was no practical difference among the Jews. The following statistics (1936) are of infants who died out of every 100 born alive:

Nationality	Riga Boys	Riga Girls	Latgale Boys	Latgale Girls	Latvia as a whole Boys	Latvia as a whole Girls
Letts	5.5	2.9	9.0	7.1	6.7	5.3
Jews	3.2	3.9	3.1	3.9	3.3	3.2

Average for all groups in the whole country: boys - 8.6; girls - 14.1. There was also a much higher mortality of boy infants than girls among the Letts, whereas no such discrepancy existed among Jews.

The progress made by the Jews in combating infant mortality is shown by the figures for 1927. The Jewish infant mortality rate (the number of infants who died out of every 100 born alive) for 1927 was 4.22, showing a drop of 25% in 9 years.

Latvian official statistics cite nationality in relation to death causes only with regard to tuberculosis and other pulmonary ailments:

Nationality		Total No. of deaths		Death due to Tuberculosis			Other illnesses of the respiratory organs		
		Absolute	Percent	Absolute	Percent	% in relation to total deaths	Absolute	Percent	% in rel. to tot.no.
Letts:	1933	3,052	58.92	419	65.16	13.73	266	60.18	8.72
	1938	2,933	60.33	315	70.16	10.74	301	60.68	10.26
Germans:	1933	704	13.59	66	10.26	9.38	42	9.50	5.97
	1938	649	13.35	33	7.35	5.08	63	12.70	9.71
Russians:	1933	476	9.19	70	10.89	14.71	48	10.86	10.08
	1938	443	9.11	38	8.46	8.58	43	8.67	9.71
Jews:	1933	530	10.23	38	5.91	7.17	47	10.63	8.87
	1938	474	9.67	24	5.34	5.11	41	8.27	8.72
Poles:	1933	218	4.21	33	5.13	15.14	25	5.56	11.47
	1938	196	4.03	21	4.68	10.71	27	5.44	13.78
Lithuanians	1933	95	1.83	12	1.87	12.63	9	2.04	9.47
	1938	87	1.79	9	2.00	10.34	11	2.22	12.64

Housing.

For 1935 the following figures on housing conditions in Latvian cities and towns according to nationality are available.

Housing conditions in Latvian towns according to ethnic groups in 1935 (in percentages)

Number of Rooms	Jews	Letts	Russians	Germans
Room-kitchen	5.1	13.1	15.3	5.4
1 room	11.5	44.3	40.7	23.08
2 rooms	24.9	23.6	22.5	23.2
3 rooms	26.6	11.2	12.8	19.6
4 rooms	17.0	4.5	4.7	12.6
5 rooms	9.6	2.0	2.2	7.8
6-7 rooms	4.5	1.0	1.4	6.1
8 and over or unknown	0.8	0.3	0.4	1.5

Education.

Before the establishment of the Ulmanis regime, the educational facilities for Jews were provided as part of the minority set-up of the country. Schools in which Yiddish and Hebrew was the language of instruction were maintained by the municipalities or the state, and there was a Jewish Department under the Ministry of Education. Under Ulmanis the Jewish schools were affected by a law promulgated on July 24, 1934, abolishing the minority school departments and substituting individual officials ("referents"). The Jewish schools of all types were turned over to the Agudath Israel which did its best to transform them, with the help of state machinery, into Orthodox schools. A number of Jewish parents who disliked this return to religious schooling reminiscent of the Heder (Hebrew school), preferred to transfer their children to Lettish schools. Nevertheless it must be emphasized that the right of the Jews to have their own tax-supported schools in their own languages (Yiddish or Hebrew) was maintained even under the dictatorship, but a number of Jewish schools were closed for reasons of "economy" or "efficiency" in the general course of school reforms. In 1932 the total number of Jewish schools was 122; in 1939 it had fallen to 77. The corresponding figures for Lettish schools in these two years were 1,679 and 1,672.

Elementary Schools: Of the 1,904 elementary schools in existence in the country in the academic year 1937-1938, 62 (3.3%) were Jewish (Yiddish or Hebrew was the language of instruction). They were attended by 9,715 (4.2%) children out of the total of 231,533 children of school age. Since there were 11,372 (4.87%) Jews by nationality in the elementary schools that year, only 1,657 Jewish children attended Lettish schools. In preceding years the number of children attending Yiddish and Hebrew elementary schools had been:

1936-1937	10,205
1935-1936	10,562
1934-1935	10,998

The proportion of Jewish children in the elementary schools of the country during the preceding years had been:

Year	Total number	Jews
1925-26	173,099	11,804
1935-36	223,483	12,347
1936-37	231,591	11,912
1937-38	231,533	11,572
1938-39	229,825	11,127

An average Jewish elementary school had 157 children. For an average Lettish school the corresponding figure was 124; for a German, 86; for a Lithuanian, 48; and Estonian, only 29.

The number of teachers in Jewish (Yiddish and Hebrew) elementary schools in the academic year 1936-37 is given as 544. Most of them were undoubtedly Jews, but no exact figures are available.

Trade Schools: In the elementary trade schools, the number of Jewish students in 1936-37 was 465, or 10.4% of the total attendance. During the next year, the number dropped to 463.

High Schools: There were 11 high schools (9.67%) in Latvia where Yiddish or Hebrew was the language of instruction (it should be noted that the Latvian high school Vidusskola which prepared students for the university was roughly equivalent to the American high school plus the first two years of college.) These 11 schools had 1,626 students in 1937-38. The total number of Jews by nationality in high schools was 2,367(10.0%), which means that 742 Jews attended other than Jewish high schools.

In contrast to the elementary school population, the number of students in Yiddish and Hebrew high schools had increased almost constantly during the preceding years:

1920-21	664	1935-36	1,561
1933-34	1,549	1936-37	1,550
1934-35	1,400		

For the academic years 1936-37 and 1937-38, the following figures are available:

Jewish High Schools belonging to	Number of Schools		Number of Students		Number of Teachers	
	1936-37	1937-38	1936-37	1937-38	1936-37	1937-1938
the State	2	2	267	273	29	28
Municipalities	2	2	375	363	49	48
Organizations and persons	6	7	908	989	100	105
Total	10	11	1,550	1,625	178	181

In 1936-1939 there were the following Jewish high schools in Latvia:

Name of School	No. of Students	No. of Teachers
Riga		
1. Yiddish City H. S. (Municipal)	225	32
2. Jewish H. S. of Arts and Letters	153	18
3. Jewish Society H. S.	212	17
4. Ezra H. S.	244	20
5. Kheder Mesukon H. S.	66	17
6. J. Rauchvarger H. S.	217	18
Liepaja (Libava, Libau)		
7. Jewish State H. S. (State-maintained)	154	16
Ventspils (Vindava, Windau)		
8. Jewish Association H. S. (State-maintained)	16	10
Daugavpils (Dvinsk, Dünaburg)		
9. Jewish State H. S. (State-maintained)	150	17
Rezekne (Ryezhitsa, Rositten)		
10. Jewish State H. S. (State-maintained)	113	13

The Jewish high school students (2,367, in 1937-38; 2,311 the previous year) were distributed in different types of high schools as follows:

Type of H.S.	1936-37	1937-38
General (gymnasium)	2,156	2,192
Commercial	90	107
Teachers training	28	29
Technical	22	21
Agricultural	1	1
Others	14	17

There was also one Jewish school for nurses, with 15 students (1936-37 and 1937-38). In 1936-37, eight girls were graduated from this school. The ORT Society for the promotion of trade and agriculture maintained a vocational school for agricultural and technical instruction.

Private courses: On December 1, 1937, private courses in the following subjects were attended by Jews:

Subject	Men	Women
Bookkeeping, typing, etc.	17	58
Technical	15	4
Languages	68	153
Home economics	1	--
Sewing	18	87
Arts and crafts	753	99
Dancing, athletics	21	122
Music	50	118
Dramatics	--	--
Painting, drawing	5	5
Religious courses	399	39
General	87	81
Medicine	1	43
Total	1,435	809

Higher education: In the three institutions of higher learning in Latvia, the Jews were represented as follows in the academic year 1937-38: University, 432 Jewish students (6.4% of the student body); Conservatory, 45 Jewish students (16.2%); Academy of Arts, 1 Jewish student (0.5%). In the Latvian University the ratio of Jewish students had decreased steadily. In 1936-37 the percentage had amounted to 6.83; in 1924-25 to 8.84; in 1919-20 to 19.57.

Within the university, the Jewish students were distributed as follows (1936-1937): architecture, 16; philology, philosophy, 38; engineering, 28; chemistry, 62; agriculture, 19; mathematics, science, 52; mechanics, 76; medicine, 34; law, economics, 130; veterinary art, 8; total, 463.

According to the degree of their economic independence, the university students were distributed as follows:

	Total no. of students	Jewish students
Completely independent	3,226	152
Partly independent	929	80
Dependent	3,092	212

The number of Jewish students at the Conservatory was as follows:

1927-28	34	1936-37	50
1931-32	56	1937-38	45
1935-36	48	(Salnītis, op. cit., p. 183)	

The number of Jewish students attending the Academy of Arts was:

1935-36	3
1936-37	4
1937-38	1

There are also available figures concerning Jewish attendance in the following institutions classified as higher vocational schools, both public and private (1936-37).

Institution	No. of Jewish students	Total no. of students
Commerce Institute	3	108
2nd Commerce Institute	31	222
Herder Institute (German)	4	220
State English Institute	34	378

Under the democratic government the teachers for the different types of Jewish schools were selected by the respective teachers' organizations and appointed by the Jewish department of the Ministry of Education. The practice was so liberal as to allow even the appointment of a number of aliens who by the regular procedure of naturalization became Latvian citizens after five years had elapsed. Under Ulmanis the training and selection of teachers was entrusted to the Agudath Israel.

Welfare Institutions.

Exact data on Jewish welfare organizations in Latvia are practically unavailable and no reports of such institutions can be traced for the time being. It may be said, however, that under the democratic regime, Jewish institutions were not discriminated against as far as participation in state and municipal funds was concerned.

History of Anti-Semitism.

In the Czarist days an outspoken anti-Semitic faction was led by Fridrichs Veinbergs, whose mouthpiece was the paper Latviešu Avize. It did not survive the First World War, but the anti-Semitic ideas continued to permeate the ideology of several social and political groupings in independent Latvia. They were particularly recognizable in the Peasant's Union headed by Ulmanis, although this does not apply to Ulmanis himself, who freely associated with Jews in his numerous business enterprises and seemingly had no personal prejudices. Anti-Semitic doctrines were also noticeable among the Union of New Farmers, who were granted land under the agrarian laws of the early 1920's; their leader was Margers Skujenieks, a former Socialist who repeatedly advocated the abolition of the economic "privileges" of minorities, including the Jews. In 1934 Skujenieks, as Vice-Prime Minister, joined Ulmanis in the proclamation of the authoritarian state under the slogan "A Lettish Latvia".

During the first years of Latvian independence there was much hostility against the Jews which led from time to time even to outbursts and kept alive a feeling of insecurity in the Jewish population. The reasons were partly of an economic nature; young Lettish bourgeoisie and professionals, imbued with pride in their newly-won independence, viewed the Jew as an undesirable competitor. There was also a feeling that the Jews, with their leaning toward German or Russian -- the languages of two powerful adjacent cultures -- menaced the development of a strong Lettish culture. When, however, Latvia succeeded in overcoming the attempts of the Russians and the Germans to deprive her of her independence, and conditions became stabilized, the anti-Jewish feelings gradually subsided. During the 1920's, before Nazi doctrines penetrated into the country, there was never a thought of encroaching upon Jewish rights and even the cooperative movement was as a rule not supported by the state to the detriment of the Jewish population engaged in trade and commerce. The meticulous regard of the governments and the municipalities for the school rights of minorities aided in the development of the general feeling that the Jews were equal citizens.

Particularly close cooperation existed in the labor organizations. The Bund -- the Jewish Socialist organization -- and its youth division from the very beginning constituted a section of the Social Democratic party of the country. No separate Jewish trade unions were in existence.

With the rise of National Socialism in Germany, Hitlerian ideas also spread to Latvia and no doubt Nazi money rather early became active in the country. At the beginning of the 1930's or somewhat earlier, an organization sprang up called Pērkankrusts (Lightning Cross), patterned after the Nazi model in both name and ideology. Small in size, it exercised considerable influence. Its first adherents were probably drawn from the ranks of university students who anticipated Jewish competition in their later professional life. They were supported by some professionals and intellectuals. Some higher-rank military, administrative and police officials also lent the Pērkankrusts their support. The actual strength of the organization was never revealed because it preferred to veil itself in secrecy, but in the early 1930's it started to stage street demonstrations directed against Socialists and Jews, and to publish pamphlets and leaflets against both of them. One of the pamphlets (published in 1934) was significantly called Socialdemokratija Kā Žīdu Privatā Armija (Social Democracy as a Private Army of the Jews). With the rise of Hitlerism in Germany, the movement seemed to gather momentum; rumors about close ties between the Pērkankrusts and the Nazis never ceased to circulate. Ulmanis cited the alleged preparations of the Pērkankrusts to seize power as one of the reasons for his coup d'état, and indeed the Ulmanis regime suppressed this movement together with all other forms of political activity. During the summer of 1934, Gustavs Celmiņš and a number of other persons connected with him in the leadership of the Pērkankrusts were arrested and never heard of again.

In the early 1930's, the Protocols of the Elders of Zion and several other Nazi publications were translated into Lettish. The following anti-Jewish publications of 1933-1934 may also be quoted:

Nostradamus Redivivus, Arcanum revelatum (astsegtais noslēpums) jeb Patiesība par žīdiem (The Revealed Secret or the Truth About the Jews) Riga, 1933, 112 pp; Dr. M. Luters, Par žīdiem un uinu meliem. Tulkojis un apgādajis J. Dāvis (Luther, About the Jews and Their Lies), Riga, 1934, 15 pp; J. Dāvis, Rabins Pauls kā kristietības pār žīdotajs (Rabbi Paul, the Judaizer of Christianity); J. Dāvis, Kapēc vecā derība nav mācama skolas un baznīcas? (Why the Old Testament Should Not Be Taught in Schools and Churches); G.A. Kalniņž, Žīdu loma cilvēces vēsturē (The Role of the Jews in Human History), Riga, 1934, 178 pp.

J. Dāvis, previously a leader in the anti-alcoholic movement, seems to have been particularly active in publishing anti-Jewish literature. The pamphlet on the Social Democrats as Jewish mercenaries mentioned above, which significantly ends in a eulogy for Ulmanis, also bears his name.

These anti-Semitic publications, as indicated by their titles are strikingly reminiscent of the German literature of the Theodor E. Fritsch brand. Fritsch is profusely quoted in most of these pamphlets. In some cases Christianity is identified with Judaism, though simultaneously the Jews are pictured as the worst enemies of Christendom. The Jews in Latvia are only casually referred to, which is additional proof that the ideas contained in these publications were imported.

With the establishment of the totalitarian regime, the attitude toward the Jews became more aggressive. Though no law was promulgated that explicitly discriminated against the Jews and though the other minorities also felt the meaning of the "Lettish Latvia" policy, the situation of the Jews as a whole and of every Jew in particular tended to become more precarious. The object lesson of the Social Democratic organization in practicing partnership had disappeared; the new unions established on a fascist model by Ulmanis' propaganda minister, Alfrēds Berzinš, always stressed the predominance to be accorded the Lettish element. The whole economic policy of the state, with its candid intention to eliminate all non-Lettish groups, succeeded in creating within the Jewish population a sense of being doomed to poverty and disappearance. This apprehension grew more acute with the growth of Hitler's international power and the imminence of the war.

Among the outspoken anti-Semites in the 1920's and 1930's may also be mentioned: Arveds Bergs, a lawyer and editor of the newspaper Latvis, and the politician Breiks.

Attitude of Government: Before 1934.

There is little to be said about the attitude of the Latvian government toward the Jews before the establishment of the authoritarian regime in 1934. The government scrupulously fulfilled its obligations in regard to maintaining the Jewish school systems. No limitations were imposed on the Jews in the political field or in free business enterprise. There were limitations to Jewish participation in officialdom and in the allotment of government orders to private business firms. Even more restricted was the admission of Jews in the Latvian University, where rigorous entrance tests in the Lettish language were used to keep away a considerable portion of Jewish applicants. Only one or two Jews were admitted to professorships at the University during the whole period of Latvian independence.

There is one particular point in the situation of the Jews in Latvia which may be understood only through an intimate knowledge of the situation. It is connected with the name of Mordecai Dubin, the leader of the Agudath Israel. A powerful and genial personality, this businessman, without any general education and with a knowledge of only colloquial Lettish, became involved in politics and was elected to the Diet where, among the 100 members split into an endless series of factions, every vote counted. Dubin easily found his way around in the different party maneuvers and soon was at home in every government office from the ministries down. Every Jew in Riga and all over the country became aware that Dubin's intervention could help him toward confirmation of his citizenship, toward the lease of a lot belonging to the government, the extension of permission to conduct a certain kind of business, or the grant of a visa for a relative. In the afternoons and late evenings Dubin's reception room was crowded with visitors and several secretaries had to be employed to cover all the work.

Never did Dubin accept any remuneration for his services. On the contrary, he rendered assistance in the payment of government fees, as well as by encouragement. This personal charm of Dubin's was to a considerable extent responsible for his successes during elections, but from the point of view of the political development of the country and the Jews in it, grave fears were voiced even before the establishment of the dictatorship. Dubin's way of managing things, it was said, amounted in effect to converting rights to which the Jews were entitled into favors that might or might not be granted. His influence was maintained until the outbreak of war, although it had by that time become limited to matters of no material importance.

With the advent of Hitler in 1933 and the dictatorship in Latvia itself a year later, the nationalistic course was strongly emphasized and made a matter of pride instead of evasive apologies. State officials were forbidden to answer questions in any language other than Lettish, except when the person in question was a foreigner who had proved his status by his passport. On June 5, 1934, Ulmanis assured a Jewish delegation that his regime would not limit the rights of the Jews. In all subsequent enunciations of the dictator (who soon was given the name of Vadonis, an exact translation of Führer) and his followers, constant reference was made to the necessity of making Latvia a Lettish country and of eliminating "alien" influences. The economic policy of the Latvian government in crushing minorities was second only to Hitler's anti-Jewish measures, but the word "Jew" was never explicitly mentioned in any law and in this respect Ulmanis kept his word. Whether such linguistic delicacy was of any practical significance is another question.

After the cancellation, in October, 1938, of the Polish citizenship of many thousands of Polish Jews living abroad, Latvian consuls were advised not to grant even temporary visas to Polish Jews. The influx of Jewish refugees from Germany, Austria, Memel and Danzig was severely curtailed; some refugees who had not been able to leave Latvia after the expiration of their temporary visas were said to have been put to forced labor in the summer of 1939.

Extra-Legal Discrimination.

Extra-legal discrimination against the Jews was practiced chiefly in the economic sphere. Some students of Latvian life believe that nowhere else except in Soviet Russia had the state assumed such power in the economic life of the nation as in Latvia. In view of the avowed intention of the authoritarian regime to make Latvia Lettish, the Jews had nothing to hope for. It is nevertheless significant for the general trend of development in Europe in the years preceding this war that the initial anger of the Jewish population quickly changed into sad gratefulness for what little was left. When Ulmanis came into power, Hitler had been dominating Germany for more than a year and the inauguration of full-fledged Nazism in Latvia was justly feared. There was considerable relief when it turned out that although Hitlerism was spreading and increasingly ominous news came from Poland, Hungary and Roumania, Ulmanis intended to impose "only" dispossession and poverty.

The first year of the war, before the Soviet occupation, saw no essential change in the policy of the authoritarian government although in official pronouncements more stress was laid upon the necessity of the unity of all citizens.

The Soviet authorities of occupation did not differentiate between Jews and non-Jews in nationalizing property and industrial or commercial enterprises, or in prosecuting non-Communists and so on. On the other hand, Jews were admitted to employment in the nationalized enterprises, though the Latvian Soviet government exercised great caution in putting Jews in conspicuous posts on the ground that the impression should be avoided that the Soviet regime was a Jewish one. Some Jews, however, believed that anti-Semites had remained in or were given key positions.

Appropriation of Immovable Property.

The appropriation of immovable property under the authoritarian regime was also subject to governmental authorization; practically, only Letts were granted this right. Lettization of Latvian economic life may be gauged by the fact that as early as 1937 all nationalities lost in the number and value of immovable properties in favor of the Letts.

The number of immovables which changed hands in cities or towns in 1937 was:

Nationality	Increased no. of immovables	Value in 1,000 lats
Letts	+ 338	+ 11,536
Germans	- 185	- 4,119
Jews	- 119	- 3,898
Russians	- 90	- 772
Others	- 25	- 2,746

Reconstruction Agencies.

Among the foreign agencies which will be able to cooperate in the rehabilitation of the Jewish population are the American Jewish Joint Distribution Committee; the American Joint-Reconstruction Foundation; the ORT Society for the promotion of trade and agriculture among Jews; the OSE World Union for health protection, the HICEM (Hias-Ica Emigration Association) and the Jewish Agency for Palestine.

JEWS OF LITHUANIA

JEWS OF LITHUANIA

Index

Agriculture	11	Health Services	17
Anti-Semitism	15	Industry	11
Attitude to the United States	18	Labor	11
Attitude to the War	18	Languages	5
Banking	12	Leaders	18
Bar, The	12	Marriage	4
Birth	7	Minority Rights	13
Church	14	Mortality	7
Citizenship	13	Occupation Measures, German	17
Commerce	9	Occupational Distribution	8
Communal Organization	2	People, Attitude of	13
Cooperatives	9	Population	1
Criminality	4	Press	7
Divorce	4	Reconstruction Agencies	18
Economic Position	8	Religion	2
Education	6	Social Services	17
Family	4	Sovietization	17
Government, Attitude of	12	Trade	9
Government, Jews in	13	Women	4

THE JEWS OF LITHUANIA

Population

In 1925 the 154,321 Jews of Lithuania constituted 7.15% of the total population of slightly more than 2,000,000. Varying estimates were made in subsequent years, but it is probable that in 1939 the Jews numbered about 155,000, a little more than 6% of an estimated total 2,500,000. Vilna (Lithuanian -- Vilnius; Polish -- Wilno) was added to Lithuania in 1939 and increased the Jewish population of the country by about 55,000, to total approximately 210,000, or something less than 7.3% of 2,880,000. In 1897 there had been 257,000 Jews in Lithuania, exclusive of Vilna. The drastic decrease was the result of two prime causes: emigration, especially to the United States and South Africa; and deportation to the Russian interior by the Tsarist authorities in 1915.

There was practically complete identity between the number of those who considered themselves Jews by religion and those who considered themselves Jews by ethnic nationality. In 1939 the number of births of both sexes to mothers of the Jewish religion and of the Jewish nationality was the same.

In 1923, 52% of the Jews were urban (living in towns and cities) and 48% were rural (living on farms and in villages). In 1897 only 28% had been urban; 72% had been rural.

The districts most important from the point of view of Jewish population, together with approximate 1923 figures, were as follows: Kaunas, 30,000; Šiauliai, 13,500; Panevežys, 12,500; Ukmerge, 8,200; Raseiniai, 8,200; Utena, 8,000; Alyta, 7,800; Vilkavižkis, 7,200; Marijampole, 6,500; Telšiai, 6,300; Taurage, 6,200. Memel was ceded to Germany in 1939; in 1930 it had a population of 42,000, of whom at least 3,000 were conservatively estimated to be Jewish, as against the 578 Jews in Memel in 1924.

Towns and cities with important Jewish population, together with approximate 1923 figures on Jewish and total population for each, were as follows: Kaunas (Polish-Kowno; also known as Kovno), 25,000 Jews of a total of 154,000; Panevežys, 6,900 of 26,600; Šiauliai, 5,400 of 31,650; Ukmerge (Yiddish -- Vilkomir), 3,900 of 12,400; Vilkaviškis, 3,200 of 8,700; Jonava, 2,700 of 5,450; Marijampole, 2,550 of 15,800; Kedainai, 2,500 of 8,660. Vilna in 1931 had a total population of some 208,000, of whom about 55,000 were Jews.

While no exact figures are available for the Jews who escaped into the Soviet Union from the Nazi armies, it is safe to say that they were not many; the German advance was too swift. A few thousand escaped, and a few hundred Jews deported into the interior of Russia by Soviet authorities who considered them untrustworthy elements also survived. Most Lithuanian Jewish refugees in Russia were in the Chkalov (Orenburg) region in the Southeast and the Barnaul region in Central Siberia.

No large number of Jews were able to escape to other countries. After war hit Lithuania a few halutzim (trained pioneers) were able to reach Palestine. Under Soviet rule only non-Lithuanian nationals (Poles, etc.) were permitted to leave; a few Jews escaped in this guise to Palestine and the United States.

Under German occupation a very large proportion of the Jewish population was killed. Of those deported to Poland it is safe to say that the majority died. In 1944 there were few Jews left in Lithuania.

Religious and Communal Organization

By the constitution of 1922 Lithuania more than fulfilled its commitments to minorities in its declaration to the League of Nations. The Jews established an autonomous system based on local communities (Heb. -- Kehillot; sing., Kehillah) and on a national council of the Kehillot. A 1920 law provided for the establishment of a united Jewish community on a basis wider than religion alone, which was to have charge of education, social work and health. Representation in the various communal bodies was to be democratic and there was to be compulsory taxation of all Jews for the community. An elected Jewish National Council, although not called for in the law, received the recognition of the government.

Complete freedom of worship and religious instruction prevailed even after the dictatorship came to power in 1926. Before that date, however, the Kehillah system, despite the guarantees of the 1922 constitution, was gradually weakened; it was finally abolished by the Christian Democratic Party regime in 1924. The centralization and coordination of Jewish communal activities was thus made impossible, and the right to impose taxes for communal purposes was annulled. A 1924 law reintroduced the old Tsarist system of "synagogue councils" on a narrowly congregational basis. For some years the Jewish population refused to accept the new regulation, which went so far as to deny recognition even to purely religious Kehillot. The assumption of power by the dictatorship in 1926 put an end to the hope that the liberal principles which had prevailed immediately after the cessation of the war would return, and the Jews had to reconcile themselves to the knowledge that the Kehillah system would not be reinstituted. Two organizations, of a private character, were established: the Adat Yisrael (Heb. -- Congregation of Israel) for religious affairs, and Ezra (Heb. -- Aid) for welfare activity. In 1940, after Vilna passed from Poland to Lithuania, the Lithuanian government formally recognized the Vilna Kehillah, which had been in existence during the entire period of Polish rule.

Shehitah (ritual slaughter of meat-animals) was never banned, although attempts were made to have the government outlaw it, especially after Hitler rose to power in Germany. In 1939 a local ordinance banning Shehitah was declared null and void.

Vital statistics were the concern of the various religious officials, including rabbis. In 1931 there were 40 "essential" and 134 "auxiliary" Jewish offices of vital statistics registration. Rabbi B. Sapiro of Kaunas was considered the Chief Rabbi of Lithuania. In 1931 the government gave Jewish religious institutions 116,510 lits, 5.06% of the total distributed for religious purposes; in that year the Jews constituted 7.26% of the total population.

The East European adherents of Orthodox Judaism can generally be classified as either Hassidim or Mitnagdim. The doctrine of the Hassidim (sing. -- Hassid) is Hassidism; they are pietists who follow any of a number of rabbinical dynasties. Mitnagdim (Heb. -- Opponents; sing. -- Mitnagged) are opposed to specifically

Hassidic doctrine; their emphasis in religion is more intellectual and scholarly and less emotional than that of the Hassidim; they have no rabbinical dynasties. Lithuania was the traditional stronghold of the Mitnagdim, and Hassidism was not strong. Hassidim, however, constituted the bulk of the Jewish population of Rakiskis and about half of that of Kupiškis; they were mostly of the Habad school, an intellectual and scholarly subdivision within Hassidism.

Judaism preaches loyalty to the state. In Lithuania Jewish religious leaders were particularly friendly to the government, which contributed to the support of institutions of Jewish learning and otherwise encouraged them; the government looked on the religious element among the Jews as the most conservative and therefore the most "reliable."

Unorthodoxy grew between the two World Wars. An increasing number of Jewish stores, for example, were open for business on the Saturday Sabbath. Nevertheless religious learning and observance were both widespread and held in much esteem. Even the secularists were influenced by religious tradition. No matter how "leftist" in ideology, no secular Hebrew or Yiddish school included Saturday as one of the six school days of the week; Saturday was the weekly holiday, and classes were held Sunday.

Since no elections, general or Jewish, were held after 1926, the comparative strength and influence of the various tendencies in Jewish life were not precisely known. The Zionists of various schools were dominant. The <u>Yiddishe Shtimme</u> (Yid. - "Jewish Voice"), for a long time the only Jewish daily in Lithuania, was a Zionist newspaper. The Agudath Israel (very Orthodox, non-Zionist) had considerable influence, to judge by the educational institutions it built and maintained. The Folkists were non-Zionist Yiddishist nationalists whose strength in the Jewish community was substantially less than that of the Zionists and the Agudath Israel; they published the <u>Folksblat</u>. The Bund (General Alliance of Jewish Workers; socialist, anti-Zionist and Yiddishist) was active in the early days of Lithuanian independence, but some of its members became more and more pro-Communist and others less and less political, until the party disappeared in Lithuania. The Communist party was severely repressed by the Smetona dictatorship; since it was an underground organization its influence was even harder to gauge than that of other groups. It is likely that with the deterioration of the Jewish position during Smetona's rule Communism gained some popularity, especially among the youth. (It is to be noted that despite his persecution of the Communists Smetona maintained good relations with the Soviet Union.)

All political movements (and the cultural organizations which frequently served as a disguise) had youth affiliates. Scouting was very popular.

Throughout the year Zionist celebrations and observances were fairly numerous; participation in them by the school youth made them particularly impressive. May Day celebrations were forbidden after 1926; even in 1940, when the Red Army had bases throughout Lithuania, the celebration of workers' holiday was still prohibited.

Family; Women

Jewish tradition tended to make for family stability. In the last two generations emancipation and westernization gave women equality with men. Elementary and secondary education was for girls as well as for boys, and to an increasing degree women were to be found among the gainfully employed.

Marriage; Divorce

Marriage and divorce were the province of the various religious bodies.

In 1939 5.5% of all marriages were Jewish. In absolute numbers, the 1939 figure for Jewish marriages was 995; of these, 741 were concluded in urban centers and 254 in rural settlements.

In 1939 there were no mixed marriages in the rural settlements; in the urban centers there were six mixed marriages, three entered into by men and three by women. In 1935 there were seven mixed marriages, of which five took place in Memel.

Jews tended to marry a little later than the average for the Lithuanian population as a whole. The following table is for 1939. It indicates the percentage of each group married at various age intervals.

Age	Jews		Men Total population		Jews		Women Total population	
Under 17	-		2.3		.2		2.4	
17-19.9	2.4)		2.3)		6.3)	28.8%	16.4)	48.5%
20-24.9	13.2)	51.1%	17.3)	58.3%	22.3)		29.7)	
25-29.9	35.5)		38.7)		35.9)		27.1)	
30-34.9	24.8)		21.5)		20.6)	64.8%	12.8)	45.6%
35-39.9	10.6)	42.6%	9.7)	37.6%	8.3)		5.7)	
40-49.9	7.2)		6.4)		4.0		4.5	

Criminality

Crimes committed by Jews were in a smaller proportion to the total number of crimes than the proportion of the Jewish population to the total.

	Total crimes	Crimes committed by Jews, in numbers and %ages	
1937	12,274	383	3.1%
1938	11,193	240	2.1
1939	11,610	247	2.1

The 1939 crime statistics are divided into four categories.

Category	Total	Committed by Jews, in numbers and %ages	
Against public order (including political offenses)	2,386	54	2.3%
Violation of laws for the protection of the person (crimes of violence, prostitution and procuring, slander and libel)	1,719	43	2.5
Violation of property laws (theft, embezzlement, forgery, etc.)	7,375	145	2.0
Crimes committed by civilian officials, military offenses	130	5	3.8

The Jewish population at this time constituted a little more than 6% of the total.

Languages

The 1923 Lithuanian census did not include language data, probably because the new government was reluctant to reveal the inroads which the Russian and Polish languages and cultures had made among Lithuanians.

In Lithuania there was less language assimilation among Jews than in any other country. The number of Yiddish-speaking Jews amounted to very nearly 100% of the Jewish population. It is not improbable, indeed, that after 1920 Yiddish had a stronger position than before 1914; Russian, a language and culture with a strong attraction, weakened greatly with the cessation of Russian rule, and the Lithuanian language and culture did not exercise nearly the same attraction. All Lithuanian Jews knew and used Lithuanian, and the younger generation, which had been schooled under the Republic, had a thorough command of it. Still, Lithuanian never attained any importance in Jewish social and communal, let alone private, life.

In the early days of Lithuanian independence, Yiddish was recognized as one of the official languages. Street signs in the provisional capital of Kaunas were in Lithuanian, Polish and Yiddish; Yiddish was also allowed to be used in matters relating to administration and the courts. The policy of language toleration soon changed, however; Yiddish and Polish street signs disappeared, Lithuanian was proclaimed to be the only official language and, about 1925, even private signs in languages other than Lithuanian were banned from the streets. Minority languages continued to be allowed in the various school systems.

As concerns the Jewish school system, Zionists were strongly in favor of Hebrew, while such groups as the Folkists and the Bund were partisans of Yiddish. In the Yeshivot (sing.; Yeshivah; Talmudical academy) the East European Orthodox tradition of using Yiddish in the elucidation of the sacred text was continued, but in the general school system of the Orthodox element Hebrew was favored. Early in the 1930's the Hebrew school system of the Tarbut (Heb. -- Culture) organization had grown to the point where it maintained 17 gymnasia, partially subsidized by the government, all recognized as suitable preparatory institutions for entrance to the University of Kausas. (These schools were similar to the German Gymnasien and the French lycées; their course of studies would correspond roughly to that offered in the American high school plus junior college.) The Yiddish gymnasium, at Ukmerge, ceased functioning about that time. The Yiddish Komertsgimnazye (Commerce Gymnasium) in Kaunas was a large school with a good reputation.

Education

Education was partly treated under "Languages."

The Lithuanian school system included: 1) kindergartens; 2) elementary schools (four years); 3) "middle" schools (four years, similar to the first four years of the gynmasium curriculum); 4) gymnasia (eight years); and 5) the University. All elementary and middle schools were state institutions; none could be conducted by private persons or organizations.

Short of the University, the only discrimination practiced against Jews was that the state's financial aid to Jewish kindergartens and gymnasia was less than they were proportionately entitled to receive.

In 1937, 15 of the 109 kindergartens were Hebrew or Yiddish; they employed 18 of the total 116 teachers, and were attended by 427 of the total 4,317 pupils.

In the same year the elementary schools had 17,090 Jewish pupils, of the total elementary school population of 276,675. 13,607 pupils attended 108 state schools in Hebrew and Yiddish.

In 1935-36 there were 60 gymnasia in Lithuania, of which 28 were government institutions and 32 were private. All the Jewish gymnasia (14 in that year) were private. 18.9% of gymnasium students were Jewish.

There were four Yeshivot, in Kaunas, Panevezys, Telsiai and Kelme. In 1935-36 they had 25 teachers and 893 students.

The rise of anti-Semitism was reflected in the attitude of the government to Jewish educational institutions. In 1935 the state subvention for the Yavneh (Orthodox, Hebrew) Teachers Seminary, in the amount of some $4,000 was cancelled. In 1936 the Ministry of Education announced that all Jewish normal schools were to be closed, and that teachers would be trained in Lithuanian institutions only, no provisions being made for teaching Jewish subjects in those schools. Financial aid was not withdrawn form other Jewish schools which had been receiving it.

The University practised discrimination against Jewish applicants for admission. In 1935 there was not one Jew in the entering class of the medical school. The proportion of Jews to the total student body of the University dropped from 41.8% in 1922 to about 20% in 1937. Discrimination was strongest in the technical and professional schools -- law, medicine, engineering, etc. This led to the concentration of Jewish students in the humanities faculty. Students of philosophy, history, philology, and the like, could not compete in economic life on terms of equality with graduates of technical and professional schools.

In 1940, during the brief Lithuanian rule in Vilna, a chair in Yiddish language and literature was created in the University of Vilna. The University of

Kaunas already had an assistant professor of Hebrew.

In 1930 there were about 19,500 Jewish students on all levels of education. 16,000 attended Jewish institutions, and 3,500 did not. Of the latter figure, 1,100 were students at institutions of learning higher than the gymnasium level and 300 were in vocational schools, for neither of which there was a Jewish equivalent. In all, only 2,100 Jewish students attended non-Jewish schools of a kind that was duplicated among Jews. Five thousand children attended heder (old-fashioned full-time religious school), 8,000 attended Jewish elementary schools, and 3,000 Jewish secondary schools; 1,500 were in non-Jewish elementary schools, and 600 in non-Jewish secondary schools.

Private organizations founded and maintained Jewish kindergartens and gymnasia. The most important were Tarbut (Zionist, Hebrew), Yavneh (Orthodox, Hebrew) and the Yiddishe Bildungsgezelshaft (Jewish Education Association; Yiddish).

Press

The following daily newspapers were published in 1939: Yiddishe Shtimme (Jewish Voice; Zionist); Haintikke Nais (Daily News; Zionist); Dos Vort (The Word; Labor Zionist); Folksblat (People's Press; Folkist); Ovntblat (Evening Journal; Folkist). All were in Yiddish.

A very extensive periodical press existed, representing every variety of ideology within the Jewish community. In 1930 there were 13 Yiddish and 14 Hebrew periodicals; in 1939 there were 18 Yiddish and 25 Hebrew. Between 1930 and 1939 the number of Yiddish periodicals had ranged from 13 to 63, and the number of Hebrew periodicals from 11 to 30. (The above is exclusive of Vilna.)

The Association of Jewish Participants in the Fight for Lithuanian Independence published a Lithuanian-language monthly, Apžvalga (Review), intended primarily to be read by non-Jews. Otherwise the extent of Lithuanian-language journalistic activity by Jews was negligible.

The Russian-language Echo was published in Kaunas and probably had a number of Jewish readers.

Birth; Mortality

In 1939, of the 54,184 births in Lithuania, 1,776, or less than 3.3% were Jewish. Jews then constituted somewhat more than 6% of the population.

Of all religious groups, the Jews had the lowest illegitimacy rate.

Year	General illegitimacy rate	Jewish illegitimacy rate
1937	9.4%	2.3%
1938	8.2%	.9%
1939	8.2%	1.2%

(These figures are for the urban population.)

In general, Jewish mothers gave birth to their children at a higher age than was average both for the country as a whole and for the urban elements. This was in accordance with the average higher age of Jewish women at marriage.

The number of children in the Jewish family was lower than the average for the rural and urban populations. In 1939, 45.5% of Jewish mothers giving birth had no previous children; the corresponding figures for the total and urban populations were respectively 28% and 40.4%.

The data on deaths according to ethnic and religious origin are limited. In 1939, of 32,983 deaths, 1,668, or 5%, were Jewish.

Infant mortality among Jews was lower than among the rest of the population.

Infant mortality

Year	General population	Urban population	Jews
1923-27	28.6%	?	7.4%
1937	12.0	10.9	4.5
1938	11.2	11.0	5.8
1939	12.2	9.8	4.1

Occupational Distribution; Economic Position

The following is the occupational distribution of the Jews in 1923:

	Men		Women	
Trade and commerce	16,881	(23%)	8,251	(10.3%)
Industry and handicrafts	13,414	(18.2%)	4,693	(5.9%)
Agriculture	2,659	(3.6%)	2,337	(2.9%)
Civil service and professions	3,430	(4.7%)	750	(1%)
Transport	2,318	(3.1%)	30	--
Others	3,579	(4.9%)	25,449	(31.7%)
Dependents	31,241	(42.5%)	38,670	(48.2%)
Unknown	25	--	16	--
(Total)	(73,547)	(100%)	(80,196)	(100%)

Despite the poverty of large sections of the Jewish population, especially in the smaller towns, the Jews of Lithuania managed to get along. It was the prospective, even more than the actual, situation that was black. They saw clearly that in their economic activities, within the framework of scarcity of jobs and goods, the full weight of the state's economic (and political) power would be brought into play against them. As the 1930's progressed the only two alternatives facing them in Lithuania seemed to be the German policy of elimination and extermination or the Polish-Roumanian policy of gradual but complete exclusion.

The lack of confidence in their own future in Lithuania was clearly shown by the eagerness with which Jews attempted to emigrate. That the figures presented below are not larger is to be explained solely by the barriers to immigration throughout the world.

Year	Total Lithuanian emigrants	Jews	%age of Jews
1932	1,001	725	72.5%
1933	1,300	1,020	75.5
1934	1,521	1,099	71.6
1935	1,911	1,425	74.6
1936	1,707	1,008	59.1
1937	979	447	45.7
1938	811	426	52.5
1939	604	439	72.7

Cooperatives; Commerce and Trade

In 1938 a pro-Nazi Lithuanian economist wrote: "If the former economic power of the Jews in Lithuania is now on the verge of disaster, the reason for this is to be sought not in the State's economic policy, as the Jews always maintain, but in the highly developed cooperative system already in existence before the (First World) War, and in the national consciousness of the Lithuanians." He neglected to say that only the decisive help of the state enabled the cooperatives to proceed with their program of ousting Jews from their economic positions.

In the field of importing, various state-owned and state-supported cooperatives dominated. Lietukis, one of these cooperatives, in 1936 imported 100% of fertilizers, 100% of salt, 50% of cement, 50% of oil, and a large proportion of coal, iron, glass, etc. Lietukis alone did more business than all other importers together. If we add to its activities those of the state factories, the Klaipeda (Memel) port administration and the like, we can see that the sphere of private business in general, and of Jewish-owned business in particular, was limited. Within the category of private trading enterprises Jews were dominant.

Jewish business firms were at a disadvantage in the internal wholesale trade as well. Lietukis had an annual domestic business of approximately 50,000,000 lits (ten lits being worth one pre-1934 dollar) in grain and sugar. Maistas dominated the meat trade, and Pienocentras the trade in milk, butter and eggs. Other cooperatives, also excluding Jews from their employ and management, were powerful in other phases of the wholesale trade. In the mid-1930's the Verslininki (or Verslas), an organization of anti-Semitic artisans and traders, were preparing the creation of a large-scale wholesale agency to "protect" Lithuanian retailers from "exploitation" at the hands of Jewish wholesalers.

In the retail trade, from 1923 to 1936 the number of businesses owned by Jews decreased 9% absolutely and 29% relatively, while Lithuanian firms increased by 30% absolutely and 300% relatively. In 1923 there had been 16,585 independent retail firms, exclusive of the Memel region. 15,959 of these belonged to Jews and 2,160 to ethnic Lithuanians. By 1936 the number of firms had risen to 23,400, exclusive of 304 stores belonging to 186 consumers' and farmers' cooperatives, from all 304 of which Jews were barred. Of the 23,400, 12,000 belonged to Jews and 9,900 (plus the 304 cooperative stores) to ethnic Lithuanians. In 1936, 54% of retail businessmen were Jews and 43% were Lithuanians, with Germans, Poles, etc., making up the remaining 3%. Many of the Jewish "businessmen," however, could not support themselves and had to be helped by remittances from relatives in the United States, Palestine and South Africa. (In South Africa the majority of the Jewish community were themselves immigrants from Lithuania or descended from them.)

The total value of Lithuanian exports in 1936 was about 190,000,000 lits, of which 140 to 150 million lits' worth of business had been done by state, state-owned or state-supported institutions. A fourth or a fifth of the export business was done by Jews, Poles, Germans, etc. The years after 1936 saw a continued decline in the status of the Jews in this area of the Lithuanian economy.

Lithuania's exports were almost entirely agricultural, pastoral and forest products: cattle, meat (including processed meat), hides and skins, butter, eggs, grain, timber, etc. In the early days of the Republic the bulk of the export trade continued to be in the hands of Jews. The government was intent on removing the Jews from export activity, and proceeded to that end by a system of rigid export quotas and centralization of export agencies. By 1938 the export of meat and cattle (exclusive of horses) was almost solely exercised by Maistas, a cooperative with a capital of 9,000,000 lits, of which 7,000,000 belonged to the Ministry of Finance. Even if its large capital had not allowed it to maintain a series of modern and efficient processing plants, its position as a de facto government agency would have given it practically full control over its sphere of activity. Pienocentras did 100% of the export business in dairy and eggs. Lietukis exported grain, flax, linseed, clover seed, potatoes, etc. These three cooperatives, which were in effect organs of the state, were closely connected with each other, making common use of their storage and shipping facilities, etc. They founded and exclusively controlled the Lietuvos Baltijas Lloydas to further the cause of a Lithuanian merchant marine.

In 1938 these organizations did 80% of the total export business in their fields. The remaining 20%, in the amount of 30,000,000 lit per annum at the outside, was mostly done by Jewish export firms trading in horses, horse hair, hides and skins, goose feathers and flax. In 1937 Lietukis already controlled 25% of the flax-exporting business. It seemed clear that as soon as sufficient personnel was trained and other preparations were made, it would take over the rest of the flax-export trade, representing two-thirds of the value of all exports of agricultural products still in private hands. (Linas, a cooperative for processing flax in Lithuania, was being formed at this time.)

Timber was the last important export in which Jews were able to remain active. Even there, however, about 20,000,000 lits of the 33,000,000 total annual income from timber export went to the State Forestry Department. By 1939 only the final touches had yet to be applied to the ousting of the Jews from the timber export business, which they had done so much to create and develop.

The exclusion of the Jews from the Lithuanian economy was gradually being accomplished by state measures in support of cooperatives. This policy was intended to accomplish "Lithuanization," and it was succeeding. The authoritarian government continued to pursue a program which, while it resulted in some undeniable advantages to the Lithuanian population as a whole, could have accomplished the same purpose without stifling the Jews economically. The exclusion of Jews from any role in the cooperative system showed that their elimination from the economy was one of the aims of the government's policy.

Industry

The difference between industrial and artisan activity was not clearly marked, especially in statistical reports. The term "industry" is here to be understood as comprising the activity of artisans as well as industry proper.

The following table shows the 1936 distribution of ownership of industrial enterprises according to ethnic origin; it does not include the armaments industry, in which Jews were not represented at all.

Ownership	Number of enterprises	% age of total enterprises	Number of persons employed	% age of total employed
Lithuanians	9,600	60%	22,500	52%
Jews	5,300	32	17,700	40
Others	600	8	3,200	8
(Total)	(15,500)	(100)	(43,000)	(100)

Artisan establishments made up a significant proportion of the Jewish total.

Among the large Lithuanian industrial firms were the cooperatives Maistas, with five large plants for curing bacon, and Pienocentras (which exported butter and eggs), with power plants throughout the country.

At that time, according to the pro-Nazi economist from whom our figures on the distribution of industrial property were taken, the Jews were dominant in chemicals, leather, textiles and clothing.

Most of the industrial enterprises in Lithuania came into existence after World War I and were therefore fairly modern.

The government intervened to meet the scarcity of capital. It founded several large corporations, such as Elektra, for the electrification of the country, and Auto, for establishing bus communications. In these cases the government supplied 51% of the capital, with the balance coming from banks and private investors; Jews were almost completely excluded.

Great care was taken by the government to explain the exclusion of Jews from participation in the industrial and other economic activities of state and quasi-state organs by reasons other than anti-Jewish discrimination as such.

Labor

No labor unions were allowed under the authoritarian regime.

Agriculture

The land reform of the early 1920's was the basis for the entire further development of the Lithuanian economy. The large estates, formerly owned mostly by Poles, were partitioned among the Lithuanian peasantry. Jews received little land to speak of. The rural Jews of Lithuania were not primarily farmers but inhabitants of the villages engaged in trade with the farmers.

There were a number of hachsharah (Heb. - training) farms accommodating several hundred halutzim (Heb. - pioneers; sing., halutz) preparing themselves for emigration to Palestine. These farms were run by Hechalutz (The Pioneer), the Zionist agricultural training agency.

Banking

The Union of Jewish People's Banks (Yid. -- Tsentrale fun Yiddishe Folksbenk) had 85 member banks in the last years before the war; in 1931 it had had 101 member banks. Only a few, like those in Kaunas, Šiauliai and Panevežys operated on a relatively large scale; most were loan kassas (credit organizations). These kassas, though mostly small, played a very important part in the economic life of the Lithuanian Jews.

The Lithuanian Commercial Bank (Lith. -- Lietuvos Komercbanka) was predominantly in Jewish hands, as was the Braun banking house.

The following table refers to the Union of Jewish People's Banks.

	1935	1936	1937	1938	1939
Number of constituent members	85	85	85	85	85
Balance as of December 31 (in lits)	104,447	72,545	34,465	47,163	182,642

The sharp rise of 1939 was due to the comparatively large amounts of American money sent into Lithuania for the benefit of the newly acquired Vilna region and for the "Jewish Poland-in-exile" that found refuge there. A good share of that money was sent through the People's Banks and the Braun firm.

The Bar

In 1933 ethnic Lithuanian lawyers succeeded in having a law promulgated which authorized the government to reexamine the eligibility of all lawyers for the bar. Sixty-six, of whom 58 were Jews, were disbarred. Of the eight non-Jews disbarred every one was later readmitted to the bar or given a government post; of the 58 Jews only three were readmitted.

In subsequent years the number of Jewish students admitted to the Faculty of Law of the University decreased very sharply; no Jews were allowed to obtain the preliminary court experience which was a requirement for admission to the bar.

In the 1930's there were no Jewish judges, public prosecutors or notaries.

Jews in the Government

In the first Seimas (Parliament) of 1919 the Jews had seven representatives; in the second (1924) gerrymandering reduced their number to three.

Gerrymandering also reduced substantially the number of Jewish members of the Kaunas city council, even before 1926, when the dictatorship established itself through a coup d'etat. After that year the not inconsiderable group of Jewish members of municipal councils throughout the country was removed entirely. "Equality" of taxation for Jews remained, however, even after equality of representation had disappeared. Appointment of a Jew to the post of mayor, no matter of how small a town, was completely out of the question.

In December 1935 the Kaunas city council for the first time failed to make any provision in its budget for allocations to Jewish social and cultural institutions. In previous years the allocations had been discriminatorily low.

After 1926 there were no Jews in the civil service. The last Jewish judge ceased exercising his function about 1933. Gross discrimination by the judiciary against Jews was not frequently charged.

Citizenship

The Jews on Lithuanian territory when the Republic was established had no difficulty about being recognized as citizens. In the 1930's obstacles were put in the way of German Jewish refugees, some of them stateless, when they tried to obtain Lithuanian citizenship. Some Jews from Memel who left for the interior of Lithuania when the Germans took over in 1939 had some trouble in having their citizenship recognized.

Isaiah Rozovsky, Hias (Hebrew Immigrant Aid Society) director in Kaunas, was of great help to many Jews involved in citizenship tangels. His pro-Lithuanian initiative and conduct during the First World War and after gave him great prestige and a large measure of influence with the Lithuanian governments before 1926 and even with the dictatorship after that year. His entirely unofficial intervention with officials who were able to exercise a good deal of discretion had very beneficial results for many Jews.

Minority Rights

This subject is discussed throughout the present report, mostly under the headings "Religious and Communal Organization" and "Education."

Attitude of the People and Government to the Jews

Under Tsarist rule and after, relations between Jews and Lithuanians were traditionally good. No conflicts between peasants and village Jews occurred of the kind that was known in the Ukraine, nor were there pogroms in Lithuania (and White Russia) even at a time when the Tsar's government was energetically stirring up "popular wrath" against the Jews.

In the revolutionary movements starting in 1905, very cordial relations were established between Lithuanian and Jewish organizations and leaders. Their friendly relations continued through German occupation during the First World War and the final struggle for Lithuanian independence. The Lithuanians recognized that the Jews at home and abroad, the latter through their support and advocacy of independence, had been of significant help in its attainment. Relations between Lithuanians and Jews continued good even under the domination of the Christian Democratic Party, which drastically limited Jewish minority rights. During the short-lived Grinius regime, just before the dictatorship's coup d'etat in 1926, some Jews were even appointed to relatively high posts in the administration.

In the latter 1930's the general feeling of the Jews about their own situation was not that it was good, but that "things could be much worse." The anti-Jewish trend could not be mistaken, but it was still possible to mitigate some evils by appealing to one or another official who was more liberal than the fact of his holding office might have led one to expect. President Smetona himself, "Leader" of the authoritarian regime, whose philosophical writings had suggested his title of "Lithuanian Plato," at times displayed a kind of benevolently paternalistic attitude which served to improve somewhat what might otherwise have been a dangerous social climate for Jews.

In February 1938, on the twentieth anniversary of Lithuanian independence, a new constitution was promulgated which gave even more emphasis to the authoritarian spirit than the facts since 1926 had given. Although minorities as such were not mentioned in the new constitution, equality of rights was provided for all citizens, irrespective of race or creed. Among the celebrations held in honor of the event, some were arranged by Jewish organizations; in response to their greetings Smetona and some of his ministers praised the Jews for their patriotism and promised them fair treatment.

While the scarcity of reliable information from German-occupied Lithuania does not permit generalization about the attitude of the population as a whole, it is known that fairly large numbers of Lithuanian guards (together with Ukrainians and others) were used by the Nazis in the reduction and annihilation of the ghettos in Poland. They appear to have been recruited from the ranks of the "riflemen" (Siaulis) organization, which for many years had enjoyed the protection and financing of the government and had long been considered the shock troops of Lithuanian anti-Semitism.

The Church and the Jews

Lithuania was a predominantly Catholic country. Before the dictatorship came into power the Christian Democratic Party carried through measures disadvantageous to the interests of the Jews. It may be presumed that the party represented the point of view of the clergy. The authoritarian regime was not clerical and, although in principle it was not opposed to the Church, some of its leading figures were strongly anti-clerical. With respect to the Jews, however, both clergy and members of the dictatorial regime resembled each other in generalized anti-Jewish feeling coupled with reluctance to proceed to extreme measures and with occasional manifestations of friendliness.

It was reported in August 1943, Bishop Brizgis had ordered the excommunication of all Lithuanians guilty of participation in the persecution of Jews and Poles.

Anti-Semitism

The Christian Democratic Party was anti-Semitic. When the Tautininki (Nationalist Party) took power in 1926 anti-Jewish tension was in some ways actually lessened. With the rise of Nazism in Germany, however, "Lithuanism" began to be understood increasingly in a racist sense, and Nazi racial terminology came into increasing use. The desire for autarchy, the policy of reducing imports to a minimum and attempting to make the country as "self-sufficient" as possible, led to intensification of the drive to eliminate "foreign" elements from the national economy. The Jews were considered a foreign element, although they were very active in furthering the establishment of Lithuanian industry before and after the high protective tariffs of the 1930's.

The Tautininki regime completed the elimination of Jews from public office begun by the Christian Democrats. The suppression of Parliament and of political activity worked to the disadvantage of the Jews; it is to be noted, however, that there was less interference with the press than under other dictatorships. Active anti-Semitic propaganda as such was not encouraged, but with the development of the Versla (Verslininki) anti-Semitic artisans' movement and its expansion after 1933 it was not unusual for government officials to take part in its anti-Jewish meetings and conferences.

The young Lithuanian intellectual class was the backbone of the Tautininki. Young professionals -- lawyers, physicians, etc. -- invoked the support of "their" government against their Jewish competitors. As early as 1933 drastic action was taken against Jews already admitted to the practice of law; simultaneously it started to become increasingly difficult for a Jewish student to be admitted to one of the professional or technical faculties of the University.

In 1934 there were anti-Semitic excesses in Siauliai and two other places, and windows were broken in five Kaunas synagogues. The government seized several Jewish newspapers which charged it with being too lenient.

As the situation of the Jews deteriorated in neighboring countries tension mounted in Lithuania. In August 1938 the newspaper Lietuvos Aidas, the government's mouthpiece, advocated the establishment of special bathing beaches for Jews. Although the article was disavowed and the editor punished, its publication was the signal for a number of anti-Jewish incidents in several towns.

In 1938 the Lithuanian society for the prevention of cruelty to animals urged the passage of a law to prohibit shehitah. Local ordinances with that intent have been discussed under "Religious and Communal Organization."

In 1938, too, the Union of Lithuanian Engineers petitioned for the restriction on Jews in their profession based on the Nazi-model "Aryan paragraph," already in force in Germany and vigorously advocated in Poland. The simultaneous introduction of the Aryan paragraph in Germany and agitation for it in neighboring countries must be considered more than a coincidence; a German organization was in all probability behind it. At the same time, while the Nazi "racial scientists" were quite pleased with the anti-Jewish trend of events in Eastern Europe, they felt that its ideology was not sufficiently racist.

Anti-Semitism continued to grow during 1939. In January leaflets distributed in Kausas called for workers and consumers to boycott Jewish firms in order "to throw off the influence of aliens." In February the organ of the Fascist-style Labor Chamber championed a law "for the protection of Lithuanian honor," which, like its German model, would forbid Jews to employ Christian female domestic workers.

It cannot be said that in all this the attitude of the government and all intellectuals was decisively anti-Semitic. In June 1939, after anti-Jewish riots had occurred throughout the country, the Minister of the Interior expressed the belief that anti-Semitism was not, at least yet, deeply rooted in Lithuania. Indeed, the government intervened against the rioters during the course of the riots. In July a group of professors, clergymen, etc., made public their protest against the advertisement by a hotel that Jews were not admitted.

Economic anti-Semitism was perhaps the most serious aspect of all. (Compare "Cooperatives.") In this the Verslininki, or Verslas, the society of artisans and tradesmen, was in the forefront. It was founded in 1930 for the express purpose of combatting Jewish competition and by 1935 had already engaged in noisy anti-Jewish demonstrations.

In April 1936 a law was promulgated requiring all artisans, businessmen and shop assistants to qualify for certificates of proficiency in their trades and mastery of the Lithuanian language. The measure was obviously directed against Jews, and caused all the more disquiet among them since the government had issued the law after consultation with the Verslininki and without seeking to know the opinion of Jewish artisans.

Almost simultaneously the Jewish Artisans' Association was astonished at being approached by the Verslininki for the creation of a joint committee. Of the seven members of the committee, as finally constituted, three were Jews. The mistrust of the Jewish artisans proved to be justified when, in November 1936, the Verslininki conference in Panevezys called on the government to "rescue the Lithuanian people from the hands of the aliens." During the following month the ministers of the Interior and of Finance, as well as the mayor of Kaunas, condemned the Verslininki's agitation.

Early in 1937 the Verslininki petitioned the government to forbid entirely keeping shops open on Sunday. In February the government replied that for the convenience of the peasants, whose custom it was to do their shopping after church attendance in town, no ban would be put on Sunday business after church hours.

In 1938 the Verslininki launched several vigorous boycott campaigns against the Jews, which in some localities led to riots. The government declared itself opposed to this policy, but did nothing to suppress the anti-Jewish campaign.

In March 1939, after the cession of Memel to Germany, Prime Minister Černius assured the minorities that nothing would be done to violate their rights. In May, however, after the Verslininki conference had adopted a series of resolutions directed against the Jews, the Prime Minister promised the government's support and declared that the cities and towns of Lithuania had to be "Lithuanized." Although other high officials sounded the same note, the government ended by rejecting the Verslininki's program.

At their conferences in July 1939 and March 1940 the Verslininki again demanded that anti-Jewish measures be taken, including a numerus clausus in industry and commerce. Government officials who attended spoke out against the disunity advocated by the organization; at the same time, however, messages of congratulations and encouragement were sent.

A considerable part of the Lithuanian press enthusiastically supported the Verslininki movement. The organization itself published two periodicals, Verslas and Amatininkas.

Sovietization

In economic Sovietization during the period of Soviet rule Jews fared equally with others in the same situation. In accordance with the long-standing Communist hostility to Hebrew and Zionism, Hebrew and Zionist institutions, organizations and organs were suppressed. Religious activity was not interfered with to any great extent. The Folkist Folksblat, considered by some a crypto-Communist newspaper, continued publication.

German Occupation Measures

The large majority of the Jewish population were killed or deported. Deportation was to Poland especially, where it is likely that perhaps most of the deportees were exterminated by starvation or acts of violence.

The economic policy of the Nazis with respect to the Jews was fairly stable. In 1939 they confiscated in Memel property belonging to Jews in the amount of some $17,000,000. In October 1941 the following decree was published in the Deutsche Zeitung im Ostland (East European German Journal): "At the beginning of the German-Soviet War private property did not exist in the countries under Soviet rule, so nobody can claim legal ownership. Through the sacrifice of the blood of German soldiers all those countries were liberated. The German Reich therefore becomes the legal heir to the Soviet inheritance." The property of Jews was, of course, included.

Social and Health Services

Since no all-embracing Kehillah was recognized, the Jewish population had to rely on a multitude of welfare societies of a purely voluntary nature. Some, like the Ose (Society for the Protection of the Health of the Jews), were large organizations, with dispensaries, hospitals, playgrounds and camps in several communities. Most were much more modest, conforming to the old-fashioned hevrah (Heb. -- [charitable] society) pattern.

The only city for which data on voluntary organizations are available is Vilna; almost a hundred names appear on the list of Jewish organizations of all types in that city. Vilna was probably not entirely typical of the cities of pre-1939 Lithuania, since conditions under Polish rule were somewhat more favorable to the development of private organizations than under the Lithuanian dictatorship; nevertheless the trend was similar in the pre-1939 Lithuanian cities.

Ose was the most important Jewish health agency, and it did an excellent job. It maintained 44 institutions throughout the country and particularly distinguished itself late in 1939 when the large influx of Polish Jews, both as residents of Vilna and as refugees, strained the existing resources of the Jewish community.

No statistics are available for the number of Jewish physicians and other medical personnel. In the 1930's Jewish students desiring to enter the University's medical school were very strongly discriminated against.

Attitude to the United States; to the War

The Jews had an entirely positive attitude to the United States, not only as a bastion of democracy and equality, but also as the home of many relatives and friends able to help relieve the distress of those who stayed behind in Lithuania, and who constantly wrote of its virtues.

As late as June 1944 there were reports of Jewish partisan action against German troops. The partisans were apparently mostly from the Vilna area.

Leaders Who Escaped

It was extremely doubtful whether any considerable number of leaders of the Jewish community would survive German occupation, any more than the more undistinguished members of the community. The following arrived in the United States before or during the war: Jacob Robinson, authority on minorities, director of the Institute of Jewish Affairs of the American World and Jewish Congresses; Yudel Mark, Folkist, Yiddish philologist and educator, associated with the New York Yiddish Scientific Institute (Yivo); Isaiah Rozovsky, formerly of the Kaunas Hias; and Mendel Sudarsky, head of the Federation of Lithuanian Jews.

It was announced early in 1944 that Reuben Rubinstein, editor of the Zionist Yiddishe Shtimme, who was arrested and deported by the Communists in 1941 and later reported to have died in a Russian prison, was still living.

Reconstruction Agencies

Among the foreign agencies which will be able to cooperate in the rehabilitation of the Jewish population are: the American Jewish Joint Distribution Committee; the American Joint-Reconstruction Foundation; the ORT Society, for agricultural and industrial retraining; Ose, for health; HICEM (Hias-Ica Emigration Association), and the Jewish Agency for Palestine.

THE JEWS OF POLAND

THE JEWS OF POLAND

Index

Agriculture	29	Industry	30
Alcoholism	12	Labor Unions	33
Anti-Semitism, History of and Parties	50	Languages	11
Army-in-Exile, Jews in	19	Leaders, Jewish	
"Aryanization" and Expropriation	32	In Exile	15
Badges and Other Identification	53	In Poland	14
Banking	27	Liquidation	55
Bar, The	24	Marriage	9
Birth Rate	43	Medicine	
Catholic Church and the Jews	50	Physicians and Other Practitioners	41
Celebrations	7	Mortality	43
Citizenship	15	Motion Pictures	36
Commerce	31	Narcotics	12
Communications	53	Natural Resources	28
Communities, Religious, Jewish		Notaries, Public	25
After the Invasion	4	Observance, Religious	5
Assets	5	Occupational Structure	26
Before the Invasion	3	Patriotism	13
Cooperatives, Agricultural	30	People, Attitude of	
Criminality	11	After Invasion	21
Curfew	53	Before Invasion	20
Disease and Sanitation, Post-War	46	Police	52
Divorce	10	Population	1
Economic Condition	26	Press	
Education	37	General and Anti-Semitic	34
Epidemics	44	Jewish	35
Family Life	10	Prostitution, Forced	54
Food Control		Reconstruction Agencies	55
Before the War	45	Social Service	
During Occupation	45	Child Welfare	48
Functionaries, Religious	6	Jewish Welfare	47
Funerals	10	Public Welfare	47
Ghetto	3	Welfare Workers	49
Government, Attitude of	51	State, Attitude Toward	13
Government, Jews in		Stateless	16
Civil Service	22	Sterilization	55
County Posts	26	Suicides	45
Government-in-Exile	17	Travel, Regulations of	54
Judiciary	23	Underground	19
Municipal Posts	26	United States, Attitude Toward	13
Parliament	16	Vermin	45
Groups, Communal	7	War, Attitude Toward	13
Groups in Exile, Jewish	19		
Health Services	40		
Hospitals	42		
Supplies, Medical	42		
Vaccinations	42		

THE JEWS OF POLAND

Population.

According to the last official Polish census (1931), there were in the country 3,113,000 Jews by religion out of a total population of 31,915,000 (9.8%). Of these, 2,732,000 declared their mother tongue to be either Yiddish or Hebrew. Classification by mother-tongue was introduced into the 1931 census to replace the provision in the 1921 census which allowed Jews to claim Jewish nationality. The mother-tongue classification became the criterion of distinction between those who considered themselves Poles by nationality and those who thought of themselves as members of a national minority.

According to an official estimate on August 31, 1939, Poland had 35,339,000 inhabitants (31,915,000 in 1931), of whom 3,351,000 (or 9.7%) were Jews by religion.

The 1931 census showed that 2,300,000 Jews, or more than 75% of all the Jews by religion, resided in cities and towns. Less than 25%, or 733,000 Jews, lived in villages and on farms. The Jews constituted 27.3% of all the inhabitants of cities and towns and only 3.2% of the rural population. The largest portion of Jews lived in the central and southern provinces, where they formed from 10% to 14.5% of the total population. The smallest proportion of Jews was in the western and southwestern provinces, where they constituted 0.2% to 1.5% of the population.

By provinces the ratio of Jews in 1931 was as follows:

	Jews	% of total population
Warsaw city (considered as a province by the census)	352,659	30.1
Lodz	378,495	14.4
Lublin	314,340	12.8
Bialystok	197,365	12.0
Lwow	342,405	10.9
Kielce	317,020	10.8
Polesie	113,988	10.1
Volhynia	207,792	10.0
Stanislawow	139,746	9.4
Warsaw (province)	219,124	8.7
Vilno	110,796	8.7
Tarnopol	134,117	8.7
Novogrodek	82,872	7.8
Cracow	173,618	7.6
Silesia	18,938	1.5
Pomorze	1,663	0.2
Poznan	4,249	0.2

In the most important cities the ratio of Jews to the total population in 1931 was: Warsaw 30.1%, Lodz 33.5%, Lwow 31.9%, Poznan 0.6%, Cracow 25.8%, Vilno 28.2%, Katowice 4.5%, Lublin 34.7%.

In September 1939 Poland was partitioned between Nazi Germany and the Soviet Union. The territory occupied by the Germans was inhabited, according to the official 1939 estimate, by 2,042,000 Jews, while the territory that came under Soviet domination contained 1,309,000 Jews. The Germans subdivided the territory under their rule; one part was incorporated into the Reich, the other converted into the so-called Government General. On August 31, 1939, there were 641,000 Jews in the territory subsequently incorporated into Germany, and 1,401,000 Jews in the territor. that became the Government General.

Immediately after the occupation of Poland by Nazi Germany, the Jews were ordered to register, but were permitted to remain in their former place of residence. The Germans first attempted to set up a Jewish reservation in the Lublin district; later, however, they abandoned the idea. In the middle of 1940 another plan was substituted -- the Ghetto plan. Jews were ordered to leave many small towns and to concentrate in large cities where ghettos were being set up.

The Warsaw ghetto at one time contained about 500,000 Jews; the Lodz ghetto, nearly 180,000 Jews; and the Lwow ghetto, about 120,000. By the end of 1942, about half of the Jewish population was concentrated in the ghettos of the larger cities. The situation changed in October 1942, when a decree was issued ordering all the Jews to move into fifty-five cities and towns in Poland. All other places were barred to the Jews. These fifty-five localities consisted of so-called Jewish cities, in any parts of which Jews could reside, and the Jewish ghettos in the larger cities, where the Jews were confined to special districts. In 1943 practically all Polish Jews were concentrated in these fifty-five localities.

Underground authorities in Poland estimate that at the beginning of 1944 there were fewer than 2,000,000 Jews left, including about 600,000 Jews who had been deported into Poland from west and south European countries. It was estimated that between September 1939 and January 1944 more than 2,000,000 Jews were either killed by the Nazis or died of starvation, disease or other causes.

Between 1939 and 1941, about 400,000 Jews were deported by the Soviet Government from the eastern territories then occupied by the Soviet, to the interior of Russia, mostly to Siberia. After the Polish-Russian pact of July 1941, most of the deported Jews left Siberia and settled in the southern part of Asiatic Russia. Tashkent became a center of settlement. Several agricultural colonies were set up there. It is estimated that of the Jews deported into Russia, about 100,000 have died of hunger, disease and other privations.

The number of Polish Jews who escaped to countries other than the Soviet Union, either before the Nazi occupation of the country or after, is very small. They were almost all relatively wealthy individuals or political leaders who were able to secure transportation through influence or special circumstances, when the Polish railway transportation system broke down during the Polish-German campaign. Precise figures cannot be given but it is assumed that no more than 10,000 Jews escaped. Of these between 2,500 and 3,000 are in the United States and between 2,000 and 2,500 in Palestine.

The Ghetto.

The first special area for Jews, or ghetto, was established in the city of Lodz shortly after the German occupation. At the beginning of December 1939 the Jewish Community there was given the order to organize a speedy redistribution of the Jewish inhabitants, to be completed before January 15, 1940. All the Jews of Lodz, who then numbered 160,000 -- including 55,000 children -- had to move into the poorest section of the city -- the crowded and dilapidated area known as Baluty. The ghetto was separated from the rest of the city by a barbed wire fence, and no one was allowed to enter or leave the area without a special permit from the German authorities.

The Gestapo also attempted to establish a ghetto in Warsaw in November 1939, but following the intervention of the Jewish Community Council, the German military authorities recognized that the Gestapo plan would be impracticable at that time and ordered a postponement. In the spring of 1940, however, the Germans began the construction of a wall eight feet high. On August 7, 1940, the Warsaw Nazi authorities issued an ordinance forbidding all Jews who arrived in Warsaw from the provincial towns from which they had been expelled to settle outside the sections surrounded by the walls. The final decree definitely setting up a ghetto for the Jews in Warsaw came on October 17, 1940, when the city was divided into three parts. All the Jews living outside the Jewish district were to move into the ghetto within a month. The limits of the Jewish area were changed several times, but the ghetto as finally set up covered an area about 3/4 of a mile square. Into this small space were crowded 400,000 Jews; later the number was increased to more than 500,000. Leaving the ghetto brought a fine of 1,000 zlotys or three months imprisonment. Subsequently the penalty was death; any Jew leaving the ghetto without a permit could be shot on sight.

In November 1940 a ghetto was established in the city of Radom; here 30,000 Jews were crowded. Ghettos were also established in Lublin and Cracow; and after the attack of the Nazis against the Soviets and the occupation of the eastern part of the country, in Lwow, Stanislawow and other cities. Liquidation of the ghettos started in July 1942.

The famous Battle of the Warsaw Ghetto, waged in April and May 1943 by the inhabitants of the ghetto against the German police and military, with weapons supplied by the underground, was the defiance of the Jews against the liquidation orders. Full military equipment had to be resorted to by the Nazis, and the ghetto destroyed virtually house by house before the resistance of the insurgents was broken. By the middle of 1943, the Warsaw ghetto was reported liquidated, and the elimination of the other ghettos was proceeding rapidly.

Jewish Religious Communities: Before the Invasion

The legal status of the Jewish religion and the Jewish religious communities was determined by a Presidential decree of October 14, 1927. The Jewish population of Poland was constituted a public corporation, at the head of which there should have been a religious council of 34 laymen and 17 rabbis. This council, however, was never organized. Membership in the local community was compulsory. A Jew was able to step out of the community, however, by a simple declaration before a Judge.

In cities with fewer than 5,000 Jews, the community was governed by an elected executive council of eight; in larger cities, an elected executive committee chose an executive council. The rabbi was an ex officio member of the council. Elections were held every four years by secret ballot. All males above the age of 25 could vote; all males above the age of 30 were eligible for office. Election rules were issued by the Minister of Education and Cults on October 24, 1930.

The law of 1927 imposed on the Jewish communities the obligation to support the religious functionaries (each community was supposed to have a rabbi and a dayan, a rabbi who acted as judge), the synagogues and the ritual baths; the communities were also supposed to provide religious instruction for the young, supply kosher meat, keep watch over community assets, supervise welfare institutions and maintain cemeteries.

Communities had the right to tax members; funds were derived from direct taxation, from the provision of kosher meat, and from the sale of cemetery plots. The budget and the finances were under government control, and the communities were released from tax obligations. Synagogues were protected by government authority; punishment for defilement was the same for religious structures of all faiths.

Shehitah (ritual slaughter) was restricted on April 17, 1936, by a law limiting the ritual slaughter of animals to a percentage to be determined by the local authorities. Where the Jews constituted less than 3% of the population, Shehitah was entirely forbidden. Poznan fell within this classification.

Jewish Religious Communities: After the Invasion

A decree was issued by Governor General Frank on November 28, 1939, turned the Jewish communities into deputizing agents for the Nazi occupation authorities, whom all the Jews were constrained to obey. The community executive was henceforward to be known as the Judenrat, which was to consist - in communities with fewer than 10,000 Jews -- of 12 representatives, and in larger communities, of 24. The law provided for an election of these representatives, but actually they were appointed by the German authorities.

On October 26, 1939, Shehitah was forbidden, with minimum penalties of a year in prison or concentration camp for violation of the law. On January 26, 1940, gathering in synagogues for the purpose of prayer was forbidden; the excuse offered was that the measure was intended to prevent epidemics. (The same excuse was offered on October 16, 1940, for the establishment of the Warsaw ghetto.) Persons participating in public prayer were subject to punishment. Various orders were issued to prevent Jews from observing their holidays; in Cracow, for instance, Jews were ordered to work and to keep their businesses open on Yom Kippur in 1940.

On November 23, 1939, all tax exemptions previously enjoyed by the Jewish communities of Poland were removed.

An order of August 31, 1940, decreed that the Judenrat was to provide elementary, professional and trade schools for the communities, and teachers' training courses. Jewish children could attend only these schools. Actually, few councils were able to establish schools. The provision of Jews for forced labor was also turned over to the councils. A decree of December 12, 1939, had ordered the communities to register all men between the ages of 12 and 60; heavy penalties were provided for failure to fulfill these demands. A further decree, dated January 20, 1940, commanded the communities to furnish tools for Jews drafted into forced labor, and to submit to the authorities information regarding the private possessions of Jews in the labor battalions.

Community Assets

The older synagogues of Poland possessed religious objects of great worth: silver crowns for the scrolls, scrolls which were themselves valuable, candelabra, pointers and heavily-embroidered mantles. Every synagogue also had its own library. The library attached to the Warsaw synagogue, in 1928, contained 19,386 works, in 24,860 volumes. Some of the synagogues, built during the 16th and 17th centuries, were of great architectural significance. Among the newer structures were massive houses of worship, such as the two synagogues in Lodz and the synagogue in Tarnow. There were also archives and museums of considerable value, as well as large immovable property holdings, including orphan asylums, hospitals, etc. The average wealth of a synagogue in Poland, exclusive of the building itself, might be appraised at $20,000. About 3,000 such synagogues were ravaged by the Nazis, bringing the loss to $60,000,000. Many synagogue buildings were burned; of these the value was approximately $40,000,000. Some of the larger libraries, including that of the Warsaw synagogue, were removed to Germany. The Straszun Library in Vilna (25,000 volumes) and the Yeshivah Library in Lublin (25,000 volumes) were burned. The value of the libraries and other movable properties destroyed may be assessed at $100,000,000.

Religious Observance

The religious divisions within the Jewish community were largely those between the Orthodox and the non-observant groups. Orthodoxy was itself subdivided into Hassidim and Mithnagdim. Hassidim were distinguished by their attachment to any one of a number of rabbis, each of whom maintained headquarters in a particular city and was the scion of a long dynasty. There were 23 such dynastic seats in Congress Poland and 20 in Galicia. Mithnagdim, while as observant as Hassidim, have no attachment to any rabbinic dynasty, but make the letter of the law their guide in interpretation. Non-observant Jews, even if they fulfilled none of the ritualistic obligations, were nevertheless obligatory members of the Jewish community.

The distinctive beards, sidelocks, black plush hats and long coats, which had once distinguished Orthodox Jews, had fallen into considerable disuse. Major Jewish holidays were largely observed by the Jews. According to a law of December 18, 1919, all citizens of Poland were obliged to rest on Sunday, and on Christian holidays. This imposed a choice on the Jews: they were forced either to observe a two-day rest during the week and take doubled holidays, or to work on the Sabbath and on Jewish holidays. Because of the Orthodox tradition, the former alternative was chosen by at least half the population. The right of Jews not to appear as witnesses in court on the Sabbath was recognized in the Minorities Treaty of 1919. Jews in the army were permitted to observe the major holidays.

Under the Nazis, the Jews had to violate Jewish laws of observance. The Jewish communities, as deputizing agents for the occupation authorities, were compelled to enforce the orders which forced these violations. On the other hand, observance of the Sabbath replaced Sunday observance. A decree of January 20, 1941, transmitted by the Warsaw council on April 15, 1941, made observance of the Sabbath and of the major Jewish holidays obligatory for all Jews of the Warsaw ghetto. Observance of Sunday as a day of rest was forbidden, but the important Christian holidays still had to be observed. Beginning with June 28, 1941, virtually the same regulations went into effect for the Jews of Cracow. Those Jews who worked outside the ghetto had to continue their observance of Sunday, and to work on Saturday.

Religious Functionaries

Rabbis supervised the religious life of the community, especially Shehitah and other regulations regarding kosher food; Shohetim (ritual slaughterers) had to be appointed by the rabbi. Rabbis supervised religious instruction, performed marriages and issued divorces. Provision of kosher meals and holiday observance for the military also came within the scope of the rabbi's activities. In the section of Poland which once belonged to Russia, the rabbis kept the official birth, mortality and marriage records. In other than religious matters, the rabbi was also important, often making political suggestions to the community.

Hassidic rabbis were influential in both religious and secular spheres. During the high holiday season, Hassidim journeyed to the centers in which their rabbis held court, though these centers, following the migrations of the post-First World War period, did not always remain in the towns or villages of origin. During the rest of the year, the Hassidim had their own houses of worship, called kloisen in Galicia and stiblech in Congress Poland. The influence of the Hassidic rabbis was noted in communal as well as government elections. Occasionally special lists of candidates for communal posts were offered by the Hassidic groups; largely, however, they were united in the Orthodox organization, Agudath Israel.

Although there was no Reform movement as such, and therefore no Reform rabbis, there were a number of liberal rabbis in the larger cities presiding in synagogues where organ music was played (in the Orthodox code, the playing of musical instruments is forbidden on the Sabbath and holidays). Some of these rabbis were employed and paid by the communities, others were privately engaged by the separate synagogues. Their functions also included supervision of education, and they were usually active in social work.

The Jewish Din Torah (Court of Arbitration), which offers the opportunity for the settlement of civil suits according to the Talmudic law, functioned fairly wide in Poland. Almost every larger community detailed a rabbi and one or more dayanim to form such a court. A defendant, however, had the right to demand that the court consist of two alternates, one nominated by each of the participants in the suit, and a third chosen by the two. The Din Torah was resorted to frequently even by non-religious Jews, because it offered a chance for the quick settlement of disagreements.

Celebrations

Some of the Jewish family and communal celebrations were held in public, sometimes in public squares. The traditional way of celebrating a wedding among the strictly Orthodox Jews, especially in the smaller towns, was to have the ceremony outside the synagogue. This custom, which was quite general in previous generations, gradually disappeared, and only very Orthodox Jews still kept it up. If the son or daughter of an extreme Orthodox rabbi was married in a smaller town it was customary to have the wedding ceremony outside the place of worship with practically the entire community congregated. Only the ceremony was held out-of-doors; the wedding reception was held in the house of the bride. After the ceremony, the wedding guests paraded in a colorful procession from the synagogue to the bride's house.

In some smaller towns, the tradition persisted according to which the community on Rosh Hashonah (New Year), marched towards a river or some other body of water. There they would say appropriate prayers, the whole ceremony symbolizing the purification of the soul and the throwing off of the sins committed during the year. This ancient tradition was followed only in the very Orthodox communities in smaller towns.

In some cities, especially during the first few years after the issuance of the Balfour Declaration promising Palestine as a national home for the Jews, street demonstrations were held on November 2, the anniversary of the Declaration. Meetings were organized by the Zionist groups, followed by parades. However, the observance of this day gradually diminished in importance.

Jewish labor unions and socialist parties celebrated May 1st together with the Polish labor movement. In the larger cities, and especially in the industrial cities like Warsaw, Lodz and Bialystok, the Jewish labor groups organized special groups within the general labor parade. In the last years of the Republic, during the labor day parades, many clashes occurred between the workers and the police who objected to the slogans and speeches. Clashes occurred also between the police and the Jewish groups who participated in the parades. Some labor leaders, Jewish and others, were arrested the day before May 1st, to prevent their participation.

One of the slogans of the labor-day parade was usually a call to fight against anti-Semitism and a call on the working people of all nationalities and religions in Poland to cooperate for the overthrow of the reactionary regime and for the establishment of a liberal and democratic government.

Communal Groups

Most of the Jews, like the other national minorities in Poland, were organized into political parties of their own. Some Jewish intellectuals and radicals belonged to the general Polish parties; the various democratic small groups had a number of Jews among their leaders. However, the majority of the Jews belonged to specifically Jewish groups which participated in the political life of the country. These Jewish groups can be divided into three blocs: 1) the Orthodox bloc; 2) the various Zionist factions; 3) the labor and radical organizations.

1. The most influential Orthodox group was the Agudath Israel. Organized in 1916, it emphasized the religious factor in Jewish life, and its political attitudes were governed by its clerical outlook. For a long time this group, favored by the Pilsudski regime, cooperated with the government bloc in Parliament. At its inception, the Agudath Israel was bitterly anti-Zionist and especially opposed to political Zionism, believing that in God's own time the Messiah would deliver the Jewish people and restore them to Palestine. More recently, under the pressure of its younger members, the attitude of the Agudath towards the secular upbuilding of Palestine underwent considerable change. Some of its younger members have settled in Palestine. Generally it may be said that although it is still anti-Zionist, the Agudath Israel was in 1939 pro-Palestinian.

    In 1931 a new Orthodox group called Machzikay Hadas was formed under the influence of the Hassidic rabbinical dynasty of Belz. This group was even more religious than the Agudath Israel. Its opposition to Zionism was extreme; however, its influence was limited to eastern Galicia.

2. Polish Jews were the backbone of the world Zionist movement between the two wars, and Zionists in Poland were also active in the internal politics of the country. During the existence of the Polish Republic there were always Zionist members in the Polish Parliament, and this had considerable influence upon the Jewish communities. The Zionists of Poland were divided into the following groups:

    a. Mizrachi, an Orthodox group, distinguished itself from other Orthodox factions by furthering a nationalist and pro-Palestinian Jewish policy. In domestic affairs it usually cooperated with other nationalist Jewish groups and had some influence among the religious Jews.

    b. General Zionists were divided into two groups -- one conservative; the other -- more progressive -- had a working alliance with the Labor Zionists. The General Zionists were not united in a common organization including the whole Polish territory. They retained their pre-First World War divisions with three separate party headquarters in Warsaw, Cracow and Lwow, respectively. Socially and economically they held "Centrist" views, upholding middle-class and professional interests particularly, since they represented the rather modern Jews who knew at least some Polish and who had developed a national Jewish consciousness. Politically they were the most influential among the Zionist groups; most of the Jewish deputies in Parliament represented the General Zionist faction.

    c. Labor Zionists were concerned mostly with furthering the upbuilding of Palestine along labor and cooperative lines and had comparatively little interest in internal Polish politics. Although considered a very moderate Labor group, they were members of the Second International. Within the Zionist movement they were probably numerically the largest group although their influence in the Jewish community in Poland was not in proportion to their numerical strength.

d. The Revisionist Zionist group seceded from the World Zionist Organization in 1935 and created its own world body. In Poland its hold was mainly among the young people. It was considered anti-labor and used some of the militaristic approaches of totalitarian movements, appealing especially for the support of the Jewish War Veterans. It was very friendly to the Pilsudski regime, and was the only Jewish group openly advocating the "evacuation" of Jews from Poland. For this reason it was favored by the post-Pilsudski regime which, following the anti-Semitic propaganda line that there were too many Jews in Poland, was officially demanding Jewish mass evacuation.

3. The most important Jewish labor group in Poland was the Bund, the General Jewish Workers Union. Formed in 1897, the Bund played an important role in the movement against Czarist oppression. Later it joined the Second International, cooperating closely with the Polish Socialist Party and with the Socialist parties of other nationalities in Poland. It was always strongly anti-Communist, and was also opposed to Zionism, which it considered reactionary and capitalistic; its program called for cultural autonomy for Jews and support for Jewish schools and cultural institutions in Yiddish. The influence of the Bund increased during the last few years of Polish independence; in some of the city council elections, the Bund succeeded in obtaining a majority of the Jewish votes. The Bund was strongly against mass emigration from Poland and in favor of collaboration between the Jewish and Polish labor and democratic elements.

In all the Jewish organizations -- political, economic, social and cultural -- membership was voluntary and mostly based on membership dues. In some organizations, membership was quite restricted and was based on social or economic considerations. The B'nai B'rith, which in the United States is a fraternal organization of a quite popular character, was in Poland an exclusive body.

Marriage

A religious marriage ceremony was obligatory in Congress Poland and Galicia. In Poznan, civil marriage was required, but in Congress Poland and Galicia a marriage was valid when performed by a rabbi, whether or not civil steps had been taken. This caused complications in the case of remarriage -- following a religious divorce -- of either husband or wife. The deserted spouse, accusing the other of bigamy, had to depend on the interpretation of the judge, who might or might not decide that the previous religious marriage was tantamount to a civil marriage and that the remarried spouse was therefore a bigamist. Children born of marriages where a religious ceremony alone had been performed were considered illegitimate; they were registered under the mother's name, with the father's name given after the word false (alias). When they used the father's name, the mother's name was inserted following recte (rightfully). The Agudath Harabanim (Union of Rabbis) had asked the rabbis of the country not to officiate at religious marriages unless civil registration had first been complied with. Since religious marriage was obligatory in Congress Poland and Galicia, intermarriage was impossible there, unless one of the parties had been converted to the religion of the other.

During the first ten months of 1938, 1,431 Jewish marriages took place in Warsaw. During the entire year, there were 21,000 Jewish marriages throughout Poland.

No statistics are available for marriages under the Nazi occupation. Almost no civil marriages are known to have occurred; and although there may have been some religious marriages, the number is unquestionably far smaller than before the war.

Divorce

A religious decree in divorce was obligatory in Poland. A legal divorce could be granted only after the reading of the Jewish divorce writ -- in Polish translation -- in the court. Although until about two years before the war, when the law was unified for all of Poland, civil divorce had been independently obtainable in Poznan, this method was rarely resorted to.

The <u>Agunah</u> (deserted wife) problem was very serious in Poland because of the religious marriage requirement. According to Jewish law, a woman whose husband disappeared and to whose death no one can testify may not remarry. The problem may be reconstituted with unprecedented seriousness after this war for people of Orthodox conviction because of the numerous unwitnessed murders at Nazi hands. The few <u>Rabbiner</u>, or moderate liberal rabbis, in Poland, had practiced a modified interpretation of this law.

Funerals

Every Jewish community in Poland had a <u>Hevra Kadisha</u> (Burial Society), which took care of the fulfillment of Jewish burial regulations. These include quick burial, burial in individual graves, and -- customarily -- honor to the dead through the presence of friends and relatives at the obsequies. The Nazi occupation from the very beginning made the fulfillment of most of these regulations and customs impossible. For a time funerals during daylight hours were prescribed in Warsaw, to keep the non-Jewish population from seeing how many deaths occurred. With the beginning of mass extinction in 1942, all disguises were dropped. Burial in individual graves became impossible, as did the use of shrouds.

Family Life

The position of the father in the Polish Jewish family was traditionally very strong; the lives of the mother and of the children were determined entirely by paternal decision. In the past few decades, however, there has been a movement toward sex equality. This was true even in Orthodox Jewish households, where the woman -- although expected to remain pious -- was no longer uneducated. Even in ultra-Orthodox households, both daughters and sons went out to earn a living. In less Orthodox and comparatively irreligious households, the process of emancipation moved faster and to greater extremes.

Jewish family relationships, as a whole, had the unity and stability which result from obedience to Talmudic precepts, but the admissibility of divorce was one of the chief points of difference between family life among Jews and family life among the Catholic non-Jewish population of Poland.

Languages

For centuries the vernacular of the Jews of Poland was Yiddish -- a language based on medieval German mixed with Hebrew and Slavic expressions. In their dealings with non-Jews, they spoke Polish, Ukranian, White-Russian or Lithuanian, according to region. But the knowledge of those languages among the great majority of Jews was rather limited.

The situation changed considerably during the last few decades, and especially after the resurrection of an independent Poland. Jews, especially in the larger cities, increasingly accepted the language of the country. A growing number of Jews used Polish in their every-day life, particularly among the younger generation. Even many of those who still used Yiddish became bilingual, speaking Yiddish with the older generation and Polish with schoolmates and friends. In the large cities, with the possible exception of Vilno, Polish became the language of the Jewish youth and Jewish white-collar and professional classes. In smaller towns the situation was somewhat different; Yiddish was still largely the dominant language, particularly among the Orthodox elements of the population. But even there many changes occurred during the twenty years of Polish independence and a great number of young Jews became bilingual. The situation varied according to region. While in the central and southern provinces the influence of Polish culture and the Polish language was very great, in the eastern and northeastern provinces, inhabited mostly by non-Polish majorities, the Jews to a larger extent kept Yiddish as their medium of expression.

In all Jewish religious schools Hebrew was taught as the language of the Bible, which was read in the original; it was not taught as a conversational language. The revival of Hebrew as a living language in Palestine brought about attempts by some Zionist circles in Poland to introduce Hebrew as a conversational medium of expression, and a comprehensive secular school system in Hebrew was established. Some clashes between the so-called Hebraists and Yiddishists developed. However, most responsible Jewish leaders and groups tried to avoid these clashes and favored the support of both school systems, Yiddish and Hebrew.

Criminality

In cities there were twice as many crimes and infractions against the law as in rural centers; every type of crime was more prevalent. Practically all movements directed against the political or social order originated in the cities, while the peasants, who were fundamentally conservative, only occasionally took part in such activities. It is therefore significant that the Jews, although an urban population and therefore expected to have a crime ratio in proportion to their ratio in the city population, comprised no more than 5% of those who were sentenced by the courts, for any reason, while in Poland as a whole Jews constituted 9.8% of the population and in the larger cities between 25% and 30%. In crimes committed in the larger cities they participated to the extent of only one-fourth their population ratio. Most of the infractions committed by the Jews against the law were of a minor nature. According to the official Polish statistics for 1936 (the latest crime statistics available), out of 1440 condemned for murder, there were only 42 Jews. The proportion of Jews in petty crimes and felonies was higher but still it never exceeded 5%, or half of the general ratio in the population. In infractions committed against the safety of the state, their participation was slightly higher than their population ratio, but smaller than the ratio of criminality in the city as compared with the countryside. Of 37,300 crimes and infractions committed against the state or public order, Jews committed 3,805. Most of these infractions were of a political nature, directed against the dictatorship.

This generally low rate of criminality can be explained by the mode of life of most of the Polish Jews and by the adherence to Jewish tradition, which was still an important factor with the great majority of the Jewish population. What the effects of the Nazi regime may be upon the outlook and morale of the Jewish population is of course at present unknown. Jews are participating actively in the underground movement and it may be assumed that some elemental violence unknown previously has been introduced into the pattern of Jewish life. It is also possible that constant humiliation and persecution have brought about a desire towards violent reactions and acts against the oppressors which may leave serious moral scars on many Jews, especially the youth. On the other hand, however, the sufferings under the Nazi regime might bring about a resurgence of idealism and social consciousness among the Jews in Poland. From the information emerging from Poland we know that the ghetto has considerably intensified Jewish as well as human solidarity, and the consciousness of a common faith -- regardless of previous class and social differences.

Alcoholism; Narcotics

Among the important sources of income in the Polish government budget were the liquor, tobacco and salt monopolies, of which the prices were very high compared with the income of the people. Beer was a popular drink; the majority of the poorer population, especially the peasants, could afford little more than beer which was comparatively cheap because its manufacture was a highly competitive industry in Poland. However, alcohol was used in large quantities at most festive occasions and family celebrations. Peasant weddings often ended with shootings among the guests because of the excessive consumption of alcohol.

Jews also consumed large quantities of alcohol and beer at family festivities and during some of the holidays, but among them, the occasions seldom terminated with fights or violence. Beer was generally less popular among Jews than among the Gentile population; few Jews frequented the taverns found by the thousand throughout the country. The white-collar and middle classes were seldom found in bars. The type of bar existing in the United States for the middle-class was practically unknown in Poland, where there were either taverns for the poorer working people or restaurants where liquor was served.

Jews played a considerable part in the alcohol industry although the state monopoly gradually tried to eliminate them. To a large extent Jews were eliminated from all monopolized industries, especially from the wholesale trade. It was more difficult to eliminate the Jews from the retail trade but even here progressive "Aryanization" was taking place.

Tobacco consumption in Poland was high, especially during the last two decades when women, particularly of the middle and upper classes, also became heavy tobacco consumers. Among peasants and lower-income groups women usually did not smoke; the consumption of tobacco was therefore considerably lower than in the West European countries or in the United States. The use of narcotics was practically unknown in the villages and smaller towns and was limited to a very small group even in the larger cities. This of course is only an estimate because the consumption of narcotics was illegal but it is safe to assume that it was very small as compared with the western countries.

Jews and the State

Jewish precepts emphasize devotion to the State. In the history of Poland, this devotion was expressed in many patriotic acts. When Polish independence came to an end at the end of the 18th century, Berk Joselowicz gathered a separate Jewish regiment, which fought under Kosciuszko (1794), and was almost entirely annihilated. During the first Polish rebellion (1831), the students in the Warsaw rabbinical seminary volunteered for military service. The Warsaw community, at its own cost, finally recruited a separate Jewish cavalry squadron. In answer to a call from the Warsaw Jewish community for Jews to participate in the rebellion, 350 Jews joined the National Guard.

Jews were active in the 1846 independence movement in Galicia, which was supported by Berisz Meisels, rabbi of Cracow. A number of Jews were arrested. In 1862, a group of Jews were sentenced to Siberia for their activities in the cause of Polish independence. The second Polish revolt (1863) saw even greater Jewish participation. Berisz Meisels, then rabbi of Warsaw, was arrested and had to leave the country. A number of Jews who were officers in the revolutionary armies fell in battle. Many more Jews were privates. The Jewish population as a whole contributed greatly to the uprising, and a Jew named Wahl served as minister of finance in the revolutionary government.

In 1905 many Jews lost their lives for revolutionary activity against the Czarist government under the flag of the Polish Socialist party. At the outset of the First World War, many Jews fought in the Polish Legion; many fell in battle. During the period of Polish independence (1918-1939) Jews participated generously in government loans and other patriotic undertakings.

Attitude toward War: toward the United States

The majority of the Jews were consistently opposed to the foreign policies of Mr. Beck, which they considered as being pro-Hitler. However, they hesitated to express their opinions lest they be accused of being swayed not by the interests of Poland but by a hatred of Hitler based on his attitude towards the Jews. Throughout the period of alliance between Poland and Hitlerite Germany the Jewish press and public opinion favored cooperation with the Western powers and collective security against the aggressors, especially against Germany. Jewish public opinion was unanimously opposed to the Polish policy of annexing Teschen (until then Czechoslovak) after the Munich agreement. When Polish policy changed and the British-Polish agreement was concluded, the Jews enthusiastically supported the new trend. The ratio of Jewish subscriptions to the defense loans was considerably higher than the ratio of the Jewish population in the country. When the war broke out Jewish soldiers, together with all other Polish soldiers, fought the Nazi armies although they knew that if taken prisoner they would be treated differently from non-Jews. During the defense of Warsaw the Jews played a conspicuous role in the civil defense council of the city, which held out against the Nazi armies for more than three weeks. All Jewish political groups were enthusiastically behind the war effort and were ready to forget the anti-Semitic policies of the government in order to achieve national unity in defense.

There are in the United States an estimated 2,000,000 Jews of Polish extraction; nearly half of the Jewish population in the United States comes from Poland or is of Polish descent. Few Jews in Poland have no near relatives in the United States. Since the beginning of this century and especially since the First World War the United States Jewish community has greatly contributed to the welfare of Polish Jewry; the bonds between the Jews of Poland and those in the United States are close and intimate. Polish Jews also remember the role that America played in the securing of equal rights for Jews during the Versailles peace conference. For the Polish Jews the United States has become a symbol of human equality and of hope for the future, although quota restrictions allowed very few to immigrate to the United States during the last 20 years.

Jewish Leaders in Poland

Most of the prominent Jewish industrialists, community leaders, etc., remained in Poland. A few did escape to the Soviet occupied territory, to be later imprisoned. A few of the most prominent have died since 1939, either under the Nazi occupation or somewhere in the Soviet Union. Among them was the prominent Jewish communal leader Professor Moses Shor, Chief Rabbi of Warsaw, who died in a Soviet prison. Dr. Emil Sommerstein, former head of the Jewish Deputies Club in the Polish Parliament, was also reported to be in a prison somewhere in the Soviet Union

The two most prominent Jewish labor leaders in Poland, Henryk Ehrlich and Viktor Alter, were killed by the Soviet authorities in December 1941. Among the most important communal leaders who remained under the Nazi occupation, Adam Czerniakow, who became the mayor of the Warsaw Ghetto, committed suicide in July 1942. Dr. Henryk Schipper, prominent Zionist leader and Jewish historian, was executed by the Germans; Professor Mayer Balaban of Warsaw University, renowned Jewish historian, was also killed.

Rabbi Aaron Lewin, the most important leader of the Agudath Israel, the Orthodox party, and former Deputy of the Polish Parliament, remained in Poland. Among the industrialists remaining in Poland, the most important are Abraham Gepner, one of the leaders of the metal industry; Solomon Graff (iron), Michael Friedbert (textiles), Solomon Levinsohn (chemicals) and Emile Spaet (banking).

Among the most prominent lawyers of Poland were Ignatz Baumberg and A. Margolis of Warsaw, and Leib Landau of Lwow. Among the prominent doctors were Ludwig Abramowicz, Paul Goldstein and Fryzberg.

Jewish Leaders in Exile

Of the Jewish leaders who escaped the Nazi occupation, many found their way to the United States, some went to Palestine, others to Great Britain, and a few are in Latin America. Among the industrialists in exile are Karl Sachs, an important figure in the pre-war Polish sugar industry, and at present Consul in Cuba; and Mr. Nahum Eitingon, one of the greatest textile industrialists of Lodz, now in the United States. Among the important bankers, Mr. Rafael Szereszowski, the head of the private banking house in Warsaw, is in the United States.

Among the most important political figures and communal leaders now in exile are Apolinary Hartglas of the General Zionists (Palestine); Louis Levite, Zionist (Palestine); Henryk Rosmarin, former Sejm Deputy, at present Polish Consul General in Tel Aviv, Palestine; Engineer Reiss, Labor Zionist leader (Palestine); Ignacy Schwartzbart, former Sejm Deputy from Cracow, a member of the Polish National Council in London; Rabbi Isaac Rubenstein, former Deputy, and Mizrachi leader (United States); Shloime Mendelsohn, leader of the Jewish Socialist Party Bund (United States); Emanuel Szerer, Bund leader, now a member of the Polish National Council in London.

Among the prominent scholars are Professor Taubenszlag, professor of law, University of Cracow (United States); Dr. Bychowski, professor of psychoanalysis at the Warsaw University (United States); and Professor Henryk Tennenbaum, renowned economist (Great Britain).

Citizenship

The minority treaties with Poland provided that all the inhabitants of the country would automatically receive citizenship without regard to race, creed or nationality. All Jews who at the time of the conclusion of the peace treaties found themselves on Polish territory were therefore granted Polish citizenship. No distinction between the citizenship status of Jews and other citizens was ever officially introduced during the 20 years of Polish independence. However, a law was passed by the Polish Parliament in 1938 which deprived all Polish citizens who remained outside Polish territories for more than five years of their Polish citizenship. The law was directed mainly against Jews living outside of Polish territory, and in fact, affected a considerable number of Jews.

The passing of this law had important international consequences; it was used by the Hitlerite regime as an excuse for the expulsion of Polish Jews from Germany. Before the law entered into effect the Nazis rounded up 8,000 Polish Jews and sent them to Poland on the pretext that they would soon lose their citizenship and that the Nazis did not want to harbor stateless Jews. The Polish authorities refused to permit these Jews to enter, because according to their legislation they were no longer Polish citizens. For months several thousand Jews lived under deplorable conditions in a "no-man's land" near Zbonszyn, on the frontier between Poland and Germany. Only after great effort was their fate finally settled. Most of them were ultimately readmitted to Poland, but not given citizenship, and obliged to remain stateless.

In 1941 the Government-in-Exile annulled the law which deprived citizens who had lived over five years outside of Polish territory of their citizenship.

Under the Nazi regime, the Jews of the incorporated area were granted the same status as those in Germany; they were not citizens, but subjects of the German Reich who received special identification papers indicating clearly that they were Jews. All the restrictions and discriminations introduced in Germany were automatically extended to the incorporated areas, which were considered provinces of the Reich.

In the Government General the situation was somewhat different. The Government General was not considered a part of the Reich, but a Nebenland, which is tantamount to a European colony of the Reich. Poles as well as Jews were considered, not citizens, but natives of the country and subjects of the German administration. A customs frontier was retained between Germany and the Government General; theoretically the Government General was supposed to be "the home of the Polish people." In 1941, after the occupation by Germany of the section of Poland formerly occupied by Russia, Eastern Galicia was added to the Government General. While the Ukrainians here enjoy a privileged status they are not considered German citizens either.

The Soviet Union, during its occupation of the eastern sections of Poland, proclaimed that all those who resided there in November 1939, when a plebiscite was held, had become Soviet citizens. At present the Polish Jews who are in the Soviet Union are considered Soviet citizens although some of them were permitted to join the Polish army and subsequently to leave the Soviet territories.

As for Jews of other countries who have been deported by the Nazis into Poland, their citizenship status varies according to the laws of the countries from which they came. The Jews of Belgium, Holland, Norway, etc. have retained their former status. The status of naturalized French Jews who were later deprived of their citizenship by the Vichy regime and eventually sent to Poland by the Nazis, is very complicated; they probably may be considered stateless. The Polish Government-in-Exile does not recognize any of the Nazi laws concerning citizenship; Polish Jews in all the former Polish territories are considered Polish citizens.

Stateless

The number of stateless Jews in Poland was small. The problem of statelessness became important throughout Europe after the First World War and the establishment of the Soviet regime in Russia, when millions of emigrés were deprived of their citizenship status. However, all residents of the Polish territories were given Polish citizenship as the result of the Versailles treaty; the number of Jews who had succeeded in escaping Soviet territories and settling in Poland after 1919 was small. In many cases the citizenship status of individual Jews was in doubt, but most of these were settled during the early years of Polish independence.

Jews in Parliament

Jews participated from the beginning in the political and parliamentary life of independent Poland. In the first Polish Sejm (House of Deputies) there were 11 Jewish members. The first Sejm voted the constitution of 1921 which introduced universal elections and guaranteed secrecy of the ballot. To the second Parliament (1922-1927) the Jews elected 35 deputies and 12 senators, the Senate having been established by the 1921 constitution. During the 1922 elections the Jews formed a bloc with all other national minorities except in Eastern Galicia where the Ukrainians, who still did not acknowledge Polish sovereignty, refused to participate in the elections and the Jews were the only minority taking part in the elections. After the coup d'état by Pilsudski in May 1926 the importance of the legislature decreased considerably. In the elections of the third Sejm (1928) the so-called "Non-party Bloc for Cooperation with the Government" was created, and won more than 25% of all the seats in the parliament. Some of the Jewish moderates cooperated with the bloc and were elected from it to parliament.

The Jews also elected deputies independently (these deputies formed the Jewish Club in Parliament), but the number of Jews in the third Sejm decreased. Instead of the 35 Jewish deputies and 12 senators who had served in the second Sejm there were only 15 Jewish deputies and six senators in the third.

During the two years of the third Sejm's existence (1928-30) the breach between the executive and the legislative departments widened until parliament was dissolved and the important opposition leaders were imprisoned for alleged conspiracy against the regime. The elections of 1930 were dominated by administrative pressure and corruption; the non-party bloc succeeded in electing a majority to parliament. The elections of 1930 really marked the end of the parliamentary regime in Poland and the disappearance of an independent legislature. In the fourth Sejm (1930-1935) the Jews had 10 deputies and one senator. The Jewish representatives were divided as follows: six deputies belonged to the Jewish Club, three deputies and one senator belonged to the "Non-party Bloc for Cooperation with the Government," and one deputy, representing the Orthodox Agudath Israel, did not belong to either group.

During the last years of the republic, the legislature was little more than a rubber stamp. The constitution of 1935 abolished universal and direct voting; all the opposition groups boycotted the elections of that year. Some of the Jewish groups also boycotted the election, but the more conservative elements did participate. The number of Jewish representatives in the legislature continued to decrease and in the last years of the Polish republic there were only four Jewish deputies, and two Jewish senators appointed by the president of the republic. The number was of no consequence because the legislature lacked any real power.

Government-in-Exile

The Mikolajczyk government, organized after the tragic death of General Sikorski in July 1943, included one Jew, Dr. Ludwig Grossfeld, who represented the Polish Socialist party, as Minister of Finance. Dr. Grossfeld had been undersecretary of the Ministry of Labor and Social Welfare in the Sikorski government. The representation of Polish Jews abroad, composed of representatives of all the Jewish political parties in Poland before the war except the Bund, and also the representation of the Bund abroad, have asked for the inclusion in the cabinet of a Jew representing the Jewish community in Poland. This request was not met and no representative of the Jewish community is to be found in the Polish Government-in-Exile. In the Polish National Council, which is only a consultative body, there are two Jewish members: Dr. Ignacy Schwartzbart, representing the Zionists, and Dr. Emanuel Szerer, succeeding the late Schmuel Zygilbojm (who committed suicide as a protest against the indifference of the democratic countries towards the suffering of Polish Jewry), representing the Bund.

Very few Jews are employed by the Polish Government-in-Exile, and several protests made by the Jewish groups have been of no avail. There are only a few Jews serving as honorary consuls without pay, a few experts in the departments dealing with economic and financial problems, very few in the Ministry of Information and in the Polish telegraphic agency and practically none in the department of foreign affairs or other political departments. There is a special bureau dealing with minority problems in the Ministry of Home Affairs, headed by one of the most liberal and enlightened Poles in exile -- Dr. Olgierd Gorka. General Kukiel, Minister of War, announced that a special bureau would be set up to improve the relations between the Jewish and Gentile soldiers in the army. It was also suggested that a special department for Jewish affairs should be instituted by the Polish government; however, this suggestion has to date not been realized.

When the Soviet government, after the agreement with Poland of July 30, 1941, permitted relief to be sent to the Poles in the Soviet Union, relief agents were appointed by the Polish government in many cities of the Soviet Union. Among them were several Jews who were entrusted with the administration of relief sent by the Polish government and by private organizations in the United States and Great Britain. Nevertheless, complaints (which later proved to be justified) were reported of discrimination against Jews in the distribution of relief. As Polish-Soviet relations worsened, all the relief agencies were closed.

The Polish Government-in-Exile has been from the beginning a government of national unity composed of four main parties: The National Democrats, the Peasant Party, the National Labor Party and the Polish Socialist Party. In addition, a few independent ministers were appointed, including some former followers of the Pilsudski regime. After the conclusion of the Polish-Russian agreement, the Pilsudski followers resigned from the government and the extreme wing of the National Democrats also refused to support Sikorski. A split occurred in the National Democratic Party, the moderate faction remaining in the government while the extremist group went over to the opposition. Thus at present the government still represents the four main parties, while the opposition is composed of the extreme nationalists and the followers of Pilsudski.

Parties comprising the government coalition are of course bound by official statements. The government has repeatedly promised complete equality to all citizens of Poland, including the Jews. It condemned the anti-Semitic policies instituted by the pre-war Polish government and declared itself in favor of a democratic Poland. However, the only parties who can be relied upon to support a democratic regime are the Polish Socialists and the Peasant Party. The National Democrats, even those who are represented in the government, have not discarded their anti-Semitic tradition; while supporting official governmental declarations, they have frequently made important reservations in regard to Jews. The extreme nationalist groups which have refused to enter the government coalition are openly anti-Semitic and have been continuing their anti-Jewish propaganda even in England, publishing several newspapers. Not a few of them are quite in agreement with the anti-Jewish policies of the Hitlerite regime.

It should be noted that the Poles who have succeeded in escaping and are now in exile do not represent a complete cross section of the nation. Liberal and democratic elements have remained chiefly in the country; former governmental officials and many of the nationalist elements succeeded in escaping.

All Polish Jewish groups have their representatives in exile; the same party division that existed in pre-war Poland is found among the Polish Jews who have succeeded in escaping the Nazi occupation. Some Jewish leaders have found their way to Palestine where they have formed a group called the General Polish Jewish Representation. The Representation claims the right to speak in the name of Polish Jews abroad and to represent the interest of all Polish Jews who at present cannot be heard from. A branch of the Representation was established in New York, composed of representatives of the Zionist factions and the Orthodox Agudah. The Bund, the most important Jewish labor organization in Poland, has refused to join the Representation and has established its own body in the United States called the American Representation of the General Jewish Workers Union of Poland.

Jews in the Army-in-Exile

It is impossible to give exactly the number of Jews in the Polish army. The strength of the army is a military secret and no statistics arranged by religion are available. However, on the basis of statements made by Polish military leaders it may be estimated that the Jews form about 10%, a little more than their ratio in pre-war Poland, of the Polish army-in-exile. According to General Anders, the head of the Polish army that was formed in the Soviet Union, Jews constituted 15% of his forces. The percentage of Jews in the Polish army in Great Britain is probably considerably lower.

The Polish army since 1939 has contained more officers than the size of the army itself would demand. Most of these officers were reserve officers or in active service in pre-war Poland, where there had been marked discrimination against Jews in the army as a whole and especially in the officers' corps. It is therefore not surprising that the Polish army in Great Britain, which included so many officers, does not have a high percentage of Jews. The ratio of Jews in the Polish army in France until the fall of France was considerably higher but most of that army has been lost. Only a relatively small number of Polish soldiers, especially officers, were saved at Dunkerque. There would have been a higher percentage of Jewish soldiers in the army evacuated from Russia had there not been considerable discrimination against accepting Jews in the army there. Some anti-Semitism was to be found in the army-in-exile. According to the official Polish statistics, 32,000 Jewish soldiers fell during the Polish-German campaign in September 1939.

Underground

Jews have developed an active underground movement in Poland, divided into two main groups: Bundist and Zionist. The Bundists publish three underground papers, the Zionists one paper. While the Polish underground had to fight such collaborationist tendencies as might have arisen among some Polish groups, Jews naturally have no such problem.

The chief tasks of the Jewish underground movement are to inform the people about the progress of the war and to maintain morale and resistance against Nazi oppression. It also tries to help as many Jews as possible to escape from the ghettos and to hide among the Gentile population in towns and villages. The Bundist group is in close collaboration with the democratic groups of the Polish underground movement, particularly with the Polish Socialist party.

Some Jews are participating in the guerrilla and sabotage units of the Polish underground. After July 1942, when the Hitler regime started the policy of mass extermination, the Jewish underground repeatedly appealed for arms. At first some Jewish groups refused to accept a policy of desperation in the hope that the terror would be lessened. But instead, it constantly increased until all the Jewish groups realized that they must demand arms from the Polish Government. After some hesitation the Polish Government consented.

In April 1943, in the battle that developed between the Jews in the Warsaw ghetto and the German police and military forces, in resistance to extermination squads, the Nazis had to use heavy artillery and to burn a large part of the ghetto before the Jews submitted. Similar resistance subsequently developed in other cities, where many Jews were in possession of arms and ready to resist the German extermination squads.

Attitude of People: Before Invasion

Jews have lived in Poland for about a thousand years, as long as the Poles themselves. Throughout the Middle Ages Poland was the most liberal of all countries in the treatment of the Jews. Since Poland lacked a native middle class the Jews were invited by the Polish authorities to develop the commercial and industrial life of the country. For centuries the Jews formed a necessary and useful component of the Polish social structure, which was based on a sharp division between the only existing two classes of population, the landowners and nobles on the one hand and the peasants deprived of all political rights on the other. Towards the Jews the attitude of both groups was on the whole friendly. Although, because of his religion, the Jew was considered different and a little odd, he was nevertheless generally accepted as an important part of the social structure of the country, performing essential economic functions. The relative liberalism of Poland towards the Jews as contrasted with other countries, including those of western Europe, is demonstrated by the fact that at the end of the 18th century, at the time of the partitions of Poland, the great majority of the Jews in the world lived on Polish territory.

During the 19th century the Jews participated in all the Polish insurrections to regain independence. Polish writers of the period, among them the greatest Polish national poet Adam Mickiewicz, depict the Jews in a very sympathetic light. However, after the last unsuccessful insurrection of 1863 and even more toward the end of the century, anti-Semitic tendencies began to grow, particularly among the expanding native middle class. Many impoverished landowners and members of the gentry went into commerce, industry, and the professions where they had to compete with Jews. Anti-Semitism found a fertile ground among these elements, which became the backbone of the reactionary National Democratic Party (Endeks), created in 1897.

As long as Marshal Pilsudski was alive he kept the National Democrats in check and prevented anti-Jewish pogroms and riots. But after the death of the Marshal, his followers -- in order to maintain themselves in power against the opposition of the democratic forces -- began cooperating with the anti-Semitic and pro-fascist elements. The Polish workers and most of the peasants generally refused to play the anti-Semitic game, and the workers in particular often defended the Jews against their assailants. The Polish Socialist Party, representing the majority of workers, always stood for equality of all citizens, Gentiles and Jews alike. The powerful Peasant Party also generally favored the principles of democracy and opposed anti-Semitism, at least in its violent forms. Some of the peasant leaders, especially in the last few years of Polish independence, partly fell victims to anti-Semitic propaganda, but generally speaking the great majority of the rural population refused to follow the reactionary Jew-baiting leaders. In the country at large, part of the landowning and industrial and business classes were against the Jews. The landowners believed that through anti-Semitism they could divert toward the Jews the wrath of the people who were demanding agrarian reform. The business classes saw in the Jews competitors whom they desired to eliminate, while a large section of the white-collar groups, especially the university youth, was fascinated by the success of fascism and Hitlerism, in which anti-Semitism was one of the most important factors and a wedge for obtaining power.

Attitude of People: After Invasion

In the defense of Warsaw and other cities, Jews participated and fought side by side with the Poles, and a better understanding between the two peoples seems to have been evolved during the Polish campaign. However, it was reported that when the Germans first occupied the country some Polish anti-Semitic groups collaborated with the Nazis in their anti-Jewish policies. This was limited to a relatively small group of young people who had formerly participated in the various pro-fascist anti-Semitic campaigns. The majority of the Polish people refused to collaborate with the Nazis on any score, including that of anti-Semitism.

Some elements of the Polish underworld were used by the Nazis for anti-Semitic riots, and given a free hand in looting Jewish-owned business establishments. However, the great mass of Polish workers and peasants consistently refused to be swayed by the Nazi anti-Semitic propaganda and, generally speaking, the Polish underground movement has collaborated with the Jewish underground movement and in many instances sympathy and help were given to the Jews by various Polish groups. Although even among the underground groups there are still some who have anti-Semitic tendencies, the majority are more democratic and resist anti-Semitism. When the ghettos were introduced, many manifestations of sympathy with the Jews were shown by the Poles and the ghettos were to a large extent supplied with food by Polish peasants and workers.

It is interesting to note that when the Nazis embarked on a policy of complete destruction of the Warsaw ghetto they used German and Ukrainian police, believing that the Polish police could not be trusted in carrying out their orders. In various documents and statements that have come out of Poland, the fact is emphasized that a great majority of the nation understood that anti-Semitism was before the war partly inspired by Germans in order to divide the nation and to weaken its resistance against German invasion. All the underground statements stress the harm that anti-Semitic propaganda did to the unity of the nation and favor the elimination of all anti-Semitism in the future Poland. When the Jews, facing a desperate situation, decided to resist the complete destruction of the ghettos with arms, the Polish underground movement provided them with weapons. Thousands of Jews, according to reliable reports, have succeeded in escaping the ghettos and have fled to the small towns and villages. The peasants are reported to have hidden them from the German executioners, and a general feeling of sympathy and solidarity with the Jews is prevailing throughout the country.

Civil Service

During twenty years of independence, Poland developed state capitalism to a greater extent than did most European countries. The state owned about 100 industrial establishments consisting of more than 1,000 units, and including railroads, mines, factories and banks. Many of the important industries in the country were either directly or indirectly under the control of state institutions. There were five state monopolies: alcohol, match, tobacco, salt and lottery. In the last few years before the war the state institutions wrote almost half of all insurance policies. State banks dominated the financial market. Thus about one million people were on the public payroll of the state and the communities. Including their dependents, about 3,000,000 people, or some 10% of the entire population, derived a livelihood from state enterprises.

There are no general statistics on the number of state employees who were Jews, but it was so small as to constitute probably less than 1% of all state employees, although the Jews made up about 10% of the population and 25% to 35% of the urban population. Official statistics in Warsaw, for instance, indicate that in the administration of Warsaw, where the Jews formed about 1/3 of the population, only 1.9% of all the municipal employees were Jewish. The percentage among the employees throughout the country was even smaller.

The consequences of such a state of affairs were extremely harmful to the economic position of the Jews in Poland, and the inevitable result of the nationalization and government control of an industry was the gradual elimination of Jews from that industry. On the other hand, Jews were forced to crowd the industries and professions which were still left to the private competitive system. They formed about 50% of all the privately-practicing lawyers of Poland, but practically no Jews were admitted to the judiciary, appointed public notaries, or allowed to occupy any of the government positions for which they were qualified by legal training.

The same policies of discrimination against the Jews that prevailed in other governmental services also obtained in the police force. There were practically no Jews either in positions of importance or even among the lower ranks. A few Jews might have been found serving as officers or police department employees in Galicia once under Austrian regime, but most of them were retired after reaching the age limit. Virtually no Jews had ever been appointed to the police department in Poland.

Immediately after the Hitler occupation, all Jews were dismissed from civil service and deprived of pensions. The Jewish community was given extensive powers to perform many functions which formerly belonged to the state. After the establishment of ghettos in the larger cities, the community was made responsible for the maintenance of order as well as for the economic and social life of the Jews within the ghettos. The Jewish communities became the centers of Jewish economic, social and cultural life; the budget of the community councils was considerably increased and the bureaucracy greatly extended.

Under the Hitler regime a special Jewish police force was established in Warsaw and other larger Polish cities, composed of young Jews with college and some military training. They were armed with rubber truncheons and wore special insignia on their caps and sleeves, but as members of a volunteer civilian body they had no right to act without instructions from the Nazis. Their main task was to keep order and to see that the commands of the German authorities were carried out by the Jewish population. They also regulated traffic in the ghettos, supervised demolition and construction work, and supplied the Nazis with Jewish labor.

Other services that are usually within the powers of the state or city were taken over by the Jewish communities in the ghetto. They instituted special arbitration boards to deal with cases between Jews and organized a post-office system. Mail reaching the ghetto was distributed by Jewish mailmen, most of them war veterans. Some of the Jewish professionals and white-collar workers who lost their jobs after the German occupation were now able to earn a meager livelihood as community employees. When the policy of exterminating the Jews began, a special police force composed of Germans, Ukrainians and Lithuanians, was sent into the ghettos to carry out the orders.

The Judiciary

Generally speaking, Polish courts were fair and did not discriminate against Jews. However, in some instances, especially in cases growing out of anti-Jewish riots, anti-Semites would escape with light sentences or with acquittals. This was largely the result of interference on the part of the government in power, especially during the last few years of the Republic, and cannot be considered as typical of the behavior of Polish judges. Under the dictatorial regime, the judiciary lost most of its independence, and therefore had to follow the general government policies in cases involving political problems.

Soon after the occupation of Poland, a decree dated October 26, 1939 introduced the principle of two judicial systems -- one for Germans, the other for Poles and Jews. Two groups of German courts were set up: 1) martial and police courts; 2) general German courts.

The jurisdiction of the martial and police courts, which was in most cases not subject to appeal, covered the illegal possession of firearms, food speculation, use of railroads without permission, offenses against forced labor legislation, acts committed against the German civil and military authorities, acts against German individuals and damage to German property. All cases between Germans and Poles, or Germans and Jews, came before the general German courts, regardless of whether the German was defendant or plaintiff. German courts followed Nazi law and procedure.

The Germans also established so-called "special courts" (Sondergerichte) which tried all cases so designated by the authorities and any case, if it "appears advisable because of the obvious gravity of the offense." These courts passed judgment without preliminary investigation.

Polish courts were retained and theoretically had jurisdiction over all civil law cases except those in which Germans were involved, and over all criminal cases with no political implications. But in fact the division of jurisdiction was so vague that most criminal cases were dealt with by the German courts. The Nazi authorities could at any time transfer a case from the Polish courts to the German courts, even if the case obviously fell within the jurisdiction of the Polish court. The maintenance of Polish courts was therefore more a matter of convenience than a limitation of German powers.

In principle the Polish courts applied Polish law, unless otherwise stipulated. However, many changes were introduced insofar as Jews were concerned. One of the most important changes was that no decision could be rendered on the basis of testimony given by a Jew, but only on the basis of documents and evidence presented to the courts. Thus the Jews were not only discriminated against by the German courts, but the German authorities imposed anti-Jewish discriminations even on the Polish courts, which usually dealt almost exclusively with civil law and minor criminal cases.

Officially, there were no special Jewish courts, but in practice the discrimination practiced by the German courts and the various discriminatory rules imposed by the Nazi authorities upon the Polish courts prompted the Jews, in litigation among themselves, increasingly to refer their cases to the arbitration boards established by the Jewish community councils. Such arbitration boards had always existed in Poland, but their importance grew after the Nazi occupation of the country.

Jews as Judges

The number of Jewish judges decreased as discrimination intensified. Before the First World War, there were many Jewish judges in the Polish provinces under Austria and also a few under Germany. These judges were retained by the Polish regime, but very few new appointments of Jews were made. One of the members of the Supreme Court, Rapaport, was a Jew; he was also one of the authors of the new Polish civil and penal codes. Artur Miller was a high official in the Ministry of Justice and there were a few Jews in the Courts of Appeal. However, it became increasingly difficult for a Jew to become a judge in Poland and the number of Jewish judges, prosecutors, etc., at the outbreak of the war in 1939 was insignificant.

The Bar

The proportion of Jews among the privately-practising lawyers in Poland was estimated at 50%, although in the law schools Jewish students formed a small minority. In 1936-1937, only 9.4% of the law students were Jews, but even in 1928-1929, the most prosperous year in Poland, they had constituted only 27.7% of the total. The disparity between the percentage of Jewish students in the law schools and the number of Jews who were lawyers in private practice can be found in the fact that Jews were virtually excluded from government judicial and administrative positions requiring legal training, of which there were about 12,000 in the Polish civil service. Only about 5,000 of these posts were held by qualified lawyers; the remaining positions were distributed among comparatively untrained men while fully-trained lawyers who were Jews were denied public employment. Since the

Jewish graduates of the law schools could not become judges, public notaries, or government employees, they engaged in private legal practice.

After 1935, when anti-Semitism -- to a large extent supported by the government -- increased considerably in Poland, a movement to eliminate Jews from the legal profession was begun by the Polish Lawyers Associations with the cooperation of the government. In March 1937 the government introduced a bill in the Sejm to regulate the legal profession. It provided obligatory clerkship in the courts for young lawyers in addition to the equally obligatory clerkship at a lawyer's office; it empowered the Minister of Justice to limit or to close the list of lawyers by an administrative decree. After the Minister closed the lists, he could make any exceptions he wished. As a result, admission to the Bar was denied to young Jewish lawyers, while Poles were admitted through the rule of exceptions. Government officials frankly confessed that the purpose of the law was to reduce the proportion of Jews in the legal profession. Several decrees were issued to implement the law.

The Polish lawyers who until 1936 were divided in two main groups, The National Association of Lawyers, dominated by the anti-Semitic national democrats, and the Union of Polish lawyers, dominated by government supporters, united. On May 9, 1937, they accepted the so-called "Aryan" paragraph and decided "to fight for the protection of the legal profession against the influx of aliens" (meaning Jews). The Association asked for the reduction of Jewish lawyers to the ratio of the Jews in Poland, and passed a resolution recommending that Polish lawyers should not employ Jewish clerks. All Jews were to be excluded from the organization. The resolution met with the approval on the part of some local associations, but strong opposition developed in the local lawyers' organizations in Warsaw, Cracow and Lwow, and the Polish Socialist Lawyers Union issued a statement condemning it. However, the Association remained the most important body of lawyers in the country and enjoyed the support of the government.

A law of May 4, 1938, destroyed the self-government of the Bar; the district Bar councils were dissolved and replaced by new councils nominated by the Supreme Bar Council. Only a few Jews were appointed to the district board councils throughout the country.

According to the decree of the Governor General, after the invasion, Jews were excluded from the Bar and forbidden to practice law; practice was declared open only to holders of special permits; even a great number of non-Jews were refused such permits because they were not considered politically safe enough. The situation of the Jews who were lawyers was probably worse than in any other profession. It was reported that after the establishment of the ghetto in Warsaw, when about a thousand janitor vacancies existed because Christian janitors had to move out of the ghetto, hundreds of Jewish lawyers applied for the jobs. Lawyers also found employment with the Jewish communities, some joining the ghetto police force. Most of them, however, became manual workers or were forced to ask for charity.

Public Notaries

There were a few Jews serving as public notaries in Galicia at the time of the establishment of the Polish Republic. These were, however, soon retired by the Polish authorities and no other Jews were appointed. In the last few years of the Republic there were practically no Jews serving as public notaries.

Municipal and County Posts

In theory, the Jews enjoyed equal rights with regard to municipal government posts. In 1939 there were 4,650 Jews serving in municipal councils throughout the country, or about 32% of the total. Since Jews formed between 30% and 35% of the total urban population, this proportion was about fair. On the other hand, there were only 212 Jews in the county councils, or about 4%, and very few Jews in the councils of the rural districts.

After the elections of 1934, about 25% of all the members of the municipal councils were Jews, less than their proportion in the city population. Subsequently the most important municipal councils were dissolved by the authoritarian government; government commissars and appointees took their place. This brought about, first, a decrease in the number of Jews in the important municipal councils and, second, the selection of only those Jews who were favored by the government.

The Jews never took advantage of their strong position in some of the municipal councils. In none of the important cities have the Jews either elected or tried to elect a Jew as mayor.

Economic Condition

The anti-Jewish discriminations, the economic boycott and the increase of state control in various industries and commerce aggravated the bad economic condition of the Jews, already made hazardous by the effects of the First World War and the economic depression. During the last few years before the Nazi invasion, approximately one-third of the Jewish population was at one time or another forced to appeal to public welfare agencies. In the large cities the situation was even worse; about 40% of the Jewish population of Bialystok and Lwow applied for Passover relief in 1937. In Warsaw, 53% of the Jewish families were exempt from paying even the minimum community tax of 5 zlotys ($1.00), and almost the same percentage of exemptions prevailed in other cities. Even those whose incomes qualified them to pay the minimum tax, at which 18% to 20% of all the taxpayers were rated, were close to impoverished. Estimates indicate that just before 1939, about one-third the population, though representing middle-class elements, had an income which provided less than a bare subsistence level; another third earned the bare subsistence level. They did not appeal to local philanthropies, but many received aid from overseas. About 10% or 15% of the Jewish population may have been considered as living on a comfortable level; very few were wealthy. After the invasion, these few were for a while able to exist by selling jewelry and valuables, but eventually the entire Jewish population of the country was pauperized.

Occupational Structure

The first Polish census of 1921 showed 33.8% of the Jews to be engaged in industry, 41% in commerce, 5.8% in agriculture, 3.2% in transport and 16.2% in other professions and occupations. In 1931 the proportions had changed as follows: 42% in industry and handicraft, 37% in commerce, 4% in agriculture, 4% in transport and 13% in other occupations, including liberal professions and civil servants. Partial figures for the years after 1931 showed an even greater trend toward industry and handicraft, and a drop in the number of Jews in commerce. Participants in the liberal professions and civil service also decreased in number during the last years of Polish independence.

Banking

The most important banks in Poland were either owned or controlled by the state; practically no confessing Jew was employed in any position of importance in these banks.

Before the First World War some of the larger private banks were owned or controlled by foreign capital. Banks located in the former German or Austrian part of Poland were usually branches of German or Austrian banks, with headquarters in Berlin or Vienna. After the formation of the Polish Republic most of these banks either disappeared or were Polonized. In some of these institutions a few Jews occupied important positions, but their number constantly decreased so that in 1939 only a handful of Jews were left, even in the banks which were formerly branches of foreign institutions. There were practically no large banking institutions in Poland that were either owned or controlled by Jews or Jewish-owned capital. Of the smaller institutions, the Lodzki Bank Depozytowy (The Deposit Bank of Lodz) was controlled by the textile manufacturer, Mr. Nahum Eitingon, and was largely in Jewish hands.

Of the private banks owned by Jews, the most important were: D. M. Szereszowski, owned by the Brothers Raphael and Michael Szereszowski in Warsaw; and Wohl of Cracow.

After the Nazi occupation, all banks owned by Jews were closed and all stocks blocked. There were no Jews left in banking; most of the Polish banks were taken over by the Germans. Steps were immediately taken to deprive Jews of their property and economic resources. Without waiting for the complete occupation of the country, the Nazis issued at first local and then general decrees forbidding Jews to withdraw funds from banks. A currency regulation, issued in Lodz on September 19th and in Warsaw on October 13th, 1939, prohibited individual Jews from having more than 2,000 zlotys in their possession. The surplus had to be deposited in blocked bank accounts (Sperrkonto). Jews were not allowed to withdraw more than 250 zlotys a week. But for such withdrawals, they had to present special permits, which the German authorities were not eager to issue. In the Danzig-West Prussia area a similar regulation was issued on November 20, 1939. Jews were ordered to deposit with a bank or credit institution all currency in their possession exceeding 2,000 zlotys.

A decree of November 20, 1939, finally regulated the situation of the Jewish bank accounts in the entire Government General territory. All accounts belonging to Jews or managed by Jews were in principle blocked. Jews were ordered to concentrate all their deposits, credits, safes, etc. in a single bank before December 31, 1939. Banks were forbidden to pay more than 250 zlotys weekly to a Jewish depositor, but could make payments for current needs of industrial or commercial enterprises if such needs were proven authentic to the satisfaction of the authorities. All payments in excess of 500 zlotys made to Jews for business purposes were to be made to a bank and put in a blocked account.

The transfer of money from the incorporated area to the Government General was in principle forbidden. This rule was of great importance to the thousands of Jews who fled or were deported from the incorporated area into the Government General. The owner of a blocked account in the incorporated area had to ask for special permission to transfer any funds at all. But it took months before such permits were granted and in the majority of cases they were refused altogether. All violations of rules were punishable by imprisonment (in some instances the sentences were for 10 to 20 years) and fines amounting to ten times the value of the amount involved. Jurisdiction over all currency problems was given to the special German tribunals, the Sondergerichte.

In regard to banking regulations, the Jews of Poland were treated worse than the Jews of Germany or of other German-occupied countries. While the general German decree established a rule that no Jew could draw more than 500 marks a month, which would correspond to the 1,000 zlotys a month which he was allowed in the Government General, exceptions were made in Germany for individual cases. In Poland no exceptions were permitted; the general rule allowing the withdrawal of only 250 zlotys per week was categorically applied without regard to the previous standard of living of the individual. Insofar as postal checking accounts were concerned, the situation was still worse. According to an ordinance of March 1940 all withdrawals of funds by Jews from postal checking accounts, whatever the sum, required special permits from the currency bureau. Postal checking accounts, which were extremely popular in Poland, especially with people of modest means, were completely blocked as far as the Jews were concerned. To receive a permit for withdrawal weeks and sometimes months of red tape had to be gone through; in practice, Jews of modest means, who often had all their savings in postal checking accounts, were left penniless overnight.

Natural Resources

Jews were the pioneers in developing the oil industry in Galicia at the end of the 19th and beginning of the 20th century. At the beginning of the Polish Republic, Jews still owned quite a number of smaller oil fields, but control of the larger fields and most of the refineries were in the hands of foreign capital. By 1939, the Jews had become a very small factor in oil production; 84% of the capital invested in the oil fields and refineries in Poland was foreign.

The share of the Jews in the ownership and exploitation of mines in Poland was insignificant. In the exploitation of other natural resources, Jews also played no important role. The most important natural resources of Poland are coal, iron, salt and zinc, in all of which Jews were practically unknown. On the other hand, Jews led in the development of Polish forests, having been active for centuries in the timber and sawmilling industries. Timber and timber products held a leading place in Poland's exports and were important in the Polish balance of trade. During the last years of the Polish Republic, however, timber exports dropped considerably. While their value amounted to 589,000,000 zlotys in 1926, or 26.4% of the total value of all Polish exports, it was only 163,000,000 zlotys in 1936, or 15.9% of the total. A large share of the cause for the decline in timber export can be attributed to the anti-Jewish policies of the Polish government. Official or semi-official government organizations were set up, whose purpose was the elimination of the Jews. Jews who had contacts and experience in the foreign timber trade were not admitted by these bureaucratic organizations; as a result, export decreased considerably.

Agriculture

Poland is primarily an agrarian country. This is true not only in the economic sense, agriculture providing a livelihood for the majority of the population, but it is also true to a large extent of the psychological, political and social outlook of the country. Traditionally Poland was dominated by the landowning class, who despised commerce and industry as inferior callings. Whatever commerce and industry were necessary were left to outsiders - to the Germans and to the Jews, who were specifically invited for that purpose by the Polish kings.

In view of those historical factors it is not surprising that the Jews have played a secondary role in Polish agriculture while they were dominant in the development of commerce and industry. According to official Polish statistics, only 1% of all the people in agriculture were Jews, and 4% of all the Jews in Poland derived their livelihood from agriculture. The ratio varied greatly according to provinces. In the Galician provinces, which before the First World War belonged to Austria, the percentage of Jews in agriculture was considerably higher than in the other Polish provinces. In the Stanislawow province, 10% of the Jews were in agriculture; in the Lwow province 9%; in the Tarnopol province 9%; and in the Cracow province 5%. In the eastern provinces (Kresy) the percentage of Jews in agriculture was: Vilno 6%, Novogrod 6%, Polesie 7%, Volhynia 5%, and Bialystok 3%. The smallest percentage of Jews in agriculture was in the central and western provinces: Lublin 3%, Kielce 2%, Warsaw 1%, Lodz 1%, and in Poznan, Pomorze, and Silesian provinces less than 1%.

The total number of Jewish agricultural holdings amounted to about 20,000, which constituted 0.6% of all the agricultural holdings in Poland. Only in two provinces, Lwow (1.5%) and Stanislawow (1.2%) did the Jewish agricultural holdings equal or surpass the 1% Jewish ratio in agriculture.

Under the system of extensive cultivation that prevailed in Poland a holding had to contain at least 7 hectares (about 17½ acres) to provide a modest livelihood for the average peasant family. In most cases, especially in the eastern Galician provinces where most Jewish holdings were concentrated, 10 hectares (25 acres) was the minimum. According to the 1931 official statistics, 89% of all the Jewish holdings contained less than 10 hectares (43.9% were of less than 2 hectares) and were therefore too small to support a single family; 7.6% of the Jewish holdings contained between 10 to 50 hectares and 3.4% consisted of more than 50 hectares (125 acres). In 1921 there were in Poland 286 Jews who owned estates consisting of more than 100 hectares each. These totalled 154,557 hectares, or 1.3% of all the large estates. After 1921 the number as well as the acreage of the Jewish-owned large estates decreased greatly, being more affected by agrarian reform than the large estates owned by non-Jews. By 1939 the number of Jewish-owned large estates was estimated at less than 1% of all large estates, or about the same ratio as that of Jews in Polish agriculture in general.

According to Nazi concepts, Jews were not fit to possess or to cultivate land. To find Jews in agriculture was quite a new experience for the Nazis, because this was practically unknown in Germany; when they occupied the western and central provinces of Poland they immediately decreed that trustees (Treuhänder) be appointed to manage the larger Jewish-owned estates. From many towns and villages the Jews were expelled or deported, and their land was appropriated by the German authorities.

However, there were very few Jews engaged in agriculture in the provinces occupied by the Germans in 1939. Most Jews in agriculture were in the eastern and southeastern parts of the country, which in 1939 came under Soviet control. There the Soviets confiscated the Jewish-owned large estates as well as others, either dividing them among the peasants or establishing agricultural collectives. When the Nazis in 1941 occupied this part of Poland, Jews, unlike Gentiles, were not given back their land. The Jewish owners of small agricultural holdings also lost their possessions when the decree of October 1942 ordered all Jews to move to 55 cities and towns and forbade them to reside in any other locality.

Agricultural Cooperatives

Jews did not participate in the general cooperatives. According to official statistics in 1936, there were eight Jewish agricultural cooperatives with a total membership of 1,000, composed of Jewish farmers selling their products (mostly milk and milk-products). In addition, about 6,000 Jewish farmers were members of the Jewish credit cooperatives. Since there were only about 20,000 Jewish-owned farm holdings in Poland, about 35% belonged either to an agricultural or a credit cooperative. Under the Nazis, the Jewish agricultural and credit cooperatives were destroyed.

Industry

The great textile industry of Lodz and Bialystok was built chiefly by Jews, starting with modest means. Their personal labor and ability made the city the most important textile center of Eastern Europe. Before the First World War Lodz supplied most of the needs of the large Russian market. When, after the war, the Russian market was lost a crisis developed, but it was soon weathered and new export possibilities were found. Jews, to a large extent controlled the textile industry until the downfall of the Polish Republic in 1939.

They were also important in the garment industry, which occupied about 15% of all Polish Jews. About 50% of all workers in the garment industries were Jews. Here again the small-scale enterprise predominated. Large garment factories of the type to be found in the United States were very rare in Europe and practically unknown in Poland. Most of the undertakings were in fact custom order craft work shops, rather than factories for mass production.

In industries where large factories and mass production prevailed, the Jews were much less important both as manufacturers and managers or as workers. No precise figures are available, but according to the best estimates Jews owned or managed about 15% of the sugar industry, 25% of the chemical industry and about 20% to 25% of the fat and soap industries. They were pioneers in the rubber industry in Poland and by 1939 still controlled between 40% and 50% of it. In all industries, however, the importance of the Jews was decreasing because the policy of the Polish government was towards increased state control of economic life accompanied by the progressive elimination of the Jews from management and ownership.

Commerce

The 1921 census showed that 41% of the Jews were in commerce and trade, but in 1931, only 37% were in that listing, while the percentage of the population as a whole thus engaged was 6.1%. Jewish participation goes back to the invitation extended by the rulers of Poland to the Jews, largely in the 14th century, to develop the commerce of the country. The lack of economic equilibrium in post-1919 Poland provoked contradictory governmental attitudes, all of them, however, directed at ousting the Jews from their major livelihood. Disproportionate taxation was imposed, so that in 1937 it was estimated that two-thirds of all direct taxes were paid by medium-sized and petty enterprises, which comprised the bulk of enterprises owned by Jews. The Jewish population of Poland, constituting 10% of the total, paid between 35% and 40% of all taxes, and commerce paid in taxes more than double its proportion in the national income.

There were five state monopolies, established in the early 1920s: salt, tobacco, alcohol, matches and lottery. In both the production and distribution of the products involved, the Jews had been important, but after the establishment of the monopolies the Jews were either eliminated or had to carry special burdens to remain in business. Some 3,000 Jews were engaged in the tobacco trade before the monopoly, subsequently only 102 remained. The alcohol monopoly allowed a privileged class to live at the expense of the Jews, who were enabled to maintain their concerns by renting them from the monopoly owners. Polish war veterans enjoyed monopoly privileges, but being in most instances unable to provide credits or offer business experience, they employed the very Jews who had been deprived of their businesses to handle the affairs; the Jews were thereby obliged to carry on their own shoulders the support of the war veterans, who should have been the charge of society as a whole.

The establishment of government purchasing agencies in the fields of export and import also affected the Jews, especially in the wheat and meat trades. A system of government export premiums was set up for wheat, but these were in most cases granted to official or semi-official agencies. The experienced Jewish traders had to purchase these premiums, export was seriously handicapped thereby, and the Polish trade balance subjected to a disadvantage.

Difficulty in obtaining credits also cooperated in reducing Jewish participation in commerce, and in forcing those Jews who were active into the lower categories. Business enterprises were divided into five categories; the first three included large or medium-size establishments, the fourth was the small retail store and the fifth the market stand or street-vending. In 1933, of the licenses procured by Jews, 62.9% were in the fourth and fifth categories, and 37.1% in the first three. Non-Jews, on the other hand, obtained 46.8% of their licenses in the last two categories and 53.2% in the first three.

A study made of 1,475 villages showed that in 1914, out of 2,187 stores, 1,574, or 72%, were owned by Jews. In 1935, out of 3,715 stores, only 1,281, or 34.5% were owned by Jews. While the total number of shopkeepers had increased, the enterprises owned by Jews had decreased not only in percentage but numerically. A survey made of 92 small towns with a population of 500,000, of whom 200,000 were Jews, showed that between 1932 and 1937 the number of stores owned by non-Jews had more than doubled, and in some regions quadrupled, while the number of shops owned by non-Jews decreased by as much as 15% in some regions.

With official approbation of the economic boycott against the Jews in a statement by Premier Skladkowski in 1936, and Church approbation through a pastoral letter by Cardinal Hlond in the same year, the already impoverished Jewish business man became even poorer. A call to boycott the Jews economically was inserted in the official program of the Camp of National Unity on February 21, 1937, under the auspices of the President of the Republic and Army Chief Marshal Smigly-Rydz. Picketing, which was banned in the matter of labor disputes, was tolerated by the courts in the case of economic picketing of Jewish-owned shops. Peasants were encouraged to come to the cities and to engage in business, with the alleged aid of direct or indirect government subsidies. Riots and pogroms during the last years of the Republic, resulting in the outright ruination of tens of thousands of Jewish business men, were the culmination of all these tactics.

"Aryanization" and Expropriation

Expropriation of Jewish property began immediately after the German occupation of Poland. For the incorporated area a decree was issued on September 17, 1939, by Marshal Goering, in principle confiscating all property owned by Jews. Jews were immediately deprived of all large properties and industrial establishments, which were turned over to so-called Treuhänders, or trustees. The Haupttreuhandstelle Ost, known as H.T.O. (the Chief Trustee Office for the East) was set up by Marshal Goering early in 1940; one of its main functions was the administration of confiscated property. Trustee management was also applied in real estate, especially in larger cities. All Jewish-owned real estate in the cities of the incorporated area was put under trustee managements, as well as all Jewish-owned real estate outside the Ghetto in the Government General. For the administration of the great number of buildings confiscated by the Germans, a special company was organized which supervised the administration of all the real estate in the hands of Germans.

In the Government General, a trustee headquarters was created and attached to the Governor General's office. Its tasks were officially defined as "the direction of the general economic policy of the country and creative intervention in individual enterprises."

Immediately after the incorporation of the western provinces to Germany, general registration of Jewish-owned property was ordered. The order to register was soon followed by the appointment of German trustees to all Jewish-owned property of some value. Former Jewish owners were theoretically allowed to derive a maximum income of between 250 and 300 marks per month, no matter what the value of the property.

In the Government General the situation was slightly different. While the registration of all Jewish-owned property was ordered, outright confiscation did not invariably take place. The most important industrial and commercial establishments were given German trustees and management. Lesser establishments of medium importance were given either German or Polish trustees. Most of the smaller establishments remained in the hands of their former Jewish owners; the Germans showed little interest in enterprises which even before the war could hardly maintain themselves. In the cities where ghettos were established, the Jews had to give up all enterprises, whatever the size, situated outside the ghettos. Within the ghettos, jurisdiction over the Jewish-owned business establishments was turned over to the Jewish Community Councils. All enterprises connected with products that were rationed suffered greatly; only a few stores in the ghettos were allowed to sell food or clothing; all the others were practically expropriated or forced to close. Whenever the Jews were expelled in numbers from the cities like Cracow, they were refused the right to take most of their belongings with them. These were left for sale to the German trustees, which virtually meant confiscation of Jewish property.

Special central control offices were created for the most important industries. By a decree of April 12, 1940, a central office was set up to supervise and control the textile industry and the textile trade, regulating not only the production of textile goods, but also its purchase, sale, export, etc. The textile industry office supplied the raw material for production; by refusing supplies it could, without actual confiscation, stop all work in a factory belonging to a Pole or a Jew. The office also issued permits for managing textile factories and stores. Prices were strictly controlled by the government office. All the Jewish-owned textile factories of importance were quickly confiscated and German trustees put in charge. Similar offices were set up for the coal, metal, leather, fur, oil and practically all other important industries in the country.

In the incorporated area, a special institution was created to put German merchants in enterprises taken away from Poles and Jews. The institution, called Handelsfbau, (commercial reconstruction), had branches in the important cities of the annexed areas. Preference was given to the racial Germans of Poland, then came the Baltic Germans, then the Germans of Bessarabia and Bukovina, and finally the Germans of the Reich.

In order to bring about greater immigration of German business men to the East, German authorities issued special tax decrees. Liberal credits were granted by the Reich Government to German business men wanting to settle in the East. A system of special subsidies and loans was instituted; the German business man could obtain almost any amount of money at an annual interest of 1% or 2%. Furthermore, the Reich Commissioner of prices issued a decree forbidding all price increase in Poland to maintain that country at a lower price level than the Reich and thus make settlement in the East more attractive. Also, the trustees appointed for the commercial and industrial establishments taken away from the Jews were given all attendant facilities

Labor Unions.

Of the 42% of the Jewish population engaged in industry, about 81.5% worked in enterprises where there were fewer than five employees (as against 42.2% of the Poles engaged in industry), 15% were in medium-sized enterprises (Poles, 20.4%), and only 3.5% in large-scale enterprises (Poles, 37.4%). The Jews were largely concentrated in the textile, leather and food industries and in personal services (barbers, photographers, waiters, etc.). The consequences of this special structure of Jewish labor was that the Jews were an insignificant factor in industrial labor unions, but an important element in the organization of craft unions.

Since labor unions were illegal in the Czarist regime, the first Polish and Jewish trade unions appeared in important industrial centers in 1915 and 1916. The first conference of Jewish labor unions, at which a Trade Union Council was elected, took place in June, 1921. In November of that year the Jewish and Polish unions united, with the Jewish groups retaining the autonomous right to use Yiddish and to carry on educational and cultural activities. The Jewish Trade Union Council, through its educational department, issued several publications in Polish and Yiddish, the most important of which was Der Ruf (The Call), with a reported circulation of 70,000.

The trend of the Jewish masses away from commerce and towards industry during the last years of the Polish Republic resulted in an enormous increase in the influence of the Jewish labor unions, particularly the Bund factions. By 1928, about 72,000 Jewish workers were represented at the Trade Union Congress; by 1939, there were already 98,000. The Jewish Trade Union Council was dominated by the Bund, with the Communists and Left Wing Labor Zionists in the minority. The Right Wing Labor Zionists, refusing to affiliate themselves with the Council, set up their own organization in 1934, and in 1939 claimed a membership of 22,000.

After the German occupation, all unions were dissolved and their properties confiscated or destroyed. Forced labor was introduced, and the Jewish Community Councils were compelled to organized workshops in the ghettos, to produce material for the Nazi war machine. Jewish workers were excluded from all social security benefits.

General Press.

A large section of the Polish press was either openly anti-Semitic or in favor of anti-Jewish discriminatory policies. The National Democratic press repeatedly called on the Poles to boycott the Jews economically and to eliminate them from the political, economic and cultural life of the country. The most important National Democratic newspaper in the country was the Gazeta Warszawska (The Warsaw Gazette), to which leaders of the National Democratic party like Roman Dmowski, Professor Rybarski and others were contributors. The press of the National Democratic party was important in Poland; several outstanding dailies and magazines were under the influence of the party. The outstanding anti-Semitic National Democratic newspaperman was Adolf Nowaczynski.

During the last few years before the outbreak of the Second World War, several pro-fascist groups like the Falanga, the O.N.R. or Nara (Oboz Narodowy Radykalny), and others, were formed because the anti-Semitic policies of the National Democrats were not sufficiently extreme. These groups also controlled a number of dailies and weeklies, most of them of a sensational nature. The most important of these papers was the A.B.C., a daily published by the Naras in Warsaw.

After the death of Marshal Pilsudski (1935) the government press became openly anti-Semitic and began to propagate an economic anti-Jewish boycott. The government papers were not as rabid in their anti-Semitic propaganda as the Nara press, and did not advocate violence and pogroms. However, they favored mass immigration of Jews from Poland and the elimination of Jews from the political and cultural life of the country. The most important paper of the pro-government bloc was the Gazeta Polska (Polish Gazette) edited in its last years by Mr. Mieczyslaw Miedzynski, who was influential in high government circles and vice-speaker of the Sejm. The popular Ilustrowany Kurjer Codzienny (Illustrated Daily Courier) of Cracow also supported the regime; during the last year; before the outbreak of the Second World War it propagated anti-Semitic policies, although in a mild form.

In general, the majority of the Polish press was anti-Semitic, while only a few of the Democratic and Socialist papers with limited influence and circulation directly opposed anti-Jewish policies.

Immediately after the occupation of the country, all the Polish newspaper plants were confiscated; several editors were arrested or sent to concentration camps. Some of them were repeatedly offered positions with the Nazi-controlled papers in the Polish language. Four such Quisling papers were known to have appeared: Nowy Kurjer Warszawski (New Warsaw Courier), Goniec Krakowski (Messenger of Cracow), Kurjer Czestochowski (the Courier of Czestochow), and Gazeta Lwowska (The Gazette of Lwow). In addition, a Polish weekly, Ilustrowany Kurjer Polski (the Illustrated Polish Courier) was published in Cracow. The Krakauer Zeitung, the official daily paper of the Government General, and various weeklies and periodicals were published in German.

According to the most reliable information, only one of the former Polish editors has agreed to cooperate with the Germans in their Quisling press; all the papers published in Polish are in the hands of former editors of German papers in Poland.

Jewish Press.

On September 1, 1939 when Hitler attacked Poland, there were 27 Jewish dailies and over 100 Jewish weeklies in Poland, and many other Jewish periodicals of various types. The Jewish press in Poland exerted its influence not only on the Jewish community of Poland, but throughout eastern and central Europe and even overseas.

The first Jewish newspaper, Der Beobachter an Der Weichsel (Observer on the Vistula), was issued on December 3rd, 1823. From this modest sheet, the Jewish press developed into a great instrument for molding public opinion and for fighting for the rights of Jews in Poland. The first Yiddish daily was Der Weg (The Way) of Warsaw, which appeared in 1905. Der Hajnt (Today) founded in 1906, reached a circulation of 200,000 copies by 1914, and became the largest Jewish newspaper in Europe. In 1910, the second largest Yiddish daily in Europe, Der Moment, was founded in Warsaw. With the Folkszeitung, the official organ of the Socialist Bund, Warsaw had three important and influential Yiddish dailies. In addition, several important Yiddish newspapers were appearing in practically every large city of Poland that had a substantial Jewish community.

After the resurrection of Poland, an important Polish-Jewish press came into existence. Large groups of Jews in the cities, especially among white-collar and professional classes, could not or would not read Yiddish newspapers. In Warsaw, Lwow, Cracow and other cities, a Jewish press in the Polish language was established; several Polish-Jewish dailies, weeklies and magazines appeared throughout the country. The most important Jewish dailies in the Polish language were: Nasz Przeglad, (Our Review), of Warsaw; the Chwila (Moment) of Lwow and the Nowy Dziennik (New Daily) of Cracow.

Poland also had a Hebrew press; the first Hebrew daily, Hatzefirah, was founded in Warsaw in 1875. It was suspended with the outbreak of the First World War and all later attempts to revive it proved futile. Another Hebrew daily, Hayom (The Day), which was founded in 1920 did not last either. Between the two wars the Hebrew press in Poland included only weekly and monthly publications.

During the last years of the Polish Republic, the total of 27 Yiddish and Polish-Jewish daily newspapers published included 10 in Warsaw, 5 in Vilna, 4 in Bialystok, 2 in Grodno, 2 in Lwow, 2 in Lodz, 1 in Cracow and 1 in Rowno. There were more than 100 Jewish weeklies, 24 bi-weeklies, 28 monthlies and 16 irregularly published periodicals. While the exact circulation figures are not known, it is estimated that the Jewish and Polish-Jewish press in Poland had an average daily circulation of 500,000. Allowing three or four readers for every copy sold (Jewish families in Poland were large especially in the smaller towns), it was estimated that the majority of the Jewish population in Poland was reached by the Yiddish and Polish-Jewish press.

Immediately after the occupation of Poland by the Nazis, all Jewish publishing houses and newspapers were closed and taken over by the Germans. However, the Nazis permitted the establishment of one Polish-language newspaper for the Jews, to print all official notices concerning Jews. This paper, the Gazeta Zydowska (the Jewish Gazette) was established in December, 1940, in Cracow, the capital of the Government General. At first it appeared twice a week, later three times. No other periodical for Jews was permitted and the Gazeta Zydowska was of course under Nazi control and censorship.

Until the middle of 1942 the Gazeta Zydowska could be sent out of the country then this right was withdrawn. The reason for the ban was that in spite of the strict censorship, the mere publication of official German measures and statistics conveyed such a picture of misery and destruction to public opinion abroad, that the Germans decided it was against their interests to have the paper reach the outside world. As far as is known the Gazeta Zydowska is still being published three times a week in Cracow and is the only publication for Jews permitted by the German regime in Poland.

Motion Pictures.

The motion picture industry in Poland was very little developed; there were only two or three companies of any consequence producing a few pictures a year. Among these, the most important was the Sfinx Company; founded and owned by two Jews. Forbert Films, another important company, was also founded and owned by Jews, and Jews were connected with several lesser companies. During the last few years, the state had become interested in the production of motion pictures and supported a company from which Jews were practically excluded. The agents of foreign, and especially of American, companies, were mostly Jewish.

Under the Hitler regime all the motion picture companies formerly owned or controlled by Jews were liquidated. In Cracow a new company was set up entirely under the control of the government and for propaganda purposes. With one exception -- Igo Sym, who was later killed by the underground -- no prominent Polish actor cooperated with the Germans.

The motion picture houses were all "Aryanized" and showed exclusively German or Axis pictures. Underground newspapers constantly called on the Polish population to stay away from the motion picture houses because the taxes on theatre tickets helped the Germans to finance the war.

Education.

During and after the First World War the Jews of Poland developed a comprehensive school system of their own. Most of the Jewish schools were situated in the eastern provinces where the Poles formed a minority and Polish culture had made little headway. The Jews established their own schools partly as the result of the lack of Polish schools and also because of their desire to educate their children in their own culture and traditions. In the more Polonized sections of the country, the number of the Jewish schools was relatively small, although some had been set up as the result of discrimination against Jews in the general educational system. The various Jewish schools were usually directly controlled or promoted by the political parties and trends that prevailed in Jewish life. The most important among the Jewish school organizations were:

1. The Choreb Schools Associations and the Beth Yakob Society (devoted to the schooling of girls), both representing the Jewish Orthodox movement. Together, these organizations maintained and directed about 600 schools, including Orthodox religious schools (Hedorim), rabbinical seminaries and special schools for girls, all attended by about 75,000 children of school age. The Orthodox movement also controlled a large number of privately-owned religious schools.

2. Jabne Schools Association, controlled by the Orthodox Zionist group, the Mizrachi. It maintained elementary schools, four secondary schools and one teachers' training college.

3. Tarbuth Educational Society, which promoted the teaching of the Hebrew language wielded considerable influence among the Zionist youth. This Hebrew Zionist school system, attended by about 25,000 pupils, included nurseries, primary and secondary schools, teachers' training colleges and extension courses.

4. The Central Jewish School Association, supporting schools in which the language of instruction was Yiddish, was under the influence of the General Jewish workers Alliance -- the Bund. The association maintained over 200 schools attended by more than 23,000 pupils.

5. Mixed-type Jewish schools, supported by various organizations which were bilingual, either Polish-Hebrew or Hebrew-Yiddish.

In spite of the provisions of the Minorities Treaty between Poland and the principal Allied and Associated powers, not a single primary Jewish school in Poland was supported either by the government or by the local authorities. Primary schooling in Poland was compulsory for all children. The 425,566 Jewish children in all primary schools in 1934-1935 formed 9.1% of the primary school population. But while they were only 7.6% in the public primary schools, they constituted the majority (59.1%) of all the pupils in the private schools, which included the schools maintained by the various Jewish organizations. Of the total, 37,400 Jewish children attended primary schools in which Yiddish or Hebrew was the language of instruction.

Considerable restrictions were applied in the admission of Jewish pupils to the public secondary schools. In all secondary schools (1934-1935), there were 30,000 Jewish pupils, or 18% or the total. But in the state-owned schools, the ratio of Jewish pupils was only 10.2% in the municipal-owned schools even less -- 7.2%. The ratio of Jewish pupils in the private secondary schools was 30.2%. Official statistics indicated that about 2/3 of Jewish secondary school students attended schools privately maintained by the Jews themselves; 1,800, or about 6% attended Yiddish or Hebrew schools.

A similar situation prevailed in the trade schools. In 1934-1935, there were 29,948 pupils in the industrial and crafts schools, of whom 4,803 (or 16%) were Jewish. But the number of Jewish pupils in state-owned industrial - artisan schools was 694, or 6.9% of the total. In the schools owned by the municipalities their percentage was even smaller -- 83 Jewish pupils, or 3.9% of the total. The situation was entirely different in the privately-owned schools. Here the Jews comprised 31.2% of the total. The 32 Jewish trade schools were overcrowded, having 4,026 pupils. That meant that all the other 165 schools together had only 777 Jewish pupils or less than five Jewish pupils per school. This is significant because even the so-called privately-owned non-Jewish trade schools were really semi-public schools, receiving large government subsidies which in some instances constituted the bulk of the incomes. On the other hand the subsidies to the Jewish schools given by the government were insignificant, amounting to about 3% of the cost of instruction. Thus, 91% of all Jewish pupils in trade schools were in the private schools owned and supported almost entirely by the Jews themselves.

The restrictions against Jews in the Polish universities constituted one of the notorious features of the Jewish situation in Poland. Thousands of Jewish students were compelled to leave the country and to live in foreign lands under the most difficult conditions. In the last years of the Republic, the economic situation of the Jewish population was such that few could afford to send their children to foreign universities and the majority of the Jews who desired to go to universities were deprived of higher education.

Restrictions had existed in the Polish universities since the establishment of the Republic. But the numerus clausus was considerably aggravated after 1933. The figures of Jewish students in the institutions of higher learning in Poland for the period between 1921 and 1938 are as follows:

Schoolyear	Total number of students	Jews	in % of total
1921/2	34,266	8,426	24.6
1922/3	38,132	9,130	24.0
1923/4	39,255	9,579	24.4
1924/5	37,984	8,173	21.5
1925/6	37,456	7,768	20.7
1926/7	40,734	8,198	20.1
1927/8	41,734	8,258	19.8
1928/9	43,607	8,711	20.0

Schoolyear	Total number of students	Jews	in % of total
1929/30	45,486	8,796	19.3
1930/1	48,155	8,923	18.5
1931/2	49,770	8,982	18.0
1932/3	51,770	9,694	18.7
1933/4	49,599	8,425	17.0
1934/5	48,071	7,114	14.8
1935/6	47,161	6,207	13.2
1936/7	48,198	5,682	11.8
1937/8	48,018	4,790	10.0
1938/9	49,987	4,113	8.2

These figures show that while in 1921-1922 the Jews formed about one-fourth of the student body in the universities, in 1938-1939 they were only 8.2%, or less than the ratio of the Jews to the total population in the country. Not only had the anti-Semitic demand of a numerus clausus for Jews based on the ratio of the Jewish population of the country been fulfilled, but the number of Jews in the universities was actually below that ratio. Until 1932-1933 the restrictions applied to the Jews reduced the percentage of Jewish students with relation to the non-Jewish students, but the absolute number of Jewish students remained almost the same. After 1933 the absolute number as well as the relative proportion of Jewish students decreased to such an extent that although the Jews were essentially urban and the cities in Poland provided two-thirds of all the university students, they actually became a small factor in the universities. With the approval if not encouragement of the government and the university authorities, so-called ghetto-benches were established. Jewish students were relegated to the left side of the classrooms and thus segregated from the other students. Instead of submitting to such humiliation, Jewish students preferred to listen to the lectures standing. The anti-Semitic professors and students completely dominated the universities; during the last few years of Polish independence, it was actually dangerous for Jewish students to go to a university, where they were constantly exposed to moral humiliation, physical assault and even danger of life. Several murders occurred at universities.

According to official data, of 81,353 teachers, only 1,831 or 2.3% were Jewish, or about one-fourth the ratio of the Jewish population in the country. Of the 1,831 Jewish teachers, 778 were teachers of Jewish religion, which means that there were only 1,059 Jewish teachers of secular subjects in Polish public primary schools. The Jewish teachers in the elementary schools were almost exclusively employed in the so-called Sabbath schools -- special schools maintained by the government for Jewish children -- which had Saturday as the day of rest instead of Sunday. Among the principals of public elementary schools, the percentage of Jews was even lower -- 1.3%.

Of the 4,429 teachers in public secondary schools, 125 (or 2.8%) were Jewish. However, they were almost exclusively in Galicia, where they had been teachers under the Austrian pre-First World War regime. Outside of Galicia, there were fewer than a score of Jewish teachers in the public high schools. Not one Jewish principal was found in a public high school in Poland.

At the outbreak of the war all Jewish schools were closed, and the Nazis never permitted the reopening of any of them. A decree issued by the Government General on August 31, 1940, established a segregated school system to be maintained by the

Jewish Community Councils; but no permit was ever issued to a community council actually to open a Jewish school. In connection with the relief and assistance work for children, some teachers tried to give a little instruction to children and some schools even worked underground. The number of teachers and of the underground schools could of course not be determined.

Health Services: General Survey.

Health services were the responsibility of state and municipal authorities. But in view of the general inadequacy, which was aggravated by certain restrictions against the Jews, and prompted also by special Jewish religious requirements, the Jewish communities and welfare organizations voluntarily established and partly supported a network of medical institutions. In addition to Jewish community councils, the Towarzystwo Ochrony Zdrowia (Union of Societies for Health Protection among Jews), known as TOZ, and several charitable groups engaged in health work.

The community councils concerned themselves mainly with providing direct medical aid, maintaining general hospitals, small clinics and public baths. Larger population centers had hospitals with modern equipment, competent medical personnel and a wide range of services; smaller communities had poorly-equipped and understaffed clinics. Public baths were found in nearly every town and village, their size and facilities varying with the size of the community. Municipalities cooperated in the support of the larger Jewish hospitals; the general Jewish hospitals in Warsaw, Vilno and Byalystok were maintained entirely by the municipalities. Smaller clinics received but negligible municipal support.

TOZ rendered large-scale preventive and therapeutic aid; it maintained numerous institutions for child and adult health care (dispensaries for infants and expectant mothers, day nurseries, camps for school children, children's clinics, vaccination centers, TB dispensaries, trachoma clinics, hospitals, polyclinics, dental institutions and X-ray clinics). Before the war, TOZ supervised 368 medical and hygienic institutions in 112 Polish localities. In 1936 the government contributed 5.4% of the TOZ budget, the municipalities 4.1% and the Jewish community councils 1.1%.

Special child care service was rendered also by the Towarzystwo Przyjaciol Dzieci (Society of Friends of Children) and Kropla Mleka (Drop of Milk); tuberculosis therapy was provided by Briuth (Health) and Marpe (Treatment); mental diseases were treated at Zofiowka and elsewhere. The Lipas Hazedek (Attending the Sick) groups in many communities provided medical aid to patients at home, including first-aid treatment, physician's services and home nursing.

Among the foreign agencies offering financial support to Jewish health activities in Poland were the American Jewish Joint Distribution Committee and the World Union OSE (Obshestwo Ochravinenia Zdorowia -- Society for the Protection of the Health of the Jews). They contributed chiefly to TOZ, which, before the war, had received from 20% to 30% of its entire budget from the American Jewish Joint Distribution Committee, and from 5% to 7% from the OSE. The local charitable health institutions were supported by the municipalities and by private donations.

Physicians and Other Medical Practitioners.

There were between 3,000 and 3,500 Jews practising medicine in pre-war Poland, about 2,000 as dentists, 600 as registered nurses and 100 to 120 as veterinarians.

Requirements for physicians' licenses were the same for Jews and non-Jews. Graduates of recognized domestic or foreign schools were admitted to practice. Polish citizens who had graduated from medical colleges in Austria and Germany before 1919 and from Russian medical colleges before 1917 were automatically admitted, but those who had graduated from foreign medical colleges later than the given dates had to apply to the Department of Education or to specially designated medical colleges in Poland for examination. Numerous restrictions were imposed which sought to limit the number of foreign graduates admitted to practice; these were aimed largely at the Jews, who were forced to study at foreign medical schools because of restrictions on their admission to schools within the country. Dentists were admitted to practice if they had graduated from government schools or from private schools recognized by the government.

Licensed nurses had to be graduates from government schools or from private schools recognized by the government. A large group of practical nurses, not possessing the necessary qualifications, were nevertheless admitted (1922-35) on the basis of many years of experience and special examinations -- a measure made necessary by a scarcity of nurses. There were two Jewish schools for nurses in pre-war Poland -- the school of the Jewish Hospital in Warsaw and the TOZ school in Vilno, each with a two-year curriculum. Seventy-five nurses were graduated from both of these schools annually.

Licensed veterinarians had to be graduates of Polish or foreign veterinary colleges, and registered with the Government Health Board.

About 40% of the Jews who were part of Poland's medical personnel were lost in the first few months of the war, either as casualties, prisoners of war or through joining the refugee flow to the east. Of the remaining 60%, about 3/4 were within the boundaries of the Government General and 1/4 in the section incorporated in the German Reich. How many of these are still alive cannot be ascertained.

The first Nazi decree regulating the rights of the Jewish members of the medical profession, issued March 6, 1940, by Dr. Samuel Wolfbaum, chief of the Health Board of the General Government, forbade Jews to treat non-Jews, and vice versa. On May 7th an amendment allowed Jews to apply for special permits to treat non-Jews, the permits to be valid for four weeks and renewable. At the end of 1940, Jews were excluded from the general medical guild and forced to establish their own professional organization under the supervision of the German Health Board. At the same time, Jewish physicians were ordered to put the Star of David on their shingles. All decrees and regulations referred to Jewish members of the medical profession not as physicians but as <u>Krankenbehandler</u> (attendants of the sick), a form of humiliation imported from Germany proper. These "attendants," however, were subsequently called in to minister to German army casualties.

Jewish members of all branches of the medical profession were barred from governmental, municipal and sick-benefit institutions and posts. Numerous acts of violence, including confiscation, looting and destruction of medical property, were practiced on them, and they were subjected to arbitrary arrest and confinement in concentration camps.

Jewish Hospitals.

There were 700 hospitals in pre-war Poland, with a total of 75,000 beds. Of this number, 47 were Jewish hospitals, with a total of between 4,500 and 5,000 beds. The largest were: General Hospitals: Warsaw General Hospital - 1,200 beds; Lodz - 250; Lwow - 200; Cracow - 200; Vilno General Hospital - 200; Vilno Welfare Hospital - 80; Lublin - 150; Byalystok - 200; Grodno - 120; Sosnoviec - 120; Piotrkow - 100; Biendzin - 100; Radom - 100; Special Hospitals: Warsaw Children's Hospital - 400; Warsaw (Otwock) Hospital for Mental Diseases - 400; Warsaw (Otwock) Hospital for Tuberculosis - 250; Cracow Hospital for Tubercular Children - 50; Vilno (Antokol) Hospital for Tuberculosis - 90; Worochta (Galicia) Hospital for Tuberculosis - 60; Rabki (Galicia) Children's Hospital for Joint Diseases - 80. Almost every hospital had at least one laboratory and one clinic; in addition there were numerous independent clinics and laboratories maintained by private charities, and the 159 clinics maintained by TOZ.

With the deportation of Jews from many localities in Poland, all the buildings, equipment, medical supplies and stores of the Jewish hospitals in Lodz, Plotzk, Kalish, Poznan, Lublin and other cities were confiscated by the Nazis and converted to military use. The two large Jewish hospitals in Warsaw, and those of Cracow, Vilno, Lwow and other cities where Jewish populations remained were largely confiscated, the property expropriated, and the Jewish patients ejected. Temporary hospital accommodations had to be set up by the Jewish communities within the newly-created ghettos. Jewish hospitals were known to have been operating in the following cities under Nazi rule: Warsaw, Cracow, Lwow, Sonsnowice, Lublin, Radom. The property of clinics and laboratories in localities from which Jews were deported were confiscated; elsewhere, the number of clinics and laboratories grew because of increased need and decreased medical aid of other kinds.

Medical Supplies.

The Jewish medical institutions functioning under the Nazi regime in Poland were cut off from serum supply sources, such as the Warsaw State Board of Hygiene, the Bacteriological Institute of Professor Weigel of Lwow University and private chemical concerns. Such serums as were obtained came through the OSE in Switzerland, with the cooperation of the International Red Cross, German authorities rejected requests made by the International Red Cross, the Swiss Red Cross and the Swedish Red Cross, to ship and distribute serums.

Drugs and medical supplies were also cut off. The Jewish communities sought to replenish their stocks via the black market or through shipments sent from Switzerland by the OSE and other Jewish welfare organizations with the cooperation of the International Red Cross. Reports from various Jewish hospitals and from TOZ indicate that the lack of drugs and medical supplies has been a factor in the catastrophic death rate.

Vaccinations.

Before the war, vaccination against smallpox was compulsory for Jews and non-Jews. Children had to be vaccinated twice --during the first six months of life, and at the age of six, before being admitted to schools. In 1934 there were only five smallpox cases in Poland, in 1935, four (two fatal) and in 1936 only one. Vaccination against diphtheria, scarlet fever and typhus was voluntary, but obligatory for soldiers, school children, medical personnel and -- during epidemics -- large sections of the population. The Public Health Service had also inaugurated the attempted immunization of infants against tuberculosis -- during the first few weeks after birth -- with solutions of weakened cultures of B.C.G. (Bacillus Calmette Guirin). Approximately 500,000 infants received this treatment.

Compulsory and voluntary vaccination continued under the occupation, perhaps even on a wider scale. TOZ reported 238,595 injections of various kinds administered in Warsaw alone from January to September, 1941. 10,177 Jews were vaccinated in the same period in 32 small towns. The Jewish communities and many welfare institutions participated in this preventive work.

Birth Rate.

The birth rate among Jews, between 1931 and 1936, was 19.3 per thousand. The birth rate among the Polish population as a whole during this period varied from 27.6 to 26.3 per thousand. In 1936 there were approximately 62,000 births among the Jews of Poland.

No exact data for the occupation period are available, but from reports on Jewish population changes in various localities, it would seem that the birth rate among the Jews of Warsaw declined by 20% and in the rest of the country by 27% in 1940. In 1941 the decline was 29% in Warsaw and 40% in the rest of the country; in 1942, 40% in Warsaw and 54% in the rest of the country. The total deficit in births for these three years is approximately 55,000. The probable number of births among the Jews in Poland was therefore about 34,000 in 1940; 28,000 in 1941 and 22,000 in 1942, as against the annual average of 62,000 just before the war.

Mortality.

Prior to the outbreak of the war, the mortality rate among Jews averaged 100 to 105 per 10,000. The general mortality rate in Poland was 159 per 10,000.

With the Nazi occupation, the mortality rate in Poland, particularly among the Jews, took an abrupt upward turn. In the spring of 1940, there were 239 Jewish deaths per 10,000 Jewish inhabitants in Warsaw. In the spring of 1941, the number was 859; the following September it was 1,368, or 14 times as high as the pre-war mortality rate among Jews in Warsaw, which had been 97 per 10,000.

In the first half of 1941, 20.3% of the patients in the General Jewish Hospital in Warsaw died; in the Children's Hospital, 23.4%. In the Central Children's Home in Warsaw, 125 out of 607 children died (20.6%). (The hospital death rate in the United States in 1941 was 3.9%; in 1942, 3.5%).

In 1940, Jewish mortality comprised 45% of the general mortality in Warsaw; in 1941, it was 75%, while Jews made up only 30% of the entire population. The annual mortality rate for those years among Jews in the whole country, excluding Warsaw, seems to have been 4.5% to 5%; in Warsaw, it ranged from 9% to 14%. During the first three years of the occupation, the natural deaths among the Jews of Poland reached

400,000. This does not include the victims of extermination and mass murder, which began in 1942; the number of these cannot be estimated with any degree of exactness.

The biological deficit among the Jews for the first three years of the war, taking into consideration only births and deaths from "natural" causes, was about 300,000. But the actual decline for that period, which does not yet include the mass extermination that began in the latter half of 1942, included other serious extraordinary losses. Among these were: 32,000 Jews fallen in battle, 30,000 civilian victims of the blitz, 150,000 executed and murdered in pogroms, 150,000 victims of deportation, and 24,000 deaths in concentration camps. The addition of this total of 386,000 brings the biological deficit -- until the latter part of 1942 -- to approximately 700,000.

Epidemics.

Lack of sanitation, an acute shortage of soap, disinfectants and medical supplies, an insufficient number of physicians, nurses and hospitals aggravated the disastrous effect of undernourishment and inadequate clothing to help spread infectious diseases. Official Polish records showed that the average weight per person in the ghettos under Nazi control is 30 to 40 pounds below normal. Epidemics of typhus, typhoid fever, dysentery and scarlet fever, while occuring frequently in Poland even during the country's period of independence, had nevertheless decreased in severity with the improvement in living conditions. Between 1921 and 1931 the number of sufferers from such diseases annually had dropped from 42,367 to 14,259. Then, during the depression years, there was a renewed rise, to 17,739 in 1935 and 19,664 in 1936. With the invasion, conditions took a drastic turn for the worse.

During the first six months of the occupation, from October 1, 1939 to April 1, 1940, there were 13,000 cases of tyhpoid fever in Warsaw, 8,000 among Jews and 5,000 among non-Jews. During all of 1937, there had been only 17,490 cases of typhoid throughout all of Poland, or 55 to every 100,000 inhabitants. Even allowing a doubled proportion for Warsaw, because of crowded conditions, the rate for the first six months of occupation was still 20 times the normal rate. The proportion of sufferers among Jews in Warsaw for the first six months was 61.5%, while they constututed only 38% of the population. During the last week of March, 1940, there were 281 cases of typhus in Warsaw, 268 among Jews and 13 among non-Jews. The first week of April brought 305 new cases, 293 among Jews and 12 among non-Jews.

For the year 1941, the total number of all cases of typhoid and typhus recorded in Warsaw was 17,800, of which 15,749 were among Jews and 2,051 among non-Jews. The percentage of Jewish sufferers was 84, while in the population they still constituted about 38%. Before the war, on the contrary, there had been 331 cases of infectious diseases among non-Jews and 145 among Jews out of every 100,000 residents respectively of Poland.

The provinces fared no better than Warsaw. During the first half of 1941, there was a severe typhoid fever and spotted typhus epidemic in Lodz. In the first three weeks of May, 1941, 1,080 Jews died in Lodz, or seven times as many as the average before the war. In Lublin, after the deportations, there were 801 Jews in the hospital with typhus. In Cracow, where the Jewish population had also been greatly reduced by deportation, mortality nevertheless exceeded the pre-war rate three and a half times. Epidemics forced the opening of new hospitals in Ostroviec, Nowy-Soncz, Chmelnik, Otwock and other towns, mostly for refugees from other regions.

Tuberculosis took a similar rise. Reports of health agencies show that during the war there was a significant increase in the number of tuberculosis patients, both in the larger cities and the smaller towns.

Suicides.

A high incidence of mental disease was produced by the specific persecutions imposed on the Polish Jews. Apathy, resignation, lack of will power and suicide occurred frequently, as did psychic collapse and insanity. Suicide epidemics usually came with waves of deportation or other acts of extreme oppression. In 1941, five times as many Jews committed suicide in Warsaw as in normal times. At the end of the summer of 1942, with the beginning of mass executions, there was a new wave of suicides. In lwow entire families put an end to their lives; in Lublin, in March 1940, 32 suicides were buried in a single day.

Vermin.

Vermin had always constituted a serious hygienic problem in the crowded living conditions of Poland. The occupation made matters worse. A report on the medical inspection of children in the TOZ polyclinic in Warsaw indicates that of 12,164 children examined during August 1941, 19% suffered from lice; of 11,580 children examined in September 1941, 20% had lice. Jewish community councils and health and welfare organizations, agitating for cleanliness in public shelters and private homes, managed to achieve some improvement of conditions, even under the handicap of the occupation.

Food Control : Before the War.

Nominally there was control and sanitary inspection of the sale of foods in Poland before the war, but the regulations were poorly enforced, as a result of the decentralized system of distribution. Peasants brought milk to the cities, where it was ladled out to small dairies and individual consumers. Pasteurization and tuberculin tests were therefore impossible. The same freedom of action rested with butchers who slaughtered their own cattle.

Housing and Hygiene: During Occupation.

Housing in the ghettoes, or even in the small towns, was dangerously overcrowded during the occupation. In small towns, the number of deportees from other localities sometimes exceeded the number of regular inhabitants. Throughout the country, and especially in larger cities, conditions were aggravated by bombing. Municipal regulations permitted three to four persons per room; in actuality, five, six or even more shared a room.

Private baths were rare in Poland even before the war, and were found only in better-class homes in larger cities. War, the occupation and the lack of fuel put even these out of commission. Despite the fact that the whole population now had to depend on public bathing establishments, the number of these establishments was also reduced. Jews could use only bathhouses located in the ghettos. Before the war there were 216 bathhouses maintained by the Jewish communities; how many remained functioning during the occupation is not known. TOZ reports indicated that some new bathhouses were constructed during 1941, administered by the community councils and by TOZ. TOZ also reported that from January to November 1941, 31,598 persons passed through Jewish bathing establishments in small cities, not counting centers like Warsaw, Lwow, Cracow and Lodz.

The disruption of the water and sewage systems destroyed toilet facilities. Temporary outhouses were constructed in courtyards. In smaller cities outhouses had always provided the only toilet facilities.

Even during the occupation, the Jewish community councils made an effort to maintain a system of garbage control in the ghettoes through the appointment of special sanitary inspectors, house committees and block wardens. School children and former employees of the sanitation department assisted. Great improvement was achieved.

Disease and Sanitation: Post-War Aspects.

Diseases caused by undernourishment or starvation will present the gravest health problem of the Jews in Poland after the war. Infectious diseases, such as typhus, typhoid fever, scarlet fever, trachoma and favus, will also have a high rate of incidence, especially in the central and eastern sections of Poland. Even after the First World War, the eastern districts were most seriously affected by these diseases; at one time, more than 22,000 favus patients were recorded in the area.

Tuberculosis, a classic companion of war and hunger, will offer a difficult problem. All these conditions will be aggravated by the miserable sanitary and living conditions in the overcrowded ghettoes, particularly when these areas are reopened and the populations wander back to their original places of domicile. A scarcity of hospitals, epidemiological facilities and isolation wards will also have to be coped with.

Special sanitation problems confronting reconstruction workers will include: fumigation, disinfection and water purification in areas previously affected by epidemics; restoration of existing bathing and laundry facilities and establishment of new ones; surveillance of water supply; sewage disposal and public lavatories and out-houses; enlargement and improvement of existing disinfection facilities and the establishment of mobile disinfecting units; inspection of public institutions, especially schools, asylums and orphanages; preparation of new resettlement areas through the construction of living quarters, sanitation facilities, and preventive and therapeutic medical units.

Water sewage disposal systems were completely destroyed in those towns and villages of Poland which lay in the direct path of active military operations. Between 30 and 40 towns were destroyed by bombardment and fire, and between 70 and 80 were severely damaged. Of the large Jewish population centers, Warsaw suffered most; its center -- a concentrated Jewish residential section -- was heavily hit. Lack of construction material and technical facilities prevented rebuilding. Winter worsened the situation by cuasing numerous pipes in both the water and sewage disposal system to burst. In many buildings temporary measures permitted the drawing of water in a common courtyard from a single outlet. Temporary outhouses were also constructed. Hot water facilities, which had never been widespread, were completely disrupted.

Public Welfare.

The most important general public welfare organizations in Poland were the Public Welfare Committees (Komisje Opieki Spolecznej) acting through special welfare guardians, who were voluntary social workers; the Union of Societies for the Protection of Mothers and Children (Towarzystwo Opieki nad Matka i Dzieckiem); the Union of Anti-Tuberculosis Associations (Zwiazek Przeciwgruzliczy); and the Union of Associations for Summer Camps (Komisje Kolonji Letnich). There were also a number of Foundations. Jewish welfare organizations were constitutent members of these groups.

There were more than 3,000 public welfare committees throughout Poland, with 20,000 voluntary guardians cooperating. Their purpose was the care of indigents, and the dispatch of these indigents to proper social agencies. Some 300 welfare societies concerned with the care of children and young people belonged to the Union of Societies for the Protection of Mothers and Children; in 1935 they maintained more than 900 institutions and fully supported more than 43,000 children. More than 200 organizations working in the field of tuberculosis belonged to the Union of Anti-Tuberculosis Associations. The union of Associations for Summer Camps, in 1938, maintained 1,800 summer camps providing a month's vacation for 300,000 children. In addition there were some 1,200 day camps, where 135,000 children were cared for during the summer months. Foundations acted separately, in accordance with the specific wishes of their respective founders; in 1937, there were 1,554 such foundations in Poland.

Discrimination and favoritism were undoubtedly practiced in some localities in the allocation of the funds which were at the disposal of these committees, despite the membership of Jewish welfare organizations. However, since the major part of their work was done in the cities, where Jewish population was concentrated and initiative greater, Jews did derive considerable benefit from them.

Jewish Welfare.

The main Jewish private relief organizations in Poland were the Central Committee for Interest--Free Loans (Centralny Komitet Bezprocentowych Kas Pozyczkowych), known as the Cekabe; the Alliance of Societies for the Care of Children (Centralny Komitet Opieki nad Sierotami i Dziecmi), known as Centos the Union of Societies for Health Protection and Child Care among Jews (TOZ) and numerous specialized smaller services. These organizations received aid from the Joint Distribution Committee. Before the war, Cekabe had loan offices in 960 localities, served nearly a quarter of a million persons, and had outstanding loans to the total of 20,000,000 zlotys ($4,000,000). Centos will be dealt with later, under child welfare, and TOZ has been discussed earlier, under health and sanitation. The JEAS, which was the Polish equivalent of the HIAS (Hebrew Immigrant Aid Society) and was affiliated with HICEM, maintained offices in eight main districts, and annually aided some 8,000 immigrants. Prospective immigrants to Palestine were served by the Palestine Immigration Board, a branch of the Jewish Agency in Palestine, which handled between 15,000 and 20,000 persons annually.

Despite the enormous difficulties, private relief among the Jews did not stop with the occupation. On the contrary, the scope of work was extended wherever possible to include soup kitchens, tea distribution wagons, shelters, ambulance service, public laundries, etc. With outside aid cut off, support for these services depended entirely on the Jewish community councils, and was derived from forced taxation and voluntary contributions. The American Jewish Joint Distribution Committee had made preliminary arrangements for some degree of assistance by empowering the local communities to borrow money which the JDC would later repay.

Under the Nazis, all Jewish welfare organizations had to merge into a Central Board for Jewish Self-Help (Samopomoc Spoleczna), which consisted of the following departments: finance, health, labor and economics, food supply and organization. A representative of the Board served on the Central Committee for Welfare Action, consisting of four Poles, two Ukrainians and one Jew. The Board, which was entitled to special funds for relief work obtained by special taxation, was under the supervision of several departments of the Nazi administration in the Government General.

Child Welfare.

Child Welfare assistance was rendered by municipalities, the Social Security Board and various welfare organizations. In 1937 there were 488 consultation centers in which 128,000 children and 15,299 mothers received advice, and through which 2,605,000 quarts of milk were distributed. In 1937, 138 infant-care centers attached to large factories cared for 6,445 children. Some 3,000 infants were handled in nurseries, 36,000 pre-school age children were maintained in special homes and 87,300 children were given kindergarten instruction. Foster care was widely resorted to, especially in Lodz. Homes and schools for blind, crippled, sick and retarded children cared for 4,000 children. Juvenile courts handled child delinquency, with a representative of a welfare agency usually present for advice and consultation. Special correction homes, under the Department of Justice, housed 1,152 children in 1937. That same year there were 5,444 illegitimate children being cared for in homes run by the municipalities or welfare institutions.

Theoretically, all the above facilities were supposed to serve the entire population, but intensifying anti-Jewish feeling had forced the Jewish population to turn more and more to its own welfare organizations.

The most important Jewish institutions engaged in child care were the Centos, and TOZ, both of which maintained a network of institutions. The Friends of Children maintained polyclinics in Warsaw, several homes, and summer camps. The Drop of Milk ran infant consultation centers in Warsaw, where there was also a large orphanage under the direction of a special society. The Central Jewish School Organization

(Zentrale Yiddishe Shule Orgenizatzie) had a sanatorium for weak, convalescent, or tuberculosis-suspect children, which cared for 5,000 children.

Centos, operating in 293 localities, maintained 187 institutions, caring for 15,428 children. Among its institutions were 83 orphanages, 90 day nurseries, and several food kitchens. In 1937-38, the 190 summer and winter camps supported by Centos accommodated 20,488 children, while 21,652 children were fed in its food kitchens and 6,097 were supported in private homes. The Centos budget for 1937 was 3,146,000 zlotys ($629,200), 74% of which was covered by local contributions, 13% by municipalities and the balance by the Joint Distribution Committee.

TOZ maintained 22 infant consultation centers, 15 homes for pre-school children, 28 children's clinics, and 1,100 camps for school children, which in 1938 accommodated 26,000 children. TOZ also provided breakfasts and lunches for 35,000 school children in 1938-39.

Under the occupation, Centos and TOZ took over the bulk of child welfare work among the Jews; lesser organizations merged with them. According to reports, Centos in 1941, cared for 35,000 children, 26,000 of whom were maintained in so-called children's corners (Kinder Vinkel), of which there were 827, with 1,738 guardians. These children's corners made an effort to provide organized play, gardening and generally wholesome surroundings. The 35,000 also included 7,500 refugee children in shelters. The remainder were homeless children, beggars, and children whose parents were in labor battalions. Centos also maintained 122 child feeding stations serving 23,000 children, and provided cod liver oil for 25,000 children. Both Centos and TOZ were affiliated with the Central Board for Jewish Self-Help, which coordinated welfare work under Nazi control and functioned especially in the larger cities, such as Warsaw, Cracow, Lublin and Lemberg.

The Youth Sector of Emergency Aid (Pogotowie Ratunkowie) provided emergency aid to children, through 867 special guardians recruited from youth organizations, sport and cultural societies. Emergency Aid was supported by special emergency taxation of the Jewish community council.

Welfare Workers.

Welfare workers in Poland were trained in special training schools, the State School for Public Health (Panstwowa Szkola Hygjeny) and the Faculty for Social Sciences at the Liberal School for Higher Learning (Wolna Wszechnica Polska) which, in 1937-38, had 1,400 students, 1,300 students and 700 students respectively. Training schools required a high school diploma for admission and the other schools two years of college work; all offered a two-year course. No statistics are available on the number of welfare workers.

Jewish workers were trained in the same schools, where the percentage of Jewish students was higher than the population proportion. Many workers in the Jewish welfare field were teachers who had been unable to receive licenses.

Municipal citizens committees for welfare aid and charities, chosen from among influential citizens and representatives of welfare agencies, existed throughout Poland before the war. Although without legal status, they performed valuable service, particularly in emergency situations. Jews were invited to participate, but not in proportion to the size and influence of their welfare organizations; in some localities they were not represented at all. In the western sections of the country, the citizen committees disregarded the needs of the Jewish population and practiced discrimination in the allocation of funds. Charges of discrimination were made to the authorities, and although redress was promised, little occurred.

With the war, citizens committees for aid to war victims were set up in the municipalities. Jews participated and cooperated. But after the Polish retreat, and with the beginning of occupation, the composition of the committees changed; the Jews were isolated and then forced to drop away. Their work was taken over by the Judenraten, the Central Board for Jewish Self-Help, and Emergency Aid.

Catholic Church and the Jews.

The attitude of the Catholic Church, prior to the Nazi invasion, was almost entirely anti-Semitic. Catholic education was anti-Jewish in implication. Many priests belonged to the National Democratic (Endek) party, which was strongly anti-Semitic. Others were adherents of the Christian Democratic (Chadek) party, or, later, of the government party known as Ozon (Oboz Zjednocoenia Naradowego), both of which had anti-Semitic tendencies. It was believed that much violence could have been forestalled or prevented by priests. Pilsudski's agreement with the Conservatives was partly prompted by the desire to hold the Catholic Church, which, however, wanted a more anti-Semitic attitude. Cardinal Hlond, Primate of Poland, in 1936 gave written approbation to the economic boycott of the Jews. Several years before the outbreak of war in 1939, Cardinal Kakowski of Warsaw, in a conference with a group of rabbis, openly expressed anti-Semitic convictions, as had the Archbishop of Lwow during the student riots in 1937. During the parliamentary debates on the limiting of Shehitah in 1936, a Catholic priest named Trzeciak testified in its favor. Cases of pro-Jewish actions were largely unknown. After the invasion, however, there were reports of such attitudes. The archbishop of Vilno is said to have excommunicated the Catholics who appeared as witnesses against the Yeshivah teachers who were charged with black magic.

Anti-Semitic Parties.

The oldest anti-Semitic party in Poland, the National Democratic Party (Endeks), was organized in 1897 and represented the conservative middleclass and white-collar elements. It was largely an urban party, one of whose main objectives was the elimination of Jews from business, industry and the professions. Opposing all federalist ideas and all autonomy or equality of rights for national minorities, the party had considerable influence, especially in the cities. During the early years of the Republic the National Democrats dominated the government.

There were also small rightist groups such as the National Christian Party, which represented the great landowners and in a measure the aristocracy. This party was also reactionary, anti-Semitic and opposed to all progressive social legislation, especially agrarian reform. Another rightist group, the Christian Democrats, were dominated by the Catholic Church, and were also strongly anti-Semitic. They had no influence outside of Upper Silesia.

After the Pilsudski coup d'état, the rightist parties were eliminated from the government, but their anti-Jewish agitation not only continued unabated but was considerably increased during the last years of Polish independence. The youth elements of the National Democratic Party, however, were not entirely satisfied with its traditional anti-Jewish policies and asked for even more radical and aggressive anti-Semitism along the lines of Hitler Germany. They accepted Hitler's racial theories and asked for the complete elimination of the Jews from Poland. In 1934 some of the younger people seceded from the National Democratic party and created the National Radical Party (Nara) an openly pro-fascist and anti-democratic group. Other pro-fascist groups were formed, of which the most rabid was the Falanga. These groups advocated complete cooperation with Germany and racialism and fascism in Poland.

The government, which after the death of Pilsudski in 1935 lost all popular support, attempted to gain the support of these pro-fascist groups. It collaborated with the Nara and the Falanga and while officially opposing the excesses and anti-Jewish pogroms it accepted the anti-Jewish program of the extreme Nationalists. The Camp of National Unity, created in 1937 under the sponsorship of the President of the Republic, Prof. Moscicki, and the chief of the army, Marshal Smigly-Rydz, accepted the Nationalist program of eliminating the Jews from the economic and cultural life of the country and favored mass evacuation of Jews from Poland. Thus the government party hoped to win the Nationalists, especially the pro-fascist Nationalist youth groups. The Camp refused admission to the Jews and even Jewish war veterans were not accepted as members.

During the last years of the Republic, therefore, the anti-Semitic groups could have been divided into three distinct sections: (1) the National Democratic Party and the other old Nationalist groups representing, largely, the Polish middle class and gentry, (2) the pro-fascist and authoritarian factions, representing mostly the youth and especially the university students favoring a racial and fascist government, and (3) the Camp for National Unity, the official party of the regime composed of followers of the late Marshal Pilsudski who accepted and advocated anti-Semitism in order to win support they otherwise lacked.

Attitude of Government.

After the death of Marshal Pilsudski in May 1935 the Government lost the popular support that the Marshal had personally commanded. No important political party was behind the government which was dominated by the followers of the late Marshal, mostly military men. The policy of rapprochement with Germany and of balance between Germany and Russia had been inaugurated in 1934 with the Polish-German agreement, and was now transformed into a policy which was generally interpreted as favoring Germany.

This friendship with Germany also influenced the policies of the government toward the Jews. The group in power felt that the anti-Semitic factor could serve as a means to acquire popular support for the government. Also the youth which had previously left the National Democratic Party might, in the opinion of the government leaders, be led to support the regime if anti-Semitism became an integral part of government policies. While some of the government leaders who were following the tradition of the late Marshal refused to appease the nationalistic youth by engaging in a brutal anti-Jewish campaign, others who eventually became the decisive factors in the government did not shrink from using the Jews for their own ends. Parliament, which had since 1935 been hand-picked by the government, was used as a platform for anti-Semitic discussions. The Jewish problem suddenly assumed the proportions of a first-rate political question; more time was spent in Parliament discussing it than considering the important economic and political problems which were facing the nation. The results were anti-Jewish riots in many towns and cities during the last few years of Polish independence.

The government also officially endorsed the policy of an economic anti-Jewish boycott, and Parliament, in contradiction to the minority treaties and stipulations of the constitution, attempted to introduce legislation directed against the Jews. Introduction of ghetto benches for Jewish students in the universities was permitted and Parliament adopted a bill prescribing the ritual slaughter of animals, which was a blow not only to the economic position of a large number of Jews but to the religious sentiments of that great majority of Jews who in Poland were still Orthodox. The government also permitted various semi-official organizations to introduce the "Aryan" paragraph excluding Jews from membership.

The last years of Polish independence brought an increasingly anti-Jewish official policy. While not openly accepting Nazi racial theories, the government did everything in its power to reduce the Jews to second-class citizenship. Racialism could not very easily be introduced into Polish political and social life because of the predominant Catholic character of the nation. However, within those limitations a progressive policy of discrimination against Jews was followed and Jews were eliminated from political, economic and social life under the direct or indirect inspiration of the government or of groups connected with the regime.

Police: After the Occupation.

Early in the occupation, the Gestapo and the regular German and Polish police were in charge of the execution of the policies towards the Jews.

When the Germans invaded the eastern parts of Poland in June 1941, they organized a special Ukrainian police which dealt with the Jews under the supervision of the Gestapo. In 1942, when the policy of mass extermination of Jews began, these Ukrainians were used, together with policemen brought in from Latvia, Estonia and Lithuania. Later, Estonians, Latvians, Luthuanians and Ukrainians were being used in the extermination camps as well as in most of the forced labor camps.

According to the reports from Poland, the most brutal elements were incorporated in the police force. Among the Ukrainians, especially, only pro-fascists and extreme nationalists who had great hatred for Poland were being recruited. Graft and corruption were widespread among the Gestapo officials as well as the police force. To be appointed to Gestapo service in Poland was considered a reward for services to the Fatherland because it was known that here, in a relatively short time, any Gestapo official could enrich himself by graft and corruption. This was more or less officially sanctioned. The turnover of Gestapo officials was large. Once an official was judged to have sufficiently enriched himself, he was sent back to Germany and another took his place to begin the same procedure all over again.

In all Jewish ghettos a special police force was formed under the control of the Gestapo. This force was to maintain order and to execute all the decrees of the German authorities concerning the Jewish population. Most of the men on this police force were college graduates. When the mass extermination of Jews began in July 1942, daily deportation quotas were set by the Germans, and the Jewish police were responsible for the fulfilment of those quotas. At the slightest infraction of the Gestapo orders, the Jewish policemen were executed. The Jewish police also enforced all the orders of the Jewish Community Councils.

Curfew.

Curfew regulations were usually much stricter for Jews than for the rest of the population. In the ghettos the curfew was usually from 9:00 P.M. to 5:00 A.M. Outside the ghettos, Jews who had permission to move about were also subjected to stricter curfew regulations than others. Jews could easily be distinguished by their armbands. A few Jewish doctors had the right to be on the streets during curfew hours, but those were very exceptional cases. Usually, the German police shot on sight any Jew who dared appear after curfew hour.

Identification Badge.

A decree of November 23, 1939, imposed on all male and female Jews over the age of ten the wearing of a white band, at least ten centimeters wide and containing Star of David, on the right sleeve of their outer clothing. The Jews had to provide themselves with these armbands. Violation of the decree was punishable by imprisonment. Later, according to an ordinance of February 1940, the violaters became liable to imprisonment and unlimited fines.

Even before the general decree was issued some local authorities ordered the wearing of armbands, and the Jewish Community Councils were made responsible for carrying out the orders. Even after the ghettos were established, and Jews were practically forbidden to leave them, they had to continue wearing the armbands. Christians of Jewish descent -- who, according to the German definition of a "Jew," belonged to the Jewish community -- were compelled to wear the distinctive signs. This sometimes included Catholic priests.

A decree of February 23, 1940, regarding the names of business firms in the Government General, ordered that Jewish-owned firms were to be distinguished by a Star of David clearly visible from the streets.

Communications.

A decree of November 15, 1939, stated that letters sent by mail in a script other than German or Latin would be destroyed before transmission. This decree imposed great hardship on a large number of small-town Jews (especially of the older generation) who could not write German or Latin script. Even before the establishment of the ghetto, Jews were forbidden to mail their letters in most of the post-offices. In Warsaw Jews could mail their letters abroad only in the general post-office. After the establishment of the ghettos, post-offices were set up in them under the supervision of the Jewish Community Councils.

Immediately after the occupation of Poland, the Germans confiscated all radio sets belonging to Jews. Failure to comply with the confiscation order was punishable by prison and fine. The destruction of, or damage to, a radio set before it was delivered to the police was considered sabotage and was severely punished. Other Poles could in principle be given special permits to own a radio set and to listen to radio programs. Jews could not obtain such permits. Listening to radios without permits was punishable by a prison term of not less than six months. Listening to foreign stations was strictly forbidden under penalty of death.

Travel Regulations; Public Conveyances.

By a decree of January 26, 1940, Jews were prohibited from using the railroads without a written permit of the governor general, his deputies or district chiefs. Violation of this order was made punishable by an unlimited fine, an indeterminate prison sentence or both. The reasons for this decree were not given in the official text, but the Nazi newspapers and several official statements have indicated that the Jews were forbidden to use the railways because they (the Jews) were dirty and a menace to health. Only in special cases were permits given. Requests for permits had to be made through the Jewish Community Councils which examined them and prejudged the necessity of the journey. If the Council believed the journey to be necessary, the request was submitted to the authorities who either agreed with the Council or rejected the application.

This decree brought considerable hardship on the Jews who were forced to resort to primitive means of transportation, such as peasant carts and buggies. The situation became even worse when a new decree was issued on February 20, 1941, forbidding Jews to use not only railways but all inter-city transportation facilities, except by special permit, as of April 1, 1941. The question of use of local transportation facilities, such as trolley cars, busses and taxicabs, was left to the local authorities.

Permits, to be issued by the county authorities, were valid for only the lowest class of facilities except for express railways. Violation of the law was punishable by a fine as well as by one year in prison.

Forced Prostitution.

In spite of the fact that according to the racial theories of Nazi Germany all sexual intercourse between "Aryans" and non-"Aryans" was considered a criminal offense it has been reliably reported that Jewish women had been repeatedly forced into prostitution and sent to public houses visited by Nazi soldiers. The military authorities in Warsaw even went so far as to suggest to the Jewish community, shortly after the occupation of Warsaw, that it provide Jewish women for this purpose. The women were to be maintained in special houses from which the community was offered a profit. The suggestion was rejected with indignation. The Nazi authorities did not press the point further and gave up the idea of having the community promote prostitution. But reports have persisted that Jewish girls have been abducted by the Nazis and sent into public houses, either in Germany or in Poland. Eye witness reports of Jews and non-Jews who succeeded in escaping German-occupied Poland have testified to the rape of hundreds of Jewish girls by German soldiers. The Germans sometimes forced their way into Jewish houses and raped women and young girls in front of their husbands and parents. Other women were sent to the barracks where the private soldiers were housed, or to the officers' rooms. According to statements of doctors who have succeeded in leaving Poland, many of these girls were infected with venereal diseases. Some of them, unable to withstand the moral and physical tortures, committed suicide.

Sterilization and Liquidation.

No accurate information is available regarding sterilization practiced on the Jewish population of Poland by the Germans. Reports from Holland and Belgium, however, that Jews in those countries were given the choice of sterilization or deportation to Poland indicate that sterilization was not practiced in Poland itself.

Some data seem to indicate that liquidation was practiced on the inmates of insane asylums, homes for the aged and orphan asylums, either through deportation to unspecified places or through wholesale execution. Incurables and cripples were removed from the hospitals in Warsaw, Lublin, Radom and other cities and sent to unknown destinations. Orphans in the large orphanage in Warsaw and tuberculosis-suspect children in the sanatorium in Medzeszyn were also sent to parts unknown, with their nurses and guardians.

Reconstruction Agencies.

It is impossible to determine what has been left of the Jewish welfare personnel in Poland.

Among foreign organizations which may cooperate in reconstruction, the most important is the American Jewish Joint Distribution Committee, which carried on large-scale activity during the entire interval between the two wars, and into the beginning of the present war. Between September 1939, and June 1941 the Joint Distribution Committee spent $1,540,000 for relief in Poland, collaborating with Cekabe, Centos, and TOZ. Other American Jewish relief organizations which may cooperate in reconstruction are the American Federation for Polish Jews, the Federation of Galician Jews, which also were active between the two wars, the HICEM (Hias-Ica Emigration Association), the OSE Union for health protection, the ORT organization for the promotion of trade and agriculture among Jews, and the Jewish Agency for Palestine.

By the middle of 1936, however, the permeation of National Socialist influence into all administrative branches had brought about the abrogation of all democratic rights for the population as a whole. The Jews were confronted with additional disabilities, including expulsion from public service, administrative discrimination, defamation and maltreatment by Nazi stormtroopers and mobs, elimination from the judiciary, the Bar, the medical professions, educational segregation and persecution, banishment from all branches of cultural activity, ousting from economic life, boycott, and the suppression of the only Jewish newspaper, the Danziger Echo.

The right of recourse through appeal to the League of Nations was prevented by a Senate Ordinance of July 16, 1936, authorizing the dissolution of any group "disseminating news detrimental to the interests of the State." The enforced dissolution of the Catholic Center Party on October 21, 1937, gave the Nazis absolute control of the city. Pogroms, mass arrests of Jews, and "Aryanization" were introduced. When the German anti-Jewish laws were formally enacted in Danzig in November, 1938, a large part of the Jewish population had already left the city. On January 1, 1939, there were 2,938 Jews left; on August 1, 1939, only 1,666. The remainder lived an isolated life, without religious or other institutions, until, after the outbreak of war in 1939, they were deported to Eastern Poland.

The Jews of Roumania

THE JEWS OF ROUMANIA

Index

Agriculture	10	Industry	11
Anti-Semitism, History of	18	Insurance	10
Parties and Organizations	21	Jewish Leaders	
Leading Fascists	23	In Roumania	26
"Aryanization"	12	In Exile	26
Attitude of People and Government	20	Judiciary, The	8
Attitude toward War and toward		Languages	6
the United States	7	Marriage and Divorce	6
Army, Jews in	7	Medical Practitioners	15
Banking	10	Minority Rights	5
Bar, The	8	Mortality Rate	16
Birth Rate	16	Motion Pictures	15
Child Care	18	Municipal Governments	8
Christian Churches and the Jews	20	Natural Resources	9
Civil Service, Jews in	7	Occupational Structure	9
Commerce	11	Parliament, Jews in	7
Communications	25	Passports	24
Communal and Fraternal Groups	4	Police	24
Concentration Camps	25	Political Structure	7
Cooperatives	12	Population	1
Credit Banks	13	Press	
Criminality	5	Anti-Semitic	14
Cultural and Social Background	5	General	14
Discriminatory Measures	21	Jewish	14
Divorce	6	Rationing	25
Education	17	Reconstruction Agencies	26
Employment	13	Regulations, Travel	24
Family Life	6	Religious Community Organization	1
Fire Department	24	Assets	3
Forced Labor	13	Divisions	2
Gerrymandering of Jewish Districts	7	Functionaries	4
Groups in Exile	25	Observance	3
Health	15	Taxation	23
Hospitals	15	Trade Unions	13
Hygiene and Sanitation	16	Transportation	24
Identification Cards	25	Welfare, Jewish	18

THE JEWS OF ROUMANIA

Population.

The government census of 1930 showed a total of 756,930 Jews in Roumania, or 4.7% of the total population. Allowing for possible minimization of the significance of minority groups, the actual number may have been nearer 850,000. In 1937, the Goga regime claimed that there were more than 1,500,000 Jews in Roumania, but the population probably remained at about 850,000 until the outbreak of the Second World War.

During the period between the two World Wars, Greater Roumania consisted of the following provinces: 1) Old Roumania, 2) Bessarabia - which was formerly Russian territory, 3) Transylvania, the Banat and the district of Marmarosh-Sziget - formerly Hungarian territory, and 4) Bukovina, which formerly belonged to Austria. The latter three were annexed by Roumania after the First World War.

In 1939, there were some 280,000 Jews in Old Roumania (4% of the total local population), 250,000 in Bessarabia (nearly 10%), some 200,000 in Transylvania (4%) and more than 120,000 in Bukovina (over 12%). The largest Jewish communities in 1939 were in Czernovitz (Bukovina); Bucharest, the capital; Marmarosh-Sziget and Oradea Mare (Transylvania); Kishinev and Beltz in Bessarabia; and Jassy in Old Roumania. Bucharest had about 100,000 Jewish inhabitants and the other cities mentioned contained at least 30% of the Jewish population. Including Jews living in smaller towns, about 70% were urban; the rest lived in villages, largely in Bessarabia.

The changes brought to the Jewish population by the Soviet occupation of Bessarabia and Northern Bukovina (June, 1940) were upset by the German advance of 1941. The transfer of Northern Transylvania to Hungary under the "Vienna arbitrations" of August, 1941, and of Southern Dobrudja to Bulgaria at the same time, reduced the Jewish population of Roumania by some 160,000 Transylvanian and 5,000 Dobrudjan Jews. About 100,000 Jews from Bessarabia and Bukovina either escaped or were evacuated to Soviet Russia, and were settled largely in the republics of Uzbekistan and Azerbaijan. The rest are scattered through European Siberia and Central Russia. By August, 1943, at least 185,000 Jews had been deported from Bessarabia and Bukovina to Transnistria, the Roumanian-occupied part of Southern Ukraine. Here they were largely concentrated in the almost ruined city of Mohilev-Podolsk. Practically no Jews were reported to be remaining in Bessarabia and only some 16,000 in Bukovina. An announcement in the German semi-official Krakauer Zeitung in August 1942 stated that the total number of Jews left in the Roumanian territory was about 272,000, about 98,000 of whom were in Bucharest, 34,000 in Jassy, 16,000 in Czernovitz, 13,000 in Galati, 13,000 in Bacau and 11,000 in Timisora. Of some 230,000 unaccounted for, about 80,000 are supposed to have escaped to Soviet Russia and at least 20,000 to have perished during the Iron Guard pogroms in 1940 and subsequent excesses. About 10,000 Roumanian Jews got into Palestine. Only several hundred managed to escape to the United States.

Religious Community Organization.

Before the Second World War, the Jewish religion was recognized by the Roumanian Government as a lawful religious confession. The Jewish communities were organized according to the regulation formulated in 1929 by the first Peasant Party cabinet; communities supervised not only religious observance, but philanthropic institutions and a comprehensive system of education. Although the establishment of federations was permitted, only the communities of Old Roumania took advantage of the right. Old Roumania was, therefore, the only province that had a Chief Rabbi, (until March 1939, the late Dr. Jacob Nemierover; from then until the Antonescu regime, Dr. Alexander Shafran), who was the official Jewish representative in the Senate.

Most of the Roumanian Jewish communities had a monopoly on shehitah (ritual slaughter); like the rabbi and other religious functionaries, the shohetim were employees of the community. The Din Torah (religious tribunal) was resorted to only by the most Orthodox groups in northern Transylvania.

Like all officially recognized religions, the Jews were given an annual subsidy by the state, provided for in the government budget. However, as social and official anti-Semitism grew stronger the subsidies grew smaller. The last government under King Carol stopped payment entirely.

The decree which was issued by Marshal Antonescu's regime on September 11, 1940, changed the status of the Jewish religion from an officially recognized religion to a tolerated one. The number of synagogues was limited to one synagogue for every 400 families in the cities and one for every 200 families in the villages. Special permission had to be obtained from the Ministry of Culture for the establishment of a new synagogue. Shehitah was eventually forbidden.

By the decree of December 16, 1941, Antonescu set up a Jewish Central Organization to replace the Jewish communities. All Jews came within the jurisdiction of this Central Organization. The term Jew was also given a broader racial definition, including converted Jews and their children. Membership in the Central Organization was thus arbitrarily increased by about five or six thousand. The Central Committee in Bucharest is appointed by the government and the local committees by the Central Committee. The Central Committee functions as the sole representative of the Roumanian Jews to the government, and acts principally as a collector of regular and extraordinary Jewish taxes. It also publishes the only official weekly in the country, the Jewish Gazette (Gazeta Evreeasca). Heinrich St. Streitman, the well-known Jewish-Roumanian author, was the government appointee as the first president of the Central Committee. He remained in office until January, 1943, when Dr. N. Gingold was made president. The real leader and general-secretary is the operetta composer Matei Grunberg, known as Ben-Eli or Yosef Wilman. Under the Goga regime, he played a questionable role as organizer and stimulator of Jewish emigration. Under government orders, the Central Committee established a Jewish cataster, which was completed on July 30, 1942.

Religious Divisions.

In Bessarabia and in Bukovina, there was only one Jewish community consisting of Jews representing every religious group, from the strictly Orthodox down to the non-observant.

Old Roumania had an Ashkenazic (following the German or Polish ritual) as well as a Sephardic (following the Spanish or Portuguese ritual) community. The Jews that had settled near the shores of the Danube after the expulsion of the Jews from Spain (1492), built their own communities and several cities in Wallachia, the western part of Old Roumania. The leading Sephardic communities were in Bucharest (the most important Sephardic temple was burned during a pogrom in January, 1941), in Craiova, in Turnu-Severin and in Giurgiu.

The dominating Ashkenazic community was divided into a smaller Orthodox (conservative) and a larger Progressive group. Transylvania (formerly a province of Hungary) offered an example of religious differentiation. For more than a century, there have been three groups in most Transylvanian cities: Orthodox, Reform, and the so-called Status Quo groups, the latter consisting of those who were opposed to a division. The Status Quo group has been the smallest and is gradually disappearing because the descendants of the original peacemakers have become affiliated with either the Orthodox or the Reform group (Neologs). The Orthodox stronghold lay in northern Transylvania and in the Marmarosh-Sziget district, which in 1941 was reannexed by Hungary. The Reform group is strong in southern Transylvania, both in the parts that were in 1943 under Roumanian and under Hungarian rule.

During the 19th century, the influence of the once powerful Hassidic center in Sadaguora (Ruzhiner Rabbi), was felt not only in Bukovina, but in Old Roumania as well. (Hassidim are Orthodox Jews who remain attached to rabbinic dynasties). Hassidic dynasties were established in Boian (Bukovina), and in Stefanesti, Ajud, and Buhusi (Old Roumania). Their spiritual influence was felt until the First World War, but hardly any signs of it remain now, except in northern Transylvania and in the Marmarosh-Sziget district.

Religious Observance.

Jewish holidays were carefully observed in Orthodox circles everywhere and in the smaller cities generally. In addition to Rosh Hashonah (New Year) and Yom Kippur (Day of Atonement), the most widely-observed holidays were Pesach (Passover) and Succoth (Tabernacle). In the larger cities and in the provinces of Transylvania and Old Roumania, the only Jewish holidays whose hold even economic urgency could not weaken were the two days of Rosh Hashonah and Yom Kippur. Even in Bucharest all Jewish-owned business concerns and offices were closed on these three days.

Community Assets.

Almost every large Jewish community in Roumania had a synagogue, a culture and administration building, and public welfare and educational institutions. The Moorish-styled Temple in Czernowitz, the Choir-Temple and the Sephardic Temple in Bucharest were of architectural significance. In Czernowitz there was a Culture and Administration building which occupied a square block, and which the Goga government expropriated by a decree of January 21, 1938. The Caritas Hospital in Bucharest, the Jassy Children's Hospital and the Jewish Hospital in Czernowitz were not only fairly important medical institutions, but post-graduate schools for Jewish doctors as well.

There were community schools, homes for the aged, and orphan asylums in almost every large city. Ancient cemeteries were found in Jassy, Bucharest, Czernowitz, Beltz, Arad, Sziget, and in other cities and villages; the old Czernowitz cemetery was known for its examples of tombstone engraving.

By the decree of July 3, 1942, the Antonescu government confiscated all the property owned by the Jewish communities, except the synagogues and the cemeteries in use. All Jewish communal institutions, such as schools, bathhouses, slaughterhouses, hospitals, homes for the aged, orphan asylums, and the residence of the rabbi, shohet, and synagogue sexton, were confiscated and transferred to the National Center for Roumanization (Centrul National de Romanizare).

Religious Functionaries and their Influence

Rabbis wielded a significant social influence. The Chief Rabbi, the late Dr. Nemierover and Dr. Yacob Nacht, were well-known Zionist leaders. The leading rabbi of Czernowitz, Dr. Avrom Jacob Mark, was a Mizrachi (Orthodox Zionist) leader, and the noted rabbi of Kishenev, Reb Yehuda Leib Tsirelson, was an important personality, serving as deputy and senator for several years. In July, 1941, Tsirelson and Mark died as martyrs to their faith. Cantors or shohetim in Roumania were generally not known beyond the narrow limits of their profession and had little significance whatever in Jewish life.

The most influential among the Hassidic rabbis was the Rabbi of Satu-Mare, Reb Youlish Teitlebaum, who held religious sway over the majority of the Jews in North Transylvania and the Marmarosh-Sziget district. The Rabbi of Vishnitz, now dead, who lived in Oradea Mare between the two World Wars, also exercised considerable spiritual and social influence. The smaller Hassidic dynasties scattered through Old Roumania, Transylvania and parts of Bessarabia had practically no influence at all, because they were too dependent economically on their followers and their rabbis lacked the personality to compensate for this economic dependence.

The most noted progressive rabbi in Transylvania had been Dr. Leopold Kesckemeti of Oradea Mare (today, under Hungarian rule, Nagyvarad), a leader of Hungarian-educated Jews in Transylvania. In Transylvania, even conservative Hassidic Jews voted in large numbers for candidates of the Hungarian minority party, instead of Roumanian candidates. This was the result of a Roumanian policy which had in the early 1920's already started a systematic policy of eliminating Jewish intellectuals and businessmen from their long-held positions in the provinces then newly-won from Hungary.

Communal Organizations.

The two most important Jewish groups in Roumania were the Union of Roumanian Jews (Uniunea Evreilor Romani) and the Jewish Party (Partidul Evreesc). The Union, whose objective was to obtain equal rights for Jewish citizens, was the older of the two groups, and derived its membership mainly from among the Jews of Old Roumania, and the Neolog (Reform) groups of Transylvania. Its leader was Dr. Wilhelm Filderman, first deported to Transnistria and recently reported released from internment. The Jewish Party stressed Jewish nationalism; its demands were more radical than the Union's, and its following was larger in Bukovina, Bessarabia and Northern Transylvania. Twice, at parliamentary elections, this group succeeded in electing four or five deputies. Its leaders were Dr. Theodore Fisher and Dr. Yosef Fisher of Transylvania, Dr. Meyer Ebner of Bukovina, and Sami Singer and Misu Weissman, well-known lawyers in Old Roumania.

Zionists had a non-political organization to which members of both the Union and the Jewish Party belonged. A second Zionist group, of the Poale Zion (Labor Zionist) division, and called <u>Zeire Zion</u>, supported the Jewish Party. The Orthodox Agudath Israel, under the leadership of Rabbi Reb Yehudah Leib Tsirelson, had a limited membership.

There were B'nai B'rith lodges in all the larger cities of Roumania, combining to form a union headed by a Sanhedrin (executive body) whose presiding officer was -- until his death in November, 1939 -- Dr. Jacob Nemierover, the Chief Rabbi. Fraternal orders and mutual aid societies, organized on occupational or district lines, were significant; in Bucharest they were organized into a union. All such organizations were dissolved under Nazi influence.

Cultural and Social Background.

The Roumanian Jew generally was not so well schooled in Jewish matters as the Polish Jew, nor did he possess the general education which Jews in central Europe had. The Jewish sections of Roumania were not lands of Jewish learning, nor of general higher culture. Only the Bukovina and southern Transylvania, with the Banat, form an exception to this rule. However, Jewish sentiment prevailed, and campaigns for Zionist and other funds generally met with relatively more success in Roumania than in the surrounding countries.

The standard of living of the Roumanian Jews between 1920 and 1930 was higher than that of the Polish Jews, but there was an increasingly large lower stratum being reduced to pauperism.

Criminality.

There was a low rate of criminality among Jews in crimes of violence, and a somewhat higher rate in the civil categories.

Minority Rights.

The minority treaty which Roumania signed on December 9, 1919, remained only a scrap of paper as far as the Jews were concerned. The Jews were in practice not given even a modicum of cultural rights. According to the Private School Law of December 22, 1925, the Jews were entitled to establish private schools, with Hebrew as the official school language. But this was never translated into reality. Private Jewish schools had to be conducted in Roumanian, and to follow the curriculum of the Roumanian school system.

The Roumanian Ministry for the Interior had no departments for national minorities. The Jorga government (1931-1932) established a subsecretariat for minorities, under the directorship of the German deputy of Transylvania, Rudolph Brandsh, but its plans did not get far. The subsecretariat was in existence about a year.

The Ministry for Culture included a department to deal with the recognized religions, excluding the Greek Orthodox, which was the State religion.

Family Life.

The traditional patriarchy in the Roumanian Jewish family practically disappeared between the two World Wars, although remnants of the system could still be found in the district of Marmarosh-Sziget, where the older pietistic form of Jewish life remained. In the other provinces, and especially in Old Roumania and part of Transylvania, where the Neologs (Reform Jews) were a leading social force, paternal discipline had disappeared even more. Roumanian women, including many Jewish women, had made considerable progress toward emancipation, being represented in various spheres of vocational life.

Marriage and Divorce.

In both marriage and divorce, civil ceremonies were obligatory, and religious solemnizations or decrees optional. Derived from the section on Personal Rights in the Roumanian Civil Code, the law applied to Jews as well as non-Jews.

Languages.

In Bessarabia, Bukovina and northern Transylvania, the majority of the Jewish population (about 90%) spoke Yiddish. Hungarian assimilation prevailed in Transylvania before the First World War; between the two World Wars, the Jews still considered Hungarian an important social and cultural factor. Even the youth, attending Roumanian schools, respected Hungarian culture. Hungarian newspapers and various other expressions of Hungarian cultural life maintained by the 1,500,000 Hungarians living in Transylvania, also influenced the Jews. A nationalist Jewish daily newspaper Uj Kelet, was published in Hungarian in Cluj, the capital of Transylvania (now Hungarian and called Koloshvar).

German, which was once the official tongue in Bukovina, was not as influential as the Hungarian tongue in Transylvania. In Bukovina, there were only 70,000 Germans; the German press was for the most part antagonistic to Jews even before Hitler. Nevertheless, two small German daily newspapers, Morgenblatt and Allgemeine Zeitung, were published by Jews and had only Jewish readers.

Romanization was strongest and most successful in Bessarabia, which had the only daily newspaper printed im Yiddish in the whole country, Unser Zeit, published in Kishinev and edited by Zalmen Rosenthal. The Bessarabian Jews did not read the Russian newspapers, and were open to Romanization. In Bessarabia, the assimilated Jewish youth spoke Roumanian, but the majority of the Jews spoke Yiddish.

In Old Roumania, the Jews most frequently read Roumanian newspapers. In Wallachia, the region near Bucharest, Roumanian was also generally spoken. Yiddish was the language of all immigrants from Bessarabia and Bukovina. It was kept alive for the rest of the Jewish population in the Yiddish theatre, which retained a strong appeal, even for the assimilated intelligentsia. In the second part of old Roumania, Moldavia, near Jassy, a great deal of Yiddish was spoken. But there were no Yiddish newspapers.

Attitude Toward War; Toward the United States.

There is no Jew within Roumania who is not wholeheartedly pro-Ally. The United States of America was always an object of admiration for the Jews, and Roumanian Jews who emigrated to the United States fostered this attitude. The diplomatic intervention of American ambassadors more than once proved helpful to Roumanian Jews. To them America represents succor for all oppressed peoples.

Political Structure.

Jews were not generally active in the larger political parties. Besides the Jewish Party, the only one to which Jews were freely admitted was the weak Social Democratic Party. The Socialist Bund, in Bukovina, had a purely Jewish membership, but was really the Jewish branch of the general Social Democratic Party. The majority of the votes cast by Jews went to the National Peasant Party as the most liberal of the major groups.

Jews in the Roumanian Army.

According to Marshal Antonescu's decree of December 4, 1940, Roumanian Jews were barred from service in the army.

Jews in Parliament.

In the last elected parliament (1933-1937) to function in Roumania, under the government of Georges Tatarescu, the only Jewish representative was the Chief Rabbi, Dr. Jacob Nemierover, who represented the Old Roumanian Union of Communities in the Senate. To the parliament preceding the last, under the rule of Jorga (1931-1932), five Jewish deputies were elected. This was the largest number of Jews ever to have served in parliament.

Gerrymandering of Jewish Districts.

Elections to Parliament took place by district, but even in districts densely populated by Jews, Jews were always in the minority. Gerrymandering was resorted to in elections to city councils, particularly in the smaller towns of Bessarabia, Bukovina, and Transylvania. Where there was a Jewish majority in a town, and the election of a Jew as mayor became a possibility, several outlying villages were attached to the town, relegating Jews to the position of a minority. Examples of this occurred in Bessarabian cities of Falesti and Bacau, among others.

Jews in Civil Service.

Jews in Civil Service were found mostly in Transylvania and in Bukovina, where they were taken over from the Austrian and Hungarian governments. Even in the 1920's the Roumanian government ousted Jewish judges, high school teachers and postal and railroad employees. Most Jewish judges were forced to retire on pension; teachers who did not know Roumanian were transferred to remote towns in Old Roumania, and thus coerced into resigning. Even before Goga, therefore, there were no Jewish judges to be found, and only a few Jewish teachers in the high schools. Some physicians functioning for fraternal groups and in the villages retained their rank in the Civil Service, until the time of Goga. In 1942-43 there were no Jews at all in the Civil Service.

Municipal Governments.

Jews often comprised 40% and 50% of the general population in the larger cities of the new eastern provinces; in the smaller towns of Bessarabia they were often in the majority. However, the government found ways to weaken, and then to eliminate, Jewish influence in municipal governments. In the 1930's, the autonomy of municipal governments was restricted and so many appointed government representatives were granted the right to vote in city councils that Jews were invariably in the minority.

Where opposition was encountered in a municipality some pretext was always found to suspend the city council and to appoint a provisional regency to govern until the next elections. This regency was made up solely of government supporters, among whom were often found one or two compromising Jews. New elections were usually put off indefinitely.

The Judiciary.

It is difficult to speak of the spirit of the judiciary in a country where, during the major part of the period between the two wars, martial law and military censorship prevailed. Political processes were dealt with by military courts, acting always on political instructions from the government. In ordinary civil and penal matters, civil courts retained their powers, but here, curiously enough, it was the jury system which injected the political tendencies of the ruling regime. Juries, notably those dealing with civil or criminal offenses against Jews, were influenced by overt or indirect political pressure. Even in the 1920's men accused of assassinating Jews were repeatedly acquitted by juries. In several instances, such trials became the points of departure for political careers for the assassins; this was true in the cases of Zelea Codreanu, Prefect Robu, Lungu and Rakovita. Rakovita was elected to parliament solely by virtue of having shot to death a Transylvanian Jewish timber industrialist in the courtroom at Cluj, after the industrialist had won a civil trial against the state, which had illegally confiscated his forest.

Although the Antonescu regime instituted discriminatory laws against the Jews, no discriminatory treatment of the Jews by the judiciary is provided for. Until 1942 or 1943 judges were not allowed private interpretations outside the realm of discriminatory laws. For instance, a judge could not discredit a witness just because he was a Jew.

The Bar.

A movement to oust Jews from the Bar started in the early 1930's. In 1937 a group of Cuzist and Codreanist lawyers, protected by Ion Inculet, then King Carol's Minister of the Interior, and led by Istrate-Micescu, later Foreign Minister, took command of the Bucharest Bar by force. They arbitrarily revised the

Jewish membership and did not accept Jews as new members. Many provincial Bar associations followed the example of the Bucharest bar. Hundreds of Jews were thus ousted from the Roumanian Bar. According to a decree issued by the Antonescu regime on October 16, 1940, Jews were barred from the practice of law. Exceptions were an insignificant number of pre-First World War citizens and decorated War veterans, who were allowed to represent Jewish clients.

Occupational Structure.

According to the official census of 1930, there were 318,000 economically active Jews in Roumania. Of these 106,000 (about 33%, as against 11.3% of the general population) were engaged in industry and trade; 157,000 (about 49%) in commerce and credit; 13,000 (4%) in agriculture; 9,000 ($2\frac{1}{2}$%) in the liberal professions (including a very small number of public servants), and 8,000 (2%) in communications and transportations.

After the crisis of 1930-31, about 20% of the previously economically active Jews were so impoverished that they were forced to seek aid from public charities. The anti-Semitic laws, and even more the anti-Semitic practices of the decade between 1930 and 1940, forced almost all the Jews out of agriculture and more than half out of the liberal professions; it also radically diminished the number of industrialists and merchants. These effects were produced mainly by the Citizenship Revision Decree of January 21, 1938, enacted by Goga and carried out by the Cristea government, denaturalizing some 300,000 Jews and barring them from participation in gainful occupations; and by the General Jewish Statute enacted by Carol II's dictatorial government on August 9, 1940, barring 90% of the Jewish population from most occupations. Corruption in official circles somewhat mitigated the immediate full execution of this law. It devolved upon the Antonescu regime to complete the task of eliminating the Jews from economic life. Mass revocations of trade licenses, exclusion from the Bar and professional chambers, forced labor, "Aryanization", large-scale special taxation and property confiscation were resorted to.

By December 31, 1941, only 17,134 Jews were engaged in any kind of gainful occupation. Since then the number has been diminished by more than half, despite German pressure to keep expert operators on the job, whether they are Jews or not. Except for approximately a hundred lawyers, and several hundred physicians, the balance of Jews are in a state of permanent unemployment, unless engaged in forced labor. In Transnistria between 170,000 and 180,000 Jews live in a gigantic penal colony.

Natural Resources.

The brothers Auschnitt-- Max (a convert, who remained in Roumania), and Edgar (now in the united States) were the chief stockholders of the iron-mines in Resita, Transylvania. The Poper and Shein families, Bucharest, owned small oil-wells in the district of Prahova. The Anhauch family of Czernowitz was the largest private owner and lease-holder of timberland and in the heavily forested territory of Bukovina.

Banking.

The largest Jewish banks in Roumania before the crisis in the early 1930's were:

1) Banca Marmarosh, Blanc & Co., founded by Mauriciu Blanc, who was succeeded by his son, Aristide Blanc, formerly a member of King Carol's entourage. The government let this bank fail in the early 1930's.

2) Lobl Bercovitz and Son, headed by the brothers Eli and Adolph Bercovitz, who were friends and supporters of the Bratianus. The government also allowed this bank to fail. What was left of the estate was managed by the son of Eli Bercovitz, Dr. Joseph Bercovitz.

3) Banca Moldovei, with headquarters in Jassy. Its largest shareholder was Moritz Wachtel, and after his death his son-in-law Willy Dinerman, who committed suicide. The government let the bank fail.

4) The only important Jewish bank to remain active was the Banca de Credit Roman, supported largely by foreign capital from the Nieder-Österreichische Escompte Bank in Vienna. The leading stockholder and general director was Oscar Kaufman, who was reported to have died in London in 1941.

No laws proclaimed by the Antonescu regime limited Jewish bank deposits; confiscation ("Aryanization") was directed at fixed assets. Credit bonds issued as "payment" for confiscated houses were frozen on the day of issue. Withdrawal of bank funds by Jews was under the supervision of the police, to prevent the money from being sent to Switzerland and the currency devaluated. Jews who sent money to relatives deported to Transnistria had to pay 60 lei per mark; the recipents got 23 lei per mark.

Insurance.

Even before the Antonescu regime, Jews were not well represented in the insurance business. The important insurance firms, Dacia, Romania and Generala, and even smaller ones, were in Roumanian hands. A few were under Italian control. There were relatively few Jewish officials, but Jews were active as brokers. Insurance branch officials as well as brokers came under the Romanization of Employees Law of November 12, 1940. According to reports, however, Romanization in insurance is proceeding relatively slowly, because there are not enough qualified Roumanians to replace the Jews. By the end of 1943 there had been no new regulations relating especially to Jewish policy owners.

Agriculture.

According to the census of 1930, more than 4% of the Jewish population was engaged in agriculture. Bukovina and Bessarabia had many Jewish landowners and farmers. In northern Transylvania (Marmarosh-Sziget district), there were a number of Jewish peasants. Official and unofficial anti-Semitism and the revision of citizenship decreased Jewish population in agriculture; Jews sold their land and migrated to the cities. Marcu Fisher and his son, of Czernowitz, were considered the most important landowners in Bukovina and Moldavia.

On October 5, 1940, a month after taking over the government, Antonescu issued a decree forcing Jews to sell their farm property to the government at a price to be set by the government and paid in bonds at 3-1/2%, which were frozen on the day of their issue. Land surrounding factories was also considered farmland. On November 17, 1940, a similar decree was issued concerning Jewish-owned forest property.

The Jewish Colonization Association had colonized Jews in Bessarabia, where there was a Jewish agricultural colony, originally called Lambrievka and later Ungarovka. Every family in the colony owned 15 to 20 hectares (37½ to 50 acres) of land, several cows and a team of horses. The colony had its own public school, a park, a cooperative store, a milk farm, and a wine-press. Dairy products and the wine from the Lambrievka-Ungarovka colony were well known throughout that section. The land was worked individually.

This colony was no longer in existence in 1942-43. There were then no Jews left in Bessarabia.

Industry.

Jews were once well represented in the textile industry. Jews from Lodz, who were forced to leave Poland in the middle 1920's as the result of Polish taxation policies, established a number of textile factories in Roumania. At that time the Roumanian government, interested in industrial development, approved of such initiative and even granted certain privileges. Discrimination against the Jews began in the 1930's, in taxes, government-contracts, rate of exchange for foreign raw materials, work granted to foreign specialists, and bank credit. Nevertheless, Jews managed to retain leadership in the manufacture of textiles. The general-director of the factory in Buhusi (Bacau) for instance, was the noted Zionist, Lazar Margulies. Jews were also important in the manufacture of soap, controlling the Stella and Singras factories in Bucharest and Noah Ler in Czernowitz. The big railway car factory Astra in Arad was also partly in Jewish hands.

Commerce.

Retail trade was largely in Jewish hands. The largest department store in Bucharest, Socec, was owned by Jews. The exclusive retailer for several of the larger oil associations was Micu Tzentler, who was the leading stockholder of the firm Distribution. The central sales organization of the sugar factories in the country was largely managed by Jews. Discrimination was practiced mostly in matters of taxes, credit and exchange. In the 1930's overt anti-Semitic campaigns were instigated in the press against large and popular firms. Subsequently, as anti-Semitism was aggravated, the Chamber of Commerce began to hamper the registration of Jewish firms, and to "review" the credentials of those already registered.

Jews were very well represented in the export of domestic products. In the 1920's, the export of eggs was almost exclusively controlled by Jews. Jewish-owned export firms were eventually ruined, because the government favored the Roumanian domestic cooperatives and granted them exclusive export rights. The later

1930's offered additional opportunities for discrimination against the Jews, since foreign trade was based on the principle of compensation for exported goods with essential imports.

Until then, a large portion of the import agency firms had been controlled by Jews. In 1935, the Nazis barred Jewish agents for German factories in foreign countries, and many Jewish agents in Roumania lost their means of livelihood. Others saved themselves temporarily by camouflaged partnerships with non-Jewish agents. In 1942-43, Jews were completely excluded from Roumania's export and import trade.

Cooperatives.

The subsidies which the Roumanian government gave to the Roumanian village producer and consumer cooperatives helped to drive the Jewish storekeeper out of the villages, even in the 1920's, by making him superfluous.

"Aryanization."

According to a decree of October 4, 1940, the Antonescu government appointed "Aryanization" commissars for all Jewish enterprises. These commissars were under the supervision of the Ministry of Commerce and Industry. A special sub-ministry for "Aryanization," Ministrul subsecretar de stat al Romanizarii, Colonizarii si Inventarului, was not formed until June 11, 1942, under the direction of Titus Dragos. One of its departments is the Centrul National de Romanizare (Committee for Romanization, popularly known by its initials C. N. R.)

General control of "Aryanization" lies with the Minister of Justice, Constantin Stoicescu. In Bessarabia it is directed by the military Governor, General C. Voiculescu; in Bukovina by the military Governor General C. Calotescu.

The Commissariat for Jewish Affairs was under the chairmanship of Minister Marinescu. Radu Lecca was general secretary. Lecca was the factotum for the government's anti-Jewish activities, and is known as the Commissar for Jewish Affairs.

Creditul Romanesc (Roumanian credit), is an institution to subsidize Romanization by means of loans, and is financed by the Roumanian National Bank. By the middle of 1943, 287 million lei ($1,246,600) had been loaned for the Romanization of industry, and 289 million lei ($1,260,000) for the Romanization of trade. Alexandru Studza is the head of the office for Jewish forced labor. By June, 1943, almost all Jewish firms had been "Romanized", together with some 92,000 buildings and about 500,000 hectares (1,250,000 acres) of land belonging to Jews. Those Jews permitted to work were subjected to a special tax amounting to 1.2 billion lei.

Employment.

There were approximately 100,000 Jews engaged in proletarian occupations in Roumania. Statistics regarding their trade classifications are lacking, but the majority were employed in the needle trades, in weaving, printing, and as goldsmiths. The average working day of the Jewish worker before the war was between 40 and 48 hours a week. The chief concentrations of Jewish workers were in Bucharest, Buhusi (Bacau), Czernowitz, and Satu Mare (Transylvania).

On November 12, 1940, Marchal Antonescu decreed the Romanization of private enterprise employees. Jewish employees had to be ousted by December 31, 1941. This proved difficult, because of a lack of essential workers with even half the qualifications necessary to replace the Jewish employees. However, according to a report of the sub-ministry for Labor, published in the Deutsche Zeitung of Budapest in July 1942, Romanization had already made considerable progress when the decree was published. In Bucharest, which had once been the center of Jewish employment, there were on November 30, 1941, only about 10,000 Jewish employees and about 134,000 non-Jews. In Transylvania, there were only 2,000 Jews as compared to more than 35,000 non-Jews. Jews could work for the army if they possessed the necessary skills. For the rest, the only hope lay in unskilled forced labor.

Trade Unions.

The trade union movement in Roumania was connected with the Social Democrats. Since the Communist party was illegal, no trade unions could be connected with this group. The attitude of trade unions to Jews, or more accurately, to anti-Semitism, was that of the sponsoring party. Anti-Semitic propaganda seeped into the Social Democratic unions here and there because of laxity in principle.

There were no separate Jewish unions in Roumania. In Bukovina certain unions (such as the tailors' and barbers') had an exclusively Jewish membership, but they belonged to the Social Democrat Trade Union Central, whose leaders were for the most part non-Jews.

Credit Banks.

After the First World War the American Jewish Joint Distribution Committee and the ICA (Jewish Colonization Association), first working separately and then together through the American Joint-Reconstruction Foundation, established a network of cooperative credit banks in Roumania. Initial capital was provided, and subsidies to the banks were continued in the form of loans. Most of the banks' membership was derived from small merchants and private employees. The bank cooperatives, especially in Bessarabia, also served as centers of Jewish culture and social education. There were no Jewish workers' banks in Roumania.

Forced Labor.

The organization and management of Jewish forced labor, involving all Jews between the ages of 18 and 50, was--according to the decree of July 5, 1942,--taken over by the military general-staff. Jews in the above classification were taken from civilian jurisdiction and placed under military discipline. This is tantamount to martial law. For Jews who try to evade forced labor, the punishment, according to an order of the general-staff, is deportation to Transnistria. If the evader cannot be found, his family is deported. The number of Jewish forced laborers (in excess of those in Transnistria) cannot be established. In August, 1942, of the 98,000 Jews of Bucharest alone, 28,177 were engaged in forced labor. In December, 1943, a report stated that even Jews over 50 years of age would be drafted for forced labor if they are found engaged in private enterprise without special permission.

The Press.

The Roumanian newspapers owned by Jews were: 1) The daily Adeverul, the leading political afternoon newspaper and Dimineata, the informative morning newspaper; the chief stockholders of both were the journalists Constantin Graur, who died in Bucharest in 1940, Jacob Rosenthal, now in New York, and Saniel Labin, now in New York; 2) Lupta (The Struggle), a political afternoon newspaper, owned by Emil Fagure and Albert Honigman. Goga banned all three newspapers.

Other newspapers of a general nature owned by Jews were the two German dailies in Czernowitz: Morgenblatt, edited by Julius Weber, and Allgemeine Zeitung, edited by Dr. Adolph Niederhoffer.

Newspapers that were Jewish in content were: 1) Unser Zeit, a Yiddish Zionist daily, published in Kishenev, and edited by Zalman Rosenthal; 2) Uj-Kelet, a Hungarian Zionist daily, published in Cluj (Transylvania); 3) Ost-Jüdische Zeitung, published three times a week (German Zionist) in Czernowitz, and edited by Dr. Meyer Ebner; 4) Curierul Israelit, Roumanian weekly, Bucharest, the organ of the Union of Roumanian Jews, edited by M. Zelter-Saratianu; 5) Renasterea Noastra, Roumanian Zionist weekly, Bucharest, edited by L. B. Wechsler; 6) Czernowitzer Bletter, appearing three times a month in Yiddish, edited by A. S. Soifer.

The only Jewish newspaper appearing in 1942-43 was the Gazeta Evreeasca, the organ of the Jewish Central Committee, which the law of December 16, 1941 made the official Jewish representative body.

Fascist Press.

The chief anti-Semitic newspapers in Roumania were: 1) Universul, the largest morning newspaper in Roumania; its director and owner was Stelian Popescu, former judge, and Minister of Justice; 2) Perunca Vremei (Law of the Times), edited by Dr. Ilie Radulescu; 3) Buna Vestire (Good Message), organ of the Iron Guard; 4) Curentul (The Trend), edited and owned by Pamfil Seicaru; 5) Cuvantul (The Word), once edited by the late Prof. Naie Ionescu; 6) Opararea Nationala (National Defense), edited by Prof. Cuza. The first five publications were dailies, the last a weekly. Of the six, the only one not being published in 1942-43 was Cuvantul. All those appearing in 1942-43 were Quisling newspapers, because they served the Antonescu government.

Important members of the Universul Staff are the well-known journalist Romulus Seisanu and the lawyer-journalist Ion Nedelescu, both violent anti-Semites. Another important Quisling writer is Nichifor Crainic, author and former Minister. An important "Guardist" journalist is the English-speaking Prof. Dragos Protopopescu; a pro-German and anti-Semite of long standing is the German connoisseur and Goethe scholar, Ion San-Giorgiu.

Motion Pictures.

Motion picture distribution and exhibition were largely in Jewish hands. Jews imported German, French, and American films to Roumania.

According to King Carol's law of August 9, 1940, which established a new racial status for Jews, the non-privileged Jews in categories 1 and 3, or 90% of the Jewish population, could not own motion picture theatres. This resulted in a voluntary "Aryanization" of the industry. In 1942-43 Jews were absolutely excluded from this means of livelihood. Motion pictures as an important propaganda weapon were receiving special attention from the German army leaders in Roumania. The films were furnished by the Roumanian Propaganda Ministry, under the censorship of the German Military Gestapo.

Health and Hospital Services.

The hospitals and people's clinics maintained by Jews in the larger Roumanian cities were not subsidized by the government, but were private or communal institutions. The Antonescu government took over all private and communal Jewish hospitals, and later also all health institutions belonging to the Jewish communities.

The largest Jewish hospitals in Roumania were: Caritas, maintained by the Jewish community of Bucharest, containing about 200 beds; Caritas and Nova Maternitate, Bucharest, of which the building was completed, but not the furnishings (it would have been the largest Jewish maternity hospital in the country, with 300-400 beds); the Jewish Hospital in Czernowitz, with about 150 beds; Iubirea de Oameni (Love of Human Beings) with more than 100 beds maintained by a hospital society in Bucharest, under the direction of the noted Socialist leader, Dr. L. Gelerter; Central, a private sanitorium, in Bucharest, with about 150 beds; (owners: Drs. Rosenthal and Cuten); The hospital Shuler in Ploesti, with more than 100 beds.

Almost every Jewish community had its own hospital, which was run on a non-sectarian basis. All Jewish hospitals were taken over by the Antonescu government and were, for the most part, turned into military hospitals. Jewish doctors are as a rule not admitted to the hospitals, unless particular qualifications make their presence imperative. These doctors are mobilized for a period of 90 days and placed under the military hospital-command.

Physicians and Other Medical Practitioners.

There were approximately 1,500 Jewish doctors, dentists, and veterinarians in Roumania before the war, and between 300 and 400 trained Jewish nurses. Jewish doctors were for the most part well-trained; many had graduated from the best universities in Europe, and then received additional diplomas in Roumania. Distinguished diagnosticians and surgeons were found on the roster, but not one occupied a professional chair in a university.

In Bucharest, there were four Jewish university lecturers; one internist, Dr. Fuffer, one dermatologist, Dr. Blumenthal, and two neurologists, Drs. Kreindler and Sager. The number of Jewish doctors has since decreased only through emigration and personal accidents, which cannot amount to a great deal.

Today Jewish doctors may treat only Jewish patients. For treating a non-Jew, a doctor is liable to a fine and the loss of the right to practice. The same applies to Jewish nurses and dentists. Jews are not allowed to be veterinarians.

Birth and Mortality Rates.

In the 1930's there were about 17,000 live births a year among Roumanian Jews. No exact statistics are available for 1942-43, but the birth-rate probably fell about 60%.

The number of deaths among Jews in Roumania in the 1930's was estimated at about 10,500 a year. The ten principal causes of death were: cancer, heart disease, senility, arterio-sclerosis and other circulatory diseases, respiratory diseases, contagious diseases, suicide, diabetes, paralysis, infant mortality.

General reports indicate that the mortality rate among the Jews of Roumania has risen significantly in the past few years. In the first three months of 1940, there was no surplus of births over deaths, but rather a shortage of more than 1,000. From December, 1941, until February, 1942, spotted typhus was prevalent among the Roumanian Jews deported to Transnistria. According to semi-official reports, 13,000 died in the course of two months. Another report states that toward the end of 1941 an average of 180 Jews died every day in the Transnistrian city of Mchilev-Podolsk.

Hygiene and Sanitation.

In the occupied sections of the Ukraine, the deported Jews live in ruined cities. Almost all the houses are dilapidated, offering no protection against the cold. Sanitation is deplorable. Living accommodations are bad, one room often sufficing for two and three families. Undernourishment and starvation play their part. The prevalence of epidemics is not surprising; the mortality rate of children is terrifying.

In Bucharest, which in 1942-43 contained more than 1/3 of the Roumanian Jewish population, in Jassy, with 34,000 Jews, in Czernowitz with 16,000 and in Temeshvar, with 11,000, there are water supply systems, and no special prohibitions which make it difficult for Jews to obtain water. But in the ghettos of Transnistria, where there is no water supply system and where even the most primitive means of transportation to facilitate the procurement of water are lacking, conditions are bad.

Even before the war, there was a great deal of tuberculosis among the Jews in the smaller towns of Bessarabia, Bukovina and Old Roumania, largely the result of unhygienic living conditions. Rickets, produced by the same unhygienic conditions, was widespread among children.

Education.

There were no legal restrictions against Jews in Roumanian schools, except that Jewish medical students were allowed to dissect only the corpses of Jews. In practice, however, at the end of the 1920's, there were no Jewish medical students in Bucharest. In the medical schools at Jassy and Cluj, there were very few. Jewish students could study only jurisprudence and the sciences because here discrimination could take effect when the student came up for the Bar examination, or tried to become a government employee. In the 1930's, secondary schools started to refuse to accept Jewish students because "there wasn't any room."

Private Jewish schools with public privileges were virtually Roumanian schools whose program did not deviate from the government schools, except that Jewish religion, Hebrew reading and some Hebrew songs were taught. Even in the Jewish private schools, which were all elementary, history and Roumanian had to be taught by non-Jewish Roumanians. Jewish private schools were most frequently maintained by the community. Private schools without public rights had to have permission from the Ministry of Education, which was seldom granted.

There were several Jewish vocational schools in Roumania, the most important of which were Morgenroit, supported by the Jewish socialists in Czernowitz (Yiddish was included in the curriculum), and Ciocanul (the Hammer), supported by the Bucharest community. Northern Transylvania, Bukovina and the smaller cities of Bessarabia also had Hebrew schools and Talmud Torahs but without the official knowledge of the national government.

In principle, the curriculum and the text books used in pre-war schools were supposed to be free of religious and racial discrimination, but were not. Discrimination was practiced by many teachers also. Propaganda among teachers stressed the danger of frontier revision, the importance of Romanizing the sections containing minorities, anti-Semitism, anti-Socialism, anti-Bolshevism and, during the era of Hitler-influence, anti-democracy. Roumanian teachers in the minority sections (Bessarabia and Bukovina) were paid Romanization premiums. The selection of teachers was largely dependent on the opinion of the Minister of Education. In 1942-43, teachers were officially anti-Semitic.

There were between 200 and 300 Jewish elementary and secondary school teachers in Roumania, and between 500 and 600 teachers in Jewish schools with public rights. This number probably increased in 1942-43, with the addition of those teachers who were ousted from the Roumanian schools.

The elementary schools, in 1938, had between 80,000 and 90,000 Jewish pupils; the secondary schools between 10,000 and 12,000, and the universities 3,000 to 4,000. The few Jewish elementary and secondary schools in existence had between 3,000 and 4,000 students.

Jewish children were excluded from government schools by the decree of October 7, 1940. The Jewish schools in 1942-43 were supported and directed by the Jewish Central Committee under the supervision of government inspectors. Their program had not been changed; it taught Roumanian patriotism, but the teachers were not anti-Semites. Jews were not admitted to universities in 1942-43, and the government had closed all but one Jewish technical school. An order of January 30, 1943, forbade the teaching of Hebrew in Jewish schools, and a later dispatch indicated that in Czernowitz schools for Jews were entirely banned.

Social Welfare.

Sick benefit insurance for all employees has been in effect in Roumania since the early 1930's. Before the war it also applied to Jewish workers.

The most important government relief work was unemployment insurance, from which the Jews got very little benefit. There was no other large-scale organized relief work in Roumania. Municipalities and regional governments maintained hospitals, old-age homes, and orphan homes. The relief work for Jews was carried by the Jewish communities and by foreign aid societies.

Every larger community had an orphan asylum, a home for the aged and kitchens for the poor. These were supported by the community budgets, by special charity funds and to a great extent by bequests. Between the two World Wars, Jewish philanthropic institutions were aided by the American Jewish Joint Distribution Committee. The credit cooperatives established with the aid of the Joint-Reconstruction Foundation had to adjust themselves, in the 1930's, to the Roumanian Corporation Law which tried to eliminate them. The Jewish small-loan banks suffered, but held on until the Antonescu regime.

The fate of the Jewish credit cooperatives in 1942-43 is not known. The only source of income for all philanthropies rests with the Roumanian Jews themselves; the only authorized philanthropy control is the Jewish Central, under government supervision.

Child Welfare.

Public child welfare was comparatively undeveloped in Roumania, being restricted to village doctors, orphan homes, and several educational establishments for juvenile delinquents. Among Jews, the only form of welfare was the orphan asylum.

History of Anti-Semitism.

Both the international recognition of Roumania's independent statehood in 1878, and her territorial acquisitions after the First World War, contained specific conditions and treaty obligations to grant absolute equality to all her subjects. In both cases, the main objective of these stipulations was the assurance of rights to the Jewish population. But so thoroughly was the anti-Semitic tendency a part of the official attitude that various arbitrary handicaps were placed in the way of the fulfillment of these obligations. After 1878, non-Christians could be naturalized only through a special grant of citizenship by both houses of parliament; consequently, until 1919, no more than a few hundred Jews had been able to obtain citizenship, the rest were stateless. The post-First World War obligations regarding equality were subjected to the Citizenship Law of 1924, requiring documentary proof of residence in the same community for ten years prior to 1918 -- a condition that few Jews were able to meet because official records were scarce. Other prejudicial administrative measures regarding trade licenses, public officials and education came subsequently. Nevertheless, the need to retain the good will of the Western Powers somewhat restrained the anti-Semitic procedure.

The ambiguity in the official attitude, however, weakened government resistance against the extreme anti-Semitic agitation of the Iron Guardists of Codreanu, the National Christians of Cuza, the Goga group, and other anti-Semites. In the early 1920's, Cuza was elected to Parliament through government and church support. During the next decade, the Iron Guard was condoned and encouraged throughout the country as a counter-weight against the liberalism of the National Peasant Party. Premier Vaida-Voevod's "Roumania to the Roumanians movement" enjoyed the full approval of the Crown. In 1936, during the regime of the Liberal Party, an attempt was made to pass a revision of the National Labor Act, which would have forced employment rosters to contain 50% or 75% "ethnical" Roumanians. French opposition prevented the passage of this bill, but Valer Pop, Minister of Industry and Commerce, attempted to force private firms to apply the same percentage principle. In December, 1937, King Carol, having merged the Cuza and Goga groups into the National Christian Party, turned the government over to the new combination, although the party had polled less than 10% of the votes a week before. The regime was short-lived, but the Citizenship Revision Law of January 31, 1938, passed under its auspices, and enforced by Goga's successor, Patriarch Premier Miron Cristea, reviewed the citizenship of all Jews naturalized after 1924 and made another 300,000 of them stateless. A law of September 15, 1938, put these "stateless" Jews under control of the Alien Office and barred them from employment.

On August 9, 1940, Jews were divided into three "estates": one of which, including war veterans and their descendants, and numbering about 15,000, was privileged to full equality with the general population; the rest, in the other two categories, were barred from military service, from most occupations, and from the ownership of rural property. On August 31, 1940, intermarriage between Roumanians and Jews was prohibited. Under Antonescu's dictatorship there was the following additional discriminatory decrees and actions: total Romanization of private enterprise, except for a few indispensable posts (November 12, 1940); expropriation of property owned by Jews (March 28, 1941); forced labor; special Jewish taxes; expropriation of property owned by Jewish religious communities (July 4, 1942), and mass deportations.

Pogroms and Other Excesses.

In keeping with an old tradition, physical violence against the Jews remained a feature of Roumanian life even after the creation of Greater Roumania. In the early 1920's, the practice was more or less confined to the eastern provinces, but with the growth of reactionary movements, the disturbances spread throughout the country. Jewish homes, synagogues and whole districts were devastated. Large numbers of Jews were assaulted, some fatally.

The most horrifying events took place in the summer of 1940, under the encouragement of Hitler's aggressive successes. In Suceava, Radauti and Dorohoi, as well as in a large number of smaller places in eastern Roumania, Jews were driven by the thousands to concentration points, where they were massacred. In July the Gigurtu government took over. Under this regime, tens of thousands of Jews were driven across the Russian border. Jews were thrown out of speeding trains, and torture and massacre spread to the center of the country. After the abdication of King Carol on September 6th, the rift within the Antonescu -- Sima Iron Guard regime brought about a climax. By November, terrorism had engulfed the capital and most of the country to the extent that Antonescu himself intervened by removing General Petrovicescu, director general of the Iron Guard and Minister of the Interior.

This led to the Iron Guard rebellion of January, 1941. On the night of January 22d, the most violent pogrom in Roumanian history broke out in Bucharest. The Jewish quarters were wrecked, looted and burned, hundreds of Jews were killed, thousands beaten up and tortured. Some of the victims were murdered in the slaughter-house, in bestial parody of the Jewish ritual of animal-slaughter; others were set aflame, like living torches, in the open streets and squares. Serious disturbances occurred also in Radauti, Bradow and Arad. The exact number of victims cannot be established. Later, the mass expulsion of Jews to Transnistria was also accompanied by physical excesses.

Christian Churches and the Jews.

The Greek Orthodox Church, comprising 73% of the population, and considered the national church of Roumania, was consistently inimical to the Jews. Although not all its high dignitaries participated, large numbers of the clergy were increasingly active in the Iron Guard and the Goga-Cuza movement. Patriarch Miron Cristea, a member of the Regency Council between 1927 and 1930, and Prime Minister from February, 1938, until his death in March, 1939, issued an official patriarchal proclamation on August 18, 1937, calling on the Roumanian people to liberate themselves from the "Jewish parasites". Lay leaders in the Greek Catholic Uniate Church, second in importance, were also anti-Semitic. The Roman Catholic minority remained aloof, and the Hungarian Protestant churches in Transylvania remained traditionally liberal. Reports in 1943 indicated that Patriarch Cristea's successor, Patriarch Nikodem, was beginning to appeal for more humane treatment of the Jews.

Attitude of People and Government.

Roumanians cannot be said to have had traditional, innate anti-Semitic sentiments; anti-Semitism always had to be roused by the government. Inherently, the Roumanian peasant is not anti-Semitic. He considers the Jew a "non-believer", but nevertheless respects him for his own "beliefs".

In the 1920's, Cuza was successful in electing a deputy to Parliament only with the help of the government, which was in need of a diversion. In the late 1920's and early 1930's, the followers of Codreanu were given financial and organizational assistance by the Minister of the Interior, and later also by Premier Alexandru Vaida-Voevod. The merging of the Goga and Cuza parties into one powerful anti-Semitic party was accomplished with King Carol's consent. Anti-Semitic sentiment in the country from 1930 until the establishment of the Antonescu regime (September 5, 1940) was sponsored by the government of Georges Tatarescu (1933-1937), and after the fall of Goga, by the government of the Patriarch Miron Cristea (February 1938-March 1939).

During the depression years, the anti-Semitic demagogery of Cuza and Codreanu was acceptable to the poverty-stricken and despondent peasantry, among whom the propaganda was easily disseminated because the successive governments were in sympathy with it. The Roumanian intelligentsia, unfortunately, remained silent. But the warnings of the democratic surge which inevitably must come, stirred the conscience of finer and more discerning natures. The Patriarch Nicodem protested against Antonescu's brutality, and threatened to resign. The greatest living Roumanian poet, Tudor Argezi, was arrested for his criticism of the deportation of Wilhelm Filderman, former president of the Union of Communities of Old Roumania, and an ex-deputy. An important Roumanian political figure in Bukovina, he protested, in a memorandum published July 14, 1942, against the methods used to deport the Jews from Bukovina.

Anti-Semitic Parties and Organizations.

Until early in the 1920's, there was only one anti-Semitic party in Roumania, the League for National Defense (Liga Apararii Nationale), under the leadership of the veteran anti-Semite, Prof. Alexandru Cuza of Jassy. Many business people, students, intellectuals, priests and officials were adherents of the party.

In 1925, Corneliu Zelea Codreanu, a student at the Jassy Law School, left Prof. Cuza's party to form a student nucleus of the new anti-Semitic movement. His prestige as a national leader was based upon the fact that he shot and killed the police prefect of Jassy for alleged pro-Jewish sympathies (1924). His group was first called The League of the Archangel Michael (Leguinea Archangelui Mihail). Out of it finally emerged the Iron Guard (Garda de fer), which was formally but not actually dissolved in 1933 after the assassination of liberal premier Duca by its members. To conceal its identity, it was for some time called The Party All for the Fatherland (Partidul Totul pentru Tara).

This group actually modelled itself after the German National Socialist party. In contrast to the Cuzist group, it was totalitarian and anti-Carlist; besides being anti-Semitic and pro-German like the Cuzists. It adopted the entire Nazi political and social program, disguised by local trimmings, and demanded absolute political alignment with Nazi Germany.

The Cuzists were theoretically in favor of Roumanian democracy, and their only projected solution to all problems was to deprive the native Jews of their rights, and to deport the "alien" Jews. The Cuzists, who were much weaker than the Codreanists, came into power on New Year's eve of 1938, having merged with Octavian Goga's group. In the early 1930's the latter faction split from the People's Party, which was under the leadership of General Alexandru Averescu, a popular hero of the First World War. The union of Goga's National Agrarian Party and Cuza's League for National Defense took place at the expressed desire of King Carol. The new party was called the National Christian Party (Partidul National Crestin) and was in power under the premiership of Octavian Goga between December 28, 1937 and February 10, 1938. At the end of this 44-day incumbency, the nationwide economic crisis precipitated by its disruptive anti-Semitic measures, forced this first openly totalitarian government to resign. The Codreanists participated in Marshal Antonescu's regime from September 5, 1940 until the revolt in January 1941 which was coordinated with the most bestial pogrom in Roumanian history.

Official and Unofficial Discrimination Before and After the Outbreak of War.

The most important legal discrimination against the Jews during the years immediately before the Antonescu regime were:

a) The law of January 21, 1938, revising the citizenship of all Jews. A government report of November 24, 1939, publishing the results of the revision, stated that of the 620,000 Jews who had submitted their legal papers, some 300,000 had lost their citizenship and their right to earn a livelihood.

b) The law of September 15, 1938, placing all the disenfranchised Jews under the control of the Alien Bureau and forbidding their participation in the professions for which citizenship is a prerequisite (lawyers, certified accountants, and rural property holders).

c) The decree of August 9, 1940, dividing the Jews into three categories, the first and third of which dealt with the non-privileged and consisted of 90% of the Jewish population. They were barred from most of the important occupations. They were also deprived of the right of military service. All Jews lost the right to own rural property. The second category dealt with privileged Jews-- war veterans, the sons of veterans, etc., altogether some 15,000 people.

d) The law of August 31, 1940, forbidding inter-marriage of pure Roumanians and Jews.

The most important of many extra-legal discriminations against the Jews before the Antonescu regime were:

a) The attempt of the Minister of Commerce and Industry of the "liberal" Tatarescu government to blackmail all major firms in Roumania into firing huge numbers of employees belonging to ethnical minorities in order to obtain, within three months, a 50% share in all qualified, and a 75% in non-qualified jobs for racial Roumanian employees. The plot was foiled only by a Hungarian diplomatic appeal in Geneva to Messrs. Eden and Delbos, although the original action was directed much more against the Jews than against the Hungarians.

b) The review of the qualifications of Jewish lawyers in 1936 and 1937.

c) Goga's order to suspend the publication of the two big newspapers Adeverul (Truth), and Dimineata (Morning), because they were owned by Jews.

d) Under the regime of the Patriarch Cristea (1938-1939), Jews were barred from all public bids and government contracts; Roumanian newspapers were not permitted to hire Jews; Jewish citizens living in other countries were not permitted to return to Roumania. In certain localities (Czornowitz), the speaking of Yiddish was banned, in others (Ismaiel) fines were imposed, and in many cities, the Jewish Shehitah ritual was forbidden.

The most important legal discriminations against the Jews under Antonescu in 1942-43 were: a) Romanization of all the employees in private enterprise (law of November 12, 1940); b) expropriation of Jewish capital (decree of March 28, 1941); c) forced labor for all Jews from 18 to 50 years of age); d) special Jewish taxes (clothing taxes, war-debt taxes, etc.); e) expropriation of the wealth of all Jewish communities, except the synagogues and cemeteries in use (Decree of July 4, 1942).

The most important extra-legal discrimination against the Roumanian Jews was the deportation of the Jews from Bukovina and Bessarabia in the fall of 1941. According to Roumanian-German statistics, (Krakauer Zeitung, August 13, 1942), 185,000 Jews were exiled to Transnistria. The exile of individual Jews to Transnistria was the most abominable and most arbitrary administrative act of the Antonescu regime.

Taxation.

The Roumanian system of taxation tried to spare the agrarian and place the burden on the urban population. Since the comptroller and the local tax authorities fixed the amount to be paid by merchants and professionals, on the basis of flexible criteria, there was opportunity for both discrimination against Jews and for corruption. Certain taxes, such as the tax on turnover, would, if paid honestly, have prevented a merchant or industrialist from carrying on his affairs. Here discrimination against Jews was especially noticeable. Jewish merchants and industrialists were under constant control. Non-Jews were treated with more sympathy. Jews were mulcted by comptrollers, agents and mainly by the tax authorities themselves.

By a decree of June 11, 1942, the government sub-secretariat formed to control romanization, colonization, and inventory, was also given management over wealth confiscated from the Jews. The sub-secretariat, under the direction of Titus Dragos, a journalist, was to ascertain whether Jews, with the cooperation of Roumanians, concealed their wealth (decree to prevent Jewish wealth deception, March 14, 1942), and to arrange the transfer of confiscated property to Roumanians. Jews were represented by the Jewish Central Committee (decree of December 16, 1941), which also collects the prescribed Jewish taxes.

The most important special taxes imposed on the Jews are:

a) Military taxes (according to a decree of January 20, 1941). Jews between the ages of 18 and 50, are required to pay taxes which amounted to from 1000 lei (about $6.50) a year and 20% of their income, to 6,000 lei (about $40) a year and 30% of their income.

b) The Reunion Tax (decree of March 12, 1942). Jews were forced to pay four times as much as non-Jews.

c) The clothing tax, imposed in the Spring of 1942, forced the Jews to give to the army all but their most essential apparel.

Leading Roumanian Fascists and Anti-Semites.

Apart from Iron Guard leaders hiding in Germany, no leading Roumanian fascists are to be found outside of Roumania now, unless we include in this category the former Roumanian Minister to London, Viorel Virgil Tilea, who was the Vice President of Alexander Vaida-Voevod's semi-Fascist and anti-Semitic party, Frontul Romanesc (Roumanian Front).

Within Roumania, in addition to the head of the government, Marshal Ion Antonescu, the most important Fascists are the following: Prof. George Alexianu, governor of Transnistria; the Vice Premier and Minister of Justice, Mihai Antonescu, Bucharest; Ion Zelea Codreanu, father of the murdered leader of the Iron Guard, Corneliu Zelea Codreanu; Prof. Alexandru C. Cuza, professor in Jassy, son of Alexandru Cuza; Nichifor Crainic, poet, author, and former Minister in King Carol's cabinet; Ion Gigurtu, industrialist, and King Carol's last Premier; Stelian Popescu, owner and editor of the largest Roumanian daily newspaper Universul (Bucharest); Valer Pop, lawyer in Transylvania, and many times Minister in King Carol's cabinets between 1930 and 1938; Dr. Ilie Radulescu, editor of the anti-Semitic newspaper Porunca Vremii (Bucharest).

Jews and the Police.

There were no Jews in the Roumanian police force between the two World Wars. Only a few higher officials, remnants of Austrian rule and several detectives in the criminal police remained as functionaries in the Bukovina. Corruption had always been known in the dealings of the Roumanian police with the Jews, who were in desperate need of documents, certificates, naturalization, etc. Between September 1940 and the end of January 1941 the special legionary assistant-police handled Jewish affairs. They led the pogrom on Jews in January 1941. When the Iron Guard stepped out of Antonescu's government, the legionary police was liquidated.

In 1942-43 the secret government police, known as Siguranta Statului, handled Jewish affairs. This corps, known throughout Roumania for its brutality, was under the supervision of the Gestapo-Commandant Ernst Kaltenbrunner, who was sent to Roumania when an Allied invasion of Europe began to seem probable.

Fire Department.

Before the war, the fire departments were attached to the military garrisons in most of the large cities, such as Bucharest and Jassy. A Jewish soldier might have served in them by chance. In the smaller cities, where there were municipal fire departments, they had Jewish members (more in the new provinces), but relatively few. In the Jewish quarters of Czernowitz, and in the Transnistrian camps, there were in 1942-43 no separate Jewish fire departments.

Passports.

In 1942-43, Jews obtained their passports and travel permits through the Jewish Central. An order of the Minister of the Interior required Jews to pay 1,000 lei (about $6.50) in advance to the Jewish Central for every day of travel. The Jewish Central forwarded the request to the government; if the Ministry did not approve of the trip, the deposited money was returned. According to an order of February 15, 1942, a Jew may obtain a passport if he leaves the country forever, and has valid visas.

Transportation.

An order issued by the Ministry of Communications early in January 1943 forbids the use of motorized means of transportation of which Jews are the owners, even if the vehicles are not privately owned, but the property of a corporation.

According to a decree of December 4, 1940, all water conveyances belonging to Jews were taken over by the government.

Curfew; Travel.

In Czernowitz, the military commandant barred the Jews from appearing on the streets except between 10 A.M. and 1 P.M. Punishment for violation was not mentioned in the order, but it would probably mean deportation to Transnistria.

The Jews of Czernowitz are not allowed to leave the city. From Old Roumania, Jews could not go to Bukovina or to Bessarabia. Punishment for violation was Transnistria.

Communications.

In 1942-43, Jews were forbidden to have telephones or any radio apparatus. Even Jewish doctors were not allowed to have telephones.

Identification Cards.

The official agency for issuing Jewish identification documents is the Jewish Central, which was formed by the law of December 16, 1941. Although there have been scattered reports about the imposition of yellow-badge regulations, no definite information is available.

Concentration Camps.

Jewish concentration camps, in 1942-43, were located in the ruined cities of Transnistria. Before the exodus from Bukovina and Bessarabia, there was a temporary concentration camp in the Bessarabian city of Hotin. An internment camp for Jews and "disloyal" non-Jews is situated in the Old-Roumanian city, Targu Jiu, in Gorj. All camps are under the jurisdiction of the general-staff; their commandant is General Cipeanu.

Rationing.

Jews are under the same rationing system as non-Jews, but there are several known exceptions. According to an order issued by the Bucharest city council on November 13, 1941, Jews may buy only between 10 A.M. and noon on weekdays, and between 9 A.M. and 10 A.M. on Sundays and holidays. Jews are forbidden to buy directly from farmers. According to a decree published in the newspaper Timpul on August 20, 1942, Jews must pay thirty lei (20 cents) for a loaf of bread weighing somewhat more than a pound while non-Jews pay only fourteen lei. This supplementary tax was reported lifted in December 1943. Non-Jews get 500 grams of sugar a month, while Jews get only 200 grams. In Transnistria, Jewish forced-laborers receive 1/8 the amount of rations allotted the Roumanian soldier.

A report in July 1943 stated that certain categories of Jews (foreign Jews, disabled war veterans, and widows of Jews who were decorated in the First World War) would receive regular food cards.

Roumanian Jewish Groups in Other Countries.

The most important groups of Jews of Roumanian origin in other countries are:

1) The Union for Roumanian Immigrants (Palestine), under the presidency of Dr. Meyer Ebner; 2) United Roumanian Jews (United States and Canada), under the presidency of Leo Wolfson and Charles Sonnenreich (this group has been in existence for more than thirty years and practically all of its members are American and Canadian citizens); 3) the Roumanian division of the Advisory Committee for European Jews of the World Jewish Congress, consisting mainly of refugees and recent immigrants, under the chairmanship of Jacob Rosenthal, former press attaché

of the Roumanian Embassy in Washington.

The only Jew known to be active in the "Free Roumanian" groups under the leadership of ex-King Carol was Leon Fisher, of New York.

Jewish Leaders in Roumania and in Exile.

The important Jewish leaders and influential persons who are still in Roumania are: Uri Benador, noted Jewish Roumanian author, of Bucharest; Dr. Lazar Bickel, noted physician and author; Aristide Blank, banker; Dr. Max Diamond, author, former deputy, lawyer, Czernowitz; Abraham Feller, a leading Zionist, and printer, in Bucharest; Dr. Wilhelm Filderman, a former president of the Union of Communities in Old Roumania and a former deputy, who was deported to Transnistria by the decree of June 1st and later reported released; Dr. Yosef Fisher, former deputy, Cluj (Transylvania); Dr. Theodore Fisher, former deputy, Cluj (Transylvania); Dr. Ludwig Gelerter, Socialist leader who was very popular in all Old Roumania, Bucharest; Jacob Groper, noted Jewish poet, Bucharest; Rabbi Dr. Meyer Halevi, noted rabbi and historian, Bucharest; Philip Chefner, noted Bucharest lawyer; Barbu Lazareanu, famous Jewish Roumanian author and savant, of Bucharest; Ilie Moscowitz, Socialist leader; Dr. Manfred Reifer, former deputy, historian, Czernowitz; Dr. Alfred Ramler, former director of Psychiatric Institute, Czernowitz; Dr. Gabriel Rosenrauch, noted lawyer in Czernowitz; Mr. Seltzer-Saratianu, former secretary of the Union of Roumanian Jews and editor of the weekly Courierul Israelit in Bucharest; Dr. Alexander Shafran, chief Rabbi of Old Roumania, Bucharest; Reb Yoelish Teitelbaum, famous Hassidic Rabbi, Satu Mare, Transylvania; Dr. Meyer Teich, noted Nationalist leader in Bukovina, lawyer, journalist, now in Transnistria; A. L. Zisu, industrialist, financier, author.

Many important and influential Jews found it possible to escape from Roumania. Moishe Altman, noted Jewish novelist, formerly of Bucharest, is now in Tashkent (Uzbekistan); Dr. D. Avram, noted lawyer and Bucharest social leader, in Havana, Cuba; Dr. Shlomo Bickel, lawyer and author, formerly of Bucharest, in New York; Dr. Meyer Ebner, former deputy and senator from Czernowitz, in Tel Aviv; Wilhelm Ippen, industrialist and Socialist leader in Czernowitz, in Novosimbirsk; Michael Landau, former deputy from Bessarabia, in Tel Aviv; S. Labin, former co-director of Adeverul, in New York; Leon Misrachi, Bucharest Zionist leader, in Tel Aviv; Jacob Rosenthal, former press-attache of the Roumanian Embassy in Washington, now in New York; Dr. Israel Shefler, Bucharest industrialist and important Jewish cultural leader, in Tel Aviv; Dr. Sami Singer, former deputy and lawyer in Bucharest, in Tel Aviv; Jacob Sternberg, noted Jewish poet and author, formerly of Bucharest, in Tashkent; Dr. Theodore Weiselberger, noted Zionist leader of Czernowitz, in Novosimbirsk; Misu Weissman, former deputy and noted Bucharest lawyer, in Tel Aviv.

Reconstruction Agencies.

Foreign relief organizations which may assist in reconstruction activities include the American Jewish Joint Distribution Committee, the American Joint Reconstruction Foundation, the ORT Society for the promotion of trade and agriculture among Jews; the OSE World Union for Health Protection, the HICEM (Hias-Ica Emigration Association) and the Jewish Agency for Palestine.

THE JEWS OF YUGOSLAVIA

THE JEWS OF YUGOSLAVIA

Index

Anti-Fascist Yugoslav Jews...............19-20

Anti-Semitism
    History..........................12-13
    Leaders............................19
    Publications.......................18

Catholic Church and the Jews............13

Child Care..........................11-12

Citizenship..........................6-7

Civil Service and Government Posts.......7

Community Organization..................2-3

Concentration Camps.....................17

Cultural and Fraternal Groups............8

Discriminatory Measures..................13-16

Education..............................12

Family Relationships....................1-2

Guerrilla Fighters......................1

Health...............................9-10

Marriage and Divorce....................3

Occupational Structure..................4-6

Population.............................1

Press and Periodicals...................9

Public Welfare........................11

Reconstruction Agencies.................20

Social Security........................11

THE JEWS OF YUGOSLAVIA

There were 76,654 Jews in Yugoslavia in 1931 (census of March 31), including between 1,000 and 2,000 First World War refugees from Poland. In addition, some 2,000 or 3,000 refugees from Germany, Austria and Czechoslovakia entered Yugoslavia between 1933 and 1940. Thus the number of Jews at the time of the Nazi invasion (April 6, 1941) was about 80,000 (0.55% of the entire population). They were concentrated largely in cities: Belgrade (8,389), Zagreb (12,315), Sarajevo (8,090), Skoplje, Novisad, Osijek, etc.

The Nazis established the puppet "Independent State of Croatia," where concentration camps, massacres, deportation and starvation ruthlessly destroyed about 80% of the Jews. In Serbia proper the Jews were almost all killed or deported to Poland. In Bulgarian-occupied South Serbia, all Jews were reported to have been deported by August, 1943. Where towns and cities were inhabited by people of German origin (Volksdeutsche), the Jews were mostly exterminated. The Hungarians killed about 2,500 Jews in Novisad and other cities in reprisal for participation in guerrilla warfare; in the parts occupied by Hungary (Vojvodina, Medjimurje), about 10,000 Jews were left. In Slovenia, partly occupied by Italy and partly by Germany, there were no Jews left in 1942-43. Almost no Jews remained in Yugoslav cities. According to a report via Switzerland to a South American country, some 400 Jews remained in Zagreb, Croatia (February, 1943).

Many of the Jews saved their lives by escaping to Italy or to that part of Yugoslavia occupied by Italy (the entire Adriatic coast, Dalmatia, Montenegro). Delassim, a voluntary relief organization founded originally by Italian Jews with the aid of the Joint Distribution Committee, altered its activities during the war and aided some 8,000 Yugoslav Jews on Italian territory. About 1,000 Yugoslav Jews escaped to Hungary; several hundred to Palestine. No more than 50 reached the United States between 1941 and 1943. There were about 50 in Cuba and several hundred in South American countries.

Many Jews joined the guerrillas under Draja Mikhailovich and the Partisans. Some estimates stated that about 5,000 Jews were fighting in Yugoslavia in 1942-43, but other reports cited a considerably higher figure. The Bulletin of the Yugoslav Information Center, New York, stated that there were about 15,000 Jewish guerrilla fighters. More than 1,000 officers, and a greater number of ordinary soldiers, were prisoners of war in Germany.

The position of the father in Yugoslav Jewish families differed according to religious observance and origin. In Sephardic (practicing the Spanish and Portuguese ritual) and extremely Orthodox Ashkenazic (practicing the German and Polish ritual) families, the father had much more authority than in the Neolog (modern liberal) families. Among the Sephardic and the Orthodox Ashkenazim, full obedience and devotion was paid him as the religious head of the family. This patriarchal tradition was bound up with a strict general observance of religious ceremonies and holidays.

The position of women in the southern parts of Yugoslavia did not differ from that found among Serbian non-Jewish families; 80 per cent of them were dependent and almost entirely unemancipated. In Belgrade, however, many emancipated younger women were employed in offices, and served as teachers or physicians.

In the cities, traditional Jewish family relationships assumed the form manifested among the general population, except in the matters of religious ritual and holiday observance. In villages, family life retained a more individual character. After the First World War, most of the Jews migrated from the villages to the cities, leaving a small percentage in the provinces.

The Jewish religion was officially recognized by the state and given equal rights with other religious groups. Freedom of religion was guaranteed in the Constitution, and was strictly followed in practice by all state officials. Observance of all religious ceremonies and customs, including Shehitah (ritual slaughter) was protected by law.

The Federation of Jewish Religious Communities (Savez Jevrejskih Veroispovednih Opstina) was the official religious body, subsidized by the state, and maintaining a central office in Belgrade. In religious affairs, the Chief Rabbi represented the Federation before the government; in other matters, the president was the spokesman. The religious communities had the right to levy taxes, in the collection of which the government administrative authorities aided.

The Chief Rabbi ranked with the highest government officials, as did the religious heads of the Serbian Orthodox, Catholic and other recognized churches; he was a member of the Senate. Frequently rabbis served as teachers in the elementary schools maintained by the Jewish communities and as teachers of religion -- an obligatory subject -- in the state high schools. Religious services were conducted by the cantor, who -- in smaller communities -- also acted as shohet (ritual slaughterer) and mohel (one who performs circumcisions). Additional functionaries were the teachers in the Jewish elementary schools. The synagogue shamas (sexton) assisted at funerals and other religious ceremonies and also generally in the synagogue, as a lower-bracket employee.

Within the Jewish religious communities, there were Sephardic, Ashkenazic, extreme Orthodox (also Ashkenazic) and Neolog components. The Neologs drew their adherents from both the Sephardic and Ashkenazic groups. The 1931 census indicated the following numerical division: Ashkenazim - 47,244; Sephardim - 26,459, and extreme Orthodox - 2,951. Among the refugees from other countries there had been a few Hassidim, but they were inconsequential in the Jewish communities. Without regard to their particular ritualistic affiliations, the Yugoslav Jews observed all the Jewish holidays. The Sabbath was strictly kept by the Orthodox Jews and by many of the Sephardim.

Since the majority of Yugoslav Jews belonged to the lower middle-class, the Jewish communities did not have much wealth. In Belgrade, Zagreb, Sarajevo, Novisad, Skoplje, Osijek and other centers, the Jewish communities owned some real estate, consisting of synagogue and school buildings, homes for the aged, hospitals and similar welfare institutions. The total wealth represented by these properties was perhaps between three and five million dollars.

Toward the state, the Jewish religious community had an attitude of unequivocal cooperation and loyalty. Jews participated in political life and were appreciated for their patriotism. In the Balkan War (1912-13) and in the First World War, numerous Serbian Jews became noted heroes. Skoplje, the largest city in South Serbia, has a street named after Mosha Amar, a hero in the Balkan War. Dr. Albala and Chief Rabbi Alkalay were sent to the United States during the First and Second World Wars to represent the Yugoslav cause. Although devotion to the state characterized the Jewish communities throughout Yugoslavia, it was in Serbia that the Jews were most active politically. In elections, they invariably voted for the democratic parties.

The Nazi invasion destroyed Jewish life. The occupational authorities and the puppet governments utilized the communal organizations to obtain data about the Jews and to facilitate plunder. Subsequently, the community organizations ceased to exist; their funds were confiscated. In Zagreb, Sarajevo and other cities the synagogues were demolished. Such Jews as remained in Yugoslav territory had no legal status. All Jewish organizations were dissolved. In Belgrade, the Secretary of the Federation of Jewish Communities (who was later killed), and in Zagreb, the vice-president of the Federation, Dr. Drago Rosenberg, its secretary, Aleksa Klein, and the Rabbi Dr. Shalom Freiberger, under the protection of the Archbishop, devoted all their efforts to the work of Delassim, the organization which was aiding as many Jews as possible in Italian-occupied territories.

The marriage and divorce laws of Yugoslavia, as applicable to Jews, and others, were complicated. At the end of the First World War, Yugoslavia did not invalidate such laws as had existed in the territories which were incorporated in the new state. Consequently, five separate laws concerning marriage and divorce obtained in the country. Serbia retained the old Serbian Civil Law; Croatia had an old law requiring religious marriage and divorce ceremonies; Vojvodina (Banat, Bacska) and Medjimurje, had a modern Hungarian law demanding a civil wedding and a judicial divorce; in Bosnia a special application of Austrian Civil Law and religious ceremony was practiced, and in Dalmatia and Slovenia new Austrian statutes prevailed.

After the Nazi invasion, Jewish marriages could not be publicly performed. Rabbis performed ceremonies secretly, without witnesses. Because some puppet government leaders had wives of Jewish origin, the usual Nazi practice of voiding mixed marriages was not followed. New marriages, however, between Jews and non-Jews were barred; all mixed relationships were punishable by death.

The _Agunah_ (deserted wife) problem had no significance in Yugoslavia except among the Jews practicing the Orthodox form of ritual. Orthodox Jews do not permit the remarriage of a woman whose husband has disappeared.

There was no _Din Torah_ (religious court of arbitration) or any other form of Jewish judiciary before or after the Hitler invasion, but in the Croatian Banat, divorce proceedings, leading to a _get_ (Jewish divorce), had to be instituted with the Rabbi before the regular court would hand down a judgment.

Funeral customs, before the Hitler invasion, did not differ from Jewish funeral customs elsewhere. Every Jewish community had its own cemetery, and also a Hebra Kadisha (Burial Society) which provided funerals for the poor. After the invasion, Jewish cemeteries were largely desecrated, the Hebra Kadisha were dissolved and Jewish burials took place secretly and often in common graves.

Most of the Yugoslav Jews belonged to the middle-class, gaining their livelihood as small merchants, traders and white collar employees. Before the First World War, there were more Jews living as farmers and merchants in and around the villages throughout the country, but after the plundering of their properties by the dismissed remnants of the Austrian army and military deserters, most of them moved to the cities.

A class of industrialists existed, consisting of large-scale merchants and some bankers, and exercised considerable influence in the development of newly-created industries. To a great extent, Yugoslavia's economic development was aided by the initiative and enterprise of Jews. A number of Jews were employed as white-collar workers in banks and factories, but some were also civil service employees, although here they rarely rose to the higher brackets. In the free professions, Jews were more numerous.

The general aspect of the economic structure of the Jews in Yugoslavia varied regionally. In Croatia and Vojvodina, the Jews were comparatively well off, with a small proportion of poor. In Bosnia, small trading prevailed, and the standard of living was lower. In Serbia, the middle-class was strongest, but in South Serbia there was a great deal of poverty and a low standard of living.

Statistics taken in the 1930's show the following occupational distribution for the Jews in Yugoslavia as a whole: commerce, 37%; white-collar workers, 25%; handicraft, 13%; liberal professions, 8%; industry and finance, 2%; agriculture 3%; other professions, 7%; unemployed, 5%.

There were not many banks in Yugoslavia owned or controlled by Jews. Some small private banks did come under this heading, but were without influence in Yugoslav banking. Among these were the Jugoslovenski Creditni Zavod in Belgrade, the Merkur Banka, Trgovacka Banka and the Depozitna Banka in Zagreb.

Jews were not prominent either as the owners of mines or of other natural resources in Yugoslavia, although they aided in the introduction of foreign -- mostly British -- capital into the development of Yugoslav natural resources. Several small coal mines were owned by Jews. Not long before the invasion a modern iron foundry was established in Caprag, near Zagreb, by a Jew.

The first paper mill in the country was established in Zagreb by a Jew named Friedfeld; a family named Stern founded the first and largest leather factory in the country; the Sauerbrunn family owned the first textile factory; the Alexander, Walkenfeld and Mauer families were the owners of breweries and distilleries; a large machine and railroad car factory was established by Jews in Brod (Sava) and was later taken over by the Croatian Savings Bank (Prastediona); the first electric bulb factory was established by Jews in Pancsevo, near Belgrade; a furnace, radiator and dynamo plant was founded in Petrovgrad (formerly Becskerek). All these industries were put under the direction of Nazi commissioners after the invasion.

Before the invasion, there does not seem to have been discrimination against Jews in industry by the government or in government-owned cartels.

Yugoslav Jews participated to a significant degree in domestic commerce, especially in the timber, corn, textile and clothing trades. Later, their influence in many of these fields declined, as the result of the establishment of cooperatives for agricultural products and the centralization of export in state institutions. Only in 1940-41 did special discriminations become evident, when political nationalistic groups in the Chambers of Commerce and the Stock Exchanges succeeded in weakening the position held by the Jews in these bodies. This was especially true in Croatia.

The Nazi policy of excluding Jews from industry and commerce was efficiently carried out after the invasion with the help of the puppet governments.

In foreign trade, Jews were originally active in timber, export, and the food, grain and cattle fields. After government centralization, as mentioned above, they remained important only in timber and food commerce.

Under Nazi control, Jews in foreign trade were ousted from their firms, just as were the Jews engaged in domestic commerce.

Participation of the Jews in the economic life of Yugoslavia as employees and workers was not great, but even so the economic depression of the 1930's increased unemployment. The Jewish communities tried to meet the situation by various retraining programs. After the invasion, all employment possibilities were destroyed. During the first month, young Jews between the ages of 16 and 21 were taken for forced labor, but most of them were eventually killed.

In industry, wages paid to Jews were the same as those paid to non-Jewish workers. In the few years just prior to the invasion, the average wage was from 3 to 6 dinar per hour (8 to 16 cents). The work week averaged 40 hours; a license had to be obtained for overtime work, paid at time and a half.

No labor camps as such existed in Yugoslavia for Jewish workers in 1942-43, only concentration camps. Even of these, the majority were being liquidated and the remaining Jews deported to Poland.

Before the invasion, there were two kinds of labor unions in Yugoslavia; The Ujedinjchi Radnicki Sindikati (United Labor Federation), known as the U.R.S., and nationalistic labor organizations which differed in various parts of the country. Of the latter group, Slovenia had a Slovene Catholic organization, Croatia a Croatian Labor Party, etc. Although, during the first ten years of the existence of independent Yugoslavia, the labor unions had complete independence, increasing restrictions were subsequently imposed by the state authorities.

The agrarian reforms which were instituted in Yugoslavia after the First World War, and which divided the larger estates into smaller farms for individual farmers, almost eliminated the participation of Jews in Yugoslav agriculture. A small number of Jewish farmers and large-scale landowners remained. No Jewish agricultural cooperatives were in existence. In conjunction with the other confiscations, agricultural properties owned by Jews were also taken from them by the Nazis.

There were two large agricultural cooperatives in Yugoslavia, the Savez Srpskih Zemljoradnickih Zadruga (Federation of Serbian Agricultural Cooperatives) in Serbia, and the Seljacka Sloga (Peasant Union) in Croatia. A small labor bank existed in Slovenia; there were no large labor cooperatives.

There were three small Jewish cooperatives in Yugoslavia; one in Sarajevo; the Ezra, a cooperative bank for middle-class people and small traders, in Zagreb; and one in the Vojvodina.

The only government subsidy which affected the Jews of Yugoslavia was that given to the Federation of Jewish Religious Communities. The state authorities assisted the respective communities in raising the taxes which they were entitled to levy.

The major burden of general taxation in Yugoslavia was borne by the urban and commercial sections of the population, in which the Jews were most frequently represented. Only in this way did the Jews happen to bear a disproportionate, though not unfair, tax burden.

Jewish citizens had equal rights with all others. Citizenship could be applied for after ten years of continuous domicile in the country, but the Minister of the Interior could grant or reject the application without giving a reason. This possibility sometimes made it more difficult for Jews to obtain citizenship; during the period that Father Anton Koroshetz was Minister it was almost impossible for a Jew to be made a citizen. Unequivocal rights to citizenship, except for reasons specifically mentioned in the law, was granted after 30 years of continuous domicile in the country.

The only stateless Jews in Yugoslavia were Polish refugees who had been deprived of Polish citizenship because of five years residence outside of Poland. These Jews, mostly refugees from Germany, were without passports, and had no recognized rights to remain in Yugoslavia. After the Hitler invasion all Jews were deprived of citizenship by special law.

There were no minority rights for Jews, no Jewish bureaus in the Ministry of the Interior and no office of Minorities.

Between 1918 and the Hitler invasion there were no more than 2 or 3 Jews in the Yugoslav Parliament (Skupshtina) and Senate. The Chief Rabbi was an appointed member of the Senate.

Although the Yugoslav Jews were not notably active in political life, they were frequently represented in the municipal governments; in Belgrade and Zagreb there were Jews in the city council. The smaller towns sometimes had Jewish mayors.

Before the Hitler invasion, Jews served in all departments of the Yugoslav civil service; but largely as physicians, engineers and teachers. After the invasion, there seem to have been a few physicians retained.

There were Jews serving in the judiciary in many of the larger cities. Among those in Zagreb were judges Hoenigsberg of the Supreme Court, Gotlieb of the Court of Appeals, Hirshl of the District Court, Bozho Gruenwald, a District Attorney and I. Gold of the Magistrates Court. Judge Kerner was a magistrate in Gjurgjevac, Croatia. All these were ousted after the invasion. Except for Gotlieb, who escaped to Italy, and Gruenwald, who was in a concentration camp, the fate of the others was unknown. Under the puppet governments, the Jews had no recourse to the courts.

There was no discrimination against Jews in the Yugoslav Bar. Many Jews served on its executive committee, and a Jewish lawyer, Dr. Siebenschein, was for several years its president. Notaries had virtually the same qualifications as lawyers, and the same conditions regarding the Jews prevailed. One of the first measures to be instituted by the Nazis was the exclusion of Jews as lawyers. All the Jewish lawyers in Belgrade were sent to concentration camps in Kerestinec. No special lawyers were empowered to plead for Jews.

Within the Jewish community itself, the main division, on other than religious grounds, was between Zionists and non-Zionists. The only time that they opposed each other openly, however, was at community elections. The Yugoslav Zionists were in the majority and virtually controlled Jewish life. In addition to general Zionists, there were various labor factions, including the Histadruth, Hashomer Hazair, and Poale Zion. The New Zionist Organization (Revisionist) was not strong and had little influence. The Agudath Israel was also small and uninfluential. There was no specific Jewish communist group, although some Jews had communist views. All communist groups in Yugoslavia were illegal.

Jewish youth organizations were united in the Federation of Zionist Organizations, including all factions of the Zionist movement. They did a great deal toward training the youth for new occupations and supported a well-founded Hachshara (training) movement for Palestine pioneers.

Except for the Jewish community itself, in which membership was obligatory, affiliation with all groups was on a voluntary basis.

Among fraternal organizations, the B'nai B'rith, which had five lodges in Yugoslavia and a grand lodge with headquarters in Belgrade, was outstanding. It helped in the establishment of many social institutions and assisted the welfare work of other Jewish organizations. The first attack of the Nazis was against the B'nai B'rith.

There were also many charitable organizations and welfare institutions. Women were especially active in social welfare groups. One of the leading women's organizations in Yugoslavia was the WIZO (Women's International Zionist Organization). Refugee work resulted in the creation of suitable organizations and institutions in Yugoslavia.

Except for religious holidays, celebrations were usually limited to events of importance to the Zionist movement, such as Balfour Day (May 1st) and the anniversary of the death of Theodore Herzl.

The general orientation of the Yugoslav Jews was determined by whether they were under Western influence or -- as in the case of the Sephardim -- more attuned to Byzantine cultural life. But the tradition which prevailed in all segments of Jewish life, and which included a strong religious ethical force, was the determining factor. Yugoslav Jews were known for their readiness to offer aid wherever needed, and to support communal and civic undertakings of all kinds. Comparative crime statistics showed a low percentage of Jews; in robbery, murder, rape and other crimes of violence, Jews were almost unknown. Where they did appear in crime statistics, it was usually under the classifications of fraud, larceny and various commercial illegalities. The use of alcohol was very uncommon, and the use of narcotics almost non-existent.

About 90 per cent of the Yugoslav Jews used the native Serbo-Croat language. Most of them knew at least one additional language: in Croatia it was German; in Vojvodina and Medjimurje, Hungarian; in Bosnia and in Serbia, Ladino (15th century Jewish Spanish). The intellectual classes knew French. In the 1930's, the study and use of English became popular, many Jews joining English-speaking clubs. Yiddish was used by only very few Jews. Hebrew was popular among Zionist members of the younger generation.

The Jewish press in Yugoslavia was not well developed. A Jewish weekly, Zidov (Jew), was published by the Zionist organization in Zagreb in Serbo-Croatian and read throughout Yugoslavia. Sarajevo had a weekly, Jevrejski Glas (Serbo-Croatian). There was also a magazine Omanuth (Serbo-Croatian). All these ceased publication under Nazi rule.

Jewish participation in the ownership of the general Yugoslav press was small. A few Jews (mostly baptized) had some financial interest in two or three newspapers, but no editorial influence.

The general health service in Yugoslavia was extended to Jews and non-Jews alike. There was only one small Jewish hospital, in Subotica, a city in Vojvodina, later under Hungarian rule. A department of the Jewish asylum for the aged in Zagreb was also utilized as a hospital. Several private sanitoriums were managed by Jews in Belgrade, Subotica and other cities. After the invasion, the asylum for the aged in Zagreb, including the hospital beds, were seized; all the inmates were placed in barracks in a nearby village.

There was a high percentage of Jews in the health services of Yugoslavia, engaged chiefly as physicians, dentists, veterinarians and pharmacists. Relatively few Jewish women worked as nurses in Yugoslavia; the profession as a whole was not well developed and in many hospitals nuns performed nursing service. As physicians, Jews contributed a great deal to the development of medical science and health service in Yugoslavia, and were very much appreciated for it. Dr. Rabinowitz was physician to the King and the Court; Dr. Kohen, physician to the Queen, was subjected to a great deal of suffering at the hands of the Nazis, but finally escaped to London via Italy and Spain. Two of the best-known surgeons in Yugoslavia were Drs. Kostich of Belgrade and Gottlieb of Zagreb, both Jews, and General Dr. Mandel was one of the chief physicians in the army. Dr. Lavaslov Shick wrote a study of the important role Jewish physicians have played in Yugoslav history.

The only Jews who could work as physicians after the invasion were a few who were manifestly needed in small towns to fight disease, and in Bosnia, where no other physicians were available, to treat endemic syphilis. The number cannot be estimated because they were dispersed and working under miserable conditions, but it is known that many prominent Jewish physicians were killed in concentration camps. Most of the Jewish physicians in Bosnia were reported to have joined the guerrilla fighters.

Except for the physicians referred to immediately above and for the few who were considered indispensable in certain city hospitals, Jews were not admitted to practice medicine after the invasion.

Access to medical treatment was practically barred to the Jews after the invasion; medicine for the sick was obtainable only with the greatest difficulty and often secretly.

In pre-invasion Yugoslavia, vaccination against smallpox and immunization against other diseases was general in the cities; therefore almost the entire Jewish population was so protected. Vaccination against smallpox was obligatory in all the schools.

Health conditions for the Jews surviving in Yugoslavia in 1942-43 were extremely bad. They were doomed to starvation; in concentration camps, where 80% were estimated to have died for lack of medical aid, decimation continued from typhus, typhoid fever and other diseases.

Before the invasion, there had been no epidemics among Yugoslav Jews except influenza, followed by pneumonia. Sections which had been heavily populated by Jews during Yugoslavia's independence were largely in the cities; therefore the Jews were afforded the usual urban sanitary and hygiene protection. No ghettos were established after the Nazi invasion and consequently there was no special ghetto sanitation problem. Hygienic control over milk, meat and other foods was general throughout Yugoslavia and there was no danger of disease from spoilage. South Serbia had a kind of mosquito which caused dengue fever. Flies, fleas and lice were less common among the Jews than among the rest of the population.

The housing, bathing and toilet facilities enjoyed by the Jews in independent Yugoslavia equaled those of the rest of the population with a higher standard of living. Jews were known to have spent about 1/3 of their income for good apartments with facilities as modern as were available.

Birth statistics for the Jewish population of Yugoslavia before the invasion are not available; after the invasion births virtually ceased.

Mortality statistics are equally unavailable, but the rate among Jews was known to be relatively low, because of their higher living standards and more rigid hygienic observance. Deaths among Jews were most frequently caused by angina pectoris, pneumonia, diabetes, cancer and tuberculosis; diphtheria and scarlet fever were causes among children.

The net loss in the Jewish populations of Yugoslavia between the invasion and the middle of 1943 could probably be estimated at about 50,000; the remaining 30,000 include those still living in concentration camps or in points of deportation.

Sterilization and liquidation of incurables was not practiced on Yugoslav Jews after the invasion.

Social reforms established in independent Yugoslavia included compulsory social security and unemployment insurance, a 40-hour labor week, aid for small farmers, the expropriation and distribution of large farming estates, a system of public sanitation and public health institutions, free hospitalization for the poor, etc. Jews shared the privileges of all Yugoslav citizens in these respects.

Relief and public assistance was provided for old age as well as for the unemployment and medical care mentioned above. No discrimination was apparent in the distribution of any kinds of relief. Beginning with 1940, however, some tendency to avoid the employment of Jewish physicians in social security institutions was noticeable.

Jews were exceedingly active in the support of non-sectarian welfare institutions. Prehrana (Merisa), Uboski Dom (Home of the Poor), and Covjecnost (Humanity) -- all well-known organizations in Zagreb -- were under the chairmanship of Jews at one time or another.

There were many Jewish relief organizations. Every Jewish religious committee had a welfare department maintained from the budget established by the compulsory levy. All other organizations were maintained by private voluntary contributions. Considering the number of Jews in the country the contributions were very high. The amount spent on behalf of refugees after the beginning of the Nazi regime in Europe were so commendably high that the American Joint Distribution Committee and other welfare institutions expressed their appreciation. There were also organizations, largely maintained by women, for childrens' camps and other charities; student aid organizations, health organizations, organizations for productive retraining, and homes for the aged. The five lodges of the B'nai B'rith carried on a broad social welfare program. Government authorities co-operated with the various groups, but gave no financial assistance.

The following were some of the leaders in Jewish welfare work in independent Yugoslavia: Chief Rabbi Dr. Isak Alkalay, head of the Federation of Religious Communities in Yugoslavia, who was living in New York in 1943; Aleksa Klein, Secretary of the Jewish religious community in Zagreb, who escaped to Italy; Otto Heinrich, vice-president of the Zagreb community, who escaped to the United States; Dr. Drago Rosenberg, also vice-president of the community; Dr. Makso Pscherhof, president of the Refugee Committee, who escaped to Italy; Dr. David Furman, who led the retraining program; Julije Fischer, last president of the B'nai B'rith, who went to Palestine; Dr. Paul Neuberger, vice-president of the B'nai B'rith, who came to the United States; Dr. Richard Bauer, also its vice-president, who went to London; and Riki Kohn, head of the Palestine Bureau in Zagreb, who went to Italy. Most of the welfare workers were killed, died in concentration camps or were deported.

All provate relief work among the Jews in Yugoslavia had practically ceased by the middle of 1943.

The general juvenile court and probation system in Yugoslavia concerned the Jews very little, because of the almost non-existent percentage of Jewish juvenile delinquency. Nor were there any but a nominal number of Jewish illegitimate children.

Recreation for children was privately provided. The Jewish communities maintained kindergartens and various other recreational facilities. The Maikabi, a well-organized sports organization, had separate sections for children. Various youth groups, especially the Hashomer Hazair, maintained summer camps. In Zagreb a special welfare group, the Ferijalna Kolonija, sent poorer children to the seashore and to the mountains for vacations.

About the only child welfare accomplishment in 1943 was the sending of about thirty Yugoslavian children to Palestine.

Until October, 1940, when a law restricting the admission of Jews to high schools and universities was promulgated in Yugoslavia under German influence, there were no restrictions whatsoever in the Yugoslav school system. The educational system was free and progressive, and the curriculum was also devoid of any racial or religious discrimination. After the invasion, racial discrimination was introduced according to the Nazi tenets.

In independent Yugoslavia, there were a number of elementary Jewish schools supported entirely by the Jewish religious communities, without state subvention. These elementary schools, employing about 100 teachers, had four grades and were recognized as public schools by the state educational system. There were no Jewish high schools, but students in the public high schools were obliged to take religious instruction. There were several Yeshivath (rabbinical seminaries) in the country, and a school for cantors in Sarajevo. No statistics are available for the number of Jewish students in any branch of the school system. After the invasion, all educational possibilities for Jews were eliminated.

There were a certain number of Jews serving in the Yugoslav school system as elementary and secondary school teachers, but the percentage was not remarkable. The requirements for appointment to the elementary school system were graduation from high school and a three to four year course in pedagogy. High school teachers had to be university graduates. Education was on a nationalistic, patriotic and classical basis.

After the invasion, teachers were selected for political and party standing, so that education dropped to a low standard. German schools for the German natives (Volksdeutsche) were established and were frequented by other children as well. Hatred for the Jew and mutual hatred between Serbs and Croats were propagated in all the schools under Nazi influence.

There was no specific anti-Semitic party in Yugoslavia. Several groups, financed by the Nazis, carried on increasing anti-Semitic propaganda, but had little influence on the democratically-minded people of the country. Zbor, a movement headed by Dimitrije Ljotich, was clearly fascistic and included anti-Semitism in its program, but it made little headway and had no representatives in parliament. A group centered around the Zagreb newspaper Hrvatska Straza (Croatian Guard) was more successful because it operated in Croatia, where German influence had always been stronger than elsewhere in Yugoslavia. The Pavelich movement in Croatia, also called the Frankovci or Frank party, and eventually known as the Ustashi, was led by Ante Pavelich from Italy. As German power and influence increased, the anti-Semitic incitements of this group made some progress, although the movement remained illegal. Anti-Semitism had some sympathizers among reactionary intellectuals and the middle-class. From these groups were subsequently drawn the supporters who aided the quisling Pavalich when -- after the invasion -- he was made head of the puppet government.

Before the Hitler attack, the Catholic clergy in Yugoslavia, generally speaking, was tolerant and liberal. A small group of clergy, however, and some Catholic associations, especially in Croatia, were openly anti-Semitic. The Hrvatska Straza, organ of the clerical Catholic party, often published reactionary and anti-Semitic articles. Although the official clergy did not participate in these actions, they took no steps to suppress them. After the invasion, the Archbishop and the higher clergy were friendly and helpful toward the suffering Jews, saving many lives and trying to obtain relief. On the other hand, Catholic priests in some instances served as local leaders of the Croatian quisling party, Ustashi, and were guilty of many persecutions. Some were responsible for excesses against the Jews in provincial towns.

Friendliness and tolerance toward the Jews marked the attitude of the Yugoslav people, especially in Serbia. When, under German pressure, the Yugoslav government in October 1940, promulgated a law restricting the admission of Jews to high schools and universities, non-Jewish students and even professors participated in public protests and threatened to go on strike.

The attitude of the government was similarly friendly and the equality of the Jews granted in the Constitution was vigilantly safe-guarded. However, with the growing Nazi influence of Europe, some restrictions against Jewish refugees were instituted. These had been introduced by the Minister of the Interior Koroshetz, a Slovenian Catholic priest, and sanctioned by the majority of the Council of Ministers.

In October, 1940, insistent German demands resulted in the introduction of three anti-Jewish laws in Yugoslavia. These were: (1) A law prohibiting Jews to deal in food articles; (2) the law restricting the admission of Jews to secondary schools, technical schools, and universities; (3) regulations regarding the transfer of business enterprises and stocks owned by Jews.

Before the Hitler invasion, unofficial discrimination against the Jews was virtually non-existent.

With the establishment of the Pavelich puppet government in Croatia, and the rule of the Ustashi guards and the Gestapo, the vicious instinct of the very scum of the Yugoslav population was released. In addition, there were many who, to further personal interest or to please the new Nazi masters, joined in the attacks on the Jews. Generally speaking, the attitude of the urban populations was worse than that of the peasants.

In Serbia the population behaved itself better, except for a few officials and others in the service of the invaders. There were reports of non-Jews helping Jews wherever they could.

Under Nazi rule, legal discriminations against the Jews covered every aspect of life, leaving no room for extra-legal discrimination, except insofar as legality itself was extended to justify pillaging, torture, and ruthless murder.

There was no special legislative department for the Jews of Yugoslavia under the Nazi regime. A special section set up in the police department eventually became obsolete, because there were no more Jews to deal with. This department, under the direction of the Gestapo, excelled in the usual cruelties. Its notorious head was Eugene Kvaternik, son of Marshal Kvaternik.

The puppet government of the "Independent State of Croatia" imposed a collective contribution of six hundred million dinar in gold ($16,000,000) on the Jews. Subsequently it was raised to 800,000,000 dinar and finally to 2,000,000,000 dinar. To collect this tax, a committee for self-taxation was chosen to submit a list of individuals and their respective financial possibilities. The Jews who were not assessed were regarded as hostages. Most of them were imprisoned without a hearing, and released only when they and their families had been stripped of their last possessions and valuables. All this plundering, however, did not raise more than 900,000,000 dinars ($24,000,000).

The Jews in Yugoslavia had to pay 100 dinar (About $3) apiece for the Star of David badge.

The collections extracted by the Nazis after the invasion could hardly be called taxation. They simply took everything the Jews had. Jews who were leaving their homes were permitted to carry along only a minimum number of personal habiliments, such as one shirt, one pair of stockings and one handkerchief.

A decree prohibiting the free disposition and transfer of Jewish property was promulgated in October, 1940.

After the invasion, all bank deposits owned by Jews were confiscated. In the beginning, it was possible to withdraw small amounts for living expenses. Because of exchange regulations which had been in effect earlier, and which had prevented the transfer of money or stock without special permission from the Yugoslav National Bank, the greater part of the assets loaned by Jews fell into Nazi hands.

All Jewish enterprises were put under the control of commissars; their signs and stationery had to contain the legend: <u>Jewish enterprise</u>. As the owners were imprisoned, deported or killed, these enterprises became "Aryanized" through sale and transfer by the authorities. There was no special "Aryanization" corporation. The process was practiced with special speed in Croatia, although Serbia, Bosnia and other parts of the country achieved the same results somewhat more slowly.

There were many Jews in the insurance business in Yugoslavia, but after the invasion they were ousted from this as from all other occupations. No special rules prevailed regarding insurance policies owned by Jews, but new policies could not be obtained by Jews nor could they collect insurance claims on old policies. Since most of the insurance companies in Yugoslavia were affiliates of British, French and Italian corporations, recovery of claims may be possible after the war.

Jews were not active as motion picture producers in Yugoslavia. They were engaged in distribution, and some of the theaters were owned by Jews. After the invasion, all these enterprises were taken over by German commissars; it was reported that Franjo Gundrum, known as an admirer of Hitler, was made commisar for the motion picture theaters of Zagreb. The presentation of German propaganda films was at once instituted. Among the first to be shown were "Jew Suss" and "Baptism by Fire", the latter dealing with the invasion of Poland.

No special Nazi or quisling police departments were detailed for Jews, but in the first few months after the invasion special referees handled Jewish affairs in the police department. No special qualifications were necessary for those chosen to serve in the police force under the Nazi regime; they had only to be followers of the new regime and ready to work under Gestapo orders. They were of low moral standing and the program instituted against the Jews demanded plunder and elimination.

Sometimes five different authorities were empowered to handle Jewish affairs after the invasion; the regular police, the Jewish referees, the Gestapo, the Ustashi, and the Ministry of the Interior. They vied with each other to see who could achieve greater severity and cruelty. The Gestapo came to Yugoslavia wearing the same uniforms they used in Germany. The Ustashi had military uniforms, including a cap marked with the letter "U". The regular police were given new insignia for their uniforms.

Jews, like other citizens, participated in the voluntary fire departments in independent Yugoslavia. No specific rules regarding protection were instituted after the invasion.

Immediately following the invasion, Jews had to register with the police for the yellow Jewish badge for which they had to pay 100 dinars (about $3). Disobedience was punishable by concentration camp. There were no other identification cards.

Certain areas in all the cities were declared barred to the Jews, and Jews living within these areas often had to move out of their apartment at an hour's notice, leaving all the furniture. Jews were also barred from cafés, restaurants, motion picture and other theaters and public parks. Violation of the law was punishable by concentration camp or death.

A general curfew was established throughout Yugoslavia after the invasion. In Belgrade anyone found on the street after 7 p.m. was shot; in Zagreb the curfew hour was 6 p.m. Jews did not dare to leave their homes even during the permitted hours.

Under Nazi rule, the death penalty was imposed for the possession of fire arms, explosives or ammunition. This applied to the whole Yugoslav population.

Immediately after the invasion, the Jews were deprived of their citizenship, and thereafter could not obtain passports. There were occasional exceptions; some Jews, after paying substantial contributions, were given passports for Italian-occupied territory. In April and May of 1941 the passports still bore no distinguishing marks, but afterward a "Z", standing for Zidov (Jew) was stamped on them.

After the invasion, Jews were not permitted to travel on railroads without special permission, but as stated above, bribery often obtained for them the right to go to the Italian-occupied Adriatic coast.

The use of public highways became practically impossible for the Jews, because of the efficient ruthlessness of the Ustashi, who would have killed any Jew trying to escape via the public highways. From the very moment of the invasion, the use of busses or trucks was proscribed for Jews.

All motor cars and horse-drawn carriages owned by Jews were confiscated. Jews were not allowed to move from that part of the city where they were first allowed to live.

Waterways communication was also barred to the Jews after the invasion. Although no specific regulations regarding air travel were imposed, Jews could not get permission to engage in such travel or even to reach an air field.

Shortly after the invasion, all telephones in Jewish homes were disconnected. To use cable facilities special permission had to be obtained. All radios were confiscated within a few days. A Jew caught listening to the radio would face the death penalty.

The rationing program instituted after the invasion allowed the Jews only one-half as much food as the non-Jews had. They could not get milk, meat, and other staples. Marketing was permitted for them only after 10 a.m., sometimes only after noon, and they could buy what had been left by the non-Jewish population. Even these regulations were applicable only at the beginning of the Nazi regime; later it became difficult for a Jew to buy anything legally.

When the arrests of Jews first began, after the Nazi invasion, the majority of those arrested were taken to police prisons. But the number of prisoners was so great that they had to be put into temporary barracks and camps near the cities, including Belgrade and Zagreb. From here they were transferred to concentration camps. Jews from Belgrade and from Banat were sent to labor camps in Tashmajdan and Topovska Shupa. From Croatia they were brought first to the mountainous section of the Lika (Gospich); the youth were taken to a former factory building in Drnje, ostensibly for forced labor, but most of them were killed. Later, Croatian Jews were brought to the Adriatic island of Pag, where they lived in salt mines under terrible conditions. Another group was sent to Karlobag. These camps were subsequently liquidated, and half of the Jews and Serbs imprisoned there were reported killed and thrown into the sea.

There were large concentration camps in Jasenovac, in Nova Gradiska and in Hruscica. From Hruscica women were later sent to Lovorgrad. Other camps for women were in Gornja Reka and Diakova in Slavonia. All camps in Croatia and Bosnia were controlled and guarded by Ustashi, those in Serbia by German natives (Volksdeutsche) and some renegades.

Wooden barracks, without any protection against weather, provided the only living quarters in the camps. Food was at starvation level, there was no medical care, and no communication with the outside world was allowed. During a short period in 1942, some relief was achieved through the intervention of the Pope on the appeal made by the Association of Yugoslav Jews in the United States and the American Friends of Yugoslavia, but this did not last long. The Gestapo, the Croatian puppet government and the Ustashi party exercised supreme control in the camps in Croatia and Bosnia; the Gestapo and the renegade Nedich police in Serbia.

The inmates in the concentration camps were in no way criminals; the latter were confined in regular prisons. The Jews were imprisoned not as political culprits, but only as Jews. Juveniles and women were at first kept together with the men, then separated.

Officially, Jewish women could not be forced into prostitution by the Axis, because of the racial pollution laws. But in the concentration camps sexual violations and rape against Jewish women were prevalent. A report brought out of the camp at Hruscica, in Bosnia, by a woman who succeeded in escaping, told of unimaginable beastiality by the Ustashi guards. When some of the women were transferred to Lovorgrad, near Zagreb, examination by physicians disclosed the fact that nearly all of them were suffering from venereal disease, exhaustion and apathy. Many of the women in Hruscica and other Croatian camps committed suicide.

It is impossible to speak of an organized underground movement specifically among the Jews who remained in Yugoslavia, because of their dispersion and the control to which they were subjected. The guerrilla fighters previously referred to constituted the real underground movement.

The Jews of Yugoslavia, without exception, welcomed the overthrow of the Cvetkovich government, which signed a pact with the Axis on March 25, 1941. They approved the government of General Simovich, established two days later, and joined the armies with enthusiasm.

To Yugoslav Jews, the United States had always seemed the homeland of democracy and of equal rights. They studied American history and read American literature; during the World's Fair many Yugoslav Jews spent their savings in coming to the United States. They have always believed that the United States would be a determining factor in rescuing Europe from the Nazi yoke. Refugees who have succeeded escaping Yugoslavia report that this belief in the United States has grown even stronger.

There are no Jews in the Yugoslav Government-in-exile.

There are no special Jewish parties or groups among the Yugoslav Jews in exile. The association of Yugoslav Jews in the United States is not properly a group-in-exile.

There were very few anti-Semitic publications in independent Yugoslavia, and these had little influence. The Balkan, edited by Krsta Cicvaric in Belgrade and the Zagut Hrvatska Straza, edited by Dr. Janko Simrak, were openly anti-Semitic. Slobodna Hrvatska (?), edited in Belgrade by Dr. Ivan Cicak, was sponsored and supported by the Nazis.

After the invasion, the most important quisling journalists congregated around the Novo Vreme and the Hrvatski Narod in Zagreb. Among those in Belgrade, however, were Danilo Gregorich, editor of Novo Vreme and a known anti-Semite even before the invasion; Krsta Cicvarich, editor of Balkan; Grgur Kostich; ...... Stefanovich, secretary of Novo Vreme; Milan Tokin; Stanislav Krakov, a pro-fascist of long standing; Dr. Bajkich; Predrag Milojevich; ..... Ivanich; Dr. Spalajkovich; and M. Radulovich.

In Zagreb: Dr. Ante Budak, editor of Hrvatski Narod and ambassador of the puppet state of Croatia in Berlin; Dr. Janko Shimrak, editor of Hrvatska Straza; Ivo (?) Lentich, co-editor of Hrvatska Straza; Dr. Ivan Cicak, editor of the Coratian Stürmer paper, Slobodni Narod, now in Zagreb; Mirko Glojnarich, former collaborator of Hrvatski Dnevnik; Janko Tortich, director of the former Yugoslav newspaper agency Avala; ..... Kloss, member of the staff of the former Morgenblatt; Ivo Malinar, editor of the former Jugoslavenski Lloyd in Zagreb; Dr. Filip Lukas, former president of Matica Hrvatska and a notorious racial propagandist; ..... Drajach (?) the director of the Quisling Croatian trans-Ocean radio station Rakovica; in Bari, Italy; ..... Kovachevich; ..... Bogdan; Dr. Vilko Rieger; ..... Orshanich; Franjo Rubina; Stanislav Florio; Franjo Bubalich; ..... Zidovec; ..... Fuis. With the exception of the German Morgenblatt, all these publications appeared in Serbo-Croatian.

Both the Croatian and Serb puppet governments were openly fascistic and anti-Semitic. Among the anti-Semites best known even before the war were:

Serbia: Dimitrije Ljotich, president of the fascistic Zbor organization; Danilo Gregoric, editor of Novo Vreme; Krsta Cicvarich, editor of the anti-Semitic newspaper Balkan; Milan Achimovich, puppet minister of Interior; Dragi

Jovanovich, mayor of Belgrade under the Nazi regime.

Zagreb; Croatia: Dr. Ante Pavelich, leader of the Ustashi Party and chief of the "Independent State Croatia", Croatian Quisling; Dr. Andrija Artukovich, Pavelich's minister of Interior; Dr. Benzon, physician and first Croatian ambassador in Berlin; Dr. ..... Koshak, minister for Pavelich; Dr. Josip Vragovich, director of the Zagreb police while it was under Yugoslav authority and later under Pavelich; Dr. ..... Sarich, Catholic bishop of Sarajevo, responsible for the anti-Semitic excesses inspired by priests in Bosnia; Dr. Mile Budak, Vice-"Poglavnik", Croatian Ambassador to Berlin; Kvaternik junior, son of Croatian Marshal Kvaternik, and responsible for many cruelties during his regime as chief of the Jewish department of the Zagreb Police; Vladimir Kren, former colonel of the Yugoslav Army, who three days before the invasion flew to Germany with the plan of all Yugoslav secret air bases, and was later made marshal of the Croatian Air Fleet; Leonardo Grivicich, merchant, president of the Association of Friends of Germany; Dr. Ivan Andres and Dr. Frangesh, both former Yugoslav ministers; Dr. Filip Lukas, president of the Matica Hrvatska and a Croatian racist; Ivo Wenner, the Ustashi Mayor of the city of Zagreb; Dr. ..... Buch, president of the Federation of the Hotel and Restaurant Owners in Zagreb; Dr. ..... Ruzhich, former Banus of Croatia; Dr. Aleksandar Hribar, lawyer and member of the German Technische Union; Dr. Milorad Kozjak, lawyer in Zagreb; Dr. Mirko Lamer, former Secretary for commerce at the Croatian Banat, and later in the same position under the Croatian puppet government (perhaps in Switzerland in 1942-43); Dr. Marijan Drazich, lawyer and president of the Association of Friends of Germany in Zagreb; Dr. Boris Zarnik, professor at the University in Zagreb, and propagator of the "scientific" racial theory; Dr. .... Smokvina, professor at the University in Zagreb; Dr. Ivan Pernar, Zagreb politician, Janko Tortich, deputy of the Croatian peasant party, director of the Yugoslav News Agency "Avala", and reputed to be a Hitler spy; Dr. Vulco Mrshulia, Zagreb lawyer, later lawyer in Fiume; Dr. Vitomir Tordoni, Zagreb lawyer, fascist and anti-Semite. In the Zagreb Auto-Club, in the late 1930's, a group started to propagate fascistic, nazistic and especially anti-Semitic ideas. The most noisy were: ..... Hugo, Velimir Vrankovich, and the Brothers Vernich. All these obtained good posts under the Nazi regime.

There was no anti-Semitic propaganda among Yugoslavs in exile, but some Yugoslav-American circles showed anti-Semitic tendencies before Pearl Harbor.

Since in 1943 communication with Yugoslavia was practically impossible, detailed information about the few Jewish leaders who had managed to escape with their lives and were still in the country can hardly be given. However, in June, 1943, the Vatican transmitted a letter stating that the Rabbi of Zagreb, Dr. Shalom Freiberger, the former president of the Jewish community there, Dr. Hugo Kon, and the vice president, Dr. Drago Rosenberg, were all still living in Zagreb, despite earlier reports of their deportation to Poland. Dr. Bukich Pijade, president of the Sephardic religious community of Belgrade, was believed still to be in the latter city.

A number of Yugoslav Jewish leaders escaped to other countries. In the United States, in 1943, were the Chief Rabbi of Yugoslavia, Dr. Isak Alkalay; Otto Heinrich, vice president of the Jewish religious community of Zagreb, who was serving as president of the association of Yugoslav Jews in the United

States; Dr. Paul Neuberger, once member of the executive of the Federation of Jewish communities in Yugoslavia and Zionist leader, who was vice-president of the association of Yugoslav Jews in the United States; Alfred Bondy, textile manufacturer; Milan Freund, paper manufacturer; Frances Hubert, banker; Roman Schmutzer, textile manufacturer, and Manfred Sternberg, distiller.

Dr. Adolf Weissmann, mining industrialist and former Uraguayan consul in Yugoslavia, was in Mexico. Dr. Richard Bauer, physician and former president of the B'nai B'rith in Zagreb, was in London. Among the Yugoslav Jewish leaders who made their way to Palestine are Dr. S. Steineler of Belgrade; Dr. Zwi Rotmuller, Dr. Joel Rosenberger, Lav Stern, Julije Fisher, of Zagreb; Mayer Weltmann of Novisad; Dr. Zigo Bauer of Sarajevo. Dr. Aleksandar Licht, president of the Central Yugoslav Zionist Organization, escaped from German internment to Italy, and was living as a civil internee in the province of Modena. Dr. Ziga Neumann, former president of the Keren Hayesod in Yugoslavia, and Aleksa Klein, secretary of the Jewish community of Zagreb, were also in Italy.

No relief personnel which might cooperate in post-war reconstruction was left in Yugoslavia in 1943. Organizations outside Yugoslavia which might cooperate include, in Palestine: the Committee of Yugoslav Jews, whose president is Lav Stern and whose former presidents were Zwi Rotmuller, Julije Fischer, and Dr. Meir Weltmann; in the United States: the Association of Yugoslav Jews in the United States of America, of which the president is Otto Heinrich, acting chairman, Dr. Paul Neuberger, vice president, Avram Judich and secretary, Roman Smutzer. The organization which was most intensively active before the war was the American Jewish Joint Distribution Committee. The Jewish agency for Palestine and the Hicem (Hias-Ica Emigration Association) may also be turned to.